Managerial Economics: Theories and Analysis

Managerial Economics: Theories and Analysis

Edited by
Rex Henson

Willford Press
www.willfordpress.com

Published by Willford Press,
118-35 Queens Blvd., Suite 400,
Forest Hills, NY 11375, USA

ISBN: 978-1-68285-599-7

Cataloging-in-Publication Data

Managerial economics : theories and analysis / edited by Rex Henson.
p. cm.
Includes bibliographical references and index.
ISBN 978-1-68285-599-7
1. Managerial economics. 2. Management. 3. Industrial management. I. Henson, Rex.
HD30.22 .M36 2019
338.5--dc21

For information on all Willford Press publications
visit our website at www.willfordpress.com

Willford Press

Printed in China.

Contents

Preface

Every book is a source of knowledge and this one is no exception. The idea that led to the conceptualization of this book was the fact that the world is advancing rapidly; which makes it crucial to document the progress in every field. I am aware that a lot of data is already available, yet, there is a lot more to learn. Hence, I accepted the responsibility of editing this book and contributing my knowledge to the community.

Economics aims to analyze and predict the patterns of production and consumption of diverse goods and services. Managerial economics is the application of economic principles to business scenarios to resolve management issues. Managerial economics is significant in the development of efficient methods of risk analysis of pricing and decisions, etc. by using economic tools like regression analysis, calculus and more. This book is a valuable compilation of topics, ranging from the basic to the most complex advancements in the field of managerial economics. The data collated herein explores the fundamental theories and concepts associated to this branch of study and their applications. This book presents researches and studies performed by experts across the globe. Easy to comprehend language and extensive use of examples make this book an ideal reference text for students and researchers alike.

While editing this book, I had multiple visions for it. Then I finally narrowed down to make every chapter a sole standing text explaining a particular topic, so that they can be used independently. However, the umbrella subject sinews them into a common theme. This makes the book a unique platform of knowledge.

I would like to give the major credit of this book to the experts from every corner of the world, who took the time to share their expertise with us. Also, I owe the completion of this book to the never-ending support of my family, who supported me throughout the project.

Editor

Allocation of Innovative Human Resources: A Case Study of Suzhou in Jiangsu Province

Zhaofeng Chen* and Huihui Chen

Science and Technology Policies and Innovation Management Research Institute, Nantong University, Nantong, Jiangsu, PR China

Abstract

The transformation, upgrading, and sustainable development of local economies have all created the intrinsic need to increase regional indigenous innovation. Furthermore, the capacity of local self-dependent innovation should be determined based on efficient innovative resource aggregation and allocation. To those with a developmental tendency, the competition of mechanism and paths of innovative resource allocation has become a new target for regional competition in the new era. Many developed regions in China not only have considered efficient innovative resource allocation as one of the goals of their government function, but they also have established diversified path systems of innovative human resource aggregation allocation in their practice.

Keywords: Innovative abilities; Resource allocation; Agglomeration allocation; Diversified paths

Introduction

The endogenous need of economic transformation is more urgent in developed regions than developing regions due to the unbalanced development of economy in China. Objectively, many developed areas in China have reached the advanced stages of local economic development; therefore, these regions are under high demand and pressure in upgrading, transformation, and sustainable development when compared to traditional regions. Innovative and entrepreneurial talented people (hereafter refer as talents) have their intrinsic characteristics of mobility and agglomeration. Hence, the developed regions focused on the aggregation of innovative human resources and explored diversified paths of innovative human resource aggregation allocation and efficient allocation. From the viewpoint of developmental tendency, the competition of mechanism and pathways of innovative resource allocation have become the new target and task in current era of regional competition in developed regions. Moreover, the formation of regional competitive advantages of innovative resource agglomeration allocation and efficient allocation orientate new strategies of advantage competitiveness in the developed regions.

Correlation Studies

Studies on the concepts, current situation, problems and causation of innovative resource allocation

Jian Chen and Guoxiang He proposed the concept of regional innovative resource allocation [1]. Albert Guangzhou Hu pointed out that the agglomeration of China's high-technology firms in technology parks does not fit into an industrial endogenous growth model [2]. Fengchao Liu et al. analyzed the distribution properties and differences of global innovative resources based on OECD national data [3]. The causations of low efficiency innovative resource allocation are that the infrastructure for science and technology is not brought into government's project for scientific and technological development, and that the managing system of the research and development is fragmented and segmented and so on [4]. The theory of human capital threshold concludes that a host country needs to exceed a minimum human capital threshold level to reach foreign R&D spillovers [5]. There exists great subjectivity and blindness for the allocation of innovative resources solely derived from state planning, which results in low efficiency of allocation of limited innovative resources [6]. Bottazzi and Peri proposed that the stock of knowledge has a very significant impact on innovation in the study of OECD member countries [7]. The size of domestic market demands is of great importance for the innovation and development of machine tool builders [8]. The science and technology innovative resource allocation during the transitional period in China shows coexisting "government-led" and "market-led" performance which leads to the dilemma that both government and market lose their efficacy in the national innovative resource system [9].

Studies on the paths and patterns of regional innovative resource agglomeration

Romer's study showed that the more R&D invested, the higher probability of innovation will be achieved [10]. Alliances and cooperation are the basic capacities for biotechnology industrial development [11]. Furman et al. proposed that the national innovative capacity also includes the factors of innovative infrastructures, industrial innovative environment and the connection quality between scientific departments and industrial departments and so on [12]. The optimal allocation and effective utilization of science and technology innovative resources using science and technology programs have become important strategies to support science and technology innovation in many countries or local governments [13]. Fuhua Li concluded 5 modes of local innovative resource integration: public science and technology innovative platform establishment; scientific parks; establishment of research and development institutes by enterprises; joint establishment of laboratories or engineering technology centers; achievement transformation and cooperative research and so on [14]. Aitken and Harrison studied Venezuela and found that domestic firms with more foreign ownership are significantly less productive in R&D than those with a smaller foreign presence [15]. Reddy showed that globalization of R&D is highly relevant with its corresponding environmental quality of innovation [16]. Government-venture capital investors, as stand-alone investors, have no impact on invention and innovation. However, government-venture capital investors boost the impact of independent-venture capital investors. Government-

***Corresponding author:** Zhaofeng Chen, Professor, Nantong University, Science and Technology Policies and Innovation Management Research Institute, Nantong, Jiangsu 226009, PR China, E-mail: czf8080@163.com

venture capital investors are an ineffective substitute, but an effective complement of independent-venture capital investors [17]. Multiplex mechanisms are important for the increase of innovative capabilities of enterprises. Recruitment from universities, research institutions and higher education institutions has increased the capacity of firms to generate technical inventions [18].

Diversified Paths of Efficient Allocation of Innovative Human Resources

Path of government promotion

The formation of top-level design is one of the most important strategies in government promotions for innovative human resource regional agglomeration in developed cities. Suzhou strengthens the top-level design of "City Revitalization Relied on Talents" strategy by establishing an interactive mechanism by combining "City Revitalization Relied on Talents", "Innovative Cities", and transformation and upgrading of economic development strategies. The well-established top-level design of Suzhou guarantees its rising prosperity of innovative human resource agglomeration. The main features of the top-level design contain several aspects, of which the first is to take the lead in establishing and carrying out. "The Strategy of Human Capital Accumulation First" in local development. Suzhou emphasizes "The Strategy of Human Capital Accumulation First" and focuses on promoting the transformation of supporting elements from "material resources first" to "human resources first". <The outline of medium & long-term program for talent development in Suzhou (2010-2020)> points out that the implementation focus is to carry out "the recruitment program of global experts" ("1010 Talent Project"), namely in key and emerging industries, from 2010 to 2020, Suzhou will annually introduce one research and development group with the international advanced level, introduce and train 10 national talents from the "The Thousand Talents Plan" and 100 high-level leading talents of innovation and enterprising, and introduce 1000 high-level overseas talents; Second, Suzhou established the talent work leading group office and the talent work joint meeting which take charge of the selection and management of professional and technical talents and the management of special fund for human resource development and so on. Third, Suzhou implemented the transformation from supportive "talent policy" to "major projects for talent development". The goal of the national "Thousand Talents Plan" is to support a group of strategic scientists and leading talents who are capable of breaking through key techniques, developing high-tech industries and promoting the development of other new subjects to come back to China for innovation and enterprising. The scale of the talents who are selected by the national the "The Thousand Talents Plan" in which Suzhou declared independently has been on a continuously rising trend. There was one talent selected in Suzhou in 2008, 11 in 2009, 18 in 2010, 24 in 2011, 51 in 2012, 20 in 2013, 15 entrepreneurial talents in 2014. At present, the total number of selected talents is 140 (34% of the whole province) including 95 entrepreneurial talents. This number, for the first time, outcompeted Beijing and ranked highest comparing with all other cities in China. The fourth aspect is the formation of effective management means. In 2011, Suzhou financially invested more than 4 billion Yuan in science and technology and reduced taxes of 3.78 billion Yuan for enterprises to promote science and technology innovation, because of which, the effective management levered more than 26 billion Yuan investment into research and development from the whole society. The research and development fund of Suzhou was close to 30 billion Yuan in the year of 2012 (2.6% of the Gross Regional Product (GRP) of Suzhou). The amount of patent authorization in Suzhou was 98,276,000 (27.2% year on year), which ranked first in China in two consecutive years. In 2010, Suzhou municipal party committee and government published <Implementation opinions of assessment of objective responsibility for talent science and technology work of the party and government leading bodies and leading cadres at county level> by which 6 assessment systems that talent work takes priority over science and technology work were established for the party and government leading bodies and leading cadres at county level in evaluating talent investment, talent policy, bank work and environmental optimization.

Path of enterprises

The establishment and improvement of agglomeration mechanisms and institutional arrangements of high-level innovative and entrepreneurial talents that take an enterprise as the main body are fundamentally guaranteed to establish market-oriented agglomeration allocation mechanisms of innovative and entrepreneurial human resources. Developed cities support and lead the agglomeration of high-level innovative and entrepreneurial talents towards the aggregation of enterprises through corresponding policies, plans and institutional arrangements; which highlight the principal statue of enterprises in agglomeration allocation of innovative and entrepreneurial human resources. It was a successful attempt for Suzhou to cultivate enterprise carriers of innovative talent agglomeration allocation that enterprises have grown into the most important micro subjects for innovative human resource agglomeration allocation.

Advantage establishment of enterprise agglomeration of doctorial talents: Suzhou insists on aggregating talents by considering enterprises as the main body of agglomeration. Suzhou also profoundly implements "Doctor of Enterprise Allocation Plan" and leads talents moving towards the frontier of production and research work of enterprises. On the grants list of the "Doctor of Enterprise Allocation Plan" of Suzhou in 2013, 75 innovative and entrepreneurial talents in Suzhou (Tao Yuan from Suzhou Hongchuang High-frequency Induction Heating Equipment Co., Ltd and others) were listed. At present, in 296 individuals in Suzhou have been selected, this number reaches close to 1/5 of the total amount in Jiangsu province and ranks first in the whole province. There are currently 240 enterprise postdoctoral research stations in Suzhou, ranking number one amongst prefecture-level cities in China. Since 2013, Suzhou introduced 90 post-doctorates (400 post-doctorates in cumulative number including 195 post-doctorates at the station). In 2013, there were 6 national innovative (pilot) enterprises, 300 provincial innovative enterprises, 133 Suzhou innovative pioneer enterprises, 209 science and technology listed enterprises, 2502 high technology enterprises, 131 National Torch Plan high technology key enterprises, 153 advanced technology service enterprises, and 7700 private science and technology enterprises in Suzhou. This is now the most energetic enterprise carrier for the regional agglomeration of doctorial high-level innovative and entrepreneurial human resources. In addition, Suzhou provides an efficient platform for the agglomeration of high-level science and technology innovative and entrepreneurial talents by establishing Suzhou the "The Thousand Talents Plan" specialist association and Suzhou leading-talent club.

Advantageous establishment of enterprising agglomeration of entrepreneurial talents: Entrepreneurial human resource allocation has become the focal point of innovative resource allocation in developed regions and the important preference of regional innovative resource allocation. Objectively, the focus and the goal of the regional innovative resource agglomeration allocation are very dissimilar with that in national key cities. This is because the aim of the regional innovative resource agglomeration allocation is to adapt to the upgrading and transformation of local development, thus the local innovative resource agglomeration allocation must focus on application. The establishment of advantages of enterprise agglomeration allocation of entrepreneurial talents meets such endogenous need. The Organization Department of the Central Committee of the CPC has published the 10th version of "The Thousand Talents Plan" in which there are 15 talents selected in Suzhou accounting for 16% of the total number in China and 52% of Jiangsu province.

Implementation of the oriented policy in which innovative resources, particularly innovative human resources, are focused towards enterprises: Suzhou, on the one hand, guides and motivates enterprises to accumulate independent innovative capabilities through policies, which enlarges the needs of enterprise innovative and entrepreneurial human resource agglomeration allocation. On the other hand, it shapes the structure that innovative talents, funds, programs and techniques and so on. Innovative resources are aggregated towards enterprises, especially towards science and technology enterprises by the implementation of the oriented policy in which innovative resources; especially innovative human resources are aggregated towards enterprises and the preferential policies in which innovative human resources are guided towards enterprise agglomeration allocation. According to the corresponding policies of Suzhou, the innovative and entrepreneurial doctors who have been selected via the "Doctor of Enterprising Agglomeration Plan" will be funded no less than 200,000 Yuan individually (free of income tax) including 150,000 Yuan from provincial finance and no less than 50,000 Yuan from local finance. Until now, there have been 125 talents in total who have applied and obtained the high-level overseas talent residential permits accounting for 1/4 of the provincial amount. Suzhou fostered science and technology innovation-led enterprises and small and micro-growing enterprises as important bodies via a serial of policy stimuli. Suzhou implemented the most supportive policies for science and technology innovation-led enterprises when compared with any other similar policy in China. Suzhou also applied preferential policies to support innovative pioneer enterprises and innovative pioneer cultivation enterprises. Innovative pioneer enterprises, since the first year, will be rewarded via the policy of refund for collection of added-value tax, business tax and corporate income tax (annual new tax of the remaining local portion). (100% refund in the first two years, 50% refund in the following three years (maximum 5 million Yuan per year)) The incentive policy for Innovative pioneer enterprises that Suzhou applies is the supportive policy when compared with any other similar policy in China.

Path of carriers

The establishment of carrier platforms of different kinds of innovative and entrepreneurial talents has provided a platform system for regional agglomeration allocation. The platform system offers a reciprocal competition and cooperation environment for the agglomeration allocation of innovative and entrepreneurial talents.

Carriers of universities: Jaffe proposed the geographic coincidence index and explored the spillovers from university research on commercial innovation [19]. Thus, the advantages of universities on the establishment of paths of efficient allocation of innovative and entrepreneurial human resources and the spillovers of universities on the development of local economy should not be underestimated. Besides, Suzhou focused on the establishment of talent foster carriers with an accumulative investment of 26 billion Yuan by planning and setting up Suzhou Dushu Lake Science and Education Innovation District and Suzhou International Education Park. University of Liverpool, University of Science and Technology of China, Nanjing University, Renmin University of China, Fudan University, Xi'an Jiaotong University, Xi'an Jiaotong-Liverpool University and so on. have settled down in the higher education district in succession; Wenzheng College of Soochow university, Suzhou Vocational University, Suzhou Art and Design Technology Institute and so on. Thirteen institutes have been introduced to the education park in succession. The innovation district and the education park have introduced and fostered accumulative 22,000 industry talents (including 8500 masters, 40% obtained employment in Suzhou), which increases the capability of talented person transports. Soochow University applied the systems of "One Person One Discussion", "Wage contracts", and "Annual Salary", for outstanding high-level talents. The "Settling-in Allowance" and "Scientific research Foundation" for high-level talents were set individually, and gave competitive payment compared with other universities in China. The aggregation of talents drives significant development of discipline constructions of Soochow University. Chemistry, material science, clinical medicine, physics, engineering, biology, and chemical biology at Soochow University were ranked in the top 1% of the Essential Science Indicators (ESI) globally and amongst the best nationally. In May 2013, the Collaborative Innovation Center of Suzhou Nano Science and Technology which is under the auspices of Soochow University was selected in the "2011 Plan" as one of the first 14 cooperative innovation centers [20]. Soochow University obtained 301 projects from The Natural Science Foundation of China in 2013 with total funds of 17,068,970,000 Yuan. The project number was ranked 18th among all universities in China and ranked in second place within Jiangsu province after Nanjing University.

Carriers of national research institutes: While Suzhou focused on national research institute carriers such as Suzhou Institute of Nano-Tech and Nano-Bionics (SINANO), Chinese Academy of Sciences and Nano-Vacuum Interconnected Scientific Station and so on., it also set up public rental housing and central enterprise service centers for high-level talents to provide a full ranges of services covering settling down, payments, relatives, schooling for offspring and entry and exit control for high-level talents [21]. The institute of SINANO, Chinese Academy of Sciences insists on the concept of "human resources as the first resources" and has become one of the most dynamic institutes for the agglomeration allocation of global high-level talents in Suzhou. There were five talents selected in the "The Thousand Talents Plan", and 7 talents selected in the "The Thousand Youth Talents Plan". There were nine researchers entitled "Gusu Leading Talents", and 15 entitled "Science and Education Leading Talents", "High-level Oversees Leading Talents" and "Science and Technology Leading Talents" in the fourth "Jinji Lake Double Hundred Talents" with adding up to 71 leading talents (Table 1).

Carriers of leading-talent-based innovative groups: The leading-talent-based aggregation of innovative talent groups is the basic form of aggregation allocation and efficient allocation of innovative and entrepreneurial talents. In the past 5 years, Suzhou introduced 1339 leading talents total and attracted more than 3000 innovative groups. The accomplishment rate of talent's goals, and talent group projects' goals, ranks highest in Jiangsu province. Suzhou earlier implemented promotion plans and policies of agglomeration of innovative talent groups based on leading talents. Since 2006, Suzhou carried out the

	Suzhou
National research institutes	2 (Suzhou Institute of Nano-Tech and Nano-Bionics (SINANO), Chinese Academy of Sciences; Suzhou Institute of Biomedical Engineering and Technology, Chinese Academy of Science)
Provincial research institutes	11 (Suzhou Nuclear Power Research Institute (SNPI), Suzhou Electromachining Machine Tool Research Institute(SEMTI), China National Building Waterproof Material Company Suzhou Research and Design Institute companies, Sunan Industrial Technology Research Institute, National Biomedicine Incubator Research Platform, China Electronic Product Reliability and Environmental Testing Research Institute (CEPREI, east China), Suzhou Technology Research Institute of Physics CAS, National Software and Integrated Circuit Public Service Platform (CSIP), Jiangsu sub-center, The 22nd Research Institute of China Electronic Technology Company, The 214th Research Institute of China North Industries Group, China Data Technology Development Center)
City and county research institutes	37
Provincial foreign invested R&D centers	243
Enterprise academician stations	41
National key laboratories	3 (Soochow University National Engineering Laboratory for Modern Silk, Jiangsu Key Laboratory for Stem Cell and Biomedical Material, Jiangsu Key Laboratory for Nano-devices)
Provincial key laboratories	15
National public service platforms	25
Provincial public service platforms	39
National engineering technology research centers	2 (National Engineering Technology Research Center For Non-metal Minerals Deep Processing, National Engineering Technology Research Center For Nuclear Power Plant Safety & Reliability)
Provincial engineering technology research center	335

Data source: From the website of Suzhou Science and Technology Bureau and Nantong Science and Technology Bureau.
http://www.szkj.gov.cn/cxzt/20100414/c4c1c8d3-009e-4e45-ae00-a86d36d3b2d5.htm

Table 1: Agglomeration situation of national and provincial science and technology innovative and enterprising platforms in Suzhou.

introduction project for limited high-level talents and the innovative and entrepreneurial leading talents plan. In 2007, Suzhou initiated "The Gusu Talents Plan" in which Suzhou annually selected a batch of leading talents of science and technology from applicants who met the requirements of industrial development. According to policies, the settling-in allowance for innovative and entrepreneurial talents in Suzhou reaches to the highest 2.5 million Yuan. Besides all corresponding "Talents Introduction" policies of county-level cities' and districts', the talents also benefit from the policies as below: The ones who are selected in the "The Gusu Leading Talents of Innovation and Enterprising Plan" will get 0.5 to 2.5 million Yuan settling-in allowance, 1 to 4 million Yuan scientific research funds, no less than 100 square meters workplace with free rent for 3 years and no less than 10% of the total amount of the initial investment of venture capital funds. According to the annual investigation of data of above-city-level enterprises of leading talents in Suzhou from Suzhou Science and Technology Bureau, the enterprises of leading talents acquired sales revenues of 11.43 billion Yuan in the year of 2013 (20% year-on-year growth), scientific research funds of 1.65 billion Yuan (16.6%% year-on-year growth), 6291 patent applications (including 4034 invention patents) and 2303 authorizations of patents (including 762 authorizations of invention patents). Besides, Suzhou encouraged and supported leading talents to expand their enterprises to be stronger. Suzhou provided an extra 1 million Yuan in scientific research funds and a maximum of 10 million Yuan secured financing loans for enterprises of leading talents, which had gotten projects, supported and had achieved sales revenues of more than 50 million Yuan within 3 years. Suzhou preferentially supported enterprises that implemented policies with additional deduction for research funding and governmental purchases of products of independent innovation [22]. As a result, the policies applied by Suzhou promoted the growth of a series of enterprises InnoLight Technology Corporation, Suzhou Silikron Semiconductor Technology Co. Ltd., Suzhou Robot Corporation and so on.

Carriers of science and technology business incubators: In 2013, four enterprises from Suzhou were added to the list of national science and technology business incubators; they were the ones that ranked highest in Jiangsu province. The establishment of science and technology business incubators in Suzhou has been transformed from a single carrier establishment to the incubation chain establishment of local science and development incubators of innovation and enterprising. This transformation created favorable conditions for the fast growth of small and medium-sized science and technology enterprises and provided efficient platforms for the agglomeration of high-level innovative and entrepreneurial talents. According to the statistics of the implementation of policies of innovative pioneer enterprises, 68 enterprises in Suzhou matched the criteria of reward policy of innovative pioneer enterprises and received total funds of 0.12 billion Yuan accordingly. Suzhou preferentially provided multiple policies supporting science and technology finance supermarket platforms for recorded and confirmed enterprises, financing services for small and medium-sized science and technology enterprises to integrate science and technology resources, and especially, technological innovative activities for the enterprises. Suzhou "Science and Technology Loans" has offered loans of 8.09 million Yuan in total for small and medium-sized science and technology enterprises [23].

Path of development zones

The developmental zone carriers, especially the national development zone carriers are not only the most important growth poles for local economic development, but they are also the most important platforms for the aggregation allocation of innovative and entrepreneurial human resources. Suzhou had successful trials of development zones. Based on the fact that the areas of the development zone of Suzhou have reached 90% and the reality that the constraints on resource space have been fully uncovered, Suzhou industrial park proposed the transformation-oriented strategy in which Suzhou was supposed to transform into the new stage of "Development of new industries, construction of a new city, aggregation of new talents" and the "Composite business parks" would replace the manufacturing functions of traditional industrial parks by "Innovation drive" and "Business entities". The percentage of financial allocations of science and technology for Suzhou high technology districts exceeded 10% of the general budget expenditures and the research investment of the society exceeded 3% of the gross regional domestic product. The output value of high technological industries and the output value of strategic new-developing industries accounted for more than 50% of the total industrial output value, this ranked highly in technology districts in China. Since 2012, Suzhou industrial park has been increasingly abundant in innovative resources: more than 3 million square meters science and technology carries, more than 20 public technology service platforms, 20 national innovative bases and the International Science and Technology Park, the Creative Industry Park, the China-Singapore Suzhou Industrial Park, the Nanolis Suzhou, a batch of innovative groups, have been established. In Suzhou industrial park, the energy consumption per 10 thousand GDP and the chemical oxygen demand (COD) and the emission of SO_2 have been decreasing continuously and are currently only in proportion of 1/2, 1/15 and 1/26, respectively, of the average level of Jiangsu province. The high-end industries, high-end commercial industries and the high-level talents are accelerating in accumulation, the output value of high technology industries and the output value of emerging strategic industries account for 63.6% and 55.7% of the total industrial output value separately [24]. According to the statistical data from the Torch Center of Ministry of Science and Technology, the number of independent brand enterprises increased from 800 in 2006 to more than 3000 in 2011. In the year of 2013, the total number of the innovative talents in Suzhou industrial park who were selected in the "The Thousand Talents Plan" (produced by the Organization Department of the Central Committee of the CPC) and added up to a total number of 48, which, for the first time, surpassed Shanghai and Beijing. In addition, by the year 2013, a cumulative 23 post doctorial research stations were licensed in Suzhou high technology district, the number of talents who were selected in the "The Thousand Talents Plan" reached up to 32, and the number of high-level talents exceeded to 12,000. The proportion of talents who have obtained college degrees or higher to the employed population and the total number of introduced leading talents of innovation and enterprising both ranked top among high technology districts in China.

Conclusions

Maximizing the efficiency of regional innovative resource allocation, particularly innovative and entrepreneurial human resource allocation

The creation of advantages in various conditions to improve the agglomeration capacity of local innovative resources, particularly the agglomeration capacity of innovative and entrepreneurial human resources, and to increase the efficiency of the allocation of scarce innovative resources in China is not only the endogenous need for the establishment of a sustainable development mechanism of independent innovative capabilities, but also is an important prerequisite to further release other innovative resources. Essentially, only the establishment of the mechanisms and the systems of efficient allocation of innovative resources can eventually enhance the competitive advantages of the agglomeration of innovative resources and consequently, can create local and national competitive advantages for talents. Regarding the boost of the establishment of the mechanisms and systems of efficient allocation of innovative resources as core strategies with the design and the support of diversified paths is not only an effective way to implement the strategy of the allocation competition of innovative human resources, but also an endogenous need to improve the allocation efficiency of innovative human resources. Therefore, developed regions should explore the mechanism and the system of the efficient allocation of innovative resources by the help of the design and the practice of diversified paths, to provide institutional arrangements for the diversified paths. However, we must also be aware of that the allocation efficiency of innovative resources in China is not ideal due to various reasons. Because of the "Local state corporatism" that resulted from the fiscal reform of China, there exists a great gap between the promotion work of the agglomeration allocation of talents led by the local government and the final goal of the efficient allocation of innovative resources [25]. Thus, the negative effects of low efficient allocation of innovative resources on the practical work of the agglomeration allocation of innovative resources in different regions must be fully assessed. Although many regions begin to realize that innovative resources are the most important competitive resources in local development and competition, the establishment of the mechanism and the system of the efficient allocation of innovative resources is a long term process and a complicated social system task; it not only needs policy guidance and innovative promotion and supports from local governments, but also requires comprehensive reform and deepening reform of economic system, technology system, education system, talent system and social security system as well as practical support from diversified channels and so on. The efficient allocation of innovative resources, particularly innovative and entrepreneurial human resources depends not only on the scale of the agglomeration of innovative resources but also on the quality of the agglomeration of innovative resources (in this respect, it is a process of quantitative changes to qualitative changes), and also on the intrinsic fusion degrees between the allocation of innovative resources and the mode of the regional economy development. Taking the lead in establishing diversified paths of innovative resources will provide valuable practical exploration for the establishment of the mechanism and the system of the efficient allocation of innovative resources, which is a core strategy to master first chance of regional development and regional competition in the new era. This requires overall planning governance and discretionary approach on the cultivation of demands, the improvement of supply capacities and the equilibrium management of supplies and demands of innovative resources, particularly innovative and entrepreneurial human resources.

Establish a new integration system that introduces, cultivates and utilizes innovative resources, particularly innovative and entrepreneurial talents based resources, to improve the organization and level of support for talent introduction and for cultivation of local governments to foster "Permanent" and "Localized" innovative and entrepreneurial talents

Introduction, cultivation and utilization are the main objectives of the efficient allocation of innovative resources, particularly the growth of the innovative and entrepreneurial talents. It was proposed in the <Key points of Suzhou talent work in 2012> that Suzhou needs to put emphasis on the regularity of study of the introduction and cultivation of talents and pinpoint the conspicuous contradiction and bottleneck of the constraints on talent development, especially the constraints on the agglomeration of key industrial talents. On the one hand, we need to develop mechanisms, carriers and paths for the introduction, cultivation and utilization of talents to promote the accumulation and utilization levels of innovative resources, particularly innovative and entrepreneurial human capital; On the other hand, we need to promote the localization of innovative and entrepreneurial talents. It is necessary to set up good living, working and enterprising environment, to establish clear paths for the integration of introduction, cultivation and utilization of innovative resources and to improve the abilities of the integration of introduction, cultivation and utilization of innovative and entrepreneurial talents relying on key disciplines and key majors in colleges and research institutes, on college science and technology parks and innovation-enabled enterprises and on key research laboratories and industry-university-research alliances. The establishment of the collaborative innovation and confident relationships in the industry-university-research alliances facilitates the deep cooperation of social capital [26]. Finally, with the help of science and technology parks and diverse incubator platforms, it is necessary to provide a favorable environment and advantageous conditions for the commercialization and industrialization of innovative achievements and for the enterprising development of entrepreneurial talents. It is believed that, with the support of a "nutrient-rich soil", they will take root and blossom, and yield rich fruits.

Acknowledgement

The article was funded by the National Social Science Foundation of China under the project "Research on efficient allocation paths of innovative resources of strategic emerging industries" (Grant No. 13BGL024), the Key Projects of Philosophy and Social Sciences Research 2016 "Research on strategies and effect factors of the development of cultural industries in Suzhou" (Grant No. 2016ZDAXM003), the Educational Programming Projects of Jiangsu 2013 "Research on mechanisms of collaborative innovation of industries, schools and research institutions in colleges and universities based on endogenous cultivation of strategic emerging industries" (B-a/2013/01/10), the Nantong Soft Science Project 2015 "Research on strategies for the acceleration of agglomeration of scientific resources outside Nantong based on competition"(Grant No. AR2015007) and the Programs Foundation of Ministry of Education of China under the project "Research on the endogenous mechanism of strategic emerging industry cultivation in China: an integrated view of independent innovation and national value chain" (Grant No.12YJAZH007).

References

1. Chen J, He G (2005) Research of the regional innovation resources allocation ability. Studies in Dialectics of Nature 21: 78-82.
2. Hu AGZ (2007) Technology parks and regional economic growth in China. Res Policy 36: 76-87.
3. Liu F, Xu Q, Han Z, Sun Y (2011) Distribution characteristics and spatial differences of global innovation resources- An analysis based on data from OECD. R&D Management 23: 11-16.
4. Tan Q (2004) On the efficient allocation of regional innovation resources. Studies in Science of Science 22: 543-545.
5. Borensztein E, De Gregorio J, Lee JW (1998) How does foreign direct investment affect economic growth? J Int Econ 45: 115-135.
6. Zhou H (1993) Market structure and innovation resource allocation. The Journal of Quantitative & Technical Economics 1: 29-35.
7. Bottazzi L, Peri G (2005) The International dynamics of R&D and innovation in the short and in the long run. NBER working paper No. 11524.
8. Mazzoleni R (1997) Learning and path-dependence in the diffusion of innovations: comparative evidence on numerically controlled machine tools. Res Policy 26: 405-428.
9. Wang X (2006) The market and government in national innovation system in Chinese transformation period: the analysis based on the function of innovation resource allocation. Industrial Technology and Economy 25: 6-9.
10. Romer PM (1994) The origins of endogenous growth. J Econ Perspect 8: 3-22.
11. Al-Laham A, Tzabbar D, Amburgey TL (2011) The dynamics of knowledge stocks and knowledge flows: innovation consequences of recruitment and collaboration in biotech. Ind Corp Change 20: 555-583.
12. Furman JL, Porter ME, Stern S (2002) The determinants of national innovative capacity. Res Policy 31: 899-933.
13. Wang X (2008) Research on regional science and technology innovation resources allocation system optimization based on science and technology program. PhD thesis, Harbin University of Science and Technology.
14. Li F (2009) Analysis of local innovation resource integration modes and policy suggestions. Journal of the Party School of C.P.C. Qingdao Municipal Committee (Qingdao Administrative Institute) 10: 24-28.
15. Aitken BJ, Harrison AE (1999) Do domestic firms benefit from direct foreign investment? Evidence from Venezuela. Am Econ Rev 89: 605-618.
16. Reddy P (2000) Emerging patterns of globalization of corporate R&D and implications for innovation capability in host countries. Science, Technology, and Innovation Policy 1: 219-241.
17. Bertoni F, Tykvova T (2015) Does governmental venture capital spur invention and innovation? Evidence from young European biotech companies. Res Policy 44: 925-935.
18. Herstad SJ, Sandven T, Ebersberger B (2015) Recruitment, knowledge integration and modes of innovation. Res Policy 44: 138-153.
19. Jaffe AB (1989) Real Effects of Academic Research. Am Econ Rev 79: 957-970.
20. Ding S (2013) The secret of being far ahead in Jiangsu province of the "Dual-creative Talents" of Soochow University. China Science Daily.
21. Huang Z (2012) Suzhou industry park is a first choice for creating high-level talents. Conference of The Third Jinji Lake Double Hundred Talents, Suzhou.
22. Qian Y (2010) Suzhou high-level talents will become quadrupled in 10 years. Suzhou daily.
23. Zhou N (2014) Suzhou governmental work report. Third session of the 15th National People's Congress.
24. Ministry of Science and Technology (2014) Suzhou industrial park: Innovation drive, priority to talents, exploration of establishing national innovation and enterprising districts.
25. Oi JC (1992) Fiscal reform and the economic foundations of local state corporatism in China. World Politics 45: 99-126.
26. Carayannis EG, Alexander J, Ioannidis A (2000) Leveraging knowledge, learning, and innovation in forming strategic government-university-industry (GUI) R&D partnerships in the US, Germany, and France. Technovation 20: 477-488.

2

Effects of Leadership Style on Health Care Organizational Performance: A Survey of Selected Tertiary Care Hospital in Karachi, Pakistan

Raza Khan*, Adeel Bukhari and Zahid Ali Channar
Department of Management Sciences, Institute of Business and Technology (IBT), Pakistan

Abstract

Our study has explored the effects of leadership traits on organizational performance in hospitals and health care industry. The core objective of this study was to examine the effect of leadership traits and behavior on performance of hospitals. Transactional and transformational leadership traits were measured. Transformational leadership traits and performance/results measured relevantly in the study was leaders charisma, individual consideration and their inspirational motivation; extra effort, effectiveness, and satisfaction, in that order. Transactional leadership traits and performance/result variables were positive/contingent incentive or rewards and corrective actions/ management by exception; and effort, productivity and commitment/loyalty, correspondingly. In this study we adapt a survey questionnaire, and employed evaluative quantitative analysis method. Analysis was based on primary data generated through a planned Multifactor Leadership Questionnaire (MLQ) administered on participants. The answers to research questionnaire were scaled on likert's scale and converted to quantitative data to enable segmentation of the data responses into the independent and dependent variables assumed on leadership traits and connected performance variables. The model which was used in the study was OLS linear regression model to estimate and evaluate the results. The result illustrates that although transformational leadership traits had positive effect on performance but it is insignificant while transactional leadership trait had an important constructive effect on organization and employees performance. The study also analyzed that transactional leadership trait was more suitable in inducing and enhancing performance in hospitals than transformational leadership style and, as a result, transactional leadership trait/behaviors is recommended for the health care organization/hospitals with integral policies and strategies for evolution to transformational leadership style as the hospitals matured, grew and developed.

Keywords: Leadership traits; Transactional and transformational leadership; Effects; Performance; Hospitals/Healthcare organizations

Introduction

The concept of leadership and trait may vary from one to other. The term "leadership" has been used in various human effort for example businesses, politics, academics, social works etc. where previous views about leadership show it as personal skill. Messick and Kramer [1] explore that the on which level of leadership traits it depends not only on his characteristics and personal abilities, but also it may affect characteristics of the circumstances and culture of organization. So the purpose of human beings to become members of an organization to achieve specific tasks, the degree to which they are active members depends upon how he is influenced that his membership will facilitate him to accomplish his predestined objectives.

That is why, a personality will sustain an organization if he thinks that all the way through his personal task and objectives may be achieve; if he did not, then his interest will be down. Leadership technique in an organization is the main foundations that affect it in very significant way in attraction or retard of the interest and his commitment with the organization. So, Glantz [2] emphasizes on the need for a manager to find his leadership trait.

Among the objectives of any health care organization are primarily to serve humanity, increase health level and secondly is the profit making and to maintain its status. To achieve it health care organization allocates insufficient resources to challenging ends. During this process they maintain humans' health and provide employment, provide services, purchase equipment, drugs and other goods and services and, therefore, contribute to in increasing health status and the growth of the society and economy at large. Unamaka observes that in most hospitals settings, the effectiveness of this process is greatly determined by the patient satisfaction and availability of access to employees, operation departments, equipment, supplies to their immediate community and the nation at large.

The research support the concept of leadership as defined by Taffinder and, therefore, reflect on leadership within the context of a hospitals as the action of managers of hospitals to contribute their best to the purpose for the organization. This study was conducted in three large health care organizations of Karachi and ten employees from each hospital.

From this point of view, this paper is proposed to estimate the effect of leadership trait on the performance of health care organization, contribute to observed researches on leadership traits and organization performance, and will suggest the policies and procedures through quantitative approach for the hospitals in order to contribute in society and nations economic growth.

Literature Review

Leadership approaches and performance

In the field of organizational literature, leadership is recognized as a vital subject when considering literature. During individual and organizational interaction, leadership has the most dynamic effects where the ability of the management to execute "collaborated efforts" depends on leadership capability. Leadership can be explained as the

***Corresponding author:** Raza Khan, Department of Management Sciences, Institute of Business and Technology, Pakistan, E-mail: razaphd87@gmail.com

behavior of an individual to guide a group to achieve the common target.

"Excellent leader does not only inspire potential of subordinates to increase their efficiency but also fulfill their requirements in a process of obtaining and achieving organizational goals" [3].

There are many reasons that leadership approaches and organizational performance must have relationship. Foremost because today, the market is dynamic and demanding and features novelty based struggle, price/performance competition, diminishing revenues, and inventive demolition of modern competencies.

Organizational performance mean the ability of an organization to achieve the objectives of increased profits, enhanced quality product, greater market share, financial results, and survival using relevant strategy for action.

Organizational performance also explains the role of enterprise in terms of level of profit, market share and product quality as compared to other enterprises in same industry. Basically it is a reflection of efficiency of members of an enterprise measured in terms of revenue, profit, development and growth of the organization. To identify and realize the effects of leadership on performance is important because leadership is observed by some scholars as one of the dynamic forces for improving the performance of a firm.

Effective leadership is seen as a potent source of management development and sustained competitive advantage for organizational performance improvement [4,5]. Transactional leadership helps organizations achieve their current objectives more efficiently by linking job performance to valued rewards and by ensuring that employees have the resources needed to get the job done.

Visionary leaders create a strategic vision of some future state, communicate that vision through framing and use of metaphor, model the vision by acting consistently, and build commitment towards the vision. Visionary leadership will result in high levels of cohesion, commitment, trust, motivation, and hence performance in the new organizational environments.

Team leaders are understood to play a vital role in determining collective standards, helping teams manage with their situations, and organizing collective accomplishment. A longstanding approach for an effective organization is to focus on the effects of their leadership. This leader-centered approach has provided cherished understandings into the association between leadership and team performance.

The planned role of leadership can be used to examine on how to engage leadership models and use leadership behavior to progress organizational performance. The intangible assets such as leadership styles, culture, skill and competence, and motivation are key sources of strength in firms that can combine people and processes and organizational performance. The missing liaison in understanding the connection between leadership and organizational functioning conclude that despite a theorized leadership-performance relationship proposed by some scholars, current findings are unconvincing and hard to understand.

From the above discussion, it is clear that although some scholars propose that leadership augments organizational performance while others contradict this, different ideas of leadership have been employed in different studies, making direct judgments almost impossible. Consequently, the current study is envisioned to again inspect the proposed leadership-performance relationship.

Theories on Leadership

The most prominent among the various theories of leadership and motivation relating to effective organizational change management is the "transformational-transactional" theory of leadership. As per the theory, there are two factors to differentiate "ordinary" from "extraordinary" leadership: transactional and transformational leadership.

Transactional leadership is based on conventional exchange relationship in which follower's attitude; his efforts, productivity, and loyalty are exchanged for anticipated rewards, whereas transformational (extraordinary) leaders raise follower's awareness levels about the status and worth of designated results and ways of accomplishing them. They also motivate followers to exceed their own immediate self-interest for the sake of the goal and vision of the organization. Such engagement (emotional, intellectual and moral) boosts followers to progress and perform beyond expectations.

Transformational leadership implicates the process of manipulating major changes in organizational attitudes in order to achieve the organization's goals and objectives. While Transactional leaders work their organizational cultures following prevailing rules and procedures, transformational leaders modify their cultures based on a new vision and a revision of shared expectations, values and norms. A leadership of an organization is a critical factor in determining its successful change when it must adapt to changes in technology.

Transformational leadership

A transformational leader's behavior instigates in the personal values and beliefs of the leader and motivates people to do more than expect. Transformational leadership is a process where, "one or more persons engage with others in such a way that leaders and followers raise one another to higher levels of motivation and morality".

In transformational leadership, the devotee feels faith, respect, loyalty and admiration towards the leader, and is motivated to do more than what was actually expected of him to do. The transformational leader motivates by making follower more aware of the importance of task consequences, encouraging them to exceed their own self-interest for the sake of the organization or tea. He encourages followers to think critically and seek new ways to approach their jobs, resulting in intellectual stimulation. Consequently, their level of performance, satisfaction, and commitment to the goals of their organization is increased.

Charismatic behavior also persuades followers to go beyond self-interest for the good of the group, providing reassurance that problems will overcome. Followers place an inordinate amount of confidence and trust in charismatic leaders. Due to their charismatic attributes, the leader is characterized by vision and a sense of mission, gaining respect and trust from their followers.

Inspirational motivation is concerned with a leader defining higher standards. Followers look up to their inspirational leader to increase awareness and understanding of mutually desirable goals. It is characterized by the communication of high expectations, using signs to focus on struggle, and expressing central purpose in much simpler ways. The leader always talks optimistically about the future; he articulates a compelling vision for the future and provides an exciting image of organizational change. The motivation occurs by providing meaning and challenge to the followers work; individual and team spirit are aroused and enthusiasm and optimism are displayed. The leader encourages followers to envision attractive future states, for the organization and themselves.

Intellectual stimulation delivers followers with challenging new concepts and encourages them to break away from obsolete ways of intellectual. The leader is characterized as one promoting intelligence, wisdom, cogent, and cautious problem solving. The leader encourages the followers to be pioneering and creative by questioning assumptions, reframing problems, and approaching obsolete situations in new ways.

Individual consideration is another dimension of transformational leadership which is concerned with developing followers by training and mentoring. The leader pays understands inter-individual differences among his followers and acts as a mentor to his follower. He preaches and assists his followers to develop their strengths, and pays close attention to their concerns. Followers are treated individually in order to increase their stages of maturity and to improve effective ways of addressing their goals and trials.

Transactional leadership

An exchange procedure in which follower agree with leader's request but is not likely to make enthusiasm and commitment to task goal can be defined as Transactional leadership. The purpose of the transactional leader is to make sure that the path to accomplishment of objective is clearly understood by the people, to eradicate potential hindrance within the system, and to inspire the people to achieve the scheduled goals.

The leader focuses on having internal actors perform the tasks required for the organization to reach its desired goals [6]. Both constructive behavior and corrective behaviors are exhibited by transactional leadership. Constructive behavior involves conditional reward, and corrective dimension includes management by exception. Conditional reward involves the clarification of the work required to obtain rewards and the use of incentives and empirical reward to employ influence. Followers expectations and offers recognition when goals are achieved are considered in conditional rewards.

The clarification of goals and objectives and providing of recognition once goals are achieved should result in individuals and groups achieving expected levels of performance [7]. Active management by exception refers to the leader setting the criteria for deference as well as for what constitutes ineffective performance, and may include punishing followers for non-compliance with those standards. This style of leadership implies monitoring for eccentricities, mistakes, and faults and then taking remedial action as quickly as possible when they happen.

Hypotheses

Hypothesis 1: There is no relationship between leadership style and performance in health care organizations.

Hypothesis 2: The leadership style does not any significant effect on performance in the health care organizations.

Research Methodology

This research paper is on based on primary data generated through a structured questionnaire. The instrument used is the Multifactor Leadership Questionnaire (MLQ) developed by Bass in his research: 'Leadership and Performance beyond Expectations. Mostly this instrument is used for measuring the effects of leadership styles and outcomes. The version which was used in this research is the well-liked MLQ Form 5x-Short. The dependent variables are the outcomes: extra effort, effectiveness and satisfaction while the independent variables are the transformational and transactional leadership styles. So, the questions in the questionnaire are those relating to leadership styles or traits and performance as calculated by extra effort, effectiveness and satisfaction; effort, productivity and loyalty or commitment which are projected by Bass and House et al. [8,9]. The study provides all these variables to estimate the effect of leadership traits or behavior on performance of health care organizations in the city of Karachi (survey area). In the MLQ, each dependent and independent variable is given equal weighting on likert's scale. Each research question has five possible answers, ranging from "strongly disagree" to "strongly agree" and is scaled from 1 to 5.

Three health care organizations were initially selected through stratified random sampling technique, 10 from each hospital and total 30 samples from health care organizations of Karachi [10-13]. The health care organizations which were selected were tertiary care. Ten respondents were randomly selected from each of these three organizations for a sample size of thirty (30) respondents. A test which was conducted on sample demonstrated that leadership style in two hospitals was transactional, while the leadership style in the third hospital was transformational. The study concerted on the two leadership styles. The questionnaire was administered to the Participants with directions to how fill them. All were returned filled out and the response was with return rate of 100%.

Correlations and ordinary least squares (OLS) linear regression analysis models were used to examine the hypotheses on the subject of the relationship among the respective leadership style and performance procedures of the health care organizations [14-18]. The hypotheses are examined through evaluation of relevant information related with the statistical values of model parameters in the tables.

Research hypotheses

In this study the null hypothesis was that there is no relationship between leadership style and performance, and that the respective leadership styles do not any significant effect on performance in the health care organizations.

So, the first hypothesis relates to relationship between leadership style and performance in the health care organization, while the second and third relate to effects of transformational and transactional leadership styles on employee/organizational performance.

Pros and corns' relationship, model specification and the correlation coefficient

Regression model of the functional relationship between leadership style and performance assist assessment of effect of leadership style on organizational performance.

Function relationship

From the supposed relationship among leadership style and performance, functional relationships and associated regression models were particularly selected for the transformational and transactional leadership traits, correspondingly.

$PSE_{TFLS} = f(CHM, ISM, ISC)$

$PSE_{TSLS} = f(CCR, CME)$

Where:

PSE_{TFLS} = Performance in health care organizations with the transformational leadership style. It is a compound of Effectiveness, Extra Effort and Satisfaction.

PSE_{TSLS} = Performance in health care organizations with transactional leadership style. It is a composite of Effort, Productivity and Loyalty/Commitment.

CHM = Charisma

ISM = Inspirational motivation

ISC = Intellectual stimulation/individual consideration

CCR = Constructive/contingent reward

CME = Corrective/management by exception

$= \alpha_0 + \alpha_1 CHM + \alpha_2 ISM + \alpha_3 ISC + \mu = \beta_0 + \beta_1 CCR + \beta_2 CME + \mu$

Where α_0 and β_0 are the constants, which represent performance of health care organizations which is independent of the particular leadership traits, α_1, α_2, and α_3; β_1, β_2 and β_3 are the model coefficients representing effect of the particular leadership traits on the organizational performance.

μ is a sample error or random variable commenced to hold effect of other factors that affect organizational performance within or outside the leadership traits which are not related or not included in the model.

Data Analysis

Effect of leadership style on performance

To determine the relationship between leadership style and organizational performance, and subsequently evaluate the effect of leadership style on performance, average performance response variables are regressed on leadership behavior variables shown in Table 1.

Kurtosis

The Kutosis shows peakness of a curve. The value of kurtosis is positive for Charisma (CHM), Individual Consideration (ISC), Performance through Transformational Leadership Style (TRANSF) and Corrective/ Management by Exception (CME) and Performance through Transactional Leadership Style (TRANSAC), therefore we can say that data is spread towards upward for these variables as shown in Table 2.

The value of kurtosis is negative for Inspirational motivation (ISM) and Constructive/contingent reward (CCR), therefore we can say that data is spread towards downward for these variables.

Skewness

Skewness shows scatterness of curve. If it is positive then rightly skewed means more values on left and vice versa. If kurtosis and skewness are 0 then data is not normally distributed. Charisma (CHM), Inspirational motivation (ISM) and Performance through Transactional Leadership Style (TRANSAC) values are positive therefore, it shows that these are positively skewed mean more values on left.

Individual Consideration (ISC), Performance through Transformational Leadership Style (TRANSF), Constructive/contingent reward (CCR) and Corrective/ Management by Exception (CME) values are negative therefore; it shows that these are negatively skewed mean more values on right as shown in Table 3.

If Konglomorov score is less than 0.05; then data is not normally distributed. In this data set all variables have a Konglomorov score of more than 0.05; therefore, we can say that the data is normally distributed.

Correlation

a. Transformational style: The outcome of the correlation analysis shows that the Performance with Transformational Leadership Style (PSE_{TFLS}) has a positive but weak relationship with the Charisma (CHM) in the context of private hospitals in Karachi. (Here r = 0.123, significant $p<0.05$ as shown in Tables 4-6 and Figures 1-4.

The outcome of the correlation analysis shows that the Performance with Transformational Leadership Style (PSE_{TFLS}) has a moderately

PSE (TFLS)	CHM	ISM	ISC	PSE (TSLS)	CCR	CME
3.27	3.6	3.6	3.4	2.13	3.5	3.86
3.47	3.6	3.4	2.6	2	3.75	3.14
3.4	3.4	3.4	3.4	2.4	3.63	3.71
3.6	3.6	3	3.4	2.13	3.75	3.86
3.47	3.8	4	3.6	2.07	3.88	3.86
3.53	3.6	3.2	3.4	2.2	3.75	3.57
3.6	3.6	3.6	3.6	2.13	3.63	3.57
3.6	3.6	3	3.8	2.13	3.63	3.71
3.67	3.6	3	3.8	2.33	3.75	4
3.53	4	3.6	3	2.73	3.75	3.57
3.27	3.6	3.6	3.4	2.13	3.5	3.86
3.47	3.6	3.4	2.6	2	3.75	3.14
3.4	3.4	3.4	3.4	2.4	3.63	3.71
3.6	3.6	3	3.4	2.13	3.75	3.86
3.47	3.8	4	3.6	2.07	3.88	3.86
3.53	3.6	3.2	3.4	2.2	3.75	3.57
3.6	3.6	3.6	3.6	2.13	3.63	3.57
3.6	3.6	3	3.8	2.13	3.63	3.71
3.67	3.6	3	3.8	2.33	3.75	4
3.53	4	3.6	3	2.73	3.75	3.57
3.27	3.6	3.6	3.4	2.13	3.5	3.86
3.47	3.6	3.4	2.6	2	3.75	3.14
3.4	3.4	3.4	3.4	2.4	3.63	3.71
3.6	3.6	3	3.4	2.13	3.75	3.86
3.47	3.8	4	3.6	2.07	3.88	3.86
3.53	3.6	3.2	3.4	2.2	3.75	3.57
3.6	3.6	3.6	3.6	2.13	3.63	3.57
3.6	3.6	3	3.8	2.13	3.63	3.71
3.67	3.6	3	3.8	2.33	3.75	4
3.53	4	3.6	3	2.73	3.75	3.57

Table 1: Average leadership behavior and performance measure variables.

	N	Mean	Skewness		Kurtosis	
	Statistic	Statistic	Statistic	Std. Error	Statistic	Std. Error
CHM	30	3.64	1.146	0.427	1.589	0.833
ISM	30	3.38	0.335	0.427	-0.719	0.833
ISC	30	3.4	-1.095	0.427	0.706	0.833
TRANSF	30	3.514	-0.804	0.427	0.157	0.833
CCR	30	3.702	-0.336	0.427	-0.007	0.833
CME	30	3.685	-1.031	0.427	0.971	0.833
TRANSAC	30	2.225	1.492	0.427	1.631	0.833
Valid N (listwise)	30					

Table 2: Descriptive statistics.

	Kolmogorov-Smirnov[a]			Shapiro-Wilk		
	Statistic	Df	Sig.	Statistic	df	Sig.
CHM	0.404	30	0	0.718	30	0
ISM	0.182	30	0.013	0.874	30	0.002
ISC	0.3	30	0	0.834	30	0
TRANSF	0.177	30	0.018	0.898	30	0.007
CCR	0.282	30	0	0.857	30	0.001
CME	0.212	30	0.001	0.857	30	0.001
TRANSAC	0.278	30	0	0.79	30	0

[a]Lilliefors Significance Correction

Table 3: Tests of Normality.

	CHM	ISM	ISC	TRANSF
CHM	1	0.440*	-0.231	0.123
		0.015	0.218	0.518
	30	30	30	30
ISM	.440*	1	-0.22	-0.540**
	0.015		0.244	0.002
	30	30	30	30
ISC	-0.231	-0.22	1	0.348
	0.218	0.244		0.059
	30	30	30	30
TRANSF	0.123	-0.540**	0.348	1
	0.518	0.002	0.059	
	30	30	30	30

*. Correlation is significant at the 0.05 level (2-tailed).

Table 4: Correlations (a. Transformational style).

		CCR	CME	TRANSAC
CCR	Pearson Correlation	1	-0.058	0.027
	Sig. (2-tailed)		0.763	0.888
	N	30	30	30
CME	Pearson Correlation	-0.058	1	0.114
	Sig. (2-tailed)	0.763		0.548
	N	30	30	30
TRANSAC	Pearson Correlation	0.027	0.114	1
	Sig. (2-tailed)	0.888	0.548	
	N	30	30	30

Table 5: Correlations (b. Transactional style).

PSE_{TFLS} = 2.647	+ 0.371CHM	- 0.243ISM	+ 0.1ISC
SE	(0.111) *	(0.052) *	-0.044
T-statistic	-3.339	(-4.634)	-2.268
Prob (t-stat)	-0.003	0	-0.032
R2 = 0.543			

*Confidence Interval 95%

Table 6: Transformational style.

negative relationship with the Inspirational Motivation (ISM) in the context of private hospitals in Karachi. (Here r = 0.54, significant $p<0.05$)

The outcome of the correlation analysis shows that the Performance with Transformational Leadership Style (PSE_{TFLS}) has a positive but weak relationship with the Intellectual stimulation/individual consideration (ISC) in the context of private hospitals in Karachi. (Here r = 0.348, significant $p<0.05$)

b. Transactional style: The outcome of the correlation analysis shows that the Performance with Transactional Leadership Style (PSE_{TSLS}) has a positive but weak relationship with the Constructive/contingent reward (CCR) in the context of private hospitals in Karachi. (Here r = 0.027, significant $p<0.05$ as shown in Tables 5 and 7

The outcome of the correlation analysis shows that the Performance with Transactional Leadership Style (PSE_{TSLS}) has a positive but weak relationship with the Corrective/management by exception (CME) in the context of private hospitals in Karachi. (Here r = 0.114, significant $p<0.05$) and Figures 5-7.

Estimated models and discussion

The estimated models are showing that the coefficients are consistent with expectations, except for inspirational motivation (ISM). These are showing that while other leadership behaviors are having a positive effect on performance, Inspirational Motivation (ISM) is having a negative effect.

Consequently, it can be extracted in the health care organizations that transactional leadership style has significant positive effect on performance. A possible reason for this is that the employees of health

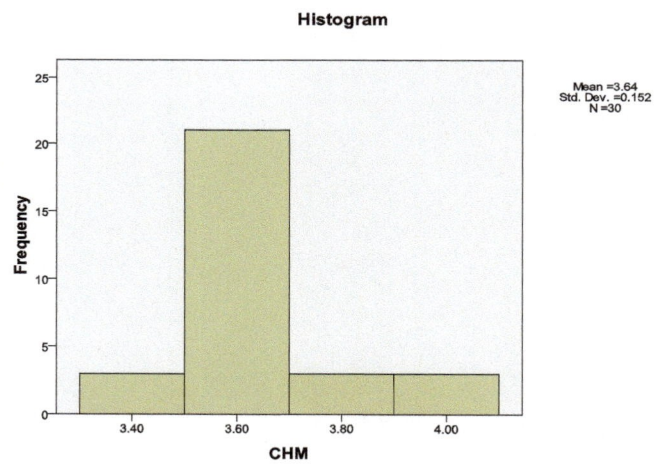

Figure 1: Histogram representing CHM vs Frequency.

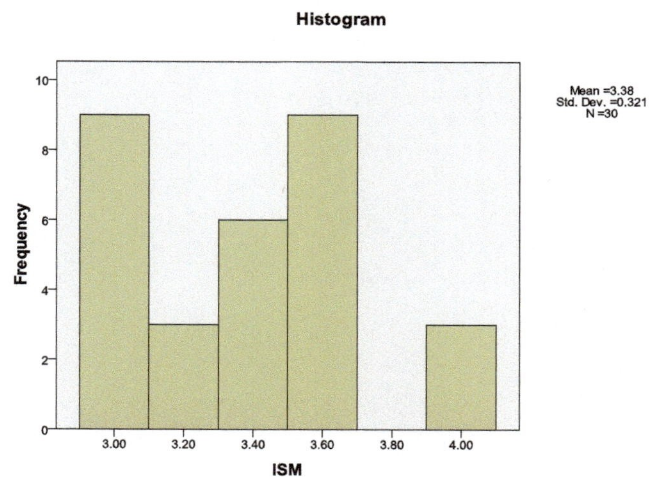

Figure 2: Histogram representing ISM vs Frequency.

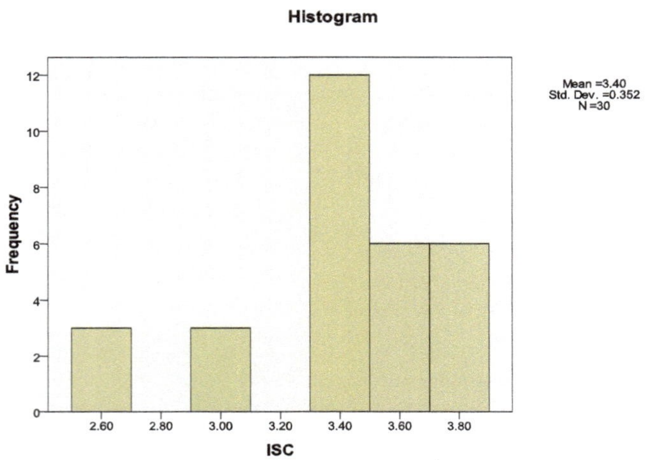

Figure 3: Histogram representing ISC vs Frequency.

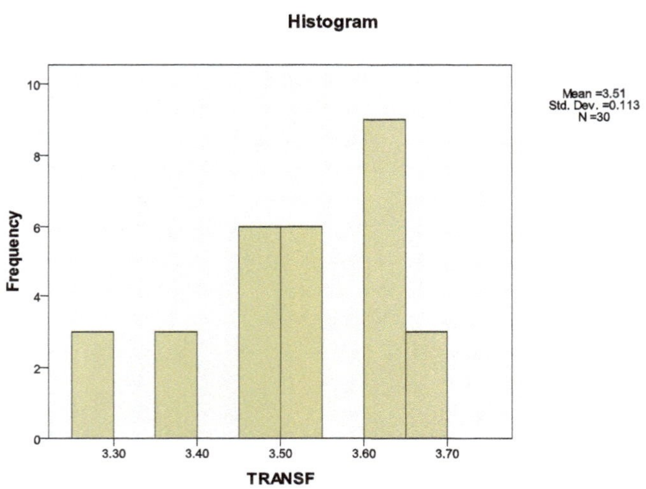

Figure 4: Histogram representing TRANSF vs Frequency.

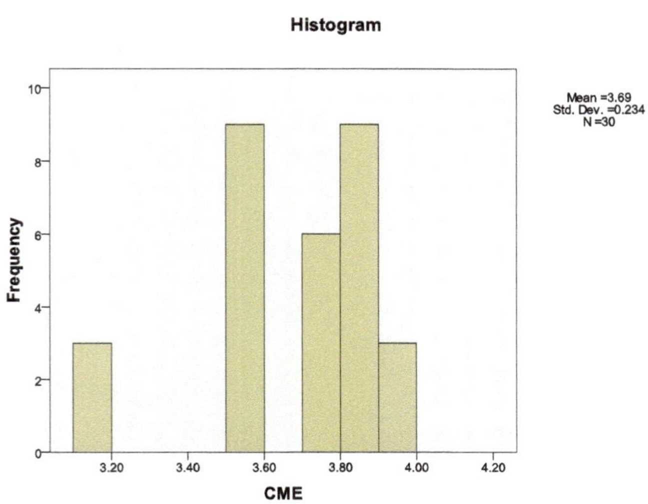

Figure 5: Histogram representing CME vs Frequency.

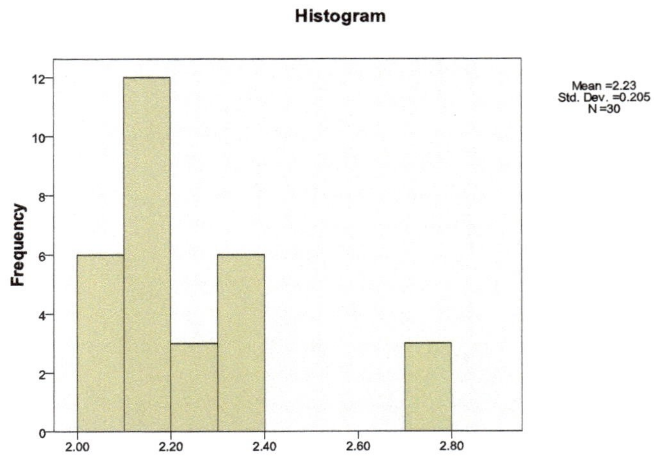

Figure 6: Histogram representing TRANSAC vs Frequency.

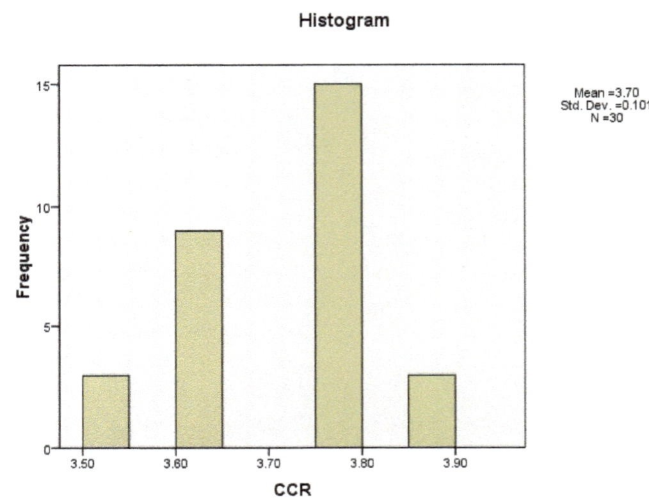

Figure 7: Histogram representing CCR vs Frequency.

PSE_{TSLS} = 1.598	+ 0.068CCR	+0.102CME
SE	(0.387) *	(0.168) *
T-statistic	(0.175)	(0.607)
Prob (t-stat)	(0.325)	(0.549)

*Confidence Interval 95%

Table 7: Transactional style.

care organizations are usually experienced professionals. Therefore, contingent recognition/reward and management by exception rather than charisma, inspirational motivation and intellectual stimulation/individual consideration could be appropriate leadership behaviors and strategies to induce them to perform [19-23].

Conclusion

In this study we calculate and analyzed the effect of leadership traits on organizational performance in selected three hospitals. The investigation has find that each one of traits like charisma and individual consideration or intellectual stimulation of transformational leadership style are positive but has very low effect so it has insignificant effect on employees and organizational performance while the other traits like inspirational motivation was negative and also insignificant for the performance. So, these traits are not explaining the variations in performance while on the other side, each trait of transactional leadership style measured in this research were significant, constructive/contingent reward and corrective management by exception has very important and strong effect on employees and organization performance, and both are defining very big section of variations in the performance. Consequently, it can be extracted in the health care organizations that transactional leadership style has significant positive effect on performance. A possible reason for this is that the employees of health care organizations are usually experienced professionals [24,25]. Therefore, contingent recognition/reward and management by exception rather than charisma, inspirational motivation and intellectual stimulation/individual consideration could be appropriate leadership behaviors and strategies to induce them to perform. The study also implies that the transactional leadership style is an appropriate and more suitable in obtaining results and inducing performance in hospitals rather than transformational leadership style. As a result, the study makes recommendation that hospitals should adopt the transactional leadership traits and style but strategies to transfer and reflect the transformational leadership style as their organizational development and boost.

Recommendations

This study recommends and suggests that more researches can be conducted in the Karachi to examine the effect of leadership traits and behavior on performance of other industries in Karachi and to explore primary and secondary health care centers. There is also need to check the effect of leadership traits on Patient satisfaction, services quality and employee's satisfaction in hospitals, as these areas can help to increase the health care quality and will emphasize of the provision of effective, monitored and safe care in Karachi. The study also implies that the transactional leadership style is an appropriate and more suitable in obtaining results and inducing performance in hospitals rather than transformational leadership style. As a result, the study makes recommendation that hospitals should adopt the transactional leadership traits and style but strategies to transfer and reflect the transformational leadership style as their organizational development and boost. The finding of study can also be used as a guideline for health care managers and administrators as it will help them in performance improvement.

References

1. Messick DM, Kramer RM (2005) The Psychology of Leadership: New Perspectives and Research. Lawrence Erlbaum Associates Publishers.
2. Glantz J (2002) Finding Your Leadership Style. A Guide for Educators; Association for Supervision and Curriculum Development.
3. Lee, Chuang (2009) The Impact of Leadership Styles on Job Stress and Turnover Intention: Taiwan Insurance Industry as an Example.
4. Avolio BJ (1999) Full Leadership Development: Building the Vital Forces in Organizations. Human Resource Development 12: 99-102.
5. Rowe WG (2001) Creating Wealth in Organizations: The Role of Strategic Leadership. Academy of Management Executive 15: 81-94.
6. Boehnke K, Bontis N, Distefano J, Distefano A (2003) Transformational Leadership: An Examination of Cross-national Differences and Similarities. Leadership and Organization Development Journal 24: 5-17.
7. Bass BM (1985) Leadership and Performance beyond expectations. New York Free Press.
8. Bass BM, Ralph MS (1990) Bass and Stogdill's Handbook of Leadership: Theory, Research, and Managerial Applications, (3rdedn). New York: Free Press, London.
9. House RJ, Aditya RN (1997) The Social Scientific Study of Leadership: Quo Vadis? Journal of Management 23: 409-473.
10. Ashibogwu M (2008) Common Failures of Family Business. Business Day, Accessed on: 18 May 2008.
11. Bass BM, Avolio BJ (1997) Multifactor Leadership Questionnaire, Mind Garden.
12. Bass BM, Avolio BJ (1994) Improving organizational Effectiveness through Transformational Leadership. Sage publications.
13. Conger JA (1999) Charismatic and Transformational Leadership in Organizations: An Insider's Perspective on these Developing Streams of Research. The Leadership Quarterly 10: 45-169.
14. Conger JA, Kanungo RN (1987) Towards a Behavioral Theory of Charismatic Leadership in Organizational Settings. Academy of Management Review 12: 637-467.
15. Fenwick FJ, Gayle CA (2008) Missing Links in Understanding the Relationship between Leadership and Organizational Performance. International Business and Economics Research Journal 7.
16. Fry LW (2003) Towards a Theory of Spiritual Leadership. The Leadership Quarterly 14: 693-727.
17. Guzzo RA, Dickson MW (1996) Teams in Organizations. Annual Review of Psychology 47: 307-338.
18. Humphreys JH, Einstein WO (2003) Nothing New under the Sun: Transformational Leadership from a Historical Perspective. Management Decision 41: 85-95.
19. Howell JM, Avolio BJ (1992) Transformational Leadership, Transactional Leadership, Locus of Control, and Support for Innovation: Key Predictors of Consolidated-Business-Unit Performance. Journal of Applied Psychology 78: 891-902.
20. Howell J, Frost P (1989) A Laboratory Study of Charismatic Leadership. Journal of Organizational Behaviour and Human Development Processes 43: 243-269.
21. Judge TA, Piccolo RF (2004) Transformational & Transactional Leadership: A Meta-analytic Test of their Relative Validity. Journal of Applied Psychology 89: 755-768.
22. McGrath GR, MacMillan IC (2000) The Entrepreneurial Mindset: Strategies for Continuously Creating Opportunity in an Age of Uncertainty. Harvard Business School Press.
23. Meyer GD, Heppard KA (2000) Entrepreneurial Strategies: The Dominant Logic of Entrepreneurship. New York, NY: Irwin University Books.
24. Podsakoff PM, McKenzie SB, Bommer WH (1996) Transformational Leader Behavior and Substitutes for Leadership as Determinants of Employee Satisfaction, Commitment, Trust, and Organizational Citizenship Behaviors. Journal of Management 22: 259-298.
25. Purcell J, Kinnie N, Hutchinson S, Rayton B, Swart J (2004) Understanding the People and Performance Link: Unlocking the Black Box. Research Report, Chartered Institute of Personnel and Development.

A Study of Consumer Awareness towards e-Banking

Amutha D*

Department of Economics, St. Mary's College, Tuticorin, India

Abstract

The paper deals the consumers perception towards e-banking system related to consumer awareness towards e-banking system with special reference to Tuticorin District of Tamilnadu. Data for this investigation were collected from primary as well as secondary sources. The sampling is random. The data was collected during the months between April to June, 2015. The data collected from the primary source were analysed with the help of various statistical measures such as simple percentage analysis, averages, F-Statistic, chi square test and probability analysis were used. Secondary data have been collected from books, journals, newspapers, internet and periodicals. It is inferred that 36.67% of the respondents income levels are up to Rs. 1,00,000, 52.22% of the respondents are Rs. 1,00,001 to Rs. 3,00,000 and 11.11% respondents are belonging to above Rs. 3,00,000 and the average income is 167222. The study reveals that, the opinion of customers on future expectations. Out of the total respondents, Majority (i.e.) 58.89% of the sample respondents have mentioned that they would like operate their banking transactions in a core banking environment which is free from neither technical intervention such as computer connecting nor 23.33% of the samples respondents expect the bank will provide security. 17.78% of the sample respondents have stated reasonable charges have to be imposed on their banking transaction. The main difficulty for using the E-banking facility is less knowledge about the operations of banking facility (50%). Respondents also feel the services of E-banking too complex to use (30%) and respondents also believe the E-banking to be risky (12.22%). The research report is based on primary data. According to the study, the researcher concludes that the most of the bank customers are aware about all the banking services in Tuticorin District of Tamilnadu. The banks further have to take necessary steps to educate the customers regarding the new technology and other services offered by the banks.

Keywords: Electronic banking; Internet banking; Credit/debit cards; Transparency; Accuracy; Cost saving; Customer's awareness and Satisfaction

Introduction

The Internet has changed the operations of many businesses, and has been becoming a powerful channel for business marketing and communication American Banker [1]. The banking industry has followed this trend in recent years, and sometimes called "*e-banking*" referring to all banking transactions now completing through Internet applications [2,3]. The advance of communication and computer technology and the availability of the Internet have made it possible that one can do most banking transactions from a remote location even without stepping into a physical financial structure i.e., the emerging of e-banking Bruene [4]. Today, less than 30% of the same consumer financial transactions run through a branch office or the lobby of a main bank office (Online Banking Report. As a result, the banks, as an industry, are formulating strategic plans to fight back in winning their customers suggested by Healy [5].

E-banking has been viewed as an advanced upgrading from previous electronic delivery systems to open many new business opportunities for the banking industry [6]. A survey revealed that at that time there was a planned $2 billion new investment in the new electronic banking technology within the banking industry Radeki [7]. Among surveyed banks at the time, about two third (66%) planned to invest in telephone banking technology, and the remaining one third (34%) already targeted e-banking options. Some key issues addressed in the recent literature about the e banking include: customer acceptance and satisfaction, services rendered, value added for consumers and banks, privacy concerns, profitability, operational risks, and competition from non-banking institutions Boss et al. [8]. In addition to previous electronic banking delivery systems-automated teller machine (ATMs) and telephone transaction processing centers, online banking provides banks a new and more efficient electronic delivery tool Costanzo [9]. There have been several major challenges and issues faced to the e-banking growth and the e-business in general. One major obstacle addressed most is the security concern [10,11]. Another issue challenged e-business (including e-banking) is the quality of delivery service-including both delivery speed (i.e., short advance time required in ordering) and delivery reliability i.e., delivery of items/services on time Furst et al. [12]. Limited payment options available to online customers are also being complained by Furash, [13]. Additionally, customers (who are non-computer "*genius*" like most senior citizens) have been reluctant in their choice of doing business (including banking transactions) online and worried their unfamiliarity about the computer placing them in a disadvantageous position [14]. The paper deals the consumers perception towards e-banking system related to consumer awareness towards e-banking system with special reference to Tuticorin District of Tamilnadu.

Objectives

1. To know the socio economic characteristics of the customers of E-banks
2. To identify the reasons for preferring E-banking.
3. To study the consumer's service quality in E-banking System.
4. To find out the opinion of the respondents regarding the various problems of E-banking
5. To give valuable suggestions to improve awareness and satisfaction about E-banking services.

***Corresponding author:** Amutha D, Associate. Professor of Economics, St. Mary's College, Tuticorin, India, E-mail: amuthajoe@gmail.com

Research Methodology

The study is intended to cover the awareness and satisfaction about E-banking facility provided by commercial banks in Tuticorin district of Tamilnadu. Data for this investigation were collected from primary as well as secondary sources. The sample chosen consisted of 90 sample respondents representing the customers of E-banks. The sampling is random. The data was collected during the months between April to June, 2015. The data collected from the primary source were analysed with the help of various statistical measures such as simple percentage analysis, averages, F-Statistic, chi square test and probability analysis were used. Secondary data have been collected from books, journals, newspapers, internet and periodicals (Table 1).

Results and Discussion

From the above table it is clear that 40% of the respondents belong to up to 25 years, 43.33% of the respondents belong to between 26-50 years and 16.67% of the respondents are in the age group of above 50 years and the mean age group is 33.41667 (Table 2). From the above table it is clear 61.11% of the respondents belong to male group and 38.89% of the respondents belong to female group (Table 3). From the survey the above table reveals that 64.44% of the respondents are married and 35.56% of the respondents are unmarried (Table 4). From the above table out of 90 respondents, it is clear that 13.33% of the respondents are illiterate, 22.22% of the respondent's educational qualification is school level and 26.67% of the respondent's educational qualification is college level and 20% of the respondent's educational qualification is professionals and 17.78% of the respondent's educational qualification is diploma (Table 5). From the above table it is clear that 54.44% of the occupational status of respondents are belong to employee, 13.33% of the respondents belonging to business, 8.89% belonging to agriculture, 12.22% belong to professional 18.89% belonging to student (Table 6). From the above table it is inferred that 36.67% of the respondents income levels are up to Rs. 1,00,000, 52.22% of the respondents are Rs. 1,00,001 to Rs. 3,00,000 and 11.11% respondents are belonging to above Rs. 3,00,000 and the average income is 167222 (Table 7). The table highlights the customer preference towards E-banking services. Out of the total respondents, Majority (i.e.) 93.33% of the customers are satisfied about the mobile banking as most of the customers prefer to adopt the mobile banking services in the near future. 88.89% of the customers are satisfied with the ATM and 78.89% of the customers are satisfied about internet banking. 86.67% of the customers are satisfied about credit/debit cards service and 81.11% are satisfied about the Electronic fund transfer services by the customer. The chi-square analysis (χ^2=53.1, df=8, P=0.000) result shows there is relationship between the customer preference towards E-banking services and their level of satisfaction. Thus, most of the respondent is aware and satisfied with the services provided by the bankers (Table 8). Easy and convenient access, confidentiality, service quality and time saving are the factors influencing the respondents to prefer e-banking services at 75.56%, 55.56%, 74.44% and 81.11% respectively in Tuticorin district. 70%, 54.44%, 85.56%, 34.44%, and 97.78% of the respondents are influenced by factors such as transparency, accuracy, cost saving, ubiquity, and speed respectively to prefer e-banking services of the commercial banks. Social status, security, control over funds, time out feature and exchange of information are the motivating factors for the customers at 95.56%, 50%, 40%, 58.89% and 90% respectively to prefer

Age in Group (in years)	No. of Respondents
Up to 25	36 (40)
Between 26-50	39 (43.33)
Above 50	15 (16.67)
Total	90 (100)

Table 1: Distribution of sample respondents according to their age. Source: Primary Data. Figures in brackets represent percentages to total.

Gender	No. of Respondents
Male	55 (61.11)
Female	35 (38.89)
Total	90 (100)

Table 2: Distribution of sample respondents according to their gender. Source: Primary Data. Figures in brackets represent percentages to total.

Marital Status	No. of Respondents
Married	58 (64.44)
Unmarried	32 (35.56)
Total	90 (100)

Table 3: Distribution of sample respondents according to their marital status. Source: Primary Data. Figures in brackets represent percentages to total.

Educational Qualification	No. of Respondents
Illiterate	12 (13.33)
School level	20 (22.22)
College level	24 (26.67)
Professional	18 (20.00)
Diploma	16 (17.78)
Total	90 (100)

Table 4: Distribution of sample respondents according to their educational qualification. Source: Primary Data. Figures in brackets represent percentages to total.

Occupation	No. of Respondents
Employee	49 (54.44)
Business	12 (13.33)
Agriculture	8 (8.89)
Professional	11 (12.22)
Student	17 (18.89)
Total	90 (100)

Table 5: Distribution of sample respondents according to their occupation. Source: Primary Data. Figures in brackets represent percentages to total.

Income	No. of Respondents	Percentage
Up to Rs.1,00,000	33	36.67
Rs 1,00,001 to Rs 3,00,000	47	52.22
Above Rs 3,00,000	10	11.11
Total	90	100.00

Table 6: Distribution of sample respondents according to their income. Source: Primary Data.

Customer preference	Satisfied	Percentage	Not Satisfied	Percentage
Mobile Banking	84	93.33	6	6.67
E-Cheques	69	76.67	21	23.33
Phone Banking	61	67.78	29	32.22
Credit /Debit cards	78	86.67	12	13.33
ATM	80	88.89	10	11.11
Electronic fund transfer	73	81.11	17	18.89
Tele banking	54	60	36	40
Internet Banking	71	78.89	19	21.11
SMS Banking	59	65.56	31	34.44

Table 7: Customer preference of E-banking services (n=90). Source: Primary data.

Motivating Factors	No. of Respondents	Percentage
Time saving	73	81.11
Accuracy	49	54.44
Ubiquity	31	34.44
Easy and convenient access	68	75.56
Cost saving	77	85.56
Transparency	63	70.00
Social status	86	95.56
Confidentiality	50	55.56
Exchange of information	81	90.00
Service quality	67	74.44
Security	45	50.00
Speed	88	97.78
Control over funds	36	40.00
Time out feature	53	58.89
Total	90	100.00

Table 8: Motivating factors to prefer E-banking services (n=90).

Service Quality Factors	Average Score Respondents	F-Statistic
Time factor	3.1032	1.1361
Reliability	2.1736	3.1432*
Queue management	2.1438	1.6413
On-line bill payments	2.3710	1.4351
Easy to use and user friendliness	3.2134	0.4751
Anytime and anywhere banking facility	3.6415	3.2185*
Convenience way of operating banking transactions	2.8124	3.6141*
*Significant at 5% level.		

Table 9: Customer perception on service quality factors.

e-banking services of the commercial banks in Tuticorin district of Tamilnadu.

Customer Perception on Service Quality Factors

The convenience of online banking is helping people gain greater control of their finances and contributing to changing patterns in cash withdrawal and day to day money management. [15,16] identified one of the very important service quality dimensions of i-banking service quality is reliability. Saving time is an importance factor which influences the customers prefers to use i-banking [15]. The most popular online transaction through internet banking is funds transfer/ bill payment [15]. Ease of use is another important determinant for the customer preferring the internet banking [15]. Online banking users say that convenience is the most important factor, online banking lets them access their accounts from anywhere and at any time [17]. One among the important dimensions of e-banking service quality is queue management Joseph et al. [18]. The attitude towards the above said customer perception on service quality factors is measured at a five point scale highly satisfied, satisfied, moderate, dissatisfied, highly dissatisfied which carries 5, 4, 3, 2, and 1 mark respectively. The mean score in the attitude towards various customer perceptions on service quality factors are measured by the customers separately is shown in the following table (Table 9). The customers are asked to rate each SQFs five point scale according to their order of satisfaction. The mean score of each SQFs and F-Statistic is given in table. According to the table customer perception on service quality factors was found high in the variables namely reliability, anytime and anywhere banking facility and convenience way of operating banking transactions. The mean score values of these variables are 3.1432, 3.2185 and 3.6141 respectively [19].

Future Expectations	No. of Respondents	Percentage
Reasonable cost	16	17.78
Expected neither technique intervention nor quality services	53	58.89
Security	21	23.33
Total	90	100.00

Table 10: Respondent's response with future expectations with E- banking services.

Difficulty	No. of Respondents	Percentage
Risky	11	12.22
Less Knowledge	45	50
High Fees	7	7.78
Complex to use	27	30
Total	90	100.00

Table 11: Difficulty for using the E-banking facility.

The significant differences among the different customers are noticed in the case of service quality factors namely reliability, anytime and anywhere banking facility and convenience way of operating banking transactions since the respective 'F' values are significant at 5 per cent level (Table 10). The table reveals that the opinion of customers on future expectations. Out of the total respondents, Majority (i.e.) 58.89% of the sample respondents have mentioned that they would like operate their banking transactions in a core banking environment which is free from neither technical intervention such as computer connecting nor 23.33% of the samples respondents expect the bank will provide security. 17.78% of the sample respondents have stated reasonable charges have to be imposed on their banking transaction (Table 11). The main difficulty for using the E-banking facility is less knowledge about the operations of banking facility (50%). Respondents also feel the services of E-banking too complex to use (30%) and respondents also believe the E-banking to be risky (12.22%).

Conclusions

The research report is based on primary data. According to the study, the researcher concludes that the most of the bank customers are aware about all the banking services in Tuticorin District of Tamilnadu. The banks further have to take necessary steps to educate the customers regarding the new technology and other services offered by the banks. Banks may extend customer meeting time with bank officials and also friendly approach is necessary. Definitely it will help to retain the existing customers and to attract new customers. It will automatically improve the banking service and development of banks in India and also in abroad. The research report is useful to know the consumer awareness of e-banking system and what types of risk involved in e-banking system.

References

1. American Banker (2000) Web Banks Beat Branches on Ratios but there's No Competition.
2. Beer Stan (2006) Customers Preference on Internet Banking Survey.
3. Kevin B (2001) Has dot.com Banking Peaked? ABA Banking Journal. pp: 73-75.
4. Boss S, McGranahan D, Mehta A (2000) Will the Banks Control Online Banking? The McKinsey Quarterly.
5. Jim B (2002) Online Banking by the Numbers.
6. Chris C (2000) Pioneer Internet-Only Bank Has a new Strategy. American Banker, p: I.

7. Tom E (2001) The Economics of Online Banking. Target Marketing. February, p: 67.

8. Feinman T, Goldman D, Wong R, Cooper N (1999) Security Basics: A Whitepaper.

9. Financial Services Security Lab Background (2001) Security Issues and Threats. Banking Industry Technology Secretariat.

10. Fugazy, Danielle (2002) Banking: Online Banking: To Be or Not To Be. Web Finance.

11. Furash, Edward E (1994) Payments system under siege: customers want information along with monetary transfers, non-banks are providing it. ABA Banking Journal, Vol-86, p: 55.

12. Furst K, Lang WW, Nolle DE (2000) Internet Banking: Developments and Prospects. Office of the Comptroller of the Currency.

13. Healy, Thomas J (1999) Why You Should Retain Your Customers. America's Community Banker. p: 22.

14. IAMAI's Report on Online Banking (2006).

15. Johnson JR (1999) Raising relationships: the art and science of connecting with customers. Bank Marketing, p: 16.

16. Joseph M, McClure C, Joseph B (1999) Service Quality in Banking Sector: The Impact of Technology on Service Delivery. International Journal of Bank Marketing, 17: 182-191.

17. Jun M, Cai S (2001) The key Determinants of Internet Bank Service Quality: a Content Analysis. International Journal of Bank Marketing, 19: 276-291.

18. Online Banking Report (2009) Internet Strategies for Financial Institutions.

19. Radecki LJ, Wenninger J, Orlow DK (1997) Industry structure: electronic delivery's potential effects on retail banking. Journal of Retail Banking Services, Vol-19, p: 57.

4

Corruption and the Nigeria External Reserves Management

Williams Agbara*

Department of Economics, Benue State University, Makurdi, Nigeria

Abstract

This study investigates the impact of corruption on the Nigeria external reserves management. ADF unit root test, Johansen Co-integration, ECM, granger causality and OLS were the technics implore in estimating the data for this study and it reveals that there is a unidirectional relationship between corruption and external reserves and that corruption is positively related to external reserves though corruption is a menace that has eaten deep into the nation's economy and it is embedded in the management process of our external reserves. Exchange rate has a positive relationship with external reserves. The study concluded that corruption is embedded in the management process of our external reserves. The process of managing the nation's external reserves causes corruption in the country and that corruption has grossly affected the polity of Nigeria and it is seriously affecting the ability of the country to grow.

Keywords: Corruption; Exchange rate; External reserves; Management and gross domestic product

Introduction

In Nigeria, corruption is one of the most dangerous social troubles bedeviling the economy. Its nature is thus one that is ubiquitous and endemic in modern governments. This is because corruption like a virus attacks the prominent structures that make for society's progressive functioning thus putting its existing into serious danger [1]. Corruption is a teething national problem that deserves to be study because the long history of Nigerian government and politics is characterized by endemic problem of corruption, especially in high places. Most programs and people oriented policies and projects embarked upon by successive administrations since independence has either been abandoned or shoddily executed as a result of the incidence of corruption in the polity [2]. Evidently in Nigeria today, public office holders with high impunity level loot public treasury for their private and personal interest and accumulate wealth for self-aggrandizement.

In the years past Nigeria has taken numerous policy initiatives and measures in the management of its external reserves. Although very little was achieved because the structure in place then could not support efficient reserves management, enduring lessons could be distilled from the nation's past experience (CBN) as cited by Abubakar [3]. Thus, since the 1970s, Nigerian economy has persistently depended on oil as the main source of foreign exchange earnings with the attendant cycles of economic booms and bursts.

Oil marketers tend to influence or pressurize the Nigeria government to yield to their yearnings of increasing pump price of petrol for their interest. The corrupt activities of Bureau de Change and the parallel market have impacted on the exchange rate causing the dollar to exchange at a higher rate against the naira and the possible reason behind all these anomalies was that corruption seems to have become institutionalized and enjoy official recognition, this has invariably affected the pace of socio political and economic development in the country which is giving birth to irresponsible leaders in the polity.

It is against this backdrop that this research work is anchored upon so as to ascertain the impact of corruption on the Nigeria external reserves management.

Conceptual and Literature Review

Corruption according to World Bank [4] is the abuse of public office for private gains; public office is abuse for private gains when an official receives, solicits, or extorts a bribe. It is also abused when private agents vigorously offer bribe to circumvent public policies and processes for competitive advantage and profit. Public office can also be abused for personal advantage even if there is no bribery, through a patronage and nepotism, the theft of state's assets or diversion of state revenue. In any manner corruption manifested and by whatever way it is known, Ajegi [5] admit that, it is certainly an anti-social, self-centered activity whose primary objective is to enhance the satisfaction of the perpetrator to the detriment of the larger society. It robes the society of scarce resources and weakens the efficiency and effectiveness of organizations within and outside the public realm.

IMF [6] in its Balance of Payments Manual, 5th edition defined international reserves as "consisting of official public sector foreign assets that are readily available and controlled by the monetary authorities, for direct financing of payment imbalances, and directly regulating the magnitude of such imbalances, through intervention in the exchange markets to affect the currency exchange rate and/or for other purposes".

According to Eichengreen and Adalet [7], in recent decades, currency and financial crises accompanied by reversals in capital flows have become more frequent and severe. Therefore, with increased financial integration, countries are vulnerable to infection within and outside their expanses. Consequently, central banks in developing countries have accumulated reserves to cushion extreme events, the gathering of external debt maturities, and other shocks that could affect the foreign exchange market and the local economy.

Abubakar posit that when power shifted from military to democratic based government, a lot of internal crisis and debates on

***Corresponding author:** Williams Agbara, Department of Economics, Benue State University, KM 2 Gboko Road Makurdi, Benue State 234, Nigeria E-mail: agbarawilliams89@gmail.com

external reserves was witnessed by Nigerians. For instance, between 2005 and 2006, the then president Olusegun Obasanjo was called to face a panel before the National Assembly for the illegal withdraws of billons of naira from the country's external reserves in the name of some settlements such as payments to Paris Club Creditors to remove Nigeria's debt, payment for the support of Niger-Delta power plants establishment and withdrawal for emergency fund to support Census 2006. The allegation was that these monies were not authorized by the National Assembly. In the same manner, Nwakego as cited by Abubakar observed that the Nigerian government has spent billions of dollars since 2008 to maintain an exchange rate of 150 naira to the dollar. The nation's foreign reserve which was at least 60 billion dollars in 2008 is 26.5 billion dollars today such that tens of billions of dollars has gone into propping up a depreciating naira.

Most economists in their analysis argued that a nation with mismanaged external reserve will witness crisis like retrogressive growth and development, weakness in foreign exchange, excessive external debts, upsurge poverty, rising mass unemployment, millions of workers will be struggling to have access to basic amenities, low level of living standards among others.

Empirical/Theoretical Review

Adewale [8] investigates the crowding-out effects of corruption in Nigeria, covering the periods from 1996 to 2009, he uses simulation approach to investigate the economic implications of corruption in Nigeria, employs Error Correction Mechanism (ECM) to overcome the problem of spurious regression, to ascertain the degree of stationarity of variables employed in the study and the co-integrating properties of the data; the Augmented Dickey-Fuller (ADF) test was employed. He founds that all the econometric test applied in the study show statistically significant relationship between the model, thus, he concluded that corruption retards economic growth in Nigeria, that is corruption has a crowding-out effect on growth. Fabayo et al. [9], in their study analyzed the consequences of corruption on investment in Nigeria using the Ordinary Least Square technique. They use the annual corruption perception index between the period 1996 and 2010. Their study revealed that low Corruption Perception Index ranking on Nigeria, which implies high level of corruption, leads to low investment and thus low economic growth in Nigeria.

Aliyu and Elijah [10] investigated the impact of corruption on economic growth from 1986-2007. A Barrotype endogenous growth model was adopted so also the Engle-Granger [11] cointegration and error correction mechanism (ECM) techniques were employed. The core channels through which corruption affects growth were government capital expenditure, human capital development and total employment. Results show that corruption has significant negative effect on economic growth. The study also found that corruption exerts negative impact on both human capital development and total employment, but it positively impacts on government capital expenditure. The positive effect of corruption on capital expenditure is said to be however not surprising because public expenditure figure will always be inflated with the intention of siphoning or embezzling a reasonable proportion of the total value. The paper discovers that corruption exerts both direct and indirect negative effects on economic growth in Nigeria.

This study adopts the "Economic Growth theory of corruption" because it lays more emphasis on the long-run growth rate of an economy and on the basis of endogenous factors rather than exogenous factors of the neoclassical growth theory. This theory was propounded in reactions to the deficiencies in the Solow-Swan growth theory or model by Arrow, Lucas; and Romer [12,13]. This theory as propounded lay more emphasis on the long-run growth rate of an economy and on the basis of endogenous factors rather than exogenous factors of the neoclassical growth theory. The Solow-Swan model explains that the long-run growth rate of output is based on two basic exogenous variables such as population growth rate and level of corruption in the country. The growth theory emphasizes on technical progress resulting from the rate of capital stock, human capital development, reduction in corruption and investment rate.

Research Methodology

This study investigates the impact of corruption on the Nigeria external reserves management. The data used in this study were secondary data collected from CBN bulletin. The study period span from 1996-2015 and the time series data also cover the same period. Variable were divided into dependent and independent variables. The dependent variable is external reserves (EXTR) whereas; the independent variables are corruption perception index (CPI), exchange rate (EXCR), real interest rate (INTR) and Gross Domestic Product (GDP). The estimations were carried out using Eviews8.

Model specification

The model for this study examines the impact of corruption and exchange rate on external reserves. The model is formulated as below:

$$\text{EXTR}=f(\text{CPI, EXCR, INTR, GDP}) \quad (1)$$

$$\text{EXTR}=\alpha_0\ \alpha_1\text{CPI}\ \alpha_2\text{EXCR}\ \alpha_3\text{INTR}\ \alpha_4\text{GDP} \quad (2)$$

$$\Delta\text{EXTR}_t = \alpha_0 + \alpha_1 \Sigma_{i=1}^{n} CPI_{t-1} + \alpha_2 \Sigma_{i=0}^{n} EXCR_{t-1} + \alpha_3 \Sigma_{i=0}^{n} INTR_{t-1} + \alpha_4 \Sigma_{i=0}^{n} GDP_{t-1} + \mu_t \ldots \quad (3)$$

Where:

α_0 is Constant term, α_1 - α_3 is Parameter estimate, μ_t is Stochastic disturbance term, EXTR is External Reserves, CPI is Corruption Index, EXCR is Exchange rate, INTR is Real interest rate, GDP is Gross Domestic Product. The A priori expectation provides expected signs and significance of the value of the coefficient of the model parameters to be estimated in light of economic theory and empirical evidence. It is expected that $\alpha_1<0$, $\alpha_2>0$, $\alpha_3<0$ and $\alpha_4>0$.

Estimation technique

This study employs quantitative tools of data analysis. The Augmented Dickey-Fuller (ADF) unit root test was used to test for stationary of the variables. This test is justified by Gujarati [14] that "if we are dealing with time series data, we must make sure that the individual time series are either stationary or that they are cointegrated. If this is not the case, we may open to the charge of engaging in spurious regression analysis." Co-integration test was conducted to know whether the variables have a long-term or equilibrium relationship between them. The assumption of co-integration is that if in the long run two or more series move closely together, even though the series themselves are trended, the difference between is constant. A lack of co-integration means that the series have no long relationship. The Error Correction Mechanism (ECM) is then used to correct for disequilibrium which involves reconciling the short-run behavior of the economic variable with its long-run behavior. The Vector Autoregressive (VAR) Granger Causality test is conducted to ascertain the causal relationship between corruption, exchange rate and external reserves. The granger causality test determines the causal relationship or the direction of causality between series. This test is necessary because the direction of causation between external reserves, exchange rate and corruption is not really certain. The relationship between the variables was estimated using the ordinary least square technique.

Discussion of Empirical Results

Augmented Dickey Fuller unit root test

Unit root test was carried out to determine if the variables are stationary and if not, to determine the number of times they are to be differenced to achieve stationary. The variables were tested each to see the order of integration in which they achieve stationary. This can be seen by comparing the absolute value of the Augmented Dickey fuller (ADF) test with the critical values at different level of significance.

From Table 1 above the variables are not stationary at level except for INTR that is stationary at level 1(0) indicating that it has no unit root at 1%, 5% and 10% significant level. As a result of not attaining stationary at level all the variables were tested at first difference and it can be seen that they all attained stationary at first difference hence, they are integrated of the same order. It could be observed from the same table that EXTR is the variable that is stationary at 5% and 10% significance level.

Johansen co-integration test

This test is use to check if a linear combination of the integrated variables are stationary over the long-run, and if it is so, then it means co-integration exists among the variables, this further implies that a long run relationship exist among the variables. The result is as below.

Table 2 shows that a long term linear relation is present in (Trace Staistics) and Table 3 (Maximum Eigenvalue) using MacKinnon-Haug-Michelis [15] p-values. In the co-integration tables, the trace statistic and maximum eigenvalue statistic indicate co-integration at the 5% level of significance, suggesting that there is co-integrating (or long run) relationship between EXTR, CPI, EXCR, INTR and GDP. The result of the co-integration test suggests that external reserves have equilibrium condition with corruption, exchange rate, interest rate and GDP which keep them in proportion to each other in the long run. The evidence of co-integration among the variables rules out spurious correlations which implies that one direction of influence can be established among the variables. But the existence of co-integration vectors among a group of variables may not imply that there is causal influence between pairs of variables in the model of co-integration test. The trace test rejected the null hypothesis (H_0) that there is no co-integrating relationship between the variables and the test base on the maximum Eigen value also rejected the null hypothesis. They both show that there is co-integrating equation at the 0.05 level of significance. Since the two tests are giving the same result, it shows that the variables are co-integrated.

From Table 4 the coefficient estimates can be interpreted in terms of long run elasticity and the t-statistics is used to determine the statistical significance of each variable. The rule of thumb states that, a variable is statistically significant if the absolute value of its t-statistic is approximately 2 or above. Our concern here is the relationship that exists between corruption, and external reserves. From Table 4, corruption is elastic in relation to Nigeria external reserves, meaning that in the long run, a change in the corruption index will cause a more than proportionate change in external reserves and the t-statistic of CPI shows that the coefficient is statistically significant.

Variables	Level	Order of Integration	First difference	Order of Integration
CPI	-2.189174	1(0)	-5.476396*	1(1)
EXCR	-1.351992	1(0)	-4.034843*	1(1)
INTR	-5.935054*	1(0)	-	-
GDP	0.256049	1(0)	-4.423324*	1(1)
EXTR	-1.341455	1(0)	-3.501048**	1(1)

Source: Author's computation using Eviews8

Table 1: Unit Root *Variable stationary at 1%, 5% and 10% critical values, ** Variables stationary at 5% and 10% critical values, *** Variables stationary at 10% critical values.

Hypothesized No. of CE(s)		Eigenvalue	Trace Statistic	0.05
None*	0.998454	186.8545	69.81889	Prob.**
At most 1	0.783786	70.35270	47.85613	0.0000
At most 2*	0.774453	42.78595	29.79707	0.0001
At most 3	0.459530	15.97989	15.49471	0.0010
At most 4*	0.238492	4.904190	3.841466	0.0423

Source: Author's computation using Eviews8.

Table 2: Unrestricted Cointegration Rank Test (Trace), Trace test indicates 5 cointegrating eqn(s) at the 0.05 level, * denotes rejection of the hypothesis at the 0.05 level.

Hypothesized No. of CE(s)	Eigenvalue	Max- Eigen Statistic	0.05 Critical Value	Prob.**
None*	0.998454	116.5018	33.87687	0.0000
At most 1	0.783786	27.56675	27.58434	0.0503
At most 2*	0.774453	26.80606	21.13162	0.0071
At most 3	0.459530	11.07570	14.26460	0.1505
At most 4*	0.238492	4.904190	3.841466	0.0268

Source: Author's computation usin g Eviews8.

Table 3: Unrestricted Cointegration Rank Test (Maximum Eigenvalue), Max-eigenvalue test indicates 1 cointegrating eqn(s) at the 0.05 level, * denotes rejection of the hypothesis at the 0.05 level, **MacKinnon-Haug-Michelis (1999) p-values, H0: there is no co-integrating relationship among the integrated variables, H1: there is co-integrating relationship among the integrated variables.

Variables	EXTR	CPI	EXCR	INTR	GDP
Coefficient	1.000000	-3.95989	-0.085946	0.566607	0.043552
Standard error		(0.02688)	(0.00321)	(0.01213)	(0.00107)
		-147.3173	-26.7744	46.7112	40.7028

Source: Author's computation using Eviews8.

Table 4: Normalized co-integrating coefficients.

Error correction mechanism (ECM)

ECM captures the reconciliation of the variables over time from the position of disequilibrium to the period of equilibrium [16]. The ECM coefficient is known as the speed adjustment factor, it tells how fast the system adjusts to restore equilibrium. The basic criteria for analyzing ECM are: The ECM must lie between 0 and 1; for it to be meaningful it must be negative. If it is positive there is no error correction and it diverges and the T-statistic must be significant that is, it must be greater than 2. Below is the ECM result (Table 5).

The CPI speed of adjustment coefficient is -0.417568. The ECM is negatively signed and its magnitude lies between 0 and 1. The significance of this is that it supports co-integration and it shows that there exists a long run steady equilibrium between external reserves and the explanatory variables. The error correction model in this equation means that about 41.76% of errors generated between each period are correlated in subsequent periods and also, it is significant judging from the value of the T-statistic [-4.12783].

Granger causality test

This test is conducted to ascertain the causal relationship between corruption and external reserves. If the probability is less than the critical value it means it is significant i.e. there is a causal relationship between external reserves and corruption. Mathematically it is stated as

$\Delta Y_2 \rightarrow \Delta Y_1$ or $\Delta Y_1 \rightarrow \Delta Y_2$

$H_o = \Delta Y_2 \rightarrow \Delta Y_1$ or $\Delta Y_1 \rightarrow \Delta Y_2$

From Table 6 it could be seen that there is a causal relationship between external reserves and corruption in Nigeria. The relationship between external reserves and corruption is unidirectional. We reject the null hypothesis and accept the alternative hypothesis that external reserves granger cause corruption. Also, we accept the null hypothesis that corruption does not granger cause external reserves. The above result means that external reserves management in Nigeria can cause corruption but corruption itself does not account for the increase or decrease of the Nigeria external reserves. Also from Table 6 there is a causal relationship between exchange rate and external reserves. The relationship between the two variables is significant. This means that as Nigeria naira continue to depreciate against the dollar our external reserves will continue to deplete.

EXTR=1.146096+0.002254-0.028335+0.025375

From Table 7 the relationship between corruption and external reserves is positive as against our prior expectation which suggest a negative relationship. This could be due to the fact that corruption is embedded in the management process of our external reserves. The coefficient of corruption is 1.146096 indicating that a percentage increase in corruption will increase external reserves by 14.60%. This result agrees with Ajie Etal [17-20] who in their study "Corruption and Economic growth in Nigeria" find out that an increase in corruption leads to an increase in FDI. Exchange rate and gross domestic product are positively related to external reserves. On the other hand interest rate has a negative relationship with external reserves with it coefficient being -0.028335 indicating that an increase in interest rate will reduce external reserves by 02.8%. This conforms to our expectation of a negative relationship. The correlation coefficient (R) is 0.616732 signifying that there is 62% of relationship between external reserves and corruption, exchange rate, interest rate and gross domestic product [21,22]. The coefficient of determination (R^2) is 0.544869 indicating that 54% of the total variation of external reserves is attributed to corruption, exchange rate, interest rate and gross domestic product while 46% is as a result of the error term. The Durbin Watson statistics is 0.256349 indicating the absence of autocorrelation.

Variables	ECM(-1)	S. E.	T. Statistic
D(CPI)	-0.417568	0.10116	-4.12783
D(EXCR)	-0.9063	0.7066	-1.28262
D(INTR)	-0.355323	1.82317	-0.19489

Source: Author's Computation using Eviews8.

Table 5: ECM.

Null Hypothesis:	Obs	F-Statistic	Prob.
EXTR does not Granger Cause CPI	18	3.87990	0.0477
CPI does not Granger Cause EXTR		0.54859	0.5906
EXCR does not Granger Cause CPI	18	3.80201	0.0501
CPI does not Granger Cause EXCR		2.11458	0.1603
EXCR does not Granger Cause EXTR	18	1.97567	0.1782
EXTR does not Granger Cause EXCR		2.53198	0.1179

Source: Author's Computation using Eviews8.

Table 6: Pairwise Granger Causality Tests.

Dependent Variable: EXTR	Variable	Coefficient	Std. Error	t-Statistic	Prob.
	CPI	1.146096	0.480354	2.385942	0.0297
	EXCR	0.002254	0.076432	0.029485	0.9768
	INTR	-0.028335	0.181607	-0.156022	0.878
	GDP	0.025375	0.020195	1.256502	0.227
R-squared		0.616732	Mean dependent var		26.6965
Adjusted R-squared		0.544869	S.D. dependent var		17.96511
S.E. of regression		12.11988	Akaike info criterion		8.004428
Sum squared resid		2350.264	Schwarz criterion		8.203574
Log likelihood		-76.04428	Hannan-Quinn criter.		8.043303
Durbin-Watson stat		0.256349			

Source: Author's Computation using Eviews8.

Table 7: Ordinary least squares result.

Summary, Recommendation and Conclusion

The results of this study are summarized as follows:

- The unit root test suggests that corruption, exchange rate, external reserves and gross domestic product are stationary at first difference whereas, interest rate is stationary at level. The co-integration test carried out indicates that corruption, exchange rate, interest rate, gross domestic product and external reserves have a long run relationship. Corruption is elastic in relation to Nigeria external reserves, meaning that in the long run, a change in corruption will cause a more than proportionate change in the external reserves.
- The causality test indicates that there is a unidirectional causal relationship between corruption and external reserves. That is to say that External reserves management cause corruption but corruption does not cause external reserves. Also exchange rate granger cause external reserves.
- The study also shows that corruption has a negatively positive relationship with external reserves due to the fact that corruption is embedded in the management process of our external reserves.

This study recommends that:

- Drastic measures should be put in place to check corruption in both public and private sectors. The government should not just adopt a one-sided means of curbing this menace that have eating deep into the country's economy causing huge loses and damages to the economy.
- Exchange rate should be kept low and stable avoiding too much of volatility, this could be achieved if accurate monetary policies are put in place such as allowing market forces to determine the

exchange rate in the long run and fixed exchange rate in the short run to allow for adjustments.

- Government should make policy changes that reduce corruption both at the demand and supply side.

This study investigates the impact of corruption on the Nigeria external reserves management. ADF unit root test, co-integration, ECM, granger causality test and OLS were the estimation technics implore in this study. The study found out that corruption has a positive but negative relationship with external reserves. This establishes the fact that corruption is embedded in the management process of our external reserve. The Process of managing the nation's external reserves causes corruption in the country and that corruption has grossly affected the polity of Nigeria and it is seriously affecting the ability of the country to grow.

References

1. Ameh E (2016) Corruption and the Survival of Nigeria Democracy: An assessment an unpublished B.sc Political Science project work submitted to the Department of Political Science Benue State University, Makurdi.
2. Akeem L (2015) Combating Corruption for Sustainable Democracy in Africa.
3. Abubakar J (2012) How external reserves management can hurt Nigeria's economic development. Economic confidential Nigeria export-import Bank.
4. World Bank (1997) Helping combat Corruption: The role of the world bank. Poverty Reduction and Economic Management.
5. Ajegi SO (2002) The Affluence of Poverty: A Critical Evaluation of Nigeria's Poverty Reduction Programme. Journal of Economics and Social Research 1.
6. International Monetary Fund (2003) Guidelines for Foreign Exchange Reserve Management.
7. Eichengreen B, Adalet (2005) Current Account Reversals: Always a Problem. NBER Working Paper No. 11634.
8. Adewale SB (2011) The crowding-out effects of corruption in Nigeria: An empirical study. E3 Journal of Business Management and Economics 2: 059-068.
9. Fabayo JA, Posu SMA, Obisanya AA (2011) Corruption and the Investment Climate in Nigeria. Journal of Economic and Sustainable Development 2.
10. Aliyu S, Elijah AO (2008) Corruption and Economic growth in Nigeria: 1986-2007.
11. Engle RF, Granger CW (1987) Cointegration and Error Correction: Representation, Estimation, and Testing. Econometrica 55: 251-276.
12. Lucas R (1988) On the Mechanics of Economic Development. J Monetary Econ 22: 3-42.
13. Romer P (1990) Increasing Returns and Long-run Growth. J Pol Econ 94: 1002-1037.
14. Gujarati DN (2006) Essentials of Econometrics. New York McGraw-Hill/Irwin.
15. MacKinnon JG, Haug AA, Michelis L (1999) Numerical Distribution Functions of Likelihood Ratio Tests for Cointegration. Journal of Applied Econometrics 14: 563-577.
16. Ogundipe AA, Ojeaga P, Ogundipe OM (2013) Estimating the Long-run Effect of Exchange Rate Devaluation on the trade balance in Nigeria. European Scientific Journal 9: 233-345.
17. Ajie HA, Oyegun G (2015) Corruption and Economic Growth in Nigeria: An Empirical Analysis 1996-2013. European Journal of Business and Management 7.
18. Ayua IA (2001) Overview of Corruption in Nigeria. Journal of Political and Administrative studies 1: 38-52.
19. Burke D, Lane P (2001) The Empirics of Foreign Reserves. Open Econ Rev 12: 423-434.
20. Charles-Anyaogu Nneka B (2012) External Reserves: Causality Effect of Macro Economic Variables in Nigeria: 1980-2009. Kuwait Chapter of Arabian Journal of Business and Management Review 1: 14-27.
21. Johansen S, Juselius K (1990) Manimum Likelihood Estimation and Inference on Co-integration with the Application to the Demand for Money. Oxford Bulletin of Econometrics and Statistics 52: 169-210.
22. Oluwatomisin MO, Paul O, Adeyemi AO (2013) Oil Price and Exchange Rate Volatility in Nigeria. Journal of Economics and Finance 5: 1-9.

5

E-Commerce Innovations Customer Perceptions in Qatar

Abbott J Haron*

Higher Colleges of Technology, Sharjah, United Arab Emirates

Abstract

Over the past few years, the number of online retailers has gradually climbed in the region, with the country of Qatar making up a small but growing share in the region's e-commerce market, but still selling online in Qatar has one of the lowest percentages of on-line purchase world-wide. This paper investigates the perception of the Qatari consumers on e-commerce purchasing process and how it varies among individuals due to several positive and negative characteristics of e-commerce. It is found that the demand for online marketing activities is increasing considerably; however, some individuals are anxious about the safety of online payment processing.

Keywords: Innovations; Marketing, Pricing decisions; Channel structures; Channel strategies; Standardized advertising; Localized advertising

Introduction

Business environment in Qatar is highly competitive, with increasing on-line internet transactions and a flood of all types of e-commerce by national and international companies. Electronic Commerce is the exchange of business information, goods and services, physical and digital, and all types of transactions using electronic methods. These contain internal and external computer-connected networks such as the internet, the transfer of purchase orders to suppliers via electronic data interchange (EDI), the use of telephone and fax to perform transactions, the usage of ATMs, wireless, networks and smart cards to enable payment and gain digital cash. E-commerce contains all means by which activities and transactions are conducted in 'a cyber space environment' as compared with physical 'place' environment [1].

Adoption and application of e-commerce business operation actions can benefit both the organizations and consumers. Organizations can reduce business operation expenses through the adoption and implementation of this approach. In addition to this, the organizations can bring proficiency in the overall business operation process as it aids to reduce the overall business process lead time. On the other hand, customers can save their valued consumption time and cost through online buying and payment process that are offered by the e-commerce organizations. Furthermore, some people try to avoid online purchasing and payment process due to some concerns. However, it is true that several organizations are trying to overcome these concerns in order to maintain their brand image and continuous business growth rate. The perception about e-commerce procurement is from individuals' experiences and perceptions.

Recently, several organizations are started to shift from the traditional bricks-and-mortar physical stores to online e-commerce stores in order to meet current marketing preferences. GCC e-Commerce industry is projected to grow 35 per cent year-on-year to USD 15 billion in 2015 according to Visa International, making it the world's fastest-growing market for e-Commerce [2]. The regional e-Commerce marketplace is currently valued at USD 8 billion. According to Internet World Stats, there are over 90 million Internet users through the MENA area. Over the past few years, the number of online retailers has steadily climbed in the region, with Qatar making up a decent share of the region's e-Commerce market, with the region lead by the UAE followed by Saudi Arabia.

E-Commerce Qatar is expected to reach $ 8 billion by 2018 [3]. Although selling online in Qatar has one of the lowest percentages of online purchase world-wide, e-Commerce will be growing as a main megatrend for businesses across Qatar. Currently the total value of e-commerce in Qatar is estimated at $6 billion, but this is projected to accelerate and create new businesses and job opportunities. There are many benefits and conveniences of e-commerce or on-line transactions, as the economics of time and costs and a wide variety of choices. In this, Qatar, as a prosperous economic state and Business place with global outreach is falling in line with the global business trends. What is the consumer perception of e-commerce and its economics as a marketing instrument? The consumers with an average per capita income of $55K + are amongst the globally high income individuals and enjoy the benefit of a wide range of goods and services, many of which reputed global brands. Qatar is a comparatively young Arab nation founded in 1971, with one of the world's highest incomes per capita, this has made it an interesting subject for this case study.

Literature Review

The Globalization, deregulation and information technology are clouding boundaries in an increasing range of industries. There are numerous benefits of e-commerce according to Hamel and Prahalad. It provides option to the consumers to select among a wide variety of products especially in circumstances when the product or service is not available in local markets. It also helps consumers save time and money.

The use of online shopping has developed a lot at the domestic level as compared to cross-border sales. Due to this fragmentation, consumers may fail to take advantage of e-commerce such as cheaper fees and a wide range of choices for products. The retail sector in Qatar needs a better understanding of these circumstances such as the experience of consumers with respect to online shopping and the related internet selling and marketing approaches. The main question to be answered in this regard by Qatar is whether e-commerce is delivering its full potential in respect of welfare of consumer such as choice, price, satisfactory protection and quality. If not, then Qatar has to look into the matter and find out the size of lost potential, the main barriers in this regard and the remedies. The lost potential could be the choices that are available online to consumers regarding their products

***Corresponding author:** Abbott J Haron, Higher Colleges of Technology, Sharjah, United Arab Emirates, E-mail: abbottjharon@gmail.com

and the cheap prices. Research by Quelch and Klien [4] concluded that the internet will revolutionize the dynamics of global commerce and, in particular, lead to the more speedy internationalization of small to medium - sized enterprises (SMEs).

Hamill argued that the internet can prove SMEs with a low-cost entry to global markets by helping to overcome many of the barriers to internationalization normally experienced by small companies. Research by Poulsen indicated that majority of the users of the services browse for information but do not essentially complete their transactions in the similar electronic service channel, as there have been significant concerns about the security of financial transaction. The introduction of e-retail in Qatar emerged in 2009. It has been found that Qatar is one of the top countries in the world in respect of the purchasing power of consumers of luxury accessories and clothes. Qatar has a population which is estimated at 2.2 million, 10.3% of the population is Qatari, and 89% is non-Qatari. There are many companies such as Tejari.com, Souq.com, BurjMall.com, and Brownbag.ae, which have designed approaches so as to fit the needs of online consumers in the online market in Qatar. The purchase of products online by the consumers of Qatar rose to 42% in the year 2010 against 29% in the year 2009.

According to Siddiqui, ten factors that are interrelated which contribute to online shopping behaviors and approaches in Qatar. The factors are identified as exterior environment, individual characteristics, demographics, product features, quality of website, attitudes accepted towards shopping online, intention for online shopping, decision making, online purchasing, and customer satisfaction. External environment refers to the factors that are circumstantial and have a significant effect on the online shopping behavior and attitudes of consumers. It is a three dimensional structure.

The legal framework is the first which defends the online buyers from any loss that may result on account of an online transaction. The second is the acknowledgment of third party which basically deals with the honesty of vendors that operate online. The third element refers to the number of organizations that are competing with each other. The factor demographics disclose that the online shopping market in Qatar is led by the 25 to 44 age group. Young women in Qatar are resorting to the internet to purchase goods. Personal characteristics element comprises internet knowledge of customers, their need stipulations, cultural climate, trust temperament, participation with the product, and the extent of sharing information and values with others. Product features provide information regarding the characteristics of online stores, the products that are sold by them and the support services delivered to support the transactions. Website quality refers to the content of information on the business's website, its presentation, searching instrument, navigation, technical features of the site, security and media richness. Online shopping attitudes reflect the attitudes of consumers which affect their intention to shop online and decide whether there is a transaction ultimately. The intent to shop online refers to the inclination of customers to make purchases online. It also refers to the fact whether the shopper is making repeated purchases over the net and so it is also a depiction of customer loyalty. The decision to shop online refers to the pursuing of information, comparison of substitutes, and making choices by the shoppers. Purchasing online refers to the activities of placing orders by the consumers and also paying for it. Customer satisfaction refers to the degree to which perceptions of consumers are established by a favorable experience of online shopping. When the anticipations of consumers are met, a high degree of satisfaction is attained by consumers and this influences their attitudes, decisions, objectives, and the decision to shop online.

Many people in Qatar are using their mobile phones more than their personal computers to shop online. 29% of the individuals who use internet in Qatar have purchased products using their smart phones compared to 26% individuals who have resorted to personal computers to do so. Moreover, to provide more security to shoppers while transacting online, Qatar based QNB bank has entered into a partnership with Visa to use the system of Verified by Visa which will deliver added protection to online consumers of Qatar. This partnership has led to the launch of Double Secure service. Online bookings such as booking airline tickets over the net have proved to be very popular in Qatar. The e-banking concept has increased significant recognition in Qatar and this has resulted in increasing the trust of individuals while handling their money online. This has likewise opened up growth opportunities in the region.

The most popular product which is bought online in Qatar is clothing. According to Fernandes, Qatar has seen a continuous growth in sales after the introduction of ecommerce. As customers find a wide range of products to choose from and they also save time and money, it is very advantageous for them to buy products online. There are many companies in Qatar which have designed their strategies to suit the needs of online shoppers. Every organization has to focus on e-commerce to attain more business [5]. The monitoring of the e-commerce system necessitates an organization to measure present values against the values that are expected i.e., planned values. To realize efficiency in this regard, the subsystems of the e-commerce system must be proficient as well.

There are three measurement systems within the system of e-commerce like performance measurement, success measurement, and the testing of usability. Performance measurement refers to the technical parameters which are to be measured such as loading time of the web page, the time taken to process user commands, and the speed of reporting, etc. Success measurement should provide a link between the e-commerce system and the company objectives. Testing of usability is done in a laboratory. The companies in UAE that are focusing on e-commerce as a means to increase profitability must also understand that there are negative aspects of e-commerce. There is a lack in security while transacting online as well as the inability of consumers to test the product before buying it can be considered as drawbacks of the e-commerce system. According to Blythe, the organizations that are considering ecommerce as a basis for increasing their profitability must take note of the drawbacks of the ecommerce system and design their strategies accordingly. The consumers should feel free while purchasing products online. If this is achieved, the organizations will be in a much better position to take advantage of e-commerce.

According to researchers, Qatar's e-commerce transaction need to be regulated, There is a need to bring in specific laws to administer e-commerce transactions taking place in Qatar, especially given the volumes being shipped into this country from online vendors abroad. Qatar is on the fast track in taking to e-commerce within the region. While the ranks of locally based online vendors continue to grow, a substantial portion of the transactions are still being done with overseas sites.

E-Commerce Customer Perceptions in Qatar

It is highly recommended for organizations or researchers to adopt an appropriate research method in a research work in order to get an optimistic research outcome. Research methodology can be classified into two parts, such as qualitative research methodology and quantitative research methodology, has its particular advantages and disadvantages that needs to be considered by the researchers during the application of these methods in the research work [6]. Generally qualitative research approach used to deal with inner feelings, emotions, attitudes, gestures, thoughts and behaviors of people towards the research theme [7]. On the other hand, quantitative research method is used to dealing with the analysis and evaluation of sourced and gathered data and information. It can be considered by numerous organizations to adopt and implement an effective and appropriate research approach based on the nature of the study. This particular research work is investigative in nature in which the feelings, opinions, thoughts, behaviors and attitudes of people can be considered as the source of data and evidence. On the other hand, qualitative research deals with the feelings, sentiment, views and opinions of people. Therefore, it can be stated that the implementation of qualitative research will be effective in this research due to the exploratory nature of the study. It is true that the qualitative research approach is used to focus on describing the system or procedure of defining and measuring several significant variables.

Qualitative research methodology can be categorized into three major orientations, namely, theory construction approach, informative approach and language leaning approach. However, researchers generally implement language leaning approach in the research method in order to give language and meaning of the words. Explanatory approach can be considered as a throughout the description and interpretation of several important social phenomena that are centrally focused. Lastly, theory construction approach generally evaluates the connection between several essential social phenomena. Qualitative research methodology is applied in this study due to the interpretative nature of the exercise.

Data analysis is a significant aspect in any research work. Data collection process can be classified into two parts, such as primary data collection process and secondary data collection process. Primary data collection is the process of obtaining and the collection of raw and live data directly from the field work. On the other hand, secondary data collection is collection of data from numerous existing databases. There are numerous advantages and disadvantages of these two data collection procedures. Primary data collection process can be considered as most significant data collection process that helps the researchers to source current and up-to-date data and information that can aid the researchers to enhance effective and positive research outcome. In terms of disadvantages, primary data collection process is costly and time consuming that can increase the research cost and research time. It can affect overall research result. On the other hand, a researcher can source effective, large number of data and information in limited time and cost, this can bring efficiency to the overall research process. In terms of disadvantages, validity and correctness of the collected data through secondary data collection process cannot be determined. Observing the advantages and disadvantages of both the data collection process, it can be stated that the adoption of both primary and secondary data collection process can be effective and beneficial. Several academic text books and the views of several authors have been considered as the effective secondary data collection sources for this research.

After all these methodological points, the researchers had taken recourse to primary data collection by means of open-ended questionnaire directly from a sample of individuals (50). In terms of primary data collection process, the researcher has combined an open ended interview process to source and gather nominal data. In the present study, 37 respondents out of 50 are purchasing products online. They, thereby, save buying/advertising, and execution cost and time. Their daily busy work schedule forces them to purchase products and services online for which they have necessary devices and connectivity. On the other hand, the rest of the 13 respondents were not happy with the online consumption process and purchasing activities due to several related risks. For 36, 'Yes' respondents quite happy with the organization's e-commerce business process giving them numerous products and services in a rapid period of time compared to the traditional shopping and consumption activities. On the other hand, for the 12 'No' ones, online payment procedure is a problem due to the often systems breakdown. 2 respondents had negative observations on the e-commerce business activities. Each and every respondent has specified that the organizations should try to ensure effective quality control in the online marketing actions. 2 respondents have experienced insufficient service quality as the organizations failed to maintain efficiency in the online order processing and online payment process. Adequacy and efficiency are the major aspects that need to be combined in the e-commerce business operation process in order to augment effective business performance. All the 50 respondents have responded that the organizations should try to hire or appoint skilled technological professionals who can fix the issues and glitches and ensure effective online business operation process. Order processing, order distribution and online transaction are the major features of an e-commerce business operation. Therefore, it is highly imperative for the organizations to ensure the security of the personal information of the users or business shoppers during the online payment process to sustain its strong brand image in the competitive market place [8,9].

In terms of economic stability, all the 50 respondents have responded that e-commerce purchasing action can help the people to maintain their economic stability. They have replied that organizations are implementing online business operation activities due to growing market demand. In addition to this, the organizations can decrease their overall business operation cost by the embracing and implementation of e-commerce business operation strategy. Therefore, it will aid the organizations to offer products at competitive and economic price. Apart from online hacking of personal details and security concerns, each and every respondent has replied that the cost reduction process will help the e-commerce organizations to offer goods at economic price to grab the market share of other existing organizations.

It has been argued earlier that some respondents are unhappy with the e-commerce services of some organizations. Those unhappy respondents have answered that the e-commerce organizations should consider the customer feedback concerning the online product delivery or payment services to improve proficiency in the business operation process. Last but not the least; each and every respondent has agreed the forthcoming social trend of e-commerce purchasing activity can reduce the demand of traditional shopping and consumption actions. Each and every respondent has replied that the number of internet users in Qatar is increasing at a rapid pace. Therefore, recent market demand and favorable external environment for e-commerce business can eliminate the demand for traditional bricks-and-mortar business operation process. In addition to this, low consumption effort can increase the request for online e-commerce buying activities.

In terms of answers it can be specified that several individuals among the respondents are highly concerned with the online transaction or online order delivery process. It is true that several organizations are attempting to adopt and implement effective approaches in the business operation process in order to improve effective business performance. Nonetheless, it is clear from the responses from the respondents that the organizations need to improve the security feature of the websites during the online payment process to secure the individual information and account details of the buyers.

It is obvious from the analysis and findings that the trend of e-commerce purchasing has increased considerably among the people of Qatar, with Qatar gaining a positive economic growth, which makes the Qatari Government motivate several local MNCs to position shop in the global market place and also with the launch of the Qatari government World's first store features over 100 applications and provides services to about 700 consumers in a single location. At present, several leading organizations are trying to adopt and implement cutting-edge technological processes in the business operation actions in order to enhance effective business performance and gain possible competitive advantages. In addition, the demand for online product or service consumption is significantly snowballing among the people of Qatar as it helps to decrease their consumption time and costs. It is clear from the data analysis part. However, 70 per cent of the respondents are used to purchasing products or services through online. Nevertheless, in terms of cyber-hacking and security of personal details, each and every respondent is worried. It is the responsibility of the organizations to use effective business operation assets in the business operation activities to guarantee high quality control. Therefore, it is true that several organizations need to ensure effective business operation activities to protect the data of customers and business clients to preserve their high brand images in the global market place. In addition, it is highly imperative to use advanced and high quality technological assets and tools in the business process to ensure effective e-commerce business operation activities. Notwithstanding the presence of several leading conglomerate organizations, the leading domestic firms are also trying to implement e-commerce business operation tactics in the business process in order to grab the market share of the leading multinational organizations. However, people are only apprehensive about the quality of service and security of personal details. Consequently, it is quite important for each and every organization to focus on issues and overcome them to gain effective customer following.

Conclusion

Qatar is still a fast developing country, young, active, visionary and global. This effective continuous economic growth rate is motivating several organizations to enter into the emergent Qatar market, brisk business and global reach. Demand for online marketing actions is significantly increasing among the people of Qatar. Therefore, several new competitors are also following the strategies of leading multinational organizations by presenting e-commerce business operation activities. Several individuals may have either negative or positive insight about e-commerce purchasing activities. Individuals generally prefer e-commerce purchasing process in order to decrease the consumption time and cost. On the other hand, some individuals usually have negative perceptions on e-commerce purchasing activities due to numerous problematic reasons and concerns. It is true that, in some cases several leading organizations also face issues regarding the stealing of personal information and account details of the customers and several business clients. It is highly important for the organizations to take care of the wants and demand of people. The business environment in Qatar is becoming highly competitive as several organizations are attempting to implement competitive strategies in the business operation processes in order to gain possible competitive advantages. Therefore, effective sustainability and assurance of high quality security can help the organization to uphold effective brand image among the target consumers.

References

1. Burca SD, Fletcher R (2004) International Marketing - An SME Perspective. Prentice Hall-Financial Times press, UK.
2. Gulf News (2014) Dubai sets up e-commerce hub.
3. Ekosglobal (2014) Middle-East and North-Africa.
4. Quelch J, Klein L (1996) The Internet and International Marketing. Sloan Management Review: 60-75.
5. Akaka MA, Alden DL (2010) Global brand positioning and perceptions. International Journal of Advertising 29: 37-56.
6. Patton MQ, Cochran M (2002) A Guide to Using Qualitative Research Methodology. London School of Hygiene and Tropical Medicine, London, UK.
7. Slevitch L (2011) Qualitative and Quantitative Methodologies Compared: Ontological and Epistemological Perspectives. Journal of Quality Assurance in Hospitality & Tourism 12: 73- 81.
8. Slonim-Nevo V, Al-Krenawi A (2006) Success and Failure Among Polygamous Families: The Experience of Wives, Husbands, and Children. Family Process 45: 311-330.
9. Stephens BM (2008) Dubai - A star in the east: A case study in strategic destination branding. Journal of Place Management and Development 1: 62- 91.

6

Analyzing the Influence of Sales Promotion on Customer Purchasing Behavior

Mahsa Familmaleki[1]*, Alireza Aghighi[2] and Kambiz Hamidi[3]

[1]Department of Management and Accounting, College of Humanities, Hamedan Science and Research Branch, Hamedan, Iran
[2]Department of Management, Faculty of Economics and Management, Payame Noor University, Hamedan, Iran
[3]Faculty Member of Management and Accounting, Islamic Azad University Hamedan Branch, Hamedan, Iran

Abstract

The promotion mix is a term used to describe the set of tools that a business can use to communicate effectively the benefits of its products or services to its customers. The purpose of promotion is to reach the targeted consumers and persuade them to buy. Promotion has been defined as the coordination of all seller-initiated efforts to set up channels of information and persuasion to sell goods and services or promote an idea. Sales promotion is vital element of promotional mix.

The purpose of this study is to investigate the effects of sales promotion on buyer decision making process. In other words, the general objective of this study was to find out the effectiveness of some elements on the buying behaviors of customers. Marketing activities related to the promotion of sales increased consumer purchases and indirectly to get more profit for the company.

So, the purpose of sales promotion is to reach the targeted consumers and pervade them to buy .Sales promotion has become a vital tool for marketing and its importance has been increasing significantly over the years. One of the purposes of a sales promotion is to elicit a direct impact on the purchase behavior of the firm's consumers. Firms have to rethink the relationship between attitude and behavior of their consumers. In this study, we will discuss the impact of sales promotion on consumer purchasing behavior.

Keywords: Promotion mix; Sales promotion; Buyer decision making

Introduction

Modern marketing is more than just producing good products, suitable pricing and easy access to them [1]. Today, attracting new customers has become so important in modern retailing in addition to loyal to them and efforts have been paying in that perspective as known, the cost of keeping consumers present is less than the cost of gaining new customers. World of today's world is a benefit-cost. Firms have to rethink the relationship between attitude and behavior of their consumers. All businesses need to communicate to the consumer what they have to offer [2]. Promotion refers to the motivational methods of getting the consumer to purchase the product. Promotion is referred to as "any communication used to inform, persuade, and/or remind people about an organization's or individual's goods, Services, image, ideas, community involvement, or impact on society" [3]. Promotion (also referred to as Integrated Marketing Communication (IMC)) mainly consists of messages and related media that are used to communicate with the market. IMC is defined as "a marketing communications strategy which requires that a company adopts strategies that coordinate different promotional elements and that these promotional activities are integrated with other marketing activities that communicate with customers" [4]. The basics of promotional strategy involve delivering the communicational message from the producer to the consumer. The object of the message is to persuade the audience to purchase the product or service. Therefore the consumer needs to be receptive to the message and to be able to interpret it in such a way the intent to purchase is established [5]. Companies must communicate with their present and potential customers, as well as internally, and therefore makes it very important in the marketing process. A modern company manages a complex marketing communication system.

The promotion mix includes the tools like Advertising, Public Relations, Sales Promotion, Direct marketing and Personal Selling [6]. These elements are included in the integrated marketing communications mix (Figure 1). Before companies can begin the communicational process towards the consumer, they need to define the promotional objectives. These are the objectives "which determine a firm's promotional strategy, for example, increasing sales of improving brand recognition may require a different promotional mix" [4].

Sales promotion consists of a variety of incentive tools, mostly short term, that are used to stimulate consumers and/or dealers to accelerate the purchasing process or to increase quantities of sales [7]. Sales promotion is certainly one of the critical elements in marketing mix and toolkit for the marketers. Statistics for packaging companies show that sales promotion comprises nearly 75% of the marketing budget [8]. Marketing research, both theoretical and empirical, focuses on how sales promotion impacts the behavior of consumers, particularly their purchasing decisions [8-10].

Shultz, et al. [11] says that sales promotion generally works on a direct behavioral basis rather than affecting awareness or attitude. One of the purposes of a sales promotion is to elicit a direct impact on the purchase behavior of the firm's consumers. It is continuously said that most types of sales promotions affect the decision-making and purchasing stages of the buying process directly that is affective in the long-run since it leads to increased sales and profit [12]. A sales promotion stimulates customer purchases and the efficiency of distributors through marketing activities excluding advertising, public relations and so on. In other words, a sales promotion provides the incentive for consumers to purchase some specific products, and this incentive is different from the incentive provided by advertising with respect to the reasons to purchase those specific products. The purpose of a sales promotion is to attract new customers, maintain existing customers who are contemplating switching brands and give incentives to customers who are about to use competing products. Sales promotions vary depending on the situation and need, and they have an immediate effect on product purchases.

***Corresponding author:** Mahsa Familmaleki, Department of Management and Accounting, College of Humanities, Hamedan Science and Research Branch, Hamedan, Iran, E-mail: familmaleki@gmail.com

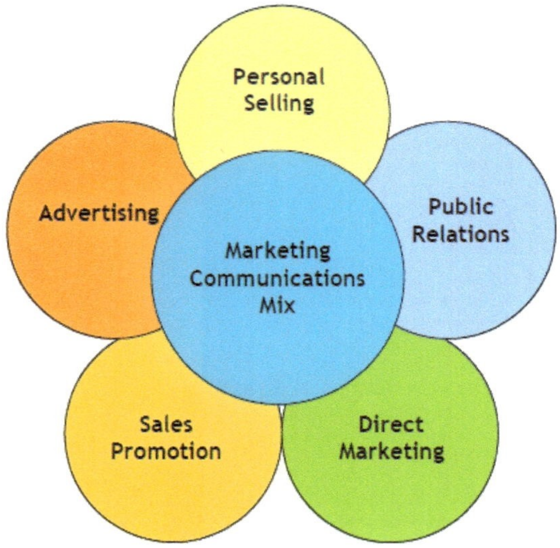

Figure 1: The elements of the Marketing Communications Mix.

According to Low and Mohr [13] manufacturers continue to spend a large amount from their communication budget on sales promotion. They allocate around 75 percent of their marketing communication budgets to sales promotion [14]. Similarly, we can see that companies spend a large portion of their budgets for sale promotion. The goal is to offer the merchandise more attractive and valuable. Buy and test consumer products direct specific goals that can be achieved through efforts to boost sales in the short term, the implementation of consumers in stores, and get to the point of retail sale displays, and encouraging stores to store products and sales support for the efforts of staff [15]. This information allows us to conclude that the institutions seek to manipulate the buying activities of consumers, and so begin a strong promotional campaigns or changes in pricing policies, with other measures. Event shows that a few consumer stand easily when they see the words of sales promotion. But price reduction, coupon or discount given by the retailer and other promotional equipment like free sample, bonus pack and "buy one get one free" were found to be encourage customer buy extra than they think [16].

The main objective of this research is to study the effect of different tools to promote sales on the buying behavior of consumers. Therefore, research on the promotional tools is actually important to understand most of the tools that affect the competition with its competitors, so they can use the most effective techniques to promote the right and attract customers. Typical tools include of free samples, price reduction, Giving advertising gifts, and Offering coupon, Offer member card, Able to pay by installments, Extend warranty period, and so on. Sampling is the process by sending the actual product or trial-sized customers. Is provided free samples of the merchandise to clients so that customers have the opportunity to try and use the products. Price promotion refers to reduction in price for a limited time, which offered to customers. The reduce in product prices play key parts in persuading customer's product test behavior and through this new customer can be paying attention [17]. Discount play an important role in today's markets and its application among retailers has been increasing during the last years and many empirical evidences confirm the use of temporary decrease of price to increase short term sales. Proper gifts are one of the best ways to transfer the message that communication is important. Oral communications are soon forgotten but gifts with company's mark on it act as a reminder and attract the customers [18]. Coupon has direct influence on increase of the sale through which consumers tendency toward the product increases [19].

Literature Review

Marketing defined

According to the American Marketing Association, quoted by Kotler and Keller [20], marketing can be defined as "an organizational function and a set of processes for creating, communicating, and delivering value to customers and for managing customer relationships in ways that benefit the organization and its stakeholders". Another simpler definition is presented as marketing "includes anticipating demand, managing demand, and satisfying demand" [3]. Marketing could also be defined in a few words with "mutually satisfying exchange relationships" [4]. The marketing mix is defined as "the specific combination of marketing elements used to achieve objectives and satisfy the target market. It encompasses decisions regarding four major variables: product, distribution, promotion, and price" [3]. The whole marketing mix is defined as "the set of controllable of controllable tactical marketing tools - product, price, place, and promotion - that the firm blends to produce the response it wants in the target market" [20].

Production and selling concept

The production concept is based on the fact that customers prefer products that are available and affordable. This means that production managers focus on the superiority of products as well as constant product development. The selling concept is based on the drive of the marketing, in other words that the customer will not buy enough of a single product unless it is constantly promoted [20]. The selling concept holds that consumers will not buy enough of the company's products unless they are stimulated through heavy selling and promotion [1].

Promotional mix

As one of the marketing mix elements, promotion includes all the activities directed to the targeted consumers, that lead to facilitate the process of contacting with them for the purpose of formatting a sense of the importance of the commodity in achieving a high degree of consumers satisfaction of their wishes and needs comparing with the competitors commodities (Mahmud I. Nour et al. [21]).

Promotion is one of the key factors in the marketing mix and has a key role in market success. Promotion is used to ensure that consumers are aware of the products that the organization is offering. The promotional mix is the combination of the different channels that can be used to communicate the promotional message to the consumers [22]. The channels to be used are; advertising, direct marketing, public relations and publicity, personal selling, sponsorship and sales promotion [23]. One of most important of channels is sales promotion.

Sales promotion

Defining the term sales promotion is rather difficult for the presence of multiple relating techniques and tactics and that sales promotion is a tool to achieve company's marketing communication objectives and an essential element in planning marketing [24]. Sales promotion is a short term strategy to derive demand and also and especial marketing offer which provides more profit than what consumers receive from the sale position of a product and also has sharper influence on sales [25].

A sales promotion consists of techniques that are aimed at increasing sales in the short run, meaning that they are mostly used for a short period of time. It offers control, and the costs can be much lower than of advertising. The main characteristics of sales promotions are that they offer better value for money and they try to cause responses immediately [26]. This tool has the ability to attract and keep loyal customers and is an excellent what to persuade them build viable link with the organization and involves all motifs applied by the producer to persuade trade with members of a channel [27]. Sales promotion has a strong ability to add value and to bring forward future sales. For sales personnel promotional tools are used primarily for motivating staff or supporting them in their selling roles. Brassington and Pettitt [28] provide a revised definition for sales promotions: "... a range of marketing techniques designed within a strategic marketing framework to add extra value to a product or service over and above the 'normal' offering in order to achieve specific sales and marketing objectives. This extra value may be a short-term tactical nature or it may be part of a longer-term franchise-building program."

Factor influencing consumer behavior

Consumer behavior is the process; thoughts, feelings and actions related to consumption process, this behavior is the dynamic interaction of the individual thoughts, feelings, actions and behavior in the environment by which the human being conducts exchange aspect of their lives. The environment refers to the external factors that influence the human being, these factors such as cultural and social forces in the society and in personal lives as well as physical and situational forces relates to the actual shopping experiences. The behavior is a dynamic interaction and communication between consumers and the marketers doing exchanges [29].

There are four main factors influencing consumer behavior each of these factors can influence a consumer action in different ways, a combination of these factors affect the decision making process differently, these factors are cultural, social and religious, personal and psychological.

Culture is an important combination of character, behavior and a self-identification of human being, these characteristics help an individual to create his or her own buying behavior, and however, isolating culture as a variable that can be studied and readily implanted is very difficult, taking into consideration that the buying behaviors of human beings consist of three phases which are the individual, societal and situational. Culture affects all these phases but the extent of the effect depends on the individual person and the circumstance [30]. Culture consists of beliefs, values and customs that serve to direct consumer behavior differently amongst the members of a particular group or society Values and beliefs are guides to behavior in such that they form and affect attitude on how to behave on certain situations, on the other hand customs are modes of behavior that constitute an acceptable way to behavior in a particular culture.

Social factors are very influential in the decision making process of the consumer, this can affect the decision making process in a positive or negative way. It may also consist of one person or few people such as spouses or someone you have never met but idealizes them, the influences of this reference or social group can be very strong in a way that a customer can change the behavior to meet the standards pushed by the reference group [31].

Gender roles have a significant effect on consumer behavior it defines what is appropriate for each gender in the form of behavior, attitude and appearance. And they are deeply integrated into the society and the people's mind, for example Male customers are interested in the café department where they meet other male friends to watch live sports or play games. And the female customers are interested in fashion, these different lifestyles help to determine consumer pattern of living which affects their purchasing behavior, if the company has an idea of the life style of its customers or a certain segments they can develop their marketing strategies to target these group of customers because consumer always chooses goods and services associated with their lifestyles. Age also plays an important role in the decision making process of a consumer for example children come and buy candy, soft drinks while adults specifically women buy fashion products, cosmetics, households keepings and food stuff [31]. Religion is a symbol which acts to establish a powerful, pervasive and long-lasting modes and motivation. It is achieved by formulating conception of a general order of existence and further, by clothing this conception with such an aural of factuality that the mood and motivation seems uniquely realistic [32].

Religion affects attitude and behaviors both directly and indirectly through religious code of conducts and value formation from birth. Religion as a culture can influence consumer's behavior by motivating them via their various interactive and related social and cultural variables. As purchasing behavior is been influenced by cognitive actions, effect and behavior, the importance of this element must be taking into consideration in explaining the differences in religious belief system [33].

Information processing is a process where a stimulus such as marketing information is received, interpreted, stored in the memory and later retrieved thus linking marketing and other external influences with the consumer's decision-making process [2,34]. It is very important to communicate as clearly as possible in order to avoid selective distortion in which the consumer misunderstands the message if it is not in accord with their beliefs and attitudes. These are important needs for sustaining the human life. Food, water, warm shelter, sleep, medicine and education are the basic physiological needs, which fall in the primary list of need satisfaction. Maslow was of the opinion that until these needs was satisfied to a degree to maintain life; no other motivating factors can work. Briefly, the first level of needs is physiologic (e.g., the need for food, air, and water). The second level encompasses safety needs. These include security, stability, protection; freedom from fear, anxiety, and chaos. The third level of need is belonging and love. These needs involve the". . . giving and receiving affection. When they are unsatisfied, a person will feel keenly the absence of friends, mate, or children."8 The fourth level is the need for esteem, which is fulfilled by mastery of the environment and the prestige that comes from societal recognition. The fifth level, the need for self-actualization, entails maximizing one's unique potential in life (Figure 2). As each of these needs substantially satisfied, the next need becomes dominant. So if you want to motivate someone, you need to understand what level of the hierarchy that person is on and focus on satisfying those needs or needs above that level [35]. Sometimes beliefs and attitude plays an important role in the decision-making process as they strongly affect the evaluation process of the alternatives. Beliefs are thoughts about the product or some of its qualities whereas attitude is overall favorable or unfavorable feeling against the purchase [2]. Attitudes are affected by three components: affect (emotional response to the product), cognition (the beliefs and knowledge of the product), the behavior (consumer's intention to purchase or use the product) Barnes et al. [31].

Figure 2. Maslow's hierarchy needs pyramid diagram (Forsyth 2002, 21).

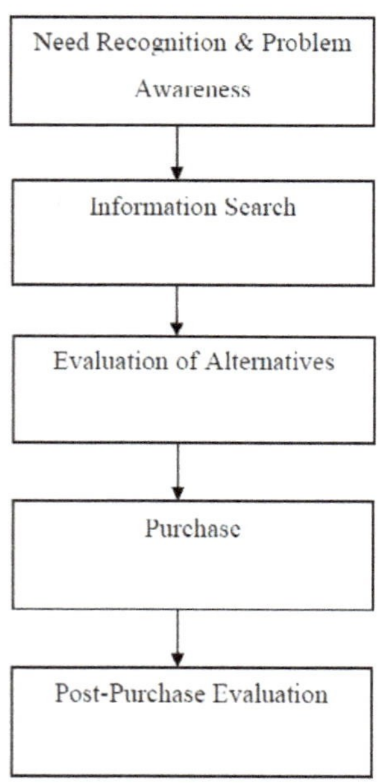

Figure 3: The buyer decision-making process.

Buyer decision-making process

Research shows that customers go through a five-stage decision-making process in any purchases made. It is a process by which a consumer makes a decision on what to buy, what quantity to buy, at what price with respect to the factors affecting consumer's attitude during the procedure. The individual stages are summarized in the diagram below followed by brief explanations.

This model is very paramount for everyone who makes marketing decisions. The model shows that customers go through five essential stages in every purchase. However, in more frequent purchases, customers sometimes skip some of the stages. For example, someone who is buying a favorite drink would recognize the need for thirst and go straight to the purchase decision, skipping information search and evaluation. However, the model is very important when it comes to understanding any purchase involving some detail considerations [2].

The buying process begins with need recognition or problem awareness. At this stage, The customer, firstly, recognizes a problem or need (example, I am thirsty, I need a new Clothe, I need a house) or attracted to an advertisement (example. you seeing a billboard Showing a chilled ice cream on scorching sunny day). After the buyer has recognized the need for something or an existing problem, the customer then moves on to the next stage; searching for information. If the need or the problem is so pressing and there is a product or service close at hand that meets the need or solves the problem, then a purchase decision is made immediately. If not, then the process of searching for information begins. There are several sources that a customer can obtain information. For example: Personal sources (family, friends, neighbors), Commercial sources (advertising, salespeople, retailers, dealers, packaging, point of sale Displays), Public sources (newspapers, radio, television, consumer organizations, specialist Magazines), Experiential sources (handling, examining, using the product). The usefulness and influence of these sources of information will vary by product and by customer. Research suggests that customer's value and respect personal sources (the influence of "word of mouth") more than commercial sources.

The next stage in the model is the evaluation stage, where the customer chooses between the alternative brands, products and services. He/she then begins to consider the alternative or substitute available in the market. The important factor which influences the extent of evaluation is whether the customer feels involved in the purchasing of the product. Involvement here means the degree of perceived relevance and personal importance that goes with the choice of a particular brand. After gathering all the necessary information about a product the next step is to make a decision on whether to purchase the product. There are three sub steps in this stage, first choosing the preferred product as previously described in the evaluation of alternative stage, then the customer decides to purchase the product that is, purchase intent and finally the implementation stage to conclude the purchase which consists of the terms of transaction payment and receiving the product. Sometimes the consumer makes the purchase intent, but never actually concludes it, or takes the implementation step and sometimes substituting product is chosen based on new information in-store, preferred product is out of stock, buyer cannot afford the product or no suitable financing terms are found.

Conclusion

Understanding the variables that affect consumer behavior and the decision-making process is not just the work of big corporations [35], but also of professionals seeking to find the key areas of marketing studies. According to [24] Sales promotion has direct impact on the consumers buying behavior, which is an action focus-promoting occasion.

According to Ghafran Ashraf [15], their study confirmed that consumers buying behavior and sales promotion can be motivated through various kinds of elements, including promotion techniques such as free samples, price discounts, social surroundings and physical surrounding.

In addition, according to Jin-Woo Park et al. [36], their study has empirically verified the relationship between sales promotions, customer satisfaction, customer value and behavioral intention, legitimizing the growth of sales promotions within the duty-free shop sector. Their results indicate that there were significant relationships between cutting price, cents off, customer satisfaction, customer value, image and behavioral intentions. From their research, they found that Duty-free shops should realize that attractive sales promotion strategies should enhance customer repurchase intention and recommendations to other customers because they raise the level of customer satisfaction, value perception and duty-free shop image formation.

According to Giuliani Isabella et al. [37], among the variables that affect the consumer's purchase decision is the price, which has a significant influence on communication factors concerning the advantages of purchasing a product or hiring a service. Price can be accompanied by a "discount," which increases the perceived value of the product for the purchaser. The value is based on the consumer's perception of the benefits of the product. Furthermore, according to price discount is well-known tool for offering a good discount in buying price, which is openly mentioned on the merchandise or point of purchase display. Ndubisi and Chiew [27] said that merchandise test can be increased through offering great price cut. According to Ehrenberg et al. [38], the short-term rises in sales were due principally to purchases made by irregular users of a brand, though they further warned that these irregular users, after taking benefit of the price discount, would most likely go back to their beloved brands in their portfolio rather than purchase the promoted brand at full price. Moore and Carpenter [39], found that price perception affects the patronage behavior. Smith and Sinha [40] determined that price level has a considerable effect on store choice. In another study, Gilbert and Jackaria [16] found that discounts significantly affect customers' purchase behaviors.

According to Ben Amor's researches [41], during the last ten years, significance of free sample as tools of promotion in the field of cosmetics has been on the rise. According to the investigation done by Denly a marketing company, 75% the companies use free samples to improve their products, whereas 52% of the companies don't advertise their new products. Although representing this method is a powerful promotion tools, it requires high costs for the organizations.

According to [42] Sampling is the technique of presenting less numbers of goods to the customers without any cost, so that they can try it and buy the product in near future.

According to Shimp [43], free sample of product effect the clients buying behavior but Jackaria and Gilbert [16] have not agree with this declaration. According to Lammers a free sample had positive relation to immediate sales of that product. Free sample had a sizeable link with product test behaviour of customer [27].

According to Fill price discount is well-known tool for offering a good discount in buying price, which is openly mentioned on the merchandise or point of purchase display. Ndubisi and Chiew [27] said that merchandise test can be increased through offering great price cut. According to Ehrenberg et al. [38], the short-term rises in sales were due principally to purchases made by irregular users of a brand, though they further warned that these irregular users, after taking benefit of the price discount, would most likely go back to their beloved brands in their portfolio rather than purchase the promoted brand at full price.

Special discounts and promotions increase customers' interest toward the store [44]. Through these results, one of the major implications of this research is that firms can increase sales by offering the right promotional tools to attract trial customers. Therefore organizations should carefully plan their promotional strategies, and allocate promotional budget over the different promotion tools, giving preference to the more effective tools.

References

1. Kotler P, Peter C, Linden B, Stewart A (2000) Marketing in Australia and New Zealand, third edition, Sydney-Australia, Prentice Hall Pty Ltd.
2. Jobber D, Lancaster G (2006) Selling and sales management, (7thedn), Harlow: Pearson Education.
3. Evans J, Berman B (1997) Marketing. New Jersey: Prentice Hall International.
4. Baker M (2006) Marketing. Scotland: Westburn Publishers Ltd.
5. Koekemoer L, Bird S (2004) Marketing Communications. Juta and Company Limited.
6. Chunnawala SA, Sethia KC (1994) Foundation of Advertising Theory and Practice, Himalaya Publishing House, Mumbai, pp.17.
7. Kotler PJ, Armstrong GM (2010) Principle of Marketing, Global Ed. New York: Pearson.
8. Neslin SA (2002) Sales Promotion. Cambridge, MA: Marketing Science Institute (MSI).
9. Neslin SA, Henderson C, Quelach J (1985) Consumer Promotions and the Acceleration of Product Purchases. Marketing Science 4: 147-165.
10. Zhang ZJ, Krishna A, Dhar SK (2000) The Optimal Choice of Promotional Vehicles: Front-Loaded or Rear Loaded Incentives?" Management Science 46: 348-362.
11. Schultz DE, Robinson WA (1998) Sales Promotion Management, Chicago: Crain Books.
12. Kwok S, Uncles M (2005) Sales promotion effectiveness: the impact of consumer differences at an ethnic-group level. Journal of Product & Brand Management 14: 170-186.
13. Low GS, Mohr JJ (2000) Advertising vs. sales promotion: a brand management perspective. Journal of product & brand management 9: 389-414.
14. Hellman K (2005) Strategy-driven B2B Promotion. Journal of Business & Industrial Marketing 20: 4-11.
15. Ghafran Ashraf M (2014) The promotional tools and situational factors' impact on consumer buying behaviour and sales promotion. Journal of Public Administration and Governance 4(2).
16. Gilbert DC, Jackaria N (2002) The Efficacy of Sales Promotions in U.K. Retail stores: a Consumer View. International Journal of Retail and Distribution Management 30: 315-332.
17. Blackwell RD, Miniard PW, Engel JF (2001) Consumer Behaviour, (9thedn). Fort Worth, TX: Harcourt College Publishers.
18. Fan, Y (2006) Promoting business with corporate gifts – major issues and empirical evidence. Corporate Communications: An International Journal 11: 43-55.
19. Meng, J, Nascom SA (2009) Cross-cultural equivalence of price perceptions across American, Chinese, and Japanese consumers. Journal of Product and Brand Management 18: 506-516.
20. Kotler P, Pfoertsch W (2006) B2B Brand Management. Heidelberg: Springer.
21. Mahmud IN, Mohammad SA, Sultan F (2014) The Impact of Promotional Mix Elements on Consumers Purchasing Decisions. International" Business and Management 8: 143-151.
22. Ansari S (2011) The effect of sales promotion on consumer interest to purchase in IKCO automotive company. Journal of knowledge management, economics and information technology.
23. Rowely J (1998) Promotion and marketing communications in the information. Library Review 47: 383-387.
24. Blattberg RC, Neslin SA (1990) Sales Promotion: Concepts, Methods, and Strategies, Prentice-Hall, Englewood Cliffs, NJ.
25. Banerjee S (2009) Effect of product category on promotional choice: comparative study of discounts and freebies. Management Research News 32: 120-131.

26. De Pelsmacker, Patrick – Geuens, Maggie – Van den Bergh, Joeri 2001. Marketing Communications. Pearson Education Limited.
27. Ndubisi N, Oly, Moi CT (2006) Awareness and usage of promotional tools by Malaysian consumers: the case of low involvement products, Management Research News 29: 28-40.
28. Brassington F, Pettitt S (2000) Sales Promotion. In: Principles of Marketing, (2ndedn), FT Prentice Hall, Harlow 642-685.
29. Peter P, Olson J (2008) Consumer behavior and marketing strategy. (8thedn). Mc Graw Hill. Singapore.
30. Usunier JC (1993) International marketing: A cultural Approach.
31. Barnes B, Marshall GW, Mitchell V, Solomon MR, Stuart EW (2009) marketing, real people, real decisions, European edition, Pearson education limited, Essex.
32. Cohen N, Dibb S (2004) Religious Influences on shopping behavior. An exploratory study. Journal of marketing management 20: 638-712.
33. Lindridge A (2009) Acculturation, Religion and Consumption in Normative Political Ideology. Advances in Consumer Research 36: 16-17.
34. Forsyth P (2000) How to Motivate People. Second edition. United Kingdom: Kogan Page Limited.
35. Ailawadi K, Beauchamp JP, Donthu N, Gauri DK, Shankar V (2009) Communication and promotion decisions in retailing: a review and directions for future research. Journal of Retailing 85: 42-55.
36. Jin-Woo P, Yu-Jin C, Woo-Choon M (2013) Investigating the effects of sales promotions on customer behavioral intentions at duty-free shops: An Incheon International Airport case study. Journal of Airline and Airport Management 3: 18-30.
37. Giuliana I, Alexandre I, Pozzani, VC, Murillo BPG (2012) Influence of Discount Price Announcements on Consumer's Behavior, Evaluated in double blind review.
38. Ehrenberg ASC, Hammond K, Goodhardt GJ (1994) The after effects of price related consumer promotions, Journal of Advertising Research 34: 11-21.
39. Moore M, Carpenter J (2006) The Effect of Price as a Marketplace Cue on Retail Patronage. Journal of Product and Brand Management 15: 265-271.
40. Sinha, I, Smith IMF (2000) Consumer Perceptions of Promotional Framing on Price. Psychology and Marketing 17: 257-275.
41. Ben A Insaf, Guilbert Francis (2009) Influences on free samples usage within the luxury cosmetic market, Direct Marketing: An International Journal 3: 67-82.
42. Pramataris KC (2001) Personal interactive TV advertising: The imedia business model. Elect Mark 11: 17-25.
43. Shimp TA (2003) Advertising Promotion and Supplemental Aspects of Integrated Marketing Communications (6thedn), USA: Thomson South-Western.
44. Grewal D, Krishnan R, Baker J, Borin N (1998a) The Effect of Store Name, Brand Name and Price Discounts on Consumers' Evaluations and Purchase Intentions. Journal of Retailing 74: 331-352.

Efficiency of Selected Sudanese Sheep Markets: A Multivariate Approach (1995-2011)

Mohamed Bushara OA[1]* and Murtada KA Abdelmahmod[2]

[1]*Faculty of Agricultural Sciences, University of Gezira, Wad Medani, Sudan*

[2]*Faculty of Management Sciences and Economics, Department of Economics, University of AL-Butana, Rufaa, Sudan*

Abstract

The main objective of this study is to investigate price movements among important sheep markets in the Sudan to explore their pricing efficiency. The short period of long-run equilibrium adjustment indicated that there are strong price linkages between Omdurman and other four markets (Elobied, Medani, Sennar and Nyala markets). The prices causality indicated unidirectional relation causality of Nyala market through Medani and Elobied markets. Nyala markets as terminal market located in production area Granger cause Medani and Omdurman as major consumption markets; this was taken as evidence that price movements were primarily driven by supply shocks. That mean the system was centred on Nyala i.e. Nyala could be considered as a supply market in sheep market which means the prices were supply driven.

Keywords: Market efficiency; Sheep; Multivariate cointegration; Sudan

Introduction

Background

The global economy witnessed a number of economic and financial crises since the late of 19th and early of 20th century, which caused a decline in consumption and private sector investment, rise in unemployment rate and slowdown in economic growth rates.

The global financial crisis of 2008, discerned with banking crisis, instability of foreign exchange and imbalances in stock markets. As the result of linkage between the international financial markets, their adverse effects outreached the performance of the international financial markets and the real sector through the slackening demand for goods and services. This engendered a decline in their prices, including oil prices during the last quarter of 2008.

The government plan toward agricultural development is to invest a part of oil revenues for the activation of agricultural sectors and to boost production to achieve the aspirations and economic goals, especially the creation of the economic boom in exports of non-petroleum resources like agriculture and livestock [1]. Unfortunately, slight progress in performance of the agricultural sector, relatively attributed to the implementing some of the development programs and the downturn in the animal resources section. In the additional; (1) reasons of this section drop is obvious the agriculture sector shares are still little and humble revenues with unstable shift, and (2) the overall state for all items of exports of non-petroleum products didn't attain the desired share of the export revenue or promote the state of the trade balance which has recently become out of deficit circle at the beginning of the year 2007 as shown in Table 1.

Table 1 above indicates high surplus with value of 2.456 Billion US$ in 2010 compared with surplus in 2008, 2007 with value 2.319, 1.1 million US$ respectively. In the last decade the government has sought to increase exports of livestock and livestock products. Sudan's livestock exports fell dramatically in 2000-2001, however, when Saudi Arabia and other Gulf countries temporarily banned imports of live animals from Sudan [2]. Since 2002 Sudan's livestock exports have rebounded, but they constitute a smaller part of non-oil exports than during the 1990s. In 2005, oil accounted for 82% of Sudan's total exports by value; livestock and livestock products were just 3-2%of exports by value (or nearly 18% by value of non-oil exports).

In 2003 President Al-Bashir issued a set of directives to spur livestock exports, putting the Ministry of Foreign Trade in charge of re-organizing and improving Sudan's livestock markets. In November 2003 the Ministry directed the creation of a pilot Cattle Auction Project at El Muwelih market in Omdurman [3]. This project would require payment in cash at the time of transaction and sale by weight and open auction, theoretically improving the overall efficiency and transparency of the marketing system [4]. If the project succeeds at El Muwelih it would be replicated at other livestock markets, but for now, the auction project is stalled owing to problems in organizing financial services to facilitate cash payments.

Sudan is among the richest African countries in term of size of its national herds. The livestock population keeps increasing through the years, in the year 2010 the livestock population comprised about 42 million cattle, 4.623 million camels, 52 million sheep and 43 million goats as presented in Table 2 below.

Period	Petroleum export	Non-petroleum export	Total export	Total import	Trade balance
2005	4187.360	636.918	4824.278	6756.820	(1932.542)
2006	5087.211	569.357	5656.568	8073.498	(2416.930)
2007	8418.258	460.722	8879.250	8775.457	1027.93
2008	11094.111	576.393	11670.502	9351.540	2318.964
2009	7131.255	702.441	7833.696	9690.918	(1857.222)
2010	9905.248	1377.351	11282.779	8839.400	2456.000

Source: (Sudan, 2012).

Table 1: The trade balance (U.S.A Million Dollar) during the period 2005-2010).

***Corresponding author:** Bushara MOA, Faculty of Agricultural Sciences, University of Gezira, Wad Medani, Sudan, E-mail: mosman@uofg.edu.sd

Year	Cattle	Camel	Sheep	Goats
1995	30077	2903	37146	33319
1996	31669	2915	37202	35215
1997	33102	2936	39835	36037
1998	34584	2974	42363	36498
1999	35825	3031	44802	37346
2000	35093	3108	46095	38952
2001	38325	3203	47043	39952
2002	39479	3342	48136	41485
2003	39669	3503	48440	42030
2004	39760	3724	48910	42179
2005	40468	3908	49797	42526
2006	40994	4078	50390	42756
2007	41138	4238	50651	42938
2008	41426	4406	51067	43104
2009	41563	4521	51555	43270
2010	41761	4623	52079	43441

Source: (Statistics, 2009).

Table 2: Livestock population (000 head) 1995-2010).

Sudan's economy is one of the fastest growing in the world. Since 1999, the country is taking advantage of vast oil reserves receiving large inflows of foreign direct investment. Yet, in spite of abundance of natural resources; agriculture remains an important sector of the economy as it contributes a third of GDP. More importantly, years of civil wars, lack of infrastructure, and a reliance on subsistence agriculture has made the majority of Sudanese to live below the poverty line.

The main livestock production sites are located far from the major consumption centres and export outlets. Economically valuable livestock populations are concentrated in northern, western and southern Kordofan and Darfur. Blue Nile and Elgadarif states are also important supply places for export sheep [5].

Allocating sheep efficiently over space should faster a sustainable use of pasture resources. It is also expected to favour the sharing of risk across regions by smoothing price variation. Thus, studying coinegration of sheep is important for optimal resource use, early warning and market and trade policy [6].

Livestock have historically been central to Sudan's overall economy, although in recent years oil production has become the dominant feature of the political economy of Sudan. Since 1999, livestock and livestock products (meat, hides and skins) have comprised approximately 20% of Sudan's annual Gross Domestic Product (Sudan, 2010). As oil production has increased, however, the relative importance of livestock and livestock product for exports as foreign exchange earners had declined. In 2005 oil was 82% (by value) of total exports while livestock and livestock product exports were just 3.2%. The international Monetary Fund attributes the recent decline in livestock exports to "supply constraints (inadequate capacity at the port, deterioration in the road infrastructure), conflict in livestock-rich areas, and higher domestic demand".

Most researchers agree that the problems of livestock marketing in Sudan are limited to the specific problems which could be summarized in a weak infrastructure especially in the area of transport and veterinary services, lack of finance led to oligopoly and oligopsony in the trade, areas of production distant from areas of consumption and together with lack of suitable transport render animals weak and meat quality low, smuggling especially across the borders to Egypt and Libya and lack of veterinary services.

One of the main problems of livestock marketing is that, the livestock markets approach is the sellers dominated market. According to ref. [7], the main constraints to animals marketing include poor marketing infrastructure, lack of marketing organization, lack of market intelligence, absence of marketing extension services and absence of grades and standards. The main problems indicated by the herders include shortage of drinking water, spread of animals' diseases, and lack of veterinary services and encroachment of agricultural activities on grazing land.

The problem statement

Despite the significant importance of sheep to Sudanese economy but its markets still not well developed. The main constraints to animals marketing include poor market infrastructure, lack of market organization, lack of market intelligence, inadequacy of market finance, shortage of drinking water, spread of animals diseases, and lack of veterinary services and transport services, these constrains are affecting marketing efficiency.

The questions of the study

To achieve the objectives of this study, the following questions need to be answered:

1. Are sheep prices data in the Sudan have stationary properties over time?
2. Is sheep price shock that happens in one market affecting the other markets?
3. Are the sheep markets integrated?
4. Is there any cointegration between these markets in the short and long run?

The objectives of study

The main objective of this paper is to investigate sheep markets in the Sudan to explore their price efficiency.

From the mentioned research problem the following sub-objectives are distinguished:

1. To investigate sheep market integration through analyzing price variation in selected markets.
2. To outline some policy recommendations, that might help policy makers to draw plans to improve the livestock marketing system.

Data and Methodology

The study focused on scrutinizing the sheep markets in Sudan by considering the prices of five livestock markets which were Elobied, Omdurman, Medani, Sennar and Nyala. The study covered the periods from January 1995 to December 2011. The data used in these prices were monthly prices which have been collected from the Animal Resources Company; these prices were wholesale price i.e. the selling price of a head of animal measure in Sudanese Pound (SDG). To attain the cointegration analysis the data should be in real terms to avoid spurious regression, so all price series were deflated by GDP deflator rather than consumer price index. The deflated prices data were transformed in term of natural logarithm so as to attain a constant variance in the series, and then this logged deflated prices data used in the empirical analysis [8]. See Figures 1-3 for visual appreciation.

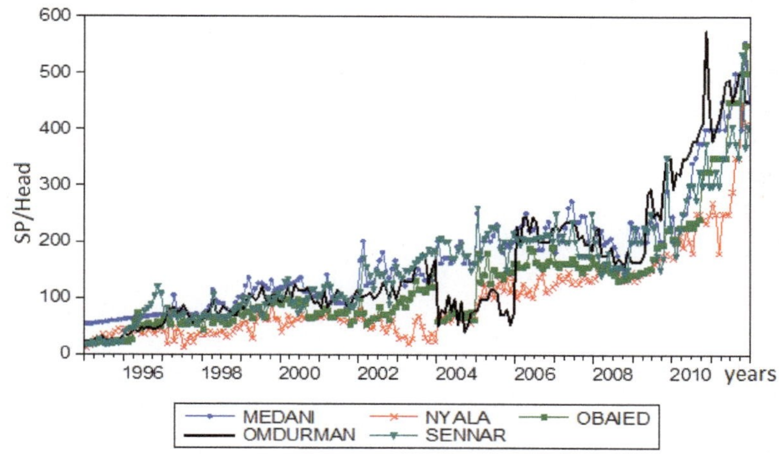

Figure 1: Monthly nominal wholesale price (Sudanese pound per head) of camels in the selected markets, January 1995 – December 2011.

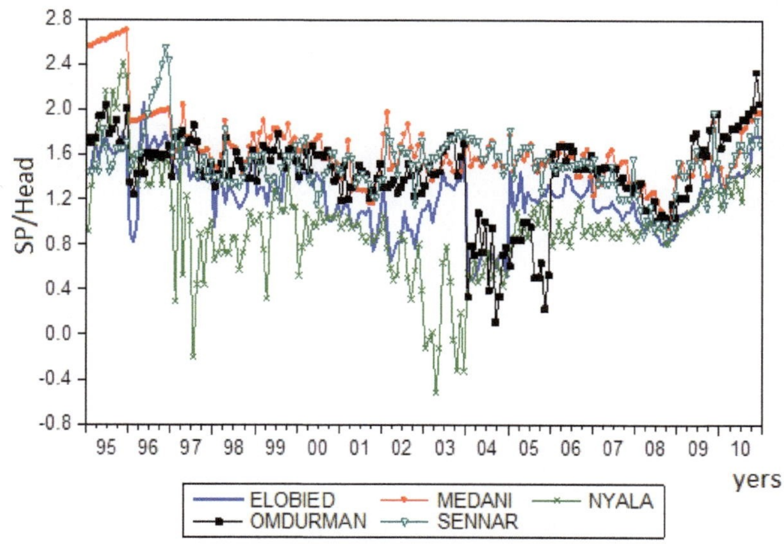

Figure 2: Monthly deflated wholesale price (Sudanese pound per head) of sheep in the selected markets, January 1995 – December 2011.

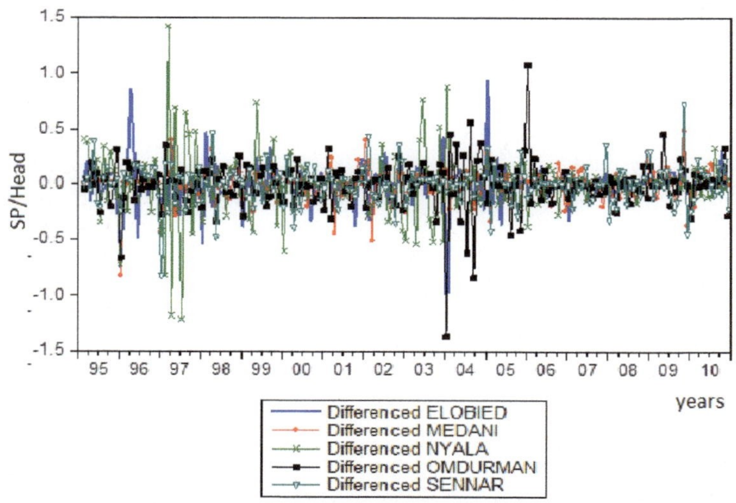

Figure 3: First difference of monthly deflated wholesale price (Sudanese pound per head) of sheep in the selected markets, January 1995 – December 2011.

Johansen Maximum likelihood ratio approach:

Johansen's methodology takes its starting point in the vector auto regression (VAR) of order p given by:

$$Y_t = u + A_1 y_{t-1} + \ldots + A_p y_{t-p} + \varepsilon_t \tag{1}$$

Where y_1 is a k-dimension vector of variables which are assumed to be I(1) series (but could also be I(0)), Ai, I=1, p is the coefficient matrix, and ε_t is a k-dimension vector of residuals. Subtracting y_{t-1} from both sides of equation (1) yields:

$$\Delta y_t = u + \prod y_{t-1} + \Gamma_1 \Delta y_{t-1} + \ldots + \Gamma_{p-1} \Delta y_{t-p+1} + \varepsilon_t \tag{2}$$

This VAR can be re-written as:

$$\Delta y_t = u + \prod y_{t-1} + \sum_{i=1}^{p-1} \Gamma_{i1} \Delta y_{t-i} + \varepsilon_t \tag{3}$$

$$\text{Where } \prod = \sum_{i=1}^{p} A_i - 1. \tag{4}$$

$$\text{and } \Gamma_1 = \sum_{j=i+1}^{p} A_j . \tag{5}$$

From equation (3) the only one term in the equation, IIy_{t-1}, is in levels, cointegration relations depend crucially on the property of matrix II. It is clear that IIy_{t-1} must be either I(0) or zero except that y_t is already stationary. There are three situations:

(a) II=**αβ**' has a reduced rank 0 < r < k,

(b) II=**αβ**' has a rank of zero, and

(c) II=**αβ**' has a full rank.

Under situation (a), α and β are both k x r matrices and have a rank of r. There are r cointegration vectors β'yt which are stationary *I(0)* series. It is equivalent to having r common trends among y_t. The stationarity of β'yt implies a long-run relationship among y_t ar a sub-set of y_t the variables in the cointegration vectors will not depart from each other over time. $\beta' y_t$ are also error correction terms in that departure of individual variables in the cointegration vectors from the equilibrium will be subsequently reversed back to the equilibrium, a dynamic adjustment process called error correction mechanism (ECM). Equation (3) is therefore called VAR with ECM. Under situation (b), there is no cointegration relation among y_t and the variables in levels do not enter equation (3), and then equation (3) becomes a simple VAR without ECM. The variables in levels are already stationary under situation (c).

Johansen proposes two different likelihood ratio tests of the significance of these canonical correlations and thereby the reduced rank of the II matrix: the trace test and maximum eigenvalue test, shown in equations (6) and (7) respectively.

The trace statistic test

The trace statistic test the null hypothesis of r cointegrating relations against the alternative of k cointegrating relations, where k is the number of endogenous variables, for r=0, 1, , k – 1. The alternative of k cointegrating relations corresponds to the case where none of the series has a unit root and a stationary VAR may be specified in terms of the levels of all of the series. The trace statistic for the null hypothesis of r cointegrating relations is computed as:

$$\pi_{trace}(r/k) = -T \sum_{i=r+1}^{n} h\left(1 - \hat{\lambda}_i\right). \tag{6}$$

Where λ_i is the *i*-th largest eigenvalue of the matrix in (4) and (5).

The maximum eigenvalue statistic test

The second test is maximum eigenvalue statistic which tests the null hypothesis of (r) cointegrating relations against the alternative of (1+r) cointegrating relations. This test statistic is computed as:

$$\pi_{\max}(r/r+1) = -TIn(1-\hat{\lambda}_{r+1}) . \tag{7}$$

Neither of these test statistics follows a chi square distribution in general; asymptotic critical values could be found in Johansen and Juselius [9] and are also given by most econometric software packages. Since the critical values used for the maximum eigenvalue and trace test statistics are based on a pure unit-root assumption, they would no longer be corrected when the variables in the system are near – unit-root processes. By default, E-views program reports the value based on MacKinnon et al., [10] p-values for Johansen's cointegration trace test and maximum eigenvalue test.

Results and Discussion of the Multivariate Cointegration Approach for Sheep

This section presents the results of the second cointegration analysis approach which is the system based tests using the vector autoregression (VAR) of Johansen [11,12] in which the joint effects of prices in all markets in concern were accounted for.

The order of vector autoregressive models

A major requirement in conducting [13,14] cointegration tests and estimation of a VAR system, either in its unrestricted or restricted Vector Error Correction (VEC) forms, is the choice of an optimal lag length. Noting that, the lag length ought to be set long enough to ensure that the residuals are white noise and considering that the study was based on monthly data. The lag structure of the estimated VAR was then examined using a combination of VAR lag order selection information criteria [15] (AIC), Bayesian (SBC), likelihood ratio (LR) and [16] (HQ) information criterion) and checking that the inverse roots of the characteristic polynomial lie within a unit circle, which is a condition for having a stable VAR system. This process led to the choice of two lags as shown in Table 3, which was used in the cointegration test and subsequent analysis.

According to Table 3 below while the SC and HQ criteria suggested the use of one lag, the AIC and LR criterion suggests the use of two lags which was used in the cointegration test and subsequent analyses.

Lag	LogL	LR	FPE	AIC	SC	HQ
0	-103.5315	NA	2.08e-06	1.107464	1.191090	1.141320
1	308.6366	799.1014	4.01e-08	-2.843230	-2.341478*	-2.640097*
2	337.0304	53.60052*	3.87e-08*	-2.877861*	-1.957982	-2.505450
3	351.9707	27.44142	4.30e-08	-2.775211	-1.437205	-2.233522
4	367.3639	27.48779	4.75e-08	-2.677182	-0.921049	-1.966216
5	384.4530	29.64446	5.17e-08	-2.596459	-0.422200	-1.716215
6	402.7316	30.77512	5.57e-08	-2.527873	0.064513	-1.478351
7	416.1288	21.87298	6.31e-08	-2.409477	0.601036	-1.190677
8	437.4491	33.72091	6.62e-08	-2.371930	1.056711	-0.983852

*indicates lag order selected by the criterion.
LR: LR test statistic (each test at 5% level).
FPE: Final Prediction Error.
AIC: Akaike Criterion.
SC: Schwarz Criterion.
HQ: Hannan-Quinn information criterion.

Table 3: Vector autoregressive (VAR) lag order selection criteria.

Examination of the inverse roots of the AR characteristic within the unit circle for the VAR specification indicates that a VAR satisfies the stability condition under using two lag. i.e. if the estimated VAR process is stationary, then all AR roots should lie inside the unit circle as showing in Table 4a and Figure 2 below. No root lies outside the unit circle. VAR satisfies the stability condition.

The stationary condition for general AR (p) processes is that the inverted roots of the lag polynomial lie inside the unit circle. There is no particular problem if the roots are imaginary, but a stationary AR model should have all roots with modulus less than one. From Table 4a above the roots computed for six lag corresponding to that VAR lag order selection criteria, and they were all less than one. This indicates that VAR satisfies the stability condition. An inverse root of AR characteristic polynomial is measuring of stability of the VAR model. According to Greene and Seaks [17] the estimated VAR is stable (stationary) if all roots have modulus less than one and lie inside the unit circle. If the VAR is not stable, certain results (such as impulse response standard errors) are not valid. Inverse roots of AR characteristic polynomial graphed in Figure 4 confirm the stability condition of the VAR model and enable to perform the impulse response analysis.

Number of cointegration vectors for sheep prices

Following the result of the previous stage was used to determine the cointegrating vectors in the models on the maximum eigenvalue, the trace of the stochastic matrix test of and the three model selection criteria i.e. HQC, SBC and AIC were also used. Table 4b below displays the result of Johansen likelihood ratio test. In this table the null hypothesis of no cointegration (r=0) among variables was rejected in both trace test statistic and the maximum eigenvalue statistic. The trace of stochastic matrix (80.60235) and the maximum eigenvalue statistic (34.01498) were above their corresponding 95% critical values of (69.81889) and (33.87687) respectively. Moreover, a hypothesis of numbers of cointegration vector in trace test under two forms, which

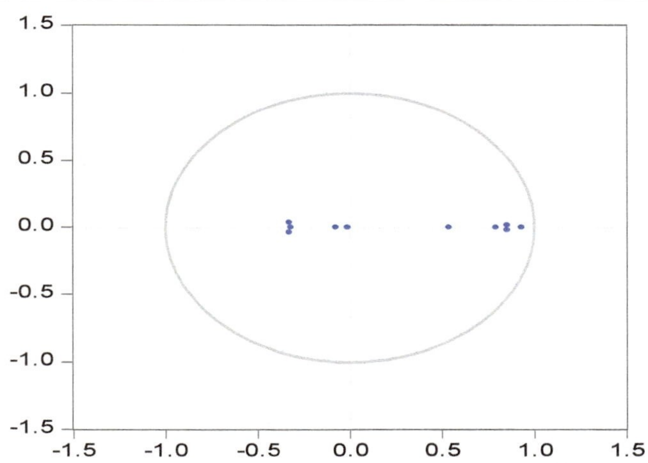

Figure 4: Inverse roots of AR characteristic polynomial.

Root	Modulus
0.931192	0.931192
0.793502	0.793502
0.540547	0.540547
-0.315481	0.315481
-0.073369	0.073369
-0.010658	0.010658

Table 4a: Roots of characteristic polynomial.

Hypothesized No. of CE(s)	Eigenvalue	Trace statistic	0.05 critical value	Prob.**
None*	0.155684	80.60235	69.81889	0.0054
At most 1	0.081920	46.58737	47.85613	0.0655
At most 2	0.071724	29.40775	29.79707	0.0554
At most 3	0.056180	14.44816	15.49471	0.0714
At most 4	0.013963	2.826300	3.841466	0.0927

Trace test indicates 1 cointegrating equation(s) at the 0.05 level.
* denotes rejection of the hypothesis at the 0.05 level.
**(MacKinnon, Haug, and Michelis, 1998) p-values.

Table 4b: Johansen tests results for number of cointegrating vector, sheep prices 1995 M1 – 2011 M 12.

Hypothesized No. of CE(s)	Eigenvalue	Max-Eigen statistic	0.05 critical value	Prob. **
None*	0.155684	34.01498	33.87687	0.0482
At most 1	0.081920	17.17961	27.58434	0.5646
At most 2	0.071724	14.95960	21.13162	0.2917
At most 3	0.056180	11.62186	14.26460	0.1257
At most 4	0.013963	2.826300	3.841466	0.0927

Max-eigenvalue test indicates 1 cointegrating equation(s) at the 0.05 level.
*Denotes rejection of the hypothesis at the 0.05 level.
**(MacKinnon, et al. 1998) p-values.

Table 5: Maximum eigenvalue test.

	Elobied	Medani	Nyala	Omdurman	Sennar
Elobied (-1)	0.613060 (7.54994)	0.090410 (1.50239)	0.311431 (2.78297)	0.091187 (1.03904)	0.032881 (0.46372)
Elobied (-2)	0.043154 (0.52055)	-0.078070 (-1.27070)	-0.151306 (-1.32434)	0.017438 (0.19462)	0.084813 (1.17159)
Medani (-1)	0.007900 (0.07254)	0.628405 (7078563)	0.141660 (0.94381)	-0.020018 (-0.17006)	0.083183 (0.87467)
Medani (-2)	-0.021268 (-0.20168)	0.228341 (2.92185)	0.065291 (0.44928)	-0.042489 (-0.37281)	-0.045833 (-0.49774)
Nyala (-1)	0.154580 (2.95996)	0.126781 (3.27577)	0.513116 (7.12946)	0.131704 (2.33339)	0.069027 (1.51367)
Nyala (-2)	-0.082681 (-1.61179)	-0.115860 (-304763)	0.227576 (3.21912)	-0.061898 (-1.11645)	-0.080753 (-1.80278)
Omdurman (-1)	0.110607 (1.58830)	0.073261 (1.41954)	-0-072923 (-0.75984)	0.563890 (7.49206)	-0.024555 (-0.40379)
Omdurman (-2)	0.024560 (0.35387)	-0.039209 (-076229)	0.061472 (0.64268)	0.246778 (3.28979)	-0.018017 (-0.29728)
Sennar (-1)	0.091231 (1.00669)	0.019972 (0.29737)	-0.085149 (-068177)	0.000184 (0.00188)	0.605897 (7.65647)
Sennar (-2)	2.53E-05 (0.00028)	-0.038050 (-056697)	-0145744 (-1.16785)	-0.032725 (-0.33437)	0.111546 (1.41066)
R-squared	0.707018	0.816817	0.714716	0.734693	0.604287
F-statistic	46.09166	85.16735	47.85076	52.89212	29.16726

Table 6: Vector autoregression (VAR) estimates for sheep prices.

is at most one cointegration relation was found (r=1) and at most two cointegration relations were found (r=2) was rejected at 5% significant level while it was accepted in hypothesis (r=3). Therefore, the trace of stochastic matrix indicates three cointegrating equations at the 0.05 significant levels while the maximum eigenvalue test suggested one cointegration relation.

According to Banerjee [18] and Dickey and Fuller, if any divergence of results between these two tests. (The maximum eigenvalue Table 5 and the trace tests Table 4b exits, it is advisable to rely on the eigenvalue test since the results of the latter test are more reliable in small samples. If rely in this argument, the sheep price data in Sudan (1995 ml – 2011 m 12) appears a stable long run relationship and suggested one cointegration vector.

Estimation of vector autoregressive (VAR) model for sheep

The lag structure of the estimated VAR was examined using a combination of VAR lag order selection information criteria with two lag length as indicated in Table 6 before. The results of the VAR model are presented in the following Table 6.

Each column in the table corresponds to an equation in the VAR. For each right-hand side variable it was reported the estimated coefficient and the t-statistic. For example, the coefficient for Elobied on Medani (-1) equation is (0.00790). The numbers at the very bottom of the table are the summary statistics for the VAR system as R-squared and F-statistic.

To examine the results presented in Table 6 above, collectively, the results significant according to the standard *F* test for each model which were (46.09166), (85.16735), (47.85076), (52.89212) and (29.16726) for Elobied, Medani, Nyala, Omdurman and Sennar models respectively. By considering the first equation of Elobied variable, only Elobied at lag one and Nyala at lag one month was statistically significant. The sings of the significant vector autoregression in the Elobied model suggest that, an increase in the level of Elobied lag one month leads to an increase in the level of prices of Nyala lag one month.

Turning to Medani equation, only Medani at lag two is statistically significant according to *t*-statistic. According to the Omdurman equation, only Nyala at lag one and Omdurman itself at lag two were statistically significant according to *t*-statistic. That means the prices of sheep in Nyala and Omdurman itself in the two previous months affected the prices of Omdurman in the current month. The positive coefficient sings explained the positive relationship between Omdurman and Nyala prices.

Sennar market affected just by its own prices in the previous month and no other market affected it. Nyala equation shows that the prices of sheep effected by its own prices in the previous two months and affected by the prices of Elobied market in the previous month.

Error correction	D(Elobied)	D(Omdurman)	D(Medani)	D(Sennar)	D(Nyala)
D(Elobied (-1))	-0127281 (-1.42999)	0.001576 (0.01605)	0.105428 (1.55952)	-1.121850 (-1.53336)	0.162604 (1.34313)
D(Elobied (-2))	-0.109718 (-1.32665)	0.007629 (0.08362)	0.014907 (0023732)	-0.023880) (-0.32341)	-0.045370 (-0.40333)
D(Omdurman (-1))	0.003431 (0.04679)	-0.353459 (-4.37004)	0.068439 (1.22900)	0.069326 (1.05906)	-0.035194 (-0.35291)
D(Omdurman (-2))	0.024603 (0.34907)	-0.132673 (-1.70639)	0.042277 (0.78978)	0.064557 (1.02594)	-0.059205 (-0.61761)
D(Medani (-1))	0.063939 (0.58112)	-0.021296 (-0.17545)	-0.325814 (-3.89883)	0.023383 (0.23804)	0.187121 (1.25037)
D(Medani (-2))	-0.075011 (-0.97988)	-0.165601 (-1.36061)	-0.165229 (-1.97178)	-0.007078 (-0.07186)	0.245021 (1.63277)
D(Sennar (-1))	-0.058338 (-0.62177)	0.079296 (0.76612)	0.003859 (0.05415)	-0.204802 (-2.44490)	0.034977 (0.27409)
D(Sennar (-2))	-0.064432 (-0.70397)	0.080315 (0.79544)	-0.041397 (-0.59550)	-0.126953 (-1.55359)	-0.247774 (-1.99030)
D(Nyala (-1))	0.077171 (1.47797)	0.104987 (1.82269)	0.124884 (3.14909)	0.115226 (2.47177)	-0.442197 (-622651)
D(Nyala (-2))	-0.064141 (-1.22032)	-0.017767 (-0.30642)	0.010852 (0.27183)	0.015668 (0.33388)	-0.278784 (-3.89963)
R-squared	0.162374	0.167111	0.137007	0.146324	0.244208
F-statistic	3.330701	3.447366	2.727750	2.945050	5.551695

Table 7: Vector error correction estimates (short run dynamics matrix (Γ)) for sheep.

Estimating vector error correction (VECM) model for sheep

After obtaining the order of vector autoregressive models, the number of cointegration vectors and estimation of vector autoregressive (VAR) model results, the next stage in the model building process requires the construction of a multivariate VECM for sheep prices in Elobied, Omdurman, Medani, Sennar and Nyala where the time series were found to be cointegrated. Using information constructed from above results, one cointegration vector and one lag lengths were imposed in estimation of Vector Error Correction (VECM) Model and the long and short run matrices were extracted and presented in Table 7 below. These matrices describe the system dynamics.

Cointegration short run dynamics matrices (Γ) for sheep

The short run test results reported in Table 7 which presents the short run matrix for sheep prices in selected markets. Again as the Vector Autoregression (VAR) estimates result in Table 6, each column in the table corresponds to an equation in the VECM (short run dynamics). For each right-hand side variable, E-views report the estimated coefficient and the t-statistic.

Elobied sheep prices were not affected by any other market price as shown in the first column. The second column in the table shows that Omdurman market was affected just by its own prices and affected by Nyala prices in the previous month, but according to F-statistics Omdurman market not affected by all other markets in the short run. Medani sheep prices affected by own prices and by Nyala market prices in the short run.

The fourth equation shows that Sennar is affected by its own prices in the previous month and by Nyala prices lag one month also. Nyala market equation shows two significant coefficients that are Nyala itself in the previous two month and Sennar lagged one month. The linkages between markets are presented in Figure 5 below.

Omdurman, Medani and Sennar were affected by their own prices and affected just by Nyala market, while Elobied market seems to be separated from the other markets, this due to feature of this market which considered as export market. Idris [19] states that the prices of sheep offered for export is higher and affect the mean prices of sheep at El Khewi. For this reason, the purchasing and the selling prices of sheep are lower in Omdurman rather than El Khewi and Elobied.

Cointegration long run equilibrium matrices (II) for sheep prices

The long run equilibrium matrices (II) describe the long run effect. These matrices are extracted from the error correction models presented in Table 8 below:

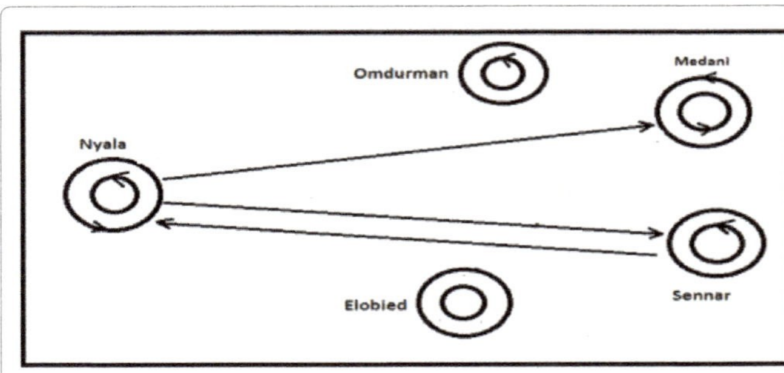

Source: drawing using vector error correction estimates, Table 7.
Figure 5: Lines connected multivariate sheep markets whose prices were cointegrated in the short run, 1995 ml – 2011 ml2.

	Medani	Elobied	Omdurman	Sennar	Nyala
D(Medani)	-0.009646 (-0.51706)	-0.028988 (-0.51706)	0.014982 (0.51706)	0.007746 (0.51706)	0.024697 (0.51706)
D(Elobied)	-0.073358) (-2.98665)	-0.220464 (-2.98665)	0.113947 (2.98665)	0.058910 (2.98665)	0.187828 (2.98665)
D(Omdurman)	0.030327 (1.11924)	0.091141 (1.11924)	-0.047105 (-1.11924)	-0.024354 (-1.11924)	-0.077649 (-1.11924)
D(Sennar)	0.059705 (2.72266)	0.179432 (2.72266)	-0.092737 (-2.72266)	-0.047946 (-2.72266)	-0.152871 (-2.72266)
D(Nyala)	0.056699 (1.69719)	0.170399 (1.69719)	-0.088068 (-1.69719)	-0.045532 (-1.69719)	-0.145175 (-1.69719)

Table 8: Cointegration long run equilibrium matrices (II) for sheep prices – 1995 ml – 2011 m12.

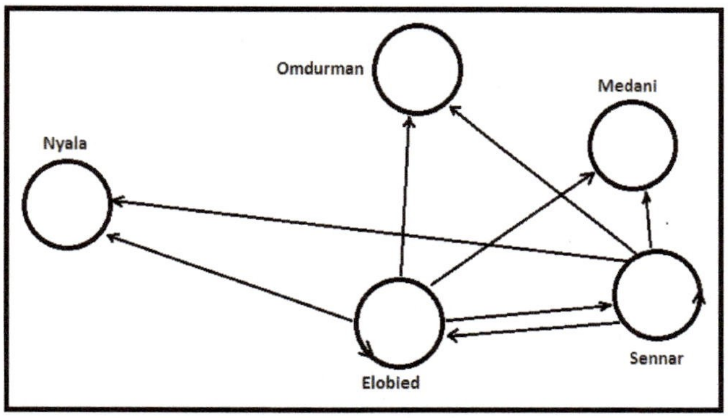

Source: drawing using the long run equilibrium matrix (II) Table 8.

Figure 6: Lines connected sheep markets whose prices were cointegrated in the long run, 1995 ml – 2011 m12.

As evident in Table 8 the error correction terms have been found to be statically significant in Elobied and Sennar markets indicating that, the level of sheep prices in Elobied and Sennar exert significant long run effect on the current development of prices of Medani, Elobied, Omdurman, Sennar and Nyala markets, suggesting the validity of the long run equilibrium relationship in Elobied and Sennar markets. But the levels of sheep prices in the other five markets have no significant long run effect on Omdurman, Medani and Nyala prices.

- Note: the coefficients in bold font are significant at 0.05 significant levels.
- The figures in parentheses are the t-ratio for the estimates.
- D stand for the changes in the variables in concern.
- Source: Calculated from appendix (B) using E-views software computer program.

The sings of the significant error correction terms suggest that the increase in the level of Omdurman, Sennar and Nyala prices in the long run leads to an increase in the level in Elobied sheep market and decrease in the level of Sennar sheep prices, while an increase in the level of Elobied itself and Medani prices in the long run leads to decrease in the level of Elobied sheep prices market and increase in the level of Sennar prices market. Figure 6 below presents these linkages between markets.

The figure shows that Omdurman, Medani and Nyala markets were not cointegrated. The lack of cointegration among these markets because of the long distances separating the major sheep production areas from the consumption areas, the slow means of transport and communication and the high marketing costs are the main reasons for this phenomenon. The trekking route from Nyala to Elobied, for instance, is about 600 kilometers, and that between Elobied and Omdurman is about 560 kilometers [20], giving a total trekking route from Nyala to Omdurman of about 1.160 kilometers. The journey along this route takes 75 to 80 days, making the total marketing costs about 24% of the total costs. The error correction model takes into account the adjustment of long-run disequilibrium in markets and time to remove disequilibria in each period.

Table 8 shows that 5-22% of disequilibrium is removed in each period. For example, for the prices of Elobied market about 7% of the disequilibrium is removed in Medani in one month, while for the prices of Sennar market about 6% of the disequilibrium is removed in Medani in one month.

Diagnostic tests

In order to select an ECM, it needs to satisfy a range of diagnostic tests. These diagnostics provide information about the data properties and evaluate restrictions on the estimated coefficients, including the special case of tests for omitted and redundant variables. The diagnostic tests usually include Lagrange multiplier test for autocorrelation, Ramsey's "RESET" test for functional form, normality and. The results of diagnostic tests of sheep prices data in Table 9 are robust as they satisfy almost all relevant diagnostic tests. But with respect of Elobied, the models suffere from normality problem as indicated in Jarque-Bera test p-value (0.34676) [21] which failed to reject the null hypotheses of non-normal distribution. One possible explanation for this problem is

Tests / Equation	Lagrange multiplier test	Ramsey's RESET	Jarque-Bera test	ARCH test
Elobied	42.32270 (0.0000)	3.481716 (0.0327)	2.11823 (0.34676)	27.58053 (0.0000)
Omdurman	88.59090 (0.0000)	11.34216 (0.0000)	126.2270 (0.0000)	34.71072 (0.0000)
Medani	128.0405 (0.0000)	9.138076 (0.0002)	36.84919 (0.0000)	74.2400 (0.0000)
Sennar	104.7137 (0.0000)	75.73425 (0.0000)	19.91321 (0.00005)	90.63660 (0.0000)
Nyala	67.08509 (0.0000)	2.631351 (0.0745)	116.6391 (0.0000)	16.43895 (0.0000)

Table 9: Diagnostic test results for the estimated equations of sheep prices, (1995-2011).

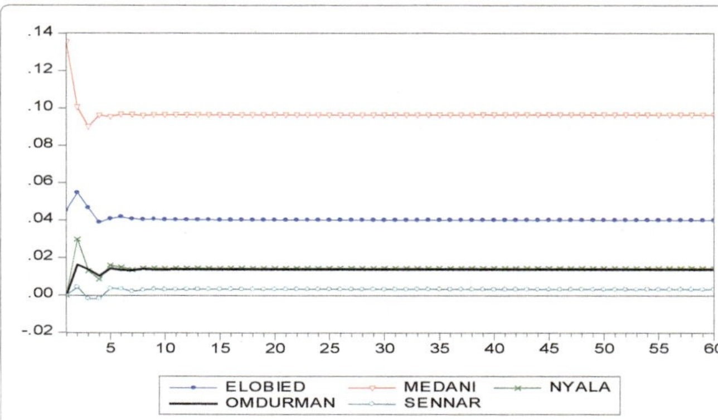

- Y axis is stander error (SD).
- X axis is months.

Figure 7: Generalized impulse response to one standard error shock in the equation of Medani sheep prices 1995 ml – 2011 m12.

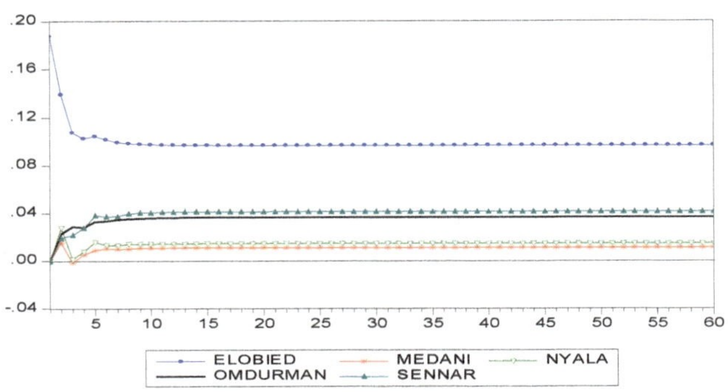

- Y axis is stander error (SD).
- X axis is months.

Figure 8: Generalized impulse response to one standard error shock in the equation of Elobied sheep prices 1995 ml – 2011 m12.

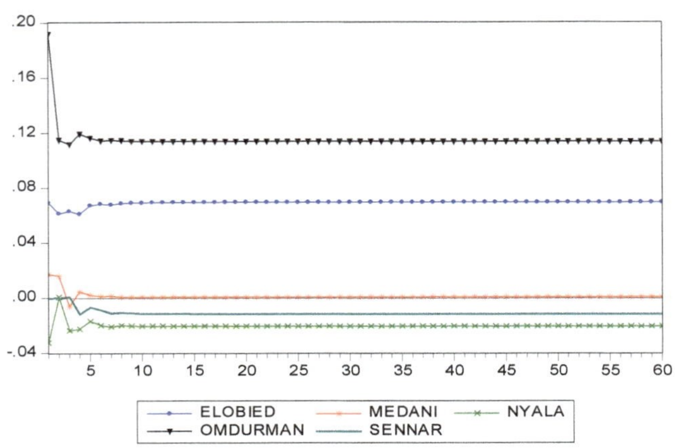

- Y axis is stander error (SD).
- X axis is months.

Figure 9: Generalized impulse response to one standard error shock in the equation of Sennar sheep prices 1995 ml – 2011 m12.

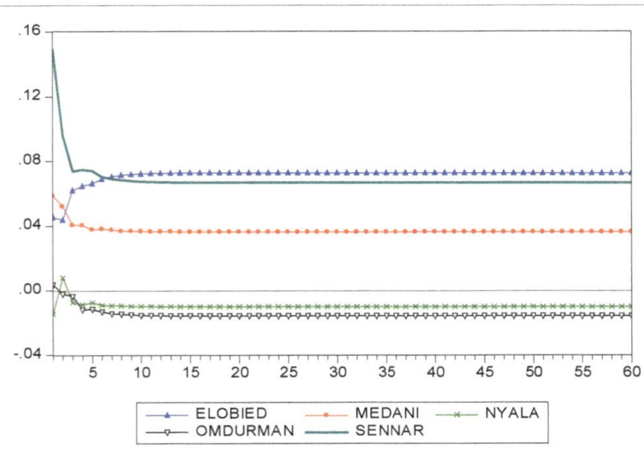

- Y axis is stander error (SD).
- X axis is months.

Figure 10: Generalized impulse response to one standard error shock in the equation of Nyala sheep prices 1995 ml – 2011 m12.

the characteristics of the data used in the models. The figures between brackets are the rejection probability.

When the series were drawn against time it was noticed that the time paths during 1990's were slightly different from previous years [22]. This is quite understandable because of the instability which has characterized the Sudanese economy during this period. Owing to this problem, the models for predicting the future path of its variables should be used cautiously.

Impulse response approach results

An impulse-response analysis was carried out to better understand dynamic price interrelationships, how price shocks were transmitted, and how long take for shocks to be eliminated in alternate markets. The Figures 7-10 below give response function to a price shock equal in size to one standard error in each market equation over a 36 months horizon.

Figure 7 below depicts the impulse response in Elobied, Omdurman, Sennar and Nyala markets due to one standard error price shock in Medani market. It's obvious that Omdurman and Nyala take eight months for Medani market to eliminate the price shock and converge onto long-run equilibrium, the long distance between Medani and Nyala justified this result while Omdurman associated with Medani as demand markets. Elobied and Sennar take six months to remove any disequilibrium and move back to long-run equilibrium. This result indicates that Elobied market is main source of sheep for Medani market in which toke the same period of Sennar market to eliminate prices disequilibrium.

Figure 8 below depicts a standard error shock in Elobied and its response in Medani, Omdurman, Sennar and Nyala, which shows that the adjustment take a five months to eliminate the price shock and converge onto long-run equilibrium for all markets. This result is reasonable because of short distance in case of Nyala and because Omdurman and Medani markets were considered as demand markets depend on Elobied market to supply them with sheep. Therefore, the information of sheep prices between these markets was continuous.

The Elobied, Medani, Sennar and Nyala markets, which in response to a shock in Omdurman markets. Elobied, Nyala and Sennar adjust within five months. While Medani market takes more than four months to converge onto long-run equilibrium, this justified by the short distance between these two markets.

The short period (5 months) of long-run equilibrium adjustment indicates that there are strong price linkages between the two markets (Omdurman with Elobied and Nyala markets individually) and also justifies the physical arbitrage adjusting for any disequilibrium between the two markets.

Figure 9 below depicts a standard error shock in Sennar and its response in Elobied, Omdurman, Medani, and Nyala markets. In response to a standard error shock in Sennar market, the above mentioned that Omdurman, Medani, and Nyala markets adjusted within four months which means there was a strong relationship among Sennar market and these sheep markets. Elobied market adjusted within five months, this may due to the same nature of these two markets as supply markets.

Figure 10 below depicts a standard error shock in Nyala and its response in Elobied, Omdurman, Medani and Sennar markets, which shows that the adjustment take four months to eliminate the price shock and converge onto long-run equilibrium for Elobied, and Medani markets. The close production areas of Nyala and Elobied justified this result for the easy information movement. Omdurman and Sennar

Direction	Obs	F-Statistic	Prob.
Medani does not granger cause Elobied	202	0.89835	0.4089
Elobied does not granger cause Medani		2.23947	0.1092
Nyala does granger cause Elobied	202	4.14190	0.0173
Elobied does granger cause Nyala		4.67885	0.0103
Omdurman does granger cause Elobied	202	2.51226	0.0837
Elobied does not granger cause Omdurman		1.81085	0.1662
Sennar does not granger cause Elobied	202	0.38267	0.6825
Elobied does granger cause Sennar		2.41048	0.0924
Nyala does granger cause Medani	202	5.62191	0.0042
Medani does granger cause Nyala		2.82837	0.0615
Omdurman does not granger cause Medani	202	1.50213	0.2252
Medani does not granger cause Omdurman		0.32690	0.7215
Sennar does not granger cause Medani	202	0.29589	0.7442
Medani does not granger cause Sennar		1.67032	0.1908
Omdurman does not granger cause Nyala	202	1.14918	0.3190
Nyala does granger cause Omdurman		4.14921	0.0172
Sennar does not granger cause Nyala	202	0.43247	0.6495
Nyala does granger cause Sennar		3.06879	0.0487
Sennar does not granger cause Omdurman	202	0.10697	0.8986
Omdurman does not granger cause Sennar		0.45528	0.6349

Table 10: Pairwise granger causality tests.

market takes more than six months to eliminate the price shock and converge onto long-run equilibrium, the interpretation behind this may due to the long distance between Nyala and these two markets.

Pairwise granger causality analysis for sheep prices

Granger causality is also estimated between pairs of livestock markets in Sudan during the period of study. Granger causality means the direction of price formation between two markets and related spatial arbitrage, i.e., physical movement of the commodity to adjust for these prices differences. If markets located in sheep production areas, tended to Granger-cause prices in major consumption markets, this is taken as evidence that price movements were primarily driven by supply shocks. If, however, terminal markets tended to Granger-cause other markets, this is taken as evidence that price movements are caused by demand shocks. Table 10 given the results of the Granger causality test.

Table 10 above show that, Medani, Elobied, Omdurman, Sennar and Nyala markets exert a causality relations, which was Nyala market created unidirectional relation causality through Medani and Elobied markets. That mean the sheep price of Nyala granger cause Medani and Elobied an on the other hand, the sheep price of Medani and Elobied granger cause Nyala. There were bidirectional relations which were Elobied market granger cause Sennar while Nyala granger causes Omdurman and Sennar, also Omdurman granger cause Elobied. Mention these results, Nyala market granger cause all other markets. The short run dynamics analysis of sheep prices holds significance results that Nyala sheep prices affecting Sennar, Medani and Omdurman markets. Nyala market as terminal market located in production area granger cause Medani and Omdurman as major consumption markets; this was taken as evidence that price movements were primarily driven by supply shocks. That mean the system was centered on Nyala i.e. Nyala could be considered as a supply of sheep market which means the prices were supply driven.

Concluding Remarks

This paper discusses the multivariate cointegration regression results for sheep prices using (Engle and Granger) test [23] and the vector autoregression (VAR) of Johansen. The first step toward cointegration tests is the stationarity tests using three approaches; these were Dickey-Fuller test, Phillips Perron test and panel unit root test. The results show that all price series are non-stationary in level, while they are stationary in first differences for all variables and then all prices were integrated of order *I(1)*. Hence these series could be tested for the existence of a long run (cointegration) relationship between them through multivariate cointegration approaches.

As the long run analysis of sheep prices in selected markets indicated, a strong evidence of cointegration of pairs of markets exists. The last month disequilibrium in prices of Medani on Sennar corrected in the next month by 5%, where it seems to adjust slowly towards the long-run equilibrium. On the other hand, with respect to Omdurman on Elobied prices relationship, the last month disequilibrium in prices was corrected in the next month by 15%.

In the long run the level of sheep prices in Medani, Elobied, Omdurman, Sennar and Nyala exert significant long run effect on the current development of prices of Elobied and Sennar markets, thus suggesting the validity of the long run equilibrium relationship in Elobied and Sennar markets. But the levels of sheep prices in the five markets have no significant long run effect on Omdurman, Medani and Nyala prices. This result indicate that Elobied sheep markets consider as leader market, The long run analysis showed that Omdurman and Nyala markets were not cointegrated. The lack of cointegration among these markets may be due to the long distances separating the major sheep production areas from the consumption areas, the slow means of transport and the high marketing costs. The trekking route from Nyala to Elobied, for instance, is about 600 kilometers, and that between Elobied and Omdurman is about 560 kilometers, giving a total trekking route from Nyala to Omdurman of about 1,160 kilometers. The journey along this route takes 75 to 80 days, making the total marketing costs about 24% of the total costs.

In the short run the sheep prices of Nyala market does not have any impact on the rest of the prices of other markets except Medani market. Babiker [24] found that the sheep prices of Nyala market are affected by their own prices only in the short run. The prices of sheep in Elobied market affect the sheep prices in Omdurman livestock market by 33% in the short run, Elobied affect Medani by 44% Omdurman affect Elobied by 34%, Medani affect Sennar by 36% and Sennar affect Medani by 46%. This coherent affecting of sheep prices may due to the active commercial movement between these markets because of the ease of transportation, as well as to the relatively near distances between these markets [25].

The periods that sheep markets need to eliminate the price shock and converge onto long-run equilibrium was fluctuated between four and five months. Elobied, Nyala and Sennar adjust the shock in Omdurman market within five months and converge onto long-run equilibrium, while Medani market takes four months to converge onto long-run equilibrium, this justified by the short distance between these two markets. The short period of long-run equilibrium adjustment indicated that there are strong price linkages between Omdurman and other four markets (Elobied, Medani, Sennar and Nyala markets). The prices causality indicated unidirectional relation causality of Nyala market through Medani and Elobied markets. Nyala market as terminal market located in production area granger cause Medani and Omdurman as major consumption markets; this was taken as evidence that price movements were primarily driven by supply shocks. That mean the system was centred on Nyala i.e. Nyala could be considered as a supply market in sheep market which means the prices were supply driven.

References

1. Corporation ARS (2004) Livestock Market Statistical. Animal Resources Services Corporation.
2. Bank World (2003) World Development Report 2003: World Bank. Washington pp: 148-161.
3. Fahey, Dan, Leonard, David K (2007) The political economy of livestock and pastoralism in Sudan. Berkeley, CA: IGAD Livestock Policy Initiative, International Resources Group and Institute for International Studies, University of California.
4. Corporation ARS (2010) Livestock Market Statistical Data Report 2010. Omdurman.
5. Bank World (2006) Diagnostic Trade Integration Study (DTIS) Productivity and Trade in Agricultural Products, World Bank, Sudan Study Draft.
6. Babiker NM, Bushara MOA (2006) The spatial integration of sheep markets in the Sudan: A bivariate approach. Gezira Journal of Agricultural Science 4: 147-156.
7. Idris B (2008) Livestock Marketing in Eastern and Central Sudan: Sector Policy Note, Sudan Multi Donor Trust Fund National.
8. Bushara MOA, Abdelmahmod MKA (2015) Efficiency of Selected Sudanese Cattle Markets: Multivariate Co-integration Approach (1995-2011). International Journal of Economics and Management Sciences.
9. Johansen S, Juselius K (1990) Maximum likelihood estimation and inference on cointegration with applications to the demand for money. Oxford Bulletin of Economics and Statistics 52: 169-210.
10. MacKinnon, James GH, Alfred A, Michelis L (1998) Numerical distribution functions of likelihood ratio tests for cointegration. Department of Economics, University of Canterbury.
11. Johansen S (1988) Statistical analysis of cointegration vectors. Journal of economic dynamics and control 12: 231-254.
12. Johansen S (1991) Estimation and hypothesis testing of cointegration vectors in Gausian vector autoregressive models. Economietrica 59: 1551-1580.
13. Johansen S (1995) Likelihood-based inference in cointegrated vector autoregressive models. OUP Catalogue.
14. Johansen S (1992) Determination of cointegration ranks in the presence of a linear trend. Oxford Bulletin of Economics and Statistics 54: 383-397.
15. Akaike H (1987) Factor analysis and AIC. Psychometrika 52: 317-332.
16. Hannan EJ, Quinn B G (1979) The determination of the order of an autoregression. Journal of the Royal Statistical Society. Series B (Methodological) 41: 190-195.
17. Greene, William H, Seaks Terry G (1991) The restricted least squares estimator: a pedagogical note. The Review of Economics and Statistics 73: 563-567.
18. Banerjee A, Dolado JJ, Henry G (1993) Co-integration, error correction, and the econometric analysis of non-stationary data. OUP Catalogue.
19. Idris B, Abdalla AM (2009) Spatial price transmission: A study of sheep markets in Sudan. African Journal of Agricultural and Resource Economics 3: 43-56.
20. Zohair MA (1970) Marketing of livestock in the Sudan. University for Reading.
21. Jarque CM (2011) Jarque-Bera test International Encyclopedia of Statistical Science 701-702 Springer.
22. Babiker NM, Bushara MOA (2006) Integration between cattle markets in the Sudan, 1980-2000. Gezira Journal of Agricultural Science 4: 130-146.
23. Robert FE, Clive WJG (1987) Co-integration and error correction: representation, estimation, and testing. Econometrica 55: 251-276.
24. Babiker NM, Bushara MOA (2006) The Spatial Integration of Sheep Markets in the Sudan: A bivariate Approach 4: 147-156.
25. David AD, Wayne AF (1981) Likelihood ratio statistics for autoregressive time series with a unit root. Econometrica 49: 1057-1072.

Does the Inflows of Foreign Aid Dampen or Stimulate FDI to EAC Members? Evidence From East African Community (EAC) Members

Masoud Mohammed Albiman*

Department Research Policy and Development, Zanzibar Revenue Board (ZRB) and Zanzibar Insitute of Business Research and Technology (ZIBRET), Tanzania, Zanzibar

Abstract

Recently, the World Bank and IMF have been more interested in understanding whether foreign aid inflows from multilateral or bilateral donors have catalyzing effect on the crowd out effect to FDI. From this fact, the paper investigates the causal relationship between foreign aid, both bilateral and multilateral aid with FDI inflows to EAC members. Using time analysis techniques of VECM and Granger causality, the results are mixed. On one hand, foreign aid (bilateral and multilateral) causes FDI in two countries. On the other hand, we found no relationship between foreign aid and FDI in other two countries. The results calls for appropriate policy implementations.

Keywords: FDI; EAC; Foreign investments

Introduction

Recently, the World Bank and IMF have been more interested in understanding whether foreign aid inflows from multilateral or bilateral donors have catalyzing effect on the crowd out effect to FDI [1]. Yet, very few studies have empirically examined the impact of foreign aid to FDI to developing countries especially the East African community members (EAC).

For long time foreign aid has become an important source of external finance to the African economics. Foreign aid as an important source of inflows especially in Africa, on average, it accounts for 12.5 percent of total GDP in Africa [2]. On the other hand, recently due to the more economic integration and promotion of open economic policies, FDI has become a second source of external finance. From this fact it is important to look for the relationship of these two variables.

According to several literatures, foreign aid has different impact of economic growth. Firstly it is argued that, foreign aid can improve the domestic infrastructures to the recipient countries [3]. Since the increase in foreign aid would necessitate marginal productivity of domestic capital thus will stimulate more FDI inflows. However, it is also argued that, when foreign aid come in the form of physical capital would increase in capital accumulation in the domestic economy as results crowd out FDI [4,5].

Furthermore, foreign aid can be used to finance budget deficits and profit outflows from FDI, as results will attract more FDI [3]. On the other hand, the increase in foreign aid can increase the supply of tradable goods and results to lower price of goods in domestic economy. From this fact, the profit of FDI would diminish due to low price of goods thus FDI will decrease or crowded out (Some time this act is tremed as "dutch diseases").

The criteria for selecting to study the EAC members are as follows lies in the argument that, the trend of foreign aid, FDI and their ration to GDP are increasing rapidly since late 1990s (Figures 1 and 2). Furthermore, the EAC members are still in the process of monetary union and political federations by 2015. From this fact, the clear and appropriate policies are needed on the determinants of macroeconomic performance of these countries. Not only that but also according to millennium development goals (MDGs), EAC members considered as poorest countries in LDCs by the World Banks. In that sense, they receive higher aid inflows in the sense that, would help to reduce levels of poverty, budget deficits and improve the social economic well-being by 2015.

On the other hand, due to the small private capital inflows like FDI, especially for the LDCs, for long time foreign aid seems to play important role in supporting FDI inflows. It suggested that, foreign aid can play the important role in mitigating the supply constraints, such as poor infrastructure and communications and low capital available for the development program. For example, the key function of the Multilateral Investment Guarantees Agency (MAG) plays an important role to ensure that FDI risks are eliminated [6].

For example, MAG, provide insurance to any risk relating to expropriation, currency, profit transfer restrictions, and political risk or any government actions against private sectors. In fact, the main assumptions here is that, the foreign aid programs would help to remove obstacles relating to the inflows and performance of FDI in developing countries especially African countries. For example, Multilateral aid (MAID) helps to reduce expropriation risk of the government. On the other hand, bilateral aid (BAID) said to reduce

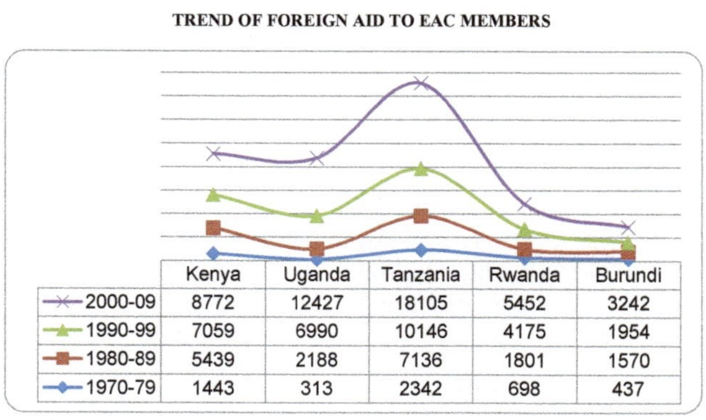

	Kenya	Uganda	Tanzania	Rwanda	Burundi
2000-09	8772	12427	18105	5452	3242
1990-99	7059	6990	10146	4175	1954
1980-89	5439	2188	7136	1801	1570
1970-79	1443	313	2342	698	437

Figure 1: The trend of Foreign aid (ODA) inflows to EAC members. (Source: UNCTAD Online database and author's calculation).

***Corresponding author:** Masoud Mohammed Albiman, Department Research Policy and Development, Zanzibar Revenue Board (ZRB) and Zanzibar Insitute of Business Reseach and Technology (ZIBRET), Tanzania, Zanzibar E-mail: Albimani1966@hotmail.com

TREND OF FDI TO EAC MEMBERS

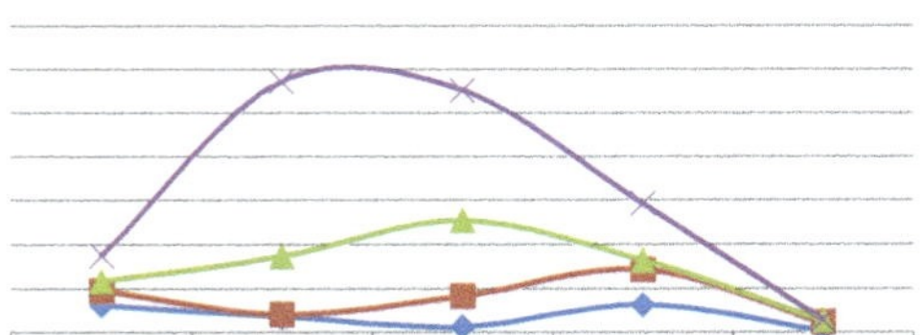

	Kenya	Uganda	Tanzania	Rwanda	Burundi
2000-09	0.6	4	3	1.3	0.02
1990-99	0.2	1.32	1.7	0.2	0.04
1980-89	0.33	0.05	0.7	0.8	0.19
1970-79	0.6	0.33	0.1	0.6	0.01

Figure 2: FDI percentage in GDP for EAC members (Source: UNCTAD Online database, 2010 and author's calculations).

the risk of FDI since it acts as good signal of the relationship between recipients and host country.

Literature Reviews

Very few literatures investigated the impact of foreign aid to FDI. This part presents the discussion of the previous empirical literatures. Karakaplan [7] argued that, found that foreign aid do not have any impact to FDI instead, financial development and good governance should be promoted to attract more FDI. Furthermore, Harmz and Lutz [3] supported Karakaplan [7], by suggesting that foreign aid does not have any impact to economic growth. In contrast, Blaise [8] found positive impact of aid to FDI in Japan. However, they pointed that aid has significant impact to FDI, when countries have unfavorable environments or when private investors faces heavy regulatory restrictions. All literatures of [3,7,8] used same proxies of total value of aid and FDI in their analysis.

Furthermore, Kosack and Tobin [9] supported Karakaplan [7] and Harmz and Lutz [3] by suggesting that, foreign aid does not have an impact to marginal productivity in host country since most of aid inflows are in the form of government budget deficits and human support. Simultaneous to that, Caselli and Feyrer [10] argued that foreign aid in most African countries substitute FDI rather than complement it. In supporting these results, Arellano et al. [11] pointed that, foreign aid substitute FDI in the host country.

Moreover, Kimura and To-do [12] after using a gravity model to investigate the impact of aid to FDI in Japan. He found that foreign aid does not attract FDI. This is indicated major difference with the results of Blaise [8] who did the same analysis in Japan.

In general, Kimura and Todo [12] supported the results of Karakaplan [7], Kosack and Tobin [9] and Harmz and Lutz [3]. Furthermore, Changsheng Xu et al. [4] suggested that, foreign aid in the form of human capital and infrastructure causes FDI in Bangladesh, India and Sri Lanka. On the other hand, they found that aid in the form of physical capital causes FDI only in India. On the other side, suggested that FDI causes aid of human capital and infrastructure only for Bangladesh. Generally, they found that aid is complement factor for FDI in five Asian countries.

Methodological Issues

The study uses time series data therefore we have to ensure that all time series technique are met before final conclusion. Therefore, the study used three unit roots test to test whether variables are stationary these tests including Augmented Dickey fuller [13] test (ADF) Philips and Perron. The standard test of ADF and PP test both relied on the null hypothesis that there is unit root, and thus they are not powerful for the alternative hypothesis [14]. From this fact, we use KPSS test which assumes that the null hypothesis of a series are stationary. Thus the KPSS test is suggested to eliminate near unit root process which cannot be detected in ADF and PP test. The method uses to test for Co integration is a Johansen and Juselius approach [15,16]. If variables are cointegrated we use a vector error correction term (VECM) to test for the long run and short run causality.VECM model will be specified in the following form:

$$InGDP_t = \phi_0 + \sum_{i=1}^{m} \phi_{1i} InFDI_{t-i} + \sum_{i=1}^{n} \phi_{2i} InBAID_{t-i} + \sum_{i=1}^{n} \phi_{3i} InMAID_{t-i} + \sum_{i=1}^{n} \phi_4 InEXP_{t-i} + \sum_{i=1}^{n} \phi_{5i} InDI_{t-i} + \phi_6 ECM_{t-1} + \mu_{2t} \quad (1)$$

$$InBAID_t = \phi_0 + \sum_{i=1}^{m} \phi_{1i} InGDP_{t-i} + \sum_{i=1}^{n} \phi_{2i} InBAID_{t-i} + \sum_{i=1}^{n} \phi_{3i} InMAID_{t-i} + \sum_{i=1}^{n} \phi_4 InEXP_{t-i} + \sum_{i=1}^{n} \phi_{5i} InDI_{t-i} + \phi_6 ECM_{t-1} + \mu_{2t} \quad (2)$$

$$InMAID_t = \phi_0 + \sum_{i=1}^{m} \phi_{1i} InGDP_{t-i} + \sum_{i=1}^{n} \phi_{2i} InBAID_{t-i} + \sum_{i=1}^{n} \phi_{3i} InMAID_{t-i} + \sum_{i=1}^{n} \phi_4 InEXP_{t-i} + \sum_{i=1}^{n} \phi_{5i} InDI_{t-i} + \phi_6 ECM_{t-1} + \mu_{2t} \quad (3)$$

$$InZ_t = \beta_o + \sum_{i=1}^{m} \beta_{1i} InZ_{t-i} + \sum_{i=1}^{n} \beta_{2i} InGDPC_{t-1} + \sum_{i=1}^{n} \beta_{3i} InAID_{t-i} + \sum_{i=1}^{n} \beta_{4i} InFDI_{t-i} + \sum_{i=1}^{n} \beta_{5i} InEXP_{t-i} + \beta_6 ECM_{t-i} + \mu_{5t} \quad (4)$$

For Equation 1 up to 4, ***INBAID*** Implies bilateral aid, ***INMAID*** implies multilateral aid. For other variables and symbols as previously defined. From the equations above ECMs' is error correction terms lagged one year period. This help to differentiate between "short run" and "long run "causality. When ECM is negative and significant we conclude that there is long run causality. This is measured through the significance of the t test of ECM. The significance of the lagged changes of all independent variables ($\alpha's, \varphi's, \delta's, \lambda's$) implies that there is short run causality. This test is performed through the significance of the F-test. However, if the variables are not Co integrated, then the Granger causality test will be conducted in first difference VAR without including the ECM In the equations.

This study used annual data with the spanning from 1970 until 2010. The data collected is as follows, Uganda (1970-2010), Burundi (1970-2006), Kenya (1970-2010)), Rwanda (1976-2010). The data collected from UNCTAD online database key indicators and World's Bank indicators (WDI). Table 1 provides the descriptions of the variables and data source.

Analysis and Discussions

Unit root tests

The results of unit root tests are presented in Tables 2-5. The results are presented in two different forms, of intercept and trend and intercept. The critical value statistics are given in response of MacKinnon values. The PP statistics are obtained through Newey West adjustment of Bartlett Kernel On the other hand, the critical

Variable	Measurement	Descriptions	Sources
Economic growth	GDP per capita	Real GDP which includes domestic productions	UNCTAD, World Bank
FDI	FDI-GDP ratio	Foreign direct inflows	UNCTAD, World Bank
Export	Export-GDP ratio	Export of goods and services	UNCTAD, World Bank
Domestic investment	Capital formation-GDP ratio	Outlays or additions of fixed assets in the economy plus net changes in inventories excludes all form of FDI	World Bank
Foreign aid (multilateral nd bilateral aid)	Net ODA –GDP ratio	Disbursement of loans and Grants for development activities	UNCTAD, World Bank

(UNCTAD refers to the United Nations Conference on trade and development

Table 1: Description of Data and Sources.

Country/Variables	ADF test		PP test		KPSS test	
Kenya	**Constant**	**Constant and trend**	**Constant**	**Constanta and trend**	**Constant**	**Constant and trend**
lnGDP	-1.731524(1)	-2.451883(1)	-1.674096(1)	-2.065574(1)	0.485651*(4)	0.112937(4)
lnFDI	-4.491753(0)*	-4.531971(0)*	-4.621104(4)*	-4.620772(3)*	0.255018(4)	0.137697**(4)
lnAID	-1.906711(0)	-1.793426(0)	-1.994703(3)	-1.888663(3)	0.175152(5)	0.141573**(5)
lnEXP	-2.470181(0)	-2.708465	-2.556325(5)	-2.819109(3)	0.274447(4)	0.104256**(4)
lnLDI	-1.298025(0)	-1.312531(0)	-1.275661(2)	-1.3254981(2)	0.413098**(5)	0.168133*(5)
LPOP	-1.843587(4)	-2.573801(4)	0.597785(4)	-2.062498(4)	0.706347*(5)	0.175043*(5)
Uganda						
lnGDP	-1.149078(4)*	-4.551953(1)*	-2.815235(9)*	-3.319285(21)*	0.376751**(5)	0.200312*(5)
lnFDI	-8.391391(0)*	-8.369213(0)*	-8.747674(3)*	-8.726228(3)*	0.551435*(5)	0.155731*(4)
lnAID	-0.727849(0)	1.019541(0)	-0.727849(0)	1.336052(1)	0.173010(1)	0.170296*(2)
lnEXP	-6.070900(0)*	-5.168852(3)*	-6.322324(13)*	-14.09970(38)*	0.2509285(4)	0.209309*(4)
lnLDI	-8.005927(0)*	-8.360548(0)*	-8.171282(2)*	-8.360548(0)*	0.647906*(5)	0.176764(4)
LPOP	-1.232883(0)	-1.714150(0)	-1.232883(0)	-1.765305(1)	0.639866*(5)	0.126875**(5)

Notes: Asteriks* and ** implies a significant level at five percentage (5%) and ten percentage (10%). Values in ( ) implies the t statistics level. ADF implies Augmented Dickey Fuller [13] and Critical values obtained in response of McKinnon. PP implies Philips and Perron. KPSS implies Kwiatkowski et al. test. The critical values of KPSS found in Kwiakowski et al. [14].

Table 2: Unit Root Test Results in Level Form.

Country/Variables	ADF test		PP test		KPSS test	
Rwanda	**Constant**	**Constant and trend**	**Constant**	**Constanta and trend**	**Constant**	**Constant and trend**
lnGDPC	-1.944762(0)	-2.054124(0)	-1.867600(1)	-1.979785(1)	0.193793(4)	0.161714*(4)
lnFDI	-4.074611*(0)	-4.037325*(0)	-4.200330(3)*	-4.177382*(3)	0.189170(4)	0.151584*(4)
LBAID	-2.760526(0)**	-2.900308(0)	-2.752944(1)	-2.911429(1)	0.241348(4)	0.094483(3)
LMAID	-0.082679(0)	-1.395741(0)	-0.082679(0)	-1.056673(2)	0.521105*(1)	0.113882(1)
lnEXP	-2.264078(0)	-0.755180(2)	-3.144161*(2)	-4.032150*(2)	0.274447(4)	0.104256(4)
lnLDI	-3.142918(0)*	-3.976006*(0)	-3.144161(2)*	-4.032150*(2)	0.166015(4)	0.167591*(4)
Burundi						
lnFDIGDP	-5.162049(0)*	-5.162049(0)*	-5.236411(3)*	-6.179674(3)*	0.513015*(4)	0.132708**(3)
lnGDPC	-0.836574(0)	-1.465642(0)	-1.064946(3)	-1.493653(1)	0.170201*(5)	0.273348(2)
LBAID	-0.821502(7)	-1.995938(7)	-1.276133(3)	-2.143425(3)	0.497656*(4)	0.061438(4)
LMAID	-2.254999(1)	-3.077111(1)	-1.748873(0)	-2.276275(0)	0.479080*(4)	0.059486*(4)
lnEXP	4.193280(0)*	-4.781145(0)*	-4.282792(3)*	-4.768487(1)*	0.424638**(4)	0.085762(0)
lnLDI	-2.354820(0)	-2.310767(0)	-2.154292(1)	-2.100319(1)	0.146934(4)	0.149821*(4)

Notes: Asteriks* and ** implies a significant level at five percentage (5%) and ten percentage (10%).Values in ( ) implies the t statistics level. ADF implies Augmented Dickey Fuller [13] and Critical values obtained in response of McKinnon (1999). PP implies Philips and Perron (1988). KPSS implies Kwiatkowski et al. [14] test. The critical values of KPSS found in Kwiakowski et al. [14].

Table 3: Unit Root Test Results in Level Form.

values for Kwiatkowski et al. [14] is given is given by Kwiatkowski et al. [13]. Special attention has been given in the process of lag length selection, so as to ensure the disturbance terms are white noise. In this consideration, we use the Schwarz Criterion method is used to select the appropriate lag length which is selected automatically using Eviews 7.

Each test among these three tests has advantages and disadvantages at different circumstance. For example the standard test of ADF and PP test fails to detect the structural break that is common in time series moving average. From this fact, we assume that variables are not stationary at level or my (0), once it is accepted for all three tests in both with intercept and intercept with the trend. Otherwise, for any conflicting results we assume that variables is not stationary at levels I (0), hence we continue with first difference "*The same reasons has been given to justify that variables are stationary after first difference by several studies and used Johansen and Juselius co integration method (See, Das and Choudhary, Malik)*".

In any conflicting results, we also assume that, variables are not stationary at levels, because most of the macroeconomic variables were found to have a unit root problem at their level form. The results in Tables 2 and 3 present the results of unit root test in level form. After

Country/Variables	ADF test		PP test		KPSS test	
Kenya	Constant	Constant and trend	Constant	Constant and trend	Constant	Constant and trend
lnFDI	-7.640860(0*	-7.539890(1)*	-11.48543(4)*	-12.00144(5)*	0.068201(4)	0.044010(2)
lnGDP	-4.116716(0)*	-4.046209(0)*	-3.985447(4)*	-3.901202(4)*	0.148200(0)	0.148200(0)
LBAID	-3.688012*(1)	-3.649542*(1)	-7.456828*(4)	-7.391203*(4)		
LMAID	-8.684503*(0)	-8.623060*(0)	-8.684503*(0)	-8.680327*(1)	0.085435(3)	0.060293(3)
lnLDI	-6.543565(0)*	-5.032387(1)*	-6.550380(1)*	-6.793171(4)*	0.163232(0)	0.129231(0)
LEXP						
Uganda						
lnFDI	-8.391391(0)*	-8.369213(0)*	-8.747674(3)*	-8.726228(3)*	0.177549**(5)	0.088330(6)
lnGDPC	-1.149078(4)*	-4.551953(1)*	-2.815235(9)*	-3.319285(21)*	0.654680(4)	0.114284(4)
LBAID	-3.985545*(3)	-3.953470*(3)	-5.540887*(3)	-5.463748*(3)	0.082933(1)	0.084072(1)
LMAID	-6.956248*(0)	-6.978830*(0)	-6.959008*(2)	-6.982372*(1)	0.168527(2)	0.047265(0)
lnEXP	-6.070900(0)*	-5.168852(3)*	-6.322324(13)*	-14.09970(38)*	0.426540(11)	0.500000(39)
lnLDI	-8.005927(0)*	-8.360548(0)*	-8.171282(2)*	-8.360548(0)*	0.279799*(1)	0.138764(2)

Notes: Asteriks* and ** implies significant level at five percentage (5%) and ten percentage (10%).Values in ( ) implies the t statistics level. ADF implies Augmented Dickey Fueller [13] and Critical values obtained in response of McKinnon. PP implies Philips and Perron. KPSS implies Kwiatkowski et al. [14] test. The critical values of KPSS found in Kwiakowski et al.[14].

Table 4: Unit Root Test Results after First Difference.

Country/Variables	ADF test		PP test		KPSS test	
Rwanda	Constant	Constant and trend	Constant	Constant and trend	Constant	Constant and trend
lnFDI	-10.24709(0)*	-10.12138(0)*	-12.50651(5)*	-14.38733(7)*	0.142941(7)	0.124823(8)
lnGDPC	-7.009409(0)*	-5.668109(1)*	-7.381535(7)*	-7.90344*(12)	0.188740(10)	0.160761(14)
LBAID	-6.826276*(0)	-6.718878*(0)	-7.257424*(5)	-7.129368*(5)	0.241348(4)	0.094483(3)
LMAID	-1.542577(0)	-1.486560(0)	-1.469814(1)	-1.357543(1)		
lnEXP	-5.702638(1)*	-6.525035(1)*	-7.712599*(0)	-18.8233*(21)	0.054959**(2)	0.048817(2)
lnLDI	-9.826658(0)*	-9.796309(0)*	-11.72239(5)*	-14.94311(7)*	0.165855(4)	0.130902(5)
Burundi						
lnGDPC	-5.294493(0)*	-5.433210(0)*	-5.318789(2)*	-5.433210(0)*	0.273348(2)	0.083974(0)
lnFDI	-7.340173(1)*	-7.280233(1)*	-18.59025(8)*	-20.29324(7)*	0.053057(3)	0.053057(3)
LBAID	-6.083343*(6)	-5.937659*(6)	-5.541868*(3)	-5.515516*(2)	0.091274(4)	0.068571(4)
LMAID	-4.745933*(1)	-4.680378*(0)	-4.645795*(0)	-4.568240*(0)	0.054166(3)	0.053749(3)
lnEXP	-9.612456*(0)	-9.459687*(0)	-12.14575*(6)	-11.90680*(6)	0.167416(8)	0.147186(9)
lnLDI	-9.543565(0)*	-9.3211662(0)*	-0.895686(3)*	-8.754315(3)*	0.164485(3)	0.145432(3)

Notes: Asteriks* and ** implies significant level at five percentage (5%) and ten percentage (10%).Values in ( ) implies the t statistics level. ADF implies Augmented Dickey Fueller and Critical values obtained in response of McKinnon. PP implies Philips and Perron. KPSS implies Kwiatkowski et al. test. The critical values of KPSS found in Kwiakowski et al.

Table 5: Unit Root Test Results after First Differences.

Rwanda (2)				
	Variables:	LFDI LGDP LBAID LMAID LEXP LDI		
Ho:	Maximum Eigen value	95% critical value	Trace test	95%critical value
r=0	57.91033	40.07757	132.5956	95.75366
r≤1	30.86456	33.87687	74.68530	69.81889
r≤2	23.95607	27.58434	43.82074	47.85613
r≤3	10.88805	21.13162	19.86467	29.79707
r≤4	6.846837	14.26460	8.976625	15.49471
r≤5	2.129788	3.841466	2.129788	3.841466

Table 6: Johansen Multivariate Cointegration Test Results.

considering all the three tests, in both conditions of intercept with and without trend, it is concluded that that, all variables are not stationary in level form. On the other hand, Tables 4 and 5 presents results of unit root after first difference.

Multivariate cointegration analysis

Before, estimating the long run relationship between Foreign aid and FDI we have to ensure that all variables in the system have Co movement towards long run equilibrium. The optimal lags selected we rely on two information criteria Akaikes and Schwarz criteria. The lag selected for each country are in brackets, Rwanda (2), Uganda(1), Burundi(2) and Kenya (1). The Co integration test was estimated in the system of six variables, namely, FDI (LFDI), economic growth (LGDP), bilateral aid (LBAID), Multilateral aid (LMAID). For six variables included, the maximum Co integrating relationship is utmost five.

From Table 6 (Rwanda), the results show that there are, one Co integrates vectors in case of maximum Eigen test (n-r) =1, whilst Trace test indicates two Co integrating vectors (n-r) =2. On the other hand, from Tables 7 (Uganda) both tests show four Co integrating vectors

Rwanda (2)				
	Variables:	LFDI LGDP LBAID LMAID LEXP LDI		
Ho:	Maximum Eigen value	95% critical value	Trace test	95%critical value
r=0	114.6813*	40.07757	256.1311*	95.75366
r≤1	57.87435*	33.87687	141.4498*	69.81889
r≤2	36.28126*	27.58434	83.57546*	47.85613
r≤3	33.77517*	21.13162	47.29420*	29.79707
r≤4	13.48425**	14.26460	13.51903	15.49471
r≤5	0.034784	3.841466	0.034784	3.8414661)

Notes: LGDP (economic growth), LFDI (FDI), LBAID (bilateral aid), LMAID (multilateral aid), LEXP (export), LDI (Domestic investment), LPOP (labor force). * and ** refers to significant at 5 and 10 percent level respectively. Number in ( ) implies the optimum lag selected by both AIC and Schwarz Criterion

Table 7: Johansen Multivariate Cointegration Test Results.

Rwanda (2)				
	Variables:	LFDI LGDP LBAID LMAID LEXP LDI		
Ho:	Maximum Eigen value	95% critical value	Trace test	95%critical value
r=0	113.6289*	40.07757	182.1067*	95.75366
r≤1	25.62332	33.87687	68.47783	69.81889
r≤2	19.34886	27.58434	42.85451**	47.85613
r≤3	14.65725	21.13162	23.50564	29.79707
r≤4	8.835404	14.26460	8.848396	15.49471
r≤5	0.012992	3.841466	0.012992	(3.841466

Notes: LGDP (economic growth), LFDI (FDI), LBAID (bilateral aid), LMAID (multilateral aid), LEXP (export), LDI (Domestic investment), LPOP (labor force). * and ** refers to significant at 5 and 10 percent level respectively. Number in ( ) implies the optimum lag selected by both AIC and Schwarz Criterion

Table 8: Johansen Multivariate Cointegration Test Results.

Rwanda (2)				
	Variables:	LFDI LGDP LBAID LMAID LEXP LDI		
Ho:	Maximum Eigen value	95% critical value	Trace test	95%critical value
r=0	30.40181	40.07757	93.82097**	95.75366
r≤1	25.34509	33.87687	63.41916	69.81889
r≤2	20.11653	27.58434*	38.07407	47.85613
r≤3	8.738821	21.13162	17.95754	29.79707
r≤4	7.248945	14.26460	9.218719	15.49471
r≤5	1.969774	3.841466	1.969774	3.841466

Notes: LGDP (economic growth), LFDI (FDI), LBAID (bilateral aid), LMAID (multilateral aid), LEXP (export), LDI (Domestic investment), LPOP (labor force). * and ** refers to significant at 5 and 10 percent level respectively. Number in ( ) implies the optimum lag selected by both AIC and Schwarz Criterion.

Table 9: Johansen Multivariate Cointegration Test Results.

(n-r) =4). Furthermore, from Tables 8 (Burundi) and 9 (Kenya) both tests of max Eigenvalue and Trace test suggest one Co integrating vectors (n-r) =1. In general both tests suggest that there is a long run relationship for all variables in FDI model. This shows that, all variables included in the model are important determinants of FDI inflows in the long run. On the other hand, data indicate that, the models are far from spurious regression.

Vector error correction model (vecm) and granger causality

As we have said earlier within VECM model we can estimate the long run and short run relationship among the variables. After having found the long run relationship between FDI and Foreign aid now, here again we consider the short run interaction among the bilateral aid, multilateral and FDI inflows.

However, we include other important variables like economic growth, domestic investment and human capital. The lag was selected using AIC and Schwarz Criterion. The results are presented in Tables 10-13. The results of error correction terms (ECTs) shown by the t statistics value whilst Granger causality is shown by Chi square statistics. For the diagnostic test most of the results show that our models are free from serial correlation and normally distributed.

In the case of Kenya, in Table 10 results show that, error correction term of bilateral aid (LBAID) and economic growth (LGDP) are significant at the five percent level of significance. This implies that, they make the adjustment towards long run equilibrium, after any short run deviations. For remaining variables do not make adjustment for any shock in the model. The results show that, at the five percent level of significance, bilateral aid (LBAID) Granger cause exports (LEXP). On the other hand, bilateral aid (LBAID) causes multilateral aid (LMAID) at ten percent level of significance. We also found that, economic growth granger causes exports.

In the case of Rwanda (Table 11) the error correction term of multilateral aid (LMAID) and domestic investment (LDI) and export are significant at the five percent level of significance. Any short run deviations from the long run, those variables which are significant will make a correction in the next period and the model will return to the equilibrium. In this model, we found that, all variables including bilateral and multilateral aid granger cause FDI. Multilateral aid

Dependent variables	Independent variables X^2 statistics of lagged first differenced term (p values)						ECT $^{t-1}$ [t-ratio]
	ΔLFDI	ΔLGDP	ΔLBAID	ΔLMAID	ΔLEXP	ΔLDI	
ΔLFDI	-	0.37(0.53)	0.22(0.63)	0.60(0.43)	0.86(0.35)	0.68(0.40)	0.05 (0.36)
ΔLGDP	0.28(0.59)	-	0.90(0.34)	0.11(0.73)	6.25*(0.01)	0.40(0.52)	0.00* (3.6)
ΔLBAID	0.21(0.64)	1.95(0.16)	-	3.39**(0.06)	1.38(0.23)	0.07(0.78)	-0.05* (-2.33)
ΔLMAID	2.55(0.10)	6.64*(0.00)	0.34(0.55)	-	0.54(0.45)	0.30(0.58)	0.01 (0.16)
ΔLEXP	0.45(0.49)	6.36*(0.01)	0.06* (0.80)	0.02(0.86)	-	1.19(0.27)	-0.02 (-1.59)
ΔLDI	1.94(0.16)	1.81(0.17)	0.00*(0.98)	0.02(0.86)	0.17(0.67)	-	-0.05 (-1.80)
GDP MODEL, AR(1)=86.84, JB=13, **FDI MODEL**, AR(1)= 86.84, JB=14, **EXP MODEL**, AR(1)=86.84, JB=19, **AIDMODEL**, AR(1)=86.84, JB =12.44, **LPOP MODEL**, AR(1)=86.84, JB =12.44, **LDI MODEL**, AR(1)=86.84, JB=83.30							

Notes: Asteriks * and ** refer to significant levels at five (5) and ten (10) significant level. Numbers in ( ) and [ ] refers to the chi square value and t statistics respectively. AR(1) refers to autocorrelation test at order one.JB refers to Jaque Berra normality test.

Table 10: Results of Vector Error Correction Model (VECM) (Kenya).

Dependent variables	Independent variables X^2 statistics of lagged first differenced term (p values)						ECT $^{t-1}$ [t-ratio]
	ΔLFDI	ΔLGDP	ΔLBAID	ΔLMAID	ΔLEXP	ΔLDI	
ΔLFDI	-	0.80 (0.66)	2.44 (0.29)	1.79 (0.40)	0.10 (0.40)	3.85 (0.14)	0.88 (1.05)
ΔLGDP	11.27 (0.00)*	-	3.11 (0.21)	5.2 (0.07)	0.01 (0.99)	5.88 (0.05)**	0.09 (1.61)
ΔLBAID	6.93 (0.03)*	0.96 (0.61)	-	2.89 (0.23)	1.14 (0.56)	5.07 (0.07)**	-0.36 (-1.68)
ΔLMAID	7.96 (0.01)*	4.92 (0.08)**	1.49 (0.47)	-	5.51 (0.00)*	1.86 (0.39)	4.97* (3.11)
ΔLEXP	4.57 (0.10)*	0.17 (0.91)	0.66 (0.71)	3.38 (0.18)	-	1.86 (0.39)	-0.23 (-1.79)
ΔLDI	7.87 (0.01)*	6.09 (0.04)	9.69 (0.00)*	3.04 (0.21)	1.43 (0.4)	-	0.33* (2.47)
GDP MODEL, AR(1)=75.84, JB=13, **FDI MODEL**, AR(1)= 75.84, JB=19, **EXP MODEL**, AR(1)=75.84, JB=29, **AIDMODEL**, AR(1)=75.84, JB =22.44, **LPOP MODEL**, AR(1)=75.84, JB =22.44, **LDI MODEL**, AR(1)=75.84, JB=43.30							

Notes: Asteriks * and ** refers to significant level at five (5) and ten (10) significant level. Numbers in ( ) and [ ] refers to chi square value and t statistics respectively. AR (1) refers to autocorrelation test at order one. JB refers to Jaque bera normality test.

Table 11: Results of Vector Error Correction Model (VECM) (Rwanda).

(LMAID) Granger causes export and economic growth. We also found that, domestic investment (LDI) granger cause bilateral id (LBAID).

On top of that, Uganda (Table 12) economic model shows that, error correction terms of the normalized variables (LFDI) are significant implies the presence of long run causality from all variables in the system including bilateral (LBAID) and multilateral aid (LMAID). Furthermore, the error correction term of economic growth (LGDP) and bilateral aid (LBAID) are significant at five and ten percent level of significance level. This implies that, all variables make adjustment to the long run, for any shocks in the short run. The results show that, only bilateral aid (LBAID) causes economic growth (LGDP).

On the other hand, we found that, multilateral aid (LMAID), foreign direct investment (LFDI) both Granger cause bilateral aid (LBAID). In turn, multilateral aid (LMAID) Granger causes bilateral aid (LBAID). This indicates that, both bilateral and multilateral aid, in the short run; they are dependent on their performance (Table 13). On the other hand, the results show that FDI (LFDI) causes export growth in the short run.

On the other hand, in Burundi, the results of error correction term show that, FDI (LFDI), bilateral aid (LBAID) and domestic investment (LDI) significantly make adjustments in equilibrium for any short run deviations. On the other hand, in the short run we found that, economic growth (LGDP), Granger cause bilateral aid (LBAID). Moreover, economic growth (LGDP), bilateral aid (LBAID), domestic investment (LDI) Granger causes exports. Furthermore, in the short run FDI, export, bilateral and multilateral aid Granger causes domestic investment (LDI).

Generally, for all countries we found that bilateral aid and multilateral aid cause FDI in two countries out of four namely Burundi and Rwanda. These results are supported by Changesheng Xu et al. [4] and Blaise [8]. This implies that the increase in foreign aid would stimulate more FDI through alleviating the constraints of FDI such as poor infrastructures and increasing more access of finance. On the other hand we found that, FDI granger cause bilateral aid in Rwanda

Dependent variables	Independent variables X^2 statistics of lagged first differenced term (p values)						ECT^{t-1} [t-ratio]
	ΔLFDI	ΔLGDP	ΔLBAID	ΔLMAID	ΔLEXP	ΔLDI	
ΔLFDI	-	1.10 (0.77)	7.66* (0.05)	5.56 (0.13)	6.59** (0.08)	16.5* (0.0)	0.09 (0.69)
ΔLGDP	0.15 (0.98)	-	5.20 (0.15)	3.65 (0.30)	0.71 (0.86)	19.2 (0.00)	0.01* (1.29)
ΔLBAID	2.28 (0.51)	6.34** (0.09)	-	14.7* (0.00)	0.11 (0.98)	7.13* (0.06)	0.37* (3.37)
ΔLMAID	2.73 (0.43)	4.68 (0.19)	8.15* (0.04)	-	2.48 (0.47)	10.1* (0.01)	-0.10 (-0.91)
ΔLEXP	1.47 (0.68)	1.79 (0.61)	6.19 (0.10)	2.29 (0.51)	-	1.79 (0.61)	-0.07 (-0.07)
ΔLDI	1.02 (0.79)	1.32 (0.73)	3.20 (0.36)	5.79 (0.12)	2.57 (0.46)	-	-0.00 (-0.19)
GDP MODEL, AR(1)=65.94, JB=14, **FDI MODEL**, AR(1)= 65.94, JB=39, **EXP MODEL**, AR(1)=65.84, JB=39, **AIDMODEL**, AR(1)=65.94, JB =22.44, **LPOP MODEL**, AR(1)=65.94, JB =22.22, **LDI MODEL**, AR(1)=65.84, JB=53.30							

Asteriks.* and ** implies five (5) and ten(10) significant level. Numbers in ( ) and [ ] refers to chi square value and t statistics respectively. AR (1) refers to autocorrelation test at order one.JB refers to Jaque bera normality test.

Table 12: Results of Vector Error Correction Model (VECM) (Uganda).

Dependent variables	Independent variables X^2 statistics of lagged first differenced term (p values)						ECT^{t-1} [t-ratio]
	ΔLFDI	ΔLGDP	ΔLBAID	ΔLMAID	ΔLEXP	ΔLDI	
ΔLFDI	-	0.30(0.85)	3.17(0.20)	0.01(0.99)	0.77(0.67)	14.0*(0.0)	-0.48* [-2.52]
ΔLGDP	3.49(0.17)	-	7.68*(0.02)	1.38(0.49)	6.06*(0.04)	32.4*(0.0)	0.00 [0.35]
ΔLBAID	0.80(0.66)	0.19**(0.90)	-	3.95(0.13)	8.65*(0.01)	6.0*(0.04)	0.15* [2.26]
ΔLMAID	3.28(0.19)	1.36(0.50)	1.63(0.44)	-	3.80(0.14)	14.8*(0.0)	-0.12 [-1.06]
ΔLEXP	0.33(0.84)	0.10(0.94)	3.03(0.21)	0.77(0.67)	-	4.49**(0.10)	-0.03 [-0.55]
ΔLDI	0.33(0.84)	1.69(0.42)	3.86(0.14)	0.39(0.82)	6.01*(0.04)	-	0.29* [5.57]
GDP MODEL, AR(1)=75.84, JB=33, **FDI MODEL**, AR(1)= 75.84, JB=79, **EXP MODEL**, AR(1)=75.84, JB=29, **AIDMODEL**, AR(1)=75.84, JB =42.55, **LPOP MODEL**, AR(1)=75.84, JB =72.44, **LDI MODEL**, AR(1)=75.84, JB=7.30							

Notes: Asteriks * and ** refer to significant levels at five (5) and ten (10) significant level. Numbers in ( ) and [ ] refers to the chi square value and t statistics respectively. AR(1) refers to autocorrelation test at order one. JB refers to Jaque bera normality test.

Table 13: Results of Vector Error Correction Model (VECM) (Burundi).

Country	FDI	Bilateral Aid	Multilateral Aid	Control Varaibles
		FOREIGN DIRECT INVESTMENT MODEL (FDI)		
Kenya	No causality	Cause multilateral aid and export	No causality	GDP causes export
Burundi	Cause LDI	Cause LFDI, LDI	Cause LFDI, LDI	Export, LDI cause FDI
Rwanda	Cause bilateral aid	Cause FDI	Cause FDI, Export and economic growth(LGDP)	LDI cause LBAID
Uganda	Cause export	Cause multilateral aid	Cause bilateral aid	LGDP cause LBAID

Table 14: Summary of Causalitry Results.

which implies that the increase in FDI would stimulate more familiarity between host countries and donors which results to more FDI inflows [17].

On the other hand we found that foreign aid both bilateral and multilateral aid do not support FDI in Kenya and Uganda. These results conform to the results of Karakaplan [7], Harmz and Lutz [3]; Kimura and Todo [12]. This implies that, the increase in foreign aid in these countries would not support FDI inflows; instead the government has to rely on alternative factors to increase FDI. In general the results are summarized in Table 14.

Conclusion

Recently, the World Bank and IMF have been more interested in understanding whether foreign aid inflows from multilateral or bilateral donors have catalyzing effect on the crowd out effect to FDI [1]. Yet, very few studies have empirically examined the impact of foreign aid to FDI to developing countries especially the East African community members (EAC). From this fact, the main intention of this research is to analyze the role of foreign aid to FDI inflows in EAC members.

Several literatures found mixed results concerning the impact of foreign aid to FDI. However at large extent, they found that, foreign aid does not have any impact to economic growth. Given that, FDI and foreign aid inflows are the large external source of EAC members it is worthwhile to determine their relationship especially in terms of causality. Using the time series techniques of vector error correction term (ECM) and Granger causality test we found mixed results for all EAC members.

Generally, for all countries we found that bilateral aid and multilateral aid cause FDI in two countries out of four namely Burundi and Rwanda. This implies that the future FDI inflows in Burundi and Rwanda largely depend on foreign aid inflows. On the other hand we found that, FDI granger cause bilateral aid in Rwanda which implies that the increase in FDI would stimulate more familiarity between host countries and donors which results to more FDI inflows. On the other hand we found that foreign aid both bilateral and multilateral aid do not support FDI in Kenya and Uganda. This implies that, the increase in foreign aid in Kenya and Uganda would not support FDI inflows; instead the government has to rely on alternative factors to increase FDI.

In the future studies, it will be important for the researchers to analyze the relationship between foreign aid and FDI in different branches such as looking the impact of human support aid and physical capital aid to FDI.

References

1. Kang SJ, Lee H, Park B (2011) Does Korea follow Japan in foreign aid? Relationships between aid and foreign investment. Japan and the World Econom 23: 19-27.
2. Pallage S, Robe MA (2001) Foreign aid and the business cycles. Review of International Economics 9: 641-672.
3. Harms P, Lutz M (2006) Aid, Governance and Private Foreign Investment: Some Puzzling Findings for the 1990s. The Economics journal 116 (513): 773-790.
4. Changsheng X, Bhavan TC, Zhong C (2011) The Relationship between foreign aid and FDI in South Asian economies. International Journal of Economics and Finance 3: 142-149.
5. Gong L, Xiaoying C (2007) Foreign aid, domestic capital accumulation and foreign borrowing. Journal of Macroeconomics 30: 1269-1284.
6. Asiedu E, Jin Y, Nandwa B (2009) Does the foreign aid mitigate adverse effects of approximation risk on foreign direct investment? Journal of International Economics 78: 268-275.
7. Karakaplan MU, Neyapti, Sayek S (2005) Aid and foreign direct investment: International evidence, JEL (Discussion paper no 5), Ankara, Turkey, Bilkent University.
8. Blaise S (2005) On the link between Japan ODA and FDI in China, Evaluation using conditional logit analysis. Applied Economics 37: 51-55.
9. Kosack S, Tobin J (2006) Funding self-sustaining development, The role of foreign aid, FDI and government in economic success. International organization 60: 205-43.
10. Caselli F, Feyrer J (2007) The marginal productivity of capital. Quarterly Journal of Economics 122: 535-568.
11. Arellano C, Bulir A, Lane T, Lipschitz L (2009) The dynamic implications of foreign aid and its variability. Journal of Development Economics 88: 87-102.
12. Kimura H, Todo (2010) Is foreign aid a vanguard of foreign direct investment? A gravity-equation approach. World development 38: 482-497.
13. Dickey D, Fuller W (1981) Likelihood ratio statistics for autoregressive time series with a Unit Root. Econometrica 49: 1057-1072.
14. Kwiatkowski D, Phillips PCB, Schmidt P, Shin Y (1992) Testing the null hypothesis of stationarity against the alternative of a unit root: How sure are we that economic time series have a unit root?, Journal of Econometrics 54: 159-178.
15. Johansen S (1988) Statistical Analysis of Co integrating Vectors. Journal of Economic Dynamics and Control 12: 231-254.
16. Johansen S, Juselius K (1990) Maximum likelihood estimation and inference on cointegration with applications to the demand for money. Oxford Bulletin of Statistics 52: 169-210.
17. Billet B (1993) Modernization Theory and Economic Development: Discontent in the Developing World, Westport, Conn. USA: Praeger Publisher.

Efficient Utilization of River Water: Constraints and Effects; Case of Alewuha Sub-basin in Raya Kobo-woreda for Irrigation Purposes

Molla DN*

Assistant Researcher, Ethiopian Public Health Institute, Addis Ababa, Ethiopia

Abstract

This research describes the findings of efficient utilization of river water; constraints and effects; case of Alewuha sub-basin in Raya-kobo-woreda. With simple random particularly lottery method, 50 samples drawn out of 3500 in proportionate representatives. Based on this, the collected data through structured interview questionnaire was analyzed with descriptive statistics analysis. It describes; land fragmentation, lack of technology, management problem, nature of channel constructed, disease and lack of skilled man power, lack of budget to maintain the channel system and repair the damaged channel, lack of interaction among the farmers, bad seed bed preparation and types of irrigation they use as a major constraints and their effects on yield reduction (-) and households emigration (+). Farmers in that river basin should convert rain fed land in to irrigable land by making a channel and they should utilize the river wisely.

Keywords: River; Water; Effects; Irrigation

Introduction

Back ground of the study

In the ancient time human population's activity on agriculture was dependent on the rain fed since rain fall scarcity was undoubted. Due to environmental problem (deforestation) the rainfall becomes erratic so that farmers tried to shift their water utilization towards both surface and ground water.

As agricultural river water use is generally accepted as the largest user of river water resource with in a given river basin, and therefore contributes at large to depletion and degradation of resource. Special attention, in the context of river water use for agriculture will be attributed to efficient use of river water at the basin level; rather than considering in the inefficiencies.

River water, once considered a free good and abundantly available resource has now become scarce and draw the attention of planners and policy makers for its optimal development and utilization.

Knuse stated that Indian farmers were preparing a plan on river water utilization in 1980 [1]. They started to construct bio-dams, reservoirs and canal networks. However, the river water resources sectors have been subjected to scathing criticism for its poor performance in increasing agricultural productivity and generating revenue from sale of water services.

As Swain stated on his research paper, Indian farmers delivered river water inefficiently and inequitably to their farms. He recognized that even if the marginal and small holdings endowed of river water resource, most of the water they take from the main canal is waste and lost.

According to Gary reported on his book, if the cultivation method (tillage and irrigation) is faulty and less efficient, resulting in the wastage of water, the duty of water will naturally be less. On many farmers, three fourth of the total irrigation water is wasted and lost [2].

Man's dependent up on irrigation can be traced to earliest biblical reference in a manner of wastage and lost. Irrigation in very early time was practiced by the Egyptians, Asians and the Indian of North American. Everyone knows that ancient Mesopotamia and Egypt were flourished on river Euphrates and Tigris, Nile respectively on irrigation activities. But, their perception towards utilization of river water efficiency was a grass-root level.

Turning to irrigation development in Ethiopia, it has a long history. Small scale irrigation started before 2000 years. It is fact that Ethiopia is the "Water Tower" of north East Africa. Although we are endowed by many big and small rivers, their economic contribution is not as such.

According to Relief Society of Tigray the major perennial rivers that pass through central Tigray such as Giba, Werie, Mereb and Tekeze are presently not utilized for agriculture efficiently. The river water distribution system in Raya-kobo woreda in general and Alewuha sub-basin in particular consists of structure built traditionally with inefficient capacity to deliver the required water reaching to the field is minimum, resulting high irrigation interval and right irrigation practices to irrigate more land area is the common experience of the farmers [3].

Conceptual frame work

Efficiency results when no resources are unemployed and no resources are misallocated. Economic efficiency is explained as equating marginal benefits obtained from the productive use of the resource to its marginal cost in water resource managements the simultaneous fulfilment of optimality conditions over space and time. Efficient utilization requires efficient water distribution and the choice of on farm irrigation technology. Efficiency means the production of any particular mix of goods and services in the least costly way. In another way efficiency is the result of full employment of the resource in this case water.

Graphically efficiency can be illustrated as follows:-

- All points on the curve are efficient i.e. no idle resource;
- At point "A" production is attainable but inefficient i.e. there is idle resource; here there is resource lost to produce the two goods.

***Corresponding author:** Molla Deribie Negash, Assistant Researcher, Ethiopian Public Health Institute, Addis Ababa Ethiopia, E-mail: mdraya3@gmail.com

- At point "D" production is unattainable; because our resources are scarce;

Efficiency depends on full employment Figure 1. So, efficiency is dependent variable but full employment is independent variable. Mathematically the concept is illustrated as follow:

Irrigation efficiency (%) = water stored in the soil for crop growth/ Water applied to the land

Justification of the study

As Kay stated basin irrigation can be very inefficiency method when it is not managed well [4]. In Alewuha sub- basin the peasants use the river unwisely, they use only small amount of its part. Even the water they distribute to their farm land is lost in different ways before reaching the irrigation land. This intern hinders agricultural production particularly crop production.

Prior to the present study, no economic study is carried out in Alewuha sub-basin. So, the problem still exists. Because of this problem; the researcher initiated to assess the constraints and their effects for efficient utilization of river water to be a solution.

The local society will benefit both economic and social aspects after accomplishing this task. This will be true if and only if different natural resource experts participate from various NGOs and governmental organization to curve or mould the behaviour of the society by reading and applying this research. If this is so, the society will become at least food secure and create employment opportunities to themselves as well as the rest of the society by handling the river water wisely.

Statement of the problem

We know that Ethiopia is the "Water Tower" of north east Africa for irrigation, drinking water and supply and development fishery. Despite the above fact only an insignificant portion of this huge amount of water resources potential is being utilized.

Since the fall of Dergue regime, the current regional government of Amhara was trying to address the problem of efficient utilization of river water by constructing a dam to the farmers. Similar to the regional government, NGOs were contributing various activities to solve existing problem. Canal from the river Alewuha was constructed to address the life of the farmers in particular Raya - kobo woreda in general. But the inefficient utilization of this river water still exists. That is why this research studies the constraints and their effects for efficient utilization of river water in this area.

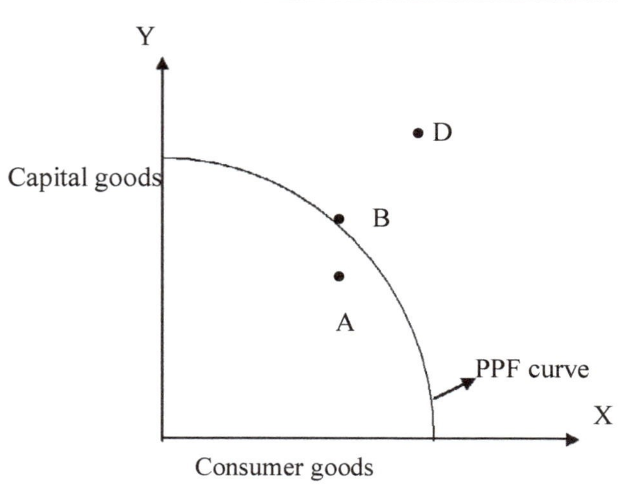

Figure 1: PPF curve.

Scope of the study

In Alewuha sub-basin there are two farmer's association that use this river for irrigation; Dur-Lebbes and Haddo. Therefore, this study was limited these to farmer's associations which are found in Raya-kobo woreda in north Wollo zone. It is highly limited to the constraints and their effects for efficient utilization of the river water.

Objective of the study

As indicated by the justification of the paper and statement of the problem the general objective is to assess the constraints for efficient utilization of river water and their economic and social effectives in Alewuha sub-basin.

Specific objectives

Apart from the general objective stated above, the paper also aims at attaining the following specific objectives:-

- To analyze the constraints for efficient utilization of river water for irrigation purposes.
- To examine the social and economic effects of the constraints on the society.
- To forward suggestions to minimize or to avoid these constraints.

Literature Review

Irrigation and water management

In the Umbeluzi experimental station, studies were done on field application efficiency the fluctuation is the river water table. The conclusion of the efficiency study was that due to the undulating characters of the fields, the field application efficiency of ferrous irrigation is very low, ranging in the four cases from 25-50%. Sprinkler application efficiencies under two treatments studded were 50 and 70%. Too long operation time's percolation losses and wind probably caused this low efficiency.

Water as a finite resource

Human consumption is obliged to share its demands for fresh water supplies with the needs of agriculture. Even if the donned community met all the funding demands of international NGOS for water and sanitation, the MDGs targets could still fail through inadequate integration with the bigger water picture.

Integrated water resource management inter-related water shad and rivers across national boundaries and oceans. In addition to educational programs for raising awareness of water conversation wise and efficient water use measures embrace water pricing.

Irrigation theory and practice

The practice of chaining water rate on area and crop basis has no relevance to the quantity of water supplied or used by the cultivator. There is always a dependency among the cultivators for over irrigation and wastage of water. This leads not only the loss of a valuable resource development at high cost but also the loss of costly nutrients through deep percolation. Further, it gives rise to problem of water logging a salt- build-up in a short period.

Climate change and water

This describes climate change as an "additional burden" to provide water services, rather an understatement in relation to the accompanying catalogued of potential impacts. The reduction in water availability caused by retreating Himalaya glaciers is possibly the impact on fresh water which carries the greatest risk to the greatest number of people to use the water efficiently and adequately. Along list of adaptation strategies in the inter government plan on climate change report concludes with a brief recognition that developing countries cannot possibly afford them and may have to resort to "unsustainable practices such as increasing ground water over exploitation".

Methodology and Data Set

Description of the study area

Alewuha sub-basin is one of the four rivers in Raya-kobo woreda of north Wollo zone in Amhara region. It is located at the south east of the woreda. It is bordered on the south by Gubalafto woreda and drainage in the mountain terrain with in the area in general to the east. It is also located, north latitude 11°30" and 12° 18" and east longitude 39° 23" and 39° 52" covering an area of 248 m^2 [3]. The area is flattened and suitable to deposition from the surrounding scraps. Small streams such as; Tikure wuha, Aba kolash, Gimbara and Belers are the major tributaries which are originated from topographically high one as of the Lasta Mountains at all average elevations of 2006 masl. The all-weather road from Addis Ababa to Mekelle passes through the basin. The local communities around this river are endowed by indigenous knowledge to prepare the local beer, the so called, "tejj".

Based on figure published by the CSA in 1994, these kebeles had estimated total population of 5482, of whom 2505 were males and 2777 were females. 86% of the total population of the woreda who live in these kebeles was agricultural population and the rest 14% live in the small town (Gobiye) as civil servant, merchants and daily labourers [3].

This area has elevation of between 1355-1640 masl and basaltic rock. And its means annual rain fall is between 800-1200 mm and average temperature is between 16-20°C. The local community's economic activity on irrigation is in this river basin and most of the time they produce teff, maize and recently sugar cane and onion.

Sampling technique

In Alewuha sub-basin, there are two farmer's associations who cultivate maize, sugar cane and onion by irrigation activity namely, Dur Lebbes and Haddo. There were 3500 households that use the river actively. But, it was tedious to draw 50 sample sizes out of 3500 households because of the societies' attitude towards this new task. Even though many difficulties arose in order to draw the sample, the local water leader /Yewuha Abbat/ provided his support by assembling the farms in the meeting hall. There by therefore drew 50 samples out of 3500 households that are active to use that arable land by proportionate representatives.

Because of time and financial budget to collect the primary data, the type of sampling was simple random particularly lottery method Table 1.

No.	Name of Kebele	Total No. of house	Let 50 = z, proportionate
		holds	sample size = (x/y)z
1	Dur – Lebbes	1750(x)	25
2	Haddo	1750	25
Total		3500 (y)	50

Table 1: Population and sample size.

Method of data collection

To get necessary data for the thesis; primary data were collected through interview to the farmers those who are the Alewuha sub – basin utilize. Secondary data from different sources like Kobo Girrana valley development study project, websites of irrigation, research thesis done in Amhara region and other parts of the world were incorporated. In general, to collect all the necessary data, interview in structured questionnaire and personal observation were conducted.

Data analysis

To get answers stated in questionnaire, both tabular and descriptive (narrative) analysis were used. The data were collected on February 14 and analyzed on February 22 Table 2.

Note:

- All the respondents gave answers.
- Households in percentage are out of the sample size (50).
- Someone can be understood from the table that utilization of river water have constraints and these constraints have negative effect on grain yield.

Note: - yield reduction is for maize production. Year is in E.C. As it can be seen from the table the constraints for efficient utilization of river water in Alewuha sub-basin had a great role for yield reduction from 1997-2001 and they had a positive impact on emigration, i.e. as the constraints become savior, the grain yield become reduced and emigration became enhance Table 3.

Results and Discussions

As Table 2 shows, 50% of the respondents gave their responses. They raised 6 major constraints for efficient utilization of river water in that area.

* Land fragmentation * Lack of technology

* Management problem * Nature of Channel constructed

* Disease * lack of skilled man power

Land fragmentation

The current Ethiopian government EFDR conducted land redistribution among the farmers in 1983 E.C for the rural people. Because of larger population size, an individual farmer had gotten small land size as a livelihood which is a state land. As a result, it was difficult to manage the river water in order to deliver water from the main canal to the irrigable arable land. Since land is small in size, it was worse off constructing wider and longer channel through the irrigable land. There by therefore as they said the water simply flows and loss. This intern created yield reduction, conflict among the farmers and emigration to another country or region. Thirty percent of the sample size gave answers.

Management problem

Because of mismanagement of the natural resource (river water), the local peasants had suffered both economic and social aspects. The zonal bureau of agriculture in general and the woreda bureau of

Responses		No. of respondents		
Constraints	Effects	House holds	Associations	Households (%)
• land fragmentation • Management problem • Nature of channel constructed • lack of technology	• Conflict • Migration (emigration) • Yield reduction	15	Dur- Lebbes	30
• lack of skilled man power • lack of Technology	• Migration (emigration) • Yield reduction	10	Dur- Lebbes	20
• lack of budget to maintain the channel system and repair the damage channel • Lack of interaction among the peasants • Bad seed bed preparation and type of irrigation.	• Night irrigation • reduction in water volume • drought • loss of nutrient	25	Haddo	50

Table 2: Responses and number of respondents in the 2 associations.

Effects	Years				
	1997	1998	1999	2000	2001
Yield reduction	20.00	17.00	6.03	10.00	8.01
Emigration	12.50	13.01	14.00	16.30	17.02

Source: kobo- Girran valley Development study project [3].
Table 3: Effects of constraints and number of peasants suffered by these constraints in different years.
Assume yield is quantified by q/ha and emigration is quantified by percentage.

agriculture in particular have no inspired confidence to manage the natural resource (river water). The natural resource managers in the woreda level and water leader (Yewuha Abat) did not implement rules and regulation properly. They did not also evaluate and monitor their doings (works). So as a constraint of efficient utilization river water; the management problem has a negative effect on economic and social aspects, yield reduction, conflict and emigration respectively. Simply supervision was not common in that area.

Nature of channel constructed

In that area the channel was constructed from traditional materials (mud, cow dung, plant remains, stones and so forth). In this, the farmers have no a common inlet/out let that connect their field because of this conflict has always arose among the farmers. Farmers considered canals as a state property and they did not take maintenance of canals. Since construction of the channels was from traditional materials/earthen/, huge amount of water loss and the field that they need to irrigate become dry and yield reduction took place. As a result, emigration happened among the farmers. Fifteen households gave this answer from Dur Lebbes farmer‘s association.

Disease

As Dur Lebbes respondents mentioned, yellow fever and malaria are available in that area, because of the elevation of the land (3000 massl). This area is preferable for reproduction of mosquitoes. There by therefore, the farmers afraid off diseases and they did not engage to irrigate their land at night. Unfortunately, the river water flows without any economic benefit and yield became down. This leads to emigration. This was answered by fifteen households from Dur-Lebbes farmer's associations.

Lack of skilled man power

Even though two research centers are available in that woreda, no economic research at all about river Alewuha. And also natural resource experts are not disseminated in that two farmer's associations to handle the problem of mismanagement of river water. Because of this constraint, the problem still up graded from day to day. And the farmers used the water unwisely; as a result their yield became less and suffered for migration to cope up with drought. Ten households raised this constraint from Dur-Lebbes.

Lack of technology

Because of land fragmentation, the farmers did not accept new technology to use the river water wisely. For example, the farmers did not allow using tractor to plough their land because land is fragmented. They feared conflict among the farmers. As a result, because of mismanagement of the natural resource (river water) by using technology, yield reduction took place which also leads emigration. Ten respondents gave this answer from Dur – Lebbes. In Haddo farmer's association 25 households or 50% respondents gave answer for the questions. These constraints are:

- Lack of budget to maintain the channel system and repair the damage channel.
- Lack of interaction among the farmers and
- Bad seed bed preparation and types of irrigation.

They gave effects for these constraints too.

Lack of budget to maintain the channel system and repair the damage channel

The peasants in those associations are not mature in terms of finance to maintain the canal and repair the damaged channel. Because of these constraints the problem of inefficient utilizations of river Alewuha sub- basin is still enhanced, therefore the volume of water through the channel is minimized as a result sufficient amount of water did not reach at the irrigable arable land. This leads yield irrigation and emigration.

Lack of interaction among the farmers

The farmers in this area had no cooperation among themselves for their common goals. They did not take maintenance of the channel before a rain had come. This is to mean that, they did not give their lion's share of maintenance in terms of monetary value and non – monetary value. If that was so, as the farmers said the river water cannot be managed well. Due to this reason the water didn't reach on the target irrigable land. It is simply loss. This by itself enhanced yield reduction, conflict and finally drought took place.

Bad seed bed preparation and types of irrigation

Aplenty of water was wasted in that sub - basin because of poor land preparation as the farmers mentioned. In that area peasants did not prepare land for irrigation or land levelling properly. That did not improve the uniformity of applied water to the irrigable land. They did not clear the bushes, grading the land finally as desired. Without confronting these constraints they irrigate the land by surface irrigation (sheet run off) method. As a result, a plenty of water cannot infiltrate to the ground. This is because of clods and aggregate soils. Therefore, this leads to yield reduction because plants on the farm don't get sufficient water supply.

In Table 3 effects of constraints and a number of peasants suffered by those constraints in different year is given.

Yield reduction

As it can be seen from the table, someone can understand that grain yield of maize is decreased from 1997 - 2001 E.C. This is because of inefficient utilization of river water.

Emigration

Because of different factors the peasants Immigrate to Arabian countries (outside of Ethiopia) and to another region (inside the country Ethiopia). As the table shows in 1997 a number of emigrate were 12.50% and in 2001 it was increased by 4.52% i.e. 17.02. This is as a result of yield reduction in that basin.

Conclusion and Recommendation

Conclusions

The overall study aims to assess efficient utilizations of river water; constraints effects in Alewuha sub - basin. As the constraints mentioned, all the constraints have a negative effect on utilization of river water that is, as the constraints become saviour, the water loss problem become higher.

As a result these constraints have negative effect on yield and positive effect on emigration. This is to mean that, as the problem become saviour, yield reduction takes place in that area. Not only the yield but also on the social aspects (emigration) those constraints have a great role.

As Table 3 shows, from 1997 – 2001 yield reduction is reflected. The population effect (emigration) became increase that is the populations emigrated from that woreda to another woreda even to outside the country (Arabian countries).

In general these constraints have a negative effect on the economic as well as on the social aspects.

Recommendations

It is difficult to give remedies for the problem and answers for the questions if the causes or constraints cannot know. But, the constraints and their effects are on hand in this study. If this is so, as a natural resource economics researcher what I need to give some suggestions here is that the farmers in that river basin should develop another area as an irrigable land around that river. In that area there is an idle land and teff cultivation by using rain fed agriculture. And they should utilize the river wisely by constructing a channel together. To avoid land fragmentation they should convert rain fed land in to irrigable land by making a channel.

References

1. Knuse (1982) Environmental science. America society, New York, USA.
2. Singh NP, Singh RA (2002) Scientific Crop Production, Nagar, India.
3. Kobo-Girana valley development study project (1996) Sustainable and rehabilitations.
4. Kay M (1986) Surface irrigation system and practices. Costs world pess, oxford, Great Britain.

A Study on Learning Styles, Gender and Academic Performance of Post Graduate Management Students in India

Ariz Naqvi* and Farah Naqvi

American University of the Middle East, Egaila, Al Ahmedi, Kuwait

Abstract

The management courses in higher education has experienced a rapid increase in the number of female students in the past decade. A number of factors were found attributing to the cause including some major social and educational factors. These factors are well studied by the scholars in the past. However, there is still considerable gap in the literature pertaining to the relationship between learning styles and gender differences in the context of management education. This paper focuses on management education using Experiential Learning Theory (ELT) and explores the effects of learning styles and gender on the performance scores of undergraduate students in three successive academic years. Results of the study indicate that the distribution of learning style type preference of the chosen sample of students was more concentrated towards assimilating and converging styles. Further results also indicate non-significant difference of learning style and gender in all groups. The performance scores of males were found higher in Finance and Marketing disciplines, whereas scores of females were higher in Human Resource and International Business disciplines irrespective of non consistency in all the groups. The study concludes that instructors should use a learning strategy matching with the style of each learner in different majors of management opted by the students.

Keywords: Learning styles; Kolb; Experiential learning theory; Gender; Management education

Introduction

The term "learning styles" is being used in educational literature since 1970s. It has been used synonymously with cognitive style and thinking style. According to Curry [1,2], till now, 21 models of learning styles have been researched in educational literature. From a generic standpoint, learning style is defined in Oxford American College Dictionary as, "A way of behaving or approaching a situation that is characteristic of or favored by a particular person." From a psychological standpoint, learning style involves more complexity, especially in the context of formal education. Therefore, a common consensus on the definition of learning styles among the scholars has never been achieved. As per ELT, learning style of a person can be defined in terms of preferred methods used by an individual for perceiving and transforming his/her learning experiences [3-5]. The person's internal goals and specific needs shape an his/her approach towards learning, resulting in a dominant learning style. The alignment between dominant learning styles of students and teaching styles of instructor has strong implications for success in academic disciplines. The cohesion and compatibility between course major and learning styles is, infact, one of the most important factors to consider when deciding on an academic major [6].

Many studies have been conducted in different disciplines using ELT as a framework. In academic literature the most published research on learning styles is on education discipline, followed by business management and computer science engineering. The focus of educational research on learning styles emphasized on matching student learning styles with curriculum and teaching styles of instructors. However, as mentioned before, little research investigates the the effects of learning styles and gender on the performance scores at different streams of courses in management education.

Literature Review

Kolb's learning theory

The work by Dewey, Lewin and Piaget have a strong influence on Kolb's experiential learning theory (ELT) and learning styles inventory (LST). Kolb's experiential learning theory emphasizes on the role of experience in individual's learning process. Kolb [7] explains experiential learning theory as a combination of perception, cognition and behavior which provides a holistic and integrative perspective on person's approach to learning. To explain the same Kolb further proposed a model, which includes four-stage cycle:

a. Concrete Experience (CE)

b. Reflective Observation (RO)

c. Abstract Conceptualization (AC)

d. Active Experimentation (AE)

Kolb (1984) further stated that the learning style of the students must comprise different abilities. To enhance the effectiveness of learning styles the learners should be able to combine at least two abilities to form their learning styles. Kolb (1976) presented four types of learning styles' combining two or more abilities under each styles:

a. Diverging Styles (CE/RO)

b. Assimilating (AC/RO)

c. Converging (AC/AE)

d. Accommodating (CE/AE)

***Corresponding author:** Ariz Naqvi, American University of the Middle East, Egaila, Al Ahmedi, Kuwait, E-mail: ariz.naqvi@aum.edu.kw; ariz.naqvi@yahoo.com

Diverging learning Style - combines feeling and watching (CE/RO), learners in this category are sensitive, and they prefer to watch rather than do, the gather information and use imagination to solve problems. Kolb refers to this style as diverging because these learners have their strength in situations that require ideas-generation, brainstorming imagination and so on. They tend to be strong in the arts and they are good listeners.

Assimilating learning style - (AC/RO) combines the ability to watch and think. Learners in this category prefer concise and logical approach to instruction. Honey and Mumford as cited by O' Neill [8] categorize learners with assimilating learning style as theorist. The learners with such style needs clear explanation of the concepts to be able to generate learning out of it. Such kind of learners are found more inclined towards ideas and abstract concepts. They excel at organizing wideranging information and interpreting it in a clear and logical format.

Converging learning style (AC/AE) - combines learners abilities to think and act. Learners in this category are more skilled in solving problems. Such learners are found generating learning by finding solutions to practical problems. They excel at technical tasks and like to experiment with new ideas, and its implementation with practical applications.

Accommodating learning style (CE and AE) - integrates learner's abilities to act and feel. Learners in this category depends more on intuition than logic. They take a practical and experiential approach while using other people's analysis. These people are attracted to new challenges and use their own experiences to carry out plans. People with such learning styles found giving preference to others as a source of information than carry out analysis by themselves.

Relationship between learning style, gender and academic performance

Since past decade the research on ELT is concentrated on the concept of learning style and using Learning Style Inventory (LSI) to examine the preffered learning styles of the individuals. However, some of the researches also aimed at investigating the relationship between gender and learning style. The research concluded that both men and women are different in their approach towards learning and use of learning styles [9,10]. The question which requires further exploration is whether or not traditional education curriculum addresses these differences in learning styles. There are evidences that traditional education curriculum does not support all preferred learning styles. As per Philbin et al. [11], traditional education curriculum supports learning styles of men more than women. However in the contemporary discipline like management education more emphasis is given on application based learning. This shift from traditional classroom education to application based learning has increased the importance of creating a culture that puts emphasis on different learning styles [12]. Most researches suggest that preferred learning styles of both the genders can be distributed equally among the four approaches of learning; however, there are considerable evidences suggesting unequality between male and female scores in the abstract- concrete dimension of learning. Studies suggest that the males score high on the abstract conceptualization whereas females tend to score high in the concrete learning mode of the continuum. Women with a preferred learning styles based on concrete experience usually rely on hands-on experiences to learn, their judgments were found mostly based on intusion and feelings, they are people oriented being, and are typically comfortable with handling ambiguity. Women were found excelling at understanding people, problem identification, brainstorming, imagining, risk taking, getting work done and leading. Conversely, men who rely on abstract conceptualization take an analytic approach to learning, they think rationally and logically, they were found enjoy working with symbols and like formalized structure.

There are also several researches that have investigated the relationship between learning style and academic performance in various disciplines. While few studies indicate a strong relationship between converging learning style and performance scores of the students [13], others explain the difference of learning styles in student performance as the function of the chosen assessment technique. When all courses across the management curriculum are taken, it is possible to propose that all learning styles should be considered in management education. However, when the characteristics of different courses (HR, Marketing, Finance and IB) are considered, different learning styles may have more effectiveness in enhancing learning of the participants. Since it is claimed that management education is interdisciplinary [14-18], all learning styles may be considered as effective in different stages of courses.

The purpose of this study is to increase the instructor's awareness of learning styles for bringing flexibility in teaching and enhance the effectiveness of the learning process between instructor and management students. Drawing on the fundamental theories of Dewey, Lewin, and Piaget, ELT provides a framework for the enhancement of management education through curriculum development and course assessment.

Research questions

Most of the recent studies which are based on the use of Experiential learning styles in management education, investigate the effects of learning styles on the performance of students with a cross sectional view. Also, very few studies attempt to investigate relationship between gender and learning style. Therefore, an attempt was made in this research to answer the following questions:

1. What is the learning style distribution of post graduate management students across two years?

2. Are there any significant differences in the performance scores at different streams (HR, Finance, Marketing and IB) of courses across learning styles and gender?

Methods

Procedure

Firstly, the objective of the study was to investigate the distribution of four original learning styles of post graduate management students. Also the nine distinct styles [19] were used to analyze the distribution of students. Secondly, it sought to determine if there was any relationship between gender, learning styles and performance scores on different streams (HR, Finance, Marketing, and IB) of the course. Since various streams in post graduate management course involve different learning activities, the performance scores of students with different learning styles might differ in these streams. Gender was selected as a second variable since it is an individual difference that can influence performance scores of management students.

Sample description

The researchers sought approval from different management institutes at National Capital Region (NCR) in India prior to embarking on this study. The protocol was reviewed by the management and the approval was given to carry it out further. Post graduate management students in the department of business administration at different institutions located across NCR region in India were the study population. The two groups of samples are chosen for the study. The samples comprised of postgraduate management students in two successive academic years at different management colleges at NCR region. The reason for selecting the first year students was the assumption that management education has not yet influenced their learning styles up to a considerable extent. The assumption is based on the conclusion taken from the longitudinal research by Kolb and Kolb which shows a considerable increase in learning style starting from reflective to active orientation through progression in higher education years. In order to examine the validity of the distribution of students on the Learning Style Type Grid, the study was conducted with two different groups who are the management students of the two successive academic years of same course. The two samples were named as the first group and second group. There were 98 management students in the first group comprises of first year management students and 87 students in the second group of second year management students. The age range was 21 to 26 in all groups. The mean age for the first group was 23.1 (std. dev. 0.15) and for the second group was 23.9 (std. dev. 1.46). In the first group, there were 50 (51.02%) males and 48 (48.97%) females and in the second group, there were 59 (67.81%) males and 28 (32.18%) females.

Instruments

The third version of the Learning Styles Inventory Test (LSI) designed and standardized by Kolb [20] was used to determine the learning styles of the selected students. At first, the scores on Concrete Experience (CE), Reflective Observation (RO), Abstract Conceptualization (AC) and Active Experimentation (AE) or each participant were determined. At second step each student's CE scores from AC scores and RO scores from AE scores were subtracted to classify learning style of each participant either as 'accommodating', 'diverging', 'assimilating' or 'converging'. In addition, the distribution of the students as per to the Nine-Region Learning Style Type Grid was also determined [21].

The semester academic performance scores (GPA) of the students in the four streams of post graduate management course, viz. HR, Marketing, Finance and IB were analyzed with respect to their learning styles and gender differences within each group. In order to bring homogeneity the performance scores of the students were converted to letter grades with pluses and minuses for performance scores. Passing grades were made range from 'A' to 'D' with 'F' a failing grade. The highest grade is 'A' while the lowest is 'F' and quality-point equivalence was provided to each grade. Total academic performances of a student including grades achieved during that semester on four different streams were determined at the end of each semester by computing the weighted-average. Finally, these four different performance scores were analyzed with respect to gender difference and learning styles.

Results

Learning styles of students

The learning styles distribution of the chosen sample was determined at first step of analysis using the Learning Style Inventory (Table 1). In both the groups of post graduate management students, there was no significant difference found between observed and expected frequency (χ^2=11.68, df=4, p=0.16) in preferred learning style of the students. The learning styles distribution in each group is produced in Figure 1. The numbers of accommodating were found lowest irrespective of no significant difference in both groups. In both the groups the majority of learners were falling between assimilating and converging learning styles. While analyzing the distribution of the students as per the nine distinct styles (Table 2), the general flow of the distribution tends towards the balancing learning style for first group (32.09%). The students of this group were found having balancing style ranging between thinking/feeling (AC and CE) and acting/reflecting (AE and RO). The most preferred learning style in the second group

Learning Styles	First Group		Second Group	
	Frequency	Percentage	Frequency	Percentage
Accommodating	10	10.20%	07	8.04%
Diverging	15	15.30%	13	14.94%
Assimilating	34	34.69%	36	41.37%
Converging	39	39.79%	31	35.63%
Total	98	99.98%	87	99.98%

Table 1: Analysis of students learning styles using learning style inventory 3.0.

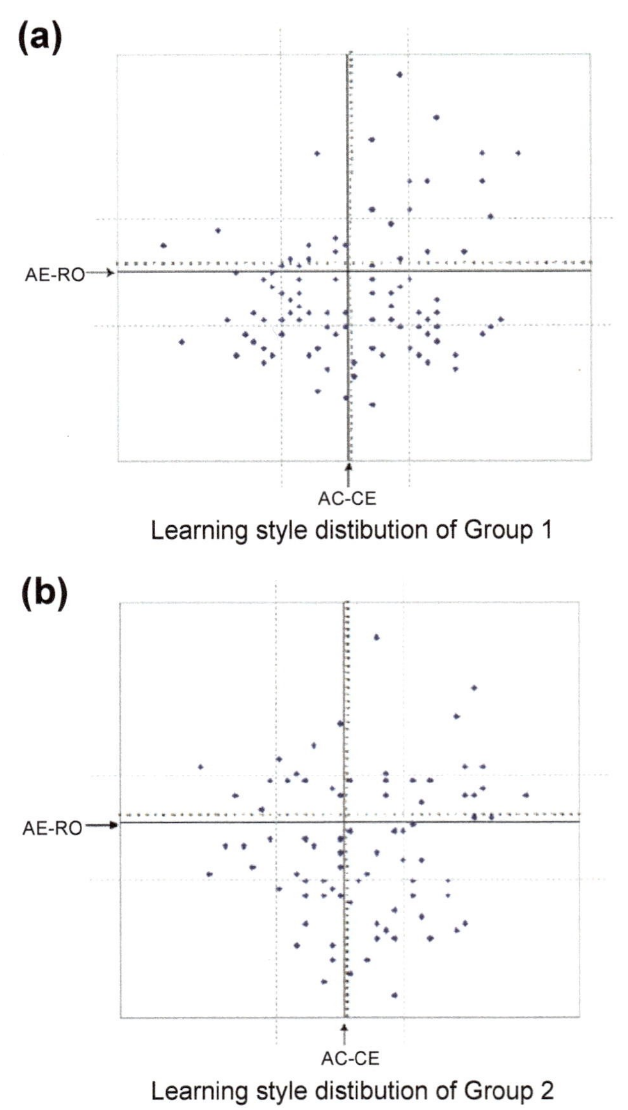

Figure 1: The distribution of learning styles in Group 1 and Group 2.

was southerner (28.89%). The focus of southerners was on thinking (AC) while balancing acting (AE) and reflecting (RO). This observation validates the research by Hunt, as these learners do not reflect their feelings in the learning process. The learning styles distributions of post graduate management students on nine distinct styles showed that in both the groups, the learning styles were generally either falling on the vertical axis ranging from AC to CE or on the horizontal axis ranging from AE to RO of the Learning Style Type Grid. This result confirmed the integration of AC and CE and AE and RO of most of the students with balancing learning style. These findings supported the assumption that the management students at postgraduate level are expected to learn through an integration of experiencing, thinking, reflecting and doing in the process of finding solutions to assigned management problems in organizational or personal context.

Cronbach alpha score of the inventory

The four basic (CE, RO, AC and AE) and two combination items (AC-CE and AE-RO) showed a approximately close internal reliability as measured by Cronbach's alpha (Table 3). The alpha values ranged from 0.56 to 0.76 for group 1 and from 0.61 to 0.76 for group 2. The values found in this study are lower than those of Kolb's study. Nevertheless, the calculated alpha scores were considered as quite satisfactory and within acceptable range in the existing study since the participants had a very constant profile as being post graduate management students, with a small age range, and sample sizes, as Schmitt (1996) argues that alpha values of 0.5 would not attenuate validity coefficient. The low reliability scores in RO, AE and AE-RO scales can be explained by the less number of learners with accommodating and diverging styles in both the groups.

First Stage	First Group	Second Group
Accommodating	0.89	2.72
Diverging	3.12	2.36
Assimilating	15.56	11.73
Converging	7.04	1.45
Second Stage		
North	4.35	11.14
East	5.46	15.08
South	15.31	28.89
West	15.37	6.88
Central		
Balancing	32.09	19.75

Table 2: The percentage distribution of participants through nine-region learning styles grid.

	First Group	Second Group
Concrete experience (CE)	0.73	0.72
Reflective observation (RO)	0.56	0.64
Abstract conceptualism (AC)	0.66	0.76
Active experimentation (AE)	0.64	0.61
Abstract-concrete (AC-CE)	0.76	0.71
Active-reflective (AE-RO)	0.53	0.57

Table 3: Cronbach's Alpha Score of the scale for Group 1 and Group 2.

Pearson correlations of the learning styles dimensions

Since the learning cycle is composed of two bipolar dimensions, the perceiving dimension measured by the combination item AC-CE and the processing dimension measured by the AE-RO combination item, they should be uncorrelated. As seen in Table 4, these items are uncorrelated in the first and second groups. The prediction is that CE and AC items should not correlate with AE-RO and AE and RO items should not correlate with AC-CE. As seen in Table 4, none of them are significantly correlating with each other in both the groups; hence the obtained result is validating the study by Smith and Kolb. The dialectic poles (AC and CE, AE and RO) of both combination items should be negatively correlated in all groups. In the second group, there was no significant negative correlation in AE and RO combination. Finally, the cross-dimensional items (CE/RO, AC/AE, CE/AE, and AC/RO) were not correlated as highly as within dimension items in both the groups.

Learning styles and gender

In this study, the chi-square tests for both the groups showed that learning styles and gender were independent. The frequencies of learning style preference were not significantly different by gender in both the groups.

Relationship of performance scores and gender

In the first group, statistically significant mean difference score of 0.35 was observed across gender and the performance scores of students in the Finance and Marketing Courses. The performance score means of males (M=1.24, std. dev.=1.05) and females (M=0.89, std. dev.=0.83) showed that males' performance scores were higher than females in the Finance and Marketing Courses.

In the first group, statistically significant mean difference score of 0.88 was observed across gender and the performance scores of students in the HR and IB Courses. The performance score means of males (M=1.36, std. dev.=1.07) and females (M=2.24, std. dev.=1.17) showed that female's performance scores were higher than males in the HR and IB Courses.

In the second group, no statistically significant difference was observed between gender and the performance scores of post graduate management students in any of the streams.

In both the groups no statistically significant difference was observed between gender and academic performance (GPA).

Relationship of performance scores to learning style

In the first group, statistically significant mean difference score of 0.72 was observed across learning styles and performance scores of students in HR, IB, Finance and Marketing streams. The Bonferroni test showed the significant difference in the performance scores of converging and diverging students (p=0.04) in a 95% confidence interval of 0.05-1.42 in favor of converging students ($M_{converging}$=2.36, $M_{diverging}$=1.64).

In the second group, statistically significant mean difference

	AC-CE/AE-RO	AC-CE/RO	AC-CE/AE	AE-RO/CE	AE-RO/AC	CE/AC	RO/AE	CE/RO	AC/AE	CE/AE	AC/RO
First Group	0.19	-0.07	0.08	-0.11	0.17	-0.44**	-0.43**	-0.32**	-0.15	-0.46**	-0.41**
Second Group	0.11	-0.11	0.04	-0.05	0.07	-0.40**	-0.13	-0.30**	-0.30**	-0.41**	-0.45**

*Correlation is significant at the 0.05 level (two-tailed).

**Correlation is significant at the 0.01 level (two-tailed).

Table 4: Pearson correlations between learning styles and combined scores.

score of 0.38 was observed across learning styles and the performance scores of students in the HR, IB, Finance and Marketing streams. The Bonferroni test showed the performance scores of converging and diverging students differed significantly (p=0.002) in a 95% confidence interval of 0.37-1.86 in favor of converging students ($M_{converging}$=2.27, $M_{diverging}$=1.89); and the significant difference in performance of accommodating and diverging students (p=0.006) at 95% confidence interval of 0.31-2.09 in favor of accommodating students ($M_{accommodating}$=2.49, $M_{diverging}$=1.92).

Discussion and Conclusion

Distribution of learning style

In the current research the Kolb's Learning Style Inventory test, was used to determine the predominant learning styles among management students. By repeating the study on two different groups who are the postgraduate management students from two successive academic years, it was observed that there was a specific distribution of learning styles for these students. The students were found to be more concentrated in assimilating and converging groups.

As per the scores, neither AC nor CE had a correlation with AE-RO, in the first and second groups (Table 5). This correlation showed that when the concrete experience (CE) score was high, learning activity on the horizontal axis of learning cycle moved towards learning by reflecting (RO) and when concrete experience score was low, the learning activity moved towards learning by doing (AE).

When considering the nine distinct styles, management students in the first group was concentrated in the balancing learning style that integrates thinking/feeling and acting/reflecting (Table 2). Kolb and Kolb have found that learners with balanced learning profiles are more adaptive and flexible learners. Management students in the second group were concentrated in the thinking oriented southern region, which was different than the art students in Kolb and Kolb study who have found that "more art students are in the eastern regions than in the western region". None of the two groups were concentrated either in the eastern or western regions, but they were balancing between acting and reflecting. This supports the proposition that management education is not only an art-oriented education, but is an integration of art and science education. To attain continuous improvements in the quality of learning in management education, departments should conduct systematic reviews of the curriculum to ensure that courses would cater for students with different learning styles.

Gender and learning style characteristics

Previous studies related to Learning Style Inventory tests concluded that males were more oriented towards abstract conceptualization (AC) than females on the perceiving dimension (AC-CE) and that there were no significant gender differences on the processing dimension (AE-RO). In our study, it is found that learning styles and gender were independent for management students both on the perceiving and processing dimensions. This study provides further empirical support for the findings in study of Smith and Kolb, on processing dimension.

Groups	χ2 scores	df	P value
Group 1	χ2=5.094	df=3	p=0.165
Group 2	χ2=1.752	df=3	p=0.625

Table 5: Chi-square scores of both groups.

Performance scores and gender

Results in this study indicate that there is a significant mean difference in performance scores across gender in Marketing, Finance, HR and IB courses. The performance scores of males were higher in Marketing and Finance courses in the first group whereas scores of females in first group were higher in the HR and IB courses as shown in Table 6. Only in the second group, no statistical significant difference was found between gender and performance scores of students in any of the courses or GPA. This can be explained by being mostly southerner learners who do not provide feedback from emotions and they are concentrated in thinking. There is no study in management education literature field to compare the findings of this study.

Implications of the study

The management education should provide the opportunity to employ different learning styles in design process. The goal of this research is to ensure that the instructors can relate concepts of learning to the specific conditions during the delivery process. Furthermore, it is important to stimulate the diverging students for bringing their range of ideas and ways of problem solving in class. These students although are not successful in performance as converging students, they play an important role in the conceptual understanding of the course material. These students are the most creative ones [22] and the other students can learn from them. Students also can be grouped into teams that made-up members with different learning styles. These teams may work on different company and field projects compared to individual student project. Besides knowing the distinct learning styles may be helpful to the instructor in giving critiques to students to overcome their weaknesses towards learning process. In management education, the courses are usually assessed through standard methods such as coursework, examination, paper and project-based work. The teachers should be encouraged to review their course and syllabi so all students have an opportunity to perform their best and be exposed to all learning styles [23-25]. Increasing the instructor's awareness of learning styles might lead to increase flexibility of teaching styles and enhance the communication between instructors and management students.

Limitations and future research

The work presented here is subject to several limitations. First, the study is based on only postgraduate management program at institutes and it should be generalized by having data from several other disciplines. Second, it should cover all two years of the course to have a general view of management education. Third, there may be cultural differences that are affecting the learning styles of students; therefore, it must be repeated in different countries.

Further work may be required to examine the change in the

Groups	Performance Scores in different streams				Total Aggregate Performance
	HR	Marketing	Finance	IB	
Group 1	F>M	M>F	M>F	F>M	No significant difference Observed
Group 2	No significant difference Observed	No significant difference Observed	No significant difference Observed	No significant difference Observed	No significant difference Observed

Table 6: Relationship between Performance scores and gender of Post graduate management students.

learning styles of the students in the following years and professional life. Furthermore, a country wise comparative analysis may be of interest to the scholars who are working in this field.

References

1. Bank B (2007) Gender and education: An encyclopedia (Vol.1) Westport, Connecticut: Praeger Publishers.
2. Curry L (1983) An organization of learning style theory and constructs. Paper presented at the Annual Meeting of the American Educational Research Association '83 Montreal, Quebec: Educational Resources Information Center (ERIC).
3. Mainemelis C, Boyatzis RE, Kolb DA (2001) Experiential learning theory: Previous research and new directions. In: Sternberg RJ, Zhang L (eds.) Perspectives on Thinking, Learning and Cognitive Styles, Mahwah, NJ: Lawrence Erlbaum Associates Publishers 227-248
4. Mainemelis C, Boyatzis RE, Kolb DA (2002) Learning styles and adaptive flexibility: Testing experiential learning theory. Management Learning 33: 5-33.
5. Lachenmayer D (1997) Learning styles: A handbook for teachers to identify and teach to all learning styles: A paper in curriculum and instruction for Pennsylvania State University Graduate School.
6. Amany S (2001) Brain hemisphericity and academic majors: A correlation study. College Student Journal 35: 193-200.
7. Kolb AD (1984) Experiential learning- Experience as the source of learning and development. Eaglewood Cliffs, New Jersey: Prentice Hall.
8. Geraldine O'Neil (2003) Personal Learning Styles Centre for Teaching and learning.
9. Heffler B (2001) Individual learning style and the learning style inventory. Educational Studies 27: 307-316.
10. Tindall T, Hamil B (2003) Gender disparity in science education: The causes, consequences, and solutions.
11. Philbin M, Meier E, Huffman S, Boverie P (1995) A survey of gender and learning styles. Sex Roles 32: 485-494.
12. Kolb AY, Kolb DA (2005) Learning styles and learning spaces: Enhancing the experiential learning in higher education. Academy of Management Learning & Education 4: 193-212.
13. Rutz E (2003) Learning styles and educational performance e Implications for professional development programs. CIEC Conference Proceedings, Tucson, AZ.
14. Bunch MA (1993) Core curriculum in architectural education San Francisco: Mellen Research University Press.
15. Demirbas OO (1997) Design studio as a life space in architectural education: Privacy requirements Unpublished Master's Thesis Ankara: Bilkent University.
16. Demirbas OO, Demirkan H (2000) Privacy dimensions: a case study in the interior architecture design studio. Journal of Environmental Psychology 20: 53-63.
17. Teymur N (1992) Architectural education: Issues in educational practice and policy. London: Question Press.
18. Uluoglu B (2000) Design knowledge communicated in studio critiques. Design Studies 21: 35-58.
19. Abbey DS, Hunt DE, Weiser JC (1985) Variations on a theme by Kolb: a new perspective for understanding counselling and super- vision. The Counselling Psychologist 13: 477-501.
20. Smith DM, Kolb DA (1996) User's guide for the learning-style. Boston: McBer and Company.
21. Hunt DE (1987) Beginning with ourselves in practice, theory and human affairs. Cambridge MA: Brookline Books.
22. Hsu CHC (1999) Learning styles of hospitality students: nature or nurture? Hospitality Management 18: 17-30.
23. Messick S (1996) Bridging cognition and personality in education: the role of style in performance and development. European Journal of Personality 10: 353-376.
24. Demirbas OO (2001) The relation of learning styles and performance scores of the students in interior architecture education. Unpublished Ph.D Dissertation Ankara: Bilkent University.
25. Teymur N (1996) Architectural history as 'educational object. In: Hardy A, Teymur N (eds.) Architectural history and the studio. London: Question Press, pp: 26-66.

Analyzing Data utilized in Process Control and Continuous Improvement

Jeffrey E. Jarrett*

College of Business Administration, University of Rhode Island, Kingston, RI 02881, USA

Abstract

Process control under the guidelines of reducing the costs of operations, production and inspection and produce high quality service and operations is examine to see if data from various parent populations can change the results and interpretations. With the purpose of achieving a minimal amount or error generation from the examination of control charts in univariate SPC, we compare data taken from three parent populations, i.e., Normal, Poisson and Exponential. Data and graphical analysis of Statistics permits one to visualize problems associated with where data comes from and whether it is satisfactory to use. We focus of univariate application but discuss multivariate application. This research will enable us to evaluate the conditions brought on by serial correlation and time series characteristics of models.

Keywords: Process control; Operations; Production costs; Data

Introduction

The powerful method to control product and service quality and to lower operations and production costs require controlling, monitoring and improving processes. The applications originally designed for industrial applications by the like of Shewhart called a process that operates under common causes of variation is in statistical control and those that operate under assignable causes of variation as being not in control (or out-of-control) [1]. Statistical process control (SPC) assumes that the quality characteristic(s) are either normal or in the case of multivariate process control are distributed according to the Hotelling T-square or in some applications a multivariate exponentially weighted moving average (MEWMA) or a multivariate cumulative sum (MCUSUM).

The assumptions of univariate SPC and multivariate SPC (MPC) is that the observations are serially uncorrelated or statistically independent over time. Previously, many (Alwan etc.) indicated that SPC and MPC applications consider the authenticated serial correlation in data for use in quality control applications. For example, many manufacturing chemical, health processes yield data containing serial correlation and in the case of multivariate processes cross-correlation of variables.

Literature Review

In the literature, two general approaches to deal with serial correlation in the process. One method for univariate processes is to fit autoregressive moving average (ARMA) models to the sampled data and then apply monitoring to the residuals. Although this approach is very promising, they may not be good enough to process mean shift. Harris and Ross [2] and Zhang and Hibler [3] may have inefficient detective power to find significant shifts in the process mean. Literature on this subject is rich and will be discussed later. A second approach is to apply changes to the MPC model to solve problems of serial correlation in set of time series data. This procedure lacks some ability to solve the problem of a time series characterized by serial correlation. Others studied this problem, including Vassilopoulos and Stamboulis [4], Alwan and Roberts [5], Harris and Ross [2], Montgomery and Mastrangelo [6] Maragah and Woodall [7], Wardell, Moskowitz and Plante [8], Superville and Adams [9], Lu and Reynolds [10], Schmid [11-14] West, Dellana and Jarrett [15] West and Jarrett [16] and Pan and Jarrett [17].

Residual Charts differ from control charts for means in that they need only one joint control limit which are based on independent and identically distributed case. Hence, residual charts have an advantage on the construction of control limits than adjusting the control limits. SPC applications focus on the residuals from the univariate serially correlated case. A number of authors have extended this analysis to the multivariate case. For example, Pan and Jarrett [18] propose using multivariate processes (VAR models) of residuals of the models having serial correlation. In addition, Kalgonda and Kulkarni [19], Jarrett and Pan [20], Wang et al. [21] and Snoussi [22] proposed other solutions to this case using multivariate analyses of residuals.

In comparison, Harris and Ross, to that of Zhang and Hibler suggested improvement to the univariate case. Hence, we propose another study where we are aware that the normality assumption may be the source of the problem. That is, we wish to compare this assumption when we know the data are distributed by another probability distribution function (PDF). In the next section, we examine the literature on assumptions of SPC control charts. Do the data result from another PDF which may characterize time series data from relatively large samples? The answer to this question will enable quality control practitioners to better understand the importance of examining one's time series data to reduce the number of false signals from control charts and improve the quality of product or service under control.

Data Analysis and Experiment

To examine the influence of the underlying PDF on the univariate SPC process, we created by simulation data from a normal PDF, Poison PDF and Exponential PDF of size 500. The purpose is to allow experimentation with univariate SPC to see if signals differ and how the differences may be avoided. The analysis will point how to process controllers whether industrial, commercial or health related professions may handle the differences when known.

First, we generate three data sets by standard simulation techniques design in *Minitab*® software producing the time series data. [Each data set contains 500 time series observations assuming the parent population was either normal having a mean of 9, the variance will vary depending on the characteristics of the variances from populations that are Normal, Poisson and Exponential.]

***Corresponding author:** Jeffrey E. Jarrett, College of Business Administration, University of Rhode Island, USA, E-mail: jejarrett133@gmail.com

Table 1 which follows the descript statistics of the three sets of time series data.

From Table 1, observe that the for the Normal distribution the mean and median are very close to each other as one may expect from having a normal parent population. In turn, for the Poison case, one may observe that the mean is 9.122 and standard deviation (2.9424) if squared (8.66) would also be very close to the to the value of the mean. This is the main characteristic of the Poisson model. Last, for the exponential model of the Parent Population the distribution is highly skewed towards greater values, that is, the data if graphed would have a very long tail to the right. All these characteristics indicate the time series are not alike but do conform the characteristics of the parent population from they were generated.

Another way in which one may examine the data simulated from each of the parent populations is to compare the Boxplots (sometimes referred to as a Box-Whisker Plot) of the time series data. Figure 1 contains the three Boxplots. Note the Normal has the greatest variation and the Poisson a smaller variation and on the same graph the Exponential appear to have very little variation.

All of this is expected when we deal with data from three very distinct parent populations. Another simple graphical analysis would be to observe the time series data.

Figures 2A-2C contains the time series plot of the foo observations of data having normal, poison and exponential parent populations. Observe the differences in the manner in which these data are distributed from left (the beginning) to the right (the ending). We know their means and variation measured previously by the sample standard deviation and noted in Table 1. We should note that measures of skewness for the distributions are 0.06 for Normal, 0.23 for the Poisson and 0.60 for the Exponential distribution. Obvious, the skewness for the Exponential is much greater in comparison to the data for the other two time series. Much of this was observed in Table 1 ad Figure 1 before but the evidence is so exemplified in Figures 2A-2C.

Residual plots- Normal probability plot of the residuals

Minitab graphs plots the residuals versus their expected values when the distribution is normal. The residuals from the analysis should be normally distributed. In practice, large sample data with moderate departures from normality do not seriously affect the results.

The normal probability plot of the residuals should roughly follow a straight line. One uses this plot to look for the following patterns:

1. Non-normality if it not a straight line.

2. U-shaped curve in the tail areas, if skewness is observed.

3. An Outlier observation is one that is very distant from the remaining observations.

4. An additional or unidentified variable is affecting the data if there is a change in the trend of the data.

If the data has fewer than 50 observations, the plot may display curvature in the tails even if the residuals are normally distributed. As

Parent Population	Mean	Standard Deviation	Minimum	Q1	Median	Q3	Maximum
Normal	8.901	5.88	-8.667	5.214	8.911	12.816	26.369
Poisson	9.122	2.9424	1	7	9	11	19
Exponential	0.411	0.0251	0	0.0232	0.0378	0.0556	0.1099

Table 1: Descriptive statistics: Normal, poisson, exponential.

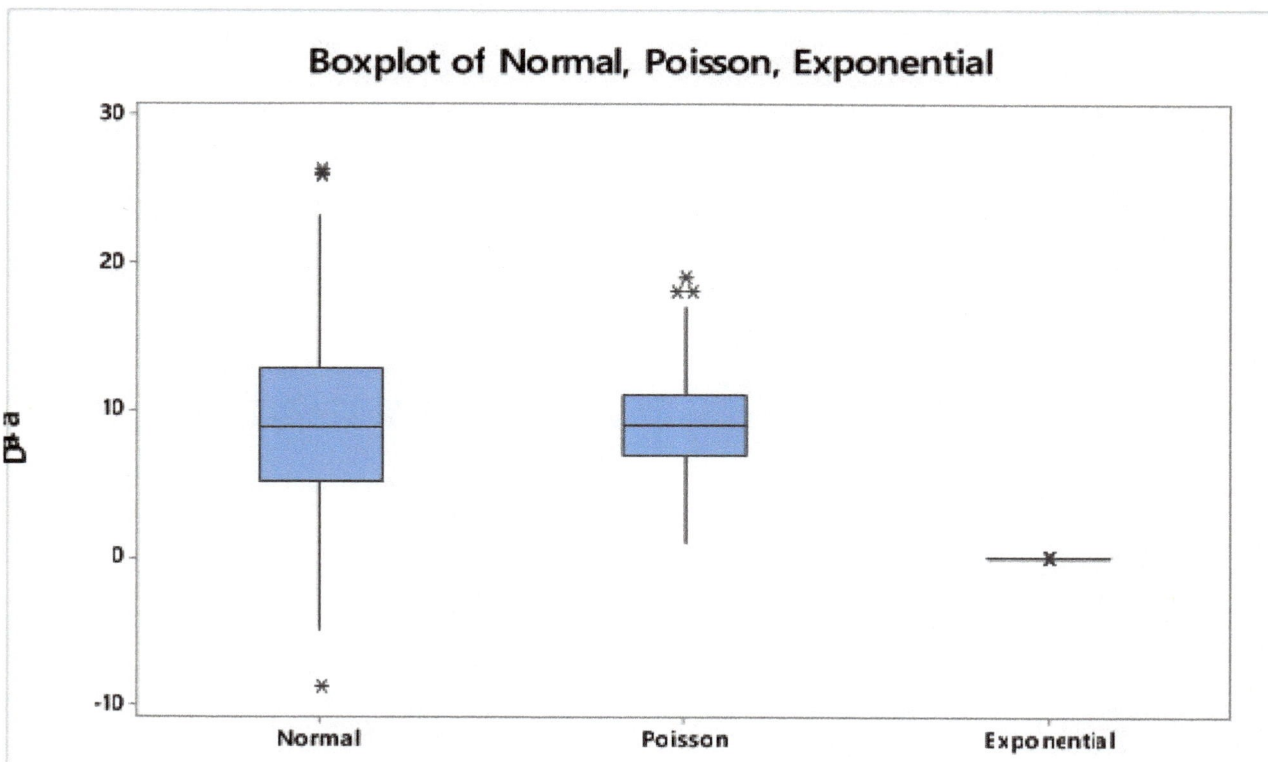

Figure 1: Box-whisker plot.

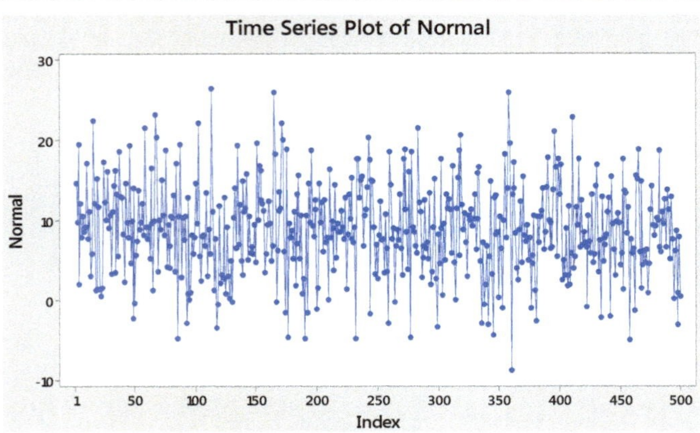

Figure 2(A): Time series plot of normal.

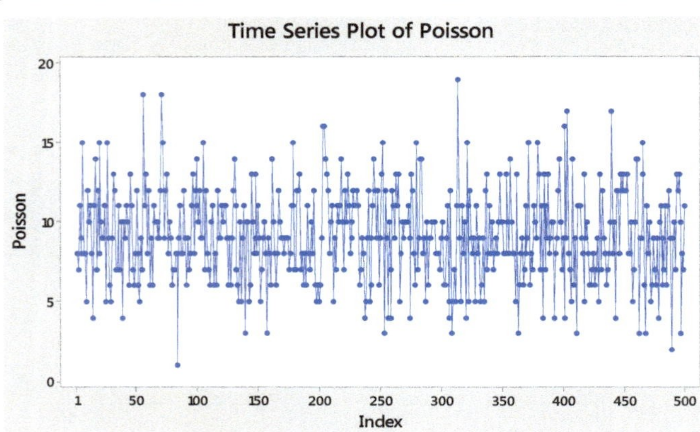

Figure 2(B): Time series plot of poisson.

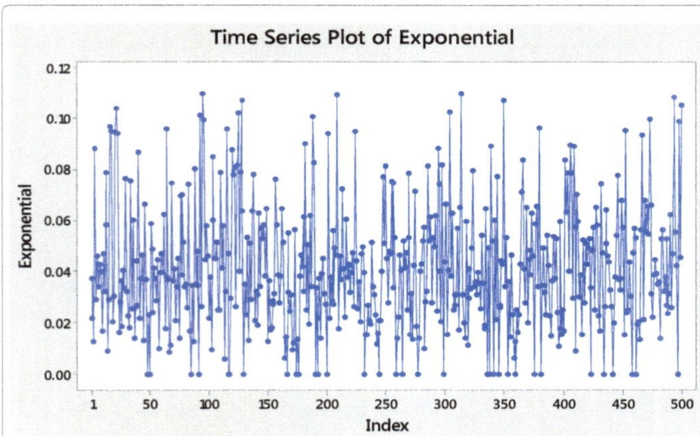

Figure 2(C): Time series plot of exponential.

the number of observations decreases, the probability plot may show even greater variation and nonlinearity. Even though probability plots perform worse with small data sets, histograms are worse. Hence, we utilize the normal probability plot and goodness-of-fit tests to assess the normality of residuals in small data sets. Our data sets contain 500 observations per set, so any tests would probably have more than sufficient robustness.

We obtain in Figures 3A-3C the probability plots for the three times series and observe the patterns in the time series. In Figure 3A we observe only two points outside the control limits at the very extremes of the graph. This would not be unusual since 95 percent control limits; one would expect 25 outside the confidence limits. Hence, the data would be near perfectly normally distributed.

By observing Figure 3B, we view a very different picture. The data points do indicate U-shaped pattern. This indicates that the data contains skewness and standard Shewhart control charts based on normal distribution of data would be inappropriate. Many points are outside the 95 percent control limits which also indicate that the data does not come from a normal parent population.

Observing the probability plot of the of the time series having an Exponential parent population provides evidence that these data are highly skewed and normal probability analysis are inappropriate. The sample observations and control limits on standard Shewhart control limits would be a fruitless undertaking with many false limits.

In the next section, we observe the use of Shewhart designed control charts.

Univariate SPC control charts

The univariate control chart that depicts the data in our sample is called the I-MR chart. This univariate chart is a is a combined chart that consists of an Individuals (I) chart, which plots the values of each individual observation, and provides a means to assess the process center and a moving range (MR) chart, which plots the range calculated from artificial subgroups created from successive observations, and

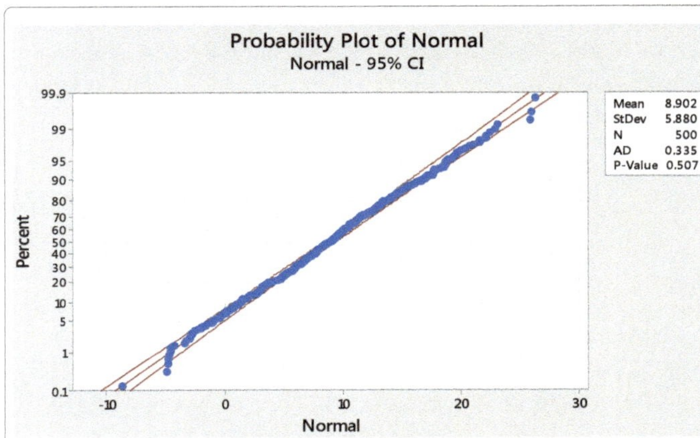

Figure 3(A): Probability plot of normal.

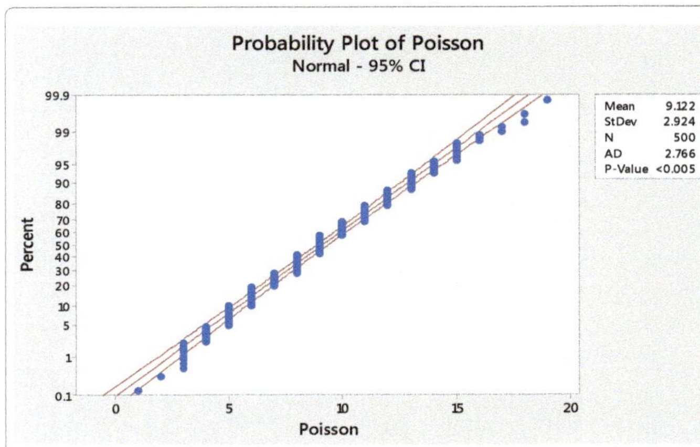

Figure 3(B): Probability plot of poisson.

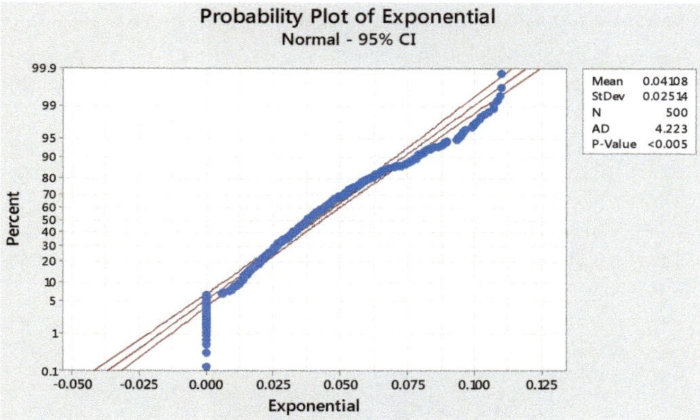

Figure 3(C): Probability plot of exponential.

provides a means to calculate the moving range (a measure of variation) in the process. Using the I-MR chart to draw a combined control chart for assessing whether process center and variation are in control when your data are individual observations. An ***in-control*** process exhibits only random variation within the established control limits. On the other hand, an ***out-of-control*** process exhibits unusual variation, which may be due to the presence of special causes. The MR chart must be in control before you can interpret the ***I***-chart. This is because the ***I***-chart control limits are calculated considering both process variation and *mean*.

When the MR chart is out of control, the control limits on the ***I***-chart may be inaccurate and may not correctly signal an out-of-control condition. In this case, the lack of control will be due to unstable variation rather than actual changes in the process mean. Similarly, when the MR chart is in control, you can be sure that an out-of-control *I*- chart is due to changes in the process mean. The results follow for these charts for data from Normal parent population.

Observe in Figure 4A there were no observations out-of-control for the I-Chart, but there were a number of points out of control in the MR-Chart indicating that there may be inaccurate limits in the I-Chart. However, since there are only few such observations, the number of observations would in turn be small. Figure 4B has three observations out-of-control for the I-Chart and five observations out-of-control for the MR Chart. Hence there probably is some inaccuracy in the control limits and more observations would be out-of-control in the MR-Chart. Figure 4C results indicate that there may be a much large number of out-of-controls for the Poisson data then for the Normal data. Finally, the exponential charts show zero observations out-of-control for the I-Chart, but five points out of control in the MR-Chart. Again, the I-Chart limits are inaccurate. Many of the observations in the I-Chart for these data that are close to the limits should be out-of-control if the limits were correctly calculated. False signals are bad because they indicate that incorrect decisions will occur when process managers make decision and incur Type I and Type II errors in total quality management. Adjustments in decision making and process control for managers to make correct decisions. Incorrect interpretation of the data analysis and decision analytics produce unsavory conditions for decision making.

Conclusions and Further Study

This study aims at understanding some pitfall in univariate SPC as applied in industrial and engineering applications as well as monitoring service application and in the field of health care and prevention, the data analysis from hospital acute care treatments and diagnosis of health care prevention and treatments. All of these analyses are utilized in these applications to achieve quality control and improvement activities often referred to as statistical process control by Deming [23,24].

Our research entailed an examination of some of the limiting assumptions of SPC and use of control charts to produce quality control and improvement. We reviewed literature on control charts both univariate and multivariate and focused on data from three sources. Stated differently, we generated samples of 500 from three sources in groups of 1 from a normally distributed parent population, a Poisson distributed parent population and an exponentially distributed parent population. In turn, we examined the descriptive statistics of three samples of time series data for its properties, the boxplots of the three time series to understand their secondary characteristics of asymmetry, variance and range. The three data sets were different in all these characteristics. The figures indicated the differences visually from normal probability plots and time series plot of each data set.

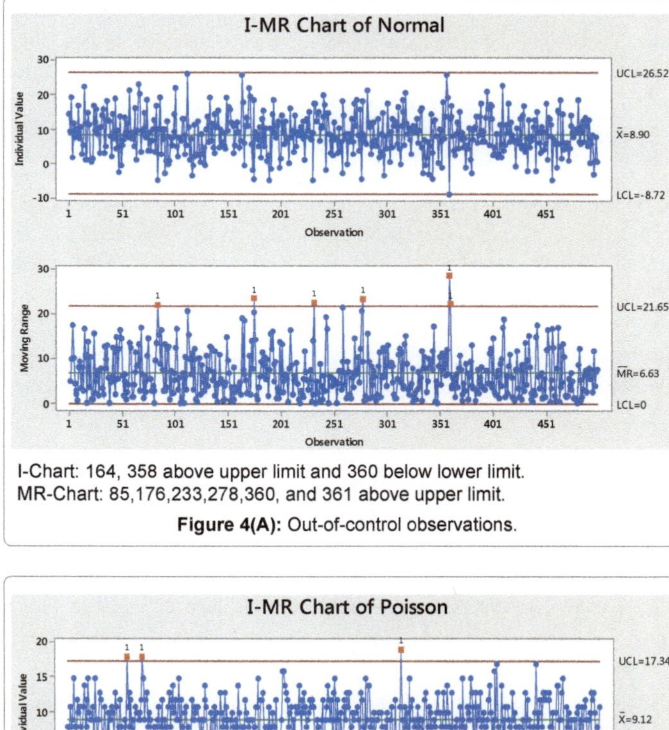

I-Chart: 164, 358 above upper limit and 360 below lower limit.
MR-Chart: 85,176,233,278,360, and 361 above upper limit.

Figure 4(A): Out-of-control observations.

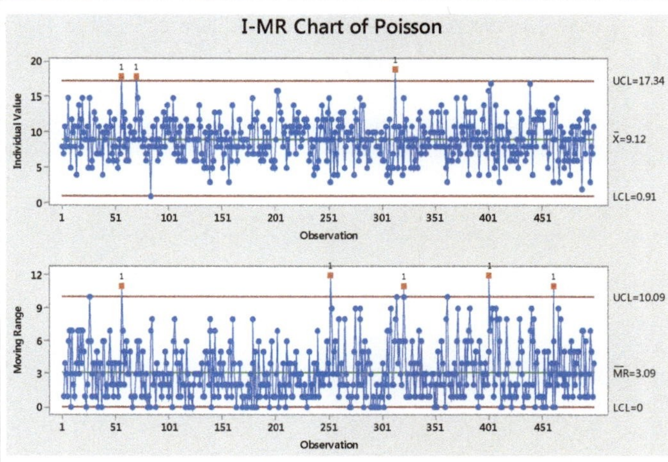

I-Chart: 56, 71 and 314 are above upper limit and none below lower limit.
MR-Chart: 56, 253, 321, and 462 above upper limit.

Figure 4(B): Out-of-control observations.

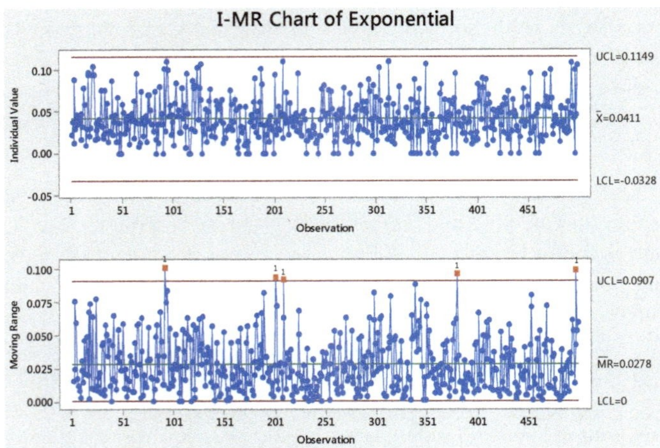

I-Chart: None are above upper limit or below lower limit.
MR-Chart: 93, 201, 210, 381 and 498 above upper limit.

Figure 4(C): Out-of-control observations.

Last, we analyzed the results after control charts based on + and - "three sigma" limits. The combinations of I_MR Control Charts indicated the fundamental difference in the results. The probability distribution of the parent populations produces varying results. Investigations into the characteristics of the parent population is necessary to insure that practitioners of SPC fully understand what it is to incur Type I and II errors.

In the future, this research will enable us to evaluate the conditions brought on by serial correlation and time series characteristics of models. As noted earlier by Alwan and later by West, Delana and Jarrett we must study the effects of autoregressive moving average models generating time series utilized in SPC. Finally, Pan and Jarrett [25,26] proposed using an operations research method called "Golden Ratio" to find an optimal solution in SPC.

References

1. Shewhart WA (1931) Economic control of quality of manufactured product. D. Van Nostrand Company, New York.
2. Harris TJ, Ross WH (1991) Statistical process procedures for correlated observations. Canadian Journal of Chemical Engineering 69: 48- 57.
3. Zhang J, Hibler WD (1997) On an efficient numerical method for modeling sea ice dynamics, Journal geophysical research 102: 8691- 8702.
4. Vassilopoulos AV, Stamboulis AP (1978) Modification of control charts limits in the presence of data correlation. Journal of Quality Technology 10: 20-30.
5. Alwan BM, Roberts HV (1988) Time Series Modeling for Detecting Level Shifts of Auto correlated Processes. Journal of Business and Economics Statistics 6: 87- 95.
6. Montgomery DC, Mastrangelo CM (1991) Some statistical process control methods for auto correlated data. Journal of Quality Technology 23: 179- 193.
7. Maragah H, Woodall WH (1992) The effect of autocorrelation on the retrospective. Journal of Statistical Computation and Simulation 40: 29- 42.
8. Wardell D, Moskowitz H, Plante RD (1994) Using run- length distributions of control charts to detect False alarms. Production and operations management 3: 219-239.
9. Superville CR, Adams BM (1994) An evaluation of forecast-based quality control schemes. Communications in Statistics - Simulation and Computation 23: 645-661.
10. Lu CW, Reynolds MR (1999) Control Charts for Monitoring the Mean and Variance of Auto correlated Processes. Journal of Quality Technology 31: 259-274.
11. Schmid W (1994) On EWMA Charts for Time Series. Proceedings and the American Society for Quality of 5th International Workshop on Intelligent Statistical Quality Control 161-184.
12. Schmid W (1997) On EWMA Charts for Time Series. Frontiers of Statistical Quality Control 5: 115- 137.
13. Schmid W (1997) CUSUM Control Schemes for Gaussian Processes. Statistical Papers 38: 191- 217.
14. Schmid W, Schone A (1997) Some Properties of the EWMA Control Chart in the Presence of Auto correlation. Anna Statist 25: 1277- 1283.
15. West D, Delana S, Jarrett JE (2002) Transfer function modeling of processes with dynamic inputs. Journal of Quality Technology 34: 315-326.
16. West D, Jarrett J (2004) The impact of first order positive auto-regression on process control. International journal of business and economics 3: 29-37.
17. Pan X, Jarrett JE (2008) Estimating σ and Improving Control Limits with RWAV for Normal and Non-normal Processes. Quality Engineering 21: 72- 78.
18. Pan X, Jarrett JE (2004) Applying State Space into SPC: Monitoring Multivariate Time Series. Appl Stat
19. Kalgonda AA, Kulkarni SR (2004) Multivariate Quality Control Chart for Auto correlated Processes. Journal of Applied Statistics 31: 317- 627.
20. Jarrett JE, Pan X (2007) Monitoring Variability and Multivariate Auto correlated Process. Appl Stat 34: 459- 469.
21. Wang F, Hwang Y, Quinn P, Wang X (2010) A Statistics-guided approach to precise characterization of nanowire morphology. ACS Nano 4: 885-860.
22. Snoussi A (2011) SPC for short-run multivariate autocorrelated processes. Appl Stat 38: 2303-2312.
23. Deming WE (1982) Out of the Crisis, MIT Center for Advanced Engineering Study: Cambridge, UK.
24. Deming WE (1993) The New Economics; for Industry, Government, and Education MIT Center for Advanced Engineering Study: Cambridge, UK.
25. Hastie T, Ribshirani R, Friedman J (2000) The Elements of Statistical Learning (2ndedn), Springer, Stanford, California.
26. Pan X, Jarrett JE (2013) Using Golden Ratio Search to Improve Paired Construction of Quality Control Charts. International Journal of Economics and Management Engineering 3: 107- 111.

Emphasize on Niche Market Strategy for Attracting Foreign Tourists in Bangladesh

Md. Sajedul Islam[1]* and Iftakhar Hossain Jubery[2]

[1]*Begum Rokeya University, Dhaka, Bangladesh*
[2]*Institute of Business Administration, IBA University of Dhaka, Bangladesh*

Abstract

Bangladesh has bright prospects of travel and leisure in future. She possesses travel and leisure possibilities everywhere. But, Bangladesh travel and leisure is experiencing so many problems including technique. By applying specialized market techniques she can earn more Forex because Bangladesh is endowed with four key travel and leisure products: Seashores, Woodlands, Mountains and islands, traditional position and Historical sites those are mostly pleasing to many visitors. This document is focusing the existing pros and cons of travel and leisure market in Bangladesh and the ways to apply specialized market technique. Results indicate that four famous items can play essential part in the total income in this industry. Finally, this document indicates how specialized market technique will help the policy maker to distinguish the visitors market and customize their service to achieve ideal promotion goals and fix existing downwards income.

Keywords: Marketing; Marketing strategy; Niche market technique; Iconic items

Introduction

Bangladesh has bright prospects of tourism in future. She possesses tourism potentials all over the country. But, Bangladesh tourism is facing so many problems including marketing strategy. By applying niche market strategies she can earn more foreign currency because Bangladesh is blessed with four key tourism products: Beaches, Forest, Hills and islands, Historical place and Archaeological Sites that are mostly pleasing to many tourists. This paper is focusing the present strengths and weaknesses of tourism industry in Bangladesh and the ways to implement niche market strategy. Findings indicate that four iconic products can play significant role in the total earnings in this sector. Finally, this paper suggests how niche market strategy will help the policy maker to differentiate the tourists market and customize their service to achieve strategic marketing objectives and solve present downward earnings.

Today's travel and leisure market has become one of the most key elements in GDP participation in globally. It plays a significant part in socio-economic growth of a nation. Most of the visitors prefer to visit in different locations for different reasons (e.g. For Company, Research, Attend globally conventions, Holidays and holidays, Treatment, Meet with members of the loved ones, to see events like globe cup, Olympic etc.). It is recognized that most of the creating countries now generate financial benefits through its travel and leisure market. In past, the federal government may have been hesitant to invest for travel and leisure growth, but in this modern age the problem has changed. Now government focuses on not only travel and leisure but also kindness management like hotels, hotels, restaurants, transport, security and entertainment etc. Bangladesh as a creating nation is moving towards experiencing difficulties of globalization. It has beautiful attractions and historical places which are able to develop attention to globally visitors. But this market failed to develop effectively because of lack of maintainable and effective travel and leisure promotion techniques and hesitant attitude of different government authorities to develop this market. Many people from other countries have negative perception toward our nation. They feel Bangladesh is a nation of hardship, beggars, flooding and governmental anxiety. Besides, secretary of state for municipal aircraft and travel and leisure, Bangladesh Parjaton Organization (Govt. Tourism Organization) and other personal tour providers did not apply promotion idea and techniques effectively to reach their vacationer item to focus on consumers (tourists).

Bangladesh, as a location, has many aspects and strong points. She is gifted with almost all the natural possibilities that attract vacationer [1]. These include; Among beaches, Cox's Bazaar, the lengthiest unbroken clean and exotic seaside in the world; Kuakata sea seaside is known as sun rising and sunset; Sundarbans, the home of the spectacular Elegant Bengal lions, Rangamati, known as the heart of the spectacular pond district; Sylhet, known as the land of twelve religious Awuilia which amazing hills and tea gardens; Chittagong, the largest port town from the and known as the town of shrines; Above all, reverie beauty, vibrant tribe culture and simple town life are the primary aspects for getting traffic [2]. Though Bangladesh has lot of attractive locations but there are some weaknesses: poor facilities, volatile governmental scenario, image crisis etc. Besides, finance allowance on travel and leisure is not sufficient; market technique would be profitable way of Bangladesh. These kind of attractions are need to be researched by the internet promotion techniques and need to come up with and apply travel and leisure promotion ideal plan either by the Bangladesh Parjaton Organization (public sector) or the public-private areas both.

Objectives

The research goals of this research are:

1. To evaluate the promotion techniques implemented by Bangladesh Parjaton Organization.

2. To identify and evaluate the niches for getting competitive advantage as a globally location.

3. To suggest recommendations for the growth of key travel and leisure items in Bangladesh.

***Corresponding author:** Md. Sajedul Islam, Begum Rokeya University, Dhaka, Bangladesh, E-mail: sajidbru@gmail.com

Conceptual Framework

Reason 1: India's perception in the international community

India's perception in the international community is not a very positive one, especially when it comes to safety. See for example, is it safe for a single American woman to travel in India? Many women have chronicled their experiences as being creepy, uncomfortable and unpleasant, to the extent of being dangerously close to sexual harassment. And this is an undeniable point. Even as a man, I have witnessed several such instances where men are clearly and unabashedly intrusive in the way they stare at women, or pass sexual comments. I remember a few years back when I was in Mumbai to meet my girlfriend and we took the local train at night. It was fairly crowded, and we got a couple of seats. A guy sat across from us and started staring at my girlfriend's chest. I noticed it and glared at him. He met my gaze, realized that he had been caught, and looked away. I didn't want to create a scene so I didn't say anything, hoping that it was over. But it wasn't. I caught him again, and then the third time. I lost my temper (not a good thing to do), caught him by the scruff of his neck and told him to get up and move away from the place. I was lucky that he was alone and that a middle aged gentleman who was aware of what was happening supported us and the guy had to move to the other end of the cabin.

Reason 2: Lack of basic tourism infrastructure like information centers, transportation etc.

At even the biggest Indian tourist spots, there is no way for someone who doesn't know the place or the language to get help and guidance. This obviously, is a hindrance to a lot of people. Plus, getting tickets in India is akin to winning a lottery. The only way people can safely travel is by air. And finally, the problem of taxis and auto rickshaws not being safe and overcharging customers is a big pain.

Reason 3: Attitude of most Indians in the tourism industry

Have you ever seen a rate card anywhere you travel? What has felt as the primary motive of all people related to the tourism industry - travel guides, taxi drivers, shopkeepers, hotel owners etc.?

I can say that their primary motive is to make as much money as possible. They will try and overcharge customers whenever possible. I faced this when I visited Matheran and Munnar a couple of years back.

Naturally, I would avoid going to places where I am surrounded by people eagerly awaiting any opportunity to loot me. And mind you, these are not officials. They are just local people trying to make money. There is no organization in a large chunk of the country's tourism industry. As such, there is no accountability and or safety guarantee.

Reason 4: Exploitation of "foreign" tourists

Point 3 is even more of a problem for "white folks". All of these people (the tourism folks) assume that white folks are far richer and they have a special price (2-3 times higher) for foreigners.

Reason 5: Lack of a proper "experience"

When I visit a place, I do not want to know only the facts that I can easily Google or wiki. I want to understand, in depth, the history of the place and some fascinating stories from the past. I want imbibe the cultural nuances and savor the local flavors.

I want it to be a fun experience where the guide is knowledgeable about the place, can build a rapport with the tourists, and ensure that they have a great time.

Reason 6: Poor planning and government involvement

A few days ago, I was cleaning up the Indian Railways topic and I realized that we have a few tourist trains in India, the most famous being Palace on Wheels (luxury train). It covers the state of Rajasthan. We similarly have Maharaja Express that runs from Delhi to Agra (main attraction - Taj Mahal) and the Golden Chariot that covers Karnataka and Goa.

Literature Review

Though there are sufficient amount of literatures highlighting the marketing aspects of tourism, but a few of them has emphasized on the discussion of the promotional aspects of tourism marketing. At the same time, the literature attempted to deal with marketing aspects of tourism is not available enough especially, on the promotional issues of tourism marketing is much neglected and the literature on the same is very limited. In this study, the literature review includes the following: Chantarachoti described that in the eyes of foreigners Bangladesh is seen as a business destination rather than as a tourist destination when in actual fact there are potentials to explore in this country if properly promoted and promotion supported by government to the outside world. Also blamed that though Bangladesh has its abundant potential for growth of tourism industry could not utilized it properly due to lack of government support as well as the right initiatives of the country's NTO to highlight, Bangladesh to the eyes of foreigners as a tourist destination instead of a business destination. Though there are lots of similarities between India and Bangladesh and even with Nepal, Bangladesh is far behind from the mentioned two other countries due to the ineffective and insufficient promotional activities. He also claimed that the high foreign travel tax discourages foreigners to visit Bangladesh. Finally, he also emphasized that government's initiative can reduce the monopoly of the five star hotels by providing the facilities of establishing more hotels of different start and improving the infrastructure support, accommodation and land arrangements to promote and sell packages. Hasan described the present situation of Bangladesh tourism industry and present marketing strategies in his research book "Problems and Prospect of Bangladesh Tourism Industry" has blamed that Bangladesh tourism industry could not achieve the remarkable progress in comparison to other neighboring (South Asian) countries though the country is endowed with different tourism attractions. His criticism was concentrated mainly on the failure of Bangladesh Parjatan Corporation (BPC) to develop and lunch any dynamic and effective promotional strategy and then he suggested creating an independent and different organization for performing the marketing activities of BPC owned tourists spots. In addition to that he strongly recommended for initiating and implementing the marketing plan and strategy effecting for the potential markets and to avoid the aimless policies to develop mass tourism at the present stage in Bangladesh. Hossain and Firozzaman mentioned that Bangladesh tourism industry failed to grow properly not merely because it lacks in enough attractions but suffering mostly due to inadequate and effective promotional activities. They also claimed that the limited promotional materials like souvenirs, brochures, travel guides, accommodation guides, hand books, tourist maps, poster, folders, etc. distributed by BPC and some other private tour operators don't reach properly to the potential tourists and in addition to that, the quality of these materials is not satisfactory which causes not to create adequate curiosity among the potential tourists. At the same time, there are lacks in government initiative to offset or correcting the country's present image prevailing to the outside of the country as the country presently is suffering a lot from the image problem. The researchers also blamed that BPC or other private tour operators have little connection with the foreign tour operators and travel agencies for promoting Bangladesh tourism abroad though they act as hidden promoters of tourism activities in any tourist destination. According to the authors, lack of coordination among the parties related to tourism sector e.g. Ministry of Civil Aviation and Tourism, BPC, Biman Bangladesh Airlines, tour operators, travel agencies, hotels, other provides, local authorities and host population also causes for not developing the industry in Bangladesh. Mitra described that Bangladesh does not have enough effort to promote the country as a tourist destination. He argued that Bangladesh has to make aware to the tourists about what to see, where to stay and what to eat. He emphasized for the development of tourism industry, Bangladesh need to develop the infrastructure like hotels, resorts, promoting more places and there should have a link of the government tourism organization with the private sector to boost up the promotional activities for the same. Siddiqui, the Marketing Communication Manager, Pan Pacific Sonargaon Hotel, Bangladesh claimed that though Bangladesh has lots of things for tourism, but the country lacks in the initiatives to expose it to the potential tourists. He added that marketing communication can play an important role to let the people abroad to know what fantastic products Bangladesh can offer to the tourists. He emphasized on the cooperative efforts of the National Tourism Organization (NTO) with the private tour operators rather than emerging as the competitor for the overall development tourism industry. He also concluded that National airlines, hotels and the foreign missions of the country or at least an officer in each mission abroad with the responsibility of encouraging the potential tourists through providing necessary information and cooperation can contribute to a great extent for promoting the tourism industry of any country.

Bangladesh Tourism Marketing Strategy

Within marketing promotion mix elements, publicity appears to be the most useful form of promotional measures of the BPC. BPC also participate in international tourism exhibitions like the ITB at Berlin through which attractive package tours are sold to international tour operators and a large number of individual visitors in the fair. During tourism month (16 October - 15 November) different cultural night 36 shows, food festivals, seminars, symposiums, audio-visual presentations etc. are arranged mainly locally. BPC also uses a web page for disseminating the information to the potential tourists. But the fact is that the web page does not contain the complete information of Bangladesh tourism and it related facilities. As a result, it is tough for a potential tourist to have the required information from the said page. In the local market, BPC advertise in different newspapers, magazines, television and radio. BPC also sometime advertises in some specialized and special interest magazines. The private tour operators also lack of sufficient fund to operate an extensive promotional activities. As a result, they also conduct some promotional activities in a traditional form by distributing the brochures, leaflets, making advertisements in the local newspapers, participation of different exhibitions arranged locally. But a limited number of private tour operators prints and distributes their brochures in Bengali (local language), English and Japanese languages and some other operators do the same either in Bengal or in English or in both. There are some operators who participate in the international tourism fairs to attract the attention and encourage the potential tourists and try to sell package tours to the foreign tour operators as well as to the individual tourist. This sort of participation helps to get the media coverage in the international level. But most of the private tour operators try to attract the local nationals and the foreign residents already living in Bangladesh or visiting Bangladesh. The private tour operators also use some sorts of sales promotion like off-season price discounts, free distribution of printed materials; organize live music programs for the visitors in destination's spot, extra service offers, group tour discounts for the packages offered and river cruise programs. Hardly two or three operators are using the web page for the promotion of the tourism in Bangladesh. Therefore, the objectives of the tourism marketing strategy in Bangladesh are now outlined:

- To consolidate Bangladesh's position as a tourist destination in the established generating markets at regional and international levels by utilizing different marketing tools such as websites;
- To target new and potential markets by identifying and monitoring changing designs and needs for various market types such as China, Japan, East European and South America, and South Asian countries;
- To enhance Bangladesh's competitive position in the intercontinental destination market by mobilizing effective promotional measures supported by attractive proposals and appealing tourism products; and
- To pay special attention (in terms of promotion and product diversification strategies in particular) to tourist arrivals from Europe, South Asia, USA, Gulf Coop.

Marketing Strategy

Marketing method is the outcome of a firm's segmentation, focusing on and placement choices (STP process) at the quality of the Strategic Company Unit [3]. This viewpoint is reinforced by promotion books (for example, Kotler, [4], where this procedure is required as the core of technique. In other words, the primary idea of technique involve the tasks of determining and choosing the focus on sections in where the actual and prospective clients are living and desired to purchase the item. In advanced stage, there are three technique, market segmentation, focusing on and placement in reaching minds of the focus on clients and offer them suitable products/services that will serve clients special interests. The term "segmentation" appears to have been initially introduced by Cruz. According to Kotler [5], market segmentation means splitting the whole market into different parts on the basis of various factors. Target Marketing involves breaking market into sections and then focusing promotion efforts on one or a few key sections. According to Kotler et al. placement is the way the item is described by visitors on essential attributes; it is the position the item consumes in tourists' mind relative to competitive items.

Niche market strategy

Niche promotion has been used synonymously with "market segmentation", "target marketing", "micromarketing" "regional marketing", "focused marketing" and "concentrated marketing" [6,7]. It is, however, none of these and all of these. From an overall firm technique viewpoint, a specialized market method described as "a focus on a particular need, or geographical, market or item segment" [8]. Kotler states that niches are usually constructed by splitting a section into sub-segments and that the key issue in internet promotion is expertise. Shani and Chalasani [9] distinguish between market segmentation and internet promotion. They define market segmentation as a top-down approach. A literary works search by Kara and Kaynak [10] came to the conclusion that internet promotion takes market segmentation one step further in terms of creating a unique group of clients.

Here are four simple strategies your tourism business can consider to bolster your appeal overseas.

Think eco-tourism/adventure travel: Canada is emerging as a global destination for eco-tourism and adventure travel. The country is a natural draw for international visitors seeking authentic wilderness, adventure and cultural experiences. Canada has a reputation as an uncrowned and unspoiled holiday destination with a wide diversity of wildlife. Its natural environment also appeals to visitors seeking an adrenaline rush with such activities as windsurfing, white water kayaking, skiing and rock climbing. Consider how you can take advantage of the eco-tourism and adventure travel opportunities in your area. Even if your business is urban based, you can appeal to foreign visitors simply by helping them find local eco-tourism activities.

Give your website global reach: You can benefit from customizing your website to your target market with simple visual aids such as country flags. Showing your prices in local currency can help you connect with international visitors and increase their ability to compare prices. In the end, you want to increase user confidence and comfort. As well, it's important to provide international travelers with basic information on Canada, such as weather, currency, local customs and cuisine.

Make your business multi-seasonal: Any tourism operator today knows that building an all-season capacity into your business drives growth and revenues. And this is particularly important for attracting international visitors. If you're looking for ways to make your business an all-season affair, the first step is to assess the potential year-round activities in your area. Are there cultural activities, such as music festivals, that would attract visitors? Are there seasonal outdoor activities year round? You might consider adding a new dimension to your tourism business, such as offering spa services in the winter season.

Consider exhibiting at tradeshows: It's a marketing rule of thumb: Person-to-person contact can generate sales. And that's precisely what attracts thousands of tourism businesses and travelers to international tradeshows. If you're shopping around for a tradeshow to exhibit your business, ensure that you choose one that gives you the best exposure and avoid untested venues. As well, prior to the show, be sure that your trade show team is properly trained to sell your business.

Methodology

To achieve the goals of the study mainly the additional details has been used for performing this analysis. Secondary details has been gathered from yearly reports, website of secretary of state for municipal aircraft and travel and leisure and Bangladesh Parjaton Organization, publications of globe trade companies, different publications and analysis documents. After collecting details scientists evaluate the prospective buyers of nice market technique for the development of travel and leisure market in Bangladesh.

Findings and Analysis

Market segmentation

Market segmentation technique performs a natural part in the achievements of travel and leisure promotion goals. A vacationer market may be recognized corresponding to each vacationer item. In that sense, we can determine companies are a set of actual and audience of each item. There are five segmenting variables: Geographical, Market, Geo-demographic, Psychographic and Behavior [11]. Bangladesh Parjaton Organization (BPC) creates the plan to control the travel and leisure market. To segmenting the focus on audience it highlight on two factors that are (i) Market segmentation and (ii) Psychographic segmentation. Market segmentation are usually huge because in that section vacationer item can entice a small variety of categories and age provides the biggest range of options for interpreting a huge amount of categories. Psychographic segmentation provides us detail details of visitors. By this segmentation could about tourists' personal passions, inspirations, ambitions and feelings etc.

(i) Demographic segmentation for worldwide tourists:

- Ethnic identification and nationality: Most of the visitors arriving from European nations, Southern Japan, USA, Beach Collaboration Authorities Countries, Eastern Japan and the Hawaiian Rim, USA, Britain, Sydney and New Zealand and others.
- Age: Tourists categories are usually young and middle age people; sometimes families with kids and even pensioners are arriving too frequented at different places.
- Family life cycle: Some Bangali UK and USA immigration like to check out Bangladesh with their kids to familiar about culture and its culture.
- Sex: Men and women both equally like to check out Bangladesh.
- Religion: Muslims, Buddhists' and Christian pilgrims are interested in their concerned spiritual websites in Bangladesh.

(ii) Psychographic segmentation for worldwide tourists:

Actually demographic segmentation deal is vast and clear and understandable but the factors of psychographic segmentation is so detail that is needed to understand more about. The living design, day to day activities and the enjoyment item absorbed by the visitors is most essential. For psychographic segmentation customer's special passions, activity, views, and behavior towards different types of holidays is significant. Therefore, BPC is trying to segmenting the marketplace on the reasons for tourists' psychographic features but not success. If they could distinguish among these sections, they would be able to select appropriate sections and create as well as apply technique for each selected focus on team.

Target marketing

Target promotion involves evaluate each market section attraction and selecting one or more sections to enter. In that stage BPC focus its promotion effort on Seashores, Mountains & isles, Woodlands & Forest, Traditional places, Historical Sites and other.

Market positioning

According to kotler et al. placement is the way the item is determined by visitors on essential attributes; it is where the item consumes in tourists' thoughts relative to competitive items. It is difficult to enhance specific visitor's item when that item have several attraction. That's why BPC enhance package of tourist's item for the visitors. According to data of MoCAT, BPC consider four major tourist's items that have attraction and demand and added competitive advantage to Bangladesh. Those items, won good placement in the visitors thoughts in the European nations, Southern Japan, Eastern

Japan and the Hawaiian Rim, USA, Britain, Sydney and New Zealand and the goods are as following:

1. Beaches
2. Forest, Mountains and isles
3. Historical position
4. Archaeological Sites

Niche sell for beaches: The Seashores item variety contains Patenga, Parki, Cox's Bazar, Teknaf, St. Martin Island and Kuakata. Among these Cox's bazaar, Teknaf and St. Martin have more regional and worldwide visitors. The visitors who want to keep relax, save from mental problem, health and fitness for body disorders and check out for open air are especially focus on team [12].

Niche sell for woodlands, mountains and islands (Eco-tourism): Mountains and Islands contain Sundarban (the home of the spectacular Elegant Bengal tigers), Rangamati (the pond district), Kaptai (the pond town), Bandarban (the roof of Bangladesh) and Khagrachhari (the hilltop town). Tourists who are looking for naturel and different societies of different tribes' everyone is especially focus on team. These websites covered visitors eco-tourism needs. So Bangladesh eco-tourism met the eye of focus on team.

Niche sell for traditional place: Mostly drawn historical position contains National Art gallery, Central shahid Minar, Curzon Area, Martyred Perceptive Funeral, Baldha Garden, Subrawardy Uddayan, World War II Graveyard, Old high Court Building, Nator-Rajbari etc. Bangladesh has rich record about its culture. Tourists who want enhance their information about record are especially focus on team.

Niche sell for historical sites: Mostly drawn archaeological websites are Mainamati, Paharpur, Shait Gombuge Mosque, Kantajis Forehead, Lalbagh Citadel, Sonargaon, Ahsan Manzil etc. Tourists (researchers and students) who want enhance their information about the archaeology of gortyn are especially focus on team. This item met the eye of focus on team [13].

Recommendations and Conclusion

Bangladesh is a developing country and it has lots of tourist's items but all goods are not gaining worldwide visitors. So Bangladesh needs to focus to create Famous items rather than to enhance the variety of offers. The following suggestions will help to the ability to create its four Famous Products: First of all, for beaches power should set up more resorts, resorts and security. Authority can encourage natives to take part for their own economic benefit. Local power should update the features of beach websites. Secondly, for eco-tourism power should secure the green environment and forest also. Local power should effort to involve tribal's in the process of eco-tourism. Additionally, for historical position power should enhance its historical places and promotion these places through marketing mix. It is essential to protect historical places. Lastly, for archaeological websites power should create interaction (transportation) features to reach these websites and set up standard hotel and restaurants closest to websites. It is necessary to train up the human resources of different websites workplace to guide the worldwide visitors properly. It is necessary to offering the key items to niches in different way in compare to competitive nations. By taking proper internet technique Bangladesh can improve the invoices and variety of visitors. Specialized market technique can be useful because most of the worldwide visitors have attention to check out the above mentioned websites and willing to keep few days and spend cash for their enjoyment. By applying this tactic BPC can distinguish its tourist's item for different focus on categories (need basis) and secure it's downwards income.

Finally, the results of this analysis will help the plan maker to apply market way to serve the focus on sub multiple worldwide visitors. By using skilled private trip providers it can have more worldwide visitors to check out its four key items Seashores, Eco-tourism, Traditional position and Historical websites in addition to marketing program, set up vacationer workplace in overseas and modified websites.

References

1. Shahid M (2004) The tourism fair contributors to Bangladesh Economy', Holiday Aviation, August 31st, Dhaka Bangladesh.
2. Hasan SR (2005) Marketing publicity and sales promotion for tourism development in Bangladesh Social Science Review 19, No. 2, Dhaka University, Bangladesh.
3. Webster FE (2005) Back to the future: integrating marketing as tactics, strategy, and Organizational culture. Journal of Marketing 69: 4-6.
4. Kotler P (2003) Marketing Management (11thedn), Prentice-Hall, Upper Saddle River, USA.
5. Kotler P (2000) Marketing Management (11thedn), Pearson Education, Inc., NJ.
6. Dalgic T, Leeuw M (1994) Niche marketing revisited: concepts, applications, and some European cases. Eur J Mark 28: 39-55.
7. Linneman RE, Stanton JL (1992) Making Niche Marketing Work: How to Grow Bigger by Acting Smaller, McGraw-Hill, Inc., New York, USA.
8. Teplensky JD, Kimberly JR, Hillman AL, Schwartz JS (1993) Scope, timing and strategic adjustment in emerging markets: manufacturer's strategies and the case of MRI. Strategic management journal 14: 505-527.
9. Shani D, Chalasani S (1992) Exploiting niches using relationship marketing. The Journal of Services Marketing 9: 33-42.
10. Kara A, Kaynak E (1997) Markets of a single customer: exploiting conceptual developments in market segmentation. Eur J Mark 31: 873-895.
11. Kotler P (1991) Marketing Management (7thedn), Englewood Cliffs, New Jersey: Prentice-Hall.
12. Saunders J (2002) Quantitative methods in marketing, Thomson, London, pp. 85-99.
13. Smith WR (1956) Product differentiation and market segmentation as alternative marketing. American Marketing Association 21: 3-8.

Career Success and Organizational Justice as the Potential Predictors of Perceived University Performance: A Study from Public Sector Universities of Pakistan

Quaisar Ijaz Khan[1]*, Abdul Shukor Shamsudin[1] and Syed Soffian Syed Ismail[2]

[1]*School of Business Management, University Utara, Malaysia*
[2]*School of Accounting, University Utara, Malaysia*

Abstract

The main aspiration of the study remained to explore and examine the predictors of perceived university performance. While career success for the faculty members of public sector universities in Pakistan is becoming the area of interest for researchers and academicians. Data were collected from 223 faculty members who are currently serving as faculty members in public sector universities of Pakistan. The results supported the significant positive association of career success and organizational justice with perceived university performance. The study applied SPSS Version 20 for data screening and Structural Equation Modelling – Partial Least Square (SEM-PLS) technique through, Smart PLS 2.0 applied to explore the results.

Keywords: Career success; Organizational justice; Perceived University Performance; Universities; Pakistan

Introduction

Current study is a smart strive towards discovering potential determinants of university performance in public sector universities of Pakistan. While, the faculty members in public sector universities of Pakistan are deemed non-productive and they contribute towards the university performance rarely [1]. As career success is an important goal for most of faculty members. However, it is deemed that Government sector organizations are not even effective, such organizations are criticised as the resource wasting institutions of the state. However, the career successes of faculty members' is in best interest of universities under public sector more than the faculty members themselves [2,3].

In Pakistan there are 179 universities recognized by Higher Education Commission of Pakistan. Currently there are 75 universities under private sector and 104 under public sector [4-7]. The performance of the 179 universities are not good enough to get place in top 500 universities of the world for the year 2015, except one which has been ranked at 496th out of 500 best universities of the world for the year 2015 [8]. Recently published QS ranking there are only 20 universities from Pakistan in top 800 universities of Pakistan. While, Pakistan's educational system was ranked the poorest in world ranking [7]. According to the universities in Pakistan are deemed like degree mills because of low employability of graduates from these institutions [9].

It is urged that the universities might have to improve their productivity to generate the employability in the professional studies, degree itself is nothing until and unless have the ability to provide proper employment for the graduates [10].

Why the public sector universities in Pakistan are not able to perform better internationally? There might be a lot of reasons including low salaries, higher workload, imperceptible opportunities of professional growth & career success and lack of organizational justice in the institutions of higher education of Pakistan. Whereas, Pakistan has been ranked at 55 in global cultural index [11-13].

The situations of law and order, justice are very poor due to the higher level of corruption by the higher leadership and parliamentarians including Prime Ministers, Presidents current and previous since independence [14,15]. According to transparency international Pakistan has been ranked 117/168 the most corrupt country of the world [16]. In such a worst situation where some nations are only progressing in corruption, the possibilities of being treated in an impartial and unprejudiced way are very rare and cannot be expected.

Statement of Problem

Public sector universities of Pakistan are not performing well as compared to the international standards, because the faculty members working in such institutions are not contributing potentially towards universities' growth, there might be a lot of reasons behind this such as feebler performance and lower contribution towards the overall university performance, hardly visible service structure for the faculty members. Upon analysing the trends of faculty members' education and research publications as shown in Table 1 below. It has been observed from the available data that there are currently 9253 faculty members having PhD degrees and 25191 faculty members have no doctoral degrees up to 2013; and could hardly published only 6507 research articles.

According to the above mentioned table only 27% faculty members have PhD degrees to teach. While, 73% faculty members require to improve their qualification. Whilst, to recap there are 25191 faculty members those have to enhance their qualification for their own growth and survival in the same field. As in the contemporary situations in Pakistan survival in the profession is not easy, it has now become highly

Description	2008	2009	2010	2011	2012	2013
PhD Faculty	3483	4975	6315	6529	7625	9253
Non-PhD Faculty	11616	12860	N/A	23141	24715	25191
HEIs	126	127	132	138	146	153
Research	3425	3939	4963	6200	6400	6507

Table 1: Statics of faculty and their contribution for universities.

***Corresponding author:** Quaisar Ijaz Khan, School of Business Management, University Utara Malaysia, Malaysia
E-mail: qaisar@gcuf.edu.pk

competitive, complex and complicated. As after the international global crises of 2008 many organizations have started following the retrenchment practices to minimize the operational cost to hedge themselves from heavy losses as well as their own survival [17,18]. Career success is deemed and necessary for the success and survival in the professional life and career [19-22].

Whilst, the organizational justice is necessary for organizational success and progress. In recent studies the importance of the career success has been focused for the institutional success (Khan, Shukor, & Soffian, 2015; Shahzad et al., 2008; Yasir et al., 2013). Career success cannot be ignored. Nevertheless, as all the human beings are not equal and the performance from all the employees at work cannot be expected the same [23-26]. Therefore the need of organizational justice is vital to allocate the workload and opportunities of progress in public sector institutions [27,28]. Human resource management practices with justice and fairness must be designed to extract higher performance from the available workforce by training them and enabling them to contribute towards their own career and development in the global market [25,29]. While, organizational justice and career success are utmost necessary for better performance of the institutions in educational sector of Pakistan and to enhance universities' performance [30,31].

Research questions

1. Does career success has relationship with university performance?
2. Does organizational justice has relationship with university performance?

Research objectives

1. To examine the relationship of career success with university performance.
2. To examine the relationship of organizational justice with university performance?

Review of the Literature

University performance has not remained the area of focus in previous studies. The ranking criteria of the international bodies specially focus the universities of developed countries [8]. These are the employees who help the organizations to achieve their desired objectives. Therefore, it can be said that employees are the backbone of organizational success but there is a strong need to motivate and maintain them to get the competitive advantage in terms of giving quality products and services to the stakeholders [32]. In this regard professionally trained workforce plays an important role for achieving competitive advantage by providing good quality output and potential contribution [33]. In the study Career has been derived from Latin word, *"Carraria"* in English like road, carriage. Career success is the permutation of two different words, Career and Success, while it can be interpreted as an individuals' journey through learning, efforts, professional experience and other aspects of life.

There are countless techniques for defining career and the term is applied in a variety of ways. So it might be construed meritoriously that it is an agenda of an individual's progress from first to last [1,23,34]. As the people are not same, their emotions about the same phenomenon can vary in different perspectives and perceptions. As according to [17] it is redundant that an individual in the age of twenty year might have different reflection or perceptions about the career while an individual at the age of thirty might be having the same reflections as the individual in the age of fifty or sixty years; it is further not necessary that both have the same perceptions about the career in same sense or meanings. There are imaginable upshots of dissimilarity of assumptions in idiosyncratic individuals may be because of diverse civilizations, learning, knowledge and physical and mental abilities. Currently, it is proposed that the current study will reveal insight into the dilemma of inclination by defining career success, through its imperative commitment in the collection of evidence and theory also. Career success has been partitioned into two reflections, (i) Intrinsic and (ii) extrinsic reflections separately, sometimes interchangeably called (i) subjective and (ii) objective in nature as well. Extrinsic reflection can be seen and observable; relatively objective in nature comprises on noticeable outcomes including (i) salary, (ii) ascendancy and (iii) professional status, while intrinsic career success stands for the internal satisfaction of the employee from his/her profession and life [1]. The neutrality of observer might be apparent while evaluating the extraneous reflections or objective achievement of the individual. While, intrinsic reflections or subjective career success means individual's own perceptions identified with his/her own profession [2,35,36].

The negligible has been observed in the area of organizational justice for organizational progress [37,38]. The psychological processes, where organizational justice have the potential to determine the attitude and behaviour of the employees' working in the organization [39,40]. Globally the organizations have been found in the strict competitive environment. The opportunities for the work or employment are scarce as well, but for high performing worker the opportunities are abundant and countless to mention [34,41]. Universities are deemed the most important and competitive weapon in contributing towards lowering down the poverty, unemployment and enhancing national income & integrity [18]. Nevertheless, the organizational justice must be in order to accommodate and facilitate the employees at work as well as to derive motivation to work and satisfaction from work; to facilitate and boost organizational functioning in the dynamically competitive and complex environment [38,42].

Organizational justice and the opportunities of professional growth are now a days getting increased influence in the academia due to the ability to manage employees' attitude and behaviour at workplace [43]. Existing literature provided the guidance about the perceptions of organizational justice that are considered more important to enhance organizational performance and retain the quality work force to produce better productivity [31,44].

Whilst, the university performance has always been desired and necessary for the development and sustainability in the competitive world, funding agencies are also concerned about the utilization of their fund either used in right way; to be utilized in extracting the maximum efficiency in productivity, otherwise the distribution of such grants can be moved to some other institution that can produce better output from these funds [45,46].

However, the heads of the institutions have to remain impartial and fair while dealing with the faculty members, all the work loads and assignments are supposed to be allocated according to the capacity and capabilities of the individuals. The discussion of legal proceedings and administrative justice are another aspect of procedural justice.

Whilst, the distributive justice is all about perturbs, a kind of a communally just to allocate goods to the society. A society where, minor inequities in outcome do not occur would be deemed as a society directed by the doctrine of distributive justice [47-51]. Individuals have the potential to contribute better towards the attainment of organizational objectives. If the individuals are given the equal opportunities of growth and progress they can contribute towards the university performance better [52].

In the organizational context as individuals' career success contributes better and enhances organizational performance. Therefore, it is necessarily required to evaluate the areas of human aspects, that are helpful in enhancing performance at work, that enable the individuals to work for their own success, which ultimately contribute better towards the organizational performance [42,53]. So it can be hypothesized that:

H1: Career success has significantly positive relationship with university performance.

H2: Organizational justice has significantly positive relationship with career success.

Research Framework is depicted in Figure 1

Underpinning Theory

The theory of dynamic capability has been found supporting the conceptual model [54-58]. According to [54] the human beings have the potential to contribute better towards the attainment of organizational objectives. If the individuals are given the equal opportunities of growth and progress they can contribute towards the university performance better and have the abilities to enhance the performance with their impending contribution [57]. The study contributed in theoretical perspective as well by enhancing the chapter of Pakistan.

Methodology and Research Design

Current study intended to explore the relationship and impact of career success and organizational justice on university performance.

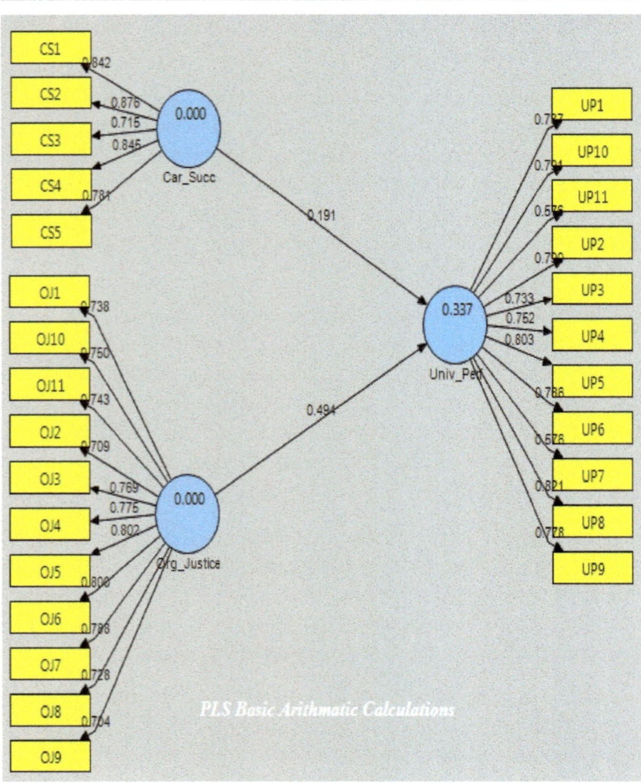

Figure1: Framework of the study.

This effort has been undertaken to enhance the existing literature by adding new chapter from Pakistan in theory and practice. The suitable approach to test theory and hypothesis has been found quantitative as the purpose of the study is to test the hypothesis and theory rather than developing new theory. For the sake of analysis quantitative tools and techniques were applied by using statistical package for social sciences (SPSS) version 20 for data validation and SMART PLS version 2.0 for assessing Reliability, Validity, Cronbach's alpha, R^2, Path Coefficient, Bootstrapping, T-statistics and standard deviation.

Sample and respondents

Sample for the study has been chosen from 104 public sector universities. 223 faculty members working in public sector universities, has participated and responded for this study. For the study a self-administrated questionnaire was personally disseminated among the respondents.

Measures and instruments

The perceptual information from respondents has been received upon the existence. However the 5 items measurement scale for career success has been adopted from the genuine source [59]. Organizational justice has been adopted from genuine source, having 11 items [60]. Whilst the perceived university performance has been adopted from [24], consisting on 11 items that has already been tested in Pakistani environment with different predictors. The questionnaire used in this study consist of 27 items overall. All the respondents were requested to articulate their adjudication by using a five point likert scale ranging from (1) strongly disagree, (2) disagree, (3) neither agree nor disagree, (4) agree and (5) strongly agree. As the measurement instrument has been tested widely in previous studies so the need of EFA has not been realised here for the study.

Results and Findings

The following Table 2 demonstrates the composite reliability and convergent validity for the latent variables of the current study. Composite reliability, Cronbach's alpha and average variance extracted (AVE) has been derived by using SMART PLS software 2.0 version. Cronbach's alpha which measures how well the variables are associate with each and other has been shown in the Table 2 as below. Table 3 represents discriminant validity of the construct. Table 4 represents the factor loading of the items, all the items remained within threshold values; as the measurements has been tested in the Asian context. Perceived university has been also tested in Pakistan earlier [24].

AVE should be above 0.5 Threshold for Convergent Validity [61,62]. The desired value for composite reliability is 0.7 and above. While for the exploratory research a value equal to above 0.6 can also be accepted [61,63].

	Composite Reliability	Cronbach's Alpha	AVE
Career Success	0.907	0.8712	0.6623
Organizational Justice	0.936	0.9247	0.5712
University Performance	0.933	0.9204	0.5617

Table 2: Reliability and the internal consistency of the variables.

	Career Success	Org. Justice	Univ.Perf
Career Success	0.8138	X	X
Org. Justice	0.2963	0.7558	X
Univ.Perf	0.3371	0.5509	0.7495

Table 3: Discriminant Validity, it is desired that the sqrt (AVE) should be above the latent variable correlation.

It is desired that the sqrt (AVE) should be above the latent variable correlation.

After verifying the basic assumptions that all are found within threshold value and standards. So the next step can be taken to test the hypothesis as visible clearly in Figure 2 below. Bootstrapping was used from sample of 223 up to 1000 to test the hypothesis.

Further details have been provided in Table 5 for making decision and testing hypothesis on threshold values and standards. As the Table 5 demonstrates the model indices fit at which the model is legitimated [61]. T-Value for two tail test is appropriate and acceptable is found equal to or above 1.96 [64]. Here T-Value has been found over and above 1.96 converted into P-Values which resulted 0.0045 and 0.0000 which are <0.05. Therefore, the hypothesis is being accepted.

Discussion and Conclusion

The study in its unique construct is exploratory in Pakistan. This research was executed for the faculty members in public sector universities of Pakistan. The study has tried to explore the impact of career success and organizational justice in predicting university performance. As the r^2 remained ***0.337*** that represents there are more than 66% other factors that determine university performance such as personality traits cultural factor that might be able to determine university performance in better and potentially significant way.

Limitations of the Study

As the scope of the study is very narrow and covers only 223 faculty members; those who are full time lecturers, assistant professors, associate professors and professors. Due to some financial constraints the data collection period also remained limited up to 45 days. The study has tested only two predictors of perceived university performance (i) Career Success (Subjective) and (ii) Organizational Justice (Procedural and Distributed), that has been remained the major limitation as well. Further, as mentioned earlier that the R^2 remained 0.337. It means there is still 66% other factor which remained unexplored in this study.

	Career Success	Organizational Justice	University Performance
CS1	0.8421		
CS2	0.8756		
CS3	0.7148		
CS4	0.845		
CS5	0.7815		
OJ1		0.7378	
OJ2		0.7089	
OJ3		0.7692	
OJ4		0.7747	
OJ5		0.8016	
OJ6		0.8003	
OJ7		0.7882	
OJ8		0.7277	
OJ9		0.704	
OJ10		0.7501	
OJ11		0.7432	
UP1			0.7874
UP2			0.7903
UP3			0.7326
UP4			0.752
UP5			0.8035
UP6			0.786
UP7			0.5756
UP8			0.8206
UP9			0.7781
UP10			0.7913
UP11			0.5762

Table 4: Factor loading.

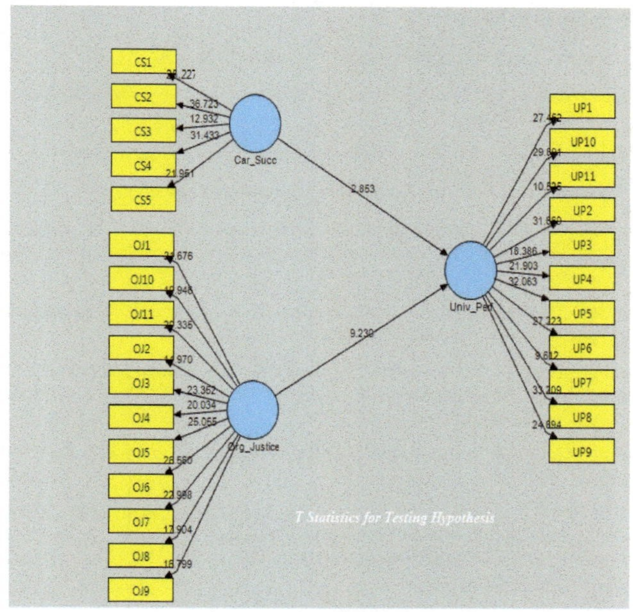

Figure 2: Results of Bootstrapping.

	Standard Deviation	Standard Error	T-Value	P-Value
Career Success → University Performance	0.0668	0.0668	2.85	0.0045
Organizational Justice → University Performance	0.0536	0.0536	9.23	0.0000
P. Value is <0.05. H1 and H2 both are Accepted.				

Table 5: T-Statistics for testing hypothesis.

Future recommendations

Future researcher may choose the larger sample and there are many other influential factors that have not been investigated in the current study. It is urged that environmental turbulence might be tested as moderator for such type of studies as the electricity shortfall, corruption, industrial setbacks are reshaping the business environment rapidly and supposed as the potential moderator for future studies. Qualitative evaluation is assumed to serve the purpose better.

References

1. Saher N, Bibi S, Farmanullah S, Abbas S (2014) Career Success in Pakistan : Human Capital and Social Networking Middle East. Journal of Science Research 19: 163-171.

2. Eby T, Sorensen KL, Feldman DC (2005) Predictors of Objective and Subjective Career Success: a Meta-Analysis. Persian Psychology 58: 367-408.

3. Ng TW, Feldman DC (2010) Human capital and objective indicators of career success: The mediating effects of cognitive ability and conscientiousness. Journal of Occupation Organ Psychology 83: 207-235.

4. HEC 2015 [Online] Available: http://wwwhecgovpk/Pages/HECMainaspx [Accessed: 30-May-2015]
5. Pakistan - Education US Library of Congress (2015).
6. Pakistan has world's weakest higher education system (2016) QS rankings Tribune The Express.
7. The Pakistani curriculum and extremism Islamabad Pakistan (2016).
8. Top 500 Best Universities Daily Dawn Islamabad - Pakistan (2014).
9. Nelofer H (2013) Quality of private universities in Pakistan: an analysis of higher education commission rankings. International Journal of Education Management 27: 775-786.
10. Pavlin S, Svetlik I (2014) Employability of higher education graduates in Europe. International Journal of Man power 35: 418-424.
11. Hofstede G (2011) Dimensional zing Cultures : The Hofstede Model in Context Dimensional zing Cultures : The Hofstede Model in Context. Online Read Psychology Culture, Vol-2, p: 126.
12. Hofstede GJ (2005) Role playing with synthetic cultures: the evasive rules of the game.
13. Minkov M, Hofstede G (2011) Is National Culture a Meaningful Concept? Cultural Values Delineate Homogeneous National Clusters of In-Country Regions. Cross-Cultural Research 46: 133-159.
14. Javaid U (2011) Corruption and its deep impact on good governance in Pakistan. Pak Economical Social Review 48: 123-134.
15. Chene M (2008) Overview of corruption in Pakistan Purpose.
16. Country Ranking in Corruption Transparency International (2016).
17. Tan FY (2010) Career Planning Individual's Personality Traits HRM Practices as Determinants to Individual Career Success: The Role of Career Strategies as Mediator. University Utara Malaysia Alore Setar.
18. Arfan S (2013) The influence of the macroeconomic variables and business environment on the foreign direct investment inflows in pakistan : the moderating role of political stability. University Utara Malaysia.
19. Praskova A, Creed PA, Hood M (2015) Career identity and the complex mediating relationships between career preparatory actions and career progress markers. Journal of Vocation Behaviour 87: 145-153.
20. Yean TF, Yahya KK (2013) The Influence of Malaysian Insurance Agents□ Career Planning on Their Career Strategies. International Journal of e-Education e-Business e-Management e-Learning 23-28.
21. Harash E, Al-Timmi SN, Alsaad FJ, Al-Badran AYZ, Ahmed ER et al. (2014) Contingency Factors and Performance of Research and Development: The Moderating Effects of Government Policy. J Asian Science Research 4: 47-58.
22. Zainal SB (2012) Influence of Rewards System to Career Planning and Success of Employee University Utara Malaysia.
23. Khan, Shukor SA, Soffian SI (2015) The influence of career planning and HRM practices on career success of faculty members in public sector universities of Pakistan. Journal of Resource Development Management 9: 68-75.
24. Shahzad K, Bashir S, Ramay MI, Khurram S, Bashir S et al. (2008) Impact of HR Practices on Perceived Performance of University Teachers in Pakistan. International Revision of Business Research Paper 4: 302-315.
25. Yasir S, Rizwan MK, Fiza S, Javed I (2013) Career Development an Imperative of Job Satisfaction and Career Commitment : Empirical Evidence from Pakistani Employees in Banking Sector. European Journal of Business Management 5: 108-119.
26. Mukhtar U, Siengthai S, Ramzan S (2011) Mediating Role of HRM in Organizational Conflict and Impact on Organizational Effectiveness : Empirical Evidence of Pakistan. Public Universities 2: 391-403.
27. Al-zu H (2010) A Study of Relationship between Organizational Justice and Job Satisfaction. International Journal of Business Management 5: 102-109.
28. Sarania H, Safania AM, Razavi MH (2013) Influence of career satisfaction and justice organization on Organizational Citizenship Behaviour in Iranian Futsal Professional League. Global Journal of Science Engineering Technology 14: 18-24.
29. Kaifi BA, Khanfar NM, Nafei WA, Kaifi MM (2013) The Need for Human Resource Managers to Understand and Prepare for Future Employees: A Study on the Perceptions of Business Students on Job Performance. Journal of Management Sustain 3: 103-109.
30. Parveen A (2011) System and Reforms of Higher Education in Pakistan. International Journal of Business Social Science 2: 260-267.
31. Arif MI, Hassan A, Ameer H (2014) HRM Practices in Public and Private Universities of Pakistan in Proceedings of 3rd International Conference on Business Management. pp: 114.
32. Khurram S, Rehman U, Shad I, Gul A, Khan MA (2011) Work-Life Policies and Job Stress as Determinants of Turnover Intentions of Customer Service Representatives in Pakistan. European Journal of Social Science 19: 403-411.
33. Amin A, Ismail WK, Rasid SZA, Selemani RDA (2014) The Impact of Human Resource Management Practices on Performance: Evidence from a Public University TQM Journal 26: 125-142.
34. Quaisar IK, Khulida KY, Tan FY (2014) The Effect of Human Capital Reward System and Career Commitment on Career Success: Mediating Role of Counterproductive Work Behaviour in Higher Education. Sector of Pakistan in 7th National Human Resource Management Conference, pp: 14-19.
35. Ng T, Feldman DC (2013) Employee age and health. Journal of Vocational Behaviour 83: 336-345.
36. Sur S, Ng ES (2014) Extending Theory on Job Stress: The Interaction Between the 'Other 3' and 'Big 5' Personality Traits on Job Stress. Hum Resource Development Review 13: 79-101.
37. Mumtaz A, Khan I, Aslam H, Ahmad B (2012) Impact of HR Practices on job Satisfaction of University Teacher: Evidence from Universities in Pakistan. Indian Engineering Letter 1: 10-18.
38. Murtaza G, Shad I, Malik WS (2011) Impact of organizational justice on employees' job satisfaction : evidence from Pakistan. International Conference on Management (ICM 2011) Proceeding, pp: 1123-1135.
39. Sabir K, Irfanullah J, Khan AZ, Siddiqui N, Dad K et al. (2010) HRM Practices a Woy for improving skills and commitment of the employees in organization (A Banking Sector in Pakistan). International Journal Asian Social Science 2: 1735-1741.
40. Raihan J (2012) The mediating effect of organizational commitment and perceived organizational support on HRM practices and turnover intention: A study of private universities in Bangladesh. University Utara Malaysia.
41. Khan QI, Shukor AS, Soffian SI (2015) The influence of career planning and hrm practices on career success of faculty members in public sector universities of Pakistan. South Asia International Conference, pp: 114.
42. Saeed RD, Mizna RN, Lodhi AA, Gill A (2014) Impact of Human Resource Practices on Deviant Workplace Behaviour A Study on Banking Sector Employees. Journal of basic Applicants of Science Research 4: 81-86.
43. Khan R, Bukhari A, Channar Z (2016) Effects of Leadership Style on Health Care Organizational Performance: A Survey of Selected Tertiary Care Hospital in Karachi Pakistan. International Journal, Vol. 5.
44. Rhee J, Zhao X, Kim C (2014) Effects of HRM Practices on Chinese Firms' Organizational Performance: The Moderating Effect of CEO Support. Asian Social Science 10: 210-221.
45. Shan S, Ishaq HM, Shaheen MA (2015) Impact of organizational justice on job performance in libraries mediating role of leader-member exchange relationship. Library Management 36: 70-85.
46. Asif M, Awan MU, Khan MK, Ahmad N (2013) A model for total Quality management in higher education Quality Quantity. 4: 1883-1904.
47. Asghar RJ, Qayyum A, Zaheer A, Mughal A, Khalid S (2011) Implementation of HR Practices in University Teachers of Pakistan. Information Management Business Review 3: 148-158.
48. Jacobs G, Belschak FD, Den Hartog DN (2013) Un Ethical Behaviour and Performance Appraisal: The Role of Affect Support and Organizational Justice. Journal of Business Ethics 121: 63-76.
49. Struyven K, Jacobs F, Dochy (2013) Why do they want to teach? The multiple reasons of different groups of students for undertaking teacher education. European Journal of Psychology Education 28: 1007-1022.
50. Dent J (2015) Evaluating your own performance in a lecture Springer link.
51. Tessema MT, Soeters J (2006) Challenges and prospects of HRM in developing

countries: testing the HRM-performance link in the Eritrean civil service. International Journal of Human Resource Management, pp: 86-105.

52. Nabi GR (2000) Motivational attributes and organizational experiences as predictors of career-enhancing strategies. Career Developement International volume 5: 91-98.

53. Stumpf A (2014) longitudinal study of career success embeddedness and mobility of early career professionals. Journal of Vocation Behaviour 85: 180-190.

54. Teece D, Pisano G, Shuen AM, Shuen AY (1997) Dynamic Capabilities and Strategic Management. Strategic Management Journal 18: 509-533.

55. Teece DJ (2009) Dynamic Capabilities and strategic management New York United States of America: Oxford University Press.

56. Fueglistaller U, Schrettle T (2010) Book review: Dynamic capabilities & strategic management Organizing for innovation and growth Oxford: Oxford University Press. International Small Business Journal 28: 522-524.

57. Teece DJ (2007) Explicating dynamic capabilities: the nature and micro foundations of (sustainable) enterprise performance. Strategic Management Journal 28: 1319-1350.

58. Helfat CE, Finkelstein S, Mitchell W, Peteraf MA, Singh H et al. (2013) Dynamic Capabilities: Understanding Strategic Change in Organizations Malden USA: Blackwell Publishing.

59. Greenhaus JH, Parasuraman S, Wormley WM (1990) Affects of Race on Organizational Experience Job Performance Evaluations and Career Outcomes. Academic Management Journal 33: 64-86.

60. Colquitt J (2001) On the dimensionality of organizational justice: A construct validation of a measure. Journal of Applied Psychology 86: 386-400.

61. Bagozzi R, Yi Y (1988) On the Evaluation of Structural Equation Models. Journal of Academic Marketing Science 16: 74-94.

62. Hair J, Sarstedt M, Hopkins L, Kuppelwieser V (2014) Partial Least Squares Structural Equation Modeling (PLS-SEM): An Emerging Tool in Business Research. European Business Review, Vol-26, pp: 1.

63. Henseler J, Dijkstra TK, Sarstedt M, Ringle CM (2014) A Diamantopoulos Common Beliefs and Reality About PLS: Comments on Ronkko and Evermann. Organ Research Methods 17: 182-209.

64. Kumar M, Talib SA, Ramayah T (2012) Business Research Methods Kualalampore Malaysia: Oxford university press.

14

An Investigation of the Impact of Foreign Direct Investment on Economic Growth: A Case Study of Mauritania

Limam Ould*

Faculty of Economics and Management Sciences, International Islamic University Malaysia, Selangor, Kuala Lumpur 53100, Malaysia

Abstract

Purpose: This paper aim to investigate the impact of Foreign Direct Investment (FDI) on the economic growth of Mauritania for the period 1976 to 1995 quarterly data. It evaluated the Gross Domestic Product (GDP) performance and the trends of FDI and Gross Fix Capital Formation (GFCF) in Mauritania.

Methodology/sample: to demonstrate the relationship between Mauritanian Gross Domestic Product (GDP) and Foreign Direct Investment (FDI) and Gross Fix Capital Formation (GFCF) Multiple-Regression-Model has been applied along side with various econometrics techniques such as Unit-Root Test, Granger-Causality Test and Ordinary Least Square (OLS). GDP in this model is used as dependent variable whereas FDI and GFCF are measured as independent variables.

Findings: According to the results, Unit Root Test indicated that all the variables included in the model were not stationary at level except FDI, whereas GDP and GFCF are stationary at first difference. The model is overall significant with the positive and significant relationship of GDP, FDI and GFCF (divya). Result also indicate a good fit for the model with R2=85%. The Granger Causality Test revealed that there was no causality between the variables since all p-value obtained are more than 5%.

Practical implications: Based on the empirical result of this paper, policy recommendation proposed that for Mauritania to generate more foreign direct investment, hard work should be made at solving problems of government involvement in business; relative closed economy; corruption; weak public institutions; and poor external image, and political instability.

Keywords: GDP; FDI; GFCF; Mauritania

Introduction

Foreign Direct Investment (FDI) is seemed to have a positive influence on the economic growth of the developing countries through direct and indirect ways. It increases the domestic investment, which is claimed to have crucial role on the sustainability of growth and development. As a result, many developing countries, including Mauritania, have presented munificent intensives in order to attract FDI inflow.

Foreign direct investment incentives may be in shape of low corporate and income tax rates, tax holidays, other types of tax concessions, preferential tariffs, special economic zones, investment financial subsidies, soft loan or loan guarantees, free land or land subsidies, relocation and expatriation subsidies, job training and employment subsidies, infrastructure subsidies, research and development support and derogation from regulations, usually for very large projects [1]. However, This important incentives offered by developing countries have been taken by foreign firms to fulfil their objective by increasing profits through numbers of advantage such as control over local market, low cost of labour.

Developing countries undertake some macroeconomic reforms to ensure investor-friendly environment. The positive impact of FDI inflow has been increasingly famous as a vital tool to encourage economic growth [2]. The pivotal effect of FDI inflow on economic growth encompass, an increase in aggregate productivity, an increase opportunities of employment, a greater outflow of export, and finally exchange technology advancement between investor and the country [3]. According to a number of studies such as [4] foreign direct investment can serve as a means of transfer of technology and knowledge [4].

In case of Mauritania, although the country being blessed with huge natural resources but it recorded very low proportion of global FDI inflow. As a part of sub-Saharan countries Mauritania has been relatively open to FDI. The attractive natural resource in mining, fishing and hydrocarbon sectors helped the country to acquire inflow. Even though FDI flows to West Africa declined by 5% to $ 16.8 billion, Mauritania mining sector helped the country to obtained double inflow to $ 1.2 [5]. Mauritania works with the International Monetary Fund (IMF), the World Bank (WB), and the international donor community to move forwards basic infrastructure projects and to update laws and regulations.

This paper aims to discover the impact of foreign direct investment (FDI) on Mauritania economic growth (GDP) for the period 1976 to 1995 quarterly data and to observe the relationship between (GDP) and Gross Fixed Capital Formation (GFCF). Mauritania is a country located at the North West Region of Africa and constitutes as part of sub-Saharan African countries. It has a total population of 3,437,610. Based on the latest Central Intelligence Agency's report Mauritania has a total GDP of $7.824 billion [6]. Mauritania economy primarily depends on mining and fishery sectors, a per capita income is low, and much of the population lives under poverty line. Therefore policies to benefit from FDI inflow in the country are the vital objectives of the macroeconomic policy makers. Mauritania is strives to fight against effects of global panic such as unemployment rise, shortage liquidity. FDI and GFCF

***Corresponding author:** Limam Ould, Faculty of Economics and Management Sciences, International Islamic University Malaysia, Selangor, Kuala Lumpur 53100, Malaysia, E-mail: limam.uia@gmail.com

play a very crucial role in its future growth and development.

Literature Review

A variety of theoretical and empirical studies are presented on the impact of Foreign Direct Investment and Economic Growth in both developed and developing countries. Majority of these studies have been done on the international level. In context of Mauritania, there is dearth of empirical studies regarding these types of economic subject. A numerous of important researches have been critically reviewed to build up objectives in the perspective of Mauritania and further to analyse it to draw important conclusion and policy recommendations.

Laura Alfaro et al., they check up the various links among FDI and GDP growth. They explore whether countries with better financial systems can exploit FDI more efficiently. The empirical analysis used data between 1975 and 1995. Result shows that FDI alone plays an ambiguous role in contributing to economic growth. However, countries with well developed financial markets gain significantly from FDI in their economic growth [7].

Frimpong [8] explored the relationship between FDI and GDP growth for Ghana for the pre and post structural adjustment program (SAP) periods and the direction of the causality between two variables. Annual time series data covering the period from 1970 to 2005 was used. The study finds no causality between FDI and growth for the total sample period and the pre-SAP period [8].

Ayanwale [9] examine the empirical relationship between non-extractive FDI and economic growth in Nigeria. The study applied Ordinary Least Square (OLS) technique. Result indicates that FDI had a positive impact on economic growth [9].

Another work by Herzer et al., [10] used a bi-variate Vector Autoregressive (VAR) Model to figure out the impact of FDI in some developing countries. The study discovered evidence of a positive FDI-led growth for Nigeria, Sri Lanka, Tunisia, and Egypt and based on weak exogeneity tests, a long-run causality between FDI and economic growth running in both directions was found for the same countries [10].

Chin-Chiang et al, [11] they check up whether the FDI promote the economic growth by using threshold regression analysis. The empirical analysis revealed that FDI alone play a vague role in contributing to economic growth based on a sample of 62 countries covering the period from 1975 to 2000 and find that initial GDP and human capital are important factor in explaining FDI. FDI is found to have a positive and significant impact on growth when host countries have better level of initial GDP and human capital [11].

Nuzhat Falki [12] explored the effect of FDI on the Economic Growth of Pakistan. She collected the data that covers the period 1980 to 2006 from the Handbook of Pakistan Economy-2005 published by the State of Pakistan and the World Bank Development Indicators. Variables of domestic capital, foreign owned capital and labour force were used in this study with the help of endogenous growth theory and applying the regression analysis. The finding revealed a negative statically insignificant relationship between GDP and FDI inflows in Pakistan [12].

Sayeed Alam and Mahmud Zubayer they founded that in SAARC FDI from outside is more important than in intra regional investments in most the countries (the only exception is Nepal) where Indian investments dominated. The concept of some region can be applicable to increase intra regional FDI. The FDI has a significant impact on GDP of SAARC countries.

Abel and Nikki [13] investigated the effect of macroeconomics variables on the foreign direct investment of 30 Sub-Sahara African (SSA) countries between 1995 and 2008. Result, showed that financial development, the size of market and infrastructural development and urban accumulations are important factors that measure the inflows of FDI to the SSA region [13].

Behname [14] used random effects model to determine the impact of foreign direct investment on economic growth in Southern Asia. The study concluded that foreign direct investment has positive and significant effect on economic growth [14].

Onakoya [15] disaggregated the economy and employed a structural macro- econometric model consisting of four blocks namely: supply, private demand, government and external sectors to measure the impact of FDI on economic growth. The findings showed that FDI has a significant impact on output of the economy, however, the growth effects of FDI differs across sectors in Nigeria [15].

Abbas et al. [16] investigated the influence of FDI and CPI on the GDP's of SAARC member nations. The findings indicated that the general model in these countries developed a positive relationship between Foreign Direct Investment and GDP while negative relationship between Consumer Price Index and GDP. This conclusion was tested using the multiple regression models. The data of the SAARC countries ranged from the year 2001 to 2010 [16]. Esther and Folorunso [17] explored the relationship between FDI inflows and economic growth of Nigeria. The findings reported that FDI influence economic growth positively to limited human capital [17].

A study by Zakia and Ziad [18] investigated the impact of FDI on the economic growth of Jordan. The empirical results revealed that there is existence of bidirectional relationship between FDI and output [18].

Kashif and Muhammad [19] investigated the impact of FDI on Pakistan economic growth. The study developed an auto regressive distributed lag (ARDL) model. The model examines long run relationship between the variables and found absence of long run relationship between FDI and economic growth [19].

Research Methodology

The purpose of this research paper is to examine the impact of FDI inflow on the economic growth of Mauritania (GDP) and the relationship between Gross Fix Capital Formation (GFCF) and GDP. Study covers the time period from 1976-1995. The quarterly data obtained form World Bank Indicator (WBI) which is considered as an authentic source of data collection. To examine the relation of Mauritania's GDP with FDI and (GFCF), the following theoretical model is used.

$$GDP=F\ (FDI\ and\ GFCF) \qquad (1)$$

The hub intention of the paper is to study the effect of FDI on GDP of Mauritania. The trend of foreign Direct Investment inflows is also observed with relevance to GDP growth and GCFCF. To examine the relation of Mauritania's GDP with FDI and GFCF, the following multiple regression model is used,

$$GDP=\alpha + \beta 1\ FDI + \beta 2 GFCF+\mu \qquad (2)$$

Where,

FDI = Foreign Direct Investment

GDP = Gross Domestic Product

GFCF = Gross Fix Capital Formation

Level of Significant: 5 to 10 percent

Method of data analysis

In analysing the dataset the following tests are expected to be employed: Unit root test for stationary, Augmented Dickey-Fuller Test (ADF), Ordinary Least Square (OLS) method, Granger causality test was applied in order to determine the presence of the relationship among variables and its direction (Granger, 1969). The study used E-views 6 software to analyse data.

Empirical Results

Descriptive statistic

The Multiple Regression Model was run on E-Views to find out the Impact of FDI and GFCF on the Gross Domestic Product of Mauritania. In this multiple regression model, GDP is used as dependent variable whereas FDI and GFCF are defined as independent variables. To estimate the effect of FDI on GDP of Mauritania, Multiple Regression Model is applied over the period of 1976 to 1995 quarterly. Descriptive statistics of GDP, FDI and GFCF are as follows.

The Table 1 showed a summary of the descriptive statistic for the three variables included in this study GDP, FDI, and GFCF. The table contains the mean, standard deviation, minimum and maximum for 80 observations covering the period 1976-1995 quarterly.

Measures the dependent variable (GDP)

In this study we used GDP as a dependent indicator in the Multiple Regression Model. Quarterly data covers the period from 1976-1995, and it is taken from WBI. GDP measured in Million US$. It is used as dependent variable. The result from descriptive statistic indicates that Mauritania real GDP recorded 24.8 Million US$. The minimum value of real GDP was 23.8 Million US$, while the maximum value was 25.9 Million US$ (Figure 1).

Measures the Independent Variable (FDI)

We used FDI as an independent growth in Multiple Regression Model. Quarterly data cover the period from 1976_1995 obtained from WBI. FDI measured in Millions of US$. The finding showed that Mauritania real FDI inflow recorded 15.52 Millions US$. The Minimum value was 14.12 Million US$, while Maximum value recorded 17.96 Million US$ (Figure 2).

Measures of Independent Variable (GFCF)

We used GFCF as an independent growth in Multiple Regression Model. Quarterly data cover the period from 1976_1995 obtained from WBI. GFCF measured in Millions of US$. The finding revealed that Mauritania real GFCF was 23.42 Million US$. The Minimum value was 22.42 Million US$, while Maximum value recorded 25.10 Million US$ (Figure 3).

	LOGGDP	LOGFDI	LOGGFCF
Mean	24.80329	15.52075	23.42091
Median	24.75002	15.52027	23.43083
Maximum	25.93635	17.96236	25.10333
Minimum	23.88494	14.12910	22.42348
Std. Dev.	0.660647	1.033912	0.655725

Table 1: Descriptive Statistic, Source: E-Views 6.

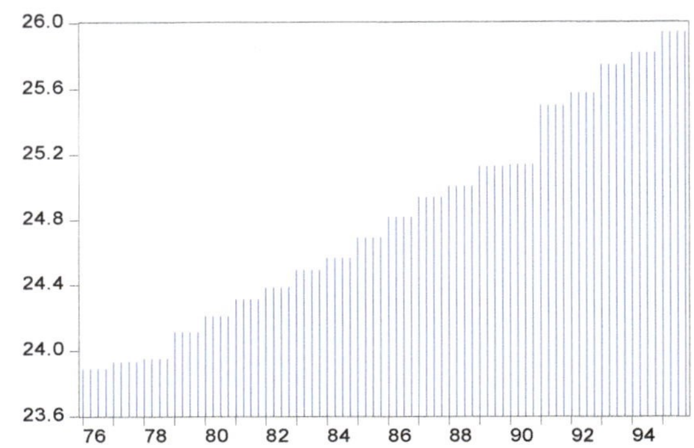

Figure 1: Mauritania's LOGGDP (1976-1995/ Quarterly).

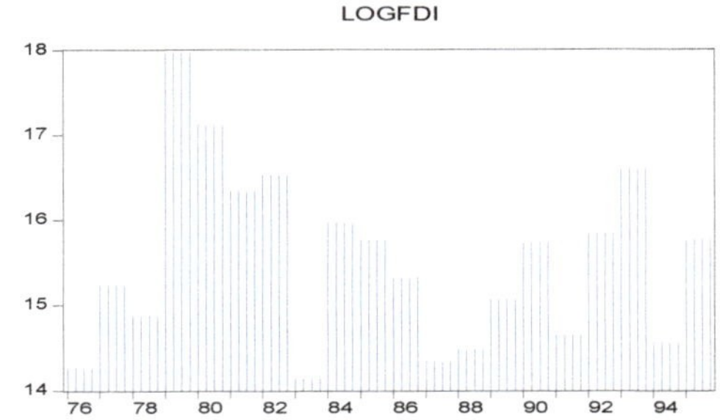

Figure 2: Multiple Regression ModelFDI (1976-1995/ Quarterly).

Figure 3: Multiple Regression ModelGFCF (1976-1995/ Quarterly).

Augmented Dickey-Fuller (ADF) unit root test

The unit root test has been applied to check whether the variables are stationary or not. The test carried out through Augmented Ducky Fuller (ADF) method as suggested by Engel and Granger (1987). The (ADF) analysis carried at both level and difference. The null hypothesis in ADF test is that there is presence of unit root. The result of (ADF) test is indicating in the following Table 2.

1% Critical Value -3.525619

Variables	Levels Data	First Differences	Status
LOGGDP	0.452219	-2.819407	I (1)
LOGFDI	-3.056340	-6.627344	I (0)
LOGGFCF	-1.209058	-6.592187	I (1)

Table 2: Augmented Dickey-Fullers (ADF), Source: Eveiws 6.

Null Hypothesis:	Obs	F-Statistic	Prob.
LOGFDI does not Granger Cause LOGGDP	78	0.11689	0.8898
LOGGDP does not Granger Cause LOGFDI		0.35370	0.7033

Table 3: Granger Causality Test Source: Eveiws 6.

Country	Variables	Coefficients	P-value	F-statistic	R-square
Mauritania	FDI	0.085614	0.0040	226.8974	0.854935
	GFCF	0.960185	0.0000		

Table 4: Summary of OLS Results GDP, FDI and GFCF, Source: E-veiws 6.

5% Critical Value -2.902953

10% Critical Value -2.588902

Interpretation of unit root test result

The result of Unit Root Test indicated that all the variables included in the model were not stationary at level except FDI. That can be seen through comparing the critical value with the ADF value, when the critical value is greater that ADF value meaning that the variable is not stationary. However, when the critical value of the variables is less than the ADF value the variable is stationary.

The granger causality test

To explain the granger causality test, we often asked questions such as "is GDP that causes FDI or is FDI that causes GDP?" We test for the absence of Granger causality by estimating the following VAR model:

$$GDP=\Sigma\alpha_{j}FDIt\text{-}3 + \Sigma\beta j\ GDPt\text{-}3+ U1t \quad (3)$$

$$FD1= \Sigma\lambda\ FDIt\text{-}3 + \Sigma\delta iGDPt\text{-}3 + U2t \quad (4)$$

α, β, λ and δ are parameters to be estimated, and Ult and U2t are the error term.

Granger causality test was applied in order to determine the presence of the relationship among variables and its direction (Granger, 1969) is carried out using E-views 6. The findings of Granger Causality Test between FDI and GDP indicated in the following Table 3:

The result in Table 3 shows that we cannot reject the null hypothesis, which means that GDP does not Grange cause FDI and vice-versa. Therefore, there was no causality between FDI and GDP of Mauritania since all P-value is greater than 5%.

Ordinary Least Square (OLS)

OLS method has applied in this study. The summary of the test indicated that the model of the study is well fitted. All the variables in the model are statistically significant. The coefficient of the constant variable recorded 3.84 which indicate a positive relationship between the constant parameter and the Gross Domestic Product. Although, the constant parameter has no significant effect on the model rather than reflecting the value of GDP when other independent variables are help constant. The summary of OLS result showed in the following Table 4.

Interpretation of OLS result

The empirical results are presented by the above table. The slope coefficients of the both inputs (FDI) and (GFCF) in Multiple Regression Analyses have positive impact on GDP. If one percent change in FDI occurs, it will bring about 0.085% change in GDP and 1 percent change in GFCF will bring 0.96% change in GDP by holding other variables constant. Estimates (FDI and GFCF) are highly significant. As the value of F is too high i.e., 226.8974 and the value of P is so small i.e., 0.000 we can deduce that model is overall very much significant and the results are not by chance. The r-square of this model is 0.85 that means only 15% variation in the model is unexplained by FDI and GFCF whereas remaining variation (85%) is explained by FDI and GDP.

Conclusion and Recommendation

The main objective of this study is to investigate the impact of Foreign Direct Investment (FDI) on the economic growth of Mauritania for the period 1976 to 1995. In an economy, direct investment is suggestive of a positive trend of investment which ultimately translates in increase in GDP and economic growth of the country. This can also be proved from the findings of this research that increasing trend of FDI also increases the GDP of the country. The Granger Causality test indicates no causality between GDP and FDI in the period under investigation. The significance of FDI in generating the target growth rate in Mauritania may be restricted by the level of infrastructure, environmental business, Economic reform, and political stability. Results of this study suggested some policy implications. The government in order to gain confidence of investors should focus on the following areas:

Improvement of infrastructure

In any economy infrastructure plays a very crucial role to develop and encourage the growth of the state. These states that have a strong physical infrastructure are considered as the best nations for attracting FDI. Thus, Mauritania government should give full consideration to improve and develop the infrastructure across the country.

Create friendly environmental business

Pleasant business environment is among the properties to attract FDI. Mauritanian in order to benefit from FDI should focus on improving human capital, and technology jobs. World Bank report 2013 released that Mauritania doing business index is 164 out of 185 which is not conducive to doing business. These factors are including, lack of world class ports, airports, road. Other problems are that of norms of registering property, protection of investors, excessive bureaucracy, lack of rationale tax structure, competition rules and time taken in enforcing contracts.

Economics reform

Economic reformation refers to the transformation of property from less productive to more productive sectors of the economy. Real growth of production is directly correlated with the effective process of economy restructuring from the less productive to the more productive sectors of the economy. FDI may be involved in the transfer of resources from less productive to more productive sectors of the economy.

Ensuring political stability

The successful and energetic market economy requires political stability for its best achievable outcomes. Political instability generates economic insecurity because of turn down in investment. Mauritania such as other African country is suffered from the political conflict. From 1976 to 2008 Mauritania has witnessed series of military coups which were enough to drag down the democratic process and create severe polarization inside political classes. This political instability has reduced the confidence of investors in the country.

References

1. Obadan MI (2004) Foreign Capital Flows and External Debt: Perspectives on Nigeria and the LDCs Group, Broadway Press Ltd, Ibadan, Nigeria.
2. Muhammad A (2007) Economic Growth and Foreign Direct Investment: The Role of Domestic Financial Sector, PIDE Working Papers.
3. Amna MG, Imran UC, Salman AS (2010) Impact of Foreign Direct Investment on Economic Growth: A Case Study of Pakistan, Journal of Management and Social Sciences, 84-92.
4. Dunning J, Hamdani A (1997) The new globalism and developing countries, United Nations University Press, New York.
5. UNCTAD (2013) Nigeria Tops List of Foreign Direct Investments in Africa, Press PR, Geneva.
6. Mahmoud MO, Limam, Abduh M (2014) The Role of Awareness in Islamic Bank Patronizing Behaviorof Mauritanian: An Application of TRA, Journal of Islamic Finance (IIUM Institute of Islamic Banking and Finance) 3: 30-38.
7. Alfaro L, Chanda A, Kalemli-Ozcan S, Sayek S (2004) FDI and economic growth: The role of local financial markets. Journal of international economics 64: 89-112.
8. Frimpong JM, Oteng-Abayie EF (2006) Bivariate causality analysis between FDI inflows and economic growth in Ghana.
9. Ayanwale AB (2007) FDI and economic growth: Evidence from Nigeria, Edited by AERC Research Paper 165, African Economic Research Consortium.
10. Herzer D, Klasen S, Nowak-Lehmann DF (2006) In search of FDI-led growth in developing countries: The way forward, Ibero American Institute for Economic Research 25: 793-810.
11. Chih-Chiang, Wu Jyun-Yi, Hsu (2008) Does Foreign Direct Investment Promote Economic Growth? Evidence from a Threshold Regression Analysis, Bulletin Economics.
12. Nuzhat F (2009) Impact of Foreign Direct Investment on Economic, International Review of Business Research Papers 5: 5.
13. Abel EE, Nikki C (2011) FDI flows to Sub-Saharan Africa: the impact of finance, institution and natural resource endowment, Department of Economics and Economic History.
14. Behname M (2012) Foreign direct investment and economic growth: Evidence from southern Asia, Atlantic Review of Economics 2.
15. Onakoya AB (2012) Foreign direct investments and economic growth in Nigeria: A disaggregated sector analysis, 3.
16. Abbas Q, Akbar S, Nasir A, Amanullah H, Naseem M (2011) Impact of Foreign Direct Investment, Global Journal of Management and Business Research 11.
17. Esther OA, Folorunso SA (2011) The role of foreign direct investment in economic development: A study of Nigeria, World Journal of Entrepreneurship, Management and Sustainable Development.
18. Zakia M, Ziad A (2007) The impact of foreign direct investment and imports on economic growth: The case of Jordan, Journal of Economic and Administrative Sciences.
19. Kashif Y, Muhammad R (2013) The Impact of foreign direct investment on Pakistan economic growth, Interdisciplinary journal of contemporary research in business 4: 287-296.

Effects of Causality and Error Correction on Volatility Modeling: A Simulation Approach

Rotich Titus Kipkoech*

Student, Mount Kenya University , Eldoret, Kenya

Abstract

Generalized Auto Regressive Conditional Heteroskedasticity (GARCH) models are usually used to analyse time series data with high volatility clustering. In this paper, we analyse the effects of Granger Causality Model (GCM) and Error Correction Model (ECM) in analysing a time series and accordingly, we simulate two series of data using the GARCH[1] model which are used for the analysis. The choice of the simulation model is based on its ability to capture volatility and heteroskedasticity. GCM[2] and ECM[3] models' parameters are investigated for adequacy. Results from Augmented Dickey Fuller (ADF), Phillips PerronPhillips Perron (PP) and Kwiatkowski Philips Schmidt Shin (KPSS) tests indicate stationarity in the data as expected. GCM is built to demonstrate all the long term relationships. The two series Granger Caused each other. A linear ECM is also fitted and there is evidence that a short-term relationship exists between these two series. A high threshold value exists at the second lag, an indication of simple smoothing in the data. The residual deviance was greater than the degrees of freedom asserting that the model perfectly fit the data, supported by high R2 value of 0.871. Residuals from the fitted linear model are also stationary. The study concludes that ECMs and GCMs are appropriate in analysing time series. It is recommended that a similar study be undertaken but with a combination of ARMA Auto Regressive Moving Average (ARMA) Process and GARCH models. Further study should also be conducted on tail clustering analysis.

Keywords: Granger causality, Error correction model, Simulation, Economics, Volatility

JEL Classification: 60K35, Granger causality, Error correction model, Simulation, Economics, Volatility

Introduction

Escalation of interest rates and exchange rates in Kenya have been a common phenomenon. Its random inter-data movements leads to the subject of volatility. It has formed the basis of most researches in time series analysis, with several scholars building various models in the attempt to exhaustively examine the sources of these volatilities and its predictions. Unfortunately, no particular scholar has been able to exhaustively determine the sources of volatilities, neither have they settled on any particular optimum model. Nevertheless, Leykam [1], Zhongjian [2], Musyoki et al. [3], amongst others, concur that modelling of these volatilities are vital for the health of an economy. It has been pointed out that the most important aspect in any volatility analysis, including others, are to be able to; predict the future volatility behaviour[4], and atleast establish the risk attached to these movements.

Volatility can be defined as the periodic displacement of a time series from its long-term mean-level. Forces that displace these time series from its mean-level is of great importance. The displacements as well occur in phases, as suggested by the definition; the short term and the long term. Most scholars have not yet done concurrent short term and long term analysis. However, there is a great need to analyze these shocks in two phases, the short and long-term, in order to capture the movements exhaustively; where imputation of the two relationships can be analyzed. Granger [4] first proposed a procedure, called granger causality, which analyses the long-term movements. On the other hand, an ECM, introduced by Granger in his work which analyses a short-term relation in existence. He was analyzing a balance in an ECM where he realized that there was an imbalance in I(0) Integration of Order 0 or stationarity[5] and I(1) Integration of Order 1[6] series, (Granger).

Earlier, Fung and Hsieh [5] had used co-integration on their study on hedge funds. They criticized the conventional approaches of model constructions for asset-class indices to be applied in hedging. Seven factors were identified from which a model was built. On analysis of parameter stability, Fung and Hsieh applies the cumulative recursive residual method and plots on a time scale to investigate the reversion of the model parameter in the risk factor model. The factors are co-integrated and hence influence each others' performance. Fung and Hsieh finally proposed a seven factor model to be applied for hedging.

Later, Leykam [1] in his work on cointegration and volatility in the European natural gas spot markets tests the Granger causality in volatily markets. Four markets were identified from which spot prices were obtained. Granger causality tests were done for different pairs of the markets. Of the four markets, one (Bunde) market indicated no association with the other three markets. All the hypotheses that the other three markets can be used in predicting volatility in Bunde were rejected at 1% significance level. This meant that Bunde could not be considered a price setter in the European gas spot market.

The study by Fung and Hsieh was further extrapolated by Zhongjian who analyzed the same hedge funds in view of further examining the validity of the method used in deriving the seven factors which had been suggested by Fung and Hsieh for the inclusion in an hedging

[1]Generalized AutoRegressive Conditional Heteroskedasticity

[2]Granger Causality Model

[3]Error Correction Model

[4]At some level of significance

[5]Integration of order 0 or stationarity

[6]Integration of order 1

***Corresponding author:** Rotich Titus Kipkoech, Student, Mount Kenya University, Eldoret-9305-30100, Kenya, E-mail: rktitus@uoeld.ac.ke

portfolio. In his research, he highlights that Fung and Hsieh did not provide enough evidence to proof that the procedure used in choosing the factors is quite different from the Sharpe and Fama-French which only relies on one characteristics of the entire market. Contrary to Fung and Hsieh, Zhongjian bases his parameter stability on the adjusted R^2 statistic. Zhongjian does not mention the reason for his selection of R^2 statistic instead of the cumulative recursive residual. He identifies nine hedge indices which can be included in the hedging strategy. A full rank co-integration in the industry was as well established, and an eight factor model to be used for hedging strategies as the most powerful model, is proposed.

Initially, Rashid [6] had applied granger causality in agriculture in a study on spatial integration of maize markets undertaken in the post-liberalized Uganda. Different markets were identified. Causality tests were conducated on different pairs of markets, and the results indicated that all pairs which included Kampala and Jinja failed to reject the causality null. This was an indication of a uni-directional causality, implying that the regional maize prices Granger caused the prices in these two large cities. Also, a two directional causality effect was established between Mbale and Hoima indicating a dependence behavior; that is, all deviances in one market affects the other.

Huang and Neftci [7] investigated co-integration relationship that existed between the swap spreads and various rates such as the LIBOR London Interbank Offered Rate[7] rates, US corporate credit spreads and the treasury yield curve; which found evidence of co-integration existence. In their study, they showed that under the ECM framework, the daily swap spreads reacted to the corrective long-run forces except from the short-term fluctuations in the variables. They concluded that the swap spread had a negative effect only on one measure, the treasury yield curve, but positive in all the other rates.

Later on, Petrov [8] applies ECM in evaluating a pairwise co-integration strategy between the South African equity market and other emerging and developed markets; using the price indices rather than MSCI Morgan Stanley Capital International[8] index, as used by Biekpe and Adjasi. There are two reasons; one, that price index is raw and two, it enabled comparisons across different markets. Petrov shows that all the markets was responding slowly to any long term disequilibrium. The integration proved to be high between most markets and hence portfolio selection was the most sensitive task to undertake. Petrov applies an ECM to analyze different portfolios of different sizes . He finds out that USA dominated in all the portfolios in which it was introduced. It was then recommended that such portfolios should be considered the most favorable for investors.

Credit risk is one of the most important type of risk which a bank will be keen to assess to ensure that it remains in business. On the other hand, most of the bank advances are made on a collateral basis. Karumba and Wafula [9] studies this collateral lending characteristic of the lending institutions[9] and their implication on the general financial equilibrium. They investigated its implication on the level of credit risk faced by the banks. Karumba and Wafula applies co-integration and error correction techniques to investigate long-run relationship. The study found over-reliance on collateral in institutional lending. A negative ECM adjustment coefficient was found indicating that advances in loans and collaterals had a short-term adjustment. With the introduction of credit referencing, the study concludes a general reduction in credit risk.

[7]London Interbank Offered Rate
[8]Morgan Stanley Capital International
[9]Banks

In Basel III accord, the main challenge is addressing rates volatility. Its evolution over time makes credit risk analysis more complex. In this research, we contribute to the bank of literature by investigating existence of short-term and long-term relation between lending and interest rates. This contributes to mitigation of credit risk analyzed by Karumba and Wafula. A procedure for modelling interbank lending rates can be seen as a milestone to the mitigation strategy. It will make the work proposed in Basel III accord much easier.

Some Theoretical Review

In this section, we review some important definitions on the various tests which will be used in section (5) for analyses. We start by reviewing definitions on granger causality in sub-section (4.1); followed by a review on ECM in sub-section (2.2), and finally defining some tests in sub-section (4.3), which are fundamental in the study.

Granger causality

In this section, we review basic concepts on granger causality. We define what is granger causality in sub-section (4.1.1), and give its mathematical representation in sub-section (4.1.2).

Definition of granger causality: Granger proposed a procedure of investigating causality using lagged series and residuals. Suppose we have a series or vector y_t from which we want to obtain K ahead predictions , y_{t+k} from an information matrix Λ . Let Λ be a vector of random variables/series $(a_t, b_t, a_{t-1}, b_{t-1}, \ldots, a_1 b_1)$. Obtaining the y_{t+k} using least squares involves calculation of the conditional mean $E[y_t/\Lambda]$. In time series, it involves regressing y_t on Λ where Λ in this case has the variables $(y_t, y_{t-1}, y_{t-2} \ldots y_1)$. This is rather complex. An easier procedure is to consider its causality.

Theoretical representation of granger causality: Let x_t and y_t be two series. x_t is said to Granger cause y_t if the lagged values of x_t has statistically important information about the future values of y_t. It is calculated for stationary series. An appropriate procedure is chosen to determine the lag to be used, to obtain optimum results. Regression is used for estimation. t-tests are used to retain the significant variables in the regression and f-test determines jointly significant variables to be retained.

The procedure involves fitting a regression of lagged values of y_t such that;

$$y_t=\lambda_0+\lambda_1 y_{t-1}+\lambda_2 y_{t-2}+\ldots\lambda_k y_{t-k}+\varepsilon_t \quad (1)$$

where ε_t are the residuals. The k statistically significant lags of y_t is augmented with lagged values of x_t such that;

$$y_t=\lambda_0+\lambda_1 y_{t-1}+\lambda_2 y_{t-2}+\ldots\lambda_k y_{t-k}+\mu_a x_{t-a}+\ldots+\mu_b x_{t-b} \quad (2)$$

The lagged values of x_t in equation are retained if it adds an explanatory power to the regression equation. F-tests are used to determine the retained lagged values of x_t. The shortest possible regression has a values where longest has b values. The null hypothesis of no Granger causality is rejected iff 3 at least one lagged value of x_t retained in equation.

Error correction model

When estimating a granger causality relationship, the requirement is to ensure the series is I (1). Making a series I (1) implies differencing. According to time series theory, differencing means removal of trend; hence loss of important information about the time series behaviour in the short-run. Also, a cointegration relationship assumes a linear relationship; which might not be always the case due to random shocks. A displacement from the equilibrium relation implies a response from one of the variables to attain the equilibrium. The rate at which either variables re-attains equilibrium is modelled by an ECM. Simply, an ECM is a model which gives an estimated response behavior of a variable upon dis-equilibrium. An ECM can be estimated as

$$\Delta A_t + \lambda \Delta B_t = \Omega + \beta (\wedge) + \varepsilon_t \tag{3}$$

Where λ and β are just coefficients, Ω an intercept which may or may not be included; ε_t random noise; and ʌ an 'error correction component'.

Empirical unit root tests

In this section we review definitions of some tests which are fundamental to the empirical analysis section.

Review of augmented dickey fuller test: This is a generalized form of the Dickey Fuller test, (Dickey and Fuller. It relies on the assumption that the residuals are independent and identically distributed. For a series y_t, ADF uses the model

$$\Delta y_t = \alpha + \lambda_t + \eta y_{t-1} + \delta_1 \Delta y_{t-1} + \ldots + \delta_{p-1} \Delta y_{t-p+1} + \varepsilon_t \tag{4}$$

which reduces to a random walk when α=0 and λ=0; and a random walk with a drift when λ=0. The ADFAugmented Dickey Fuller test[10] test thus detrends the series before testing for unit root. It uses lagged difference terms to address serial correlation. The ADF test clearly depends on differenced series. This thus possess a need for another validating test.

An inspection of the p-value also determines whether the null hypothesis of non-stationarity will be accepted. A small p-value[11] leads to the acceptance of the null hypothesis. An inspection of the Dickey-Fuller value is as well important as this indicates the mean-reverting property. It is normally a negative value. The larger its absolute value, the lower the chance of occurrence of mean-reverting property.

Review of Kwiatkowski philips schmidt shin test: Contrary to ADF test, the KPSS Kwiatkowski Philips Schmidt Shin test[12] tests, Kwiatkowski et al. [10] for the null hypothesis of level or trend stationarity. It gives a way to specify whether to test with a trend or without, in its test statistic. A regression model with linear combination of a deterministic trend[13], a random walk and a stationary residual series.

$$Y_t = \alpha + \beta t + \lambda \sum_{i=1}^{t} \varepsilon_i + \delta_t \tag{5}$$

is used where δ_t is stationary, β_t is the trend component while $\sum_{i=1}^{t} \varepsilon_i$ is the random walk. $\beta_{t=0}$ if we assume a without-trend regression. The series in equation will be stationary if λ=0. Regression is used to obtain the estimate of δ_t, that is $\hat{\delta}_t$, from which we compute

$$\Omega_{resid} = \sum_{i=1}^{t} \hat{\delta}_i \tag{6}$$

The test statistic for KPSS test is then calculated as

$$R = \frac{\sum_{i=1}^{n} \Omega_i^2}{n^2 \hat{\theta}_T^2} \tag{7}$$

where the spectral density function estimator

$$\hat{\theta}_T^2 = \hat{\sigma}^2 + 2 \sum_{=1} \left(1 - \frac{}{}\right) \hat{\omega}_t \tag{8}$$

is a linear combination of the variance estimator $\hat{\sigma}_\delta^2$ and covariance estimator

$$\hat{\omega}_t = \frac{\sum_{t=k+1}^{n} \delta_t \delta_{t-k}}{n} \tag{9}$$

The test turns to a prudential choice of T in equation above.

Review of phillip perron test: The Phillips Perron approach [11] applies a nonparametric correction to the standard ADF test statistic, allowing for more general dependence in the errors, including conditional heteroskedasticity. If there were strong concerns over heteroskedasticity in the ADF residuals this might influence an analyst to go for PP Phillip Perron test[14]. If the addition of lagged differences in ADF [12] did not remove serial correlation then this again might suggest PP as an alternative.

Empirical Results

Daily data on exchange rate of the Kenyan shilling against the dollar and the interbank lending rates are analysed in this section. The main aim is to establish if there exists any causality between the two rates. Granger causality is investigated in sub-section (5.1) while an ECM is built in sub-section (5.2) as follows:

Granger causality

The first step in granger causality analysis is to establish stationarity of the time series. A basic investigation of this property is by visual inspection of time plot. A time plot is plotted, represented in Figure 1 below, and by inspection the series is non stationary.

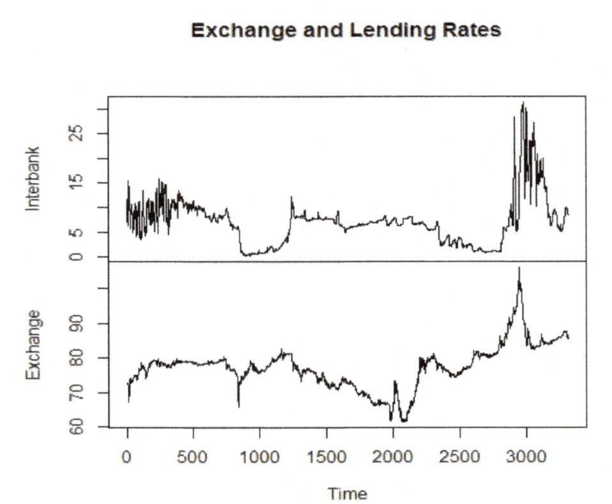

Figure 1: Time Plots of the Two Series, Dollar Exchange Rate and Interbank Lending Rate.

[10]Augmented Dickey Fuller test

[11]Less than 0.05 or 0.01 depending on the statistician

[12]Kwiatkowski Philips Schmidt Shin test

[13]If test statistic is with a trend

[14]Phillip Perron test

ACF Auto Correlation Function[15] is conventionally used in time series analysis to inspect for stationarity. If the spikes tend to be constantly high close to a value of 1, the series is non stationary. Figure 2 below represents the respective ACFs of the two rates.

An inspection of the ACFs suggest non stationarity. The respective squares of the two series helps in the analysis of heteroskedasticity, which will determine the method used to investigate for causality. Nevertheless, mathematical tests such as KPSS, ADF and PP tests are necessary to ascertain non stationarity. ADF test output of the two series is presented in Table 1 below.

The ADF test tests the null of non stationarity. From the ADF test output above, an inspection of the p-values indicates that the null hypothesis is not rejected at 5% level of significance for the Dollar exchange rate. We reject the null hypothesis at 5% level of significance for the Interbank lending rate. Conventionally, p-value indicates the amount of evidence we have against the null. It is therefore concluded that the exchange rate is non stationary while the interbank lending rate might be stationary. However, the ADF test has two weaknesses, namely;

1. The model for an ADF test uses the differenced series.

2. It assumes that the residuals are independent and identically distributed.

These weakness call for the use of KPSS test. The KPSS test uses the series to test for non stationarity without differencing. The assumption on the distribution of the residuals is not required in this test. It is therefore a tentative alternative for stationarity test.

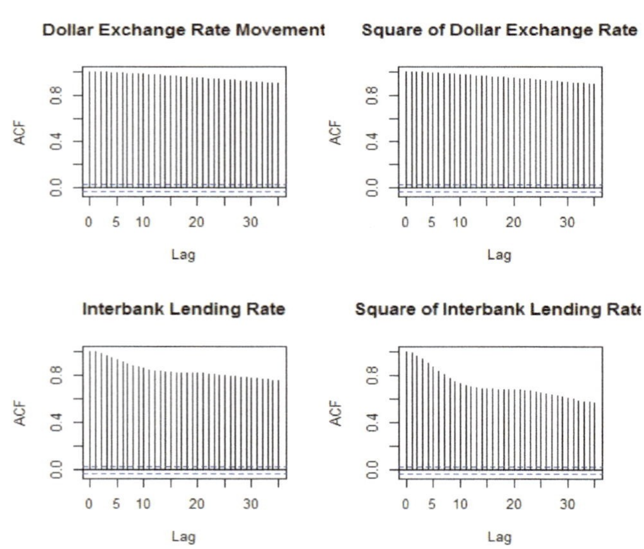

Figure 2: ACFs of the Exchange and Lending Rates.

	Exchange Rate	Interbank Lending Rate
Dickey-Fuller Value	-2.1937	-3.6382
Lag Order	14	14
P-value	0.4963	0.02897

Table 1: ADF Test output for exchange and interbank lending rates.

[15]Auto Correlation Function

	Exchange Rate	Interbank Lending Rate
KPSS Level	5.0182	1.3153
Truncation Lag Parameter	13	13
P-value	0.01	0.01

Table 2: KPSS Test output for exchange and interbank lending rates.

	Exchange Rate	Interbank Lending Rate
Dickey Fuller ( )	-7.3937	-48.5564
Truncation Lag Parameter	9	9
P-value	0.6974	0.01

Table 3: PP Test output for exchange and interbank lending rates.

Contrary to the ADF test, the KPSS test tests for the null of stationarity. Therefore, from the output presented in Table 2 above, an inspection of the p-value calls for the rejection of the null hypothesis at 5% level of significance and conclude that the two series are not stationary. This is not in line with the results obtained from the ADF output in Table 1 above, where the interbank lending rate was established to be stationary. To ascertain these results, we apply the PP test. The results of this test is presented in the Table 3 below.

Just like the ADF, the PP test tests the null of non stationarity. An inspection of the p-values indicates that the Interbank lending rate is stationary while the exchange rate is non stationary. This result is contrary to the results from KPSS test in Table 2 above, but in line with the results obtained from Table 1. This therefore calls for an informed judgement on whether to assume stationarity of the interbank lending rates. In this study, we will assume that the interbank lending rates are stationary and its only the exchange rate which is non stationary. This is because two of the three tests performed supports this judgement [13].

Following the above results, it is necessary to inspect whether the two series might be having a causal relationship. This can be investigated by superimposing the two series onto each other and checking whether their movements are similar.

Clearly from Figure 3 above, the two series have causal relationship.

The exchange rate series is thus differenced and checked for stationarity. The same tests are applied.

The null hypothesis is rejected at 5% level of significance. The exchange rate series is now stationary. Because of the weaknesses of the ADF test discussed above in Table 4, KPSS test is done and the results presented in Table 5 below.

The results are same as for ADF test. We fail to reject the null hypothesis at 5% level of significance and conclude that the series is stationary. To ascertain these results, the PP test is done and resluts presented in Table 6 below.

This tests wraps up the unit root tests and we infer that the differenced series is stationary. It is therefore concluded that the exchange rate is I(1).

Estimation of lag value to be used in the estimation of causal relation between the two series follow. AIC is the commonly used procedure in the estimation. The output of the estimation is presented in the following Table 7.

From the output, the second lag is the most appropriate for estimation. The model effects are therefore investigated and from Figure 4, it is clear that the model has a level effect except for tail values.

Since the model effects are level within the mean, the necessity of lag inclusion in the model is investigated. The results of this test is as shown in Table 8 below.

Y[16] and X[17] represents the interbank lending rate and the exchange rate, respectively. The null hypothesis of the saturated model is not rejected. Therefore, 3 sufficient evidence that the inclusion of the lagged values in causality estimation leads to the overall improvement in the model predictive ability. The coefficients for the granger causality model are presented in the Table 9 below.

The third variable[18] is found to be insignificant in the model, at 5% level of significance. The variable is dropped. A linear model is thus fit with the series itself and its second lagged value as follows (Table 10).

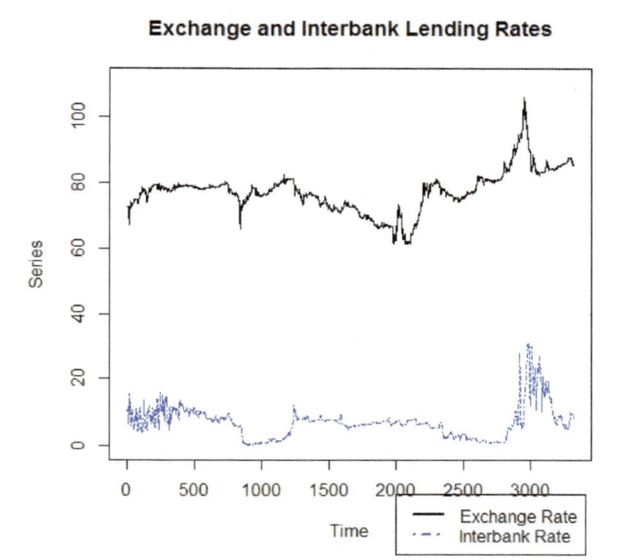

Figure 3: Superimposed Series of Exchange and Interbank Lending Rates.

Augmented Dickey-Fuller Test	
Data: diff (Exchange)	
Dickey-Fuller	-14.2119
Lag order	14
p-value	0.01
Alternative hypothesis	stationary

Table 4: ADF Test output for the differenced series of the exchange rate.

KPSS Test for Level Stationarity	
data: diff (Exchange)	
KPSS Level	0.0755
Truncation lag parameter	13
p-value	0.1

Table 5: KPSS Test output for the differenced series of exchange rate.

Phillips-Perron Unit Root Test	
data: diff (Exchange)	
Dickey-Fuller Z (alpha)	-2765.71
Truncation lag parameter	9
p-value	0.01
alternative hypothesis	stationary

Table 6: PP Test Output for the Differenced Series of Exchange Rate.

	Degrees of Freedom	Sum of Squares	RSS	AIC
			74156	10319
Diff (Exchange)	1	247.4	74403	10328

Table 7: Results for the AIC lag Estimation.

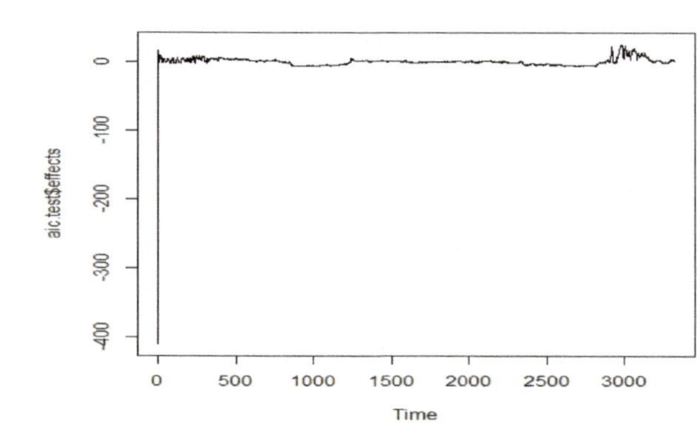

Figure 4: Exchange Rate verses.

Granger causality test	
Model 1	Y Lags(Y, 1:1) + Lags(X, 1:1)
Model 2	Y Lags(Y, 1:1)
Res.Df Df F Pr(>F) 1 3317 2 3318 -1 25.674 4.264e-07***	

Table 8: Statistical Test output on lag inclusion in the model.

Intercept	X_{11}	X_{12}	X_{13}
-7.9150651	0.1942408	0.1574291	-0.8701337

Table 9: Granger Causality Model Coefficients.

Intercept	X_{11}	X_{13}
-7.9123922	0.1942063	-0.7914011

Table 10: A Linear Model with significant lagged values.

All the model parameters were found to be statistically significant at 5% level. From the output above, the granger causality model therefore becomes:

$$y_t + 7.91239 = 0.19421x_t - 0.79140\, x_{t-2} \quad (10)$$

where y_t represents the interbank lending rate while x_t is the dollar exchange rate.

It therefore remains to check on the direction of the causality. The output is presented below Table 11.

It is clear that exchange rates granger causes the interbanking lending rates. Therefore, movements in interbank lending rates are more likely to be caused by the movements in the exchange rates. However, interbank lending rate does not granger cause the exchange rate, as could have been expected.

Error correction model

Once the granger causality model discussed above has been built[19],

[16]Interbank lending rate

[17]Exchange rate

[18]First lag of the exchange rate

[19]Equation

an ECM is easily built by considering the residuals of the model in equation above. ECM involves fitting a regression equation of the differenced series and the residuals of the fitted granger causality model. Due to the inclusion of the residuals, dynamic linear modeling is used. The fitted model will involve two main parts; the residual part which might be considered more stable than the differenced series part, hence the use of a dynamic linear model. The output of an estimated ECM is as shown in Table 12 below.

All the parameters from the model are significant at 5% level. R^2 value of 0.9308 shows that the overall model fits well to the data. The fitted ECM therefore becomes;

$$y_t = 70108730 - 0.775746 \Delta x_t + 1.000388\wedge \quad (11)$$

where y_t represents the interbank lending rate, x_t the exchange rate while $\wedge$ denotes the error correction component.

Conclusion and Discussion

Contrary to time series theory, tests on interbank lending rates return stationarity. Nevertheless, the exchange rates seem to be consistently non stationary. The stationarity of the interbank lending rate can be attributed to the fact that;

• The interbank lending rates are controlled locally and are mainly set following fluctuation of world wide economic performance. The stability of interbank lending rates is mainly determined by the central bank.

• The exchange rate is normally controlled by the overall world wide economic performance. Its fluctuation is thus not influence locally by any country, i.e, it is not controlled monopolistically.

From the above arguements, we expect the interbank lending rates to be more stable of the two.

Results of the granger causality indicate that the exchange rates granger causes the interbank lending rates. Movements in exchange rates can be used as an indication of the most probable movement in interbank lending rate. The residual sum of squares from the granger causality model is very low, an indication that the model optimally explains the variations in the data. From the superimposed plot of the two series in Figure 2, it is expected that the exchange rate and the interbank lending rate granger causes each other. However, contrary to this intuition, the interbank lending rate does not granger cause the exchange rate. This can as well be attributed to the local nature of the interbank lending rate.

	F-statistic	p-value
Exchange- Interbank	6.473963	0.00156268
Interbank- Exchange	2.992947	0.05027497

Table 11: Direction of the causality.

	Time series regression with "numeric" data: Start = 1, End = 3320				
	Call: dynlm(formula = Interbank3 Exchange4 + resid)				
	Residuals:				
	Min	**1Q**	**Median**	**3Q**	**Max**
	-4.5456	-0.6501	0.0874	0.5570	6.5569
Coefficients:					
	Estimate Std.*	**Error**	**t value****		**P_r(>|t|)**
(Intercept)	7.108730	0.021622	328.78		<2e-16***
Exchange4	-0.775746	0.055974	-13.86		<2e-16***
resid	1.000388	0.004744	210.85		<2e-16***

Signif. codes: 0 '***' 0.001 '**' 0.01 '*' 0.05 '.' 0.1 ' ' 1 Residual standard error: 1.246 on 3317 degrees of freedom Multiple R-squared: 0.9308, Adjusted R-squared: 0.9308 F-statistic: 2.231e+04 on 2 and 3317 DF, p-value: <2.2e-16					

Table 12: An Estimation of an ECM for Exchange and Interbank Lending Rates.

Finally, an ECM model is built and results presented in Table 11 in the above section. The model is presented in equation. From the output, the R^2 value is 0.9308, an indication that the model well fits to the data. Further, the adjusted R^2 value is 0.9308, same as the R^2 value, meaning the model can as well perfectly fit to any other data with similar characteristics. Therefore, the model can be used for predictive purposes. This arguement is ascertained by the very small sum of squared residuals. The model can therefore be used to analyse data with similar characterisitcs as those used in the study. It can as well be adobted by institutions for their internal hedging and as a liquidity guard.

Recommendations

It is recommended that the same study be conducted with interbank lending rates being differenced to investigate whether their will be any change in the overall model. Also, an investigation on the stationarity of the interbank lending rates should be done to establish its cause and why it occurs. Further, a study on the tail values should be done to examine the cause of the tail clustering and its impact on the overall model. Given the granger causality model, it is recommended that a cointegration model be built to examine whether the two models differ from each other; and if so, examine the reasons for the difference.

References

1. Leykam K (2008) Co-integration and Volatility in the European Natural Gas Spot Markets. University of St. Gallen, St. Gallen, Switzerland.
2. Zhongjian L (2009) Three Sections of Applications of Co-Integration: Hedge funds, Industry, and Main Global Equity Markets. Singapore Management University, Singapore.
3. Musyoki D, Ganesh P, Pundo M (2012) Real Exchange rate Equilibrium and Misalignment in Kenya. Journal of Business Studies Quarterly 3: 24-42.
4. Granger CWJ (2010) Some Thoughts on the Development of Co-integration. Journal of Econometrics 158: 3-6.
5. Fung W, Hsieh DA (2004) Hedge Fund Benchmarks: A Risk Based Approach. Financial Analyst Journal 60: 65-80.
6. Rashid S (2005) Spatial Integration of Maize Markets in Post-liberalised Uganda. Journal of African Economies 13: 102-133.
7. Huang YS, Neftci SN (2004) A Note on a Co-integration Vector for US Interest Rate Swaps. Investment Management and Financial Innovations 3: 31-39.
8. Petrov P (2011) Co-integration in Equity Markets: A comparison between South African and Major Developed and Emerging Markets. Rhodes University, Grahamstown, South Africa.
9. Karumba M, Wafula M (2012) Collateral Lending: Are there Alternatives for the Kenyan Banking Industry. Kenya Bankers Association Working paper 1-24.
10. Kwiatkowski D, Peter CB, Shin Y (1992) Testing the Null Hypothesis of Stationarity against the Alternative of a Unit Root. Journal of Econometrics 54: 159-178.
11. Phillips PCB, Perron P (1988) Testing for a Unit Root in Time Series Regression. Biometrika 75: 335- 346.
12. Dickey DA, Fuller WA (1979) Distribution of the Estimators for Autoregressive Time Series with a Unit Root. Journal of the American Statistical Association 74: 427-431.
13. CWJ (1986) Developments in the Study of Cointegrated Economic Variables. Oxford Bulletin of Economics and Statistics 48: 213-228.

16

A Qualitative Analysis of People Views of Microfinance in Lebanon

Mohammad Salhab* and Ali Abu Ali

Department of Finance, University of Bradford Leeds Teaching Hospitals, UK

Abstract

Introduction: In the Middle East and North Africa MENA microfinance struggles to find momentum. The Lebanese economy has been struggling through the years due to domestic and external, political and social instability. Although As of 2014 there are around 23 MFIs that are mainly subsidized by the USAID, operating in the country, the Lebanese microfinance market is mostly dominated by three microfinance institutions: Al Majmoua, Vitas and Al Quard Al Hassan Association.

Methodology: A quantitative approach using a standardized questionnaire would analyse the perception of the average Lebanese towards microfinance. A questionnaire was designed and validated.

Results: Almost half of the respondents earn a monthly income ranged between $100 and $600. Almost 52% of the respondents were university graduates, around 25% finished secondary and high school, and 12% hold a masters or MBA degree. Topic understanding towards microfinance differs across Lebanese areas. The highest percentage of respondents who claim that microfinance offers financial services to low income people are the residents of Beirut 35.1%, Bekaa 30.8%, and South of Lebanon 24.7%. Higher levels of topic understanding were associated with lower levels of age range. Al Quard el Hassan foundation was regarded as the most known micro financial institution operating in Lebanon. In general, Lebanese people tend to believe that microfinance can play an important role in reducing unemployment rates and poverty levels in Lebanon. When people were asked what would motivate you to get a loan from MFIs, most of the respondent 57.4% across all the Lebanese region claimed that it was the need for money to satisfy a need such as paying back a loan, to fix something at home, or for self-consideration like buying a car.

Conclusion: Our findings showed that in general Lebanese tend to have a positive perception towards microfinance. However, most Lebanese perceive microfinance as the process of just providing loans without specifying for whom it is intended. We advise that government introduces laws to regulate the microfinance market.

Keywords: Economics; Microeconomics; Finance; Business; Survey

Introduction

All that is needed for evil to triumph is for good men to do nothing: Muhammad Yunus.

Foreign aid and macro development are not enough to produce economic development or decrease poverty [1-4]. The search for effective strategies was obscure until modern microfinance was defined and was shown to decrease poverty level by awarding Prof. Yunus and the Grameen bank. The microfinance concept is not new; it has existed for more than a century. The earliest form of using the term microfinance can be traced back to 1846 when Lysander Spooner, activist and entrepreneur, theorized the extension of small credits to farmers as a way of combating poverty in rural America. Micro lending on the other hand has existed for centuries and probably is as old as the inception of buying and selling and even possibly before currency was even first used. Micro lending was mainly practiced in small villages, where family members and friends would get together in money-sharing groups. These savings clubs can be traced to all parts of the world.

The modern theory of microfinance, however; aims to deliver a program that declares to have faith in the world's poorest people to pull themselves out of poverty by providing them with financial services that were previously deprived. Other academics like Schreiner and Colombet [5,6] defined microfinance as "the attempt to improve access to small deposits and small loans for poor households neglected by banks." The basic idea behind modern microfinance is therefore that low income people, given access to credit, can build or develop their own business which is expected to provide them with a suitable income that can elevate them from poverty. On the long run, the economic status of people would improve with the help of a modern microfinance program MMP. This however, will increase the demand for more microfinance institutions' MFIs services. Thus new firms will be created to meet this increase in demand, and a multiplier-type cycle of development will begin. Although the economic and social contexts differ across countries, the basic purpose of MMP stays the same, to provide small loans and other financial services to low income people in order to help them increase their incomes through their own small businesses. In general, all MMPs target one thing; human development that is geared towards both the economic and social uplifting of the people targeted [7].

Almost 30 years after the first microfinance institutions were founded, the microfinance market is still in evolution. When microfinance started to expand during the 1980s, it was about lending to the rural poor for income-generating purposes mainly through solidarity group loans of small and smallest amounts. Since then, microfinance has evolved into a more comprehensive development tool, with the aim to supply access to financial services for all unbanked people in emerging and developing markets.

Today, most borrowers still live in rural South Asia and the East Asia and Pacific region. Over a period of time, microfinance has expanded also in Latin America and the Caribbean, in Eastern Europe and

***Corresponding author:** Mohammad Salhab, Department of Finance, University of Bradford Leeds Teaching Hospitals, E-mail: drsalhab@hotmail.co.uk

Central Asia, and in Sub-Saharan Africa. However in the Middle East and North Africa MENA microfinance struggles to find momentum despite of some forecasts expecting growth of microfinance markets in that region to be 15-20% in 2015. There are many reasons for such distorted outlook of growth of MMP in the MENA. The credit for enterprise investment is almost the sole focus of MMP in the MENA region. Credit is just one of the many financial services the poor may need. In addition governmental loan subsidiaries to various sectors of the society at very low interest rates distort the image and data even further.

In several reports by the World bank about the state of microfinance in the regions, the World Bank describes that the MENA region's microfinance industry differs from those in other parts of the world in many aspects such as: the rise of Islamic microfinance methodologies and notions, high expectations from the sector to solve the problem of unemployment and the confusion among users about the identity of the microfinance providers and other "big players" that offer lending. We therefore believe that the perception by clients of the identity and nature of MFI can lead to better services and targeted market growth of the MMP.

While microfinance seems to promote a promising new strategy, academic and empirical research has not yet acknowledged the perception towards microfinance in the MENA region, in particular Lebanon. Lebanon will be the focus of this study because Lebanon has one of 2 the lowest predicted economic growth rates of less than 2.5% for the year 2015 in the MENA region. Lebanon is also a country that has an economy mostly service oriented with banking and tourism as its main growth sectors. A research conducted by the UNDP in 2005 found that almost 1.2 million Lebanese citizens were considered to be poor. This represented around 28% of the Lebanese population. In order to develop the microfinance industry in Lebanon, it will be important for MFIs to understand the perceptions of the population regarding the impact of micro financial services provided by these firms on individual life. Analysing what Lebanese people know about microfinance and their perception towards it may help managers of MFIs to determine how they can improve their services. No study examining the perception towards microfinance on the Lebanese society has been so far published.

The main question that this study will attempt to answer is, how the average citizen in Lebanon understands the concept of microfinance and what one can expect from the MFIs and MMPs. Moreover, secondary objectives and questions will be studied.

- Does microfinance awareness differ between urban and rural residents in Lebanon?
- Have all Lebanese heard of MFIs operating in Lebanon?
- What motivates and de-motivates Lebanese people to get a loan from a MFI?

In order to answer these questions, a questionnaire will be designed to investigate these objectives.

According to the Lebanese Central Bank, the consolidated balance sheet of commercial banks has been increasing through the years, having almost 47% increase in total assets going from $115.3 billion in 2009 to reach $169.2 billion in 2014 Lebanese Central Bank Bulletin. Nevertheless, the banking regional distribution remains mainly concentrated in the region of the capital Beirut and its suburbs. A report published by Bankmed [8], one of the main Lebanese commercial banks, showed that 78% of loans are given in the region of Beirut and its suburbs, while it is only 10% in Mount Lebanon, 4% in South Lebanon El jnoub and Nabatiye, 4% in North Lebanon, and 4% in the Bekaa area Bankmed. Thus it is clear that commercial banks do not have a focus on rural areas where most of the low income population resides. A research conducted by the UNDP published in 2008 found that the vast majority of low income residents were those living in the North of Lebanon. During the last 10 years, Lebanese commercial banks started to offer microfinance products either through strategic partnership with MFIs or by issuing loans to small companies guaranteed by specialized international or domestic funds. Microfinance was mainly introduced in Lebanon in the mid-1990s. The sector has seen a remarkable growth in recent years and is expected to continue expanding. Despite all the political instability in Lebanon, the microfinance sector proved to be a success. After the 2006 war which heavily affected the sector, the microfinance industry rapidly recovered and the total number of clients increased at a compound annual growth rate of 26.2% during the years 2007 to 2014. In fact, during the period ranging from 2007 until 2014, Lebanese microfinance clients increased from 29,420 clients IFC to 150,000 clients showing an incredible increase of around 400%. Moreover, with an average loan size of $1,118, the outstanding loan portfolio stood at $23.9M in 2007. In 2014, the outstanding loan portfolio increased to $150 M approximately with an average loan amount of almost $2,000. This shift was mainly due to the increasing awareness towards the social benefits of microfinance by the Lebanese society.

According to Mr. Ali Hijazi, a microfinance researcher and microcredit program manager of the association for the development of rural capacities ADR, there is microcredit rather than MMPs in Lebanon. Moreover, according to Jawaid, different MFIs claimed that the market is very limited that it is unprofitable to provide other services than microcredit. Interviewing CFC, Jawaid stated that group loans were not widely offered as many Lebanese MFIs felt that Lebanese citizens do not like to share their personal profits or financial information with anyone. Furthermore, non-financial services like business development trainings are not provided by MFIs in Lebanon despite, housing loans, personal or consumer loans being very popular. Moreover, the author stated that different types of seasonal loans like agricultural loans, tourism loans, and Eid Islamic holidays loans were also provided. Unfortunately, no laws were put by the government in order to explicitly regulate micro lending in Lebanon.

Although as of 2014 there are around 23 MFIs that are mainly subsidized by the USAID, operating in the country, the Lebanese microfinance market is mostly dominated by three microfinance institutions like Al Majmoua, Vitas, and Al Quard Al Hassan Association. "As of September 2007, approximately 29,420 microfinance clients were being served by NGOs, MMPs, and MFIs; together, they had an outstanding portfolio of roughly $23.9 million, with 4 an average loan size of $1,118". Table 1 below shows the History of Leading Lebanese MFIs [9].

Methodology

A quantitative approach using a standardized questionnaire was used to analyse the perception of the average Lebanese towards microfinance. The same question was asked for an entire population sample and then the frequency of every response was measured to reach conclusions.

Questionnaire design

Name of institution	Type of institution when founded	Year microcredit activities started	Reason for founding	Founder	Initial source of funding	Funding status today
Al Qard el Hassan	Informal NGO; registered as an NGO in 1987	1983	Provided much needed services during the Lebanese civil war	Hezbollah	Not specified, many claimed that it was subsidized by different sources	Reported as largely self-sustaining with savings
AEP	NGO	1984	To support entrepreneurs to establish businesses and create jobs during the Lebanese civil war	Businessmen, bankers, and social workers	Businessmen, European Union, Italian and Spanish NGOs, and banks	Function as a revolving loan fund
Al Majmouaa	Registered as an NGO in 1998	1994	Social development	Administered by save the children foundation	USAID	NGOs
Vitas group	Registered as a non-profit organization in 1999, became a commercial services institution in 2003	1998	Program administered by CHF international(International NGO funded by USAID)	CHF	USAID	Funding of loans with Jammal trust bank, Lebanese Canadian bank, and USAID grants
ADR	NGO founded in 1998	1999	Targets small enterprises that do not have formal access to bank loans among other services	Microcredit program started by an imitative of bank Audi		Sustainable ; looking to become a non-bank financial institution
Emkan	NGO	2009	Social development	Hariri foundation	Hariri foundation	Continues to be subsidized by Hariri foundation

Source: Jawaid N.

Table 1: Background of the most common Lebanese MFIs.

The questionnaire was made up of both open and closed ended questions. The questionnaire consisted of 16 different questions to examine the people's understanding and perception towards microfinance services (Appendix A).

Population

According to Miners, the Lebanese population is estimated to be around 4 million people distributed on five different areas Mount Lebanon, North Lebanon, Bekaa, South of Lebanon with Nabatieh included and Beirut. A recent study conducted by credit Swiss showed that 0.3% of the population owned 48% of the Lebanese wealth estimated to be $91 billion. That being said, most of Lebanese workforce is estimated to be average to low income people that make them potential microfinance clients.

Sampling method

Cluster sampling method was used in this questionnaire. In order to assess the external validity of our study, statistical tests of inference tests like t-test, chi-squared test and correlation tests were used.

Sample size

Considering a 95% confidence level, 5% confidence interval, and 50% estimation of results, the predicted sample size to study people's perception towards microfinance was 385 individual.

N= (50% (100%-50%))/ [(2.55%)] ^2 =385

Data collection

In this study, primary data was collected through questionnaires.

The questionnaire was based on an earlier research papers conducted by Siddiqui and Gilal to analyse perception towards microfinance in Pakistan [10]. It was validated using the Cronbach's alpha, a standard test of internal consistency, using SPSS [11]. Questionnaires were distributed proportionally across Lebanon in order to tackle different Lebanese regions. In fact, the total Lebanese population was estimated to be almost 4 million people as shown in Table 3.1 in Appendix B. Mount Lebanon constituted 38.1% 1,508,658 of the total population, North Lebanon 20.6% 816739, Bekaa 13.5% 533305, South Lebanon 11.3% 446969, Beirut 9.6% 378464 and Nabatieh 7% 277686. That being said, the sample size will be divided proportionally according to the demographic distribution of the Lebanese population. For instance, 147 questionnaires should be distributed in the area of Mount-Lebanon (147 = 38.1% * 385).

Results

641 questionnaires were distributed in five different Lebanese regions as shown in Figure 1, and 397 questionnaires were collected, indicating a response rate of almost 62%. Table 2 below summarizes the distribution percentage as well as the response rate in each of the five Lebanese areas separately. For instance, 159= 38.1%×385 out of 294 distributed questionnaires were collected in the region of Mount Lebanon, indicating a response rate of around 54.1%.

Respondents' background

According to our sample size, we can conclude the following

- 45.8% of the respondents were males while 54.2% of the respondents were females as shown in Figure 2. This was almost consistent with the 0.96 males/females gender distribution in Lebanon (source: www.indexmundi.com)

- Almost half of the respondents earned a monthly income that ranged between $100 and $600, almost 32% earned between $600 and $1100, 12.3% earned between $1100 and $2000, and almost 5% earned above $2000 as shown in Figure 3. These findings were considered to be consistent with the findings of a report published by the World Bank claiming that around 70% of the population generated an annual income of around $10,000. Moreover at 30%, income inequality in Lebanon was the highest observed in the Middle East. Female participation in the labour market was 22.8% compared to 70.5 for men www. dailystar.com

- Almost 52% of the respondents were university graduates, around 25% finished secondary and high school, 12% held a masters or

Area	Population	Percent of population	Questionnaires required	Questionnaires distributed	Questionnaires collected	Response rate
Mount Lebanon	15,08,658	38.10%	147	294	159	54.10%
North Lebanon	816,739.00	20.60%	79	158	68	43%
Bekaa	5,33,305	13.46%	52	52	52	100%
South Lebanon	7,24,655	18.29%	70	100	81	81%
Beirut	3,78,464	9.55%	37	37	37	100%
Total	39,61,821	100.00%	385	641	397	61.93%

Table 2: Questionnaires distribution and response rate.

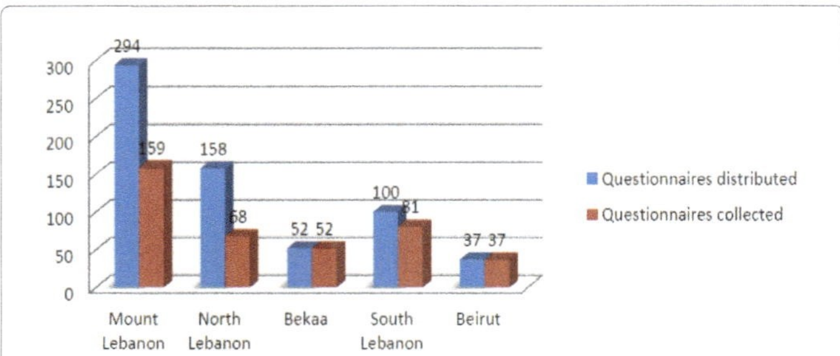

Figure 1: Questionnaires distributed through Lebanese areas.

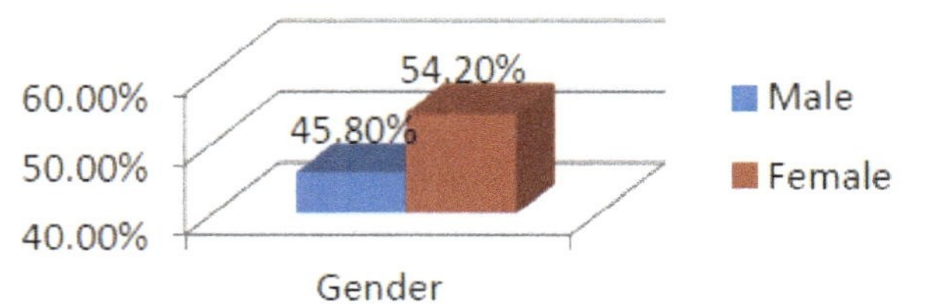

Figure 2: Gender distribution in Lebanon.

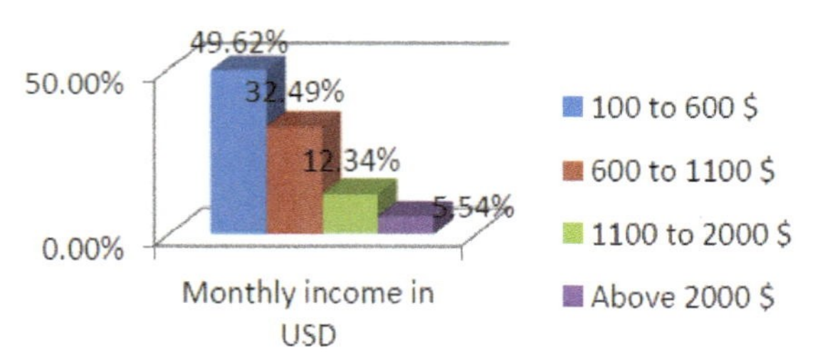

Figure 3: Distribution of income among participants in the study.

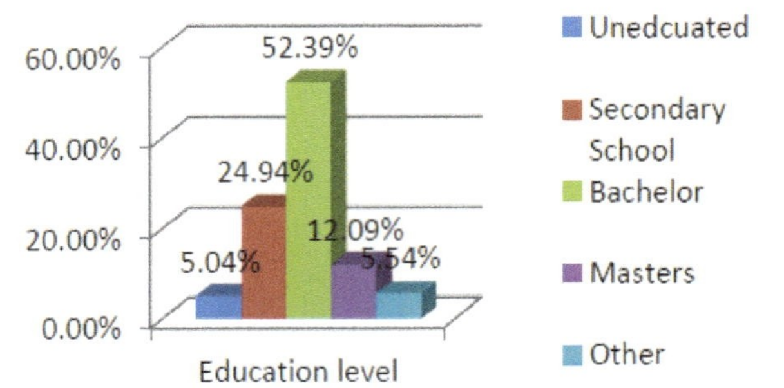

Figure 4: The percentage of participants that hold an educational qualification.

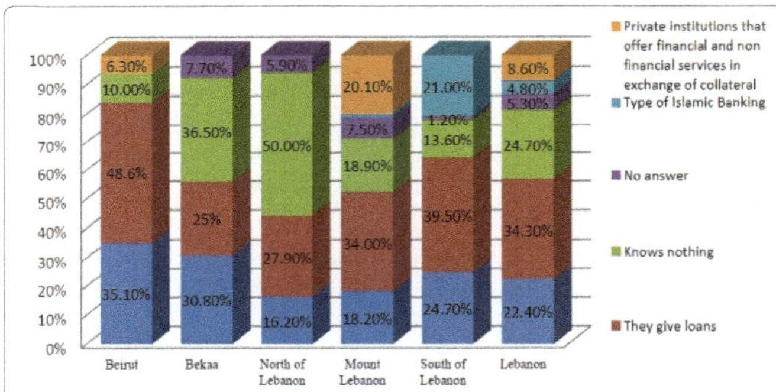

Figure 5: Respondents percentages when asked "What do you know about microfinance and microfinance institutions.

MBA degree, almost 5% had a vocational school degree, and 5% were uneducated as shown in Figure 4. This shows that most of Lebanese population was literate and educated. Hence, the respondent's level of education was consistent with the fact that almost 90% of the Lebanese can read and write (indexmundi.com). A research conducted by the united nation in 2014 showed that the average years of schooling in Lebanon was almost eight and that there was only a 0.1 per cent difference between the number of men and women who have achieved a secondary level of education

- The sample population in this study was also representative of the real population age, where most of the Lebanese population aged below 55 (www.indexmundi.com). That being said, the sample population had similar age range, gender, income range, and education level of the Lebanese population. The data collected from the field was coded and analysed using SPSS to provide pivot tables and cross tabulation analysis showing the relation between different attributes such as gender and topic understanding which were studied however, Microsoft Excel was used to draw bars, charts and pies

Current understanding of microfinance

Figure 5 shows, topic understanding towards microfinance differed across Lebanese areas. The highest percentage of respondents who claim that microfinance offered financial services to low income people were the residents of Beirut 35.1%, Bekaa 30.8% and South of Lebanon 24.7%. On the other hand, the highest percentages of respondents claiming that they knew nothing about microfinance were those living in the governorate of North Lebanon 50% and Bekaa 36%. The lowest percentages of respondents were those living in the governorate of Beirut 10% and South Lebanon 13.6%. These results confirmed the findings of a report published by Blom bank, one of the leading commercial banks in Lebanon, in which it claimed that although MFIs were spread across the Lebanese areas, the largest portion of microcredit services was seen in the areas of South of Lebanon with Nabatieh included, and Beirut [12,13].

According to Al Majmouaa annual report, most of the company's clients are those living in the areas of Beirut 39% and South Lebanon 33%, while the lowest portion of its clients were those living in the North Lebanon. This inequality of clients' distribution was mainly due to the fact that these regions had higher success and repayment rates than the other regions. That being said, the reason why the high level of unawareness towards microfinance existed in the North of Lebanon among other areas was probably because MFIs did not provide services in that region. This is probably due to the fact that this area is perceived as more risky and less profitable than the other areas. It is up to Lebanese MFIs to justify this action, as most low income people live in this area UNDP. Surprisingly, the vast majority around 92% of those unaware of the benefits or even existence of microfinance were educated, almost half of them holding a bachelor university degree as shown in Table 1.2a of Appendix B. This result clearly showed that microfinance awareness needs to be promoted more among university students. After conducting a cross tabulation analysis between topic understanding and gender as shown in Table 1.1a of Appendix B, 12.3% of males and 10% of female's respondents claimed that microfinance was the procedure of offering financial services to low income people across the Lebanese territory. Among them, almost 45% of respondents were females and 55% were males. On the other hand, respondents claimed that they have never heard of microfinance across Lebanon were more female respondents, around 14% than male respondents almost 11%. A Pearson chi-square test was conducted to examine whether the relationship between topic understanding and gender was due to chance H_0 or to a relation that existed between topic understanding and gender H_1. According to the chi-square calculation, the probability of this distribution of values happening by chance was less than 0.05. The results showed that there was a significant relationship between the two variables $P < 0.05$, as seen in Table 1.1b of Appendix B. Cross tabulation analysis between topic understanding and each of education level and monthly income showed that 95% of respondents who answered this question were educated university graduates, finished school, masters or MBA degree holders, or vocational school, and almost 20% among them claimed that microfinance was the procedure of providing loans without specifying who their target market was. However, according to the chi-square test, the answer was not statistically significant as it had few "expected count" variables. Furthermore, most respondents who answered this question were earning between $100 and $600. In fact, majority of them (33.5%) also responded that microfinance was the procedure of providing loans without specifying who their target market was. Detailed results are presented in Tables 1.2a-1.3b of Appendix B. In conclusion, 22.5% of respondents 45% females, 55% males claimed that microfinance was the procedure of offering financial services to low income people while 34.3% 48% males and 52% females said that microfinance was a procedure of providing loans to people without specifying who their target market was. Almost 25% (44% males and 56% females) stated that they have never heard of this procedure, and thus know nothing about this topic; 8.6% (26.5% males and 73.5% females) of the respondents reported that microfinance and MFIs were private institutions that offer financial and non-financial services in exchange of collaterals, and around 5% (68.4% males and 31.6% females) claimed that microfinance was a type of Islamic banking. A Pearson correlation analysis was conducted to examine if there was a relationship between topic understanding and each of education level, monthly income, and age range. As Table 1.4 in Appendix B shows, a negative weak significant correlation existed between topic understanding and age range. In other words, higher levels of topic understanding were associated with lower levels of age range. This is probably due to the fact that most of the respondents who had no idea about microfinance were older than those who claimed that microfinance offered loans, and those who claimed that microfinance provided financial and non-financial services to the poor.

Our findings concerning microfinance awareness were similar to a previous study conducted about evaluating the self-sustainability of MFIs in Yemen; the author concluded that the level of awareness towards microfinance in Yemen was considered to be low. On the other hand, other findings begged to differ. Analysing people's awareness towards microfinance in Nagpur city in India, 90% of the respondents were aware of microfinance [14].

In a study conducted in Pakistan investigating the perception towards microfinance among Pakistanis, 69% of the respondents claimed that microfinance offered small loans, while in Lebanon, almost 34% claimed that microfinance offered loans without specifying the type of loans, and around 22.5% replied that microfinance provided financial services to low income people. MFIs should therefore improve the level of awareness and perception towards microfinance and communicate its mission to the targeted segments in order to improve people's perception about the industry, using effective campaigns.

Interestingly, it was found in this study that most Lebanese mainly perceived MFIs as a social charity. When people were asked about their perception towards microfinance, almost 61% said it was regarded as a social charity, while 34% said it was a profitable activity, and 5% said it was both a social charity and profitable activity. This is a common misperception and represented an example of the bottom up approach to development by linking informal credit schemes, like intra family loans, to formal sources of capital and financial institutions that do not ask for extensive collaterals as banks do. Moreover, after evaluating the two Lebanese MFIs Al Majmouaa and Vitas, planet rating and kivas, found out that both companies showed a "clear commitment to social goals".

Microfinance institutions operating in Lebanon

Concerning the micro financial institutions operating in Lebanon, as shown in Figure 6. Al Quard el Hassan foundation was regarded as the most known micro financial institution operating in Lebanon with almost half of the respondents saying that they have only heard of this financial institution among others like Al Majmouaa and Vitas. Around 5% have only heard of Al Majmouaa, 3% have only heard of Vitas, 17.5% have heard of both Al Quard el Hassan and Al Majmouaa,

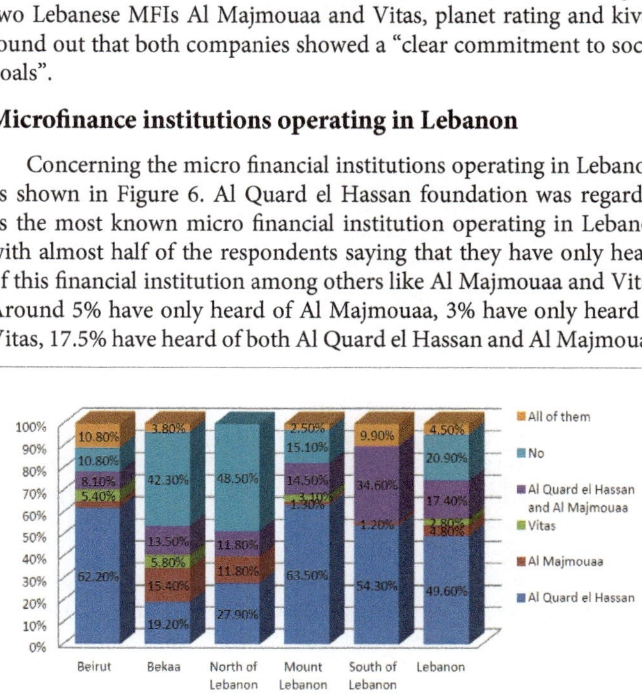

Figure 6: Top 3 Micro financial institutions operating in Lebanon.

21% have not heard of any of these institutions although they are widely known, and 4.5% heard of all these institutions.

One of the main reasons Al Qard el Hassan was widely known was because it was established after the Lebanese civil war, in which Hezbollah, one of the Lebanese parties socially active in Lebanon. Lebanon provided microcredit among other social service to help Shiite people among others in need. Moreover, after interviewing several MFIs, Jawaid claimed that many MFIs representatives admitted that the institution of Al Qard el Hassan was mainly subsidized by Iran and the wealthy Shiite Lebanese businessmen in a way that other MFIs would not be able to compete with it. Al Qard el Hassan has the largest market share among all Lebanese MFIs.

According to Al Majmouaa, its operations were mainly targeting females, and the vast majority of its clients were females; therefore the percentage of females who have heard of Al Majmouaa should be greater than the percentage of males. Table 1.5a in Appendix B shows that almost 58% of females have heard of Al Majmouaa, while around 42% of males have heard of it. According to the chi-square calculation, the probability of this distribution occurring by chance was 0.007 ($P < 0.05$). Therefore, there is a relationship between the sex of the respondent and the answer given as shown in Tables 1.5a and 1.5b in Appendix B.

Figure 6 also shows that Al Quard el Hassan was mostly known in the areas of Beirut (62.2%), Mount Lebanon (63.5%), and South of Lebanon (54.3%), and was hardly known in the North of Lebanon (27.9%) and Bekaa (19.2%). On the other hand, 48.5% and 42.3% of the residents in the North of Lebanon and Bekaa respectively have not heard of any of these micro financial institutions compared to 0% in the South of Lebanon and 10.8% in Beirut. According to the report published by Blom bank, Al Qard el Hassan occupied the largest share of microloans in Lebanon. The institution has given almost \$208.4 million in microloans in 2012 alone including repayments, having an estimated loan portfolio ranging about \$60 to \$70 million, which represented around 47% of the total microfinance portfolio in Lebanon. Besides Al Qard el Hassan, Al Majmouaa held almost 30% of the total clients, followed by Vitas (11% of the total clients), and Emkan (9% of total clients).

After conducting a Pearson correlation analysis, a weak positive relationship was found between institution knowledge and each of age range, education level, ($P < 0.05$). This means that as both the education level and the age range increased, it was more likely that the respondent knew at least one of the financial institutions. On the other hand, no relationship was found between institution knowledge and monthly income as P was > 0.05 (Table 1.6 in Appendix B).

People's overall view towards microfinance

In general, Lebanese people believed that microfinance can play an important role in reducing unemployment rates and poverty levels in Lebanon (Figure 7). In fact, when asked if microfinance can reduce unemployment rates in Lebanon, 34.5% of the female respondents and 27.2% of the male respondents gave a positive answer. On the other hand, almost 19.6% of females and 18.7% of males believed that microfinance cannot have a positive effect on the rates of unemployment. According the chi-square table this result was not statistically significant (Tables 1.7a and 1.7b in Appendix B).

A cross tabulation analysis was conducted to examine whether there was a relationship between the answers given and the respondent's education level. According to Table 1.8a in Appendix B, 61.7% gave a "yes" answer, amongst them 96% were educated, whereas, 38.3% gave a "no" answer, amongst them 93% were educated. According to the chi-square test Table 1.8b in Appendix B, the results were statically significant $P < 0.05$ (Figure 7).

Most of the respondents claimed that microfinance could have a positive impact on the Lebanese society and the educational and economical level in the country. On the other hand, respondents tended to have a perception that there was no link between political stability and MMPs.

Figure 8 below shows that almost 81.5%, 67% and 63% of the respondents claimed that microfinance could have a positive impact on the Lebanese society, Lebanese economy, and the educational level in Lebanon respectively. On the other hand, almost 60.5% of the respondents said that microfinance could have a positive impact on the political stability and thus security in Lebanon.

People generally seek microcredit to build or expand their business, and start self-employment. In order to help building the capacity of Lebanese MFIs, the IESC started in 2009 a \$15.1 million program that ended in April. It had a main objective to provide grants to create jobs and promote economic growth in Lebanon (www.dailystar.com).

In general, when more microcredit is given to poor people, poverty will be reduced. According to Wright, Khandker, Afrane, Hossain and Knight, microfinance has played an important role in income growth, reducing unemployment levels, increasing education level, and strengthening social relations and networks [15-19].

The LIM association has awarded to date \$8,299,501 in grants to Lebanese MFIs, which in turn have granted \$27,489,313 through 12,101 micro loans across the Lebanese territory. The program helped in the creation of 18,989 jobs, and 2,887 positions (www.thedailystar.com).

However, credit is not the only factor affecting income generation. Recipient's entrepreneurial skills, education, and experience are other important factors that can affect the profitability of a business. Most people do not have the vision, persistence, skills, and creativity to be entrepreneurial. In fact, Banerjee concluded that microcredit

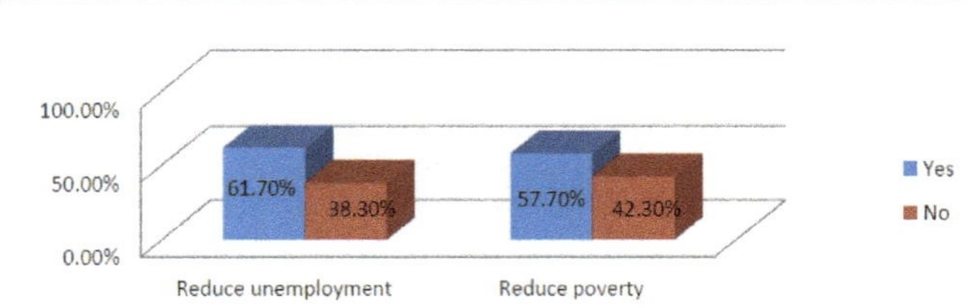

Figure 7: Unemployment and poverty reduction.

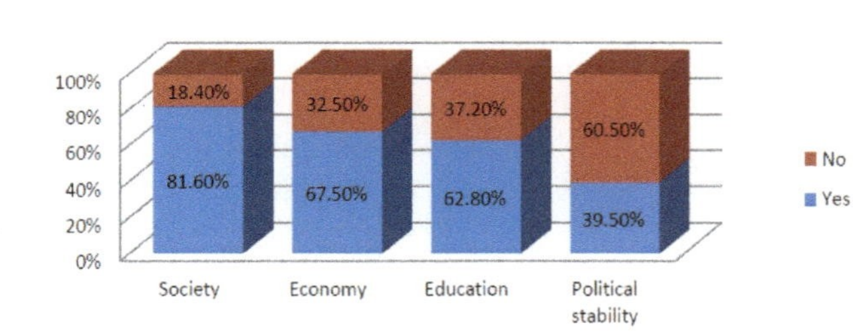

Figure 8: Can Microfinance have a positive impact on the Lebanese society, economy, education and political stability.

had no impact on borrower's health or education levels in the city of Hyderabad, India [20-22].

Many agree that access to credit by itself is not the solution to global poverty. Both Sam Daley-Harris, Director of the Microcredit Summit Campaign, and Professor Yunus, claimed that microfinance should be combined with other innovative programs that can affect economic growth in order to create one powerful tool capable to decrease poverty levels, MMPs.

Similar findings were found in Oman, when a study Murthy and Varalakshmi, showed that the majority of the respondents claimed that microfinance would have a positive impact on the society, unemployment, and poverty levels [23].

Who charges higher interest rates?

When asked who charges higher interest rates, almost 90% of the respondents said that banks charge higher interest rates, while only 10% of them responded that MFIs charged higher interest rates as shown in Figure 9. The reason why many respondents claimed that MFIs charged lower interest rates was probably because people had a negative view towards banks and believed that MFIs were a better way to get a small loan. Another reason was that most of the respondents have heard mainly of Al Qard el Hassan that follows the principal of Islamic finance. According to the Islamic Sharia, no interest rates could be charged. However, Al Qard el Hassan, charged administrative fees that take into account the cost of the loan salaries, overhead, and supplies and the cost of storing the gold which is fixed by the insurance company for 1000 grams of gold, there's a $50 fees for a period of 10 months. These types of loans were mainly granted on "gold collateral terms", in which after loan repayment, the borrower takes back his gold (Figure 9).

In fact, MFIs charge higher interest rates than traditional banks. This is mainly due to two factors: first of all, since microfinance loans amounts are smaller, the upfront commission fees are relatively greater while operating costs are constant. In consequence, these costs weigh heavier on the scale of a microcredit than on that of a traditional loan. Therefore, lending smaller amounts means a higher rate of interest. Second, loans issued by traditional banks come from the deposit and saving accounts of their clients, while in contrast, most micro financial institutions have to get their financing from local banks or from developed countries in the form of preferential rate loans from the World Bank or loans from investment funds.

After conducting a cross tabulation analysis between gender and chargers of higher interest rates, among those who gave the correct answer (MFIs charge higher interest rates), almost 69% were males and 31% were females. The findings were statistically significant ($P<0.05$) (Tables 1.9a and 1.9b in Appendix B). Therefore, we can say that male

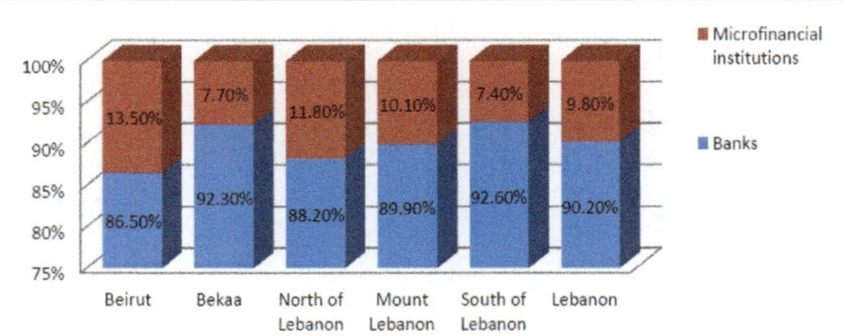

Figure 9: Who charges higher interest rates?

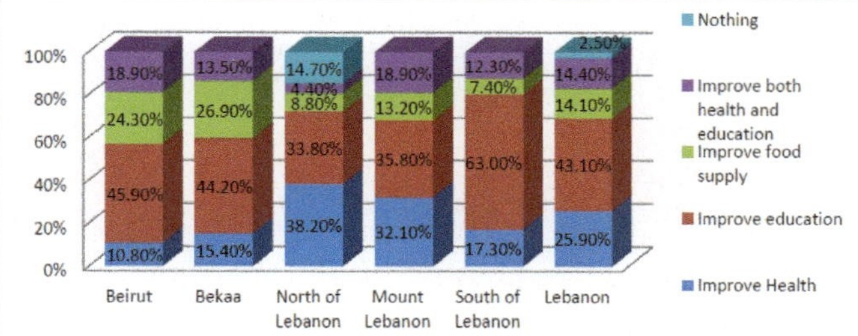

Figure 10: In what ways microfinance can help you?

respondents were more informative regarding the interest rates issues than their female's counterpart.

Moreover, conducting a cross tabulation analysis between education level and who charges higher interest rates of loans, the researcher found out that among those who gave the wrong answer, 63.7% were holding a bachelor or a postgraduate university degree. This unexpected result showed that neither the Lebanese universities nor the MFIs have built sufficient microfinance awareness among university student. A chi-square analysis could not be conducted because "3 cells (30%) have expected count less than 5" (Tables 2a and 2b in Appendix B).

How microfinance can help people?

As shown in Figure 10, when people were asked in what ways microfinance can help them, the vast majority 43.10% of the respondents across the Lebanese territory reported that microfinance can help them improve their education or the education level of their children. Among those respondents, 58.5% were females, 41.5% were males, and most of them 96.5% were educated. More than half 55.3% of the respondents that claimed that microfinance can improve their health condition were females, and the rest were males 44.7%. The vast majority among them 67% were earning a monthly income ranging between $100 and $600. In addition to the above, most of the respondents almost 55% who claimed that microfinance would help improving the food supply even for them or for their families were married. However, due to the fact that we had less than required "expected count" cells; the chi-square analysis results were not validated (Tables 2.1a-2.4b in Appendix B).

As clearly seen in Figure 10, most of the respondents in each of the five Lebanese areas believed that microfinance would help them improve either their education or the education of their children. In fact, almost 46%, 44.2%, 34%, 36%, and 63%, of the respondents living in Beirut, Bekaa, North of Lebanon, Mount of Lebanon and the South of Lebanon respectively shared the same opinion that microfinance can improve their level of education. Those living in Beirut were the least to believe that microfinance would help them in improving their health condition (10.8%), while those living in the North of Lebanon were the most to believe that microfinance can help improve health conditions (38.2%). This difference between these two areas was mainly due to the fact that those who resided in the North of Lebanon had less developed hospitals and health insurance than those living in the capital Beirut.

Table 3, compared other studies conducted in the Middle East and North Africa, Lebanese respondents perceived that microfinance had lower levels of impact on their health and food consumption. On the other hand, more Lebanese respondents than Egyptians and Moroccans respondents perceived that microfinance could have an impact on their education level excluding Jordan Planet finance. The lower perception towards the impact on their health condition is maybe due to the

Country	Food Consumption	Education their (own) or their children's	Health
Lebanon	14%	43%	26%
Egypt	50%	40%	40%
Jordan	70%	58%	48%
Morocco	62%	36%	37%

Table 3: Perception of positive impact.

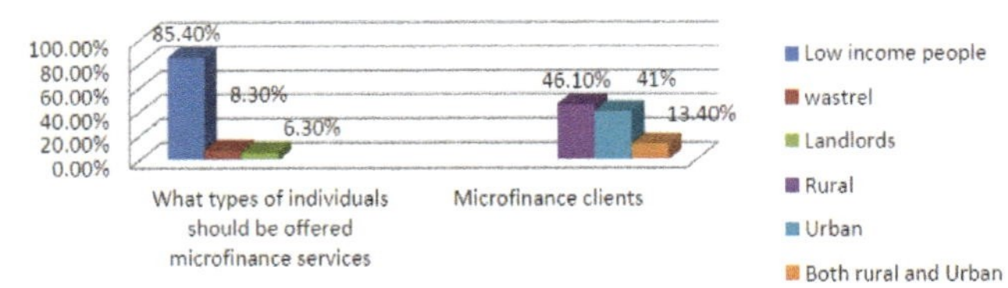

Figure 11: Distribution of microfinance potential clients.

differences in life expectancy in each of the four countries. For instance, according to the UNDP, Lebanese have a life expectancy of 80 years compared to 71.2 years in Egypt, 73.9 years in Jordan, and 70.9 years in Morocco. Moreover, in general Lebanon is well known for its medical sector as one of the most developed in the region. Therefore people search to improve other factors than heath in their lives as their health condition is already in a good situation. 14% of Lebanese respondents claimed that microfinance can improve their food supply, compared to 50%, 70%, and 62% of respondents in Egypt, Jordan, and Morocco respectively.

Interestingly, people tend to spend more time in education in Lebanon than in Egypt and Morocco. In fact, the average years of schooling in Lebanon is estimated to be 7.9 years, compared to 6.4 years in Egypt, 4.4 years in Morocco, and 9.9 years in Jordan as shown in Table 3.

Who benefit from microfinance?

When asked what kind of individuals should be offered micro finance services, most of the respondents claimed that low income people were those who should benefit the most from MFIs (Figure 11). Respondents also stated that microfinance clients were mostly rural people (46.1%). These findings support the findings of the CGAP study. In fact, studying the client base of seven MFI in Africa and Asia, CGAP found that most of the clients were moderately low income people.

What motivates you to get a loan from a micro financial institution?

When people were asked what motivates you to get a loan from MFIs, most of the respondent (57.4%) across all the Lebanese region claimed that it was the need for money to satisfy a need such as paying back a loan, to fix something at home, or for self-consideration like buying a car. On the other hand, around 20.7% of the respondents claimed that if they got a microloan, it will be to improve their own business or build a small business. A cross tabulation analysis using SPSS showed that among those who said that improving or building their businesses is what encourages them to approach MFIs, almost 54% were females, 46% were males, 94% were educated, and most of them earned an average monthly income ranging between $100 and $600 which is less or equal to the minimum wage in Lebanon. Besides having a low monthly income, most of the respondents who gave such answer (55%) were working in the private sector and 22% of them were unemployed. Therefore, being educated, earning a low income and/or unemployed, these people would seek the services of MFIs to create or develop their own businesses, and their monthly income.

On the other hand, among those who claimed that they would be motivated to get a microcredit in order to use for personal needs (57.4%), 51.3% were females and 48.7% were males; and also surprisingly the vast majority were educated.

Analysing the monthly income of those respondents, more than half of them were earning between $100 and $600 per month. Analysing the professional sector, almost 55% worked in a private company or have their own business, while around 24% were unemployed. That being said, offering a microcredit service to those people would possibly only leave them in more debt as the purpose of the loan would not be to build a business but instead to satisfy a need.

A chi-square analysis was conducted to examine the statistical significance of these answers. However, the researcher could not reach conclusion due to the fact that most of the cross tabulations tests had less than the required number of expected count (Tables 2.5a-2.7b in Appendix B).

Figure 12 shows, those who said they were motivated to get a microcredit loan in order to improve or build their own business were mostly the residents of the South Lebanon area, (28.4%) and Bekaa (23.1%) while those residents in the capital Beirut had the lowest percentage. This is mainly because most residents in South Lebanon and Bekaa might be working in agriculture or farm owners that would benefit mostly from MFI services.

Finally, when analysing the answers provided about what motivates one to get a loan and who charges higher interest rates, none of the respondents that said that MFIs services charged higher interest rates, said that that they would be motivated to get a microcredit. This was because the respondents were under the impression that MFIs offered lower interest rates. Surprisingly, 95% of those who said that microloans provided lower interest rates were educated.

Our findings were not similar to other studies Mel et al; Bruhn and Love; Banerjee; Siddiqui and Gilal; and Hagan that showed that people tend to take microfinance loans in order to expand their businesses [13].

What discourage you to get a loan from a micro financial institution?

Figure 13 shows, when people were asked what discourages them to get a loan from an MFI, almost 53% of the respondents claimed it was because of the high demands like interest rates, guarantor, or

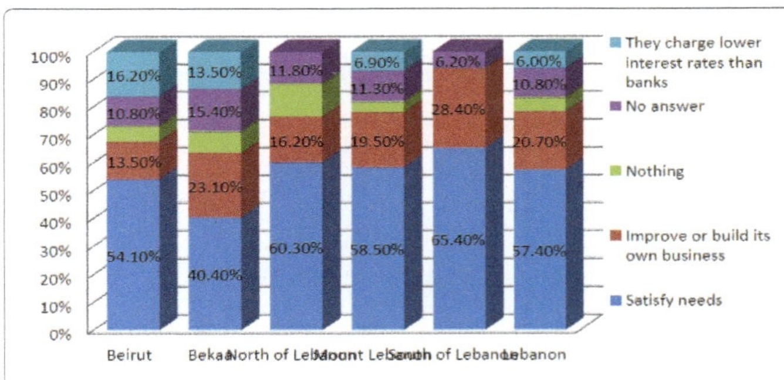

Figure 12: What motivates you to get a loan from a microfinance institution?

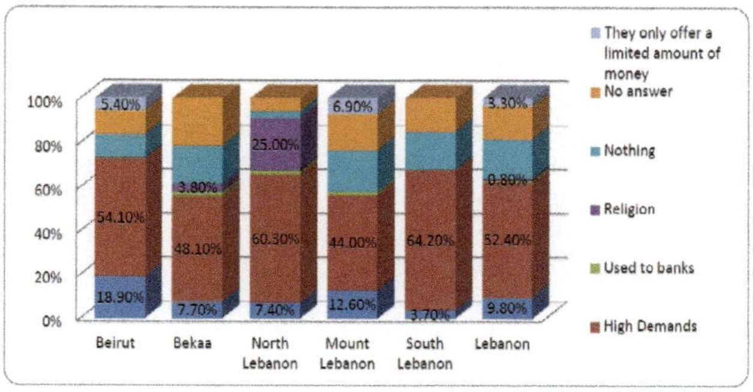

Figure 13: Which factors discourage you to get a loan from a microfinance institution?

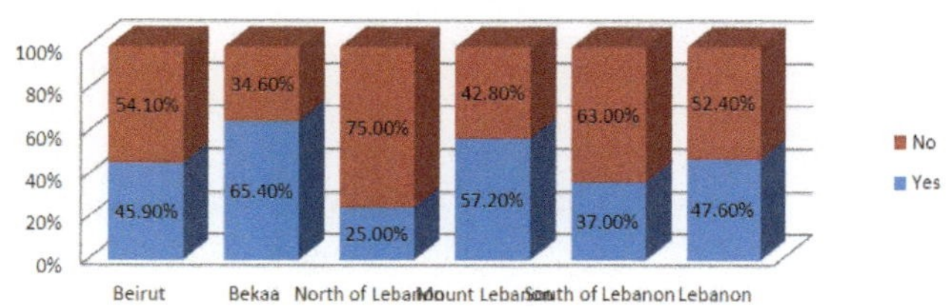

Figure 14: If you have been given the chance to get a loan, would you also consider other microcredit products like micro insurance, micro savings among others.

collaterals, almost 10% claimed it was due to trust while 17% claimed that nothing discouraged them to get a loan from such MFIs.

After conducting a cross tabulation analysis, 67% of those who said it were because they did not trust these MFIs were females. That being said MFIs should work harder in order to gain people's trust and specially the females, and assure them that there were no hidden charges in their work (Tables 2.8a-2.9 in Appendix B). Most of the respondents said that high demands requested by MFIs discouraged them of getting loans; it is up to MFIs to work on this issue in order to increase the number of their clients.

Offering other micro financial services

When asked if they would like to take other financial services like micro-savings, almost 52% of the respondents said "no", while 48% answered positively. In fact, microfinance services in the Middle East region are largely characterized by offering more microcredit than any other financial services such as savings, leasing, or insurance. Lebanese MFIs have also mainly limited their services to microcredit. A recent research was conducted, in which a number of interviews with different Lebanese MFIs were recorded. This research claimed that the Lebanese industry was not sufficiently developed in order to provide other microfinance services such as savings and insurance. Figure 14 clearly shows that the residents of Bekaa, and Mount Lebanon were more likely to take other micro financial services like micro insurance or micro-savings than the residents of Beirut, North of Lebanon, and South of Lebanon.

After analysing the respondents' average monthly income, most of the respondents earned a monthly income ranging between $100 and $600. According to a study conducted by numbeo.com, the world's largest database of user contributed data about cities and countries worldwide, Lebanon was regarded as the second most expensive country in the Arab world with an average Lebanese person earning around $1200 per month in order to have a "good life". This study showed that more than 80% of the respondents earned less than $1100. There is a need for MFIs to therefore step in and provide targeted services to those that can benefit from it the most.

Figure 15 below shows around 63%, 57% and 46% of the Lebanese living in North Lebanon, Mount Lebanon, and the Bekaa region earned an average monthly income ranging from $100 to $600. MFIs should be focusing more on these areas as most the respondents living there were low income people who are in need of such microcredit services.

Many MFIs suffer from high overhead costs and weak management structures. MFIs that operate from a social rather than a business perspective end up suffering from high rates of defaults on its loans. In an interview with an EFSD representative, EFSD claimed that "most microcredit loans were not in rural areas in Lebanon because they were not targeting the poorest of regions. Lenders want a business to generate income and that requires a critical mass ". Therefore some MFIs' goals have shifted from social focused to profitable focused activities. While microfinance assumes that access to credit leads to income generation, there has not been an extensive research focusing on how MFIs can decrease unemployment rates, sustained health conditions, and developed education levels in Lebanon. Identified as a post conflict country, Lebanese MFIs' operations are always placed under a pressure because of the high risk of political and security instability. Therefore, most of these companies prefer to build their branches in safer areas like Beirut rather than riskier ones like near the borders areas in both south and North of Lebanon.

According to Pollin, microfinance companies "need a vibrant, well-functioning domestic market itself that encompasses enough people with enough money to buy what these enterprises have to sell [22]." However, most of the Lebanese people live in Beirut, Mount Lebanon and the South of Lebanon while the North of Lebanon and Bekaa have the least number of residents that earn an average monthly income less than $600. Thus, a micro entrepreneur might be able to work in Beirut but might find it harder to work in the villages where people are fewer and have less amount of money than those living in other areas.

When cross tabulation analysis was conducted between the topic understanding and if people heard of any of these MFIs, 9% of the respondents that said that microfinance offer financial services to low income people never heard of any of the most known micro financial institutions operating in Lebanon Al Qard el haasan, Al Majmouaa, and Vitas. The remaining respondents heard at least of one of them. The majority of those who said that they know nothing about microfinance also heard of at least one of the three micro financial institutions operating in Lebanon.

This shows that people did know about the existence of these

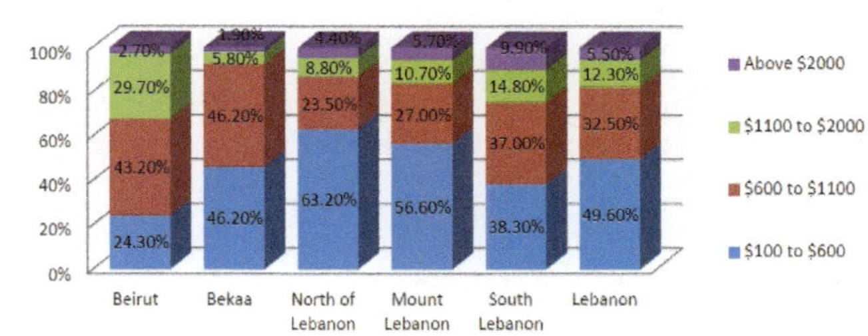

Figure 15: Average monthly income.

Reliability statistics	
Cronbach's alpha	No. of items
0.629	11

Table 4: Reliability statistics.

institutions however did not know what their main objectives of these MFIs were. After conducting cross tabulation analysis between topic understanding and who takes advantages of microfinance, almost 94% of those who said "microfinance offered financial services to low income people" also claimed that low income people were those to benefit from microfinance services.

Reliability

When analysing the reliability of questions related to perception an alpha of 0.629 as show in Table 4, statistically acceptable reliability.

Conclusion

The majority of the respondents 34.3% perceived MFIs as financial institutions that just offered loans without specifying the nature or purpose of the loan. It is clearly seen by people reactions that they had no idea that MFIs offered other services than micro credits. This may be due to the fact that MFIs operating in Lebanon restrict their financial services to micro credits only. In fact, visiting the websites of each of Al Majmouaa, Vitas, and Ibdaa, one realises that these MFIs limit their services to micro loans for individual purposes or home improvement purposes. Furthermore, most respondents perceived microfinance as a social charity 61.2% rather than a social activity 34%, with Al Qard el Hassan institution as the most acknowledged by the Lebanese respondents 49.6%.

Regarding the perception towards the impact of microfinance on the economy most respondents believed that microfinance can play a certain role in reducing both unemployment levels 61.7% and poverty levels 57.7%. Also, most respondents believe that microfinance can have a positive impact on the Lebanese society 81.6%, Lebanese economy 67.5%, and education levels in Lebanon 62.5%. However, most of the respondents 60.5% believed that microfinance cannot have a positive impact on the security and political stability levels in Lebanon.

Surprisingly, almost 90% of the respondents believed that banks charged higher interest rates than MFIs. Furthermore, most people perceived that microfinance can play an important role in improving their or their children's education level 43.1%, while almost 26% perceived that microfinance services can improve their health condition and around 14% perceived that MFIs can improve their food supply consumption. Microfinance studies focusing on Lebanon are very limited. No previous studies examined people's perception and understanding of microfinance in Lebanon.

After reviewing the relevant literature related to how microfinance impacts perceptions around the world, it seems that people tend to have a positive perception towards microfinance across the globe [24-29]. However the level of microfinance awareness differs from country to country. For instance a researcher found that the level of microfinance awareness was low in Yemen whereas it was high in Pakistan and India [30-33].

In general the Lebanese tend to have a positive perception towards microfinance as most of the respondents claimed that microfinance can reduce both unemployment and poverty levels, as well as it can have a positive impact on the Lebanese economy, education level, and society [34-36]. Despite 24% of the respondents having not heard of microfinance, the majority of the respondents including those unaware of microfinance had at least heard of one of the top three MFIs operating in Lebanon. Most Lebanese perceived microfinance as the process of just providing loans without specifying for who it is intended [37-39]. Most respondents would consider a microcredit loan for personal needs, such as paying for another due loan, buying a car, and making home improvements rather than building or improving an existing business in order to generate more income and elevate themselves out of poverty.

Study Limitations

The main limitation of this study was failure to conduct a pilot study due to time restrictions. However the questionnaire was based on previous studies questionnaires conducted on the same topic in Pakistan and sultanate Oman after the approval of their authors.

Due to security issues and military actions taking places near the Syrian borders at the time of this study, it was impossible to visit the areas in the north like Akkar, and Bekaa like Orsal and its surroundings.

Future Research

Future research should be conducted to determine how the perception of microfinance in addition to other factors can be used to improve the delivery of MFIs services. Further studies may also examine the impact of microfinance services on the Lebanese society, economy, poverty level, education level, and unemployment levels.

References

1. Al Majmoua (2007) Annual report.
2. Al-Haidi A (2009) Evaluating the Self-sustainability of Micro-finance Institutions (MFIs) Using the Balanced Scorecard Approach (BSc). Sana'a University, Yemen.
3. Yunus M (1999) Banker to the Poor: Micro-Lending and the Battle Against World Poverty, New York.
4. Erixon F (2005) Aid and development: Will it work this time?" International Policy Network Publications 1-30.
5. Leikem K (2012) Microfinance: A tool for poverty reduction? Senior Honors Projects, University of Rhode Island: 300.
6. Schreiner M, Colombel H (2001) From urban to rural: Lessons for microfinance from Argentina. Development Policy Review 19: 339-354.
7. Ghalib AK (2007) Measuring the impact of microfinance intervention: A conceptual framework of social impact assessment. The Singapore Economic Review 1: 20-50.
8. Bank med (2014) Lebanon Semiannual report.
9. FC, Grameen-Jameel Microfinance Limited (2008) Lebanon: A Diagnostic Study on the Demand for Financial Services by Micro and Small Enterprises. Washington DC, USA.
10. Siddiqui K, Gilal F (2012) Perception towards microfinance in Pakistan. Journal of Business and Management Sciences 1: 20-30.
11. Cronbach L (1951) Coefficient alpha and the internal structure of tests. Psychometrika 16: 297-334.
12. IMF (2014) World Economic Outlook.
13. Hagan L (2012) Microfinance with education in rural Ghana: Men's perception of household level impact. African Journal of Food, Agriculture, Nutrition and Development 12: 20-35.
14. Sharma S, Deshmukh A (2013) A study of microfinance facilities and analyzing the awareness level of people about microfinance in Nagpur City. International Journal of Social Science and Interdisciplinary Research 2: 30-45.
15. Khandker S (2001) Does micro-finance really benefit the poor? Evidence from Bangladesh Paper delivered at: Asia and Pacific Forum on Poverty: Reforming

Policies and Institutions for Poverty Reduction.

16. Khandker SR (2003) Microfinance and Poverty: Data from Bangladesh. The World Bank Economic Review 19: 263-286.

17. Hossain F, Knight T (2008) Financing the poor: can micro-credit make a difference? Empirical observations from Bangladesh (BWPI Working Paper 38).

18. Wright G (2001) Microfinance systems: designing quality financial services for the poor London: Zed Books. Journal of international development 13: 1194-1195.

19. Afrane S (2002) Impact assessment of microfinance interventions in Ghana and South Africa: A synthesis of major impacts and lessons. Journal of Microfinance 4: 37-58.

20. Karnani A (2007) Microfinance misses its mark. Stanford Social Innovation Review 2: 34-40.

21. Banerjee A, Duflo E, Glennerster R, Kinnan C (2009) The Miracle of Microfinance? Evidence from a Randomized Evaluation. Working paper Massachusetts Institute of Technology, Cambridge, UK.

22. Banerjee A, Chitnis UB, Jadhav SL, Bhawalkar JS, Chaudhury S (2009) Hypothesis testing, type I and type II errors. Ind Psychiatry J 18: 127-131.

23. Murthy K, Varalakshmi S (2011) Microfinance perception-A study with special reference To Salalah, Sultanate of Oman. International Journal of Multidisciplinary Research 1: 49-60.

24. Bruhn M, Love I (2009) The economic impact of banking the unbanked: evidence from Mexico. World Bank Policy Research Working Paper No. 4981.

25. Pollin R (2007) Microcredit: False Hopes and Real Possibilities. Foreign Policy in Focus.

26. Barsoum G, Shaban A (1999) Beyond Credit: An Impact Assessment of Microcredit Programs on the Livelihood of Poor Households in Egypt. Labor Market and Human Resource Development in Egypt.

27. Sengupta R, Aubuchon C (2002) The Microfinance Revolution: An Overview. Federal Reserve Bank of St. Louis Review 90: 9-30.

28. Kaboski JP, Townsend RM (2005) Policies and impact: An analysis of village microfinance institutions. Journal of the European Economic Association 3: 20-45.

29. National impact survey of microfinance in Egypt (2008).

30. Copestake J (2002) Inequality and the polarising impact of microcredit: Evidence from Zambia's Copperbelt. Journal of International Development 1: 14-35.

31. International Monetary Fund (2014) World Economic Outlook: Legacies, Clouds, Uncertainties. Washington, USA.

32. Karlan D, Zinman J (2009) Expanding credit access: Using randomized supply decisions to estimate the impacts. Review of Financial Studies 23: 433-464.

33. Lebanese Central Bank (2009) Quarterly bulletin, Beirut, Lebanon.

34. Mamari R, Ghaleb J, Majmoua A (2002) Micro-finance in Lebanon, World Bank Institute Middle East and North Africa Debates.

35. United Nations Development Programme (2005) Poverty growth and income distribution in Lebanon, Brazil.

36. United Nations Development Programme (2012) Capacity assessment of a number of Lebanese government institutions for the achievement of the MDGs.

37. United Nations Development Programme (2013) UN agencies and partners launch largest ever humanitarian appeal for Syrians: US$4.4 billion.

38. UNHCR Global Trends (2013) War's Human Cost. Geneva.

39. World Bank (2013) Lebanon: Economic and social impact assessment of the Syrian conflict, Washington DC, USA.

Growth and Development Analysis of Group Mexico in the Mining Industry

José G Vargas-Hernández*

Lic. Ángel Tomás Wong Dan, University Center for Economic and Managerial Sciences, University of Guadalajara, Periférico Norte 799, Los Belenes, C.P. 45100, Zapopan, Jalisco, México

Abstract

The aim of this research is to analyze the strategies that have taken Grupo Mexico to be Mexico's largest mining company, the largest copper producer in the country and fourth worldwide. From its founding in 1964, Grupo Mexico has grown at a rapid rate; it is now one of the leading companies in the construction industry, transport and mining. In this paper some theories of industrial organization and microeconomic analysis is used.

Keywords: Growth; Mining; Microeconomics; Econometrics; Precious metals

JEL: D21, D24, D43, L10, L11

Introduction

Mining in Mexico has been characterized as one of the most important industries throughout the history of Mexico. Since the days of New Spain to what is today Mexico has always been present in the country's economic activity. The history of Mexican mining is considered in three major stages: The colonization, the Porfiriato and North American crisis of 1929 [1]. The heyday of mining arises from the Porfiriato, when it started with the first mining extractions and minting the coin in Cananea, Sonora. This generated a great economic activity for the country and especially as a source of jobs. In 1929, mining contributed about 10% of the Gross National Product (GNP), and represented a third of the freight of the railways. From the constitutional changes of 1992, allowed ejidos and mines could be passed to the private sector.

With the implementation of the North America Free Trade Agreement (NAFTA), it was allowed foreign mining companies, especially Canadians appropriated of abandoned mines and potential ejidos for exploitation and mining. The current dominance that Canadian mining companies have in the country has marked the way of doing business in the mining industry. Currently, these mining have more than 70% of the bids in gold mines in the country. Mexican mining companies have been weakened, and there are only a few who remain within the industry.

This research aims to study the strategies used by Grupo Mexico to enter the mining industry, and use tools of microeconomic analysis to understand how they have affected the strategies of the firm in the current environment. It is very important to study this firm, for its ability to generate employment, contribution to the Mexican mining, production capacity for the country and as a role model.

Definition of the Problem

Knowing the market structure of the industry will help make this analysis more enriching, help analyze to what structure is Grupo Mexico in different markets of the mining industry and see what it is its role within the industry. As the largest copper producer in the country and has no significant competition in the market makes the structure to be monopolistic, but this is not necessarily the same for other productions such as gold and silver. The market structure of copper production is clearly marked by a single company.

By the end of 2012, Grupo Mexico produced 55% of the copper in the country. This means that at least half of the production was produced by only one company. Thus, the production of copper has a monopolistic market structure trend. Although this does not mean that in other productions of minerals has marked this trend. Production of gold and silver had only a participation of 3% and 8%, respectively [2]. But with the production capacity of the company and also it represents the most important mining country; what strategies could take Grupo Mexico to have a more dominant role in the production of gold and silver? Grupo Mexico could change the market structure of the production of gold and silver? Based on the above, microeconomic analysis of market structures and simple linear regression model to meet their elasticity will be made.

Background

First it must be understood what industry is. An industry is a conglomeration of companies engaged in the production of goods and services that have some similarity to each other [3]. For the mining industry, it is a process of using physical and human resources for the extraction of minerals from the soil. The activity of this industry in the country has its origins 200 years ago when it started the independence of Mexico, that with these resources were extracted from soil succeeded in forging the country as it is now [4]. The mining industry has always been known and characterized as one of the most important industries in the country, since it has historical memory, many jobs have left this activity, even had political overtones as the Mexican revolution or independence. One of the first companies founded for this industry was Peñoles in 1887, 50 years after the consummation of independence. Currently Peñoles is the largest producer of silver and gold in the country.

Grupo Mexico was founded in 1942. It started its first activities in construction, becoming one of the most important companies in the country. From 1965 begins to participate in the mining sector by Asarco Group, a company dedicated to the extraction and processing of copper. Grupo Mexico had acquired 51% of Asarco´s rights. The first strategy to start with these activities was the merger or acquisition

***Corresponding author:** José G Vargas-Hernández, Lic. Ángel Tomás Wong Dan, University Center for Economic and Managerial Sciences, University of Guadalajara, Periférico Norte 799, Los Belenes, C.P. 45100, Zapopan, Jalisco, México, E-mail: jvargas2006@gmail.com

of property rights (M and A), which later was to be one of the most productive and successful companies in the country. Thirteen years later, Grupo Mexico first enters the Mexican Stock Exchange as a mining company. It was when it started to grow and expand in major mining areas of the country as in San Luis Potosi, Sonora, Zacatecas and Chihuahua. The great performance that took the company was able to open up the market, through the market for corporate control (F and A) [3].

Since 1998 Grupo Mexico becomes one of the leading producers of copper and silver, thus remaining until today, although it has lost ground in the extraction of silver. Currently, Grupo Mexico is the largest extractor of copper in the country and third worldwide. He is regarded as the largest and most important mining company in the country. Currently, Germán Larrea Mota-Velasco is the chairman of board of directors of Grupo Mexico. He is also considered one of the richest man in the country, ranking third according to Forbes magazine.

The large magnitude and ability that has Grupo Mexico at the national level is of great importance. According to estimates by the Ministry of Economy through ProMéxico, it was expected that by 2014 the growth of mining production in the country is 2.0% this depending on how important was what did Grupo Mexico. Some of the strategies implemented by Grupo Mexico were vertical integration. Grupo Mexico's history is marked by the use of this strategy. Following here, a picture of the evolution of Grupo Mexico is displayed in Figure 1 above.

It is observed that in the course of time, Grupo Mexico began to grow from its beginnings as a construction company; the strategy of vertical integration that implemented the company acquired the mining railway system. Given that these three industries are closely linked allowed Grupo Mexico a high growth and development. It will be discussed in greater detail in Figure 2 below.

It can be seen how easily the three major industries that handles Grupo Mexico have a clear advantage over other companies. On the issue of mining, Grupo Mexico has competitive advantage over other companies in the transportation of minerals across the country. And in the construction industry, have mineral resources and transport.

In 2012 Grupo Mexico used the strategy of organic growth, which is a growth from the institution itself using its own resources to be leveraged for new customers or other markets [5]. Grupo Mexico plans to expand the Buenavista Del Cobre mine in Sonora, as the mine with the largest reserves of copper in the world. With investment and other growth projects developed in other countries such as Peru and the United States of America, Grupo Mexico estimated increase production at 625,000 tons to achieve a production of 1.4 million tons of copper in 2015 (Figure 3).

Mining in Mexico: gold and silver

Mexico is a geographically privileged for the development and mining country ranks first worldwide in the production of silver and is within the top 10 producers of gold and other minerals. It is very important to study the mining industry for its great contributions to the country's economy, contributing 4.9 percent to the Gross Domestic Product and generated in 2013 more than 337,000 direct formal jobs and 1.6 million indirect jobs. Mexico as the main producer of silver for its geographical advantage has had positive growth in silver production in the last 15 years, only without including the economic crisis of 2008-2009 there was a major drop in production (Figure 4).

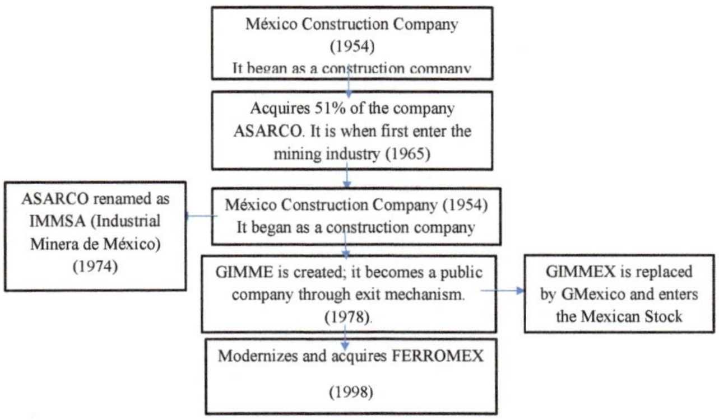

Figure 1: Evolution of Grupo Mexico. Source: Based on data from Grupo Mexico.

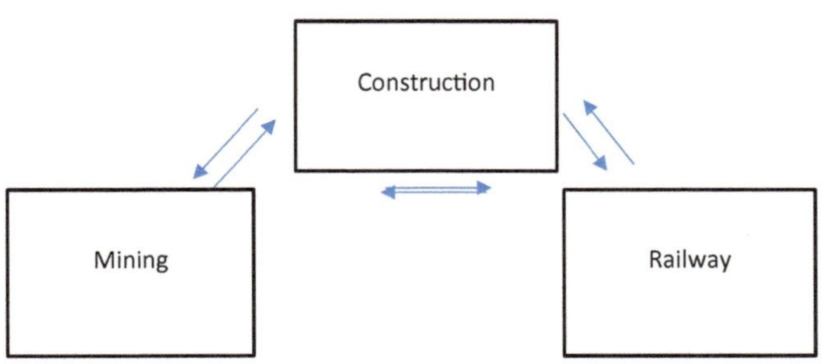

Figure 2: Industrial Interaction Group Mexico. Source: Based on information obtained from Grupo Mexico.

Figure 3: Total domestic production of silver from 2000 to 2013. Source: Data obtained from INEGI (Data in Kg).

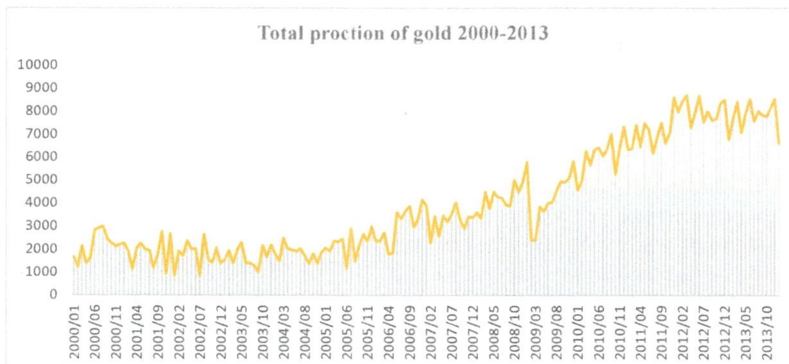

Figure 4: Total domestic production of gold from 2000 to 2013. Source: Data obtained from INEGI (Data in Kg).

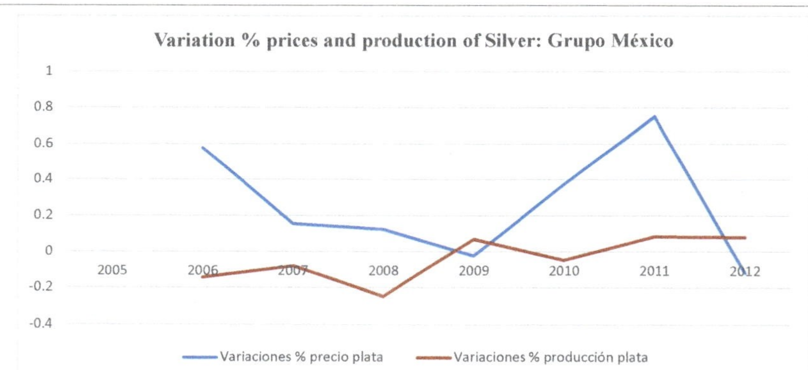

Figure 5: Percentage change in price and production of silver GRPO Mexico. Source: Based on data from INEGI and SONAMI Local-Grupo Mexico.

Although the share of silver production of Grupo Mexico is very little, only 7% of total production, it is of importance to mark this trend that could change itself, Grupo Mexico takes strategic actions to enter more strongly the silver market. Gold production in Mexico is in ninth place worldwide as a producer of gold. In 2013, Mexico produced 94,216.68 kilograms, of which 70,585.89 kilograms are produced by only 11 companies established in Mexico.

Of the total silver production there are only 8 companies that control almost 95% of the silver. The rest are distributed in small mines for gold. The interesting thing about this particular industry is that gold for its natural conditions is relatively scarce. The total amount of gold that exists in Mexico is very little compared with other minerals, and this makes the price to be stable for its production [6]; there are currently 12 companies that control gold production nationwide, of which half are Canadian mining companies. This is due to new policies to attract foreign direct investment and the Free Trade in Latin America of 1994.

Production of gold and silver from Grupo Mexico.

According to the quarterly reports of Grupo Mexico, the company produces 3% of silver production and 7% of gold production because its production strategies have focused more on copper by its geographical location which gave it an advantage, as the Cananea mine, the largest in Latin America. Many of the miners in Mexico have their production depending on market prices. In the opposite case of Grupo Mexico, the price was not a factor in silver production for the company, as its production is relatively low compared to other companies, and also that 84% of its profits come from copper.

In this graph the percentage changes between the prices of silver and variations % of silver production compared Grupo Mexico. In

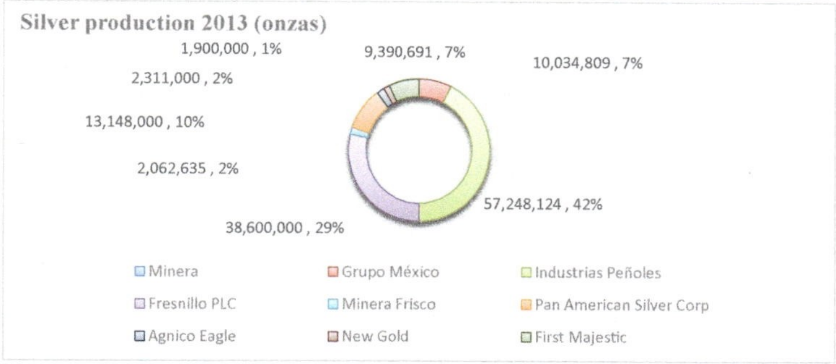

Figure 6: Market share of silver production 2013. Source: Own Calculations with data obtained from the financial reports of those undertakings.

Figure 5, it is shown that silver production of Grupo Mexico did not influence market prices. That is, that while prices are low or high, silver production will continue. Since 2009 the company had an almost constant production. It is a demonstration of how natural resources are scarce in the case of silver and gold production does not depend much the established price.

Analysis Tools

In this research are used analysis tools of market concentration and dominance, which will determine what type of market structure production of gold and silver. Besides a simple econometric model was used to analyze what kind of elasticity's have the use of capital and labor in the mining of gold and silver. Based on this analysis, it may help in creating strategies to improve resource use production.

Concentration Herfindal and Hirschmann Index

The Concentration Herfindal and Hirschmann index (HHI) shows the concentration of market participants. That is, that the greater number of participants in a market, the HHI will be smaller. If there are fewer participants in the market, the HHI would be higher. This index helps us to observe the market structure. From 0-1, where 0 is perfect competition and 1 is monopoly.

Formula:

$$VT = \sum_{i=1}^{n} x_i$$

$$H = \sum_{i=1}^{n} P_i^2$$

$$P_i = \frac{X_i}{VT}$$

$$\frac{1}{n} \leq H \leq 1$$

Where:

P_i=is the market share

X_i=value of the position of the market participant i

VT=total market value

H=Herfindal-Hirschmann Index

Econometric model

The model is a simple regression data bases using time series, thereby logarithms obtained by the capital-output elasticity and elasticity of output-labor.

STATA program will be handled for the Cobb-Douglas model.

Gold Mining	Production
Grupo Mexico	1.6%
Peñoles	28.6%
Goldcorp Mexico	19.5%
Fresnillo PLC	17.1%
Minera Frisco	2.6%
Agnico Eagle	8.7%
Alamos Gold	8.0%
New Gold	5.5%
First Majestic	0.4%
Argonaut Gold	5.2%

Source: Prepared financial statements of all companies mentioned 2011-2013.

Table 1: Market share 2013 gold.

Silver mining	Production
Grupo México	7.45%
Industrias Peñoles	42.50%
Fresnillo PLC	28.66%
Minera Frisco	1.53%
Agnico Eagle	9.76%
Alamos Gold	1.72%
First Majestic	1.41%
Argonaut Gold	6.97%

Source: Prepared financial statements of all companies mentioned 2011-2013.

Table 2: Market share silver 2013.

Econometric model $Y=AL^{\alpha}K^{\beta}$

Model expected in Stata: $\ln Y = \ln A + \sigma \ln L + \beta \ln K + u$

Where:

A=the total productivity factor

L=production factor labor

K=production factor capital (investment)

α and β are the elasticities of the corresponding factor

Results and Analysis

Based on the following tables, it will be analyzed empirically what is the market structure that might have the industry gold and silver.

Structure and market segmentation

It can be seen that on both silver and gold the production leader is Peñoles Industries besides being the oldest mining and with the greatest reputation that has made it a corporate market leader [7]. Table 1 shows that gold production companies exist and this could mean that the market could be or tends to perfect competition, while in Table 2 shows that in silver production there are fewer companies and only one company that controls almost 50% of production, so this indicates that it could be closer to the oligopoly, other than gold.

How would be the market share of the mining gold and silver industry? (Figures 6 and 7)

It is clear graphically that Peñoles dominates the production of gold and silver. It can be seen in Table 3 that the concentration index HHI is 0.28 for both years, i.e. that there has been no change in market structure from 2012 to 2013. In addition, the 0.28 says that tends to perfect competition although production of silver almost 50% has been controlled by Peñoles, but could reach the conclusion that tends to be an oligopoly.

Unlike silver production, in this table can be seen that there are more companies producing gold silver, even when the conditions of scarcity of gold are higher than silver. It can be noted that the IHH, 2012 and 2013 is about 17 and 18%. With silver can be concluded at first instance that is a perfect market competition of gold production (Table 4).

Production function of silver in Grupo Mexico (Cobb-Douglas)

Through the information provided in financial reports of Grupo Mexico, it was possible to obtain by a simple logarithmic regression for the production function of silver Grupo Mexico (Figure 8).

Although the regression of the coefficients obtained in Stata are

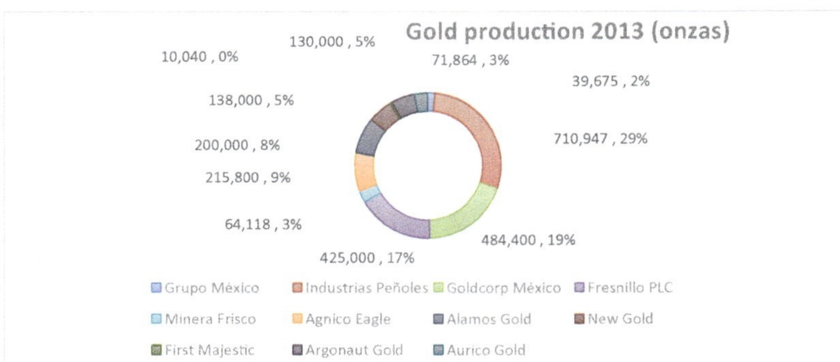

Figure 7: Market share of gold production 2013. Source: Own Calculations with data obtained from the financial reports of those companies.

Mining	Participation mining silver production (%) 2013	Silver production Participation (%) 2012	Square silver production involving 2013	Square involving silver production 2013
Grupo México	7.45%	7.79%	0.005550264	0.006071671
Industrias Peñoles	42.50%	42.70%	0.180641652	0.182344074
Fresnillo Plc	28.66%	29.15%	0.082123981	0.084954423
Minera Frisco	1.53%	1.02%	0.000234499	0.000103656
Pan American Silver Corp	9.76%	9.86%	0.009528286	0.009718959
Agnico Eagle	1.72%	1.91%	0.000294371	0.00036496
New Gold	1.41%	1.03%	0.000198977	0.000106017
First Majestic	6.97%	6.54%	0.004860607	0.004280516
Total	100%	100%	0.2834	0.2879

Source: Prepared financial statements of all companies mentioned 2011-2013

Table 3: Table of dominance and market concentration plant.

Mining	Participation mining silver production (%) 2013	Silver production Participation (%) 2012	Square of participation of silver production 2013	Square involving silver production 2013
Grupo México	1.59%	1.43%	0.000253915	0.000204128
Industrias Peñoles	28.55%	30.95%	0.081532348	0.095760495
Goldcorp México	19.46%	19.36%	0.037849847	0.037462163
Fresnillo PLC	17.07%	18.57%	0.029136254	0.034470305
Minera Frisco	2.58%	1.79%	0.000663156	0.000318785
Agnico Eagle	8.67%	9.22%	0.007512055	0.00849681
Alamos Gold	8.03%	7.46%	0.006452319	0.005561988
New Gold	5.54%	4.04%	0.003071949	0.001634547
First Majestic	0.40%	0.17%	1.62601E-05	2.74507E-06
Argonaut Gold	5.22%	4.24%	0.002726105	0.001799789
Aurico Gold	2.89%	2.79%	0.000833065	0.000779851
Total	100%	100%	0.170047273	0.186491604

Source: Prepared financial statements of all companies mentioned 2011-2013

Table 4: Index dominance and market concentration of gold.

```
. reg lproduction lpersonal lcapital if year > 2007

      Source |       SS       df       MS              Number of obs =       5
-------------+------------------------------           F(  2,     2) =    3.37
       Model |  .002888923     2  .001444462           Prob > F      =  0.2291
    Residual |  .000858351     2  .000429175           R-squared     =  0.7709
-------------+------------------------------           Adj R-squared =  0.5419
       Total |  .003747274     4  .000936819           Root MSE      =  .02072

------------------------------------------------------------------------------
 lproduction |      Coef.   Std. Err.      t    P>|t|     [95% Conf. Interval]
-------------+----------------------------------------------------------------
   lpersonal |   .1923786   .7240215     0.27   0.815    -2.922834    3.307592
    lcapital |   .1339541   .5151843     0.26   0.819    -2.082705    2.350613
       _cons |   4.781488   2.081859     2.30   0.148    -4.176027      13.739
------------------------------------------------------------------------------
```

Figure 8: Simple linear regression for Cobb-Douglas. Source: Data obtained from financial reports 2006-2012 Grupo Mexico. Regression was developed by program STATA 11.

not statistically significant, for autocorrelation and heteroscedasticity problems since there is a scarcity of data provided by the company through its annual reports, yet it allows seeing the product-labor elasticity and capital-product elasticity.

Regression Cobb-Douglas

$lny = lpersonal + lcapital$

$lny = 4.76 + 0.19 \ln personal + 0.13 \ln capital$

$lny = 4.76L^{0.19}K^{0.13}$

It can be seen that although there is not much difference in the elasticity of both factors, the labor factor is a bit more intensive in its use for the production of silver. Perhaps because the investments made for the extraction of silver are lower due to installed capacity for several years.

Conclusions

It can be concluded that the mining industry is one of the most important in Mexico, for its ability to create jobs, for its historical significance and also represents Mexico as the largest producers of raw materials, in this case precious metals.

It is observed that companies have had more time in the industry are those who have control of productive mineral market because they had the advantage of obtaining bids from the government in advance. Although in the last 10 years such calls started to pass into the hands of Canadian mining. Yet, control over 80% of the silver is hold by Mexican groups. Different case is the gold case where Canadians have managed to acquire 70% of the bids and programs of governments in gold mining.

Since 1994 when it was enacted the North American free Trade Agreement (NAFTA), Canadian and American companies have free access to establish in strategic areas for the extraction of precious minerals areas. One of the most important cases was Goldcorp in 2010 who established the Mine Mexico's largest gold mining. Goldcorp launched the Peñasquito Complex in Zacatecas, with an investment of 1,700 million dollars; the mine generates 2,500 direct jobs and 12,000 indirect jobs [8].

Finally, to emphasize that the strategy of organic growth of Grupo Mexico has been successful in recent years, which is a good model for other large companies that want to continue expanding in the market. 84% of net income of Grupo México was reinvested to continue improving and expanding its productive mines and this has generated higher yields surrendered during these years. Grupo Mexico is definitely a role model.

References

1. Muro E (2005) La minería mexicana, su evolución, retos y perspectivas. Instituto de Investigaciones Jurídicas, *UNAM*, 1-48.
2. Grupo México (2013) Reportes financieros. México.
3. Peng M (2012) Estrategia Global. Cengage Learning.
4. Gaytán E, Benita F (2014) La industria minera en México: patrones de desempeño y determinantes de eficiencia. Lecturas de Economía 103-131.
5. Tatum (2005) Cuaderno de opinión: Opciones estratégicas de crecimiento de las entidades financieras españolas. Tatum talento para tu negocio 1-18.
6. Ramón J (2009) El oro como el mejor dinero posible. El oro y la plata, activos monetarios con futuro (1-10) Madrid: Portal Oro.
7. Villafañe J (2001) La reputación corporativa como factor de liderazgo. Área abierta, 1-6.
8. Expansión C (2010) México inaugura mina de oro más grande. CNN Expansión, 1.

Relationship between the Stock Market Index and Consumer Confidence after the 2007-2008 Financial Crisis

Hanitra Rakotondramaro*

IAE-University of Perpignan, via Domitia, France

Abstract

The paper investigates potential Granger causality between the stock market index (SMI) and the consumer confidence (sentiment) index (CSI) for the period between 2007 and 2013. While studying SMI-CSI relations, the model is calibrated for US data (S&P500 and the Michigan Survey Research Centre measures of consumer confidence) and shows causality is from the stock market index to consumer confidence. This result is a consequence of the stock market index towards the consumers' attitudes, as they consider the index to be the leading indicator of the future situation, regardless of whether they own stocks or not. They also maintain a degree of optimism regarding the future economic situation.

Keywords: Consumer sentiment; Stock market index; Granger causality; Cointegration; VAR; VECM; JEL: G01; G1

Introduction

Knowledge of the prevailing relationship between stock prices, on the one hand, and macroeconomic variables, such as consumption, investment and industrial production, on the other, is predominantly postulated in a variety of economic models.

Consumer confidence (sentiment) plays an important role both in macroeconomics and finance. It is based on the "information view" [1] and it reflects the "subjective" of consumers' state of mind that cannot be deducted from the economic variables. Caroll et al. find that higher levels of consumer confidence decrease consumption today relative to tomorrow for the USA, which implies improvements in consumers' confidence stimulate consumption growth in the short run. Ludvigson [2] found that consumer confidence indicators have some forecasting power for future labour income growth. Easaw et al. [3] find that consumer confidence indices predict households' consumption of durable goods in the UK.

The relationship between stock prices and consumer sentiment has been the subject of intense research over the past three decades. Ottoo [4] showed that changes in equity values and consumer sentiment for the US are contemporaneously correlated and that increases in the equity price boost consumer confidence with a (short) lag; however, the reverse does not hold. Fisher and Statman [5] presented that consumer confidence predicts the stock market. On the other hand, results from these studies have compelled some authors to question the traditional notion of the causal chain. Meanwhile, time-series analysis has developed recently and numerous studies have investigated the connection between the two variables by using the Granger causality concept. Most previous studies have dealt with the question of temporal independence between the stock market and consumer sentiment using country panel data. For example, this is the case in both the study of eleven European countries by Jansen, Nahius [6] and the causality analysis by Chih-Chiang Hsu et al. [7]. The present paper is a contribution to this literature through analysis of several aspects of the link between stock market index and consumer confidence. Previous studies have used the consumer confidence sentiment index as the proxies of individual investors, as well as the stock market index as a stock return indicator (for example, Fisher and Statman).

Before the 2007/2008 financial crisis, all researches cited a short-term correlation between consumer confidence and the stock market index. However, the condition of the relationship after a financial crisis needs to be examined. To answer this question, consumer confidence and stock index are modelled bivariate in vector auto regressive (VAR) or vector-error (VEC) models for the United States of America and causality tests performed. The advantage of the VECM approach is that it can distinguish between long- and short-run relationships among the variables to identify sources of causation that cannot be detected by Granger causality.

The paper is structured with Section 2 presenting a description of the data, Section 3 providing an overview of the empirical analysis and Section 4 concluding the paper.

Data Source for the Study

As previously mentioned, the objective of this study is to determine the linkage between the US stock market index and the consumer confidence index. The study covers a 7-year period from January 2006 to March 2013, which was selected because it is within a jam-packed decade of financial events in the United States and around the world, including some good, some bad and all newsworthy. All of the financial events have been important for small businesses and consumers.

A. Consumer confidence

Consumer confidence, or consumer sentiment, is both an economic concept and a set of statistical measures. Alan Greespan considered consumer confidence to be a key determinant of near-term economic growth; moreover, Qiu and Welch [8] provided evidence that his index is a good proxy for investor sentiment in the US. The index is based on the responses to five questions via surveys of 500 households and is published by the University of Michigan and Thomson Reuters. The questions are:

***Corresponding author:** Dr. Hanitra Rakotondramaro, IAE-University of Perpignan Via Domitia, France, E-mail: hanitra.rakotondramaro@univ-perp.fr

1. We are interested in how people are getting along financially these days. Would you say that you (and your family) are better off or worse off financially than you were a year ago?

2. Looking ahead, do you think that a year from now you (and your family) will be better off financially, worse off or just about the same as now?

3. Turning to business conditions in the country as a whole, do you think that during the next twelve months we'll have good times financially, bad times or what?

4. Looking ahead, which would you say is more likely, that in the country as a whole we'll have continuous good times during the next five years or so, we will have periods of widespread unemployment or depression or what?

5. About the big things people buy for their homes, such as furniture, a refrigerator, stove, television, and things like that; generally speaking, do you think now is a good or a bad time for people to buy major household items?

B. The stock market index

The Standard and Poors 500 index is used as the proxy of the stock market index. It is a value-weighted index that reflects the market value of all 500 components US stocks relative to a particular base period. The Standard and Poor's Index Committee determine the selection and management of the index, which is chosen for two main reasons; firstly, the S&P500 is a better representation of the US market and, secondly, the academic community quickly adopted the S&P 500 as the benchmark used in evaluation of investment theories. As part of his work in developing the Capital Asset Pricing Model (1964), William Sharpe created the notion of the market portfolio, one of the major characteristics of which is that each asset in that portfolio is held in exact proportion to its market value. That notion also happens to be the basis upon which the S&P 500 is constructed, a fact noted not only by the researchers who used it to develop modern portfolio theory but also by the creators of indexed stock funds.

Following the research of Otoo, Jansen and Nahius and others used a monthly frequency in their work concerning the relationship between the stock market and consumer sentiment since it is the most logical option given the need to observe changes in consumer confidence over time. The two series, obtained in real values, have been transformed in their logarithmic values before modelling.

Figure 1 shows how just a quick view on the data can support a positive relation between the two variables. The analysis in this paper will show, in formal terms, the kind of relation that can be hypothesized for these two variables.

Estimation strategy

A. Vector auto regression model: In order to verify the empirical analysis, this paper uses the Vector Auto Regression (VAR) model to explore the relationship between the stock market index and consumer confidence index; therefore, according to Jansen and Nahuis, the following two equations can be specified:

$$CSI_t = \alpha_c + \sum_{i=1}^{k} \beta_{c_i} CSI_{t-i} + \sum_{i=1}^{k} \gamma_{c_i} SMI_{t-i} + \mu_{c_t} \quad (1)$$

$$SMI_t = \alpha_p + \sum_{i=1}^{k} \beta_{p_i} CSI_{t-i} + \sum_{i=1}^{k} \gamma_{p_i} SMI_{t-i} + \mu_{p_t} \quad (2)$$

Where CSI_t is the consumer confidence index of an individual investor at time t and SMI_t is the stock market index at time t,μ_{ct} is the residual of the consumer confidence index and μ_{pt} is the residual of the stock market index.

In equation (1), the stock market index Granger-causes the consumer sentiment index, if the null hypothesis that lagged coefficients, $\gamma_{c_1} = \gamma_{c_2} = \ldots = \gamma_{c_i} = 0$ (i=1,2, ,k), are zero is rejected. In equation (2), the consumer sentiment index Granger-causes the

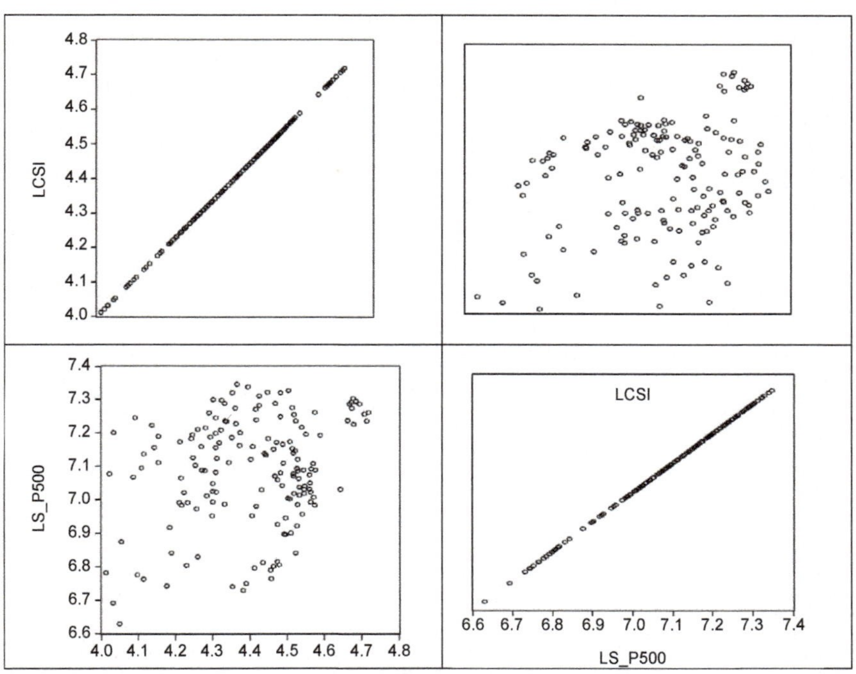

Figure 1: Scatter plot for LS&P500 and LCSI evolution.

stock market index, if the null hypothesis that lagged coefficients, $\beta_{p_1} = \beta_{p_2} = \cdots = \beta_{p_i} = 0$ (i=1,2, ,k), is rejected. Based on the estimated OLS coefficients for equations (1) and (2), four different hypotheses concerning the relationship between consumer sentiment index and stock market index can be formulated:

If $\sum_{i=1}^{k} \gamma_{c_i} \neq 0 \, et \sum_{i=1}^{k} \gamma_{p_i} = 0$, then stock prices increase the prediction for consumer confidence but not vice versa; thus, we have *unidirectional Granger-Causality from LS_P500 to LCSI.*

If $\sum_{i=1}^{k} \gamma_{c_i} = 0 \, et \sum_{i=1}^{k} \gamma_{p_i} \neq 0$, then consumer confidence increases the prediction for the stock prices but not vice versa; in this case, we have *unidirectional Granger-Causality from LCSI to LS_P500.*

If $\sum_{i=1}^{k} \gamma_{c_i} \neq 0 \, et \sum_{i=1}^{k} \gamma_{p_i} \neq 0$, then consumer confidence increases stock prices and vice versa; thus, we have *bidirectional (or feedback) causality.*

If $\sum_{i=1}^{k} \gamma_{c_i} = 0 \, et \sum_{i=1}^{k} \gamma_{p_i} = 0$, then there is *independence between LCSI and LS_P500;* in this case, there is *no Granger-Causality in any direction.*

B. Causality testing and co-integration: It should be noted that there may be some co-integrating relationship in both equations (1) and (2). Therefore, vector δ can be interpreted as a vector of adjustment coefficients that measures the strength of the deviation from equilibrium feedback into the system. Tests for co-integration are based on the estimated Eingen values of the Π-matrix, in which testing is done sequentially so that the null rank 0 is tested against the alternative of rank 1 fist, and rank 1 against rank next. Equations (1) and (2) can be rewritten after adding the co-integration assumptions, as follows:

$$CSI_t = \alpha_c + \sum_{i=1}^{k} \beta_{c_i} CSI_{t-i} + \sum_{i=1}^{k} \gamma_{c_i} SMI_{t-i} + \delta_{11} CSI_{t-1} + \delta_{12} SMI_{t-1} + \mu_{c_t} \quad (1')$$

$$SMI_t = \alpha_p + \sum_{i=1}^{k} \beta_{p_i} CSI_{t-i} + \sum_{i=1}^{k} \gamma_{p_i} SMI_{t-i} + \delta_{21} CSI_{t-1} + \delta_{22} SMI_{t-1} + \mu_{p_t} \quad .(2')$$

Where α_c and α_p are the drift components and μ_{c_t} and μ_{p_t} are white noise, the terms with summation signs represent the error correction dynamics, while the second part of the equation with δ corresponds to the long-run relationship.

The first step in the VECM test approach is to use F-tests for the existing long-run relationship among variables. The null hypothesis in the equation is $\delta_{11=}\delta_{12=}0$ for the consumer sentiment index equation and $\delta_{21=}\delta_{22=}0$ for the stock market index equation. This indicates the existence of a long-run relationship.

The alternative hypothesis is: H_1: $\delta_{11} \neq 0$, $\delta_{12} \neq 0$, $\delta_{21} \neq 0$, $\delta_{22} \neq 0$. The long run should not be interpreted in a temporal sense here; deviations from the equilibrium are, of course, partially corrected between each period in a "mechanical" sense.

The calculated F-statistics are compared with the two sets of critical values suggested by Pesaran et al. (2001). One set assumes that all variables are I(0) and the other assumes they are I(1). If the calculated F-statistics exceed the upper critical value, the null hypothesis of no co-integration will be rejected irrespective of whether the variables are I(0) or I(1). If it is below the lower value, the null hypothesis of no co-integration cannot be rejected; however, if it falls inside the critical value band, the test is inconclusive (Pesaran & Pesaran). To choose the optimal lag length for each variable, the VECM method estimates (p+1) k number of regressions, where p is the maximum number of lags and k is the number of variables in the equation. The model can be selected on the basis of the Schwartz–Bayesian Criteria (SBC) and the Akaike Information Criteria (AIC). The SBC is known as a parsimonious model that selects the smallest possible lag length; meanwhile, the AIC is known for selecting the maximum relevant lag length.

In the second step, the long-run relationship using the selected ECM model is estimated through AIC or SBC. When a long-run relationship exists among the variables, there is error correction representation. The following error correction model is also estimated:

$$CSI_t = \alpha_c + \sum_{i=1}^{k} \beta_{c_i} CSI_{t-i} + \sum_{i=1}^{k} \gamma_{c_i} SMI_{t-i} + \varphi_c ECM_{t-1} + \mu_{c_t} \quad (3)$$

$$SMI_t = \alpha_p + \sum_{i=1}^{k} \beta_{p_i} CSI_{t-i} + \sum_{i=1}^{k} \gamma_{p_i} SMI_{t-i} + \varphi_p ECM_{t-1} + \mu_{p_t} \, . \quad (4)$$

The error correction term ECMt-1 indicates the speed of adjustment back to long-run equilibrium after a short-run shock.

Empirical Results

The first step is to implement unit root tests to ensure the integration of all variables. For this purpose, the study uses the Augmented Dickey and Fuller (ADF) [9-11] and MacKinnon [12] one-side p-values tests. As evident from the results shown in Table 1, LSMI and LCSI are non-stationary but their first difference is stationary. Then, LSMI and LCSI are *integrated of order 1 I(1).*

In order to establish the direction of causality between these two variables, the Granger-Causality test has been employed and the results are presented in Table 2. F-statistic and Probability are values constructed under the null hypothesis H_0 of no causality. This is evidence that there is a causal relationship between the two variables (Jansen and Nahius) and, importantly, the one-way causality runs through the stock market index to the consumer sentiment index [13-15].

As shown in Table 3 below, there is evidence of co-integration between two variables. The stock market index is close to be stationary variable; however, the trend coefficient is significant, which means the stationary combination of the stock market and consumer confidence also need to include a time trend.

Turning to the estimated δ-coefficients and tests for long-run causality, Table 4 shows a test for significance of the impact coefficient in the stock market index equation (2') could not be rejected, whereas a corresponding test for the coefficient in the consumer confidence

Variable	ADF	Prob.*
LCSI	-0.57	0.46
LSMI	0.14	0.72
LCSI	-10.78	0
LSMI	-8.06	0

*MacKinnon (1996) one-sided p-values.

Table 1: Unit root tests.

Null Hypothesis:	F-Statistic	Probability
LCSI does not Granger Cause LSMI	0.091	0.76
LSMI does not Granger Cause LCSI	4.819	0.02

Table 2: Granger causality test.

	LSMI	LCSI	trend
Est β'	1	-4	-0.01
Trend t-stat			5.39
Coeff t-stat		6.37	

Table 3: Cointegration analysis.

Rank	Trace-Stat	Engen-Value
None	0.150649	33.33425
At most 1	0.047854*	7.698782*

Superscript* indicates that test is significant on the 5%-level.

Eq	Coeff.	Standar Error	t-statistics
(1')	0.01	0.09	0.02
(2')	0.11	0.05	26.5

Table 4: Long-run causality test.

Regressors	ΔLCSI	ΔLSMI
Constant	1.74	8.22
ECM_{t-1}	-0.02	0.05
	-0.01	-0.01
$DLCSI_{t-1}$	0.006	
	-0.08	
$DLSMI_{t-1}$	0.34	0.23
	-0.11	-0.08
R^2	0.08	
AIC	-3.55	
Schwarz SC	-3.47	

Table 5: Vector Error Correction Estimates.

index equation (1') could. Hence, the results tend to favour a long-run causality that is unidirectional from stock market index to consumer confidence. Changes in the stock market index induced by disequilibria can, through ECM, cause consumer confidence but the data does not indicate an arrow of causality in the opposite direction.

Consequently, these causal chains are the only ones that are statistically significant. The only fluctuations of the stock market index and consumer confidence that can be explained by other variables in the system are changes stemming from the error correction dynamic. The statistically positive coefficient of LCSI confirms that an increase in stock market index leads to an improvement in the consumer sentiment. This result is in line with Fisher and Statman (Table 5).

These results led us to modify equations (3) and (4) as follows:

$$CSI_t = \alpha_c + \sum_{i=1}^{k} \beta_{c_i} CSI_{t-i} + \sum_{i=1}^{k} \gamma_{c_i} SMI_{t-i} + \varphi_c ECM_{t-1} + \mu_{c_t}$$

$$SMI_t = \alpha_p + \sum_{i=1}^{k} \gamma_{p_i} SMI_{t-i} + \mu_{p_t}$$

Summary and Conclusion

This paper examined the causal relationship between stock price and consumer sentiment for the United States of America over the period 2008-2013 using a bivariate model of S&P and consumer sentiment index. To test causality, the Granger test and the VECM was used because strong evidence was found that the variables are co-integrated and the object was to study the short-run relationship as well as the long-run dynamics. The empirical study of the U.S. suggests the existence of unidirectional long- and short-run causality running from stock price to consumer sentiment. Therefore, investors seemed to follow the stock market index more closely. Although consumer confidence predicts economy, it does not predict the stock market. As it is suspected that temporal aggregation of either quarterly or monthly data to annual data may weaken causal relationships between the variables, it may well be worth studying this effect in the future.

References

1. Throop AW (1992) Consumer Sentiment: Its Causes and Effects. Federal Reserve Bank of San Francisco Economic Review 1: 35-60.
2. Bram J, Ludvigson S (1998) Does consumer confidence forecast household expenditure? A sentiment index horse race. Economic Policy Review (Federal Reserve Bank of New York) 4: 59-78.
3. Joshy ZE, Heravi GD (2005) Does consumer sentiment accurately forecast UK household consumption? Are there any comparisons to be made with the US? Journal of Macroeconomics 27: 517-532.
4. Otoo MW (1999) Consumer sentiment and the stock market, Finance and Economics Discussion Paper, Federal Reserve Board.
5. Statman F (2003) Consumer Confidence and Stock Returns. The Journal of Portfolio Management 30: 115-127.
6. Nahius J (2002) The stock market and consumer Confidence: European Evidence, Working paper 2002 July, Monetary and Economic Policy Department, De Nederlandsche Bank.
7. Chih-Chiang H, Hung-Yu L, Jyun-Yi W (2011) Consumer Confidence and Stock Markets: The Panel Causality Evidence. International Journal of Economics and Finance 3: 91-98.
8. Qui L, Welch I (2006) Investor Sentiment Measures. Brown University.
9. Johansen S (1988) Statistical methods of econometrics. Journal of Economic Dynamic Control 12: 231-254.
10. Johansen S (1992) Determination of cointegration rank in the presence of a linear trend. Oxford Bull. Econ Stat 54: 383-397.
11. Granger CWJ (1988) Some recent developments in a concept of causality. J Econometrics 39: 199-211.
12. MacKinnon J (1991) Critical values for cointegration tests. In: Engle RF, Granger CWJ (eds.) Long-run Economic Relationships: Readings in Cointegration. Oxford University Press, New York, USA, pp: 267-276.
13. Carroll CD, Fuhrer JC, Wilcox DW (1994) Does Consumer Sentiment Forecast Household Spending? If So, Why? American Economic Review 84: 1397-1408.
14. Johansen S, Juselius K (1990) Maximum likelihood estimation and inference on cointegration with applications to the demand for money. Oxford Bull Econ Stat 52: 169-210.
15. Akhtar S (2012) Stock salience and the asymmetric market effect of consumer sentiment news. Journal of Banking & Finance 36: 3289-3301.

Management Instrument in Pharmaceutical Care and Clinical Pharmacy

Mauro Luisetto[1]*, Luca Cabianca[2] and Ram Sahu[3]

[1]*European Specialist Laboratory Medicine, Hospital Pharmacist manager, Italy*
[2]*Biomedical Laboratory, Torino, Italy*
[3]*Columbia Institute of Pharmacy, Tekari, Raipur, India*

Abstract

In actual scenario of international economic cycle, rational use of drugs and medical devices has become a real priority in order to correctly use the limited economic resources available today. Healthcare government and public or private institutions, insurance company and other subject are involved in high costs management much more than past (in example cost for drugs, medical devices and, new diagnostic procedure). Healthcare managers ask the clinical pharmacist professionals to rationalize costs involved in new innovative therapy, due to medical therapy errors and also in order to have efficient logistic systems (hospital pharmacy). For this reason Clinical pharmacist every day work in healthcare setting are strongly applied to monitor high costs related to diagnostics procedures and drug therapies. But Clinical pharmacists professional need to have management instruments to be added to their classic university core curriculum (Knowledge and practice applications). A rational use of clinical pharmacist's human resource is a golden endpoint in every setting with the change from logistic to more clinical function (clinical pharmaceutical care new healthcare discipline.

According to ASHP Guidelines report: "clinical pharmacy service, in which pharmacist provide direct patient care are important foundation for successful medication utilization management program focused on managing drug cost" in this article we analyze biomedical literature involved giving some elements for improving management skills to be active part of medical team in management and monitoring costs. (Clinical pharmacist help physicians in this kind of work) clinical pharmacy competence added to management instruments can be considered the right keyword and a synergy.

Keywords: Clinical pharmacy; Clinical pharmaceutical care; Management; ICT; Human resource skills; Pharmacoeconomy; Healthcare systems; Cost containment; Business administration

Introduction

Megginson has written that management is a mix of science and art: but this is real condition also for clinical pharmacist so we think that also for clinical pharmacist University course and practical application are the right tools to adequately manage healthcare costs in efficiently way (Knowledge and practical applications) [1].

"A management tool can be defined as an entity of instruments to support implementation of concepts and ideas at all levels of conceptualization and realization, of concepts, ultimately aiming to support organizational processes." [2].

The classic theory of management by Fayol includes the following

- Planning,
- Organizing,
- Commanding (leading),
- Coordinating,
- Controlling,
- Staffing, budgetting, reporting (Gulick).

Historical Theories of Management

Scientific Management Theory (1890-1940) by F. W. Taylor,

Bureaucratic M. Theory (1930-1950) by Max Weber,

Administrative Theory by H. Fayol,

Human Relations Movement (1930-today) by E. Mayo,

X&Y Theory by Douglas McGregor.

Contemporary theories

Contingency Theory, Systems Theory by Ludwig con Bertalanffy, Chaos Theory.

Management skills include

- Conceptual and diagnostic attitude to analyze complex situations, appropriate responses to a situation.
- Political attitude to build a power, to create connections.
- Interpersonal skills to communicate, motivate, mentor and delegate, leadership, ability to lead groups.
- Technical skills to expertise in one's specifically functional area.
- Communication skills (ICT), professional social media.

Organization: General management, marketing division, administrative, technical, logistic, human resource, Mission, vision.

Planning: Middle-long term, programming in short term.

Business management: Governance system used to achieve goals (Strategic planning, budget reporting gaps analysis) Healthcare and management efficacy, economic efficiency.

Decision making systems: Identify problem, search information

***Corresponding author:** Mauro luisetto, European Specialist Laboratory Medicine, Hospital Pharmacist Manager, Italy, E-mail: M.Luisetto@ausl.pc.it

(official and not), choose the goal; evaluate alternative decision, do check. Different level top managers, middle, low manager (technical competencies are more requested in low level, conceptual Ability are more request in top management).

Steps planning: Set objectives, generate alternatives, evaluate, monitor, and obtain high level of commitment by stakeholders.

Problem solving and creative solution: Disciplines model (USA army during II world war) established the team, describe the problem implement and verify, root causes, choose corrective action and verify prevent recurrent, share knowledge

Material and Methods

This work has substantially an observational approach, we have analyzed the corpus of actual clinical pharmacy and pharmaceutical care university course in order to verify if are present or not autonomous management discipline.

Then we observed some management instrument useful for pharmacy Care practice and some pub med literature involved in pharmaceutical and health care costs management.

Results

Actual situation of the Universities of clinical pharmacy

Analyzing the actual course in clinical pharmacy and we noticed that management theory and practice are not present in the ordinary clinical pharmacy course as autonomous discipline (even if pharmacoeconomy is regularly studied into classic clinical pharmacy postgraduate course).

From literature point of view

In healthcare management field "extremely complex health care organizations, by their structure and organization, operate in a constantly changing business environment, and such situation implies and requires complex and demanding health management. Therefore, in order to manage health organizations in a competent manner, health managers must possess various managerial skills and be familiar with problems in health care. Research, identification, analysis, and assessment of health management education and training needs are basic preconditions for the development and implementation of adequate programs to meet those needs… The need for knowledge of certain areas in health management, as well as the need for mastering concrete managerial competencies has been recognized as top-priorities requiring additional improvement and upgrading." [3].

"Healthcare managers of the future will need to be prepared to accept greater accountability for the quality and efficiency of healthcare. National and state scorecards on health system performance indicate wide variation across the U.S. and across hospitals and health systems on key dimensions of performance including health outcomes, quality, access, equity, and efficiency. Benchmark data on achievable performance will be useful to healthcare managers in identifying best practices, setting priorities for improvement, and closing gaps in performance. Payment reforms are likely to reward healthcare organizations that serve as patient-centered medical homes, or assume accountability for total acute care, including hospital readmissions and post-hospital care. Health reforms to extend affordable health insurance to all, align financial incentives to enhance value and achieve savings, organize the healthcare system around the patient to ensure that care is accessible and coordinated, assist providers in meeting and raising benchmarks for high-quality, efficient care, and support greater public-private collaboration are needed to set the U.S. health system on a path to high performance." [4].

"The multidisciplinary nature of health care management requires the use of resources from diverse fields. Based on the data provided by this study, practitioners should have access to general business, applied psychology, health services research, and health policy journals, as well as health care management titles." [5].

"Although management practices are recognized as important factors in improving health care quality and efficiency, most research thus far has focused on individual practices, ignoring or underspecifying the contexts within which these practices are operating. Research from other industries, which has increasingly focused on systems rather than individual practices, has yielded results that may benefit health services management.

Our goal was to develop a conceptual model on the basis of prior research from health care as well as other industries that could be used to inform important contextual considerations within health care.

We reviewed relevant research from peer-reviewed and other industry-relevant sources to inform our model. The model we developed was then reviewed with a panel of practitioners, including experts in quality and human resource management, to assess the applicability of the model to health care settings. The resulting conceptual model identified four practice bundles, comprising 14 management practices as well as nine factors influencing adoption and perceived sustainability of these practices. The mechanisms by which these practices influence care outcomes are illustrated using the example of hospital-acquired infections. In addition, limitations of the current evidence base are discussed, and an agenda for future research in health care settings is outlined. Results may help practitioners better conceptualize management practices as part of a broader system of work practices. This may, in turn, help practitioners to prioritize management improvement efforts more systematically." [6].

"The overwhelming number of knowledge management (KM) tools on the market today and the hype surrounding them makes it difficult for knowledge managers to know which tools will provide them with the best KM value. Knowledge managers have to develop mechanisms and strategies for how best to implement and use KM tools and technologies. Using an exploratory focus group comprised of knowledge managers from a number of different organizations, this study explores the relationship between KM and technology and identifies the strategies knowledge managers use to successfully recognize where and how technology should be implemented and used to facilitate knowledge management work. Our results support the existing KM literature by highlighting the importance of delivering KM tools on a solid foundation of information technology (IT) and information management (IM) infrastructure.

Further, KM tools work best for different tasks and work groups; therefore, understanding which tool is most appropriate for the use context is critical. We also gain an understanding of the strategies that KM managers use for successful implementation and use of KM tools. These strategies embody the following principles like experimentation, iteration, adaptation of grassroots technologies and building on what works. The findings from this study suggest that when knowledge managers use these strategies for deploying KM tools, delivering success and business value from KM is much more likely." [7].

"The model of clinical pharmacy practice adopted by many

pharmacy department hospitals is no longer appropriate for the demands of today's health-care services. Reviews many new models proposed for clinical pharmacy practice including an integrated model for providing a pharmaceutical care management approach in the health-care system. This model is a response to the failures of traditional drug therapy. It is primarily an idea about how health professionals and patient should integrate their work to obtain outcomes important to patients and clinicians." [8].

"A novel clinical pharmacy management system developed by our hospital was introduced to improve the work efficiency of clinical pharmacists in our hospital and to carry out large sample statistical analyzes by providing pharmacy information services and promoting rational drug use. Clinical pharmacy management system was developed according to the actual situation. Taking prescription review in the department of general surgery as the example, work efficiency of clinical pharmacists, quality and qualified rates of prescriptions before and after utilizing clinical pharmacy management system were compared... Qualified rates of both the inpatient and outpatient prescriptions of the general surgery department increased, and the use of antibiotics decreased. This system apparently improved work efficiency standardized the level and accuracy of drug use, which will improve the rational drug use and pharmacy information service in our hospital. Meanwhile, utilization of prophylactic antibiotics for the aseptic operations also reduced." [9].

Hospital information system is widely used to improve work efficiency of hospitals in China. However, it is lack of the function providing pharmaceutical information service for clinical pharmacists. A novel clinical pharmacy management system developed by our hospital was introduced to improve the work efficiency of clinical pharmacists in our hospital and to carry out large sample statistical analyzes by providing pharmacy information services and promoting rational drug use. Clinical pharmacy management system was developed according to the actual situation. Taking prescription review in the department of general surgery as the example, work efficiency of clinical pharmacists, quality and qualified rates of prescriptions before and after utilizing clinical pharmacy management system were compared. Statistics of 48,562 outpatient and 5776 inpatient prescriptions of the general surgical department were analyzed. Qualified rates of both the inpatient and outpatient prescriptions of the general surgery department increased, and the use of antibiotics decreased. This system apparently improved work efficiency standardized the level and accuracy of drug use, which will improve the rational drug use and pharmacy information service in our hospital. Meanwhile, utilization of prophylactic antibiotics for the aseptic operations also reduced [10].

"We think that core training must include principles of Management, ICT Professional social media, psychological behavior skills for team working added to be added to the classic clinical pharmacy programs." [11].

"While in PubMed and other biomedical databases, we can rapidly find articles, in social media we can rapidly find both articles and very fine details about the authors and researchers. Researchers by publically sharing their expertise and experience, can not only network with each other, but also initiate new opportunities in multidisciplinary work, even on a long distance fashion. Nowadays, it is widespread to observe scientists in different sectors can study problems from different disciplines and thus what you have is a multidisciplinary outlook. Although these social network machines have reduced the time factor, to a light speed, which is certainly relevant to such process, still there is room for, and it is necessary, for such an instrument to engage in further improvements and developments." [12].

And in clinical pharmacy management field, "Patients with type 2 diabetes who received pharmacist-led pharmaceutical care in an outpatient diabetes clinic experienced reduction in A1c at 6 months compared with essentially no change in the usual care group. Six of 8 secondary biomarkers were improved in the intervention group compared with usual care." [10]. "Clinical pharmacy involvement in hypertension management resulted in increased BP control. Loss of long-term control after discontinuation of clinical pharmacy management supports a change in care processes that prevent patients from being lost to follow-up." [13].

The application of pharmaceutical care principle in practice settings can improve clinical outcomes, reducing therapy errors and containment cost [14]. Deep knowledge in management theory and instruments, and practice application can give positive results in clinical outcomes and also in reducing therapy errors and cost containment [15].

Priority area to cover and instruments

Costs involved in drug therapy, due to therapy errors, in drugs and medical devices logistics, Cost avoided in improving clinical outcomes (clinical pharmacist in stabile way in medical team)

Classic economical assessment and managerial instrument useful for clinical pharmacist

Principle of pharmaco-healthcare economics, business administration, Strategic management cost analysis (cost-benefit, cost efficacy, cost effectiveness, analytical way), budget impact and control, rational resource allocation, benchmarking.

Approach models

Systematic, or by project, team or task force models (high expensive or high budget impact therapy). Knowledge and Change management, HR management, communications strategy, conflict management. MBO, project management, time management, Total quality management (Problem solving, lateral thinking, SWOT analysis) ICT management (software and hardware), professional social media Process organization by function, gerarchic, matrix). Risk assessment, Total quality management, customer satisfaction data collection systems and analysis, documentation activity (access to medical patient data).

Specifically oriented pharmacy service instrument

Medication cost management (drugs, medical devices, *in vitro* diagnostics and other).

Clinical pharmacy instruments

Evidence based criteria, dose unit systems (example to reduce waste), automatized robots, informatics drugs prescription systems. ward clinical pharmacy service with advanced training in cost management, Sterile unit pharmacy drug therapy monitoring, ADR monitoring, Drugs interactions, Patients Drug and medical history TDM-pharmacokinetics, toxicology, medical laboratory data, imaging data (monitoring drug therapy) drug day (ex to reduce waste), IV OS switch (to reduce cost), IV waste reduction drug rotation (expiration day first in-first out), check list use (emergency). Committee participation (ethical and other as infectious disease, clinical risk, nutritional team) continuous medical updating activity, Lifelong learning clinical pharmacy procedure and protocols following rational drug use policy (antimicrobials, oncologic, MABS, antiviral, haemo derivate, expensive medical devices and other), antiseptic rotation, sterile procedure, isolation, vaccines, antimicrobial prophylaxis and other risk management strategy, Medication use safety, coaching activity to other professional healthcare and students Pharmaceutical care management, and Ward clinical pharmacy service assessment patient need care plan (modify or new interventions, change strategy requested) patient information sharing in medical equip follow up activity documenting activity Pharmaceutical chemistry, Structure activity relationship, clinical pharmacology, toxicology knowledge Classic and innovative drugs Epidemiology, etiology m, pathology , statistics, clinical studies clinical chemistry, molecular biology knowledge, Imaging-nuclear medicine Clinical cases, clinical and diagnostics patients data. Clinical audit antimicrobial stewardship, MDR management Medication therapy review MTM Therapy monitoring, compliance evaluation, Patient Counsuelling Preventive measure (isolation, washing hand, sterile gloves and other).

Clinical Rotations skills in clinical and surgery wards: Onco hematology, Nephrology and dialysis, gastroenterology, cardiology, neurology, pulmonary med. Critical care Psychiatric pharmacy Care, Metabolic disease and pharmacy Care, Pain management, Pediatric and geriatric, long term care, Gynecology, pregnancy and obstetrics pharmacy Care, ambulatory care and other.

High costs or critical drug and medical devices class management

Haemoderivates, antimicrobials, oncologic, biologic drugs, antidiabetics, Generics, bio similar drugs, Nutrition support, Medical devices and diagnostics *in vitro*, antiseptics and Disinfectants, contrast agents, radio diagnostics, Medicinal gas and other.

Administrative rules

Generic Drug intensive use, bio similar drug budgeting, formulary management, drug restriction policy, Regulatory affairs, administrative law Ethical committee rules, infectious disease committee.

Appropriateness, regulatory rules (central reimbursement classification, administrative prescribing limitation) centralized buying strategy, centralized logistic Legal implications management (therapy errors and insurance policy). Observing the management science we can find classic discipline to be applied by clinical pharmacist practitioner.

- Business administration (business plan, budget control, Financier patrimonial, technical and human resource, accounting activity, business management, costs analysis: fixed, variable, direct and non-direct, high costs diseconomy management).
- Project management (scope, costs, quality, time, resource, constraints, risks, monitoring).
- Knowledge management, (learning organization) Cook and J.S. Brown Bridging epistemologies explicit and tacit knowledge, Know how, Formal and non-formal communication.
- ICT management: new professional social media, communication strategy.
- Strategic management Goals, prioritizing, Mission vision governance, strategy and tactics, planning, swot analysis, make or buy, benchmarking problem solving lateral thinking, creativity, Reengineering core competences, outsourcing, competitive comparing strategy, core competencies, Scenario and Contingency Planning, strategy alliance, supply chain management, acquisitions (Outsourcing, make or buy, long term, medium, short term strategy).
- Change management (in public and private administration) burocracy administration, process business reengineering.
- Operative *Management line and staff, Gerarchic, functions, matrix systems, Performance analysis.*

Lean production input output, Planned or not planned decision, decision making systems. Ambient rumors, not sayed reality

MBO, pareto analysis, Goal setting, General management can use interference in formal, key performance indicators, organization.

- Time management (the to do list, The Eisenhower Method, delegate, Prioritize activity).
- HR management and governance coaching conflict management, team working ability, team leadership, cooperation, Team leadership, proactivity, empowerment, Team: formal and informal.

Staffing: develop human resource, Formal and non-formal chief (in some cases workers listen real expert eve in different from official chief), Human resource evaluation: knowledge, competence, motivation, HR Selection, evaluation, salary policy, administration, reward policy, penalize measure, interpersonal links formal or not formal, Butler Waldroop 4 dimensions of relational work influence, interpersonal facilitation, relational creativity, team leadership.

- Healthcare management.
- Communication management.
- Total quality management, PDCA cycle, kaizen, Kayrio, Muda, Just in time, diagnostic (procedure). Statistical performance analysis.
- Risk management (healthcare) errors, near miss event, risk assessment, incident reporting, root causes analysis, FMECA customer relationship, Market analysis Financial and Strategic marketing, Customer satisfaction (targeting, statistical analysis, segmentation).

Technology using techniques from mathematical modeling, statistical analysis, optimization, operations research arrives at optimal or better solutions to complex decision-making problems. (Instrument currently used in industrial engineering, operative management, and organization science was Originating in military field since before World War II)Operational researchers must determine which techniques is the most appropriate instrument for improvement decision making strategy under constraints, time limits or economical resource). Skills, knowledge added with practical experience.

Psychological and behavior skills

Problem solving, lateral thinking, chunking problems, focus on solution, creativity, brainstorming, open mind, collaborative working group (team, central pharmacy, hospital management).

Flexibility, to say no ability, Decision making in all situation, independence.

Leadership style: directive, supportive, participative, achievement oriented (HOUSE).

Stress management (mindfulness, resilience and other) coping strategy change strategy if not results.

Rethinking problems, searching help, take time ability to give response, communication skills, mental training, and no extreme thinking, lose comfort zone, Perseverance, resilience, self-motivation, self-control, critical thinking, and zero thinking ability.

Learning by errors, lifelong learning attitude, Serenity, assertively, positive vision.

Leadership, cooperation, Coaching, mental training, resistance to change.

Four strategic types: defender, prospector, analyzer, reactor (Miles, Snow).

Conclusion

As indicated in literature analyzed in this work there is the need to improve healthcare systems introducing classic management instruments starting from clinical pharmacist university course. This entire management instrument must be added to EBM criteria in pharmaceutical care working activities [16-19].

The clinical pharmacist presence in stabile way in medical team give general positive effects in clinical outcomes, cost containment and reducing therapy errors. Some management theory is useful, and must to be post under right light in order to efficiently manage the system.

- Business administration and management knowledge (currently offered in dedicated Master or other school after postgraduate degree but we think that introduction of an independent discipline of business administration principle and management during university period can give a more expertise useful to have a more effectiveness systems).
- New ICT instruments can give relevant contribute in management systems and in the same way Professional social media can be considered today an useful tool to meet between researcher and healthcare professional and a bases for a new kind of biomedical database (In professional social media we can find researcher curriculum, professional interest and other relevant information and an efficient systems to meet themselves) (Network economy KELLY), sharing economy [20-22].
- Psychological behavior skills for team working.

Theory and practical applications added to be added to the classic clinical pharmacy programs.

We submit to the scientific community the request to introduce this management instruments in current clinical pharmacist post graduated course at the same time we ask to public institution to strongly apply this new approach.

References

1. Luisetto M, Sahu R (2015) Clinical Pharmaceutical Care: A New Management Health Care Discipline in 2016 UK Journal of Pharmaceutical and Biosciences 4: 63-64.
2. Zlatko N, Vojko P, Marina D (2015) Current and future use of management tools. Ekonomika a management 18: 6: 3-24.
3. Osman S, Izet M (2012) Management Knowledge and Skills Required in the Health Care System of the Federation Bosnia and Herzegovina. Mater Socio medica 24: 106-111.
4. Davis K, Stremikis K (2008) Measuring and improving health system performance: what can healthcare management educators do? J Health Adm Educ 25: 5-15.
5. Meseret DG, Catherine EW, Mary KT (2007) Mapping the literature of health care management J Med Libr Assoc 95: e58-e65.
6. Garman AN, McAlearney AS, Harrison MI, Song PH, McHugh M (2011) High-performance work systems in health care management, part 1: development of an evidence-informed model. Health Care Manage Rev 36: 201-213.
7. Heather AS, James DM, Tracy AJ (2009) Journal Management System Exploring Strategies for Deploying Knowledge Management Tools and Technologies 6: 3-24.
8. Al-Shaqha WM, Zairi M (2001) Pharmaceutical care management: a modern approach to providing seamless and integrated health care. Int J Health Care Qual Assur Inc Leadersh Health Serv 14: 282-301.
9. Bao L, Wang Y, Shang T, Ren X, Ma R (2013) A novel clinical pharmacy management system in improving the rational drug use in department of general surgery. Indian J Pharm Sci 75: 11-5.
10. Luisetto M, Hemmati J, Nili-Ahmadabadi B, Cabianca L, Ibne Mokbul M, et al. (2016) Professional Social Media as an Advanced Instrument to Connect Between Researchers & Healthcare Professionals. An Innovative Model for a New Scientific Social Network, Clinicians Teamwork 1: 9-14.
11. Jarab AS, Alqudah SG, Mukattash TL, Shattat G, Al-Qirim TJ (2012) Randomized controlled trial of clinical pharmacy management of patients with type 2 diabetes in an outpatient diabetes clinic in Jordan. Manag Care Pharm 18: 516-26.
12. Kicklighter CE, Nelson KM, Humphries TL, Delate T (2006) An evaluation of a clinical pharmacy-directed intervention on blood pressure control. Pharm Pract (Granada) 4: 110-116.
13. Luisetto M, Francesca C, Giovanni B, Behzad NA (2015) Pharmacist Cognitive Service and Pharmaceutical Care: Today and Tomorrow Outlook UK Journal of Pharmaceutical and Biosciences 3: 67-72.
14. Osama MA, Amer MA (2014) Evidence-based pharmaceutical care: The next chapter in pharmacy practice. SaudiPharmaceutical Journal.
15. Mauro L, Luca C (2016) Psychological and Behavior Skills for Ph. Care Practice in Medical Team 2016. Human Journals Research Article international journal of pharmacy and pharmaceutical research 5: 1-4.
16. Bao Y, Wang T, Shang, Ren X, Ma R (2013) A Novel Clinical Pharmacy Management System in Improving the Rational Drug Use in Department of General Surgery. Indian J Pharm Sci 75: 11-15.
17. Isetts BJ, Schondelmeyer SW, Artz MB, Lenarz LA, Heaton AH, et al. (2008) Clinical and economic outcomes of medication therapy management services: the Minnesota experience. J Am Pharm Assoc 2003 48: 203-211.
18. Project Management Institute (2004) A Guide to the Project Management Body of Knowledge, (5thedn).
19. Bond CA, Raehl CL (2007) Clinical pharmacy service, pharmacy staffing, and hospital mortality rates. Pharmacotherapy 27: 481-93.
20. http://www.slideshare.net/MLuisettoWebsiteFARM/pharmaceutical-care-management-2015-dr-mauro-luisetto
21. Lyra DP, Rocha CE, Abriata JP, Gimenes FR, Gonzalez MM, et al. (2007) Influence of Pharmaceutical Care intervention and communication skills on the improvement of pharmacotherapeutic outcomes with elderly Brazilian outpatients. Patient Educ Couns 68: 186-192.
22. Luisetto M, Nili-Ahmadabadi B, Cabianca L, Ibne Mokbul M (2016) Steps and Impacts of Pharmaceutical Care and Clinical Pharmacy Development on Clinical Outcomes 2016: A Historical Analysis Compared with Results, Clinicians Teamwork 1: 4-8.

Measuring Supply Chain Coordination in Milk and Dairy Industries: A Confirmatory Factor Model

Habtamu Lemma*

Punjabi University, Business Management, Punjabi University, Patiala, Punjab 147002, India

Abstract

Coordination within the supply chain is a strategic weapon to the problem that occurs due to lack of supply chain coordination. Since supply chain consists of various organizations, it can satisfy customers' needs, only when the whole of its partners becomes coordinated. To cope up and endure in a business environment where competition is high, firms should decrease the flow of interruption within upstream and downstream supply chain activities. This kind of endurance in such business environment can only be achieved by means of organized supply chain coordination. In this paper, we investigated empirically the major factors affecting supply chain coordination in milk and dairy industries. Based on an extensive literature review, the study created 15 measured variables and offered a comprehensive model to examine four key constructs. The data were collected from 330 milk suppliers, processors, and retailers in the central part of Ethiopia and the result were validated using rigorous statistical techniques. To approach this, an exploratory factor analysis (EFA) has been applied to classify factors for major constructs. And also, Structural Equation Modeling (SEM) was employed to assess the convergent validity through Confirmatory Factor Analysis (CFA) using AMOS version 4.

Keywords: Coordination; Supply chain management; Dairy industries; Structural equation modeling

Introduction

As it is clearly seen in the business environment nowadays, effective supply chain management seems to be considered as a crucial concern that has to be dealt with in global business context [1]. In the local activities of traditional business, those involving in supply chain have been doing such activities independently. But at present, it is not advised to perform business independently considering the ever growth of the competitive market [2]. Consequently, more developed and well-organized supply chain coordination is ideal for consistent success and profitability of any business. The more convincing reason for such claim is that the ever increasing competition that is constantly influenced by business globalization, product diversity and technological advancement motivated independent firms to work in unity in a supply chain that allows them to gain mutual benefits [3]. In today's business, competition is among integrated supply chains instead of individual organizations. Hence, a supply chain shall be well coordinated and that will play a huge role in making supply chain attainable to customer demands [4].

Coordination of different business activities among units become vital as organizations pay much attention to their core activities. Thus, their fruitfulness constantly relies on their capacity to coordinate their internal and external activities in the value chain outside their own boundaries [5]. The need for coordination is evident in supply chains, as companies forming a supply chain are dependent on the performance of other organizations. Supply chain coordination is achieved when a decision maker, acting rationally, makes decisions that are efficient for the supply chain as a whole [6].

Since a supply chain consists of various organizations, it can satisfy customers' needs, only when the whole of its partners become integrated and coordinated [1]. In this way, supply chain drivers ought to jointly create value and improve supply chain performance effectively and efficiently [7]. Even if the objectives and interests of different supply chain members are varied, the coordination among them becomes undeniably crucial to determine the supply chain performance as a whole [8].

In trying to elaborate the attributes of coordination, we can say that Coordination in a supply chain involves putting the existing interdependencies in order [9]. Supply chain coordination also involves cooperation between firms a sharing of important information with each other in the process of developing, producing and distributing goods and services to end marketplaces. Coordination can also be defined as structuring the efforts of a couple or more of supply chain drivers for the outcome of achieving effectiveness and be aware of each other's tasks while working independently to achieve their actual set of goals [8]. However, lack of coordination occurs in the supply chain, when each stage has incomplete information about the flow of products, information and, funds. Such causes will reduce the supply chain performance as a whole. Thus, supply chain coordination becomes vital to achieving the all level consensus, in which different members along a supply chain can respond to market requirements in proper ways [8,10]. With regard to Ethiopian dairy industries, the concept as well as the implementation of well coordinated and supervised product supply chain management is late developed. Although it applies to industry and agriculture lead economies, the need for institutionalized supply chain coordination is indispensable. Why, because the success of such initiative, among other things, depends on the level of supply chain coordination.

The objective of this study is to identify the major determinants of supply chain coordination in milk and dairy industry. It is argued that, to sustain in competitive business environment, firms must reduce the flow of interruption within upstream and downstream supply chain process. Here, the question is how to achieve the strategic fit in the supply chain, so that the tasks of each supply chain stage can be completed in a manner consistent with a mutual goal. The reason is that firms' supply chain profitability depends on how well all supply chain members work together. Thus, this paper aims at identifying

***Corresponding author:** Habtamu Lemma, Punjabi University, Business Management, Punjabi University Patiala, Punjab 147002, India
E-mail: habtamuregassa@rocketmail.com

mechanisms for milk and dairy industries to better coordinate their product, information, and financial flow to improve the match between upstream and downstream phases of their supply chains. The studies entirely focus on supply chain coordination among supplier, processors and retailers in milk and dairy industries. The paper is organized as follows: The next section reviews prior literature on the major determinants of supply chain coordination. A research frame work developed from the literature is presented in the succeeding section. Then, the research methodology used in conducting the study is described. After that, factor analysis and confirmatory model used in data analysis is presented. Finally, Concluding remarks are explained in the last section.

Quantity flexibility

Is one of the most widely discussed forms of non-price coordination. Quantity flexibilities allow the buyer to get a different quantity than the earlier estimate [11,12] and this can be provided in various ways, such as minimum purchase quantity agreement [13], backup agreements that allow a customer to purchase higher quantities than initial amounts they ordered [14]. Quantity flexibility also considered as a major form of supply chain agreement [15].

Some popular form of supply chain contracts in the literature includes *quantity discount* and flexibility [16,17]. Also suggested different form of coordination systems for instance price changes and quantity discounts [18]. In addition, *Flexibility, solidarity, mutual benefit, harmonization of conflict,* self-control in the use of power, a kind of reputation, and information sharing are some of the norms often discussed in the coordination Zenger [19-28]. These determinants play a key role in coordinating supply chains through team-based approaches.

It is true that there are various obstacles that hinder effective coordination in a supply chain. Behavioral obstacle, quantity discounts and price fluctuations: are among the major factors that can adversely affect supply chain coordination [10,29]. On the other way, coordination in each stage of the supply can be effective during cross-functional integration. Hence, Successful supply chain coordination requires cross-functional integration in various supply chain activities [30].

Information sharing: Coordination between different stages of supply is very important for success of the global business optimization, and it is only achieved if supply chain members share their information unambiguously. Previously, the value of information sharing within a supply chain has been extensively analyzed by different scholars. These studies have been used a simulation to assess the value of information sharing in the supply chain coordination [31-36].

Simatupang and Sridharan had conducted research on the knowledge of coordination for supply chain integration [37]. In their study, four different forms of coordination has been depicted namely: logistics synchronization, information sharing, incentive alignment, and collective learning. These coordination methods are imperative to help supply chain members and enhance sustainable supply chain profitability.

Sahin and Robinson identified centralized decision-making and decentralized decision making for better-utilizing supply chain coordination [38]. As opposed to centralized decision, decentralization decision-making is the best way for better supply chain coordination as well as for prompt customer order fulfillment. Coordination mechanisms can be also classified into price and non-price coordination. Price coordination includes quantity discount and non -price coordination incorporates quantity forcing, quantity flexibility, and service differentiation [14,15]. Haghighat suggested quantity discount as a method for coordinating the order quantity between a retailer and supplier. But the motivation for giving quantity discounts might be either based on price discrimination or order quantities. On the other way, the alliance also the way of supply chain coordination in which both buyers and sellers can be benefited by providing value to each others. According to Rice and Ronchi [39], if there is alliance in the supply chain, business partners can share some mutual interest, exchange value through buyer-seller activities, and also perform some coordination mechanisms.

Xu and Beamon had conducted research on Supply Chain Coordination and Cooperation Mechanisms. They suggested that Coordination within a supply chain is a strategic weapon to the problems that occurs from inter-organizational dependencies within the chain. Whang had also conducted research on taxonomy of coordination and he suggested cross-functional and inter-organizational team as different level of coordination mechanisms [40]. Collaboration is a recent trend in supply chain management that focuses on joint planning, coordination, and process integration between suppliers, customers and other partners in a supply chain [41]. Walter et al. observed that high performing collaboration relationship requires not only a focus on the direct value creating or buyer-supplier function but also an equal focus on the indirect relationship building and sustaining function [42]. The study conducted by [43] Christopher, also shows that companies are moving towards collaborative relationship in an attempt to make the supply chains more competitive (Figure 1). A research frame work of supply chain coordination

Methodology

Research design and scale development

The methodology of the paper is quantitative in nature. A survey research design was used to collect data for the scale development. Items were developed based on extensive literature review and consulting with supply chain professionals. The items were also measured by conducting a pilot test on some other milk industries and we have strongly discussed with supply chain practitioners and with those people who have engaged themselves in milk processing.

Study area and population

The survey would be conducted mainly on the supply of milk to the inhabitants of Addis Ababa from the nearby rural districts. The study concentrated on suppliers, local milk processing industries, and retailers. To this conclusion, for methodological reasons-hence in line with the objectives, the general population of this study includes all actors in the milk industry along the chain of market. Moreover, the target population of the study would be included milk producers, processors and retail markets at various stages along the supply chain.

Sampling and data collection

The sample was drawn from suppliers, processors and retailers in bishoftu, selale, and Addis Ababa cities, Ethiopia. The data collection instrument used was a questionnaire which was administered to the total sample size of 375 respondents. Of the 375 distributed items, 15 were returned due to an unwillingness of respondents. From the sample size of 360, 342 were received, resulting in a response rate of 95%. A total of 8 questionnaires was discarded because of incomplete data. Therefore, only 330 respondents were considered as valid and the result represented an accurate response rate of 91.6%. Out of 330 respondents, the study included 225 (68%) milk suppliers, 75(23%) retailers and 30(9%) employees from 3 major milk processing plants (shola milk, mama and family dairy). A seven-point Likert scale with end points of "strongly disagree" and "strongly agree" was applied to measure the items. To approach this, purposive and stratified sampling technique has been employed.

Reliability analysis

The Cronbach's alpha was conducted to evaluate the reliability of each scale. Alpha values over 0.7 indicate that all scales can be regarded as reliable. As can be seen from Table 1, Cronbach's alpha value of coordination is 0.807 and the scale alpha values of the four factors were above the cutoff value, ranging from 0.963 to 0.979. These results imply that the theoretical constructs are good indicators of the model fit. Thus, we can state that the instrument is acceptable and used to measure 15 coordination variables.

Scale refinement

For each of the item scales, factor analysis was applied to reduce the total number of items in manageable factor. A principal component analysis is applied to extract factors with an eigenvalue greater than 1. Varimax rotation is employed to facilitate interpretation of the factor matrix. KMO (Kaiser-Meyer-Olkin) measure of sampling adequacy also examined to validate factor analysis. The KMO value was estimated around 0.819 which indicates sampling adequacy. The factor loading indicates four distinct constructs: non-price coordination (F1), relationship (F2), price coordination (F3), product development decision (F4) (Table 2).

Coordination Indicators	Theoretical background
harmonization of conflict	[19-24,26-28]
Alliance	[10]
quantity flexibility	[11-14,45]
behavioral obstacle	[10,29]
decentralized decision	[38,42]
Information sharing	[31-36,43]
Mutual benefit	[19-28]

Table 1: A brief description of reviewed papers on supply chain coordination indicators.

As we have seen in the above table, item-to-total correlation range 0.996 to 0.856 and the communality ranges above 0.5. The mean score value is 79.91 with 25.183 variance and 5.018 Std Deviation. And also, the total scale reliability alpha is 0.808, which is greater than 0.6 and confirmed reliability of the questionnaire (Table 3).

Non price coordination (F1): This factor covers five key coordination indicators (KCI). These are harmonization of conflict, alliance, behavioral obstacles, and quantity flexibility and decentralization decision. The factor loading ranges from 0.968 to 0.899 and the Cronbach's's alpha value is 0.978. Item- to- total correlation ranges from 0.873 to 0.975. Here, 92.472% of the division is explained and it covers 4.642 of the Eigenvalues.

Relationship (F2): The relationship factor covers four KCI. These are *information sharing, mutual benefit, incentives, collaboration relationship*, and *quantity discount*. The factor loading ranges from 0.948 to 0.903 and the Cronbach's's alpha value is 0.975. Item- to- total correlation ranges from 0.970 to 0.884. Here, 93.19% of the variance is explained and it covers 3.728 of the Eigenvalues.

Price coordination (F3): Three measured variables are identified in *price coordination* factor. These are quantity discount, organizational interdependencies, and price fluctuation. The factor loading ranges from 0.947 to 0.885 and the Cronbach's alpha value is 0.963. Item- to- total correlation ranges from 0.935 to 0.908. Here, 93.179% of the variance is explained and it covers 2.796 of the Eigen values.

Product development decision (F4): This factor covers three KCI. These are cross functional team, new product development, and trust. The factor loading ranges from 0.857 to 0.669 and the Cronbach's alpha value is 0.737. Corrected Item- to- total correlation ranges from 0.954 to 0.877. Here, 96.828% of the variance is explained and it covers 1.937 of the Eigen values.

Variables	Mean	S.Deviation	Corrected item-total correlation	Alpha if item delated	communality	
					Initial	Extracted
Harmonization of conflict	5.4	0.601	0.965	0.776	1	0.955
Quantity flexibility	5.41	0.624	0.996	0.777	1	0.945
Alliance	5.38	0.608	0.915	0.778	1	0.912
behavioral obstacle	5.41	0.623	0.975	0.776	1	0.949
Decentralized decision	5.37	0.681	0.873	0.782	1	0.828
Information sharing	5.28	0.69	0.97	0.789	1	0.97
Mutual benefit	5.26	0.709	0.938	0.791	1	0.933
Collaboration	5.24	0.724	0.884	0.795	1	0.87
Incentives	5.27	0.696	0.959	0.788	1	0.958
Quantity discount	5.25	0.503	0.947	0.807	1	0.955
Organizational interdependence	5.25	0.513	0.934	0.808	1	0.944
Price fluctuation	5.27	0.502	0.885	0.809	1	0.898
Cross functional team	5.37	0.762	0.937	0.818	1	0.969
New product development	5.39	0.749	0.937	0.816	1	0.968
trust	5.35	0.632	0.856	0.781	1	0.784

Scale Statistics :
Mean=79.91, Variance,25.183, Std. Deviation=5.018
No. of Variables =15, No. of cases =330,
Cronbach's alpha = 0.807

Table 2: Mean, SD, Corrected item-to-total correlation and Communality for key Coordination indicators.

		Factors			
No.	Variables	Non price coordination (F1)	Relationship (F2)	Price coordination (F3)	Product development decision (F4)
1	Harmonization conflict	0.968			
2	Behavioral obstacle	0.964			
3	Quantity flexibility	0.961			
4	Alliance	0.946			
5	Decentralized decision	0.899			
6	Information Sharing		0.948		
7	Mutual benefit		0.938		
8	Incentives		0.935		
9	Collaboration		0.903		
10	Quantity discount			0.935	
11	Organizational interdependence			0.924	
12	Price fluctuation			0.908	
13	Cross functional team				0.954
14	New product development				0.949
15	Trust				0.877
	Cronbach's alpha	**0.979**	**0.975**	**0.963**	**0.967**
	Egin value	4.642	3.728	2.796	1.937
	Percentage variance	92.472	93.19	93.179	96.828
	KMO (Kaiser-Meyer-Olkin) measure of sampling adequacy=0.819 Bartlett's Test of Sphericity (Chi-Square= 7829.503, Df=105, Sig = 0.00), mean=79.91				

Table 3: Factor analysis result for key co-ordination indicators.

Correlation between constructs and indicators								
Non price coordination	1							
Information and r/ship	0.504	1						
Price coordination	0.498	0.389	1					
Product development	-0.004	0.188	-0.08	1				
Summated 1	0.913	0.233	0.279	-0.018	1			
Summated 2	0.256	0.926	0.145	0.102	0	1		
Summated 3	0.251	0.228	0.922	-0.036	-0.009	0	1	
Summated 4	-0.004	0.118	-0.069	0.983	0	0	0	1

* Correlation is significant at the 0.01 level (2-tailed)

Table 4: Correlation.

The correlations between constructs and indicators (Table 4) show acceptable discriminant validity, as correlations between constructs (non-price coordination, relationship, price coordination and product development decision) and their defining indicators (summated1, 2, 3, and 4) are highly significant while correlations between indicators and the remaining constructs are low and insignificant.

Confirmatory factor analysis result

Confirmatory factor analysis is appropriate to analyze how well the measured variables/items clearly represent the latent construct [44]. In such instance, the confirmatory model loadings are illustrated with standardized and unstandardized results (Figures 1 and 2). This confirmatory model was estimated by maximum likelihood (ML) and the model fit results are discussed. The overall fit of the models was examined by various indices and the results for standardized and unstandardized model were x^2 =161.809, *Df*, 84, *P-value* =0.000

RMR (root mean square residual)

Lower RMR represent a better fit, but higher value indicates worse fits [44]. The RMR estimates for the present study was 0.008, meaning a reasonable fit.

RMSEA (root mean square error of approximation)

Is useful to adjust the complexity of models and to manage the tendency of the chi- square goodness of fit [44,45]. In this field, the RMSEA estimate is 0.047. GFI (goodness of fit index): the acceptable range of GFI value is between 0 to1 and the higher value indicates the better fit [45]. The GFI estimate for the current study is 0.943, which represent a good indicator of model fit.

NFI (normal fit index): ranges between 0 to 1 and a model approaching 1 represent the perfect fit [44]. In this study, the NFI value is 0.977, which is a significant and good indicator of model fit.

CFI (comparative fit index)

Is also widely used indices which help to compare the proposed model with baseline model and model values above 0.90 represents a good indicator of model fit [45]. In the present study, CFI value represents 0.989; this is another indicator of model fit (Figure 2).

Standardized confirmatory model

As indicated on the standardized confirmatory model (Figure 3), the four major constructs are non-price coordination, relationship, price coordination and product development decision. These factors are identified in the following section briefly;

Non price coordination: This construct consists of 5 (five) measured variables such as alliance (0.99), decentralized decision (0.98),

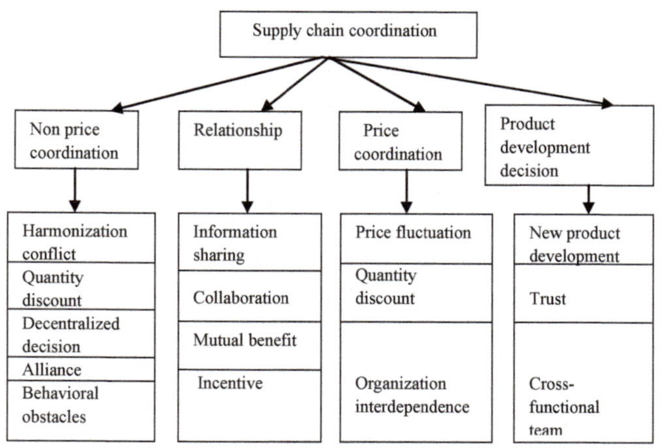

Figure 1: A research frame work of supply chain coordination.

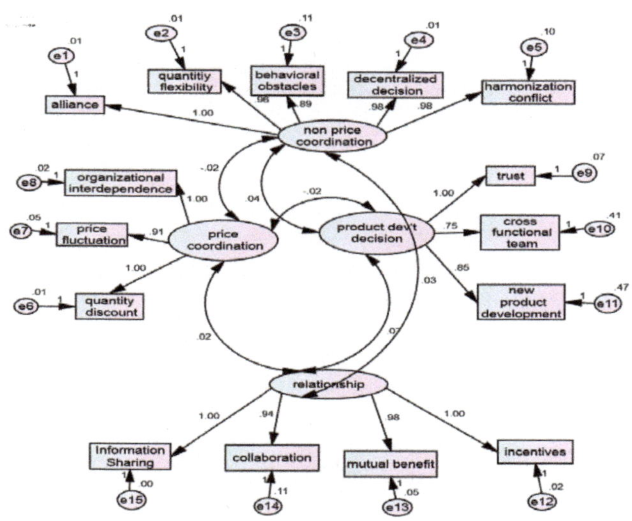

Figure 2: Confirmatory model: Unstandardized Result.

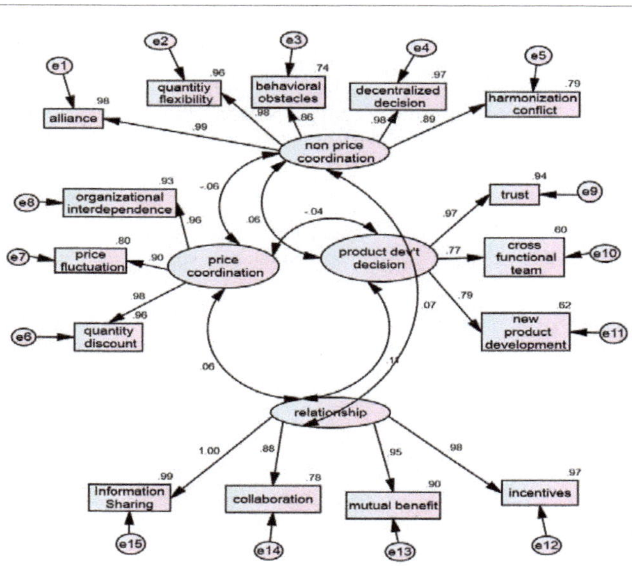

Figure 3: Confirmatory model: Standardized Result.

harmonization conflict (0.89), quantity flexibility (0.98) and behavioral obstacles (0.86). All the loading points were calculated within the range 0.86 to 0.99. This reveals that alliance, decentralized decision, and quantity flexibility play a key part for the betterment of supply chain coordination among firms 'procurement, production and distribution systems. These determinants also help to coordinate raw milk producers, processors, and retailers through team-based approaches. Hence, in supply chain coordination, suppliers and processors must have a smooth relationship with distributors/retailers that compete not only in monetary value, but also in non-price coordination manner.

Relationship: Here, the loading point of measured variables ranges from 0.88 to 1.00. In this case information sharing (1.00), incentives (0.98) and mutual benefit (0.95) are the major determinants of relationship coordination. The existence of collaboration (0.88) among producers, processors and retailers will also helpful for better supply chain coordination.

As we know that, nowadays, it is hard to do business independently in which there exist many competitors. Thus, well-organized supply chain coordination is more desirable for sustainable business profitable. In this regard, long term supply chain relationship is one of the keys to success.

Coordination: This section helps us to better understanding of financial flows within the supply chain stages through price coordination mechanism. As we have found out in the confirmatory model, the factor loading point of the quantity discount and organizational interdependencies were 0.98 and 0.96, respectively. On the other way, price fluctuation represents 0.90, meaning that all measured variables have a significant contribution to non-price coordination. In the case of milk and dairy supply chain, the volume of milk supply can be affected by seasonality of demand, shortages of supply and some other environmental elements. It is too true that price fluctuation and quantity discounts are among the major factors that can adversely affect supply chain coordination as a whole. Thus, firms' supply chain strategies should be supported by financial resource and this will create economic link and organizational interdependence between suppliers and local milk processing industries (Figure 3).

Product development decision

Here, 3 measured variables are explained under product development decision construct. As depicted in the model, the overall loading for each item range between 0.94 to 0.60 and the loading of trust was set on 0.94 and new product development as well as cross functional team explained about 0.62 and 0.60, respectively. New product development decision, trust and cross functional team activities need to be coordinated with supply chain management in a strategic level so that less competitiveness in the supply chain will be decrease (Table 5).

Concluding Remarks

In previous decades the main and crucial stages of the supply chain such as procurement, production and distribution seem to have been dominantly managed independently. But the accessibility of excess inventories, intense competition, and market globalization were forcing firms to enhance their supply chain capabilities that can promptly respond to consumer preferences [3]. To cope up and endure in a business environment where competition is high, firms should decrease the flow of interruption within upstream and downstream supply chain activities. This kind of endurance in such a business environment can only be achieved by means of organized supply chain coordination. Supply chain coordination practice attracts most firms, mainly those operating businesses independently. It is

		Fit indices for the Measurement Model	
Indices	Unstandardized Result	Standardized Result	Recommended Values
X^2	161.809	146.029	
Df	84	84	
X^2/df	1.92	1.73	<3.0
P- value	0.000	0.000	
RMR	0.008	0.008	<0.10
GFI	0.943	0.948	>0.90
AGFI	0.919	0.926	
NFI	0.977	0.978	
RFI	0.972	0.972	
IFI	0.989	0.990	
TLI	0.986	0.998	Values that approach to 1
CFI	0.989	0.990	>0.90
RMSEA	0.047	0.047	Between 0.03 and 0.08
AIC	233.809	218.029	< saturated and independence models
AIC saturated model	240	240	< saturated and independence models
AIC independent model	7139.849	6619.771	

Table 5: Model fit summary.

something that every firm needs for managing interdependent logistics activities in order to mitigate demand variability and unnecessary inventories. Giving consideration to these obvious reasons, this study was undertaken to identify the key determinants of coordination indicators in milk and dairy industries of Ethiopia. The study created 15 measured variables and offered a comprehensive model for examining supply chain coordination. Based on a scrutinized literature review, it conceptualized supply chain coordination as a major construct and 4 other latent constructs such as non-price coordination, relationship, price coordination, and product development decision. The instrument was tested using exploratory factor analysis (EFA) and confirmatory factor analysis (CFA), resulting good validity and scale reliability.

The first most important group of Key Coordination Indicators (KCI) categorized under *non-price coordination* metrics. This factor consists of 5 Key coordination variables. The other nodal point is the *relationship* construct. Supply chain relationships also play a pivotal role to create integration among each the supply chain stages. This relationship construct covered 4 Key coordination indicators, namely *Information Sharing*, collaboration, *mutual benefit, and incentive*. On the other way, we can see price coordination and this construct covered 3 key measured variables, namely *organizational interdependence, price fluctuation, and quantity discount*. Here, two measured variables relating to price coordination, such as, *sales promotion* and *price stability* were deleted from the final instrument due to unrealistic result. Therefore, price coordination construct did not include sales promotion and price stability variables. But further research shall be extended these variables by examining in a different perspective. In addition, the Product development decision presents the last nodal point for measuring SC coordination in dairy industries. *Trust, new product development*, and *cross-functional teams* were the major measured variables in product decision matrix. These outcomes can vitally be used in evaluating the major roles of milk processing industries and in identifying the gap in the problem area. This clearly indicates that the relative importance of each measured variable for improvement of supply chain coordination and it helps as imperative rules for sustainable supply chain profitability. The results can also be used as a strategic weapon to distinguish the main problem areas in which each and every change in betterment are required so that companies can easily implement their supply chain strategies in association with their business partners.

Competing Interests

The authors declared that they have no competing interests

Authors' Contributions

Habtamu. R, contributed to all data, modeling, and drafting the manuscript. Rajwinder. S also contributed to modeling and editing the manuscript. All authors have read and approved the final manuscript

Acknowledgements

The authors would like to thank Dr. Navjot Kaur, Professor in the school of management studies, Punjabi University Patiala for her suggestion and remarks. The authors would also grateful for Dr. Assegid Demissie, Associate Professor, Department of Management, University of Gonder, Ethiopia and anonymous reviewers for their valuable comments to improve the quality of the paper

References

1. Haghighat F (2008) The Impact of Information Technology on Coordination Mechanisms of Supply Chain.World Applied Sciences Journal 3: 74-81
2. Xu L, Beamon B (2006) Supply chain coordination and cooperation mechanisms: An attribute-based approach. The Journal of Supply Chain Management 42: 4-12.
3. Thomas D, Griffin P (1996) coordinated supply chain management. European journal of operational research 9: 1-15.
4. Singh RK (2011) Developing the framework for coordination in supply chain of SMEs. Business Process Management Journal 17: 619- 638.
5. Mohammad JSJ, Shemshadi TA (2009) Theoretical and practical study of supply chain coordination. Journal of Business & Industrial Marketing 24: 131-142.
6. Gupta D, Weerawat W (2006) Supplier-manufacturer coordination in capacitated two-stage supply chains. European Journal of Operational Research 175: 67-89.
7. Lewis I, Talalayevsky A (2004) Improving the inter-organizational supply through optimization of information flows. The Journal of Enterprise Information Management 17: 229-237.
8. Ning C, Zhiming Z, Kin Man T, Keng PN (2008) How are supply chains coordinated?, Journal of Fashion Marketing and Management: An International Journal 12: 384-397.
9. Li Z, Kumar A, Lim YG (2002) Supply Chain Modeling a Coordination Approach. Integrated manufacturing Systems 13: 551-561.
10. Chopra S, Meindl P (2005) Supply chain management: strategy, planning, and operation 2nd edition, Pearson Prentice Hall, India
11. Lariviere MA (1999) Supply Chain Contracting and Coordination with Stochastic Demand. International series in operations research and management science 17: 233-268
12. Fugate BS, Mentzer JT, Stank TP (2010) Logistics Performance: Efficiency, Effectiveness, and Differentiation. Journal of Business Logistics 31: 43-61.
13. Bassok Y, Anupindi R (1997) Analysis of supply contracts with minimum commitment. IIE Transactions 29: 373-81.
14. Eppen G, Iyer A (1997) Backup Agreements in Fashion Buying-The Value of Upstream Flexibility. Management Science 43: 1469-1484.
15. Andy AT (1999) The Quantity Flexibility Contract and Supplier-Customer Incentives. Management Science 45: 1339-1358.

16. Lal R, Staeling R (1984) An approach for developing an optimal discount pricing policy. Management science 30: 1524-39.

17. Parlor M, Wang Q (1994) Discounting decisions in a supplier- buyer relationship under a linear buyer's demand. IIE Transactions 26: 34-41.

18. Sharafali M, Henry C (2000) Some models for understanding the cooperation between supplier and the buyer. Int J Prod Res 38: 3425-449.

19. Ravi SA, Gundlach GT (1999) Legal and Social Safeguards against opportunism in Exchange. Journal of Retailing 75: 107-124.

20. Carson, Stephen J, Timothy M, Devinney, Grahame RD, George J (1999) Understanding Institutional Design within Marketing Value Systems. Journal of Marketing 63: 115-130.

21. Rajiv PD, SchuL PL (1992) Conflict Resolution Processes in Contractual Channels of Distribution. Journal of Marketing 56: 38-55.

22. Gregory GT, Achrol RS, Mentzer JT (1995) The Structure of Commitment in Exchange. Journal of Marketing 59: 78-92.

23. Mark HB, Johnson SA (2000) Buyer-Supplier Contracts Versus Joint Ventures: Determinants and Consequences of Transaction Structure. Journal of Marketing Research 37: 1-15.

24. Sandy JD, Ganesan S (2000) Control Mechanisms and the Relationship Life Cycle: Implications for Safeguarding Specific Investments and Developing Commitment. Journal of Marketing Research 37: 227-245.

25. Jean JL (1999) Strategic Integration in Industrial Distribution Channels: Managing the Inter-firm Relationships as Strategic Asset. Journal of the Academy of Marketing Science 27: 4-19.

26. Lusch, Robert F, James RB (1996) Interdependency, Contracting, and Relational Behavior in Marketing Channels," Journal of Marketing 60: 19-39.

27. Maloni M, Benton WC (2000) Power Influences in the Supply Chain. Journal of Business Logistics 21: 49-73.

28. Laura P, Zenger T (2002) Do Formal Contracts and Relational Governance Function as Substitutes or Complements?. Strategic Management Journal 23: 707-725.

29. Himanshu S, Moharana JS, Murty S, Senapati K, Khuntia K (2012) Coordination, Collaboration and Integration for Supply Chain Management, International Journal of Inter science Management Review (IMR) 2:2-5.

30. Lambert DM, Cooper MC (2000) Issues in Supply Chain Management, Industrial Marketing Management 29: 65-83.

31. Towill DR, Naim NM, Wikner J (1992) Industrial dynamics simulation models in the design of supply Chains. International Journal of Physical Distribution and Logistics Management 22: 3-13.

32. Bourland K, Powell S, Pyke D (1996) Exploring timely demand information to reduce inventories, European Journal of Operational Research 44: 239-253.

33. Chen F (1998) Echelon reorder points, installation reorder points, and the value of centralized information. Management Science 44: 221-34.

34. Gavirneni S, Kapuscinski R, Tayur S (1999) Value of information in capacitated supply chains. Management Science 45: 16-24.

35. Dejonck H, Disney J, Lambrecht SM, Towill DR (2004) The Impact of Information Enrichment on the Bullwhip Effect in Supply Chains: A Control Theoretic Approach. European Journal of Operational Research, 153: 727-750.

36. Ferguson M, Ketzenberg ME (2006) Information sharing to improve retail product freshness of perishables, Production and Operations Management 15: 57-73.

37. Simatupang TM, Sridharan R (2002) The collaborative supply chain: a scheme and incentive alignment for information sharing. International Journal of Logistics Management 13: 15-30.

38. Sahin F, Robinson EP (2002) Flow coordination and information sharing in supply chains: review, implications, and directions for future research. Decision Sciences 33: 505-36.

39. Rice, James B. Jr and Ronchi Stefano (2002), Supply Chain Governance. Paris, Séminaire Condor, March 28.

40. Whang S (1995) Coordination in Operations: A Taxonomy. Journal of Operation Management 12: 413-422.

41. McLaren T, Head M, Yuan Y (2002) Supply chain collaboration alternatives: understanding the expected costs and benefits. Internet Research 12: 348-64.

42. Walter A, Ritter T, Gemünden HG (2001) Value Creation in Buyer–Seller Relationships. Industrial Marketing Management 30: 365-77.

43. Christopher M (1999) Logistics and Supply Chain Management, Strategies for Reducing Costs and Improving Service. Pitman Publishing, London.

44. Hair JF, Black WC, Babin BJ, Anderson RE (2010) Multivariate Data Analysis (7th edn): A Global perspective. Pearson Education, Inc.

45. Kline RB (2005) Principles and practice of structural equation modeling, (2nd edn). New York, London: The Guilford Press.

Proposed Framework of Smart City for Gawadar, Balochistan Pakistan

Naeem Ali*, Sagheer Abbas and Maria Shahid

National College of Business Administration and Economics, Lahore, Pakistan

Abstract

Due to immense advancement in the field of technology, major portion of human's life become dependent on it. Through implementation of information and communication technologies in every field of life, things are getting easier, faster and more reliable. This paper aims to study the very challenging and innovative concept of such advancement known as Smart City (major elements of city are linked with information and communication technology) and its feasibility as well as implementation in Pakistan precisely at Gawadar Port. In proposed Smart city, smart homes, environmental sensors, vehicle networking, surveillance is dimension connected, monitored and controlled by centralized control room. This research is descriptive in nature and in the light of literature; researcher tries to check the feasibility of Proposed Smart City Model at Gawadar Port. Findings of research claims that development of Smart City at Gawadar Port highly feasible and profitable because Gawadar Port is an international route for sea trade as well as CPEC project make that location is more attractive in terms of investment. Moreover, this project is started in private-public partnership by Pakistan Government in collaboration with China.

This project introduces new dimensions of easiness, security, mobilization in human lives as well as brings drastic change in policy making, decision styles and profitability of Government. Limitation of this research is that limited work is available on Smart city concept especially in Pakistan perspective as well as population of Pakistan has low literacy of this concept.

Keywords: Smart city; Gawadar port; CPEC; Smart home; Environmental sensors; Vehicle networking; Surveillance

Introduction

Overnight technology advancement and innovation not only make the world a global village but also introduces many new amazing concepts. Smart City is also one of the innovative concepts of information and communication technology. As men's personal life is facing unpredictable changes due to such advancement in field of technology, desire to involve that technology in every dimension of life i.e., personal life, social life, economy planning, construction, transportation, hospitality industry, parliamentary decision making etc. becomes more fasten. According Harrison work in 2011, to revolutionize the above mentioned fields through latest innovations of information and communication technology, Smart City concept has emerged since 2005. Big giants of information and communication technology industry like Cisco, IBM, and HP etc. analyzed that desire and started work on Smart city project. Definition of Smart city proposed by Cisco is, "developing precise and measurable solution from emerging innovations in communication and information technology which enhances the quality of life, efficiency and cut the regulatory/ operational cost. Hatem Bin Sta work suggested that cities regulated by information and communication technologies are more efficient and cost effective in their infrastructure; living as well as utilization of scarce resources is also maximum. First smart city proposed by Cisco was in Dubai and Government, Health Care, Knowledge as well as Media were the perspectives of that smart city upgraded and regulated by information and communication technologies.

From work of Chourabi et al. [1] and Deakin [2] another definition as well as purpose of smart city is deduced as, "investment of capital on information and communication technologies to enhance the quality of living, workability and sustain that quality in urban settlement to achieve desired goals in long run." Smart city covers the different dimensions and proposed solutions as well as assist the Government/ local body for policy making. While Smart city proposed by IBM provided innovative solutions for building, security, energy conservation, public safety, traffic control and water management. Another smart city project titled SimCity project in which major focused dimensions to be controlled and regulated was transportation system of a city of Libson. It was a project initiated with collaboration of University of Minho, University of Coimbra, Massachuselts Institute of Technology along with IBM and Energias de Portugal-EDP. Through this project; not only transportation element while energy grids, building get controlled by technology and assist people and Government in decision making. Researcher defines Smart City as, "capitalization on information and communication technologies in order to engraved the latest innovations in home designing and construction, transportation system, environment protection, health and education sector, water and sewerage management, energy conservation, pollution dumping, traffic control etc. to improve living standards and strengthen the decision making of Local/ Government Body."

Gawadar port in Pakistan is the world largest international route of sea trade. China Pak Economic Corridor (CPEC) is a China Government collaboration project to develop the Gawadar port and investment done on network of roads, railway lines and wireless network connection to strengthen the trade and exchange of information. This vast network not only connects these two countries but also open the ways of trading among linked countries. So, Gawadar port is highly attractive and profitable investment opportunity for both of local and foreign investors. If smart city project initiated there it will broader the vision of Government, investors. The core purpose of this research is to inspect the monetary and non-monetary

***Corresponding author:** Naeem Ali, National College of Business Administration and Economics, Lahore, Pakistan, E-mail: naeemali@ncbae.edu.pk

feasibility of development of smart city at Gawadar port comprised of smart home, environmental sensors, vehicle network and surveillance system connected with information and communication technologies at control room. As well as explore how the usage of Information and communication technologies in these dimensions of a city enhances the living standards and security of people, planning and policy making by Government.

Literature Review

Smart city is defined as; "whole parameters and issues related to each parameter of a city is controlled, monitored and solved through usage of information and communication technology and brought flexibility, precision, cost effectiveness in allocation of limited resource to enhance quality of living environment and security." According to research of Caragliu et al. [3] a city is called smart when capitalization on modern infrastructure along with traditional one is done along with active as well as foresighted allocation of resources with collaboration of Government to attain sustainable growth in economy, profitability and standards of living. While Kanter and Litow [4] further claimed that if small smart cities are developed and these cities are connected internally and externally via latest information and communication technologies then it will enhance community collaboration and development. Communities of interlinked smarter cities can play effective role in decision making, facing any contingency due to availability of rich information via shared internet. In smart cities and smart homes, things, elements and people are connected with control rooms through wireless network and sensors.

Through sensors, data is collected, scanned at control room and immediate actions are taken in case of urgency. In smart homes, level of CO can measured, number of people in rooms and outside the rooms can be diagnose via crowd sensors [5]. Temperature sensors, wireless visitors alerts and control of electricity consumption through sensors connected with control room via wireless internet are possible.

These days damage of ozone layer due to human activities is very critical issue and major area of concern is how to control and reduce the influence of human activities on environment. According to research of Seidl et al. [6] industrial or mining untreated toxic waste water not only the reason of environmental degradation but human activities i.e. Garbage dumping at open places, untreated drainage of bathrooms etc. major reactants. So, negative influence of human activities can be monitored through wireless sensor networks. Smart city is also argued as green city and has target to minimize the bad influence on environment and it will be controlled via different ways such as development of and maintenance of zero energy buildings [7]. If Government wants to develop a highly socio-economic status conscious city then must focus on green impact of that technology. According to work of Escolar and Cellucci [8], traffic lamps, road lamps activity can be controlled by sensors. Surveillance system used to monitor security of city and defined as: "continuous monitoring of activities."Gutwirth [9] proposed surveillance definition as: "A society is smart in respect of surveillance means every activity watched by CCTV cameras with a digital record." When data related to each activity happening in a city is available to security and Government then such information can be used in more effective way to make people's life more secured. Technological advancement revolutionized the surveillance system i.e. use of algorithm analysis with CCTV cameras not only reduce manual monitoring, continuous automatic screening of hundred videos and directing attention to suspicious activities as well as keeping non-critical data in database. Infrared and microwave sensors compliment the CCTV applications. Medical sensors installed at home (e.g., smart toilets), as well as fine-grained and real time infrastructural sensing for utilities such as power, water and gas, will provide the basis for advanced data mining applications that can infer occupancy, movements and even individual activities inside buildings [10]. According to a UK home office study, "the best current evidence suggests CCTV reduces crime to a small degree [11]. Limited and unplanned parking lots cause of many other problems such as traffic jam, vehicle damage, traffic breaching, accidents etc. To overcome such issues, concept of smart parking has introduced initially in Japan, Europe and United Kingdom since 1970. Optical wireless sensor network can be used to monitor and control the vehicle traffic [12]. Shaheen, Rodier and Eaken [13] described few features of smart parking system are tracking of vehicle from entrance, guidance about nearest and feasible parking lot, assistance during parking to prevent from any damage, control of vehicle theft, reduction in traffic control staff etc. to attain above mentioned characteristics, parking guideline information system can be installed in vehicles as well as automated systems can be used.

Proposed smart city model

From literature, it is concluded that a city is considered smart when every element of that city is connected and upgraded with information and communication technologies. Researcher is proposing such smart city concept in surrounding of Gawadar port and reason to choose that area for development of Smart city is CPEC. CPEC makes that area commercialized and Gawadar port is hub of foreign sea trade in Pakistan. So, if this project started in partnership with china, it will not only strengthen the relations and roots of trade with China but also attract the foreign investment. In proposed Smart city project, Smart homes, surveillance systems, vehicle tracking network, wireless communication system and environmental sensors are initial dimensions that will be connected with control room via wired as well as wireless network connectivity. In Smart homes, security cameras will be affixed at the entrance of every home, along the roads, parks and shopping malls to monitor visitors and any other suspicious activity. These cameras will be connected to control room via Fiber Optic Cable as well as through wireless internet. Fire alarms, room temperature sensors, emergency automated hidden fountains will be implanted and connected with control room to control and provide immediate voice and physical support. Visitor's alert system will connect homes to main entrance gates and security office as well as control room through Fiber Optic Cable. Information about visitors will be provided to relevant home as visitor get clearance from main entrance. In such way, homes, residents and visitors feel more comfort and secured.

In surveillance system, security cameras both fix and pan-tilt-zoom cameras (PTZ cameras) along with temperature sensors will be installed at parks, clubs, shopping malls, along the roads, fix cameras at home entrances, Auto Focus cameras with face recognition at main gates, along the boundary walls and connected to control room. ICT based Vehicle tracking system will be installed at entrance gates and the record of all the vehicles will be maintained at the entrance and exit times. Micro sensors will be installed in the registered vehicles of the smart city and these sensors are multipurpose i.e. tracking, communication with control room. In case of accident/theft, auto lock, auto parking etc. and connected through wireless network with control room. Moreover, through such sensors traffic flow, navigation guidelines, spare parking slots information and traffic jam issue can be easily resolved by direct connection with drivers. It will provide voice guideline in case of wrong parking pattern as well as parking at wrong place. If vehicle met with any accident or parts failure, an immediate backup will be provided by regulatory authority sitting in control room. Environment sensors will be placed on automated lamp poles around the roads. These sensors will measure temperature, humidity level, wind flow, air pressure, and garbage dumping activities etc. All these sensors will connect with control room and few installed at malls and parks. In control room, relevant staff will observe each element and take corrective measures to overcome the contingencies. All these elements of smart city will be connected with control room and control further connected with local authority that will assist them in planning and decision making as well they can keep eye on every activity of smart city. In order to increase the redundancy of the system, proper power backup availability to all this system so that any sort of mishaps and disturbances may be tackled well in time. The surveillance, IP telephony, sensors data, vehicles data will be stored on cloud so that data corruption, theft and data loss chances may be minimized. In this smart city the technical teams will be available on 24/7 basis, working in different shifts. Quick decision will be taken on regular basis by the duty in charge in the best interest of the public and the policy making decisions will be taken by higher ups.

Discussion and Conclusion

According Pardo and Nam [14], smart city is organic collaboration of human, institutional and technological components of a society while Schaffers et al. claimed it as a multidisciplinary interconnected concept while Volano [15] defined it as; "efficient utilization of city technology along with citizens intelligence to develop a modern city." From literature review, it is explored that investment in technology upgrading and embedding that upgrading in every dimension of a city either it is social life of citizens, government decision and planning process, education system or transportation control etc. to make an idle living environment is known as smart city." Different giants from the of information and communication technology offered developed different smart cities i.e. in New York, smart water, building, transportation management offered in a smart city by IBM while a smart city model was presented by Siemens in Germany. But in all these models latest information and communication technologies adapted to govern economy, environment, governance, mobility, citizens living, education, resource allocation etc. Due to the use of IC technologies in decision making, regulating a city, planning by continuous flow of even minor information enhances the living standards, security, economy development, growth and profitability of a developing economy. And if such project initiated at highly attractive in respect of investment, trade base point like Gawadar port in Pakistan, such concept will pick high popularity, market acceptance and put the country on the track of rapid growth and incorporating international living standards. But starting such mega project without international financing is not feasible at initial stage. So due to high collaboration of China in economy development of Pakistan via CPEC and very fast friendship, it will be an attractive opportunity to offer partnership to China in order to start smart city project at Gawadar port. Pakistan internet system is single lane system due to which failure of network means link down of whole system with no backup. China is highly advance in technology and if smart city is started with China collaboration then such failures can be controlled and establishment of smart city will become possible.

Limitation

Limitation of this research is that limited network connectivity as in Pakistan only the major internet service provided by Fiber Optic Cable under sea water by Etisalat working with PTCL under Pakistan Telecommunication Authority, United Arab Emirates. If it is damaged then the whole internet connectivity of the country is suffered badly. So, for smart city it is very necessary that with cooperation of China another Fiber Optic Cable should be laid with CPEC project for redundancy of internet connectivity so that the smart city security and services may be maintained in the real sense. Secondly, in Pakistan imported optical fiber is used for networking. Thirdly, population of Pakistan has low literacy of technology advancement and innovations. Last but not least, lack of facts and figures related to smart city models.

References

1. Chourabi H, Nam T, Walker S, Gil-Garcia JR, Mellouli S, et al. (2012) Understanding Smart Cities: An integrative framework paper presented at the 45th international conference on system science, Maui, Hawaii.
2. Deakin M (2013) Smart cities: Governing, modeling and analyzing the transition London: Routledge.
3. Caragliu A, Del BC, Nijkamp P (2009) Smart Cities in Europe. Series Research Memoranda 0048. Free University Amsterdam, Faculty of Economics, Business Administration and Econometrics.
4. Moss Kanter R, Litow S (2009) Informed and interconnected: a manifesto for smarter cities. Harvard Business School Working Paper 09-141.
5. Yi WY, Lo KM, Mak T, Leung KS, Leung Y, Meng ML (2015) A survey of wireless sensor network based air pollution monitoring systems. Sensors 15: 31392-31427.
6. Seidl M, Da G, Ausset P, Haenn S, Géhin E, Moulin L (2016) Evaluating exposure of pedestrians to airborne contaminants associated with non-potable water use for pavement cleaning. Environ. Sci. Pollut Res 23: 6091-6101.
7. Kylili A, Fokaides PA (2015) European smart cities: The role of zero energy buildings. Sustainable Cities and Society, 86- 95.79T. Alizadeh/Cities 63: 70-80.
8. Cellucci L, Burattini C, Drakou D, Gugliermetti F, Bisegna F, et al. (2015) Urban lighting project for asmall town: comparing citizens and authority benefits. Sustainability 7: 14230-14244.
9. Gutwirth S, Rowman, Littlefield, Lanham MD (2002) Privacy and the information age.
10. Athow D (2009) Tories Promise to Slash Surveillance State Program. ITPro Portal, 17 Sept 2009.
11. Welsh, Brandon C, David PF (2002) Crime prevention effects of closed circuit television: a systematic review, Home Office Research, Development and Statistics Directorate.
12. Chinrungrueng J, Sunantachaikul U, Triamlumlerd S (2006) A vehicular monitoring system with power-efficient wireless sensor networks. ITS Telecommunications Proceedings, 2006 6th International Conference, China.
13. Shaheen S, Rodier C, Eaken A (2005) Smart parking management field test: A bay area rapid transit (bart) district parking demonstration, Final Report.
14. Nam T, Pardo TA (2011) Conceptualizing smart city with dimensions of technology, People, and institutions, in Proceedings of the 12th Annual International Digital Government Research Conference: Digital Government Innovation in Challenging Times, ACM, pp: 282-291.
15. Vanolo (2013) Smart mentality: The smart city as disciplinary strategy. Urban Stud 51.

Impact Analysis of FDI on Insurance Sector in India

Aamir Hasan*

Anuna Education Network, Lucknow, Uttar Pradesh, India

Abstract

Parliament has passed Insurance Laws (Amendment) Bill, 2015. It was first passed in Lok Sabha on 4 March 2015 and later in Rajya Sabha on 12 March 2015, which will become an Act when the President signs it. The amendment bill aims to bring improvements and revisions in the existing laws relating to insurance business in India. The bill also seeks to remove archaic provisions in previous laws and incorporate modern day practices of insurance business that are emerging in a changing dynamic environment, which also includes private participation. It is expected that the foreign investment would bring about `20,000-`25,000 crore in short funds. The amendment bill hikes Foreign Direct Investment (FDI) cap in the insurance sector to 49 percent from present 26 percent. The foreign investment in insurance would be routed under foreign direct investment,foreign portfolio investment,foreign venture capital investment,depository receipts,and non resident indians. Insurance companies are permitted to raise capital through instruments other than equity shares. Instruments would be specified through separate regulations by the Insurance Regulatory and Development Authority of India (IRDA). However, the voting rights of shareholders are restricted only to equity shares. Sale of shares over 1% of the total equity share capital and purchase of shares resulting in total equity share capital of more than 5%, requires the prior approval of the IRDA.

It also adds provision for the establishment of Life Insurance Council and the General Insurance Council. These councils will act as self-regulating bodies for the insurance sector. The bill also grants permission to PSU general insurers to raise funds from the capital market and increases the penalty to deter multilevel marketing of insurance products. There is a strong relationship between foreign investment and economic growth. Larger inflows of foreign investments are needed for the country to achieve a sustainable high trajectory of economic growth. A major role played by the insurance sector is to mobilize national savings and channelize them into investments in different sectors of the economy. FDI in insurance would increase the penetration of insurance in India; FDI can meet India's long term capital requirements to fund the building of infrastructures. The present paper focuses on the overview of the Indian insurance sector along with the opportunities due to expansion of FDI in insurance in India and the major challenges that it faces.

Keywords: Insurance; FDI; Insurance Laws (Amendment) Bill

Introduction

The insurance industry of India consists of 52 insurance companies of which 24 are in life insurance business and 28 are non-life insurers. Among the life insurers, Life Insurance Corporation (LIC) is the sole public sector company. Apart from that, among the non-life insurers there are six public sector insurers. In addition to these, there is sole national re-insurer, namely, General Insurance Corporation of India. Other stakeholders in Indian Insurance market include agents (individual and corporate), brokers, surveyors and third party administrators servicing health insurance claims [1].

Out of 28 non-life insurance companies, five private sector insurers are registered to underwrite policies exclusively in health, personal accident and travel insurance segments. They are Star Health and Allied Insurance Company Ltd, Apollo Munich Health Insurance Company Ltd, Max Bupa Health Insurance Company Ltd, Religare Health Insurance Company Ltd and Cigna TTK Health Insurance Company Ltd. There are two more specialized insurers belonging to public sector, namely, Export Credit Guarantee Corporation of India for Credit Insurance and Agriculture Insurance Company Ltd for crop insurance.

Insurance in India is a flourishing industry in India with both national and international players competing and growing at rapid rate. Together with banking and real estate it constitutes 12.9% of GDP in India. However the penetration of insurance coverage for both life and non life insurance is still very less and was 3.9% in 2013.

Indian insurance sector was liberalized in 2001. Liberalization has led to the entry of the largest insurance companies in the world, who have taken a strategic view on India being one of the top priority emerging markets. The Insurance industry in India has undergone transformational changes over the last 14 years. With raising the cap on FDI into Indian insurance companies to 49% from the 26% would allow global reinsurance companies to set up branches in India [2].

According to the insurance amendment bill (2015), the section 24 of the Pension Fund Regulatory and Development Authority (PFRDA) Act provides that the foreign investment limit in the pension sector will be linked with the ceiling in the insurance sector, which has gone up to 49% from 26%. Under the legislation, while up to 26 per cent foreign capital will be under the automatic route, the balance 23 per cent has to secure approval from the Foreign Investment Promotion Board (FIPB). According to the General Insurance Business (Nationalization) Act, 1972 (GIBNA, 1972) the four general insurance companies (GICs) had to be 100% government owned, however The Insurance Laws (Amendment) Bill, 2015 — passed by the Rajya Sabha on March 12 and by the Lok Sabha on March 4 — will change that. The GICs "are now allowed to raise capital, keeping in view the need for expansion of the business in the rural and social sectors, meeting the solvency margin for this purpose and achieving enhanced competitiveness subject to the government equity not being less than 51% at any point of time. The amendment also clearly defines health insurance business to include travel and personal accident cover. It is also expected that the proposed increase in the FDI limit will have a follow on impact on other sectors, including the pension industry creating further momentum [3].

***Corresponding author:** Aamir Hasan, Anuna Education Network, Lucknow, Uttar Pradesh, India, E-mail: aamirhasan_1@yahoo.co.in

Objectives of the Study and Methodology

The present paper focuses on the overview of the Indian insurance sector along with the opportunities due to expansion of FDI in insurance in India and the major challenges that it faces.

Global Overview of Insurance Sector

The global insurance industry is facing increasing competition, which has put significant pressure on companies to become more efficient, enhance their technology-related processes and alter their business models. Globally, most insurance companies are trying to enhance the efficiency of their underwriting process, cut their overheads and reduce claims leakage since returns from investment are shrinking [4]. With high competition in the insurance industry, companies will need to strengthen their product lines, investment strategies and corporate infrastructure (Figure 1).

According to the latest study performed by the global re-insurer Swiss Re on world insurance in 2013, India ranked 15th in terms of premium volume, from 14th in 2012. According to the swiss Re report the premiums written in the global insurance industry was 2.5 percent in 2012 and it grew by 1.4 percent in real terms to $4 641 billion in 2013 [5]. The reason behind the slowdown was mainly due to weakness in the life sector in the advanced markets. In Swiss Re's sigma study, India's life insurance penetration was 3.1 per cent, while in non-life insurance it was 0.8 per cent. A premium as a percentage of Gross Development Product is referred to as insurance penetration whereas insurance density refers to per capita premium or premium per person. The study also revealed that the insurance penetration in India fell to 3.9 percent in 2013 when compared to four percent in 2012. Also in terms of insurance density India stood at $52 when compared to $53 in 2012, thus in simple words both insurance penetration and density was low (Tables 1 and 2).

Indian insurance sector

Insurance in India is listed in the Constitution of India in the Seventh Schedule as a Union List subject, meaning it can only be legislated by the Central government. The history of insurance date backs to 1818, when Oriental Life Insurance Company was started. In 1870, Bombay Mutual Life Assurance Society became the first Indian insurer. In the year 1912, the Life Insurance Companies Act and the Provident Fund Act was passed to regulate the insurance business. This was the first statutory measure to regulate life insurance business. In 1928, the Indian Insurance Companies Act was enacted to enable the Government to collect statistical information about both life and non-life business transacted in India by Indian and foreign insurers including provident insurance societies. In 1938, with a view to protecting the interest of the Insurance public, the earlier legislation was consolidated and amended by the Insurance Act, 1938 with comprehensive provisions for effective control over the activities of insurers. The Government of India issued an Ordinance on 19 January 1956 nationalizing the Life Insurance sector and Life Insurance Corporation came into existence in the same year. The Life Insurance Corporation (LIC) absorbed 154 Indian, 16 non-Indian insurers as also 75 provident societies—245 Indian and foreign insurers in all. In 1972 the parliament passed General Insurance Business (Nationalization) Act, and consequently, General Insurance business was nationalized with effect from 1 January 1973 [6]. 107 insurers were amalgamated and grouped into four companies, namely National Insurance Company Ltd., the New India Assurance Company Ltd., the Oriental Insurance Company Ltd and the United India Insurance Company Ltd. The General Insurance Corporation of India was incorporated as a company in 1971 and it commence business on 1 January 1973.

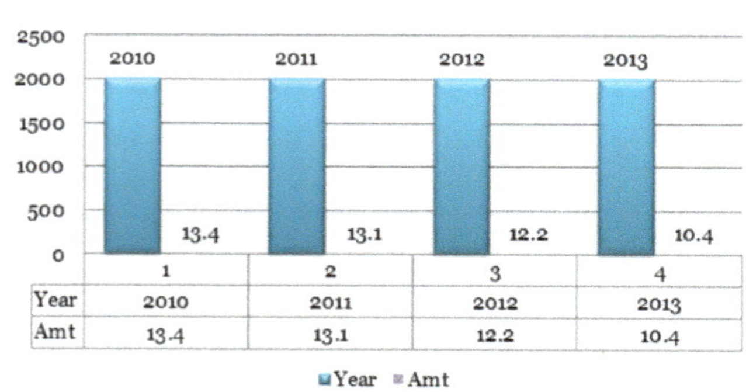

Source: Swiss Re Research and Consulting

Figure 1: Global Life Insurance Premium Volume in millions (US$).

In 1993, the Government set up a committee under the chairmanship of RN Malhotra, former Governor of RBI, to propose recommendations for reforms in the insurance sector. Following the recommendations of the Malhotra Committee report, in 1999, the Insurance Regulatory and Development Authority (IRDA) was constituted as an autonomous body to regulate and develop the insurance industry. The IRDA was incorporated as a statutory body in April, 2000. The key objectives of the IRDA include promotion of competition so as to enhance customer satisfaction through increased consumer choice and lower premiums, while ensuring the financial security of the insurance market.

The IRDA opened up the market in August 2000 with the invitation for application for registrations. Foreign companies were allowed ownership of up to 26%. The Authority has the power to frame regulations under Section 114A of the Insurance Act, 1938 and has from 2000 onwards framed various regulations ranging from registration of companies for carrying on insurance business to protection of policyholders' interests [7].

The LIC had monopoly till the late 90s when the Insurance sector was reopened to the private sector. Before that, the industry consisted of only two state insurers: Life Insurers (Life Insurance Corporation

Regions/Countries	Life	Non-Life	Total
Advanced Countries	-0.2	1.1	0.3
Emerging Markets	6.4	8.3	7.4
Asia	-6.5	2.2	-4.1
India	-1.1	2.5	-0.4
World	0.7	2.3	1.4

Table 1: Total Real Premium Growth Rate in 2013(in percent).

Region/Countries	Life	Non-Life	Total
Advanced Countries	2200.25(57.1%)	1653.02(42.9)	3853.27(100)
Emerging Markets	407.84(51.8)	379.83(48.2)	787.67(100)
Asia	898.41(70.3)	380.37(29.7)	1278.78(100)
India	52.17(79.6)	13.40(20.4)	65.58(100)
World	2608.09(56.2)	2032.85(43.2)	4640.94(100)

Table 2: Region wise Life and Non-Life Insurance Premium (USD Billion).

of India, LIC) and General Insurers (General Insurance Corporation of India, GIC). GIC had four subsidiary companies. With effect from December 2000, these subsidiaries have been de-linked from the parent company and were set up as independent insurance companies: Oriental Insurance Company Limited, New India Assurance Company Limited, National Insurance Company Limited and United India Insurance Company Limited [8].

Registered Insurers in India

At the end of March 2014, there are 53 insurance companies operating in India, out of which 24 are in the life insurance business and 28 are in the non-life insurance business (Table 3).

Insurance Premium Underwriting

Life insurance

The Life insurance industry recorded a premium income of Rs.3,14,283 crore during 2013-14 as against Rs.2,87,202 crore in 2012-13 registering a growth of 9.43%. While private sector insurers posted 1.35% decline in their premium income,LIC recorded 13.48% growth (Figure 2 and Table 4).

District level distribution of life insurance offices

As at 31st March, 2014, the sole public sector life insurer, LIC of India had its offices in 597 districts out of 640 districts (As per the Decennial Census -2011) in the country. As such, it covered 93.28 per cent of all districts in the country, whereas the private sector insurers had offices in 560 districts covering 87.50 per cent of all districts in the country. In total, both LIC and private insurers together covered 94.37 per cent of all districts in the country. The number of districts with no presence of life insurance offices stood at 36 in the country. Out of these, 23 districts belong to the six of the north eastern states namely Arunachal Pradesh, Manipur, Meghalaya, Mizoram, Nagaland and Sikkim. In 21 states/union territories (out of a total of 35 states/union territories in the country), all their districts were covered through life insurance offices (Figure 3 and Table 5).

Type of business	Public Sector	Private Sector	Total
Life Insurance	1	23	24
Non-Life Insurance	6	22	28
Reinsurance	1	0	1
Total	8	45	53

Source: IDRA, 2014

Table 3: Life Insurance Premium Underwritten in Rs (Crore).

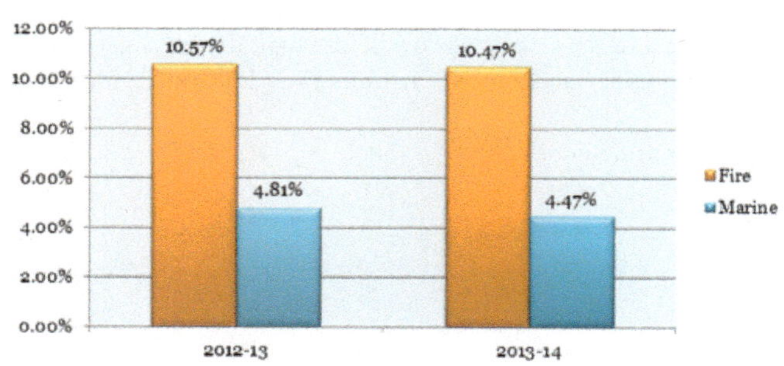

Source: IDRA 2014

Figure 2: Life Insurance Premium Underwritten.

Distribution of Offices of Life Insurers Number of Life Offices				
Insurer	Metro	Urban	Others	Total
Private	676	1926	3591	6193
LIC	372	617	3850	4839
Industry	1048	2543	7441	11032

Source: IDRA 2014

Table 4: Life Insurance Premium Underwritten in Rs(Crore).

Non-life insurance

The non-life insurance industry had underwritten a total premium of Rs.70610 crore in India for the year 2013-14 as against Rs. 62973 crore in 2012-13, registering a growth of 12.13 per cent as against an increase of 19.10 per cent recorded in the previous year. The public sector insurers exhibited growth in 2013-14 at 10.21 per cent; over the previous year's growth rate of 14.60 per cent. The private general insurers registered growth of 14.52 per cent, which is lower than 25.26 per cent achieved during the previous year (Figure 4 and Table 6).

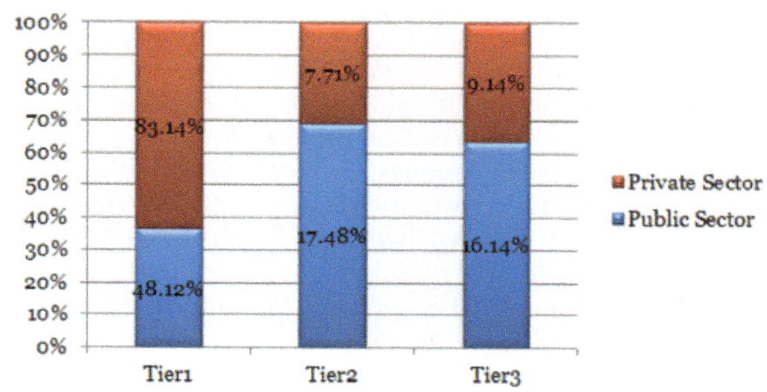

Figure 3: Distribution of Offices of Life Insurers Number of Life Offices.

Distribution of Offices of Life Insurers Number of Life Offices				
Insurer	Metro	Urban	Others	Total
Private	676	1926	3591	6193
LIC	372	617	3850	4839
Industry	1048	2543	7441	11032

Source: IDRA-2014

Table 5: Distribution of Offices of Life Insurers Number of Life Offices.

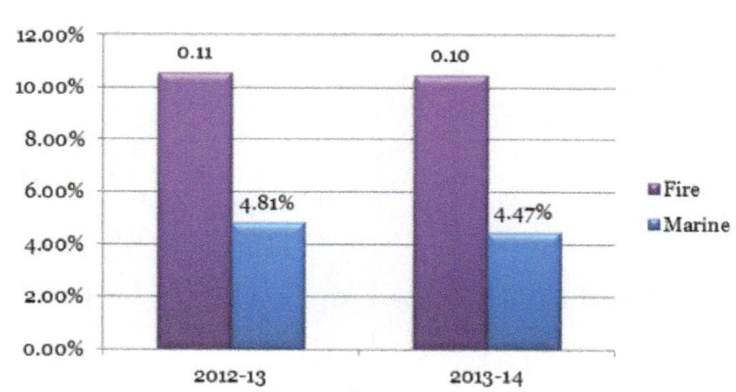

Figure 4: Non-Life Insurance Premium Underwritten in Rs(Crore).

Non-Life Insurance Premium Underwritten in Rs (Crore)		
Insurer	2012-13	2013-14
Public Sector	35022.12(14.60%)	38599.71(10.21%)
Private Sector	27950.53(25.25%)	32010.30(14.52%)
Total	62972.65(19.10%)	70610.02(12.13%)

Table 6: Non-Life Insurance Premium Underwritten in Rs (Crore).

Segment wise premium of non life insurance

The Motor insurance business continued to be the largest non-life insurance segment with a share of 47.90 per cent (47.05 per cent in 2012-13). It reported growth rate of 14.15 per cent (22.24 per cent in 2012-13). The premium collection in health segment continued to surge ahead at 15663 crore in 2013-14 from `13,975 crore of 2012-13, registering a growth of 12.08 per cent. However, the market share of health segment which is 22.18 has remained more or less at the same levels of previous year which was 22.19 per cent in the year. The premium collection from Fire and Marine segments increased by 11.01 per cent and 4.13 per cent respectively in 2013-14 whereas for the previous year the growth rate in the Fire and Marine segments were 22.63 and 5.36 respectively (Table 7, Figures 5 and 6).

Number of non life insurance offices-tier wise

When compared to life insurance, the proportion of districts covered by non-life insurers is less. While the four public sector non-life insurer has offices at 601 districts out of 640 districts in the country (94 per cent), the private sector insurers cover only 45 per cent of the districts in the country by having offices in 286 districts. There are 39 districts (6 per cent of districts) in the country, which do not have any non-life insurance office. Private sector insurance offices have not yet opened any offices in 354 districts. Further only 19 States/ Union Territories (out of 35 States/ UnionTerritories) have non-life insurance offices in all of their districts. This lower level of coverage of districts by non-life insurers might also have led to the low non-life insurance penetration in the country, as compared to penetration of life insurance (Table 8 and Figure 7).

Insurance penetration and density in India

The measure of insurance penetration and density reflects the level of development of insurance sector in a country. While insurance penetration is measured as the percentage of insurance premium to GDP, insurance density is calculated as the ratio of premium to population (per capita premium) (Table 9).

FDI in India

A foreign direct investment (FDI) is a controlling ownership in a business enterprise in one country by an entity based in another country. Apart from being a critical driver of economic growth, foreign direct investment (FDI) is a major source of non-debt financial resource for the economic development of India. Foreign companies invest in India to take advantage of cheaper wages, special investment privileges like tax exemptions, etc. For a country where foreign investments are being made, it also means achieving technical know-how and generation of employment.

Forms in which Business Can Conducted by Foreign Company in India

A foreign company planning to set up business operations in India may: Incorporate a company under the Companies Act, 1956, as a Joint Venture or a Wholly Owned Subsidiary. Set up a Liaison Office / Representative Office or a Project Office or a Branch Office of the foreign company which can undertake activities permitted under the Foreign Exchange Management (Establishment in India of Branch Office or Other Place of Business) Regulations, 2000.

Procedure for receiving Foreign Direct Investment in an Indian company

Automatic route

FDI is allowed under the automatic route without prior approval either of the Government or the Reserve Bank of India in all activities/ sectors as specified in the consolidated FDI Policy, issued by the Government of India from time to time.

Segment Wise Premium of Non-Life Insurance(Within India in crore)		
Department	2012-13	2013-14
Fire	6659(10.57%)	7392(10.47%)
Marine	3029(4.81%)	3154(4.47%)
Motor	29630 (47.05%)	33824 (47.90%)
Health	13975 (22.19%)	15663 (22.18%)
Others	9680 (15.37%)	10577 (14.98%)
Total Premium	62973	70610

Table 7: Segment Wise Premium of Non-Life Insurance (Within India in crore).

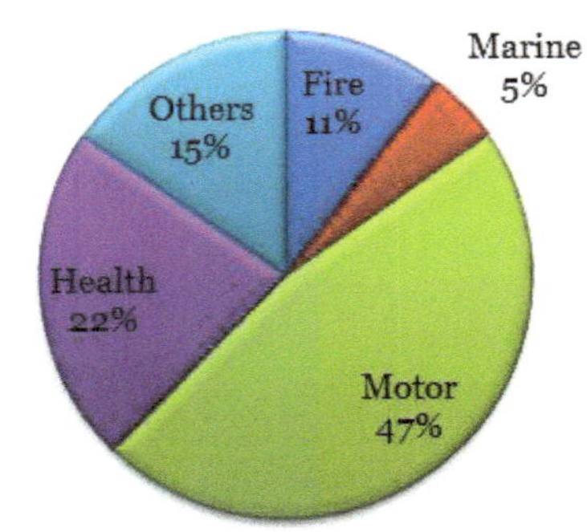

Figure 5: Segment Wise Premium of Non-Life Insurance (Within India in crore) for Year 2012-13.

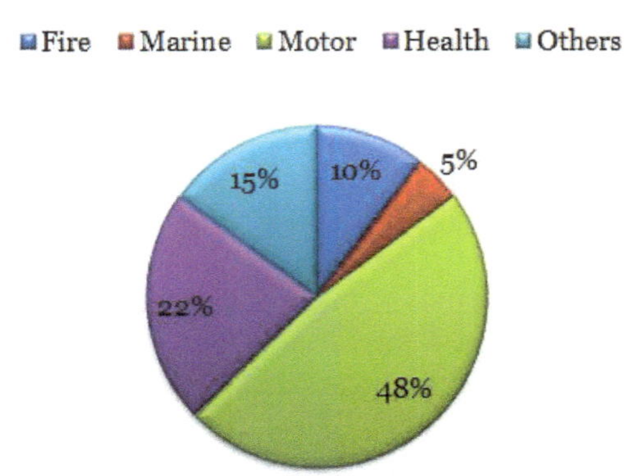

Figure 6: Segment Wise Premium of Non-Life Insurance (Within India in crore) for Year 2013-14.

Number of Non-Life Insurance Offices-Tier Wise							
Non-Life	Tier 1	Tier 2	Tier 3	Tier 4	Tier 5	Tier 6	Total
Public Sector	3747	1361	1257	1298	80	43	7786
Private Sector	1337	124	147	0	0	0	1608
Standalone Health Private	394	1	0	0	0	0	395
Specialized Insurers	82	1	0	0	0	0	83
Total	5560	1487	1404	1298	80	43	9872

Source IDRA 2014

Table 8: Number of Non-Life Insurance Offices-Tier Wise.

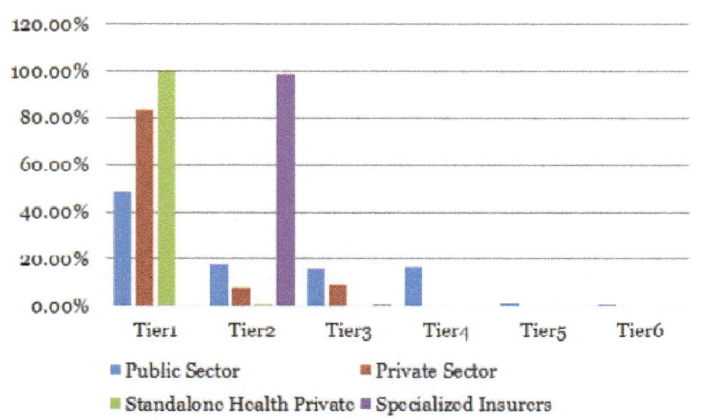

Source: IDRA 2014

Figure 7: Number of Non-Life Insurance Offices-Tier Wise.

Year	Life		Non-Life		Industry	
	Density (USD)	Penetration (%)	Density (USD)	Penetration (%)	Density (USD)	Penetration (%)
2001	9.1	2.15	2.4	0.56	11.5	2.71
2002	11.7	2.59	3	0.67	14.7	3.26
2003	12.9	2.26	3.5	0.62	16.4	2.88
2004	15.7	2.53	4	0.64	19.7	3.17
2005	18.3	2.53	4.4	0.61	22.7	3.14
2006	33.2	4.1	5.2	0.6	38.4	4.8
2007	40.4	4	6.2	0.6	46.6	4.7
2008	41.2	4	6.2	0.6	47.4	4.6
2009	47.7	4.6	6.7	0.6	54.3	5.2
2010	55.7	4.4	8.7	0.71	64.4	5.1
2011	49	3.4	10	0.7	59	4.1
2012	42.7	3.17	10.5	0.78	53.2	3.96
2013	41	3.1	11	0.8	52	3.9

Source: IDRA 2014

Table 9: Insurance penetration and density in India.

Government route

FDI in activities not covered under the automatic route requires prior approval of the Government which are considered by the Foreign Investment Promotion Board (FIPB), Department of Economic Affairs, Ministry of Finance.

Opportunities due to Expansion of FDI

Increase insurance penetration

With the population of more than 100 crores, India requires Insurance more than any other nation. However, the insurance penetration in the country is only around 3 percent of our gross domestic product with respect to over-all premiums underwritten annually. This is far less as compared to Japan which has an insurance penetration of more than 10 percent. Increased FDI limit will strengthen the existing companies and will also allow the new players to come in, thereby enabling more people to buy life cover. More companies would enter the insurance sector, which would lead to higher competition and cheaper insurance premium for the customers

Level playing field

With the increase in foreign direct investment to 49 percent, the insurance companies will get the level playing field. So far the state owned Life Corporation of India controls around 70 percent of the life insurance market.

Increased capital flow

Most of the private sector insurance companies have been making considerable losses. The increased FDI limit has brought some much needed relief to these firms as the inflow of more than `20,000-`25,000 crore is expected in the near term. This could go up to `40,000-`60,000 crore in the medium to long term, depending on how things pan out.

Job creation

With more money coming in, the insurance companies will be able to create more jobs to meet their targets of venturing into under insured markets through improved infrastructure, better operations and more manpower.

Consumer friendly

The end beneficiary of this amendment will be common men. With more players in this sector, there is bound to be stringent competition leading to competitive quotes, improved services and better claim settlement ratio.

Challenges

Foreign investment of up to 26% of the total paid up equity of the insurer would be allowed through the automatic route and the increase of FDI from 26% to 49% (i.e.23%) would be allowed through Foreign Investment Promotion Board, and not through automatic route, which means that FIPB would issue guidelines regarding the management control,which would lie with the Indian counterpart,also there are concerns about the voting rights of the foreign shareholders,which should not go beyond 26%. FIPB guidelines would also decide on the appointments of CEO's and CFO's of the insurance joint ventures. Another issue is the stability of Indian financial markets as there is a possibility of insurance companies bringing in contagion risk such as risky derivatives and contaminated balance sheet. The government is looking primarily on how much funds the insurance companies can bring with them, and not on the amount of business which these companies could generate as it is expected that their rural penetration would be low. To get listed on bourse to raise FIIs may not be attractive for all insurance companies. According to Insurance Regulatory and Development Authority (Irda) norms, companies whose embedded value is two times their paid-up capital can list on the bourses. Embedded value is a common valuation measure in the insurance industry calculated by adding the adjusted net asset value and the present value of future profits of a firm. The present value of future profits considers the potential profits that shareholders will receive in the future, while adjusted net asset value considers the funds belonging to shareholders that have been accumulated in the past. Another issue could arise when insurers list their shares on stock exchanges. Indian law requires 25 per cent of a listed company to be owned by public.

So if an insurer launches an initial public offering and the foreign partner increase its stake, then the Indian company would end up with a smaller holding in the joint venture..

Some of the Major Highlights of the Insurance Law (Amendment) Bill 2015 are

Capital availability

In addition to the provisions for enhanced foreign equity, the amended law will enable capital raising through new and innovative instruments under the regulatory supervision of IRDAI. The four public sector general insurance companies, presently required as per the General Insurance Business (Nationalization) Act, 1972 (GIBNA, 1972) to be 100% government owned, are now allowed to raise capital, keeping in view the need for expansion of the business in the rural and social sectors, meeting the solvency margin for this purpose and achieving enhanced competitiveness subject to the Government equity not being less than 51% at any point of time.

Consumer welfare

Laws will enable the interests of consumers to be better served through provisions like those enabling penalties on intermediaries / insurance companies for misconduct and disallowing multilevel marketing of insurance products in order to curtail the practice of mis-selling. The amended Law has several provisions for levying higher penalties ranging from up to ` 1 Crore to ` 25 Crore for various violations including mis-selling and misrepresentation by agents / insurance companies. With a view to serve the interest of the policy holders better, the period during which a policy can be repudiated on any ground, including mis-statement of facts etc., will be confined to three years from the commencement of the policy and no policy would be called in question on any ground after three years. The amendments provide for an easier process for paymentto the nominee of the policy holder, as the insurer would be discharged of its legal liabilities once the payment is made to the nominee. It is now obligatory in the law for insurance companies to underwrite third party motor vehicle insurance as per IRDAI regulations.

Empowerment of IRDAI

The Act will entrust responsibility of appointing insurance agents to insurers and provides for IRDAI to regulate their eligibility, qualifications and other aspects. It enables agents to work more broadly across companies in various business categories; with the safeguard that conflict of interest would not be allowed by IRDAI through suitable regulations. IRDAI is empowered to regulate key aspects of Insurance Company operations in areas like solvency, investments, expenses and commissions and to formulate regulations for payment of commission and control of management expenses. It empowers the Authority to regulate the functions, code of conduct, etc., of surveyors and loss assessors. The onus to prove that a wrong statement was not made at the time of taking the policy would lie with the policyholder and not the insurance company, i.e. if a person dies and his widow and children will have to prove why the husband or father made a wrong statement, i.e. if a person dies and his widow and children will have to prove why the husband or father made a wrong statement. An insurance policy cannot be challenged on any ground after three years. This means if a fraud is detected three years after the policy has been in force, insurance companies will have to pay the policy holder. It also expands the scope of insurance intermediaries to include insurance brokers, re- insurance brokers, insurance consultants, corporate agents, third party administrators, surveyors and loss assessors and such other entities, as may be notified by the Authority from time to time. Further, properties in India can now be insured with a foreign insurer with prior permission of IRDAI; which was earlier to be done with the approval of the Central Government.

Health insurance

It empowers the Authority to regulate the functions, code of conduct, etc., of surveyors and loss assessors. It also expands the scope of insurance intermediaries to include insurance brokers, re-insurance brokers, insurance consultants, corporate agents, third party administrators, surveyors and loss assessors and such other entities, as may be notified by the Authority from time to time. Further, properties in India can now be insured with a foreign insurer with prior permission of IRDAI; which was earlier to be done with the approval of the Central Government.

Promoting reinsurance business in india

The amended law enables foreign reinsurers to set up branches in India and defines're-insurance' to mean "the insurance of part of one insurer's risk by another insurer who accepts the risk for a mutually acceptable premium", and thereby excludes the possibility of 100% ceding of risk to a re-insurer, which could lead to companies acting as front companies for other insurers. Further, it enables Lloyds and its members to operate in India through setting up of branches for the purpose of reinsurance business or as investors in an Indian Insurance Company within the 49% cap.

Strengthening of industry councils

The Life Insurance Council and General Insurance Council have now been made self-regulating bodies by empowering them to frame bye-laws for elections, meetings and levy and collect fees etc. from its members. Inclusion of representatives of self-help groups and insurance cooperative societies in insurance councils has also been enabled to broad base the representation on these Councils.

Robust appellate process

Appeals against the orders of IRDAI are to be preferred to SAT as the amended Law provides for any insurer or insurance intermediary aggrieved by any order made by IRDAI to prefer an appeal to the Securities Appellate Tribunal (SAT).

Conclusion

The fundamental regulatory changes in the insurance sector would be significant for the future growth and would have huge impact on various sectors of economy. Active foreign participation is crucial for the sector as it would bring the best know how and implementing the best practices. India is one of the fastest growing insurance market and it is expected that Indian insurance industry can grow up to 125% in the next decade. However there is also a risk that unless given the management control the foreign insurers would be reluctant to invest in India.

References

1. Bhat R (2005) Insurance Industry in India-Structure, performance and future challenges. Vikalpa 30: 3-5
2. Budhiraja L (2010) Indian Insurance Sector Challenges and opportunities. IJRIME 3.
3. Chaturvedi I (2011) Role of FDI in Economic Development of India: Sectoral Analysis International Conference on Technology and Business Management.

4. https://www.irda.gov.in/ADMINCMS/cms/frmGeneral_NoYearList.aspx?DF=AR&mid=11.1
5. Neha S, Prachi B (2008) Distribution channels in life insurance. Bimaquest 8.
6. www.policyholder.gov.in/Annual_Reports.aspx
7. Sonika C, Priti K (2011) Life Insurance Industry in India: Current Scenario. IJMBS 3.
8. http://tsb.org.tr/images/Documents/sigma3_2014_en.pdf

Technical Efficiency Evaluation of Kenyan Sample Banking Sector

Isaiah Onsarigo Miencha[1]*, Seline AO[1], Francis KK[2], Anane E[3] and Twum A[3]

[1]*Head of the Department, Banking and Finance, School of Business, All Nations University, Ghana*
[2]*Lecturer Koforudua Polytechnic, Faculty of Business and Management, Koforudua, Ghana*
[3]*Faculties Department of Banking and Finance, All Nations University, Ghana*

Abstract

The Kenyan financial institutions structure has changed for the last two decades. The commercial banks have undergone incredible development. The study attempts to investigate technical efficiency of Kenyan commercial banks during 2004-2013 by using a Data Envelopment Analysis (DEA). The results suggests that the degree of technical efficiency was found to be lower which indicates that the inefficiency is due to producing at an inefficient scale level rather than producing below the production frontier.

Keywords: Banking; Technical; Efficiency and Evaluation

Jel Classification: C52, H21, H43, D04, E5, G24.

Introduction

The Kenyan financial institutions structure has changed for the last two decades. In addition, global trend towards liberalization in banking has led to blurring segregation of lines separating activities of the different groups of financial institutions and the removal of artificial barrier competition. At the same time, deposit taking, credit granting, investment, insurance and financial advisory services are being bundled into one financial corporation of financial supermarkets. As the financial integration of financial markets within and across borders as well as the mergers among banks, reflect an attempt to increase financial industry efficiency.

Efficiency Measurement in Banking

Efficiency is the maximum output that can be produced from any given total of inputs. It refers to the efficiency of a firm, which allocates resources to produce maximum quantity of output. The allocation efficiency of resource, Sparks, Guthrie and Shepherd [1]. This pinpointed two categories i.e. internal efficiency which referred to effective management within the firm itself like how the ways the management inspires the staff, control costs and keep the operation lean. However, when a company is increased in size, profit flows also show an increase. Hence, the management becomes less effective. Such shortcomings are known as inefficiency in management. Early research in banking industry was mainly concerned with estimating the average productivity using some sort of indices and with comparison by Farrell [2]. Researchers tended to substitute efficiency by market share. They assumed that banks with medium market shares are expected to earn higher profits because of the lower unit costs [3,4]. In other words, banks with lower cost structures could maximize profits by either maintaining the current level of prices and size or reducing the price levels and expanding a positive relationship between firms' profits and market structures being attributed to the gains made by firms that are more efficient.

Statement of the Problem

An attempt to study the efficiency in respect of return on assets of sample Kenya banks is important for benchmarking and strategic planning in the financial services sector. In Kenya, the dominance of the public sector has declined due to the use of technology and introduction of professional management by private and foreign sector banks that gained remarkable position in the Banking Industry. Private sector banks play an important role in the development of the Kenyan Economy. Many firms in the service industry, including the banks, face the problem of not producing better results in terms of return on assets efficiency. In particular, the last decade witnessed continuous changes in regulation, technology upgradation and competition in the global financial services industry and the Kenyan Commercial Banks are no exception to this. The efficiency of banks in general and technical efficiency in respect of return on assets in particular, has become an important issue in Kenya. It is therefore crucial to benchmark the efficiency of banks operating in Kenya, based on efficiency and hence this study on investigation of the efficiency (return on assets) of Kenyan Large, Medium and Small Bank groups (Table 1).

Objectives of the Study

The main objective of this study was to analyze the Total Assets of Kenyan Sample Banks

Hypothesis of the Study

The following null hypothesis was framed and tested in this study

NH01: There is no significant difference in the efficiency of Total Assets among the Kenyan Sample Banks.

Methodology of the Study

(A) Sample Selection

For the purpose of the study, the sample selection was made systematically. In Kenya, there are 41 banks, including public and private sector, as on 31 December 2013. It was found that the required data for analysis were available only for 35 banks. Finally, only six banks were selected by adopting the following criteria.

1. Sample banks were classified as medium, medium and small size for this study as used by Kenya Central Bank. The Kenya Central Bank used weighted composite index, covering assets, Total Assets, capital, and number of deposit accounts and loan accounts to classify the banks.

***Corresponding author:** Dr. Isaiah Onsarigo Miencha, Head of the Department, Banking and Finance, School of Business, All Nations University, Ghana
E-mail: drimiencha@anuc.edu.gh

Year Author/authors	Title of Study	Methodology	Findings in Brief
Keshari PK and Paul MK (1994)	Relative efficiency of foreign and domestic banks	Stochastic frontier production function	Foreign banks and domestic banks are not significantly different in terms of their efficiency
Bhattacharya A, Lovell CAK and Sahay P (1997)	The impact of liberalization on the productive efficiency of Indian commercial banks	1. DEA for calculating radial technical efficiency 2. Stochastic frontier analysis	Publicly owned Indian banks were the most efficient followed by foreign owned banks and privately owned banks
Milind Sathye (2003)	Efficiency of banks in a developing economy: The case of India	Data Envelopment Analysis	Mean efficiency score of Indian banks compares well with the world mean efficiency score and the efficiency of private sector commercial banks as a group is, paradoxically lower than that of public sector banks and foreign banks in India
Mukherjee A, Nath P and Pal MN (2002)	Performance benchmarking and strategic homogeneity of Indian banks	1. DEA 2. Multiple correlation clustering	Public sector banks are more efficient than private or foreign banks although this could be due to the fact that public sector banks have a larger number of customers and are more widespread than foreign banks, the latter generally catering for small niche markets
Ram Mohan TT and Subhash C Ray (2004)	Productivity growth and efficiency in Indian banking: A comparison of public, private and foreign banks	Data Envelopment Analysis	PSBs performed significantly better than private sector banks but not differently from foreign banks. Superior performance of PSBs is to be ascribed to higher technical efficiency
Abhiman Das, Ashok Nag and Subhash C Ray(2004)	Liberalization, ownership, and efficiency in Indian banking: A nonparametric approach	Data Envelopment Analysis	Indian banks are not much differentiated in terms for input or output oriented technical efficiency and cost efficiency. However, they differ sharply in respect of revenue and profit efficiencies
Sathya Swaroop Debasish (2006)	Efficiency performance in Indian banking: Use of data envelopment analysis	Data Envelopment Analysis	Foreign owned banks were on average most efficient and that new banks are more efficient that old ones, which are often burdened with old debts
Saha A and Ravishankar TS (2000)	Rating of Indian commercial banks: A DEA approach	Data Envelopment Analysis	Public sector banks have in general, improved their efficiency scores over the period 1991/92 to 1994/95
Sunil Kumar and Rachita Gulati (2008)	Technical, pure technical, and scale efficiencies in Indian public sector (1992–2005)	1. DEA 2. Logistic regression analysis 3. Slacks and targets setting 3. input-	Public sector banks operate at 88.5 per cent level of overall technical efficiency. Exposure of the banks to off-balance sheet activities has a strong and positive impact on the overall technical efficiency of banks.
Subroto Chowdhury (2011)	Effect of financial Crisis in efficiency and strategic homogeneity of Indian commercial banks: An empirical investigation	1. DEA 2. Cluster analysis	The global financial crisis failed to have any impact on the technical efficiency of the Indian banking sector.
Mukesh Kumar and Vincent Charles (2012)	Evaluating the performance of Indian banking sector using data envelopment analysis during post reform and global financial crisis	1. DEA 2. Malmquist productivity index 3. Jackknifing analysis	The performance of public sector banks is at par with private sector banks in terms of efficiency.
Isaiah Onsarigo Miencha and Murugesan Selvam (2013)	Financial Performance in the Banking Sector: A Study With Special Reference to Kenyan Commercial Banks Using Data Envelopment Analysis (DEA)	Data Envelopment Analysis	The extent of TE and SE varied across the commercial Kenyan banks over the study period.
Miencha et al (2013)	Relative Efficiency of Kenyan Commercial Banks	Data Envelopment Analysis	There was a small number of efficient banks and there was scope for these sample banks to improve their production efficiency.
Miencha et al (2015)	Efficiency Measurement of Kenyan Commercial Banks	Data Envelopment Analysis	The extent of TE and SE varied across the commercial Kenyan banks over the study period.

Table 1: Summary of Recent Studies on Evaluation of Banks' Efficiency.

2. Fifty percent of the total banks for which the required data were available, were selected as sample (i.e 50% of 35=18 banks). In these 18 banks, only six banks were selected from medium size.

3. According to the top index value, 6 banks from medium size (i.e. top 3 and lowest 3. The details of sample banks are given in Table 2.

(B) Sources of Data

The present study was mainly based upon Secondary Data. The required secondary data were collected from Annual Report published by Central Bank of Kenya, various reputed journals and respective bank websites. The other relevant information for this study was collected from Books, News Papers, Magazines, Articles and various websites.

(C) Feedback

The experts in the field of banking, including officials of the banking, were contacted by the Researcher. Their views and valuable information helped the Researcher to validate the findings. Consultations with the experts helped the Researcher to fine tune the research study. Some of the suggestions offered were based on the interaction with the experts.

(D) Period of Study

The study period covered a period of ten years from January 2004 to December 2013.

(E) Tools Used

For the purpose of the analysis, the following tools were used.

i) Descriptive Statistics

a) Mean

The arithmetic mean is the sum of the entire list divided by the number of items in the list. It is often simply to as the average. The following formula was used to calculate the mean.

$$\text{Mean } \bar{X} = \frac{\sum X_i}{n}$$

Where,

$\bar{x}$ =represents the mean,

Σ=Symbol of Summation

x_i=Value of the ith item x, i=1, 2, 3 ....n, and

n=total number of items

b) Standard Deviation

Standard Deviation is the square root of the mean of the squared deviation from the arithmetic mean. It measures the absolute dispersion. Greater the standard deviation, greater will be the magnitude of the deviation of the values from their mean. A small standard deviation means a high degree of uniformity of the observation as well as homogeneity of a series. The standard deviation of a random variable X is defined as below (Table 2).

$$\sqrt{E(X-E(X)^2} = \sqrt{E(X)^2-(E(X)^2}$$

$$=\sqrt{Var(X)}$$

Where,

E(X) is the expected variable of X, and

$\sqrt{Var(X)}$ =is the variance of X.

ii) Correlation

Correlation Analysis refers to the techniques used in measuring the relationship between the variables. Correlation Co-efficient indicates the direction and degree of correlation. Correlation may be positive or negative, depending upon the direction of changes of the variables. If both the variables are varying in the same direction it is called positive correlation and if the variables are varying in the opposite direction, it is called negative correlation. Coefficient of Correlation always lies between +1 and -1. +1 is perfect positive correlation, -1 is perfect negative correlation and 0 is no relationship between variables.

$\rho X, Y=cov(X, Y)/\sigma x\, \sigma y=E[(X-\lambda x)(Y-\lambda y)]/\sigma x \sigma y$

Where,

$\rho X, Y$=random variables of x and y

λx=expected value of x

λy=expected value of y

σx=standard deviation of x, and

σy=standard deviation of y

iii) Data Envelopment Analysis (DEA)

This is a non-parametric method for the measurement of the efficiency relative to various Decision Making Units (DMUs). DMUs are the homogeneous units and in the present study, DMUs are the sample commercial banks. Technical Efficiency Score is the total weighted sum of outputs divided by total weighted sum of inputs. In this model, the efficiency was measured by the ratio of weighted outputs to weighted inputs. The efficiency of bank was measured in terms of how efficiently a bank utilized its inputs by using the following formula (Charnes, Cooper and Rodhes, 1978). In the model, the condition of efficiency is $\Theta^*=1$ and all the slack variables are assumed to be zero (O). Under such conditions, DMU_O's many outputs maximized values against many inputs, which are the subject to evaluation is assumed h_0 is as follows:

$$\text{Efficiency} = \frac{\text{weighted sum of Outputs}}{\text{weighted sum of Inputs}}$$

CCR Model

Charnes et al. [5] coined the term Data Envelopment Analysis (DEA). They extended Farrell [2] piecewise-linear convex hull approach to frontier estimation by expanding multiple inputs and single output to multiple inputs and and multiple outputs and utilized linear combination to convert it to single virtual input and output. Their model assumed Constant Returns to Scale (CRS) to measure the relative efficiency of each DMU which is between 0 and 1 and can determine whether a DMU is constant, increasing or decreasing returns to scale. Following Emrouznejad and Anouze the linear programming formulation is as follows.

Minimum Θ

Subject to:

$\Sigma_s \lambda_s I\ sx\text{-}0Ikx \leq 0\ \tilde{V}$ inputs x

$\Sigma_s \lambda_s 0sx\text{-}0kx \geq 0\ \tilde{V}$ outputs y

$\lambda_s \geq 0\ \tilde{V}$ s

The value of Θ obtained will be the efficiency score of the ith DMU.

BCC Model

Banker et al. (1984) widened the CCR model to account for Variable Returns to Scale (VRS). The CRS linear programming problem can be easily modified to account for VRS by adding the following constraints to the above model [6-9].

$$\Sigma_s \lambda_{s=} 1$$

This approach forms a convex hull of intersecting planes which envelope the data points more tightly than the CRS conical hull and thus provides technical efficiency scores which are greater than or equal to those using CRS model. For the purpose of calculating data for this study, Data Envelopment Analysis Online Software (D.E.A.O.S) was used by [10,11].

Bank groups	Categories of Banks	SR. No.	Names of the Banks	Market Index Value as on 31 December 2013
Medium size Banks	Top size Banks	1	Commercial Bank of Africa Ltd	4.40%
		2	Bank of India Ltd	4.35%
		3	Bank of Baroda Ltd	4.23%
	Lower size Banks	4	National Industrial Development Bank of Kenya Ltd	4.21%
		5	I&M Bank Ltd	4.19%
		6	Diamond Trust Bank (K) Ltd	4.16%
Note: Market Index Value was calculated by the Central Bank of Kenya as on 31st December 2013				

Table 2: Details of Sample Banks (Selected based on Market Value as on 31st December 2013).

Limitations of the study

The present study suffers from the following major limitations.

- The study investigated the relative efficiency and inefficiency of Kenyan Commercial Banks and not their absolute efficiency.
- The three sample categories of banks (medium, medium and small) were selected from public and private banks.
- The study was based on only secondary data.

Analysis Efficiency of Kenyan Sample Selected Banks

8.1 Descriptive Statistics of Total Assets for Medium (Top and Lower) size Kenyan Commercial Banks

8.2 Technical Efficiency of Kenyan Commercial Banks (Top and Lower in the MEDIUM group) in respect of TOTAL ASSETS

Descriptive Statistics of TOTAL ASSETS for Medium Size (Top and Lower) Kenyan Commercial Banks

The results of descriptive statistics, for medium size Kenyan sample banks (top and lower size), during the study period from 2004 to 2013, are given in Table 3. The efficiency of sample banks was measured in terms of Total Assets as an indicator. The mean values (for total assets) of three top sample banks (Bank of India, Bank of Baroda (K) Ltd and Commercial Bank of Africa Ltd) in the medium size group, were Ksh. 15845.50, Ksh. 25159.70 and Ksh. 60677.50 respectively, during the study period. Besides, one top sample bank, namely, Commercial Bank of Africa Ltd earned a maximum total assets value of Ksh. 124882.00 which was considered by [12-15] the highest value (top rank) among the top sample banks in the medium size group. This was followed by Bank of Baroda (K) Ltd, with a total assets value of Ksh. 52022.00 and Bank of India, with a maximum total assets value of Ksh. 30721.00, during the study period. The Commercial Bank of Africa Ltd earned a high risk for total assets value of Ksh. 33220.20, with an average total assets value of Ksh. 60677.50, which was considered as a high degree of variation among top sample banks in the medium size group banks, selected for this study. The top sample bank (Bank of Baroda (K) Ltd) in the medium size group was considered for the second position, with a dispersion value of Ksh. 15728.01 for total assets and the average assets value of Ksh. 25159.70, during the study period. Another sample bank, namely, Bank of India earned a value of Ksh. 8423.64 (lowest variation) and an average total assets value of Ksh. 15845.50, with a P-value of 0.000, in the medium top group of banks during the study period [16,17]. The average assets value of sample Banks (lower size), namely, National industrial Development Bank of Kenya Ltd, I & M Bank Ltd and Diamond Trust Bank (K) Ltd in the medium size group, were to the tune of Ksh. 52517.50, Ksh. 50667.80 and Ksh. 51259.40 respectively during the study period. But the maximum of total assets values earned by Diamond Trust Bank (K) Ltd, I & M Bank Ltd and National industrial Development Bank of Kenya Ltd were Ksh. 114136.00, Ksh. 110316.00 and Ksh. 112917.00 respectively during the study period (Table 3). It is clear from Table 2 that one sample bank namely, Diamond Trust Bank (K) Ltd under lower- medium size, earned high amount (Ksh. 34704.93) for total assets variation and an average assets value of Ksh. 51259.40 during the study period. But the National Industrial Development Bank of Kenya Ltd got second rank by earning a dispersion value of Ksh [18,19]. 33547.44, along with an average assets value of Ksh. 52517.40 during the study period. The I & M Bank Ltd, with a dispersion of Ksh.33155.19 for total assets, earned an average asset value of Ksh. 50667.80 which was considered as low dispersion and low assets value, with a P-value of 0.000, which was less than 0.01 level during the study period. The overall analysis of the Table shows that the Diamond Trust Bank (K) Ltd in the lower- medium size group performed better than other two sample banks, namely, I &M Bank Ltd and National Industrial Development Bank of Kenya Ltd in the same sample group. On the other hand, one sample bank, namely, Commercial Bank of Africa Ltd in the top-medium size group, had accounted for high dispersion in the total assets, with a low mean asset value. Another sample bank, namely, Bank of Baroda (K) Ltd also earned high amount of variation in the total assets (15728.01), with a better average asset (25159.70). The Bank of India had also assumed high degree of variation, with a low mean asset value, during the study period. The total assets always act like saviours of the bank all the time. Hence it is suggested that the two sample banks, Bank of India and Bank of Baroda (K) Ltd, should encourage more total assets, without affecting the profitability [20,21].

Technical Efficiency of Kenyan Commercial Banks (Top and Lower in the MEDIUM group) in respect of TOTAL ASSETS

The results of technical efficiency for sample banks (i.e top and lower size banks in the medium group) in Kenya, in respect of their total assets, under CCR, BCC and Technical Efficiency models, during the study period from 2004 to 2013, are displayed in Table 4. The mean efficiency scores for total assets, under CCR model, were 0.651 by top medium sample bank group, 0.952 by lower medium bank group and 0.802 by all banks during the study period from 2004 to 2013. The Table reveals that the use of total assets, under the CCR model was not uniform throughout the study period. Two sample banks, namely, Commercial bank of Africa Ltd and Diamond Trust bank (K) Ltd earned an efficiency score of 1.000 in respect of total assets during the study period. This indicates that these two sample banks utilized their total assets (inputs) effectively to be at the efficient frontier level during the study period. The performance of some other sample banks, namely, Bank of Baroda (K) Ltd (0.663), National Industrial Development Bank of Kenya Ltd (0.936), and I & M Bank Ltd (0.921) was considered to be near and moderately efficient during the study period. In order to

Sr. No.	Name of the Banks	Min	Max	Mean	Std Deviation	P-value
	I. Medium –Top Banks					
1.	Bank of India	6138.00	30721.00	15845.50	8423.64	0.000
2.	Bank of Baroda (K) Ltd	8355.00	52022.00	25159.70	15728.01	
3.	Commercial Bank of Africa Ltd	20176.00	124882.00	60677.50	33220.20	
	II. Medium – Lower Banks					
4.	National Industrial Development Bank of Kenya Ltd	16636.00	112917.00	52517.50	33547.44	0.000
5.	I&M Bank Ltd	14912.00	110316.00	50667.80	33155.19	
6.	Diamond Trust Bank (K) Ltd	11037.00	114136.00	51259.40	34704.93	
Note: Raw data in Kenyan Shillings (Ksh.) were used for the statistical calculation						

Table 3: Results of Descriptive Statistics of Total Assets of (Top and Lower in the Medium group) Kenyan Commercial Sample Banksfrom 2004 to 2013.

Sr. No.	I. Medium – (top) banks in the medium group	CCR	BCC	T.E
1.	Bank of India	0.290	0.542	0.411
2.	Bank of Baroda (K) Ltd	0.663	0.705	0.584
3	Commercial Bank of Africa Ltd	1.000	1.000	1.00
	Average Score (among three top banks)	0.651	0.749	0.665
	II. Medium – (lower) banks			
4.	National Industrial Development Bank of Kenya Ltd	0.936	0.958	0.947
5.	I&M Bank Ltd	0.921	0.983	0.952
6.	Diamond Trust Bank (K) Ltd	1.000	1.000	1.00
	Average Score(among three lower banks)	0.952	0.980	0.966
	Average Score (overall among six sample banks)	0.802	0.865	0.816

Note: I) CCR: Charnes, Coopers and Rodhes Model, BCC: Bankers, Charnes and Rodhes, T.E: Technical Efficiency Models. II) Scale value of 1.000 indicates efficiency III) Scale value of 0.500 to 0.999 indicates near or moderately efficiency IV) Scale value of less than 0.499 indicates inefficiency of banks.

Table 4: Results of Technical Efficiency Total Assets (using CCR, BCC and T.E Models) for Kenyan Commercial Banks (three Top and three Lower banks in the Medium group) during the study period 2004-2013.

improve and be at the efficient level, these two banks, (namely, Bank of Baroda (K) Ltd and National Industrial Development Bank of Kenya Ltd) are required to earn a score of 0.337 and 0.064 respectively, by using their inputs perfectly. But Bank of India (an Indian origin bank) underperformed, with an efficiency score of 0.290 and it needs to earn a score of 0.710 in respect of total assets to be at the efficient frontier. The technical efficiency, under the BCC model, in respect to total assets is also represented in Table 4. The average efficiency scores were 0.749 earned by top sample banks, 0.980 by lower sample banks and 0.865 by all sample banks (overall average) during the study period. It is significant to note that all the sample banks selected for this study performed well all through, without any inefficiency score in respect of total assets, during the study period. From the analysis, it is to be noted that Commercial Bank of Africa Ltd and Diamond Trust Bank (K) Ltd gained an efficient level of 1.000 in respect of total assets during the study period (Table 4).

But banks, namely, Bank of India, Bank of Baroda (K) Ltd, National Industrial Development Bank of Kenya (Ltd) and I & M Bank Ltd earned efficiency score values of 0.542, 0.705, 0.958 and 0.983 respectively, in respect of total assets, during the study period. These sample banks, namely, (Bank of India, Bank of Baroda (K) Ltd, National Industrial Development Bank of Kenya Ltd and I & M Bank Ltd) are required to earn scores of 0.458, 0.295, 0.042 and 0.017 by using total assets efficiently, to become efficient. The analysis of efficiency score, under the Technical Efficiency model, is displayed in the Table 4. It is clear from the above analysis that the performance of Commercial Bank of Africa Ltd and Diamond Trust Bank (K) Ltd was efficient, with a score value of 1.000 for total assets during the study period. This indicates that these banks utilized their inputs in respect of total assets properly to find a place at the efficient level. Other banks like Bank of Baroda (K) Ltd, National Industrial Development Bank of Kenya Ltd and I & M Bank Ltd earned efficiency scores of 0.584, 0.947 and 0.952 respectively, regarding total assets. Hence these banks need to earn score values of 0.416, 0.053 and 0.048, by using total assets of these banks intelligently, to be at the efficient level [22-24].

Conclusion

The Commercial Bank of Africa Ltd and Diamond Trust Bank (K) Ltd maintained efficiency, in respect of its total assets satisfactorily, under CCR, BCC and Technical Efficiency models, indicating their growth. Other sample banks, namely, Bank of India, Bank of Baroda (K) Ltd, Commercial bank of Africa Ltd, National Development Bank of Kenya Ltd and I & M Bank Ltd experienced fluctuating efficiency scores all through the study period. Hence it is suggested that sample banks like Bank of India, Bank of Baroda (K) Ltd, Commercial bank of Africa Ltd, National Development Bank of Kenya Ltd and I & M Bank Ltd have to adopt the latest technology and innovations in their products and create awareness among the public to attract more customers and to earn high profits.

References

1. Sparks P, Guthrie CA, Shepherd R (1997) The dimensional structure of the perceived behavioral control construct. Journal of Applied Social Psychology 27: 418-438.
2. Farrell MJ (1957) The Measurement of Productive Efficiency Journal of the Royal Statistical Society 120: 253-290.
3. Smirlock M (1985) Evidence on the (none) relationship between concentration and profitability in banking. Journal of Money Credit and Banking 17: 69-83.
4. Evanoff D, Fortier L (1988) Revaluation of the Structure Conduct Performance Paradigm in Banking. Journal of financial services research 1: 277-294.
5. Charnes A, Cooper WW, Rhodes E (1978) Measuring the efficiency of decision making units European. Journal of Operational Research 2: 429-444.
6. Arabinda S (2008) Performance Indicators of Banking Sector in Bangradesh: A Comparative Overview of NCBs PCBs SCBs and FCBs SMART. Journal of Business Management Studies 4: 1-9.
7. Athanasoglou PP, Brissimis SN, Delis MD (2005) Bank-Specific Industry-Specific and Macroeconomic Determinants of Profitability Working Paper. Bank of Greece.
8. Badola BS, Verma R (2006) Determinants of Profitability of Banks in India: Multvariate Analysis Delhi. Business Review 7: 79-88.
9. Banker R, Charnes A, Cooper WW (1984) Some Models for Estimating Technical and Scale Inefficiencies in Data Envelopment Analysis. Managerial Science 30: 1078-1092.
10. Boris Vujcic, Igor Jemric (2001) Efficiency of Banks in Transition: A DEA Approach Croatian National Bank.
11. Christian C, Moffitt JS, Suberly LA (2008) Fundamental Analysis for Evaluating Bank Performance: What Variables Provide the Greatest Insight into Future Earnings? Journal of Bank Accounting and Finance 22: 17-24.
12. Isaiah OM, Murugesan S (2013) Financial Performance in Banking Sector: A Study with Special Reference to Kenyan Commercial Banks Using Data Envelopment Analysis (DEA). Research Journal of Social Sciences and Management 2: 48-53.
13. Isaiah OM, Murugesan S, Rajesh R, Karpagam V (2013) Relative Efficiency of Kenyan Commercial Banks. Journal of International Business Management 7: 142-150.
14. Isaiah O, Miencha M, SelvamV, Vasanth K, Lingaraja, et al. (2015) Efficiency Measurement of Kenyan Commercial Banks Mediterranean. Journal of Social Sciences 6: 621-631.
15. Isik I, Hassan MK (2003) Financial Deregulation and Total Factor Productivity Change: An Empirical Study of Turkish Commercial Banks. Journal of Banking and Finance 27: 1455-1485.

16. Kosmidou K, Pasiourass F, Doumpos M, Zopoutiidis C (2006) Assessing Performance Factors in the UK Banking Sector: A Multicriteria Methodology CEJOR 14: 25-44.

17. Ketkar K, Athanasios W, Manmohan A (2003) Analysis of Efficiency and Productivity Growth of Indian Banking Sector Finance India pp: 511-513.

18. Kumar S, Rachita G (2008) Evaluation of Technical Efficiency and Ranking of Public-Sector Banks in India International. Journal of Productivity and Performance Management 57: 540-568.

19. Lensink R, Meesters A, Naaborg I (2008) Bank Efficiency and Foreign Ownership: Do Good Institutions Matter? Journal of Banking and Finance 32: 834-844.

20. Nguyen KM, Nguyen VH (2013) Efficiency and Super-Efficiency of Commercial Banks in Vietnam: Performances and Determinants Asia-Pacific. Journal of Operational Research 30: 1250047-1-1250047-19.

21. Prasad V J, Bhalerao JV (2011) Efficiency Evaluation of Banking Sector in India based on Data Envelopment Analysis. Indian Journal of Commerce and Management Studies 2: 32-34.

22. Richard BS, Kory SF, Thomas, Sheri Z (2002) Evaluating the Productive Efficiency and Performance of US Commercial Banks Managerial Finance 28: 3-22.

23. Shanmugam, Das (2004) Efficiency of Indian Commercial Banks during the Reform Period Applied Financial Economics 14: 618-686.

24. Wei K, Wang, Hao C, Huang YZ (2005) Measuring the Relative Efficiency of Commercial Banks: A Comparative Study on Different Ownership Modes in China. The Journal of American Academy of Business Cambridge 7: 219-223.

Morbidity due to Air Pollution in Cotonou: An Assessment of the Psychological Cost

Fanougbo Avoce Viagannou*

The Benin School of Applied Economics and Management ENEAM-FASEG/University of Abomey-Calavi, 05BP 1652 Cotonou, Benin

Abstract

Atmospheric pollution is a negative externality whose health costs are significant. In this article we assessed the psychological cost or cost of suffering due to pollution-related morbidity. The Contingent Valuation (CV) method has allowed us to estimate the average monthly psychological cost of disease for a household head based on the Willingness To Pay (WTPs) of household heads to halve air pollution in the city of Cotonou. This assessment is one of the few in the city of Cotonou or even in West Africa. The analysis of the WTPs with a Tobit model has allowed us to derive the average WTP, which represents the psychological cost of morbidity whose value is estimated at FCFA 1,200/month per household head. This result can validly serve as the basis for decision-making in line with the polluter pays principle.

Keywords: Atmospheric pollution; Morbidity; Contingent valuation; Psychological cost; Generalized tobit

JEL classification: C34, I18, Q51, Q53

Introduction

Pollution is a major concern for most countries of the world. The issue of pollution is at the heart of the theory of externalities whose basic foundations are clearly laid by Pigou. Populations exposed to atmospheric pollution suffer enormous damage. The effects of this pollution on human health are the major concern in most studies that have examined the issue. Thus, Raffin [1]showed the relationship between health, environmental quality and economic development. The definition of air pollution according to Tattersfield [2], which was taken over by Nejjari et al. [3] is: 'contamination of the air by one or more substances that are either produced naturally, or result from human activity, with the consequence that the air becomes less acceptable for maintaining health'. From this definition, it is understandable that human health is threatened. This explains why studies in this area in most African countries or elsewhere focus more on the effects of air pollution (AP) on health. It is noteworthy that recently, Hunt [4] actually restated that the effects of AP range from no less important breathing problems to cases of death due to cardiopulmonary diseases. Similarly, the report on "the perceptions of indoor air pollution in Île-de-France" also specifies the effects of pollution on health.

For environmental economists, attention is often paid to the assessment of damages related to air pollution. Thus, morbidity and/or mortality profits or costs are assessed through various works [1,5-8]. It is noteworthy that two cost components allow a full assessment of the damages associated with morbidity due to air pollution: the medical-social costs and the cost of suffering or discomfort associated with the morbid condition. Indeed, Rozan [9] showed that the cost of discomfort or psychological cost is as important as the second one. But some studies (e.g. [6]) were only based on the assessment of the medical-social cost which takes into account the total expenses for treating the disease, the loss of income related to the inability (due to disease) to conduct income-generating activities, etc.

Faced with the reality of air pollution in the city of Cotonou, residents of the latter undergo health costs due to this nuisance. Given that obtaining a zero level for air pollution is almost impossible [1], the populations are exposed to the adverse effects of air pollution. In these atmospheric pollution conditions, victims would incur health expenses either for preventing diseases or for treating them. This would cost a lot to the population from a health perspective. Some expenses would be incurred to avoid premature death. Kappos et al. [10] noted that short-term studies on air pollution have shown that the relations between concentrations of dust particles (PM) and human health become less significant for low levels of concentrations. Apart from the respiratory tract, the cardiovascular system is threatened by pollutants. For this reason, there is an increase in cardiovascular pathologies or the worsening of pre-existing ones. We can also observe other symptoms outside airways such as eye irritation, headache, fatigue etc. Recently, Just [11] showed that in developed countries, when one is exposed to air pollution in youth, there is an increase of allergies and the incidence of asthma. It remains true that chronic diseases and cancers affecting the respiratory system often appear in areas with high levels of pollution. Long-term effects are more difficult to study because of their low intensity. These various works thus confirm the potential costs faced by the peaceful population being exposed to air pollutants.

Whatever the disease caused by air pollution, the affected individual suffers from it, and so depending on the severity and duration of pain. This suffering is not without consequences in terms of costs for the individual. It is these costs that Rozan [9] terms cost of discomfort or psychological cost. So what is the level of psychological cost [private cost] due to air pollution in Cotonou?

So far, no assessment of this type of cost related to air pollution has been made in Cotonou. This assessment is one of the few in the city of Cotonou or even in West Africa. The objective of this article is to assess the psychological cost of morbidity due to air pollution in the city of Cotonou in Benin. To address this concern, the article is structured as follows. In the second section, we discuss the literature and in the third section, we present the methodology used for the assessment of

***Corresponding author:** Fanougbo Avoce Viagannou, The Benin School of Applied Economics and Management ENEAM-FASEG/University of Abomey-Calavi, Benin, E-mail: fanougboisaac@yahoo.fr

the cost. The penultimate section presents results and discussions and the final section concludes.

Literature Review

Several studies have examined the question of morbidity related to air pollution [AP]. To this end, they have sought to assess damages or costs related to morbidity due to this pollution. We highlight in this section a number of works in order to take advantage from them for our assessment in the case of the city of Cotonou. First, it should be noted that in the assessment of morbidity due to air pollution, two main approaches dominate in the literature: The dose-response function (DRF) approach and the contingent valuation approach. The health production function (HPF) method approach used by Gerking and Stanley [12] seems not to have as much application in the works as the two other approaches. With this study, these authors derived an average WTP which is between $18.45 and $24.48 for a 30% reduction in ozone concentrations. To do this, they conducted a survey on a sample of 824 adults in St. Louis. The collection of information on air quality, use of medical services, prices of medical services, wage rates, sociodemographic characteristics and measurements of health stock, helped these authors make their assessment.

Regarding the dose-response function (DRF) method, it should be noted that the studies that have made use of it [13-16] were based on time series. Some of these studies [13,14] have used daily data. Based on a case study in London, Maddison [14] analyzed hospital admissions as well as PM_{10}concentrations while Laïd et al. [13], based on health variables, applied the DRF method in the city of Algiers. For assessments of this kind, the results are in terms of number of attributable cases. For example Maddison [14] found that a 1% reduction in PM_{10} levels causes a significant reduction of 0.14% in the number of respiratory hospital admissions. In a similar vein, other studies were based on annual or international data [15]. These studies took into account pollution indicators such as black smoke, fine particles, NO_2, O_3, SO_2 as well as health and socioeconomic variables. Another study, remaining in the same logic of number of attributable cases, showed that increasing pollutant from a basic level to a median level causes an increase of at least 2% of hospitalizations for each type of disease respectively. By cons, Rabl [15] found that a 10% reduction of pollutant concentrations saves 67 million of disease-related cost. These results reflect again that diseases due to air pollution cause significant costs. Whether in terms of attributable cases or monetary value, the assessment by the DRF method gives important information on morbidity costs associated with air pollution. Also, it should be noted that a study conducted in the United States [16] using the same method, was based on epidemiological and clinical data. The first allowed the authors to obtain a benefit of $ 250 million for a reduction of air pollution, and the second led them to a benefit of $ 800 million.

As for the contingent valuation method, it has had many applications since its first use in the United States by Davis [17]. This approach consists in proposing to the agents a "contingent market" in which they are asked to make a choice, the purpose of this being to determine the WTP of the surveyed individual. Thus, the studies discussed in this review [5,6,9,18] were based on field surveys. Indeed, a contingent valuation questionnaire is necessary in the conduct of such research. The various studies carried out in this context take into account socioeconomic, demographic and health variables. Thus, Alberini et al. [5] considered in their study, variables such as the nature of the disease, the length of time during which respondents have suffered symptoms, the severity of the disease, the sociodemographic characteristics. In addition to the socio demographic variables used by Chanel et al. [6], the medical expenses and the loss of income were included. Unlike other authors, the study of Rozan [9] was concerned with benign diseases due to air pollution. Also, it should be noted that she took into account variables such as prices of medicines, hospitalization costs, costs of consultancy fees, work stoppage and school absenteeism costs, as well as the socioeconomic characteristics of individuals. In these various works, the size of the sample used is not the same. The size is 262 in the work of Alberini et al. [5], 864 in that of Chanel et al. [6], and 1,000 in that of Rozan [9]. In all these studies, the WTP served as a basis for deriving the economic benefit or the economic cost. According to Berger et al. [18], the WTP increases with the pain of the disease and it has a value of $ 27 for one day spent suffering from a cold, and a value of $ 108 for a day without headaches. The economic benefit obtained by these authors totaled $ 6.79 for the case of colds and $ 3.45 for the case without headaches. Still in terms of benefit, Alberini et al. [5] found that following a pollution reduction, the value of morbidity is about US $ 262.58 million. The WTP to avoid the disease increases with the duration of the disease, the number of symptoms experienced, education and income. By cons, according to Chanel et al. [6], the morbidity costs of air pollution reach 67.8 billion francs. Rozan [9] found in her study that the average WTP amounts to F 282 and corresponds to the psychological cost of the disease. The psychological cost she obtained represents at least 50% of the total cost of the disease. She also assessed the medical-social costs per pathology [185F for Laryngitis/weakened adult]. It is noticeable that in the work of Rozan [9], a distinction is made between the psychological cost [or cost of discomfort] and the medical-social cost. And for the latter, she used the Cost-of-illness method (COIM).

It should be noted that the variables which the various authors cited above have referred to, are virtually those mentioned by Gastineau et al. [19]. Moreover, very few studies have examined the specific assessment of the psychological cost (or cost of discomfort) due to air pollution.

Cost Assessment Methodology

Sampling

In this paper, we proceeded by empirical survey. According to Ardilly [20], there are two main types of empirical surveys: -the quota method and -the standard units method. The quota method is the most frequently used empirical method. According to Gauthy-Sinéchal and Vandercammen [21], this method is based on the following assumption: *if the sample accurately reproduces certain characteristics of the study population, it will also be representative for other non-controllable characteristics but which are the very subject of the survey.* For them, the challenge in this method is to accurately determine the variables to retain, and to find in the population the exact proportions of units having these characteristics.

The sample size chosen for this purpose is 600 individuals. This size corresponds to an absolute error of about 4%. In the city of Cotonou, 74.10% of men are heads of households and 25.90% are female heads of household, out of a population of 426,220 men and 436,225 women in 2010. Account is taken of the proportions of men heads of household per area in Benin and the Littoral department (Cotonou), as well as the data of Cotonou city hall on motorcycle taxis according to which about 47.06% of men heads of household are motorcycle taxi drivers. These drivers are more exposed to atmospheric pollution because of their activity. In fact, this is also confirmed by the various research studies conducted for the city on those drivers.

The statistical units which make up the sample were randomly selected using the door to door method in the eight districts in which industrial activities are dominant in the said city.

Survey methodology

In a CV assessment method, the questionnaire is fundamental. Thus, the questionnaire was developed taking into account the main biases inherent in the method. These biases highlighted by Mitchell and Carson [22] have recently been synthesized by Bontems and Rotillon [23]. These include the strategic bias, biases related to the administration of the questionnaire, the hypothetical bias and the effect of inclusion. An effort was made to minimize the different biases.

Firstly, in the questions asked, the recommendations of the NOAA Arrow [24] have been followed. So the questions are mostly closed questions, and they are followed by some open questions at certain points. Also, the scenario described is understandable by the population which is well familiar with the problem of air pollution. To assess the cost of suffering associated with the morbid condition of individuals, the part of the questionnaire which takes into account this aspect is split into three sub-parts. The first sub-part relates to characteristics of the respondent (sex, age, educational level, socio-professional category, marital status). The second sub-part contains on the one hand, questions related to the morbid effects and those that highlight the households' perception of AP; and on the other hand questions about revealing the WTP based on the discomfort felt by the respondent. Regarding this section on the WTP, the scenario described is presented in the box below. Whatever the choice made by the respondent based on the scenario, he is asked an additional question about his maximum WTP. The third sub-part deals with other characteristics of the respondent (monthly income, being a smoker, energy sources used, and some household expenses).

Then the questionnaire benefited from the informative remarks of economicsand demographicsexperts. The contributions of health economics and environmental economics experts are rewarding. It should be noted that the questionnaire was read and corrected by the expert on field surveys, Bernard Lacombe. According to the methodological approaches to field practice which we have taken inspiration from in the work of Lacombe, the questionnaire has improved. After taking into account the various comments, the final questionnaire was used for the training of the surveyors recruited for the occasion. Finally, a pre-test was done to ensure the population's understanding of the questions. The various end-of-interview reports from the pre-test showed that respondents actually experience the phenomenon of air pollution through the nuisance it creates. These reports have allowed us to elaborate on how certain questions should be approached during the administration of the questionnaire permanently retained.

Box: Contingent scenario

Everyone has the right to breathe clean air. Yet, it has been shown that there is a relation between air pollution and the occurrence of the listed diseases such as: coughing, headaches, respiratory diseases, heart diseases, sore eyes, asthma etc. The risk of experiencing these diseases again can be reduced through a comprehensive program to fight against the degradation of air quality. This will allow improving and preserving the health of the population.

We have two cases:

***Case 1**: The air quality in Cotonou deteriorates. In this case, your health condition deteriorates because of diseases related to air pollution, and you remain without response by bearing no financial cost; but the air quality does not improve.*

***Cas 2**: You agree to help fund an air quality improvement program. Here you bear a financial cost but the occurrence of certain diseases will lessen and your health will improve as well.*

Which of the two cases do you prefer?

***If choice = Case 2**,*

We present you the following scenario:

Many of the diseases that you have suffered are due to air pollution. If pollution is reduced by half over a period of 5 years, the risk of suffering from the ills directly related to pollution will be halved too.

Will you be ready, during the 5 years of the project, to pay a monthly amount of at least [show the payment chart]: FCFA 500, FCFA 1.000, FCFA 1.500, FCFA 2.000, FCFA 2.500, FCFA 3.000, FCFA 3.500, FCFA 4.000, FCFA 4500, FCFA 5.000, FCFA 5.500, FCFA 6.000?

***If choice = Case 1**, what are the reasons for your choice?*

After the administration of the 600 questionnaires, 584 have actually been processed because of some unanswered questions. Therefore, the response rate is 97.33%. The database used in the econometric analysis traces the information on the 584 individuals processed.

Description of variables

In the works on the use of the CV method for assessments of this kind [9,25], the variables that are often taken into account are those relating to socio-economic and demographic characteristics on the one hand, and those relating to the specificities of the property to be assessed on the other hand (here, there are variables related, for example, to the health status, the fact of visiting a doctor, etc).

The main variables relevant to the estimation of the average WTP representing the psychological cost are the socio-economic variables of the respondents. We considered the following variables:

- The monthly Willingness To Pay [capmois] is a discrete quantitative variable whose values appear on the payment chart[according to the contingent scenario: FCFA 500, FCFA 1.000F, FCFA 1.500, FCFA 2.000, FCFA 2.500, FCFA 3.000, FCFA 3.500, FCFA 4.000, FCFA 4.500, FCFA 5.000, FCFA 5.500, FCFA 6.000]. This is the dependent variable.
- Sex [sexe] is a dichotomous variable. It has only two

modalities [1=0=Male and 0=Female].

- Age [age] is a continuous variable. Its modalities depend on the respondent's bygone age expressed in years. As the age of the individual increases, he is tempted to contribute more in order to have good health, to a certain degree. Note that according to Phelps the individual's health condition deteriorates with age, and so he gives more importance to his health in old age; therefore he tends to contribute more than a young man.

- Age squared [agecar]; it is a variable that takes into account the nonlinear effect of age. Beyond a certain age threshold, the individual's income decreases and the effect of age on the capmois becomes negative. It is fair to say that an individual who is aging has a low labor productivity compared to a young person, and therefore his income may be low; so his WTP may decrease.

- Duration of residence [tempshabit] is a continuous variable describing the number of years spent by the respondent in the city of Cotonou. An individual who has spent a long time in the city of Cotonou has the chance to make comparisons between ages in terms of pollution, and his contribution to improving air quality would be high.

- The profession [professionZ]; it is a qualitative variable that describes the socio-professional categories of respondents. It takes the value 1 when the individual is a motorcycle-taxi driver and the value 0 otherwise. Motorcycle-taxi drivers may be more willing to contribute because of the diseases to which they are exposed.

- The education level [nivetude] is a qualitative variable. It has four modalities [primary, secondary, higher, none]. The more the individual is educated, the more he would contribute to the improvement of air quality. Before inserting this variable in the econometric model, each modality has been dichotomized.

- The monthly income of the respondent [tranchrev]; it is a continuous quantitative variable. Incomes are grouped by income bracket. We have identified nine income brackets: 1-Less than FCFA 30.000; 2-FCFA 30,001-40.000; 3-FCFA 40,001-50.000; 4-FCFA 50,001-60,000; 5-FCFA 60,001-70,000; 6-FCFA 70,001-80,000; 7-FCFA 80,001-90.000; 8-FCFA 90,001-10.0000, 9-More than FCFA 100,000. The higher the income of the individual, the more he would be willing to contribute.

- The respondent's smoking status [fumeur] is a dichotomous qualitative variable that takes the value 1 if the individual smokes cigarettes and 0 otherwise. Given that a smoker is used to living in cigarette smoke, pollution in general may no longer seem worrisome to him and from this point of view, he will have a lower willingness to pay.

- Respondent's relocation status [projdemenagpoll] is a dichotomous variable that takes the value 1 when the individual intends to relocate due to air pollution and 0 otherwise. When an individual has such a plan, he will have a low contribution to improving air quality because of his investment in relocation.

- The variable [airpollue] reflects whether the individual recognizes that the air is polluted in the city of Cotonou. It is dichotomous and takes the value 1 when the individual recognizes that the air is polluted in Cotonou and 0 otherwise. Its effect on the willingness to pay is positive.

Table 1 presents the different expected effects of the explanatory variables on the dependent variable (monthly willingness to pay: capmois). Indeterminate effects assume that it is not easy to make a prediction on the effects of the different variables involved on the variable "capmois".

Estimation model of the psychological cost of morbidity

In view of the above, the dependent variable WTP reflecting the individuals' willingness to pay contains valid zeros. Its values are in the range [0; 6,000]. The values of this interval of the dependent variable are greater than or equal to zero. It is possible to use a censored Tobit model. This model is used when in a situation where the dependent variable is zero for a significant number of observations [25]. The use of a censored Tobit model to explain the individuals' WTP is justified. For some authors [26], the choice of the econometric model depends on the assumption made in the process for revealing the WTP. Thus, according to them, the two-step procedure of Heckman [27] can be used.

Based on the contingent scenario presented to respondents, the decision process is sequential; this leads us to estimate the two-step model of Heckman [27] or the generalized Tobit.

Presentation of the generalized Tobit model: In the scenario presented to heads of household, the choice of the WTP is made in two steps. First he chooses either case 2 or case 1, which indicates whether or not he is ready to participate; then he chooses the desired amount in the event that he decides to participate. In this process, the decision is sequential. So, formalizing this situation might look as follows:

In the first step the individual is faced with a choice situation that can be reflected by a dichotomous model based on a latent variable y_i*.

$$\begin{cases} if\ y_i^* > 0 \text{ the individual } i \text{ chooses case2 (decides to participate)} \\ if\ y_i^* \leq 0 \text{ the individual } i \text{ chooses case1 (decides not to participate)} \end{cases}$$

In the second step, if the individual chooses case 2, he also chooses his WTP. Here we have a censored data model, defined by $\forall i = \overline{1,n}$:

$$CAP_i = \begin{cases} CAP_i^* & if\ y_i^* > 0 \\ 0 & if\ y_i^* \leq 0 \end{cases} \qquad \text{[M 1]}$$

For Greene [26] 7 (taken over by N'Guessan [25]), the quality of estimators from the generalized Tobit depends on how the explanatory variables are introduced in explaining y_i and the WTP. It is important not to include exactly the same explanatory variables in both equations. Thus, we have:

$$\begin{aligned} y_i^* &= X_1\beta_1 + \varepsilon_{1i} \\ CAP_i^* &= X_2\beta_2 + \varepsilon_{2i} \end{aligned} \qquad \text{[M 2]}$$

With X_1 and X_2 designating the explanatory variables [socioeconomic or demographic characteristics]; β_1 and β_2 are parameters to be estimated, and ε_j (j=1,2) are the error terms that follow a bivariate normal distribution with ρ as correlation coefficient. After normalization [σ_1=1] we have:

$$\begin{pmatrix} \varepsilon_1 \\ \varepsilon_2 \end{pmatrix} \rightarrow N\left(\begin{pmatrix} 0 \\ 0 \end{pmatrix}, \Omega\right); \quad \Omega = \begin{pmatrix} 1 & \rho\sigma_2 \\ \rho\sigma_2 & \sigma_2^2 \end{pmatrix}$$

For reasons of simplification, a dichotomous variable D_{2i} is inserted so that we have:

$$D_{2i} = \begin{cases} 1 & if\ y_i^* > 0 \\ 0 & if\ y_i^* \leq 0 \end{cases} \qquad \text{[M 3]}$$

So the estimation of the model can be made using the two-step method of Heckman [27] or the full-information maximum likelihood method.

Variables	Expected effects
Sex	**Indeterminate**
Age	+
Professions	+
Tempshabit	+
Settle	+
Nivetude	+
Smoking	-
projdemenagpoll	-
Air pollution	+

Source: Author

Table 1: Explanatory variables and expected effects.

Variables	Coefficients	P >|z|
Settle	0.1082956***	0.000
Age	-0.017604**	0.019
Tempshabit	-0.00206	0.715
Air pollution	0.6719894*	0.085
Professions	0.2145211	0.180
Number of observations=584 LR chi2(5)=32.14 Probability>chi2=0.0000		

***significant at the 1% threshold; **significant at the 5% threshold; *significant at the 10% threshold

Source: Extract from estimation results.

Table 2: Determining variables of the participation model.

Variables	Coefficients	P >|z|
Settle	71.88752*	0.084
age	37.24831	0.207
AGE CAR	-0.3148363	0.364
smoking	320.2954**	0.042
sex	-274.5266**	0.043
projdemenagpoll	181.7703*	0.082
professions	-75.0474	0.598
niv2	-39.57184	0.747
niv3	850.3739***	0.000
niv4	-8.04537	0.962
lambda	-1516.674	0.214
Number of observations=516 F(11,504)=11.41 Probability>F=0.0000		

***Significant at the 1% threshold; **significant at the 5% threshold; *significant at the 10% threshold

Source: Extract from estimation results

Table 3: Determining variables of the WTP.

Results and Discussions

Determinants of participation in the improvement of air quality

The estimation of the participation model [M 3] gives the results presented in Table 2.

From the analysis of Table 2, it appears that the determining variables of participation in the program are: income, age and quality of air. Income is significant at the 1% threshold while age and quality of air are respectively significant at the 5% and 10% thresholds. Thus, when the individual's income increases, his probability of participating in the air quality improvement program becomes greater. Similarly, the fact that the individual recognizes that the air is polluted increases his probability of participating in the air quality improvement program.

Determinants of the monthly WTP

The second step of the estimation gives the results for model [M2] and presents the various determinants of the monthly willingness to pay (Table 3). According to the results of this table, five variables are significant. The variable "tranchrev" is significant at the 10% threshold. Its effect is positive and was expected. Thus, the willingness to pay depends positively on the income, confirming the economic theory that the willingness to pay of an individual increases with his income.

The fact that the individual is a smoker affects positively the willingness to pay. This effect was not expected. This significance at the 5% threshold of the variable "fumeur" suggests that the smoking individual knows the severity of the pollution from cigarette smoke on health. For this reason, he seems to be willing to participate in the air quality improvement program.

The negative significance at the 5% threshold of the variable "sexe" shows that males are less willing to participate than women. This could be justified by the fact that a woman would be more sensitive to the health effects of air pollution that a man. The variable "projdemenagpoll" is positively significant at the 10% threshold, which was not expected. This positive effect means that the individual who intends to relocate is more willing to participate than the one who does not. Thus, the awareness that leads the individual to undertake to relocate because of air pollution causes him to support an air quality improvement project. The education level is significant. Precisely, the effect for an individual of a higher level is positively significant at the 1% threshold compared to an individual having a primary level. In other words, a person of a higher education level is more willing to participate than a person having a primary level.

The variable "lambda" is the inverse Mills ratio. This variable is not significant, which reflects the absence of selection bias. The mean WTP predicted from the model is about FCFA 1,360. But taking into account the individuals' average predicted probability of contributing financially, the average monthly WTP is about FCFA 1,200. Thus, the annual contribution of an individual to fight against air pollution in order to reduce the discomfort due to morbidity, is about FCFA 1,200 × 12=FCFA 14,400, all else being equal.

Ultimately, the determining variables of the individuals' willingness to pay are identified and the psychological cost or cost of suffering associated with the disease, is derived and is about FCFA 1,200/month per household head. So for individuals to reduce their risk of suffering from the ills they have referred to, they are ready to contribute for FCFA 1,200/month so that the air pollution is reduced by half. This amount represents the average cost of discomfort due to diseases related to air pollution. This assumes that the annual contribution of the population to a program against air pollution is FCFA 14,400 per individual. By comparing the annual cost of discomfort obtained in this work to the one obtained by Rozan [9], we note that the result of this author (F 282 or FCFA 28,200) is FCFA 13,800 greater than that of this work. This may be justified by the fact that the conditions in which the different studies were conducted are not identical in every respect. In addition, the levels of income are not the same in these different studies. Taking into account other works, the amount obtained in our work is not exaggerated. For example Gerking and Stanley [12] calculated the WTP for a given reduction in pollution and they obtained an average annual WTP between $ 18.45 and $ 24.48 (between FCFA 10,148 and FCFA 13,464). The fact that those amounts are relatively lower compared to that of this work and the one of Rozan, may be explained for example by the reduction percentage (30%) of the average ozone concentrations suggested by the study of Gerking and Stanley, as well as by the specificities of the study environments. Ultimately, the amount of the psychological cost of morbidity considered is FCFA 1,200 per month per morbidity episode.

Conclusion

In this article, the psychological cost of morbidity due to air pollution in the city of Cotonou is assessed. This assessment is made using a contingent valuation approach. Although precaution is taken in preparing the contingent valuation questionnaire, some biases may exist given that the population's level of understanding is not uniform. But the expertise of the different experts on field surveys that have contributed to the development of the questionnaire has reduced a number of biases, enabling the validity of the results. Thus, a head of household of Cotonou city falling ill due to air pollution bears an average psychological cost of FCFA 1,200 per month. This result is one of the few assessments of this kind in Benin or even in West Africa. On this basis, public decisions could be taken in order to internalize the effects of air pollution on morbidity.

References

1. Raffin N (2009) Santé, qualité environnementale et développement économique, Revue économique 60: 831-842.
2. Tattersfield AE (1996) Air Pollution: Brown skies research. Thorax 51: 13-22.
3. Nejjari C, Filleul L, Laid Y, Atek M, El Meziane A, et al. (2003) Air Pollution: a new respiratory risk for cities in low-income countries. Int J Tuberc Lung Dis 7(3): 223-231.
4. Hunt A (2011) Policy interventions to address health impacts associated with air pollution, unsafe water supply and sanitation, and hazardous chemicals, OECD environment working papers, No 35, OECD Publishing.
5. Alberini A, Cropper M, Fu TT, Krupnick A (1997) Valuing health effects of air pollution in developing countries: The case of Taiwan. Journal of Environmental Economics and Management 34: 107-126.
6. Chanel O, Masson S, Scapecchi P, Vergnaud JC (2000) Pollution et santé : Evaluation monétaire et effets de long terme,Revue Région et Développement 12-20.
7. Sartori AE (2003) An estimator for some binary-outcome selection models without exclusion restrictions. Political Analysis 11: 111-138.
8. Muller NZ, Mendelsohn R (2007) Measuring the damages of air pollution in the United States. Journal of Environmental Economics and Management 54: 1-14.
9. Rozan A (2000) Bénéfices de santé liés à la qualité de l'environnement: Peut-on négliger les coûts privés? Revue Economique 51: 595-608.
10. Kappos AD, Bruckmann P, Eikmann T, Englert N, et al. (2004) Health effects of particles in ambient air. Int J Hyg Environ Health 207: 399-407.
11. Just J (2011) Impact de pollution sur l'asthme de la petite enfance. Revue Française d'Allergologie 51: 144-147.
12. Gerking S, Stanley LR (1986) An economic analysis of air pollution and health: The case of St Louis, Review of Economics and Statistics 68: 115-121.
13. Laïd Y, Atek M, Oudjehane R, Filleul L (2006) Impact sanitaire de la pollution de l'air par les PM10 dans une ville du Sud: le cas d'Alger. Int J Tuberc Lung Dis 10 (12): 1406-1411.
14. Maddison D (2005) Air pollution and hospital admissions an ARMAX modeling approach. Journal of Environmental Economics and Management 49: 116-131.
15. Rabl A (1999) Les bénéfices monétaires d'une amélioration de la qualité de l'air en Ile-de-France, Pollution Atmosphérique, Janvier-Mars 83-94.
16. Krupnick AJ, Portney PR (1991) Controlling Urban Air Pollution: a benefit-cost assessment. Science 52: 522-527.
17. Davis RK (1963) The value of outdoor recreation: An Economic study of the maine woods, Unpublished Ph.D. dissertation, Harvard University, Cambridge, MA.
18. Berger MC, Blomquist GC, Kenkek D, Tolley GS (1987) Valuing Changes in health risks: A comparison of alternative measures. Southern Economic Journal 53: 967-984.
19. Gastineau P, Manière D, Rotillon G (2007) Une méta-analyse de l'évaluation économique des dommages sanitaires attribués à la pollution atmosphérique. L'Actualité économique 83: 5-36.
20. Ardilly P (1994) Les techniques de sondages, Editions Technip-Paris.
21. Gauthy-Sinéchal M, Vandercammen M (2010) Etudes de marchés: Méthodes et outils, (3rdEdn) De Boeck 462.
22. Mitchell RC, Carson RT (1989) Using surveys to value public goods: The contingent valuation method, Resources for the Future, Washington D.C.
23. Bontems P, Rotillon G (2007) L'économie de l'environnement, (3rdEdn) Collection Repères, Ed. La Découverte.
24. Arrow K, Solow R, Leamer E, Portney P, Radner R, Scuman H (1993) Report of the NOAA Panel on Contingent Valuation, January.
25. N'Guessan CFJ (2008) Le consentement des ménages ruraux à payer une prime d'assurance maladie en Côte d'Ivoire, Revue d'économie du développement 22: 101-124.
26. Greene W (2005) Econométrie, Pearson Education France, Ed Française 943.
27. Heckman JJ (1979) Sample selection bias as a specification error, Econometrica 47: 1.

The Contribution of Government Expenditure on Economic Growth of Nigeria Disaggregated Approach

Eugene Iheanacho*

Department of Economics, Abia State University Uturu, Nigeria

Abstract

This study examines the long and short run relationship between public expenditure and economic growth in Nigeria over the period of 1986-2014, using Johansen cointegration and error correction approach. Two components of public sector expenditure and gross capital formation ratio are derived from Cobb Douglas production function. The result shows recurrent expenditure is the major driver of economic growth in Nigeria. Controlling for the influence of non-oil revenue, this study shows a negative and significant long run relationship between economic growth (rgdpc) and recurrent expenditure coexists with a positive short run relationship, highlighting the dual effects of recurrent expenditure on economic growth in Nigeria. For the capital expenditure, this study documents negative and significant long run effect of capital expenditure on economic growth in Nigeria. The variance decomposition confirms the collective contribution of public expenditure on economic growth. The finding of this study have some policy implications for policyholders because it could be guide on effective utilization of public funds on rightful projects rather than spending it on enormous projects that will not translate into meaningful growth of the economy.

Keywords: Recurrent expenditure; Capital expenditure; Gross capital formation; Johansen cointegration; Economic growth; Government expenditure

Introduction

For decades the relationship between public sector expenditure and economic growth has continued to occupy series of debate among researchers and policy makers. The common consensus among the researchers is that public sector expenditure has been identified as an important instrument which the government uses to influence the performance of the economy [1-3]. The channel through which public authorities satisfy the collective want of the people can be classified under public sector expenditure. Salawu observed that public expenditure is the expenses incurred by the government for the maintenance of itself, the economy and the society at large. Public expenditure is an important mechanism which the government uses to pilot significant effects on the general growth of the economy. Anyanwu [4] observed that public expenditure is simply government spending from revenue derived from taxes and other sources. Again, the study articulated that public expenditure is centered on expenses contracted on government own maintenance for the growth and stability of the general economy. Another study by Anyanwu [5] noted that public expenditure is that part of fiscal tools that embraces and puts to use judiciously, all revenue generated from all sources, for the growth and installed system in the economy.

On decomposed level, Ankrani is of the opinion that government spending on collective needs and wants of the country in different areas including pension, infrastructure, capital investment, roads etc. are categorically classified under public sector expenditure. Jhingan [6] conclusively added that public expenditure is "the beginning and end of the collection of revenues by the government".

In line with the aforementioned, there is a direct relationship between the amount of public sector expenditure and economic growth. Therefore, the policy makers place more emphasis on the roles of public sector expenditure as an instrument which the government can apply to restore some economic problems such as reduction in inequality, inflation, fall in exchange rate, unemployment, dwindling oil price and the desire to restore the economy on the part of full employment, price stability, balance of payment equilibrium and above all, increase in economic growth. No wonder Mankiw, David, and David [7] earlier reviewed that economic growth is the increase in the inflation-adjusted market value of goods and services produced by economy overtime. Ideally, economic growth brings about a better standard of living of the people and this most at times is brought about by improvement in availability of infrastructure, access to food, health, housing, education, good roads etc. These improvements are very important in stimulating economic activities as well as addressing the nation's human capital development.

Another point of interest among scholars in Nigeria economy is that total government expenditure in terms of capital and recurrent expenditures have continued to rise over the last three decades [8]. Notable studies in the likes of Abu, Abdullahi and Omoke all stressed that expenditure on defense, internal security, education, health, agriculture, construction transport and communication are rising overtime.

Judging from the above viewpoints, the various components of capital and recurrent expenditure have risen between the decades of 1981 and 2010. It has been a great debate among researchers in economic literature on the impact and contribution of this multiple increase in our economy [9] emphasized that recurrent expenditure during the last decade under review (2010) had accounted for over 50% of total expenditure, while the share of capital expenditure was relatively below 50% of total public sector expenditure. It must also be noted that the public sector capital expenditure, theoretically, is the aspect of public sector expenditure expected to drive economic growth. Out of the various categories in public sector capital expenditure, in the light of the foregoing, it could be deduced that the current state of Nigeria economy could be partly linked to the nature of public sector expenditure. Intuitively, for a developing nation capital expenditure particularly

***Corresponding author:** Eugene Iheanacho, Department of Economics, Abia State University Uturu, Nigeria
E-mail: eugene.iheanacho2016@yahoo.com

in capital projects or infrastructural development ought to constitute significant proportion of her total public sector expenditure to lay the foundation for economic growth and sustainable development, but this has not been the case in Nigeria. However, we are careful not to jump to the conclusion that the preponderance of recurrent expenditure over capital expenditure has -adversely affected the nation's economy. This is purely on the desired results in the economy to force an increasing intervention on the part of the state. This did not lead to a rapid growth in the public sector and public sector expenditure but, also fed various analytical hypotheses concerning public expenditure [10].

A question therefore, poses itself: "Is the increasing public sector expenditure influencing the rate of economic growth in Nigeria?" Specifically, Jhingan observed that some of the reasons adduced for the increase in government expenditure overtime are; inflation, public debt, tax revenue and population.

Researching further, it is a common belief that the government plays a significant role in the development of a country and the public sector expenditure is an important instrument for the government to control the economy. Also, economists have noted its effects in promoting economic growth. Meanwhile, the general view is that public sector expenditure either recurrent or capital expenditure notably on social and economic infrastructure can be growth enhancing. Jhingan stated that public sector expenditure, by increasing social welfare, helps in reducing inequalities of income and wealth and as well can be used to create trade as well as to correct externalities and regional disparities if employed judiciously, thereby fastening economic growth.

From this point that Omoke conclusively put that an increase in government expenditure will yield a positive increase in the growth of the economy by increasing the national income especially, when it is injected in development programs. For example, government expenditure on social and community services such as health and education are capable of raising the productivity of labour and increase the growth of national output. Also, an increase in infrastructural equipment and rise in salaries will motivate the lecturers and teachers to dedicate more time in equipping the students with more skills and knowledge. Similarly, Abu and Abdullah observed that the public sector expenditure on infrastructure such as roads, communication, power etc. reduces production costs, increase private sector investment and profitability of firms and fosters economic growth.

In Nigeria today, the public sector is predominant. The reason appears to lie in what the government perceived as its social responsibility or share of commitment in the growth and development process. Its largeness has been stimulated by the urge to adopt shock adjustment to economic growth for quicker realization of national aspiration. This has led to the overwhelming consistent increase in the public sector expenditure in Nigeria [11]. Specifically, the public sector expenditure in Nigeria has continued to raise for over three decades, due to the increased demand for public (utilities) goods like roads, communication, power, education and health [12]. However, it has been argued by scholars if the rising state of public sector expenditure in Nigeria has gainfully contributed to economic growth in Nigeria. Okoro pointed that increase in per capita which are a symbol of economic growth that leads to development and reduction in poverty. However, the study alarmed that many Nigerians have continued to wallow in abject poverty, while more than 50% live on less than US$1 per day [13]. Moreover, macroeconomic indicators like balance of payments, import obligations, inflation rate, exchange rate, and national savings reveal that Nigeria has not fared well in the last three decades.

Furthermore, public sector has incurred expenses in areas such as physical infrastructure, health, education, economic services, defence and general administration. Economic theory predicts that increases in productive public spending in areas like physical infrastructure, health and education leads to increases in economic growth of a country. Some governments have tried to promote public spending due to an understanding that large public sector expenditure is a source of economic growth and development, especially, in a country where public sector is predominant like Nigeria. Therefore, understanding the relationship between public expenditure and economic growth could have a significant impact on the formulation and implementation of major macroeconomic policies. It could also guide the formulation of major economic policies required urgent funding and attention.

Controlling for the influence of non-oil revenue, this study seeks to uncover the long run and short run relationship between public sector and economic growth in Nigeria using Johansen cointegration approach. By examining the effect of public expenditure on economic growth, this study contributes to a number of studies that have explored public sector contribution on economic growth [14].

The remainder of this study is structured as follows: Section 2 details the literature. Section 3 contains details of the data and methodology employed the study. Section 4 contains the presentation of results. Section 5 offers an analysis of the results presented in the previous section and Section 6 concludes this paper.

Literature Review

Theoretical review

In the past, economic literature has amongst other things, concerned itself with the research and study of the relationships between public sector and economic growth. The major consensus is public sector expenditure impacts positively on economic growth. Notable theories are Keynes [15], Wagner [16], Peacock and Wiseman [17]. Keynes, in his hypothesis draws a link between public expenditure and economic growth and concludes that causality runs from public expenditure to income, implying that public sector expenditure is an exogenous factor and a public instrument for increasing national income. Furthermore, holds that increase in government expenditure leads to higher economic growth. Wagner, Peacock and Wiseman and many other economists have formulated different theories on public expenditure and economic growth. Wagner positioned public sector expenditure as a behavioural variable that positively dictates if an economy is growing. However, the neo classical growth model developed by Solow [18] opined that the fiscal policy does not have any effect on the growth of national output. Another study by Solow [19] further argued that invention through fiscal policy helps to improve failure that might arise from the inefficiencies of the market. Similarly, Dar and Amir [20] summarized that in the endogenous growth models, fiscal policy is very crucial in predicting future economic growth. Nevertheless, Barro [21], Barro and Sali-i-Martins [22] and Roux [23] all noted that the expansion of government expenditure contributes positively to economic growth. However, Chude and Chude expressed that some researchers and policy makers do not support the claim that increasing government expenditure promotes economic growth. Instead, they assert that higher public expenditure may slow down overall performance of the economy. For instance, in an attempt to finance rising expenditure, government may increase taxes and/or borrowing. Glomm and Rarikumma [24] articulated that higher income tax discourages individuals from working for long hours or even searching for job. This in turn reduces income and aggregate demand. In the same vein, higher profit tax tends to increase production costs and reduce investment expenditure as well as profitability of firms.

Putting public expenditure into perspective, Pearce [25] noted that Public expenditure is associated with the public sector. The study emphasized that the phrase "public sector" could be referred to as that part of the economy, which is publicly owned as opposed to privately owned. It thus includes all government departments and agencies and all public corporations such as electricity boards, water boards etc. Here, the public sector is thus defined in terms of ownership. It should not be defined as the sector only, which produces only public goods although, typically, public goods are provided via the public sector. Afolabi [26] viewed the public sector the same as government sector consisting mainly of the government and government owned enterprises whether local, state or federal. In his view, Afolabi stated that the public sector is an economic agent acting on behalf of everybody generally with all its economic resources commonly owned and all its activities presumably carried out on behalf of, and for the benefit of everybody.

Meanwhile, the public sector is that portion of the society controlled by national or federal, state and local governments. The public sector encompasses defence, homeland security, public protection, firefighting, urban planning, taxation and various social programs. Nweke [27] pointed that Public ownership in key sectors of the economy were viewed as a more effective way to achieve economic growth and development since it was believed that the private sector in developing countries lacked the means (financial and entrepreneurial skill) to undertake the task of development. Anyanwu highlighted that public expenditure is usually categorized into recurrent and capital expenditure. In his view, Anyanwu noted that these are further broken down into their various compositions. For example; recurrent water supply etc. these are basis for an industrial take off which are necessary for economic growth and development.

Empirical literature

Recent evidence documents that, the size, structure and growth of public sector expenditure have increased tremendously and become increasingly complex. Olulu et al. observed that not only has recent political developments engendered expenditure growth, the challenge of raising additional and identifying alternative sources of revenue to meet the ever increasing needs of governance have made it more imperative to take a more focused look at government activities, especially its expenditures. Researchers have attempted to examine the impact of public expenditure on economic growth in different countries and periods. Alexander [28] applied OLS method for sample of 13 Organization for Economic Cooperation and Development (OECD) countries panel during the period ranging from 1959 to 1984. The results show, among others, that growth of government spending has significant negative impact on economic growth Foster and Skinner evaluated the relationship between government expenditure and economic growth for a sample of wealthy countries for 1970-95 periods, using various econometric approaches. They found a positive relationship between public sector expenditure and economic growth Devarajan et al. studied the effects of different expenditure component on growth. The study covered 43 countries for periods of 1970 to 1990. The study shows that recurrent expenditure has positive impact on growth, while capital expenditure exerts negative impact on growth. But when a subsample of developed countries were considered the result was reversed indicating that, the earlier result might be as a result of corruption and inefficiency in the use of public funds in the developing countries. Abu-Bader and Abu-Qarn employed multivariate co-integration and variance decomposition approach to examine the causal relationship between government expenditures and economic growth for Egypt, Israel, and Syria for the period 1970 to 2000. In the bivariate framework, the authors observed a bidirectional (feedback) and long run negative relationships between government spending and economic growth. Moreover, the causality test within the tri-variant framework (that include share of government civilian expenditures in GDP, military burden, and economic growth) illustrated that military burden has a negative impact on economic growth in all the countries. Furthermore, civilian government expenditures have positive effect on economic growth for both Israel and Egypt. Josaphat and Oliver [29] investigated the impact of government spending on economic growth in Tanzania (1965-1996) using time series data for 32 years. They formulated a simple growth accounting model, adapting Ram [30] model in which total government expenditure is disaggregated into expenditure on (physical) investment, consumption spending and human capital investment. It was found that increased productive expenditure (physical investment) have a negative impact on growth and consumption expenditure relates positively to growth, and which in particular appears to be associated with increased private consumption. The results revealed that expenditure on human capital investment was insignificant in their regression and confirm the view that public investment in Tanzania has not been productive, as at when the research was conducted.

Liu et al. [31] examined the causal relationship between GDP and public expenditure for United States of America using data from the period 1947-2002. The causality results revealed that total government expenditure causes growth of GDP. On the other hand, growth of GDP does not cause expansion of government expenditure. Moreover, the estimation results indicated that public expenditure raises the US economic growth. The authors concluded that, judging from the causality test Keynesian hypothesis exerts more influence than the Wagner's law in US. In Nigeria, many researchers and policy makers have attempted to examine the relationship between the two macroeconomic, variables. Fajingbesi and Odusola [32] empirically investigated the relationship between government expenditure and economic growth in Nigeria over the period 1970 to 1995. The econometric results indicated that real government capital expenditure has a significant positive influence on real output. However, the results showed that real government recurrent expenditure affects economic growth only by little.

Also, study by Ogiogio [33] revealed a long-term relationship between government expenditure and economic growth over the period 1970 to 1990 in Nigeria. Moreover, the author's findings showed that recurrent expenditure exerts more influence than capital expenditure on growth. Ighodaro and Okiakhi [34] used time series data for the period 1961 to 2007 and applied Co-integration Test and Granger Causality test to examine the relationship between government expenditure and economic growth in Nigeria. The results revealed negative impact of government expenditure on economic growth in Nigeria. Okoro investigated the impact of public expenditure on economic growth in Nigeria (1981-2011). The study concluded that Government capital spending in industries and agriculture "if properly managed" will raise the nation's production capacity and employment, which in turn will increase economic growth in Nigeria. The study advised that Government should increase its expenditure on rural roads and electricity as this will accelerate the productive sectors as well as raise the standard of living of poor citizens in Nigeria. Chude and Chude while studying the impact of government expenditure on economic growth in Nigeria (1977-2012) found that total government expenditure on education has significant effect on Gross Domestic Product (GDP). The study suggested that Government should direct its expenditure towards the productive sectors like education as it would reduce the cost of doing business as well as raise the standard living of poor ones in the country. Again, Chude and Chude concluded that Government should ensure that capital expenditure and recurrent expenditure are properly managed in a manner that it will raise the nation's production capacity. Ebiringa and Charlse-Anyaogu examined the impact of sectorial expenditure on the economic growth of Nigeria from 1977 to 2011. Their analysis viewed that government expenditure should spend more on health sector, education, Telecommunication and security since they are significant and have positive impact on the economic growth of the nation. Barro observed that empirical evidence on the relationship between government spending and economic growth is diverse, mostly on cross section studies that include a sample of both advanced and developing countries. The main conclusion in most of these studies is that government consumption spending has a negative impact on growth.

Data and Model Specification

Data

This study uses annual data covering the period from 1986 to 2014. Two widely used component of public sector expenditure are employed: recurrent expenditure and capital expenditure. Non-oil revenue is included in the study to control for the influence of other component of the economic growth or determinant. These factors have been identifying among the most significant determinants and proxies for public sector expenditure. Table 1 provides additional information on all the variables.

Model specification

In spirit with Rivera-batiz [35], and N'Zue [36], the author considers a Cobb-Douglas production function which is specified as follows;

$$Y=AL^{\alpha}K^{\beta} \quad (1)$$

Where Y is economic growth measured by real GDP per capita, K is the capital stock measured by gross fixed capital formation and A is the total factor productivity, α determines the share of output that goes to capital and the share that goes to labour. Assuming the author augment the neo classical cobb-Douglas production by incorporating recurrent, capital expenditure and non-oil revenue as: A=f (recurrent expenditure, capital expenditure and non-oil revenue), whereas L cancel out on both right and let of the equation to arrive at rgdpc and gcfr respectively. Therefore, the Neo classical Cobb-Douglas production could be re-written to give the model as thus;

$$rgdpc=f\,(gcfr, rex, ces, noilr) \quad (2)$$

The above equation can be written in econometric model and in their respective natural log form as thus;

$$lnrgdpc=\alpha_0+\beta_1\, lngcfr+\beta_2\, lnrex+\beta_3\, lnces+\beta_4\, lnnoilr+\varepsilon_t \quad (3)$$

Where lnrgdpc is log of real gdp per capita, lnrex is log of recurrent expenditure, lnces is log of capital expenditure, lnnoilr is the log of non-oil revenue, ε_t is the error term and α_0 is the intercept.

Empirical Methodology

Unit root test

In time series analysis, before running the cointegration test the variables must be tested for stationarity. For this purpose, we use the conventional ADF tests, the Phillips-Perron test following Phillips and Perron. Therefore, before applying this test, we determine the order of integration of all variables using unit root tests by testing for null hypothesis H_0:β=0 (i.e β has a unit root), and the alternative hypothesis is H_1:β<0. All the variables should be integrated at first order difference I(1) so as to avoid spurious result.

Cointegration

This study adopts a dynamic vector autoregressive regression (VAR) which explores cointegration. The essence is to capture the causal dynamics relationship between government expenditure and economic growth, and at the same time to observe the long run and short dynamics. For instance, given a VAR with possible long run cointegration amongst a set of variables.

Therefore, we start with the Johansen co-integration equation which starts with the vector auto regression (VAR) of order p is given by:

$$y_t=\mu+A_1y_{t-1+}\ldots\ldots A_py_{t-p}+\varepsilon_t \quad (4)$$

Where y_t is a (nx1) vector of variables under considertion in log form that are integrated at order one-commonly denoted 1(1), n=5 A_p are the parameters to be estimated, ε_t are the random errors. This (VAR) can be re-written as;

$$\Delta y_t=\mu+\prod y_{t-1}+\sum_{i=1}^{p=1}\Gamma_i\Delta y_{t-i}+\varepsilon_t \quad (5)$$

Where,

$$\Pi=\sum_{i=1}^{p}A_i-1$$

$$\Gamma_i=-\sum_{j=i+1}^{p}A_j \quad (6)$$

Variable	Definition	Unit	Sources
RGDPC	Represents the Real Gross Domestic Product per capita. It is derived by dividing the real GDP by total population. It captures economic growth of Nigeria 'from 1986-2014. This is consistent with the study by Okoro (2013).	InRGDP	CBN Statistical Bulletin (2014)
GFCFR	Represents the rate of domestic investment. It is derived by dividing gross fixed capital formation by total population. Its captures the rate of domestic investment which is consistent with Ajide (2014).	InGFCFR	CBN Statistical Bulletin (2014)
NOILR	It represents all the income from dgp other than oil sector	InNOILR	CBN Statistical Bulletin (2014)
CEX	Represents public sector capital expenditure which includes capital expenditure on administration. Economic services, social and community services, transfers etc. In consistent with Abu-Bader and Abu-Qarn (2003) and Josaphat and Oliver (2000).	InCEX	CBN Statistical Bulletin (2014)
REX	Represents public sector recurrent expenditure on administration. economic services, social.' and community services, transfers etc. In consistent with Abu-Bader and Abu-Qarn (2003) and Josaphat and Oliver (2000).	InREX	CBN Statistical Bulletin (2014)

Table 1: List of variables. Source: Author's design.

If the coefficient matrix Π has reduced rank r < n, then there exist n × r matrices of α and β each with rank r such that

$$\Pi = \alpha\beta' \quad (7)$$

Where r is the number of co-integrating relationship, the element is α is known as the adjustment parameters in the vector error correction model and each column of β is a cointegrating vector. It can be shown that, for a given r, the maximum likelihood estimator of β define the combination of y_{t-1} that yield the r largest canonical correlations of Δy with y_{t-1} after correcting for lagged differences and deterministic variables when present. The two different likelihood ratio test of significance of these canonical correlations are the trace test and maximum eigenvalue test, shown in equation 5 and 6 respectively below

$$\lambda_{trace}(r) = -T\sum_{i=r+1}^{n} \ln\left(1-\hat{\lambda}_i\right) \quad (8)$$

$$\lambda_{max}(r, r+1) = -T\ln\left(1-\hat{\lambda}_{r+1}\right) \quad (9)$$

Here, T is the sample size and $\hat{\lambda}_i$ is the ith ordered eigenvalue from the π matrix in equation 3 or largest canonical correlation. The trace tests the null hypothesis that the number of r co-integrating vector against the alternative hypothesis of n co-integrating vector where n the number of endogenous variables is. The maximum eigenvalue tests the null hypothesis that there are r cointegrating vectors against an alternative of r+1.

After testing for cointegration among the variables, the long run coefficients of the variables are the estimated. This study uses Akaike information criteria for selected the optimal lag length. The existence of cointegration between the variables implies that causality exists in at least one direction. The short run equilibrium relationship is tested using vector error correction model (VECM). VECM is restricted VAR that has cointegration restriction built into the specification. The VECM analysis in this study is based on equation 2 and it involves five cointegrating vector as thus:

$$\Delta lnrgdp_t = \alpha_0 + \sum_{i=1}^{n}\beta_{1i}\Delta lnrgdp_{t-1} + \sum_{i=0}^{n}\beta_{2i}\Delta lngcfr_{1_{t-1}} + \sum_{i=0}^{n}\beta_{3i}\Delta lnrex_{2_{t-1}}$$
$$+ \sum_{i=0}^{n}\beta_{3i}\Delta lnces_{2_{t-1}} + \sum_{i=0}^{n}\beta_{3i}\Delta lnnoilr_{2_{t-1}} + \lambda_1 ecm_{t-1} + \mu_t \quad (10)$$

ecm_{t-1} is the error correction term obtained from the cointegration model. The error coefficients (λ_1) indicate the rate at which the cointegration model corrects its previous period's disequilibrium or speed of adjustment to restore the long run equilibrium relationship. A negative and significant ecm_{t-1} coefficient implies that any short run movement between the dependant and explanatory variables will converge back to the long run relationship.

Diagnostic test: To ensure the goodness of fit of the model, diagnostic tests are conducted. Diagnostic tests examine the model for serial correlation, and heteroscedasticity.

Emperical Results

Descriptive statistics and graphical analysis

Table 2 above provides the summary statistics, namely, sample means, maximums, minimums, medians, standard deviations, skewness, kurtosis and the Jarque-Bera tests with their p-values. Three indictors of government expenditures: recurrent expenditure (REX), capital expenditure (CES), aggregate government expenditure, gross capital formation ratio (GCFR) and one control variable non-oil price (NOILR) over the period 1986-2014. Whilst it is clear that all the statistics show the characteristics common with most time series, for instance normality in the form of playykurtic, there are a number of noticeable differences, between the variables. Firstly, economic growth (lnRGDPC) has the largest unconditional average of 12.37 while recurrent expenditure (lnREX) has the least unconditional average of 5.201. This depicts recurrent expenditure has the lowest minimum and maximum value (7.0499 and 1.8519) respectively, while economic growth maintained the highest maximum and minimum value with 12.855 and 12.05 respectively.

The standard deviation shows the level of volatility in the variables. It displays the rate at which each variable deviates from the mean value. From the Table 2 above, public sector recurrent expenditure (non-oil revenue-NOILR) is the most volatile at 2.042 while the rate of lnGDPC is the less volatile 0.274 (approximately). The level of volatility in other variables are RGDPC 1.68% (approximately), lnREX 1.88 (approximately),lnCEX 1.85, lnGCFR 1.93 and lnAPEX 1.841.

The skewness measures the asymmetric nature of the data; Skewness is a measure of the asymmetry of the probability distribution of a real-valued random variable about its mean. A normal distribution is symmetrical at point 0. If the value is greater than zero (>0) it's positively skewed, but if less than zero (<0) it is negatively skewed [37]. Economic growth (lnRGDPC) and rate of domestic investment (lnGFCFR) are positively skewed with the values 0.6412 and 0.122 respectively while public sector expenditure (lnAPEX), recurrent expenditure (lnREX) ,capital expenditure (lnCEX) and non-oil revenue (NOILR) are negatively skewed with values -0.4763, -0.3491,-0.7544 and -0.3908 respectively.

Kurtosis measures the sharpness of the peak of a normal distribution curve. It is a measure of "tailedness" of the probability distribution of a real-valued random variable [38]. If the value is approximately equal to 3, it is said to be mesokurtic distribution implying that it is normally distribution. If approximately greater than 3, it is leptokurtic distribution which has tails that asymptotically approach zero slowly and has more outliers than the normal distribution. While if approximately, less than 3 it is platykurtic which means that the distribution produces fewer and less outliers than the normal distribution. Therefore, all the series show evidence of playtykurtic with values less than 3.

The Jarque-Bera is a test for normality of the distribution where the null hypothesis is that the distribution of the sample is a normal one. If the probability value of the Jarque-Bera test is significant, then the null hypothesis is rejected and the alternative is accepted which says that the sample is not normally distributed. If each variable is statistically significant (indicated by a zero probability), then the series are not normally distributed. Therefore the farther the probability statistic of a variable is to zero, the lower the value of its Jarque-Bera statistic and the more normally distributed it is and vice versa. From the results above,

	LRGDPC	LREX	LCES	LGCFR	LAPEX	LNOILR
Mean	12.37063	5.797012	5.201698	8.126699	6.297391	5.354993
Median	12.19823	6.134699	5.733392	7.925879	6.854027	5.750933
Maximum	12.85585	8.213127	7.049946	11.31948	8.553587	8.09411
Minimum	12.05759	2.040818	1.851992	4.943024	2.786473	1.501519
Std. Dev.	0.273519	1.885549	1.640854	1.936291	1.810001	2.042564
Skewness	0.614375	-0.349177	-0.754449	0.122129	-0.476388	-0.390855
Kurtosis	1.658278	1.872057	2.254201	2.066138	1.987984	1.882928
Jarque-Bera	3.999634	2.12661	3.423195	1.125876	2.334451	2.246194
Probability	0.13536	0.345313	0.180577	0.569533	0.311229	0.325271

Table 2: summary of descriptive statistic. Source: computed using EViews 9.

in Table 2 the Jarque-Bera tests show that the null hypothesis is strongly accepted for all the distribution. Hence, the variables can be described to be normally distributed.

Unit root test

All that data are transformed into the natural log form. To determine the order of integration of the variables, the ADF (augmented Dickey-Fuller) test complemented with the PP (Philips-Perron) test in which the null hypothesis is $H_0=\beta=0$ (i.e β has a unit root), and the alternative hypothesis is $H_1:\beta<0$ are implemented. The results for both the level and differenced variables are presented in Table 3

The stationarity tests were performed first in levels and then in first difference to establish the presence of unit roots and the order of integration in all the variables. The results of the ADF and PP stationarity tests for each variable show that both tests fail to reject the presence of unit root for lnRGDPC, lnREX, lnCES, lnGCFR, lnAPEX and NOILR data series in level, indicating that these variables are non-stationary in levels. The first difference results show that these variables are stationary at 1% significance level (integrated of order one 1(1)). As mentioned in the preceding sections, a linear combination of I (1) series could be I (0) if the series are cointegrated. We thus proceed to test for cointegration of the time series.

Result of cointegrtion test: long-run estimate

The result of the cointegration test, based on the Johanson cointegration approach is presented in Table 4. The author established lag 2 using akaike criterion (see appendix 1). Cointegration is tested on the long run relationship between the dependent variable (lnRGDPC), and independent variables; lnREX, lnCES, lnGCFR while controlling NOILR. The table indicates that tests fail to accept the null hypothesis of no cointegration at 5% level of significance. Both the trace and Maximum Eigenvalue suggest the presence of 1 cointegrating vector. The Johanson cointegration test shows this by comparing the statistic values with the critical value, a result is chosen at the value where the statistic is greater than the corresponding critical value. In this study, it is clear that there is at most 1 cointegrating equation in the model with both trace and maximum eigenvalue values suggest 5% significance level. This implies that an equilibrium relationship exists among the cointegrating variables (lnRGDPC), lnREX, lnCES, and lnGCFR In addition, no matter the fluctuation in the short run; these variables have the tendency to return to this equilibrium path in the long run.

In order to identify the true cointegrating vectors, the normalised (lnRGDPC) was estimated for the model. The result in equation 11 indicates that there is a significant negative long run relationship between public sector expenditure an economic growth. In the same vein, the equation reveals that there is a significant negative long-run relationship between rate of investment and economic growth in Nigeria. This is an indication that some of the variables studied comove. This findings are suggesting that an increase in public sector expenditures negatively on economic growth. From the findings of this study, a 1% increase in recurrent and capital expenditure decreases economic growth by 0.52% and 0.64% .This result is favour of the classical view of the classical economist that implies high government expenditure are source of economic instabilities as stated by David Ricardo. This is also in consistence with the finding of Ram, and Alexander that increased productive expenditure (physical investment) has a negative impact on growth and consumption. However, this study is in contrast with finding of Fajingbesi and Odusola.

Also, the findings of this study suggest that 1% increase in the rate of domestic investment increases economic growth in Nigeria by about 0.7%. This is consistent with the studies by Athukorala [39], Akinlo [40] and Ibrahim [41].

$$12.0513+0.007886\ln GCFR - 0.649613\ln CES - 0.527116\ln REX+1.271213\ln NOILR+\varepsilon_t \quad (11)$$

Short-run estimate: Table 5 presents the results of the multivariate error correction model with the optimal lag length chosen using Akaike information criteria (AIC). The ECM (-1) coefficient is known as the speed adjustment factor, it shows how fast the system adjust to restore equilibrium. The speed adjustment for lnrGDPC is negative and significant at 1% level. The coefficient suggests that over 13% of the short run disequilibrium is corrected in the long run equilibrium, meaning that every shock in the short run result is in a new equilibrium. Hence, economic growth adjusts the disturbances to restore long run equilibrium.

The short run effect of gross capital formation on economic growth is found to be different from the long run effect as reported in Table 5.The coefficient of lnGCFR and lnCES are negative and statistically insignificant. Surprising, public expenditure on recurrent expenditure appears to be positive and statistical significant. The coefficient is 0.1019 which shows that 1% increase in recurrent expenditure in the short run will cause the economic captured by real GDP per capital to increase by 10.19%. Foster and Skinner and Devarajan et al. found a positive relationship between public sector recurrent expenditure and economic growth. On the other side, Alexander shows, among others, that growth of government spending has significant negative impact on economic growth. Controlling for the influence of non-oil revenue lnNOILR, the coefficient is found to be negative and statistically significant contrary to the long run position with -0.1189. This indicates

Variables	In level I(0)		First difference I(1)	
	ADF	PP	ADF	PP
lnRGDPC	0.5948	0.5389	-5.2807***	-5.2585***
lnGCFR	-0.4742	-0.2321	-5.6798***	-8.6795***
lnOILR	-1.8677	-2.253	-7.0746***	-8.1002***
lnREX	-2.2041	-2.6219	-7.551***	-7.6306***
lnCES	-1.9222	-2.0757	-5.6427***	-5.6433**
lnAEX	-2.595	-2.455	-3.517**	-7.4277***

Table 3: unit root test. Note: all the variables are in the natural log form. **level of significance at 5%, ***level of significant at 1%.

Ho:no of CE	Trace stat	Eigenvalue	Critical value 5%	Max stat	Critical value 5%
R=0	132.407	0.9451	69.818**	75.484**	33.876
r<1	46.923	0.6659	47.856	26.505	27.584
R<2	28.418	.4417	29.797	15.154	14.264
R<3	13.263	0.3488	15.494	11.154	3.8414
R<4	3.8414	0.0779	3.8414	2.10877	0.077905

Table 4: Joahanson cointegration test. *Trace test indicates 1 cointegrating equ at the 0.05 level which denotes rejection of the hypothesis at the 0.05 level. **Max test indicates 1 cointegrating equ at the 0.05 level which denotes rejection of the hypothesis at the 0.05 level.

ecm (-1)	ΔlnGCFR	ΔlnCES	ΔlnREX	ΔlnNOILR	LM-stat (2)	Het (2)
-0.13232	-0.0758	0.10061	0.1019	-0.1189	27.42	0.2943
(-2.454)*	(1.778)	(1.4822)	(2.005)*	(-2.5395)**	(0.3352)	(0.7197)

Table 5: Short run error correction estimates. Note t-statistics in ( ). *level of significant at 10%. **level of significant at 5%, Source: Computation using 4.

Period	S.E.	LRGDPC	LGCFR	LCES	LREX	LNOILR
1	0.047004	100.0000	0.000000	0.000000	0.000000	0.000000
2	0.06675	91.3658	5.523861	0.007028	2.120567	0.982748
3	0.073452	86.98799	5.239935	1.602169	4.277558	1.892347
4	0.088288	62.07642	6.100357	18.14621	5.056791	8.620226
5	0.109007	40.76387	4.343065	37.55553	3.725719	13.61181
6	0.134098	28.30074	3.450967	45.42445	5.51587	17.30797
7	0.161999	21.21839	3.515998	50.82403	5.62376	18.81782
8	0.191456	17.94307	3.769715	53.00589	5.88416	19.39717
9	0.218958	16.51773	3.818249	53.91613	6.193192	19.5547
10	0.245542	15.78298	3.865193	54.42188	6.276601	19.65335

Table 6: variance decomposition of RGDPC. Source: EViews 9.

that a 1% fall in non-oil revenue will cause 11% fall in the economic growth of Nigeria and vice-vasa. Therefore, in the short run recurrent expenditure and non-oil revenue are the major drivers of economic growth in the short-run. Form the diagnostic test result (Table 5); there is no evidence of serial correlation and heteroscedasticity in the vector error correction model.

Forecasting using variance decomposition: Variance decomposition indicates the amount of information each variable contributes to the other variables in the auto regression [42]. It determines how much of the forecast error variance of each of the variables can be explained by exogenous shocks to the other variables. Therefore, Table 6 presents the variance decomposition for economic growth lnNOILR and the 10 years forecast of the contribution of the independent variables. In the first year, economic growth accounts for 100% of it its changes. In the second year, lnGCFR account for 5.52%, lnCES is 0.007%, lnREX 2.12%, lnNOILR is 0.98 of the change in economic growth. From the fourth to the tenth year, this reveals a tremendous increase in capital expenditure indicating a significant impact on the economic growth within the duration of forecast. Other the other side, non-oil revenue has also increase but at a snow rate. The same is applicable to other variables under consideration. Therefore, collective contribution of all dependent variables under consideration indicate that the impact of public expenditure on economic growth is indirect. This is in line relevant studies.

Conclusion and Policy Implication

Controlling for the possible influence of non-oil revenue, this study examines the long run and short run relationship between public expenditure proxy by (recurrent and capital expenditure) and economic growth in Nigeria using Johansen cointegration approach over 1986-2014. The results show that recurrent expenditure is a major driver of economic growth in Nigeria. A negative and significant long run relationship between economic growth (rgdpc) and recurrent expenditure coexists with a positive short run relationship, highlighting the dual effects of recurrent expenditure on economic growth in Nigeria. In general, the result is in line with documented evidence from relevant studies.

The negative significant long run effect of capital expenditure on economic growth in Nigeria confirms inverse relationship between dependent and independent variable and indeed follows the findings by Ighodaro and Okiakhi and Devarajan et al. [43]. The results suggest that capital expenditure exerts negative impact on growth due to increasing government expenditure on the sector. However, with government expenditure on areas such military rather than on economic activities will impact negatively on the economic growth of Nigeria. Surprisingly, variance decomposition suggests that recurrent and capital expenditure collectively contribute to change in economic growth.

The study provides empirical assessment of contribution of the public sector expenditure on economic growth. From the result, the long run negative relationship between recurrent, capital expenditure and economic growth holds some policy implication to policy makers and researchers. Controlling the high dependence of economic growth on non-oil revenue and gross fixed capital formation will directly improve the standard of living in the country and indeed enhance efficiency in distribution resources among competing needs. To achieve this objective, public funds must be channeled in rightful projects at the right time to meet the country's demand rather than spending on enormous projects that will not translate into meaningful growth of the economy. The government should direct its expenditure towards the productive sectors like education as it would reduce the cost of doing business as well as raise the standard living of poor ones in the country. The Government should increase its expenditure on rural roads and electricity as this will accelerate the productive sectors as well as raise the standard of living of poor citizens in Nigeria. Such strategy could lead to optimum resource utilization and indeed improve the standard of living in the country.

References

1. Okemini EB, Uranta DT (2008) Poverty and Criminality in the Niger-Delta Region: A critical analysis. Integrated Social and Management Journal 1: 1-8.
2. Omoke P (2009) Government Expenditure and National Income: A Causality Test for Nigeria. European Journal of Economics and Political Studies 2: 1-11.
3. Oni LB, Aniakam O, Akinsanya TA (2014) Joint effects of capital and recurrent expenditure in Nigeria's economic growth. European Journal of Globalization and Department Research 9: 529-543.
4. Anyanwu JC (1993) Monetary Economics: Theory, Policy and Institutions, Hybrid Publishers, Nigeria.
5. Anyanwu JC (1997) Nigerian Public Finance. Agrilakshmi Narain Educational Publishers ltd, Delhi.
6. Jhingan ML (2004) Money, Banking, International Trade and Public Finance, (8thedn) Vrinda publishers, Delhi, India.
7. Mankiw NG, David R, David W (1992) A Contribution to the Empirics of Economic Growth. Quarterly Journal of Economics 107: 407-437.
8. Abu N, Abudullahi U (2010) Government Expenditure and Economic Growth in Nigeria, 1970-2008: A Disaggregated Analysis. Business and Economics Journal 4: 237-330.
9. Ebiringa OT, Charlse- ANB (2012) Impact of Government Sectorial Expenditure on economic growth of Nigeria. International Journal of Economic Research 3: 82-92.
10. Bhatia LH (2008) Public Finance, New Delhi Vikas Publishing House, India.
11. Okoro AS (2013) Government Spending and Economic Growth in Nigeria (1980-2011). Global Journal of Management and Business Research Economics and Commerce 5: 20-30.
12. Chude NP, Chude DI (2013) Impact of Government Expenditure on Economic Growth in Nigeria. International Journal of Business and Management Review 1: 64-71.
13. Ajide BK (2014) Determinants of Economic growth in Nigeria. CBN Journal of Applied Statistics 5: 147-170.
14. Salawu RO (2005) Essentials of Public Finance, Obafeini Awolowo University Press LTD, Nigeria.
15. Keynes JM (1936) General Theory of Employment, Interest and Money, London: Palgrave Macmillian, UK.
16. Wagner A (1893) The foundation of the Political Okonomie, (3rdedn), Leipzig, Germany.
17. Peacock AT, Wiseman J (1961) The Growth of Public Expenditure in the United Kingdom. Princeton: Princeton University Press, UK.

18. Solow R (1956) A Contribution to the Theory of economic growth. Quarterly Journal of Economics 70: 65-94.

19. Solow R (1957) Technical Change and Aggregate production function. Review of Economics and Statistics 39: 748-62.

20. Dar A, Amir KS (2002) Government Size, Factor accumulation and Economic growth: Evidence from OECD countries. Journal of Policy Modeling 24: 679-692.

21. Barro RJ (1990) Government Spending in a Simple Model of Endogenous Growth, The Journal of Political Economy 5: 103-125.

22. Barro R, Martin I (1992) Public Finance in Models of Economic Growth. Review of Economic Studies 3: 645-661.

23. Roux A (1994) Defense, Human Capital and Economic Development in South Africa. African Defense review no. 19.

24. Glomm JJ, Ravikumar DJ (1997) The growth of Public Expenditure in selected developing nations: Six Carribbean countries. Journal of Public Finance/ Finances Publique 3: 57-74.

25. Pearce DW (1998) The Dictionary of Modern Economics London and Basingstore. Macinillan Press Etd. UK.

26. Afolabi L (1999) Monetary Economics, Revised Ed. Heinemann Educational Books (Nigeria) Pic. Afred, S.E & Jan, K. (2005). An Essay on Post-Keynesian Theory: A New Paradigm Economics. Journal of Economic Literature 1: 10-32.

27. Nweke J (2004) Capitalist Alternative to Resource Management in Nigeria. Nigeria Journal of Management and Social Sciences: Ebonyi State University, Abakaliki 1: 183-187.

28. Alexander AMO (1990) Public Expenditure and Economic Growth: The Case of Developing nation. Journal of Sustainable Development 2: 56-101.

29. Josaphat PK, Oliver M (2000) Government Spending and Economic Growth in Tanzania (1965-1996). CREDIT Research paper.

30. Ram R (1986) Government Size and Economic Growth: A New Framework and Some evidence from Cross-Section and Time-Series Data. American Economic Review 76: 191-203.

31. Liu C, Hsu C, Younis MZ (2008) The Association between Expenditure and growth: The Granger causality test of the US data. 1974-2002. Journal of Public Budgeting, Accounting and Financial Management 20: 439-452.

32. Fajingbesi AA, Odusola AF (1999) Public Expenditure and Growth. A Paper Presented at a Training Programme on Fiscal Policv Planning Management in Nigeria, Organized by NCEMA, Ibadan, Oyo State, 137-179.

33. Ogiogio G (1995) Government Expenditure and Economic Growth in Nigeria. Journal of Economic Management 2: 77-92.

34. Ighodaro CAU, Okiakhi DE (2010) Does the Relationship Between Government Expenditure and Economic Growth Follow Wagner's Law in Nigeria? Annals of University of 'Petrosani Economics 2: 185-198.

35. Rivera-BFL (2004) Democracy, Governance and Economic Growth: Theory and Evidence. Working Paper, Colombia University.

36. N'Zue FF (2011) Economic Freedom and Performance in ECOWAS Countries: A Dynamic Panel Data Approach. Africa Journal of Economic Policy 18:28-53.

37. Wooldridge JM (2010) Introductory Econometrics, (4thedn) Thomson South-Western, USA.

38. Hosking JRM (2006) On the Characterization of Distributions by their L-moments. Journal of Statistical Planning and Inference 136: 193-198.

39. Athukorala PP, Wasantha A (2003) The impact of foreign direct investment for economic growth a case study of Sri Lanka, 9th International Conference on Sri Lanka Studies, Matra, Sri Lanka.

40. Akinlo AE (2004) Foreign Direct Investment and Growth in Nigeria. Journal of Policy Modelling 26: 627-639.

41. Ibrahim MA (2013) Foreign Direct Investment on Economic Growth in Nigeria (1970-2011). An unpublished Research Project, Fountain University, Osogbo. Osun State, Nigeria.

42. Lutkepohl H (2007) New Introduction to, Multiple Time Series Analysis, Springer, Germany.

43. Deverajan S, Swaroop V, Zou (1996) The Composition of Public Expenditure and Economic Growth. Journal of Monetary Economics 37: 313-344.

Management Science, Economics and Finance: A Connection

Chia-Lin Chang[1], Michael McAleer[2] and Wing-Keung Wong[3]*

[1]*Department of Applied Economics, Department of Finance, National Chung Hsing University, Taiwan*
[2]*Department of Quantitative Finance, National Tsing Hua University, Taiwan*
[3]*Department of Economics, Hong Kong Baptist University, Hong Kong, China, and Department of Finance Asia University, Taiwan*

Abstract

This paper provides a brief review of the connecting literature in management science, economics and finance, and discusses some research that is related to the three disciplines. Academics could develop theoretical models and subsequent econometric models to estimate the parameters in the associated models, and analyze some interesting issues in the three disciplines.

JEL: A10, G00, G31, O32

Keywords: Management science; Economics; Finance; Theoretical models; Econometric models

Introduction

There are many studies that link management sciences, economics, and finance. In this paper, we will discuss different types of utility functions, stochastic dominance (SD), mean-risk (MR) models, and portfolio optimization (PO) as these topics are popular in the three disciplines. Academics could develop theoretical models and thereafter develop econometric models to estimate the associated parameters to analyze some interesting issues in management science, economics, and finance.

The plan of the remainder of the paper is as follows. In Section 2, we discuss interesting papers that have been published in the leading journals in management science, economics and finance. In Section 3, some theoretical models are discussed. Alternative statistical and econometrics models are analyzed in Section 4. A brief discussion of empirical models is presented in Section 5. Some concluding remarks are given in Section 6.

Brief Literature Review

The theory for different types of investors, SD, MR and OP models are popular areas in management science, economics, and finance. For example, Markowitz [1] proposes the mean-variance (MV) selection rules for risk averters. Quirk and Saposnik [2], Hanoch and Levy [3] study SD rules for risk averters. Bawa, et al. [4] develop an algorithm to obtain the SD admissible sets by stock selection. Hammond [5] suggests SD rules for risk seekers. Aboudi and Thon [6] present an equally efficient technique for third-degree SD. Gotoh and Konno [7] develop a third-order SD rule to obtain efficient portfolios associated with the efficient frontiers generated by mean-lower semi-standard deviation and mean-absolute deviation models. Post and Kopa [8] develop the theory of portfolio choice based on third-order SD.

There are different types of investors. For example, Markowitz suggests that investors' utility could be convex and concave in both the positive and negative domains. Traditional SD theory supports concave utility functions, while the theory of reverse SD supports convex utility functions. The findings from Pennings and Smidts support the existence of investors with reverse S-shaped utility functions [9].

The findings in Currim and Sarin [10] and Thaler and Johnson [11] support the existence of investors with S-shaped utility functions. Levy and Levy [12-14] and others extend the SD theory to Markowitz SD (MSD) and Prospect SD (PSD) for investors with S-shaped and reverse S-shaped utility functions, respectively.

Leshno and Levy [12] extend SD theory to the theory of almost stochastic dominance (ASD) to reveal a preference for "most" decision makers. Tzeng, Huang, and Shih [15] find that the almost second-degree stochastic dominance (ASSD) does not possess the property of expected-utility maximization, so they modify the ASSD definition to acquire this important property.

Theoretical Models

It is important to commence any rigorous research in management science, economics, and finance by developing appropriate theoretical models. We have been developing some theories to extend those that have been discussed in a number of existing literature reviews.

We will first discuss the theory developed in SD. Li and Wong [16] extends SD theory by developing some SD theorems for risk seekers and risk averters. Wong and Li [17] extend Fishburn 1974's [18] convex SD theorem by including any distribution function, develop the results for both risk seekers as well as risk averters, and including third order SD. They also extend the theory developed by Bawa, Bodurtha. Rao, and Suri [19] on the comparison between convex combinations of several continuous distributions and a single continuous distribution.

Wong [20] also extends the SD theory by introducing the first three orders of both SD and RSD to decisions in business planning and investment to risk-averse and risk-seeking decision makers, so that they can compare both returns and losses. He also introduces a MV rule for risk seekers. By incorporating both majorization theory and SD, Egozcue and Wong [21] develop a general theory for determining the diversification preferences of risk-averse investors and conditions under which they would unanimously judge a particular asset to be superior. Guo and Wong [22,23] extend the (univariate) SD theory to multivariate SD for both risk averters and risk seekers, respectively, when the attributes are assumed to be independent and the utility function is assumed to be additively and separable.

Levy and Levy develop the PSD and MSD theory for investors with S-shaped and reverse S-shaped utility functions. Wong and Chan [24]

***Corresponding author:** Wing-Keung Wong, Department of Economics, Hong Kong Baptist University, Hong Kong, China, and Department of Finance, Asia University, Taiwan, E-mail: awong@hkbu.edu.hk

extend their work by developing the PSD and MSD to the first three orders, link the corresponding S-shaped and reverse S-shaped utility functions to the first three orders, and develop some properties for both MSD and PSD. The prospect theory based on S-shaped utility functions is different from the von Neumann and Morgenstern (NM) theory based on concave utility functions.

Broll, Egozcue, Wong, and Zitikis [21] show that it is possible to convert NM theory into prospect theory. For example, unlike the NM theory, they show that the monotonicity of indifference curves depends on the underlying mean in the prospect theory. Egozcue, Fuentes García, Wong, and Zitikis [25] study rankings of completely and partially diversified portfolios and also of specialized assets when investors follow Markowitz preferences. They find that, for Markowitz investors, preferences toward risk vary depending on their sensitivities toward gains and losses.

Both expected-utility maximization and the hierarchical property are very important in SD. Leshno and Levy proposes a definition, and Tzeng, Huang, and Shih modify it to provide another definition for ASD. Guo, Zhu, Wong, and Zhu [26] show that the former has the hierarchical property but not the expected-utility maximization, whereas the latter has the expected-utility maximization but not the hierarchical property. Guo, Post, Wong, and Zhu [27] establish necessary moment conditions for ASD criteria of various orders.

Guo, Wong, and Zhu extend the ASD theory (for risk averters) by including ASD for risk-seeking investors. They also study the relationship between ASD for risk seekers and ASD for risk averters. In addition, Tsetlin, Winkler, Huang, and Tzeng [28] develop the theory of generalized ASD (GASD). Guo, Wong, and Zhu briefly discuss the advantages and disadvantages of ASD and GASD.

Wong and Ma [29] generalize the theory on the location-scale (LS) family to the multivariate setting for both risk averters and risk seekers. They also examine some non-expected utility functions defined over the LS family, and develop some properties for the partial orders and dominance relations defined over the LS family. Ma and Wong [30] establish some behavioural foundations for various types of Value-at-Risk (VaR) models, including VaR and conditional-VaR (C-VaR), as measures of downside risk. They also show that the VaR criterion is equivalent to the first-order SD while the C-VaR, is shown to be equivalent to the second-order SD.

Statistical and econometric models

Another suggestion is to develop statistical and econometric models in the areas related to management science, economics, and finance. After developing mathematical models, one might consider developing some related statistical and econometric models. We have developed several econometrics papers in SD, MR and PO theory, and discuss some contributions in the development of econometrics for SD.

The SD theory for both risk averters and risk seekers was developed by Wong and Li and others, and the SD theory for investors with S-shaped and S-shaped utility functions was developed by Levy and Levy and other, as discussed in Section 3. Subsequently, Bai, Li, McAleer, and Wong [31] extend the work of the SD test for risk averters, developed by Davidson and Duclos, to derive the limiting process of SD statistics for risk averters as well as risk seekers when the underlying processes can be either dependent or independent.

Bai, Li, Liu, and Wong develop SD tests for investors with S-shaped utility functions of the first three orders. These statistics provide a tool to examine the preferences of investors with S-shaped utility functions, as proposed by Kahnemann and Tversky in their prospect theory, and investors with RS-shaped investors proposed by Markowitz [32,33]. They derive the limiting distributions of the test statistics to be stochastic processes, and propose a bootstrap method to decide the critical points of the tests and prove the consistency of the bootstrap tests. Leshno, Levy and others have developed ASD theory, but there do not seem to be any statistical tests for ASD. In order to bridge the gap, Guo, Levy, and Wong develop tests for ASD.

In addition to SD tests, several MR tests have been developed. For example, Leung and Wong (2008) develop a multivariate Sharpe ratio statistic to test the hypothesis of the equality of multiple Sharpe ratios, and derive the asymptotic distribution of the statistic and its properties. Results in optimal stopping theory have shown that a "bang-bang" (buy or sell immediately) style of trading strategy is, in some sense, optimal provided the asset's price dynamics follow certain familiar stochastic processes.

Wong, Wright, Yam, and Yung [34] construct a reward-to-variability ratio (that is, the mixed Sharpe ratio) that is necessary for this strategy's implementation. They apply the mixed Sharpe ratio to compare the performances of the "bang-bang" and "buy-and-hold" trading strategies, and find that the former is significantly more profitable. In order to circumvent the limitations of the tests for the coefficient of variation and Sharpe ratios, Bai, Wang, and Wong develop the mean-variance ratio (MVR) statistic for testing the equality of mean-variance ratios, and prove that their proposed statistic is the uniformly most powerful unbiased (UMPU) statistic.

Bai, Hui, Wong, and Zitikis develop a MVR statistic for comparing the performance of prospects after the effect of the background risk has been mitigated. They investigate the performance of the statistic in large and small samples, and show that, in the non-asymptotic framework, the MVR statistic produces a UMPU test. Bai, Phoon, Wang, and Wong provide evidence that the MVR test is superior to the Sharpe ratio (SR) test by applying both tests to analyze the performance of commodity trading advisors (CTAs).

Tests have also been developed in portfolio optimization. The traditional estimated return for Markowitz MV optimization has been demonstrated to depart seriously from its theoretical optimal return. Bai, Liu, and Wong prove that this phenomenon is natural, and that the estimated optimal return is always larger than its theoretical counterpart. Thereafter, they develop new bootstrap-corrected estimates for the optimal return and its asset allocation, and prove that these bootstrap-corrected estimates are proportionally consistent with their theoretical counterparts.

Bai, Liu, and Wong extend the work of Markowitz [35], Korkie and Turtle [36] and others by proving that the traditional estimate for the optimal return of self-financing portfolios always over-estimates its theoretical value. In order to circumvent the problem, they develop a bootstrap estimate for the optimal return of self-financing portfolios, and prove that this estimate is consistent with its counterpart parameter. Bai, Li, McAleer, and Wong extend the theory further by developing the spectrally-corrected estimates for Markowitz MV portfolio. They find that the spectrally-corrected estimates consistently outperform the traditional and bootstrap-corrected estimates.

Empirical Studies

Yet another suggestion is to apply statistical and econometric models to examine the relationships among the variables in some important issues in management science, economics, and finance. As there are several important applications of the theories developed in SD, MR, and PO theory, several are discussed below.

Broll, Wahl, and Wong [37] apply MV rules to analyze export production in the presence of exchange rate uncertainty, and present the elasticity of risk aversion. Broll, Wong, and Wu [38] apply both MV and SD rules to examine a banking firm investing in risky assets and hedging opportunities. Broll, Guo, Welzel, and Wong [39] analyze a bank's risk taking in a two-moment decision framework. They find that the bank's optimal behaviour to a change in the standard deviation or the expected value of the risky asset's or portfolio's return can be described in terms of risk aversion elasticities.

In terms of SD relationships, Gasbarro, Wong, and Zumwalt [40] find that SD test can identify dominant iShares, which are indistinguishable when using the Sharpe ratio. Lean, Smyth, and Wong [41] use the SD statistic test to test for the existence of day-of-the-week and January effects for several Asian markets, and find the existence of week day and monthly seasonality effects in some Asian markets, but first-order SD for the January effect has disappeared.

Wong, Phoon, and Lean apply the SD test to compare the performance of different Asian hedge funds, and find both first-order and higher-order SD relationships among the funds. Lean, Phoon, and Wong [42] use the SD test to rank the performance of commodity trading advisors (CTA) funds, and find both first-order and higher-order SD relationships among the CTA funds.

However, some studies have found that there is no dominance among the different markets. For example, based on West Texas Intermediate crude oil data for the sample period 1989-2008, Lean, McAleer, and Wong [43-45] apply both MV and SD tests and find that: (i) there is no arbitrage opportunity between these two markets; (ii) spot and futures do not dominate one another; (iii) investors are indifferent to investing spot or futures; and (iv) spot and futures oil markets are efficient and rational.

Chan, de Peretti, Qiao, and Wong [45-48] apply both SD and likelihood ratio tests to examine the efficiency of the UK covered warrants market. Their SD findings suggest that neither covered warrants nor the underlying shares stochastically dominate one other, and that the UK covered warrants market is efficient. Their LR test results show that the UK covered warrants returns efficiently reflect the returns information of the underlying shares.

One could use SD to examine the preferences of both risk averters and risk seekers. For example, Qiao, Clark, and Wong [49,50] apply SD tests for risk averters and risk seekers to examine investors' preferences with respect to the Taiwan stock index and its corresponding index futures. They find that spot prices dominate futures for risk averters, whereas futures dominate spot for risk seekers.

Qiao, Wong, and Fung [51-53] apply SD tests for risk averters and risk seekers to compare the performance of stock indices and their corresponding index futures for 6 developed countries and 4 developing countries. They find that there are no SD relationships between spot and futures markets in the mature market. However, for the emerging markets, spot dominates futures for risk averters and futures dominate spot for risk seekers in the second- and third-order SD. These results suggest that mature markets are more efficient, and there are potential gains in expected utilities for risk averters (seekers) if they switch their investment from futures (spot) to spot (futures) in emerging markets.

Lean, McAleer, and Wong [54] apply SD and other tests to examine risk-averse and risk-seeking investor preferences for oil spot and futures prices. Their SD results reveal that risk-averse investors prefer the spot index, whereas risk seekers are attracted to the futures index to maximize expected utility, though not their expected wealth for the entire period or for the sub-period (pre-GFC) before the 2008 Global Financial Crisis (GFC) and the sub-period during and after the GFC (GFC).

It is also possible to apply the SD test to examine the preference of risk averters, risk seekers, and investors with S-shaped and reverse S-shaped utility functions. For example, Fong, Lean, and Wong (2008) study the preferences of investors with S-shaped and reverse S-shaped utility functions for internet versus "old economy" stocks. Gasbarro, Wong, and Zumwalt [55] examine the preferences for investors with S-shaped and reverse S-shaped utility functions on iShares.

Clark, Qiao, and Wong [56] evaluate the preferences of risk averters, risk seekers, and investors with S-shaped and reverse S-shaped utility functions for the Taiwan spot and futures markets. They find that risk averters prefer spot to futures, whereas risk seekers prefer futures to spot. Moreover, investors with S-shaped utility functions prefer spot (futures) to futures (spot) when markets move upward (downward), and investors with reverse S-shaped utility functions prefer futures (spot) to spot (futures) when markets move upward (downward).

SD can also be used to example important issues and anomalies. For example, Abid, Leung, Mroua, and Wong [57] apply PO and SD test to examine preferences for international diversification *versus* domestic diversification in the U.S. market. Their PO results imply that the domestic diversification strategy dominates the international diversification strategy at a lower risk level, and the reverse is true at a higher risk level. The SD analysis shows that: (i) there is no arbitrage opportunity between international and domestic stock markets; (ii) domestically diversified portfolios with smaller risk dominate internationally diversified portfolios with larger risk and *vice versa*; and (iii) at the same risk level, there is no difference between the domestically and internationally diversified portfolios. They do not find any domestically diversified portfolios that stochastically dominate all internationally diversified portfolios, but find some internationally diversified portfolios with small risk that dominate all the domestically diversified portfolios.

Fong, Wong, and Lean [58-62] apply the SD test to examine the momentum effect in stock returns. They find that winner portfolios stochastically dominate loser portfolios at the second and third orders. Sriboonchitta, Wong, Dhompongsa, and Nguyen [63] find that risk losers prefer losers than winners. Fong, Lean and Wong, apply the SD test to find that risk averters and risk seekers show a distinct difference in preferences for internet versus "old economy" stocks. This difference is most evident during the bull market period (1998-2000) where internet stocks stochastically dominate old economy stocks for risk seekers but not for risk averters. In the bear market, risk averters show an increased preference for old economy stocks, while risk seekers show a reduced preference for Internet stocks. These results are not consistent with prospect theory, and indicate that investors exhibit reverse S-shaped utility functions [64-68].

Hoang, Wong, and Zhu [69] examine gold, stock, and bond markets in China and find that, in general, risk averters prefer portfolios without gold, while risk seekers prefer those with gold. Their findings confirm the safe haven characteristic of gold in the Chinese context. They also obtain a very interesting finding that risk-averse investors prefer portfolios from the efficient frontier, while risk seekers prefer the equally-weighted one.

Qiao and Wong [70] adopt SD tests to compare the yields of five property size classes in the Hong Kong residential property market. They find evidence that, in general, the yields of smaller property classes stochastically dominate the yields of bigger property classes in the second order, suggesting that risk averters will obtain higher expected utility but not higher expected wealth when buying smaller properties. In addition, Tsang, Wong, and Horowitz show that, regardless of whether the buyers are risk averse or risk seeking; they will not only achieve higher expected utility but also obtain higher expected wealth when buying smaller properties [71].

SD can also be used to study income inequality. For example, Chow, Lui, Valenzuela, and Wong apply SD tests to analyze relative welfare levels of income distributions for the poor and the rich of different groups of individuals. Bai, Valenzuela, Wong, and Zhu extend the theory by applying MSD and PSD to develop SD tests for the poor (test for poorness), the rich (test for richness), and for the middle class (test for middle class) to achieve a more robust analysis of relative welfare levels in the analysis of income distributions.

Concluding Remarks

In this paper, we discussed different types of utility functions, stochastic dominance, mean-risk models, and portfolio optimization as these topics are popular in Management Science, Economics, and Finance in terms of theory and econometric analysis. Authors could also extend their work to link the three disciplines. Although we have discussed the contributions in SD, MR, and PO related to management science, economics, and finance, there are theoretical contributions in other areas that could also be useful in these disciplines. Readers may refer to Chang, McAleer, and Wong for contributions in other areas that might be useful in management science, economics, and finance [72].

References

1. Markowitz HM (1952a) The utility of wealth. Journal of Political Economy 60: 151-156.
2. Quirk JP, Saposnik R (1962) Admissibility and measurable utility functions. Review of Economic Studies 29: 140-146.
3. Hanoch G, Levy H (1969) The efficiency analysis of choices involving risk. Review of Economic Studies 36: 335-346.
4. Bawa VS, Lindenberg EB, Rafsky LC (1979) An efficient algorithm to determine stochastic dominance admissible sets. Management Science 25: 609-622.
5. Hammond JS (1974) Simplifying the choice between uncertain prospects where preference is nonlinear. Management Science 20: 1047-1072.
6. Aboudi R, Thon D (1994) Efficient algorithms for stochastic dominance tests based on financial market data. Management Science 40: 508-515.
7. Gotoh JY, Konno H (2000) Third-degree stochastic dominance and mean-risk analysis. Management Science 46: 289-301.
8. Post T, Milos K (2016) Portfolio choice based on third-order stochastic dominance. Forthcoming in Management Science.
9. Levy H (2015) Stochastic dominance: Investment decision making under uncertainty, (2ndedtn), Springer, New York, USA.
10. Currim IS, Sarin RK (1989) Prospect versus utility. Management Science 35: 22-41.
11. Thaler RH, Johnson EJ (1990) Gambling with the house money and trying to break even: The effects of prior outcomes on risky choice. Management Science 36: 643-660.
12. Leshno M, Levy H (2002) Preferred by "all" and preferred by "most" decision makers: Almost stochastic dominance. Management Science 48: 1074-1085.
13. Levy M, Levy H (2002) Prospect theory: Much ado about nothing? Management Science 48: 1334-1349.
14. Levy H, Levy M (2004) Prospect theory and mean-variance analysis. Review of Financial Studies 17: 1015-1041.
15. Tzeng LY, Huang RJ, Shih PT (2013) Revisiting almost second-degree stochastic dominance. Management Science 59: 1250-1254.
16. Li CK, Wong WK (1999) Extension of stochastic dominance theory to random variables. RAIRO - Operations Research 33: 509-524.
17. Wong WK, Li CK (1999) A note on convex stochastic dominance theory. Economics Letters 62: 293-300.
18. Fishburn PC (1974) Convex stochastic dominance with continuous distribution functions. Journal of Economic Theory 7: 143-58.
19. Bawa VS, Bodurtha JR, Rao JN, Suri MR, Hira L (1985) On determination of stochastic dominance optimal sets. Journal of Finance 40: 417-431.
20. Wong WK (2007) Stochastic dominance and mean-variance measures of profit and loss for business planning and investment. European Journal of Operational Research 182: 829-843.
21. Broll U, Egozcue M, Wong WK, Zitikis R (2010) Prospect theory, indifference curves, and hedging risks. Applied Mathematics Research Express pp: 142-153.
22. Guo X, Wong WK (2016) Multivariate stochastic dominance for risk averters and risk seekers. Forthcoming in RAIRO - Operations Research.
23. Guo X, Wong WK, Zhu LX (2016) Almost stochastic dominance for risk averters and risk seekers. Forthcoming in Finance Research Letters.
24. Wong WK, Chan R (2008) Markowitz and prospect stochastic dominances. Annals of Finance 4: 105-129.
25. Egozcue M, García LF, Wong WK, Zitikis R (2011) Do investors like to diversify? A study of Markowitz preferences. European Journal of Operational Research 215: 188-193.
26. Bai ZD, Phoon KF, Wang KY, Wong WK (2013) The performance of commodity trading advisors: A mean-variance-ratio test approach. North American Journal of Economics and Finance 25: 188-201.
27. Abid F, Leung PL, Mroua M, Wong WK (2014) International diversification versus domestic diversification: Mean-variance portfolio optimization and stochastic dominance approaches. Journal of Risk and Financial Management 7: 45-66.
28. Bai ZD, Hui YC, Wong WK, Zitikis R (2012) Prospect performance evaluation: Making a case for a non-asymptotic UMPU test. Journal of Financial Econometrics 10: 703-732.
29. Bai ZD, Li H, Liu HX, Wong WK (2011) Test statistics for prospect and Markowitz stochastic dominances with applications. Econometrics Journal 122: 1-26.
30. Bai ZD, Li H, McAleer M, Wong WK (2015) Stochastic dominance statistics for risk averters and risk seekers: An analysis of stock preferences for USA and China. Quantitative Finance 15: 889-900.
31. Bai ZD, Li H, McAleer M, Wong WK (2016) Spectrally-corrected estimation for high-dimensional Markowitz mean-variance optimization. Tinbergen Institute Discussion Paper, TI 2016-025/III.
32. Bai ZD, Liu HX, Wong WK (2009a) Enhancement of the applicability of Markowitz's portfolio optimization by utilizing random matrix theory. Mathematical Finance 19: 639-667.
33. Bai ZD, Liu HX, Wong WK (2009b) On the Markowitz mean-variance analysis of self-financing portfolios. Risk and Decision Analysis 1: 35-42.
34. Bai ZD, Valenzuela MR, Wong WK, Zhu ZZ (2016) New tests for poorness, richness, and middle class welfare: SD analysis for different types of social welfare functions. Social Science Research Network Working Paper 2742024.
35. Markowitz HM (1952b) Portfolio selection. Journal of Finance 7: 77-91.
36. Korkie B, Turtle HJ (2002) A mean-variance analysis of self-financing portfolio. Management Science 48: 427-444.
37. Broll U, Wahl JE, Wong WK (2006) Elasticity of risk aversion and international trade. Economics Letters 91: 126-130.
38. Bai ZD, Wang KY, Wong WK (2011) Mean-variance ratio test, a complement

to coefficient of variation test and Sharpe ratio test. Statistics and Probability Letters 81: 1078-1085.

39. Broll U, Guo X, Welzel P, Wong WK (2015) The banking firm and risk taking in a two-moment decision model. Economic Modelling 50 275-280.

40. Gasbarro D, Wong WK, Zumwalt JK (2007) Stochastic dominance analysis of iShares. European Journal of Finance 13: 89-101.

41. Lean HH, Smyth R, Wong WK (2007) Revisiting calendar anomalies in Asian stock markets using a stochastic dominance approach. Journal of Multinational Financial Management 17: 125-141.

42. Chan CY, de Peretti C, Qiao Z, Wong WK (2012) Empirical test of the efficiency of the UK covered warrants market: Stochastic dominance and likelihood ratio test approach. Journal of Empirical Finance 19: 162-174.

43. Egozcue M, Wong WK (2010) Gains from diversification: A majorization and stochastic dominance approach. European Journal of Operational Research 200: 893-900.

44. Ma C, Wong WK (2010) Stochastic dominance and risk measure: A decision-theoretic foundation for VaR and C-VaR. European Journal of Operational Research 207: 927-935.

45. Lean HH, McAleer M, Wong WK (2010) Market efficiency of oil spot and futures: A mean-variance and stochastic dominance approach. Energy Economics 32: 979-986.

46. Broll U, Wong WK, Wu M (2011) Banking firm, risk of investment and derivatives. Technology and Investment 2: 222-227.

47. Chang CL, McAleer M, Wong WK (2016a) Behavioural, financial, and health & medical economics: A connection. Journal of Health & Medical Economics 2: 1-4.

48. Chang CL, McAleer M, Wong WK (2016b) Informatics, data mining, econometrics and financial economics: A connection. Journal of Informatics and Data Mining 1: 1-5.

49. Chow SC, Lui FT, Valenzuela MR, Wong WK (2015) Tests for richness and poorness: A stochastic dominance analysis of income distributions in Hong Kong. Paper presented at the Sixth Meeting of the Society for the Study of Economic Inequality (ECINEQ), Université du Luxembourg

50. Clark EA, Qiao Z, Wong WK (2015) Theories of risk: testing investor behaviour on the Taiwan stock and stock index futures markets. Economic Inquiry 54: 907-924.

51. Davidson R, Duclos JY (2000) Statistical inference for stochastic dominance and for the measurement of poverty and inequality. Econometrica 68: 1435-1464.

52. De Miguel V, Garlappi L, Uppal R (2009) Optimal versus naive diversification: How inefficient is the 1/N portfolio strategy? Review of Financial Studies 22: 1915-1953.

53. Falk H, Levy H (1989) Market reaction to quarterly earnings' announcements: A stochastic dominance based test of market efficiency. Management Science 35: 425-446.

54. Fong WM, Lean HH, Wong WK (2008) Stochastic dominance and behavior towards risk: The market for internet stocks. Journal of Economic Behavior and Organization 68: 194-208.

55. Fong WM, Wong WK, Lean HH (2005) International momentum strategies: A stochastic dominance approach. Journal of Financial Markets 8: 89-109.

56. Guo X, Zhu XH, Wong WK, Zhu LX (2013) A note on almost stochastic dominance. Economics Letters 121: 252-256.

57. Guo X, Post T, Wong WK, Zhu LX (2014) Moment conditions for almost stochastic dominance. Economics Letters 124: 163-167.

58. Tsetlin I, Winkler RL, Huang RJ, Tzeng LY (2015) Generalized almost stochastic dominance. Operations Research 62: 363-377.

59. Wong WK, Ma C (2008) Preferences over location-scale family. Economic Theory 37: 119-146.

60. Lean HH, McAleer M, Wong WK (2015) Preferences of risk-averse and risk-seeking investors for oil spot and futures before, during and after the Global Financial Crisis. International Review of Economics and Finance 40: 204-216.

61. Hoang VTH, Wong WK, Zhu ZZ (2015) Is gold different for risk-averse and risk-seeking investors? An empirical analysis of the Shanghai Gold Exchange. Economic Modelling 50: 200-211.

62. Wong WK, Wright JA, Yam SCP, Yung SP (2012) A mixed Sharpe ratio. Risk and Decision Analysis 3: 37-65.

63. Gasbarro D, Wong WK, Zumwalt JK (2012) Stochastic dominance and behavior towards risk: The market for iShares. Annals of Financial Economics 7: 1-20.

64. Kuosmanen T (2004) Efficient Diversification According to Stochastic Dominance Criteria. Management Science 50: 1390-1406.

65. Lean HH, Phoon KF, Wong WK (2012) Stochastic dominance analysis of CTA funds. Review of Quantitative Finance and Accounting 40: 155-170.

66. Leung PL, Wong WK (2008) On testing the equality of the multiple Sharpe ratios, with application on the evaluation of Ishares. Journal of Risk 10: 1-16.

67. Qiao Z, Clark E, Wong WK (2012) Investors' preference towards risk: Evidence from the Taiwan stock and stock index futures markets. Accounting Finance 54: 251-274.

68. Qiao Z, Wong WK (2015) Which is a better investment choice in the Hong Kong residential property market: A big or small property? Applied Economics 47: 1670-1685.

69. Qiao Z, Wong WK, Fung JKW (2013) Stochastic dominance relationships between stock and stock index futures markets: International evidence. Economic Modelling 33: 552-559.

70. Sriboonchitta S, Wong WK, Dhompongsa S, Nguyen HT (2009) Stochastic Dominance and Applications to Finance, Risk and Economics, Chapman and Hall/CRC, Taylor and Francis, Boca Raton, Florida, USA.

71. Tsang CK, Wong WK, Horowitz I (2016) Arbitrage opportunities, efficiency, and the role of risk preferences in the Hong Kong property market. Forthcoming in Studies in Economics and Finance.

72. Wong WK, Phoon KF, Lean HH (2008) Stochastic dominance analysis of Asian hedge funds. Pacific-Basin Finance Journal 16: 204-223.

Heart Disease Diagnosis Using Data Mining Techniques

Ramin Assari[1]*, Parham Azimi[2] and Mohammad Reza Taghva[1]

[1]*Department of IT Management, Allameh Tabataba'i University, Tehran, Iran*

[2]*Faculty of Mechanical Engineering and Industrial Engineering, Islamic Azad University, Qazvin, Iran*

Abstract

In recent decades, heart disease has been identified as the leading cause of death across the world. However, it is considered as the most preventable and controllable disease at the same time. According to World Health Organization (WHO), the early and timely diagnosis of heart disease plays a remarkable role in preventing its progress and reducing related treatment costs. Considering the ever-increasing growth of heart disease-induced fatalities, researchers have adopted different data mining techniques to diagnose it. According to results, application of the same data mining techniques leads to different results in different datasets. This study tries to assist healthcare specialists to early diagnose heart disease and assess related risk factors. To this end, the main heart disease diagnosis indices were identified using experts' opinions. Then, data mining techniques were applied on a heart-related dataset. Finally, the main heart disease diagnosis indices were identified and a model was developed based on extracted rules. Visual Studio was used to write the algorithm code.

Keywords: Bayesian network; Data mining; Decision tree; Heart disease; K-nearest neighbor; Support vector machines

Introduction

In the past decade, heart disease has been the leading cause of death in different continents and countries in the world, regardless of the income level of countries [1]. According to WHO report, heart disease is the leading cause of death across the world, accounting for 7.2 million deaths, i.e., 12.8% of all fatalities in the world [2]. Figure 1, illustrates deaths from heart disease across the world (scale: 1:100000). According to recent research predictions, cardiovascular diseases will become the leading cause of death up to 2030.

Although cardiovascular diseases have been identified as the leading cause of death in the world in the past decade, they have been introduced as the most preventable and controllable diseases [3]. The complete and correct treatment of a disease depends on the timely diagnosis of that disease [4]. An accurate and systematic tool for identifying high-risk patients and extracting data for timely diagnosis of heart disease seems a critical need.

Every day, modern computer-based systems collect large amounts of data using automatic data record systems in different fields. Data mining technology is the product of the evolution of database technology, IT and storage devices [5]. The current challenge is to make data mining and knowledge discovery systems applicable to a wider range of domains [6]. Researchers are adopting data mining techniques to diagnose different diseases including diabetes [7], stroke [8], cancer [9] and heart disease [10]. Considering the high rate of cardiovascular-induced fatalities, researchers have tried to adopt data mining systems to diagnose heart disease [11].

Literature Review

Every day, modern computer-based systems collect large amounts of data using automatic data record systems in the healthcare field where data mining can extract a valuable knowledge from them. The next section briefly explains heart disease and the application of data mining techniques in treating such diseases.

Heart disease

As the leading cause of death in the world, heart disease, according to WHO, accounts for 3.8 million and 3.4 million deaths in males and females, respectively.

The symptoms and incidence of heart disease differ from one person to another. However, they commonly include chest pain, jaw pain, neck pain, back pain, stomach disorders; arms and shoulders pains and shortness of breath [12]. Different heart problems induce different heart diseases including coronary artery disease, heart failure and stroke [13].

Although heart disease has been identified as the most chronic disease across the world, it is the most preventable one at the same time. A healthy life style (primary prevention) and timely diagnosis (secondary prevention) are two main elements of heart disease control. Conducting regular check-ups (secondary prevention) plays a remarkable role in the diagnosis and early prevention of heart disease complications [14]. Several tests including, chest X-rays, angiography, echocardiography and exercise tolerance test contribute to this important issue. However, these tests are costly and require accurate medical equipment.

Applications of data mining to healthcare data

Data mining scholars have long studied the application of tools and equipment in improving the process of data analysis in large and complex datasets. Adopting data mining techniques in the medicine field is of high importance in diagnosing, predicting and deeply understanding of healthcare data. These applications include treatment centers analysis aimed at improving treatment policies and prevention of any mistake in hospitals, early diagnosis of diseases, prevention of diseases and hospital death reduction.

***Corresponding author:** Ramin Assari, IT Management, Management Department, Allameh Tabataba'i University, Iran
E-mail: assari20002000@gmail.com

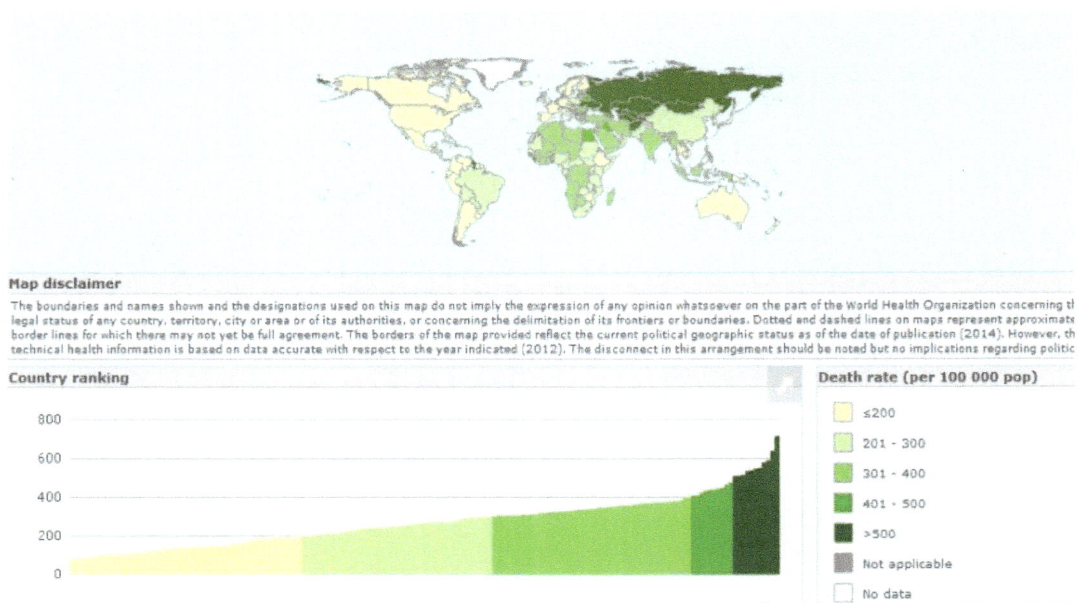

Figure 1: Heart diseases-induced fatalities across the world in 2013.

Heart specialist's record and store large amounts of patients' data. This provides a great opportunity for extracting a valuable knowledge from such datasets. Researchers are adopting statistical approaches as well as data mining techniques to help treatment and healthcare specialists diagnose and determine heart disease risk factors in patients. Statistical analyses have identified a number of risk factors for heart diseases including age, blood pressure, smoking [15], total cholesterol [16], diabetes [17], and hypertension, heart disease background in family, obesity and lack of physical activity [18]. The awareness of heart disease risk factors assists treatment and healthcare specialists to identify patients who are subject to high risk factors.

Researchers have employed different data mining techniques to help specialists and physicians diagnose heart disease [19]. Some techniques are more common such as Naïve Bayes, decision tree and K-nearest neighbor. However, there are other classification-based data mining techniques such as kernel density, neural network, bagging algorithm, sequential minimal optimization, direct Kernel self-organizing map and support vector machine. The next section briefly explains those techniques which were used in this study.

Decision tree

There are different types of decision trees. They only differ in the mathematical model they use to select the class of attribute during rule extraction. Gain ratio decision tree is the most common, successful type [20]. It is a relationship between entropy (information gain) and classified information.

In entropy technique, the attribute which minimizes entropy and maximizes information gain is selected as the tree root. To select tree root, it is first necessary to calculate the information gain of each attribute. Then, the attribute maximizing information gain should be selected. Information gain, or entropy, is derived from relation 1.3 [21].

$$E = -\sum_{i=1}^{k} p_i \, log_2^{p_i} \tag{2-1}$$

Where k is the number of response variable classes, p_i is the ratio of the number of the ith class events to total number of samples (occurrence probability of i)

Bayesian network

Bayesian network is a statistical technique predicting the membership class of the studied sample using the probability theory. Bayesian network practices classification process in accordance with Bayes' theorem. It assumes that the influence of the value of a theorem on a class is independent from the influence of other attributes. This assumption is called "class conditional independence". This assumption was made to simplify engaged calculation and this is why it was named "Naïve", i.e., simple.

This technique calculates the prior probability of the response variable and the conditional probability of other variables. The prior and conditional probabilities of the initial training are calculated. Then, for every test dataset sample, the probability of the occurrence (presence) of each case of response variable is calculated. Afterwards, the response variable with the highest occurrence probability is selected. The probability of test sample for the response variable value is derived from relation 4.3 [22].

$$P(v = c_i) = P(c_i) \times \sum_{j=1}^{n} P(a_j = v_j | class = c_i) \tag{2-2}$$

Where V, ci, aj and vj are test sample, response variable value, data attribute and the test sample value, respectively.

K-nearest neighbor

This classification technique is called a memory-based technique, since the training samples should be stored in memory during run-time [23-27].

If a is the first sample denoted by (a1, a2,..., an), and b is the second sample denoted by (b1, b2,..., bn), the distance between them is calculated by relation 2-3.

$$\sqrt{(a_1 - b_1)^2 + (a_2 - b_2)^2 + (a_n - b_n)^2} \tag{2-3}$$

Support vector machine

Given availability of support vectors, Support Vector Machine (SVM) is the boundary determining the best data classification and separation. In SVM, only those data lying inside support vectors are used as the base data for machine and building a model. This means that this algorithm is not sensitive to other data. It aims to find the best data boundary with the farthest possible distance from all classes (their support vectors). SVM transfers data to a new space with respect to their predetermined classes so that data can be classified and separated linearly (using hyperplanes). Then, it searches for support lines (or support planes in multi-dimensional space) and tries to determine the equation of a straight line that maximizes the distance between each two classes. Each support vector is characterized with an equation describing the boundary line of each class.

Dataset

This study used Cleveland Clinic Foundation dataset known as "Cleveland Clinic Foundation Heart Disease Dataset". This dataset included 13 attributes (Table 1) and 303 samples, 3 of which were incomplete and hence excluded from this study. The continuous values of this dataset were discretized using equal frequency method. This technique classifies continuous values into 5 classes.

Selected data mining techniques were applied on the studied dataset after dataset discretization. 10-fold cross-validation method was used to validate the results. This technique classifies dataset into 10 portions. 9 portions were used for training the algorithm and 1 portion was used for evaluation in each run-time. The process was repeated 10 times. This procedure is helpful specifically in datasets with small number of samples by prevention of over-fitting. Finally, the sensitivity, specificity and accuracy of each method were calculated.

Sensitivity is the ratio of true positives. Specificity is the ratio of true negatives. Accuracy is the ratio of true positives and true negatives combined (relations 2.4 to 2.6).

Sensitivity=True Positive/Positive (2-4)

Specificity=True Negative/Negative (2-5)

Accuracy=(True Positive + True Negative)/(Positive + Negative) (2-6)

Results

This section compares the accuracy, sensitivity and specificity of the employed techniques in terms of their confusion matrices.

Decision tree, Naïve Bayes, K-Nearest Neighbor and Support Vector Machine were applied to the studied dataset. Table 2 shows the sensitivity, specificity and accuracy of these data mining techniques.

Name	Type	Description
Age	Continuous	Age in years
Sex	Discrete	1=male
		0=female
Cp	Discrete	Chest pain type:
		1-typical angina
		2-atypical angina
		3-non-angina pain
		4-asymptomatic
Trestbps	Continuous	Resting blood pressure in (mm Hg)
Chol	Continuous	Serum cholesterol in (mg/dl)
Fbs	Discrete	FBS>120 (mg/dl)
		1=yes
		0=no
Restecg	Discrete	Resting electrocardiographic results:
		0=nrmal
		1-having ST-T wave abnormality
		2=showing probable or defined left ventricular hypertrophy
Thalach	Continuous	Maximum heart rate achieved
Exang	Discrete	Exercise-induced angenia:
		1=yes
		0=no
Old peak ST	Continuous	Depression induced by exercise relative to rest
Slope	Discrete	The slope of the peak exercise segment:
		1=up sloping
		2=flat
		3=down sloping
Ca	Discrete	Number of major vessels colored by fluoroscopy that range between 0 and 3
Thal	Discrete	3=normal
		6=fixed defect
		7=reversible defect
Diagnosis	Discrete	Diagnosis classes:
		1=healthy
		2=patient who is subject to possible heart disease

Table 1: Cleveland clinic foundation heart disease dataset indices.

Their accuracy ranges from 79% to 84.33%. According to Table 2, SVM achieved the highest accuracy (84.33%).

SVM and Naïve Bayes achieved the highest accuracy, followed by KNN (k=7 resulted in the best accuracy as compared to other values) and decision tree, respectively. Weka and IBM SPSS Modeler were used to implement data mining techniques.

Identification of influential factors

After implementing the above mentioned techniques and performing related analyses, the following influential indices were identified. Table 3 compares all 13 input attributes in terms of their significance based on the results obtained from each technique.

Accuracy	Specificity	Sensitivity	Method
0.79	0.8148	0.7608	Decision Tree
0.8366	0.8641	0.8043	Naïve Bayes
0.81	0.8395	0.7753	KNN K=7
0.8433	0.895	0.7826	SVM

Table 2: Results of employed data mining techniques.

Attribute	Importance degree				Avg.
	Naïve Bayes	KNN K=7	SVM	Decision Tree	
Age	0.7	0.08	-	0.01	0.04
Sex	-	0.08	0.06	0.05	0.047
Cp	0.11	0.08	0.18	0.24	0.152
Trestbps	0.04	0.08	-	-	0.03
Chol	0.05	0.08	-	-	0.032
Fbs	0.06	0.08	0	-	0.035
Restecg	0.07	0.08	0	-	0.037
Thalach	0.05	0.07	0.09	-	0.052
Exang	-	0.08	0.09	0.08	0.062
Oldpeak	0.09	0.07	0	0.04	0.05
Slope	-	0.07	0.13	0.04	0.06
Ca	0.21	0.08	0.25	0.2	0.185
Thal	0.15	0.08	0.19	0.33	0.187

Table 3: Significance comparison of input indices in each method.

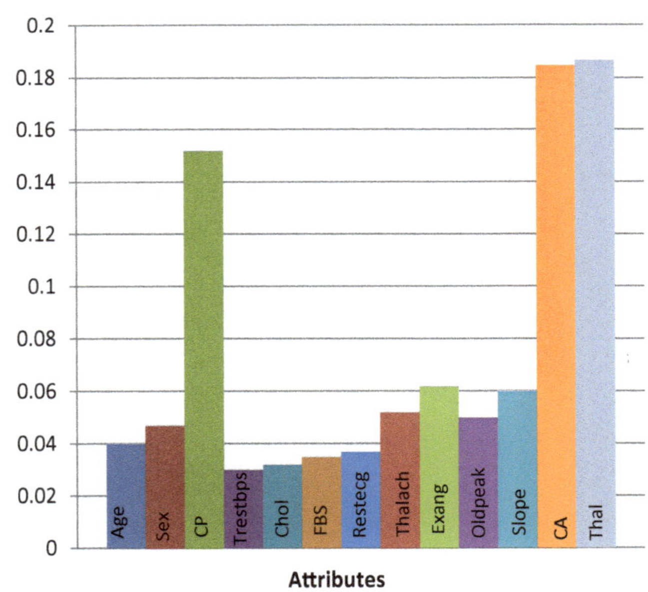

Figure 2: Comparing significance of input indices in each method.

The variables thal (0.187), ca (0.185) and cp (0.152) had the highest significance in all 4 employed techniques respectively, followed by trestbps (0.03) and chol (0.032) as the lowest. Figure 2 compares the attributes in terms of significance.

Conclusion

Heart disease is the leading cause of death across the world. It accounts for 7.2 million deaths, i.e., 12.8% of fatalities in the world. Although cardiovascular diseases have been identified as the leading cause of death in the past decade, they are the most preventable and controllable diseases at the same time. Deaths from cardiovascular diseases show an ever-increasing trend. On the other hand, their early diagnosis plays an important role in improving patients' health status and decreasing fatalities. Therefore, this study aimed to aid physicians to early diagnose such diseases and assess heart disease risk factors in studied individuals. After studying different papers, selecting different data mining techniques and implementing them on the selected dataset, SVM technique achieved the highest accuracy (84.33%). In SVM as well as the other employed techniques, thal, ca and cp were introduced as the most influential indices on average. This technique is expected to be implemented in future on a localized dataset with non-aggressive indices in general. This, in turn, imposes lower costs and complications on patients.

References

1. World Health Organization (2011) The top ten causes of death.
2. World Health Organization (2013) Deaths from coronary heart disease.
3. Center for Disease Control and Prevention (2014) Heart Disease and Family History.
4. Paladugu S (2010) Temporal mining framework for risk reduction and early detection of chronic diseases. University of Missouri-Columbia.
5. Obenshain MK (2004) Application of data mining techniques to healthcare data. Infection Control and Hospital Epidemiology 25: 690-695.
6. Shillabeer A, Roddick JF (2006) Towards role based hypothesis evaluation for health data mining. Electronic. Journal of Health Informatics 1: 1-9.
7. Porter T, Green B (2009) Identifying Diabetic Patients: A Data Mining Approach.
8. Panzarasa S, Quaglini S, Sacchi L, Cavallini A, Micieli G, et al. (2010) Data mining techniques for analyzing stroke care processes. In the Proc. of the 13th World Congress on Medical Informatics.
9. Li L, Tang H, Wu Z, Gong J, Gruidl M, et al. (2004) Data mining techniques for cancer detection using serum proteomic profiling. Artificial intelligence in medicine 32: 71-83.
10. Das R, Turkoglu I, Sengur A (2009) Effective diagnosis of heart disease through neural networks ensembles. Expert Systems with Applications 36: 7675-7680.
11. Lakshmi K, Krishna MV, Kumar SP (2013) Performance Comparison of Data Mining Techniques for Predicting of Heart Disease Survivability. International Journal of Scientific and Research Publications 3: 1-10.
12. Centers for Disease Control and Prevention (2013) Chronic Disease Prevention and Health Promotion. Accessed 27 September 2013, from http://www.cdc.gov/nccdphp/
13. U.S department of health and human services (2005) High Blood Cholesterol What you need to know.
14. Department of Health & Aging AG (2012) Seniors and Aged Care Australia websites have been replaced.
15. Heller RF, Chinn S, Tunstall Pedoe HD, Rose G (1984) How well can we predict coronary heart disease? Findings in the United Kingdom Heart Disease Prevention Project. British Medical Journal 288: 1409-1411.
16. Wilson PW, D'Agostino RB, Levy D, Belanger AM, Silbershatz H, et al. (1998) Prediction of coronary heart disease using risk factor categories. Circulation 97: 1837-1847.

17. Simons LA, Simons J, Friedlander Y, McCallum J, Palaniappan L (2003) Risk functions for prediction of cardiovascular disease in elderly Australians: the Dubbo Study. Medical Journal of Australia 178: 113-116.

18. Shahwan-Akl L (2010) Cardiovascular disease risk factors among adult Australian-Lebanese in Melbourne. International Journal of Research in Nursing 1: 1-7.

19. Helma C, Gottmann E, Kramer S (2000) Knowledge discovery and data mining in toxicology. Statistical Methods in Medical Research 9: 329-358.

20. Quinlan JR (1986) Decision trees and multi-valued attributes. In: Hayes, Michie D (eds.) Machine intelligence. Oxford University Press.

21. Han J, Kamber M (2006) Data Mining Concepts and Techniques: Morgan Kaufmann Publishers.

22. Bramer M (2007) Principles of data mining: Springer.

23. Alpaydin E (1997) Voting over multiple condensed nearest neighbors. Artificial Intelligence Review 11: 115-132.

24. National Center for Chronic Disease Prevention and Health Promotion (2013) Know the facts about heart disease.

25. Rajkumar M, Reena GS (2010) Diagonsis of Heaer Disease using Datamining Algorithm. Global Journal of Computer Science and Technology 10: 38-43.

26. Shouman M (2014) Prototype Development of a Novel Heart Disease Risk Evaluation Tool Using Data Mining Analysis. Zagazig University, Egypt.

27. Tu MC, Shin D, Shin D (2009) Effective Diagnosis of Heart Disease through Bagging Approach. Paper presented at the 2nd International Conference on Biomedical Engineering and Informatics.

The Relationship between External Debt and Economic Growth in Nigeria

Victor Ushahemba Ijirshar*, Fefa Joseph and Mile Godoo

Department of Economics, Benue State University, Nigeria

Abstract

External debt is found to be a driver of economic growth if properly managed but its servicing rather than repayment is an inhibiting factor to economic growth. This paper examined the relationship between external debt and economic growth in Nigeria for the period of 1981-2014. The study used both descriptive and econometric tools. The analysis of unit root was performed on each of the variables incorporated in the model and the result showed that, all the variables were not stationary at level but achieved stationary after first difference at 5% level of significance. The regression results showed a significant relationship between external debt and economic growth in Nigeria. However, external debt stock impacted positively while external debt service impacted negatively on the annual growth rate of the Nigerian economy both in the long run and the short run.

Keywords: Debt management; Debt servicing; Debt stock; Economic growth

Introduction

The issue of external borrowing as a policy to promote economic growth creates serious debate among economists and policy makers. The main concern is whether or not external borrowing leads to economic growth in debtor countries. This debate results in two main perspectives for explaining the relationship between external debt and economic growth. On one hand, the Neoclassical and the Endogenous growth models advocated that there is a positive relationship between external debt and economic growth. They emphasized that debt is one of the sources for financing capital formation, and if financing capital formation through this means impact positively on investment, it could promote economic growth [1-3]. On the other hand, among other scholars Krugman contradict this view by mentioning external debt as one of the factors hampering economic growth [4]. Kalonji explained that heavy external debt is the cause of poverty in the debtors' country while Chongo noted that public debt is a double edged sword [5]. This can also be seen in the mix opinion by Ojo and Sulaiman who examined the impact of external debt on the level of economic growth and the volume of investment in Nigeria and found that the current external debt ratio of GDP stimulate growth in the short-run, but the private investment which is a measure of real and tangible development shows a decline [6]. Their opinion shows a mix result indicating a positive and negative relationship between external debt and economic growth in Nigeria.

But given the ideology of the "growth-debt" nexus that a country should borrow abroad as long as the capital is inadequate and produces a rate of return that is higher than the cost of the foreign borrowing, it is generally expected that developing countries experiencing inadequate capital will acquire external debt to supplement domestic savings and investment. The rates at which they borrow depend on the links among foreign and domestic savings, investment and economic growth so that the borrowing countries increase their capacity output with the aid of foreign savings. Nevertheless, external debt can only be productive if well manage by making the rate of return higher than the cost of servicing the debt.

However, the external debt profile of Nigeria has been on the increase and has constituted a source of concern about the future. Recently, the Nigerian government has embarked on borrowing externally for the main purpose of financing increased proportion of economic activities for economic growth. It has been argued by Ali and Mshelia that in Nigeria, external borrowing is often considered the best way out of embarrassing economic situations [2]. Despite the seeming justification to borrow externally, it is soon discovered to become a perpetual lifeline burden, consequently engendering severe economic implications both to immediate and future generation economies, leaving Nigerians with an acute decline in the standard of living, high external dependence, gross social and economic overhead depreciation, currency depreciation, balance of payment disequilibria, exchange rate depreciation and rising inflationary rate. External Debt in Nigeria averaged 6375.33 Million USD from 2008 until 2015, reaching an all-time high of 10718.43 Million USD in the fourth quarter of 2015 [7]. According to Nwankwo, the Nigerian external debt has risen to $11 billion with debt sustainability ratio of 2.4% which is far below the sustainable ratio of 12.51 to the GDP [8].

Given the rising stock of external debt in Nigeria, it is important therefore that the country should undertake critical examination of the general implication of the loan on economic growth. It is against this background that it becomes imperative to assess the effect of the external debt on economic growth in Nigeria from 1981-2014.

Conceptual and Theoretical Review

External debt management

External debt is the phenomenon used to describe the financial obligation that ties one party (debtor country) to another (lender country) [6]. External debt management is a strategy design to ensure that the debt stocks does not grow to an extent that the country can no longer conveniently service her debts and also that the terms are not enslaving. In other words, it is a mechanism where a nation's debt stock and the servicing arrangement (terms of loan) do not cause severe problems for the economy and society. According to the Central Bank of Nigeria Statistical Bulletin [6], external debt management involves

***Corresponding author:** Ijirshar VU, Department of Economics, Benue State University, Makurdi, Nigeria, E-mail: ijirsharvictor@gmail.com

an assessment of the country's capacity to service existing debts and a judgment on the desirability of contracting further loans. Therefore, External debt management in this work means a mechanism used by the responsible authority (Debt Management Board) to ensure that external debt does not affect its country in terms of investment, saving and capital generation which are the basis for economic growth and development, but should be bearable and/or productive.

Debt servicing

Debt serving is a contractually fixed charge on domestic real income and savings. As the size of debt grows, or as interest rate rises, debt service charge increases. Debt services payment is made is done only with the export earning, curtailed import, or with further external borrowing. Thus if the export earning diminishes, debt-service difficulties are likely to arise.

Debt sustainability

Debt Sustainability is defined as the ability to maintain a constant debt-GDP ratio over a period of time. Sustainability is challenged when the debt to GDP ratio reaches an excessive value. Kasidi and Said thought that, a number of factors come into play when establishing if a country is able to service its debt [9,10]. These factors include the existing debt stock and associated debt service, the prospective path of its deficits, the financing mix of the debt and the evolution of its repayment capacity in terms of foreign currency value of GDP, exports and government revenues.

External debt management in Nigeria

In the face of the declining trend in world oil prices, Nigerian government has been facing difficulties in financing deficit budgets and developmental projects. This led to borrowing from external sources such as World Bank, International Monetary Fund (IMF) and Paris club amongst others. The responsibility of managing external debt among other issues led to the establishment of other departments in the Central Bank of Nigeria (CBN) to undertake the functions in collaboration with the Federal Ministry of Finance (FMF) and other relevant agencies. Since 1980s, Nigeria has devised several debt management policies in order to make the debt–service burden bearable and avoid defaulting [11]. The embargo on loans policy was placed in 1984 and 2016 to state governments from borrowing externally. The cordial objective of the policy was to check the escalation of the debt stock and to minimize the problem of additional debt burden. Prior to the 1984 policy, the Federal Government fixed the maximum level of debt commitment for both the federal and state governments. For example, an upper limit of $ 5 billion was for the federal government in 1978 and in 1982 while $200 million for the state government. The embargo was lifted in January 1989 [12]. In February 1988, comprehensive guidelines were introduced with the aim of evolving strategies for increasing foreign exchange earnings and consequently reducing the need for foreign borrowing. Various measures were undertaken to ensure implementation of the guidelines such as; embargo on new loans, limit on debt service payments, debt restructuring and debt conversion programme.

Debt restructuring policy involves the reduction in the burden of an existing debt through refinancing, rescheduling, and buy-back insurance of collateralized bonds and provision of new money. A refinancing arrangement means the procurement of a loan by a debtor to pay off an existing debt, particularly short term-trade debt so as to ease the debt burden. It should be noted that the first refinancing arrangement by Nigeria was made in July 1983, followed by second arrangements in September of the same year. In both agreements, $2.1 billion worth of trade arrears was refinanced. The rescheduling of debt involved changing maturing, tenure and terms of debt structure. For instance in 1986, debt worth $1.6 billion due to London club and payable in 1987 was rescheduled to extend to 1996 with four years grace period. Furthermore, the payback arrangement which implied the offer of a substantial discount to pay off existing debts was concluded on 21st January, 1982 when Nigeria bought 6.2% ($3.395 billion) commercial debt owed to the London club at 60% discount.

Debt conversion programme was made to complement other strategies of debt management. In Nigeria, debt conversion exercise involved the sale of an external debt instrument for a domestic debt or equity participation in domestic enterprises. The debt conversion committee was set up in July 1988 to implement Nigeria's debt conversion programme. Though the appropriation of the substantial discount offered and commission paid, the nation benefited and reduced its debt stock. As a result of the strenuous effort being made by Nigeria government to formalize its economic and political relations, the prospect for an early rescheduling of Nigerian's official debts are bright especially as the international community reposes with some measures of confidence in Nigeria. In 2005/2006, Nigeria's external debt which stood at US $32 billion was forgiven by the creditors. This has external and internal implications for the economy. On external front, Nigeria's credit worthiness increased, thereby, making the economy worthy to access short and medium term credits which enhance net capital inflows necessary for employment and growth. In the domestic economy, potential new export earnings and gains from new investment as well as the money budgeted for debt servicing are expected to be channeled into growth enhancing projects- as this result to rises in investment, employment and output [13]. External debt service on the other hand, reduces public investment funds, employment and private income. It also reduces the country's currency and compound balance of payment problems. In view of these, several policies were introduced to reduce the magnitude of public debt, ameliorate the debt service burden in order to stimulate sustained growth in the Nigerian economy. But, Henry observed that these policies have not been able to restrain the growth of foreign debt [14].

Economic growth

Ajayi perceived economic growth as the increase overtime of a country's real output of goods and services [15]. Schumpeter in Todaro and Smith defined economic growth as gradual and steady change in the long-run which comes about by a gradual increase in the rate of savings and population [16]. Freedman also in Todaro and Smith viewed economic growth as an expansion of the system in one or more dimensions without a change in its structure [16]. Thus economic growth is related to the quantitative and sustained increase in the countries per capita output or income accompanied by expansion in its labor force, consumption level, capital and volume of trade. It means an increase in a country's real gross domestic product over a period of time usually one fiscal year.

The dependency theory of underdevelopment

The theory originated from the writings of few Latin American economists whose translations began to appear in English in the mid 1960s and early 1970s. The proponents of this school according to Jhingan are Frank Gunder, Sunkel, Furtardo, Sanlos, Paul Baran, Emmanuel and Amin [17]. These scholars at one point or the other, contributed immensely to the dependency theory, though in varying capacities. The dependency theory states that the dependence of less developed countries (LDCs) on developed countries (DCs) is the main cause for the underdevelopment of the former. Though the theory has so many aspects but emphasis is on the foreign capital dependence which has a bearing to the topic under study. The resultant effect of this dependence is that foreign debt so acquired stands as an instrument through which developed countries exploit less developed countries by insisting on the choice of projects, making decisions on pricing, supply of equipment, technical knowhow and personnel. According to the theory, the developed countries use foreign capital to impose a developmental pattern that is not compatible with local needs. The theory further argued that the dependence on foreign capital leads to a much high outflow in the forms of interest payment, royalties, debt service. All these drain LDCs wealth. The theory concludes that foreign capital signifies dependence and serves as a means of exploitation of the less developed countries exploit by the developed countries.

Empirical review

Adesola in his study on the effect of external debt service payment practices on sustainable economic growth and development in Nigerian from 1981 to 2004 argued that debt payment to Nigerian creditors to affect the economic growth both positively and negatively [3]. But Ali and Mshelia found that Nigeria is indebted to several creditors which do not augur well for the country [18]. Similarly, Ayadi and Ayadi in their study on the impact of external debt on economic growth in Nigeria and South Africa using neoclassical growth model found a negative impact of debt (and its servicing requirements) on growth in the two countries while external debt contributes positively to growth up to a point after which its contribution becomes negative in Nigeria [19].

Several empirical studies found a positive impact of external debt on economic growth in Nigeria. For instance; Sulaiman and Azeez examined the effect of external debt on the economic growth in Nigeria from 1970 to 2010 [20]. The study found short and long run relationship among the variables and concluded that external debt has contributed positively to economic growth in Nigerian. Also, Chinaemerem and Anayochukwu examined the impact of external debt financing on economic growth in Nigeria from 1969 to 2011. The study also found positive impact on economic growth [21].

Methodology

The study used secondary data from 1981 to 2014. Data were sourced from Central Bank of Nigeria (CBN) Statistical Bulletin of several issues, National Bureau of Statistics (NBS), Debt Management Office and World Bank reports. The study used both descriptive and econometric tools.

Augmented Dickey Fuller Test (ADF) was used to ascertain the stationary properties of the time series. The ADF formula was specified as:

$$\Delta P_{it} = \beta_1 + \beta_{2t} + \sigma P_{it-1} + \alpha \sum_{t-1}^{m} \Delta P_{it-1} + \varepsilon_{it} \quad (1)$$

The study also used Ng and Perron (2001) which constructed four test statistics that are based upon the GLS detrended data y_t^d. The formula is stated as:

$$K = \Sigma_{t=2}^{T} (y_t^d)^2 / T^2 \quad (2)$$

The modified statistics may then be written as:

$$MZ_\alpha^d = \left(T^{-1}\left(y_t^d\right)^2 - f_0\right) / (2k)$$

$$MZ_\alpha^d = MZ_\alpha XMSB$$

$$MSB^d = (\frac{k}{f_0})^{1/2} \quad (3)$$

$$MP_T^d = \begin{cases} (c^{-2}k - \overline{c}T^{-1}(y_t^d)^2)/f_0 & \text{if } x_t = \{1\} \\ (c^{-2}k + (1-\overline{c})T^{-1}(y_t^d)^2)/f_0 & \text{if } x_t = \{1,t\} \end{cases}$$

Where

$$\overline{c} =_{-13.5}^{-7} \quad \begin{matrix} \text{if } x_t = \{1\} \\ \text{if } x_t = \{1,t\} \end{matrix} \quad (4)$$

Thus, Granger causality test was employed to determine the causal relationship between the variables under study. It is thus stated as:

$$y_t = a_0 + a_1 y_{t-1} + \ldots + a_l y_{t-l} + b_1 x_{t-1} + \ldots + b_l x_{t-l} + e_t \quad (5)$$

$$x_t = a_0 + a_1 x_{t-1} + \ldots + a_l x_{t-l} + b_1 y_{t-1} + \ldots + b_l y_{t-l} + u_t \quad (6)$$

The ECM was conducted. It incorporates both the short run and the long run effects. When equilibrium holds $[Y_{t-1}-\beta_0-\beta_1 X_{t-1}] = 0$ but in the short run when equilibrium exists, this term is non-zero and measures the distance by which the system is away from equilibrium during time t.

Model specification

Adopting the model used by Ayadi and Ayadi in analyzing the relationship between external debt management and economic growth in Nigeria [19]. The implicit form of the model shall be:

RGDPG=f(AGREXP, DSERGDP, GCAP, DEBGDP, INF, INTR) (7)

The explicit form of the model that was estimated in explaining the linear relationship between output (RGDPG) and External debt management and other macro-economic variables is stated as:

$$RGDPG = b_o + b_1 AGREXP + b_2 DSERGDP + b_3 GCAP + b_4 DEBGDP + b_5 INF + b_6 INTR + U_t \quad (8)$$

Where:

RGDPG = annual growth rate of the RGDP

AGREXP = annual growth rate of exports

DSERGDP = ratio of debt service to RGDP

GCAP = Growth in fixed capital

DEBGDP = Size of external debt stock relative to RGDP

INF= Inflation rate

INTR= Interest rate

U_t = random or stochastic error term

Data Presentation and Analysis

Result of unit root tests

The test results of the Augmented Dickey-Fuller statistic and Ng and Perron (2001) for all the time series variables used in the estimation were integrated of order one i.e. I(1) [22]. This is because the ADF statistics of annual growth rate, annual growth rate of exports, ratio of debt service to RGDP, growth in fixed capital, size of external debt stock relative to RGDP, inflation rate and interest rate were greater than their respective critical values at 5% critical level. This was evidence by the four statistics constructed under the Ng and Perrron unit root test.

Results of granger causality

From the results of the Pairwise granger causality tests reveals that DEBGDP (i.e. the relative ratio of external debt stock to RGDP),

DSERGDP (i.e. the relative ratio of external debt service to RGDP) and GCAP (i.e Gross Fixed Capital) granger causes RGDPG (i.e. economic growth rate) at 5% level of significance. More so, INFL (i.e. Inflation rate) granger causes INTR (i.e. Interest rate) at 10% level of significance.

Johansen hypothesized co-integration result

The Johansen hypothesized co-integration was carried out to determine the number of stationary long-run relationships among the variables included in the study. It offers two tests, the trace test and the Eigen values, with a view to identify the number of co-integrating relationships. The results revealed one co-integrating equation among the variables. This is because the trace statistic and Max-Eigen value of 186.3908 and 82.03992 are greater than the critical values of 125.6154 and 46.23142 respectively, at 5% level of significance. This implies that there is a long run relationship among the variables employed in the study.

The long run effect of external debt on economic growth in Nigeria

Using the normalized Johansen co-integrating equation that is based on the lowest log likelihood, the normalized coefficients present the estimates of the model (co-integrating equation).

RGDPG = 0.024197 AGREXP (0.00664) - 14.48725DSERGDP (1.29314) + 0.08966GCAP (0.01255)

+ 0.331958DEBGDP (0.08809) + 0.079347INF (0.02084) - 0.077656INTR (0.03299)

Note: Standard Errors in parenthesis.

The coefficient of growth rate of export, growth rate in fixed capital, relative ratio of external debt stock to RGDP were positive and were theoretically plausible. The coefficients were statistically significant at 5% critical level. This implies that 1% increase in the growth rate of export, growth rate in fixed capital, relative ratio of external debt stock to RGDP leads to 2% 9% and 33% respective increases in economic growth.

More so, the coefficient of relative ratio of external debt service to RGDP and interest rate were negative and obeyed their apriority expectation except inflation rate. Besides, the coefficient of relative ratio of external debt service to economic growth, inflation rate and interest rate were statistically significant at 5% critical level. This explains that Nigeria needs a digit inflation rate for economic growth.

Short run effect of external debt on economic growth in Nigeria

The short run estimates are presented in Table 1. The coefficient of $RGDPG_{t-1}$ (i.e in the previous year) and the relative ratio of external debt stock to economic growth in the previous year ($DEBGDP_{t-1}$) were theoretically plausible but not statistically significant at 5% critical level. However, the coefficient of $AGREXP_{t-1}$ obeyed its apriori expectation and it is statistically significant at 5% critical level. Thus, there is a strong positive relationship between annual growth rate in exports and economic growth rate in Nigeria in the short run. This means that growth in Nigeria's exports contributes significantly to the growth of the economy even in the short run [23-25]. This is because, it increase the country's foreign exchange earnings making it favourable for debt settlement and public financing. Furthermore, the coefficient of DSERGDP and GCAP obeyed their apriori expectations and were statistically significant at 5% critical level. This implies that servicing external debt has negative influence on the growth of the Nigerian economy. The study also reveals a significant speed of adjustment of 8.4%. This implies that the system corrects the initial disequilibrium to long-run equilibrium at the rate of 8.4%. It is obvious from the coefficient of multiple determinations (R^2) that the model has good fit as the independent variables were found to jointly explain 0.77% of the movement in the dependent variable with the R^2-adjusted (R^2) of 0.69 %. The F-statistic was significant at 15.110585% which explains the overall significance of all the variables incorporated in the model as indicated by both the R^2 and R^2 adjusted [25-28].

Variable	Coefficient	Standard errors [t-statistic]
$RGDPG_{t-1}$	0.159848	(0.19970) [0.80045]
$AGREXP_{t-1}$	0.012480	(0.01699) [0.73438]
$DSERGDP_{t-1}$	-8.517033	(2.23653) [-3.80812]
$GCAP_{t-1}$	0.008414	(0.00395) [2.13012]
$DEBGDP_{t-1}$	0.395059	(0.36575) [1.08014]
INF_{t-1}	0.029738	(0.06635) [0.44819]
$INTR_{t-1}$	-0.022320	(0.09003) [-0.24792]
C	-1.217698	(2.46639) [-0.49372]
ECM	-0.083977	(0.03173) [-2.64660]

R^2=0.769848 R^2=0.689483 F-statistic=15.110585,

Akaike information criterion=23.47637 Schwarz criterion=23.84644.

Table 1: Short-run estimates.

Summary and Conclusion

The study examined the relationship between external debt and economic growth in Nigeria from 1981 to 2014. The study used both descriptive and econometric tools. The analysis of unit root was performed using ADF and Ng and Perron on each of the variables and the result showed that all the variables were integrated at first difference. The study revealed positive impact of external debt on economic growth in Nigeria in the long-run only. However, external debt servicing had both long-run and short-run negative effect on economic growth in Nigeria.Growth in capital expenditure, growth rate of exports, and external debt stock had positive impact on economic growth while external debt servicing and interest rate were inversely related to the growth of the economy[28-30].

Recommendations

The study made the following recommendations;

i. Given that external debt stock had positive impact on economic growth in Nigeria implies that an increase in it will lead to increase the growth rate of the economy. Nevertheless, the study recommends that, the stock borrowed should be effectively managed. The federal government should laydown guidelines in terms of defining the purpose, duration, moratorium requirements and commitments, negotiation among others including conditions for external debt loans. This may guide against high external debt stock that would lead to exceeding healthy threshold.

ii. Instead of continuous debt servicing, there should be an arrangement for repayment of the loan(s) within the agreeable time. This will curtail the associated leakages from the economy.

iii. The government should adopt advanced technology in the manufacturing sector in order to make our locally made goods attractive in the international market. In order to achieve this, efforts should be made to ensure that the locally made products are of high standard so as to compete favourably both at internal and external markets as this will enhance Nigerian exports, discourage imports, and as well, lead to a decline in the country's demand for external debts. Thus, there must be vigorous promotion of the nation's exports through reviving of agriculture and industrial sector that would absorb the shock in exchange rate even if left floating.

vi. External debt loans should be used only for productive investment of highest priorities that would help in yielding returns. This would help in deriving enough money for external debt servicing; otherwise, the huge external debt would throw the economy into series and "serious" economic problems.

References

1. Siddiqui RA (2002) Debt and Economic growth in South Asia. 17th Annual General meeting of PSED, Islamabad: State of Pakistan.
2. Ali LB, Mshelia MO (2007) Effect of external debt on economic growth and development of Nigeria. International journal of business and social science 3: 297-304.
3. Adesola WA (2009) Debt servicing and economic growth in Nigeria: An empirical investigation. Global J Soc Sci 8: 1-11.
4. Krugman RP (1988) Financing vs. Forgiving a Debt Overhand. Journal of Development Economics 29: 253-268.
5. Chongo B (2013) An econometric analysis of the impact of public debt on economic growth: the case study of Zambia. An unpublished M Sc. Dessertation, University of Zambia.
6. Ojo MO, Sulaiman LA (2012) External Debt, Economic Growth and Investment in Nigeria. European Journal of Business and Management 11: 67-75.
7. DMO (2013) Annual report and statement of accounts.
8. Nwankwo A (2015) Nigeria's Foreign Debt Profile. Thisday live, p. 1.
9. Central Bank of Nigeria (CBN) Annual Report and Statement of Accounts: Various issues.
10. Kasidi F, Makame S (2013) Impact of External Debt on Economic Growth: A case study of Tanzania. Advances in Management and applied Economics. 3: 59-82.
11. Iyoha MA (2000) The Impact of external Debt Reduction on Economic Growth in Nigeria. Nigeria Journal of Economic and Social Studies 42:1-79.
12. Lucas R (1988) On the Mechanics of Economic Development. Journal of Monetary Economics 22:2-42.
13. Adam JA (2007) Foreign debt, economic growth, and Nigeria's debt servicing capacity. Doctoral Dissertation, Department of Economics University of Ibadan.
14. Henry AE (2006) External Debt burden and Macroeconomic Performance in Nigeria (1970-2003).
15. Ajayi SI (1996) Macroeconomic approach to external Debt: the case of Nigeria. AERC 8:1-78.
16. Klein MT (2009) External debt management: An introduction. The World Bank 1:1-5.
17. Jhingan ML (2002) The Economics of Development and Planning. Advent Books Division Inc.
18. Ali MA, Mshelia SI (2007) Impact of External Debt Services on Nigeria Economic MAJASS 5.
19. Ayadi FS, Ayadi FO (2008) The Impact of External Debt on Economic Growth: A comparative study of Nigeria & South Africa.Journal of Sustainable Development in Africa 10:234-264.
20. Sulaiman LA, Azeez, BA (2012) Effect of external debt on economic growth of Nigeria. Journal of economics and sustainable development 3: 71-79.
21. Chinaemerem OC, Anayochukwu OB (2013) Impact of External Debt Financing on Economic Development in Nigeria. Research Journal of Finance and Accounting 4:92-99.
22. Ng S, Perron P (2001) Lag Length Selection and the Construction of Unit Root Tests with Good Size and Power. Econometrica 69: 1519-1554.
23. Debt management department (1992) Management of external debt Nigeria's experience .Economic and financial review 30.
24. Debt Management Office (DMO) (2004) Annual reports on debt management.
25. Debt Management Office (DMO) (2006) Annual Report and Statement of Accounts, Abuja.
26. Debt Management Office (DMO) (2009) Annual Report and Statement of Account, Abuja
27. DMO (2014) Annual Reports.
28. DMO (2015) Service reports on debt management Debt Management Office.
29. IMF (2003) Debt sustainability in low income countries – towards a forward looking strategy. Policy development review department.
30. World Bank (1987-1988) World Bank debt table. External debt of developing countries, Washington, World Bank.

Measuring Competitive Intelligence as a Case of North Cyprus Banks

Mohammed HZ* and Çiçek O

Girne American University, Cyprus

Abstract

One of the greatest characteristics of the present age is the widespread changes in the human knowledge along with the increasing number of social, political, economic, and technological disciplines. As a result, it is no longer the superior quality of products and services that is the recognizing and distinguishing factor but the quality of organization knowledge that is the key variable which determines its success. In addition, all kind of organizations need information for supporting decision making process at distinctive levels in order to become competitive at the global level and retain their positions through exploiting environment opportunities. In today's world, the use of information and its conversion to applied intelligence to leading organizational decision-making has attracted increasing attention and seems to be an obligation and compulsion. Competitive intelligence plays a central role in protecting organizations against future risks and ensuring perception of concealed opportunities. Accordingly, the banking sector in North Cyprus is pivotal in developing the economy of this wonderful island. Therefore, this study seems to be the first attempt to measure competitive intelligence among 64 employees at several Cypriot banks including Turkish IS, Garanti, Ziraat, TEB, and Near East. Using Knowledge and the application of descriptive statistics. The research findings denote that there is a high level of competitiveness among the employees from the banks selected for this study.

Keywords: Benefit of competitive intelligence; Competitive intelligence; Competitive intelligence process; Effective competitive intelligence

Introduction

Competition among economic and business organizations is growing at a rapid pace. In order to stay, compete, and survive in the highly competitive environment, all types of organizations need information in addition to new tools for decision making process. One of the central principles in modern management excellence. Fact- based management can be achieved through organization's access to information. In competitive environment for all types of organizations it is important that quick access to related information is available. To account for this need, a sundry of instruments are used in different organizations. Competitive intelligence is the art of planning, gathering, processing and saving information related to decision making and make it available for the whole organization and every individual at different levels in the light of their own needs [1]. Naturally, it is important for organizations to recognize and understand the competition in order to have the capacity to adapt to changing market and environmental trends. Competitive intelligence has the ability to distinguish organizations from one another, and be equally utilized to inform an organization about developing trends within the business [2].

Literature review

The ensuing paragraphs contains a succinct review or existing literature on competitive intelligence. It begins by providing a brief definition of competitive intelligence and continues with listing the benefits of competitive intelligence for organizations. Furthermore, the literature on what affects competitive intelligence is briefly reviewed, and the main processes of competitive intelligence are discussed. Finally, it is demonstrated that undertaking this research and its finding will fill an important gap in the literature.

Competitive intelligence

In a business competitive market, the organization's success increasingly depends on gaining a decent understanding of competitive planes and activities, and utilizing that understanding to distinguish one's own products and serves in a significant way. An ever growing number of organizations have invested in competitive intelligence in order to obtain knowledge about their competitors.

Competitive intelligence could be known as the process of selecting, gathering, and explaining general information by focusing on competitors' capabilities, performance, targets, and position. In this methodology, sporadic information about the competitors and customers is replaced by strategic applied knowledge in the field of organization's threats and opportunities [3]. Consequently, continuous analysis of the organization's internal and external environment as well as explanation of information obtained from the environment significantly impact on leadership's decisions to further the achievement of the organization [4].

Kahaner [5] underscores the need to recognize and distinguish between information and intelligence in organization: Information is accurate and factual. It includes numbers, statistics, scattered data about individuals and organization. Intelligence, on the other hand, is information that has been filtered and sifted, and analyzed. It requires knowing precisely the contrasts between information and intelligence. What managers need for decision making process is intelligence and not information.

Competitive intelligence prompts organizations in both private and state sectors to make sensible decisions about marketing, investment, market expansion, and product and serves development, R&D and business approaches. To be effective, competitive intelligence must be legitimate and it must respect morality. The intelligence transfers outside knowledge to the company by adhering to specific rules and guidelines. Therefore, an alternative and more accurate definition of competitive intelligence can be "gathering information related

***Corresponding author:** Hakar Zaki Mohammed, Girne American University, Cyprus, E-mail: ha_amedy@yahoo.com

to competitors and environment to create and retain competitive intelligence". According to McGonagall and Walla [6], intelligence is a systematic process utilized by organizations to ensure updating the related and precise information of competitors. While Odenhaal [7] argues that competitive intelligence is a business process that, if managed successfully, leads to creation of organization efficiency. Additionally, CI could be utilized as an instrument for lessening operational risk. Organizational risk relates not just to its physical measurement but also to any environmental uncertainty. In summary, competitive intelligence is the best method to reduce uncertainty.

Benefits of competitive intelligence

Organizations with strong competitive intelligence programs have a superior understanding of the competitive landscape such as having a universal view to competitive threats and opportunities that helps organizations to understand and move more quickly toward devising and formulating strategies and plans in order to maximize competitive advantage [8,9].

Competitive intelligence can have the characterizing effect in the outcome of products, services, acquisitions, marketing strategies, and technology development, etc. Specific benefits of competitive intelligence include [10]:

a. Improved productivity and profit, or leveraging of the organization's knowledge assets

b. Early cautioning of competitive threats

c. An extraordinary source of impartial news, truth and analysis relevant to strategic decision-making

d. Developing functional relationships throughout the organization

e. Provision of progressing linkages with security (and ideally counterintelligence), and

f. Reinforcement of a culture of competitiveness in the organization by concentrating on external threats and influences.

Effective competitive intelligence

According to Jaworski et al. [11], we can recognize four classes of variables that seem to impact the dimension of efficacy at the organizing, search and sense-making stages of the competitive intelligent process. The four classes of variables are.

Competitive intelligence network: Given the amount of informants provided for the nurturing and development of informal networks, it may not be surprising that a number of variables pertaining to the network itself seem to influence several dimensions of the competitive intelligence efficacy.

Business environment: The second class of variables pertains to how attributes of the internal and external environment influence the organizing, searching, and Competitive Intelligence through (recognition systems, time allocation, and market pressure).

Information environment: The information environment refers to the properties of the information confronted by the competitive intelligence analyst through (richness, and information value).

Analyst characteristics: Characteristics of the individual accused of creating competitive intelligence and the strategies they use to create it additionally seemed to influence the efficacy of the competitive intelligence. According to Day and Nedungadi's [12] investigator's characteristics have largely been overlooked in the literatures of strategy and marketing.

Competitive intelligence process

Viviers et al. [13] argue that the key critical areas of Competitive intelligence are planning and focus, collection, analysis, and dissemination (communication). During this research we focused on those four processes and tried to measure them among a sample of North Cyprus banks.

Planning: The first step in competitive intelligence process is planning and focus. This stage is necessary for the identification of the problem which will be solved through a competitive intelligence process. The planning step is not about gathering all the possible information. It is initially necessary to focus on particular information that is relevant to top-level management. That is to say, "identification of needs" must first be completed. This process is a vital part of the general process to avoid collection of irrelevant information [14].

Collection: During this procedure, information is gathered from an assortment of sources - primary as well as secondary. Primary sources of information involve suppliers, customers, government agencies, employees, etc., while secondary source include analyst reports, magazines, Internet website, TV, radio, etc. The choice of a particular source is directly related to the type of information focused. According to Rouach and Santi [4], the bulk of the information, amounting to 80% at times, needed to create intelligence is already introduced inside an organization, and that this information is not shared with the people who immediately require it due to organizational, geographic, or communication barriers.

Analysis: The most difficult part of the Competitive Intelligence process is analysis [15]. Organizations need to employ different analytical tools such as SWOT analysis to analyze information (Strength, Weakness, Opportunity and Threats) for competitor profiling and Porter's Five Forces Model, and PEST analysis (political, economic, social, and technological). These analytical models if applied correctly can change dissimilar information into actionable intelligence. The analysis stage will finished by creating some intelligence products which take the shape of documents and activities like: organization profiles, benchmarking, industry analysis, technology assessments, daily reports, strategic impact analysis, customer and supplier profiles [16].

Dissemination (Communication): Dissemination is the final step of the intelligence process in which the intelligence will is delivered to the customers of the competitive intelligence or to those who request it within the organization. According to Kahaner [5] there are more than one way to disseminate intelligence. These include newsletters, intelligence reports to presentations, and meetings with the customers to name a few. As a general rule, the competitive intelligence team or professional are expected to be prepared and arranged to defend their suggestions or actions with logical arguments, utilizing presentations and persuasive skills, and suitable format or media to every case.

Research Methodology

The research combines the qualitative and quantitative method. Two instruments were used to collect data, namely, a survey questionnaire and semi-structured interviews. The questionnaire focused on identifying and measuring the process of competitive intelligence. A descriptive case study of samples of bank employees at North Cyprus was conducted. The research population consisted of 64 employees at Turkish IS, Garanti, Zeraate, TEB, and Near East banks. Questionnaire findings were analyzed through the use of the SPSS program and the data were analyzed using Percentage, Mean, Frequency, and Std Deviation. The interview method was used to support the findings and to have a better understanding of competitive intelligence among a sample of North Cyprus banks.

Significance of the research

It is important to note that this research is expected to make a contribution to both the current bank practice and academic knowledge. Secondly, from the practical perspective, this study could be used to find opportunities for improving the level of competitive intelligence in the selected banks. This process will help bank managers to develop a better appreciation of the changeable environmental factors on this wonderful island, and encourage them to exploit potential opportunities and avoid current or futures threats.

Research purpose

The main purposes of this research are as follows:

a. To assess the level of competitive intelligence applied at North Cyprus banking sectors.

b. To assess the limitation in applying competitive intelligence at selected banks.

c. To help bank managers to better understand competitive intelligence and use it as a source for decision making process.

Research questions

A wide range of research has been conducted to measure and to develop competitive intelligence and its main process. However, few studies have focused on this important topic in North Cyprus. Accordingly, this study attempted to answer two critical questions.

a. What are the levels of competitive intelligence process among the sample of North Cyprus banks?

b. How we can improve the level of competitive intelligence and its four interrelated processes?

Banking sector at north Cyprus

The Turkish Republic of North Cyprus TRNC financial system consists of three types of banks (central, commercial, and investment). The total share of the first ten banks was 79.21%. Based on ownership, TRNC commercial banks can be divided into state, private and foreign banks. State banks control 29.48% of total assets as against 39.71% controlled by private banks. Foreign banks, on the other hand, control 30.81% of total assets [17]. Currently this island has a total of 15 national, 2 state-owned, and 7 foreign banks. In terms of bank branches, domestic banks have 171 branches in total while foreign banks have 47 branches.

Data analysis and research findings

1-General information about the study sample: Table 1 shows the demographic information about selected employees. Based on the data demonstrated in Table 1, the majority of respondents were female amounting to 56.3% while Males' share was 43.8%. In addition, the data indicates that most respondents (35.9%) fall into the 26-35 age group followed by the 36-45 age group with 34.4%. Those aged 25 or less ranked third constituting 17.2% of the total number. Finally, a meager 12.5% of respondents aged 46 years and above. Accordingly, it can be inferred that youths made up the majority of respondents [18,19].

The data presented in Table 1 pertains to the respondents' level of education. While 29.7% of respondents had completed high school or less, the majority of the selected samples had bachelor's degree rating 40.6%. The ratios for diploma and Masters/PhD degree holders were were18.8% and 10.9% consecutively.

In the sample consisting of 64 respondents, 50.0% had less than 5 years of work experience. Around 28.1% had worked between 6-10 years while 21.9% had 11 or more years of work experience. The results show that majority of respondents had little work experience.

2- Measuring competitive intelligence: The researchers used descriptive statistics measurements to describe and measure the competitive intelligence between selected banks using (Mean, and Standard Deviation). A five-point Likert scale questionnaire was used to collect data. Table 2 demonstrate descriptive measurements related to competitive intelligence.

As shown in Table 2, the mean and S.D. for competitive intelligence obtained from 15 items were 3.928 and .937 respectively. According to tabulated data the highest means of 4.55 and 4.45 were obtained on Q14 and Q15 respectively. The relevant S.Ds was .733 for Q14, and .711 for Q15. That refers to the fact that banks leaders use collective information from other banks as a source in decision

Study sample according to Gender							
Female				Male			
F		%		F		%	
36		56.2		28		43.8	
Age of respondents							
25 and less		26-35		36-45		46 and more	
F	%	F	%	F	%	F	%
11	17.2	23	35.9	22	34.4	8	12.5
Education Levels for selected employees							
High school or less		Diploma		Bachelor		Master and over	
F	%	F	%	F	%	F	%
19	29.7	12	18.8	26	40.6	7	10.9

Working experience for respondents					
5 and less years		6-10		11 and more years	
F	%	F	%	F	%
32	50.0	18	28.1	14	21.9

Table 1: General information about respondents.

Q	Mean	S.D	Q	Mean	S.D
Q1	3.64	1.239	**Q9**	**3.02**	**.917**
Q2	4.34	.859	Q10	3.91	1.019
Q3	4.41	.610	Q11	3.84	1.130
Q4	4.19	.889	Q12	4.31	1.125
Q5	3.64	.982	Q13	4.03	1.069
Q6	3.78	1.061	**Q14**	**4.55**	**.733**
Q7	3.42	.956	**Q15**	**4.45**	**.711**
Q8	**3.39**	**.769**			
Total Average				**3.928**	**.937**

Table 2: Means and Standard Deviations for Competitive Intelligence.

making process to increase the validity and quality of decisions. Also based on results, it can be inferred that TRNC banks initiate marketing and communication effort to create positive relationship with other banks. Table 2 also shows that lowest means equaling 3.02 and 3.39 were obtained on Q9 and Q8. The relevant SDs for Q9 and Q8 were .917 and .769 respectively. These results point to the fact that it may be possible to measure bank employees' perception of what competitive intelligence is. However, banks don't try to hire people or other banks at TRNC to collect information on their behalf which is the clear evidence that completive intelligence at selected banks is still an ethical issue.

Conclusions and Recommendations

Competitive intelligence is a business instrument that assists all kind of organizations during strategic management processes and developing business performance through improving organization and employees' knowledge, in addition to enhancing internal and external communications. It leads organization successfully in uncertain situations at changeable competitive environments. Through this process organizations are able to forecast their markets and develop them through analyzing competitors' behavior and actions.

This research is in support of the fact that competitive intelligence and its main processes and practices have serious implications on banks performance. Through interviews with employees it was observed that the biggest limitation and threat is how to deal with other banks' plan and actions, and how we can exploit unrecognized opportunities through using available resources. Based on the findings of this research, the following outcomes and suggestions are listed:

a. Even the selected banks and its managers began to use competitive intelligence, but still there is a barrier in understanding what is competitive intelligence about and how we can exploit it to obtain organizations objectives.

b. We recommend selected banks to use a variety of resources (primary and secondary) in their decision making process.

c. The research recommends banks to organizea special training course for employees to acquaint them with competitive intelligence and its process.

d. We recommend selected banks to use most updated methods (Internet, social media, TV, newspaper, etc.) in order to communicate and explain their future projects and plans, as well as collecting relevant information from other banks.

e. We recommend banks to take into consideration customer feedback and develop customer relationship management (CRM) to collect important information which in turn will help them to have clear intelligence regarding their customer.

References

1. Mejarshin AS (2013) Competitive intelligence, Competitive advantage in the success business organizations. Reef Resour Assessment Manage Tech Pap 38: 2.
2. Johns P, Van DD (2010) Competitive Intelligence in service marketing: a new approach with practical application. Market Plan 28: 551-570.
3. Albescu F, Pugna I, Paraschiv P (2009) Business Competitive Intelligence The Ultimate Use of Information Technologies in Strategic Management. Bucharest Acad Econ Stud.
4. Rouach D, Santi P (2001) Competitive Intelligence Adds Value: 5 Intelligence Attitudes. Eur Manage J1 9: 552-59.
5. Kahaner L (1996) Competitive intelligence - how to gather, analyze, and use information to move your business to the top. Simon & Schuster, New York.
6. McGonagall JJ, Walla CM (1999) The intelligence age of competitive group, Inc, Westport, ct.
7. Odenhaal B (2003) Competitive Intelligence-Key to Corporate Risk Management. J Secur Oper Risk Manage.
8. Vedder RG, Vanecek MT, Guynes CS, Cappel JJ (1999) CEO and CIO perspectives on competitive intelligence. Commun ACM 42: 109-16.
9. Wright S, Calof JL (2006) The Quest for Competitive, Business and Marketing Intelligence, A Country Comparison of Current Practices. Eur J Market 40: 453-465.
10. Bernhardt D (2003) Competitive Intelligence. How to acquire and use corporate intelligence and counter-intelligence. Prentice Hall. Financ times 88-89.
11. Jaworski, BJ, Macinnis DJ, Kohli AK (2002) Generating Competitive Intelligence in Organizations. J Market-Focused Manage 5: 279-307.
12. Day G, Nedungadi P (1994) Managerial Representations of Competitive Advantage. J Market 58: 31- 44.
13. Viviers W (2002) Competitive Intelligence practices: a South African study. South African J Bus Manage 33: 27-37.
14. Strauss AC (2008) Competitive Intelligence Skills Needed In South Africa. Unpublished Master thesis. University of Johannesburg.
15. Toit ASD (2003) Competitive intelligence in the knowledge economy: what is in it for South African manufacturing enterprises?. Int J Inform Manage 23: 111-120.
16. Nasri W (2012) Conceptual Model of Strategic Benefits of Competitive Intelligence Process. International J Bus Commerce 1: 6.
17. Karavelioglu AM (2013) Analysis of Leadership Styles in Banking Sector in TRNC. Unpublished thesis. Girne American University.
18. Govoreanu A, Mora A, Serban A (2010) Competitive Intelligence. Stud Bus Econ 5: 101-107.
19. Calof JL (2008) Competitive Intelligence A practitioner academic and inter-disciplinary perspective. Eur J Market 42: 717 -730.

Inflation Forecasting in Ghana-Artificial Neural Network Model Approach

Yusif M Hadrat[1], Eshun Nunoo Isaac K[2] and Effah Sarkodie Eric[3]*

[1]Department of Economics, Kwame Nkrumah University of Science and Technology, Kumasi, Ghana
[2]Ghana College, Kumasi, Ghana
[3]University of Education, Winneba, College of Technology Education, Department of Accounting Studies Education, Kumasi, Ghana

Abstract

Artificial Neural Network (ANN) is a modelling technique which is based on the way the human brain process information. ANNs have proved to be good forecasting models in several fields including economics and finance. The ANN methodology is used by some central banks to predict various macroeconomic indicators such as the inflation, money supply, GDP growth etc. The use of the ANN for prediction is common in the forecasting literature but rare in Ghana. This paper forecasts inflation with the ANN method using the Ghanaian data. The monthly y-o-y data between 1991:01 and 2010:12 are used to estimate and forecast for the period 2011:01 to 2011:12. The result of the ANNs are also compared with traditional time series models such as the AR (12) and VAR (14) which use the same set of variables. The basis of comparison is the out-of-sample forecast error (RMSFE). The results show that the RMSFE of the ANNs are lower than their econometric counterparts. That is, by this comparative criterion forecast based on ANN models are more accurate.

Keywords: Inflation; Artificial neural network; Demand; Supply

Introduction

Price stability is one of the key objectives of monetary policy. To achieve such mandate, policy makers need to be forward-looking. This calls for good inflation forecasting ability for the monetary authorities. The inflation forecast is used to guide policy discussions in determining the appropriate policy stance to be adopted. In the case of an inflation targeting regime, the inflation forecast can alert policymakers to take policy response should the forecast indicate that the inflation outlook may deviate for the target. Hence, accurately forecasting the inflation is crucial for the monetary authorities.

Artificial Neural Network (ANN) model is currently a popular forecasting technique in several fields such computer science, engineering, economics, finance etc. ANNs have been used to predict variables such as bond prices, exchange rates, stock returns, money supply, electricity demand, construction demand, inflation rates etc. [1,2]. In the prediction of the inflation, in particular, scores of studies have compared the inflation forecasting performance of traditional econometric models with the neural network models and have concluded that the ANNs outperform the econometric models in the prediction of inflation [3-7].

Some central banks including inflation-targeting central banks like The State Bank of Pakistan, CZECH National Bank, Bank of Canada and Bank of Jamaica use forecasting models which are based on ANN methodology for predicting various macroeconomic indicators, like inflation, GDP growth and money supply etc [8-12]. The main purpose of this paper is to use the ANN technique to forecast inflation in Ghana for the period 2011: 01–2011:12 using the data between 1991: 01 and 2010:12.The forecast performance of the ANNs is also compared with their counterpart traditional models, AR (12) and VAR (14). The results show that the ANNs predict accurately than the econometric models.

The paper hereafter is organised in four sections. Section two presents the neural network methodology. Section three also provides the data type and source and the model specifications. The empirical results are presented in section four and the last section presents the summary of the findings.

Methodology

The Artificial Neural Network methodology was developed in an effort to model the way the human brain process information. The human brain learns by experience: It receives information and recognises the pattern; the brain then generalises and is able to predict based on the information received. It is this way of information processing by the brain that the ANN model tends to mimic. Although ANN models are too far from the way the human brain performs, by mimicking the basic features of the biological neural networks, they have succeeded in doing certain jobs very well [13-15].

The human neuron

The human brain or the central nervous system is made up of interconnected units called neurons. This system or group of interconnected neurons working together to perform the functions of the brain (i.e., learning) is the neural network. By definition, "Neurons are basic signalling units of the nervous system of a living being in which each neuron is a discrete cell whose several processes are from its cell body." Figure 1 shows the biological structure of the human neuron.

The biological neuron has four main regions to its structure: The cell body, the dendrites or membrane, the axon and the synapses. The cell body is the heart of the neuron. The human neuron receives signals through synapses located on the dendrites or membrane. When the signals received is strong enough (i.e., surpasses a certain threshold), the cell body is activated and emits another signal through the axon. The emitted signal (or action potentials) is sent to activate other neurons within the system. As similar signals continue to cross

***Corresponding author:** Effah Sarkodie Eric, M. Phil. Economics, B. A. Economics, University of Education, Winneba, College of Technology Education, Department of Accounting Studies Education, Kumasi, Ghana
E-mail: effahsarkodie@yahoo.com

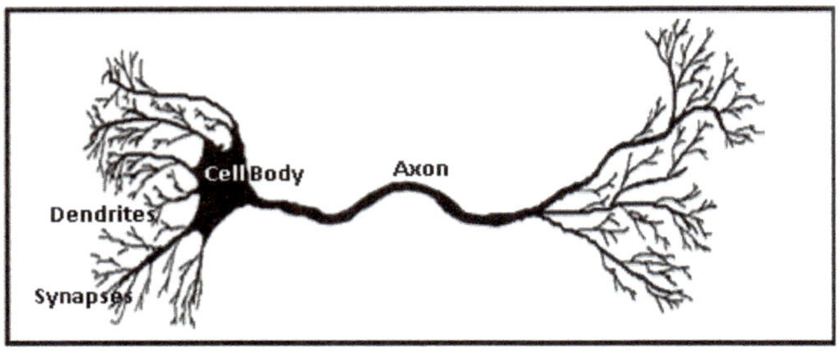

Figure 1: Biological model of human neuron (artist's conception).

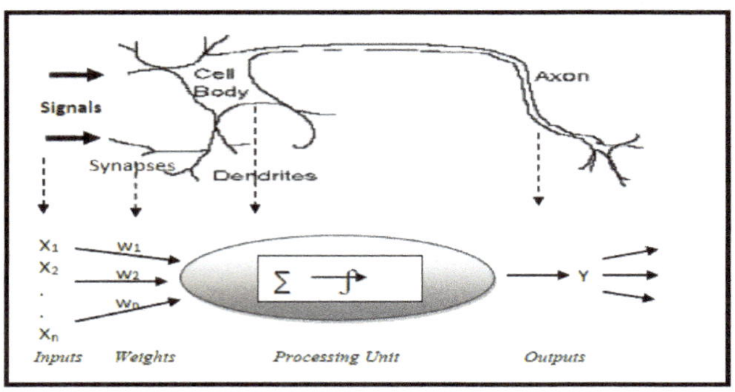

Figure 2: Natural and artificial neurons (a relational sketch).

the threshold, the network recognises the path of the signals, assumes a pattern, and as a result generalises that if the signal is like this then, the output should be that. That is, the network is able to predict based on the pattern of the signals received.

The artificial neuron

The artificial neuron is a mimic of the natural human neuron. The human brain, for example, contains approximately ten billion (10^{10}) neurons, each connected on average to ten thousand (10^4) other neurons, making a total of 10^{15} synaptic connections [16-18]. A mimic of the way biological networks perform may appear more than complex. Artificial neural networks represent an attempt at a very basic level to imitate the type of nonlinear learning that occurs in the networks of neurons found in nature.

As shown in Figure 2, a natural neuron uses the synapses located on the dendrite to gather inputs (signals) from other neurons and combines the input information, generate a nonlinear response ("firing") when some threshold is reached, which it sends to other neurons using the axon. Similarly, the artificial neuron collects inputs (x_i) from input neurons, attaches weights and combines them through a combination function such as summation (Σ). It is then activated by a function (usually nonlinear) to produce an output response (y), which is again sent to other neurons [19-24].

The mathematical model

There are three distinct functional operations that take place in a neuron. These are: the weight function, the net input function and the transfer function as shown in Figure 3.

The weight function: First, the inputs, ($x: x_1, x_2,...,x_r$) are fed into the neuron. Each input is multiplied by a random weight (w_i) to form the product and summed ($\Sigma w_i x_i$). The inputs and weights are the same as the variables and parameters, respectively, in linear regression models. For many types of neural networks, the weight function is a product of a weight times the input, but other weight functions (e.g., the distance between the weight and the input, $|w - x|$) are sometimes used.

The net input function: Next, the weighted input ($\Sigma w_i x_i$) is added to a bias (**b**) to form the net input (**n**). That is, the net input becomes: $n=b+\Sigma w_i x_i$. The bias is similar to the constant in linear models. The most common net input function is the summation of the weighted inputs with the bias, but other operations, such as multiplication, can be used.

The transfer or activation function: Then, the net input is passed through the transfer function (*f*), (Figure 4) which produces the output (y). The three processes can be shown as follows:

$$y = f(b + \sum w_i x_i) \tag{1}$$

There exist many types of activation functions. If the function is linear, it only transfers the net "n" value to the output unit that is, *f* (n)=n. This is similar to the linear regression model in econometrics:

$$y = b + \sum w_i x_i \tag{2}$$

The activation function in most applications however, takes the form of the "log-sigmoid or hyperbolic tangent sigmoid function" which is continuous and nonlinear function and generates the values between 0 and 1, and-1 and +1 respectively. One of the reasons for the popularity of the sigmoid function is that calculating its first derivative, which is needed for weight adjustment in back-propagation, is relatively simple. The sigmoid function is similar to the logit model, where the dependent variable has the logistic functional form. They have the following forms:

$$y = tansig\ (b + \sum w_i x_i) \tag{3}$$

$$y = logsig\left(b + \sum w_i x_i\right) \tag{4}$$

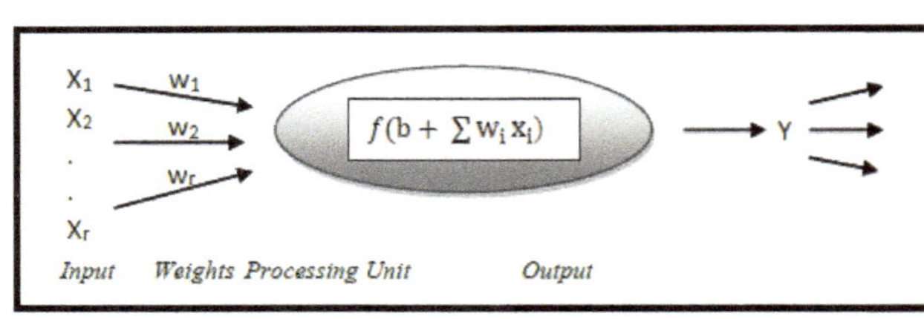

Figure 3: The basic structure of the artificial neuron model.

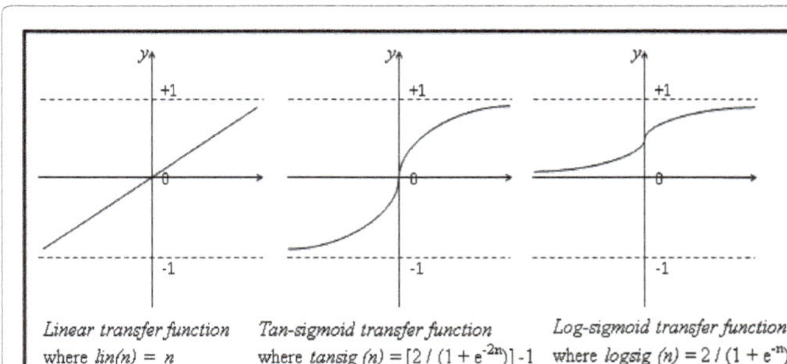

Figure 4: Three commonly used transfer (activation) function.

Finally, the output (y) generated by the network is compared with the target or desired output, the error is calculated. The objective is to minimize the error. This is done by applying a "learning" or iteration procedure through which network adjusts the weights (w_is) in the direction in which the error is minimized [25].

Multilayer neural network architecture

The basic single neuron model is very powerful in learning patterns; however, it cannot learn all types of patterns. The multilayer ANN models which have intermediate layer, called the hidden layer, are able to learn all kinds of patterns and thus, are good at prediction. In the multilayer model, the inputs are first processed in the hidden units and the outputs of the hidden units become the inputs of the output units [26]. The output units finally produce the outputs or forecasts. Figure 5 below shows the flow of network processes in the multilayer architecture.

The mathematical processes of the multilayer ANN model are as follows: First, inputs from the input layer enter the network through the hidden layer units. Each hidden layer unit receives the inputs, multiplies them by their correspondent weights and adds them all together with a bias (**b**). That is, the hidden layer unit (j) calculates:

$$\text{net}_j = b_j + \sum \gamma_{ji} x_i, \quad i = 1, 2, \ldots, r. \quad j = 1, 2, \ldots, q. \quad h = 1 \tag{5}$$

where (x_i) is the input of the unit (i) and (γ_{ji}) is a weight connecting the input unit (i) to the hidden unit (j).The output of the hidden layer unit (j), (G_j), is a transformation of the net, as follows:

$$G_j = G(\text{net}_j) \tag{6}$$

where (G) is an activation function mostly the nonlinear tan-sigmoid function. The output units receive the outputs of the hidden layer units (Gs) as their input. The process in the output layer units is exactly the same as that of the hidden layer units. That is, the output unit calculates the net, the sum of product of the inputs and weights, and bias as follows:

$$\text{net}_h = b_h + \sum \beta_{hj} G_j, \quad j = 1, 2, \ldots, q. \tag{7}$$

where "net_h" is the net value for the output unit (h), (β_{hj}) is the weight connecting the hidden unit (j) to the output unit (h) and (G_j) is the output of the hidden unit (j), which is input for the output unit (h). The output unit then applies a transfer function, (*f*), to the (net_h). The output of the output layer unit (h) is defined as:

$$F_h = f(\text{net}_h) \text{ or } F_h = f\left(b_h + \sum \beta_{hj} G(b_j + \sum \gamma_{ji} x_i)\right) \tag{8}$$

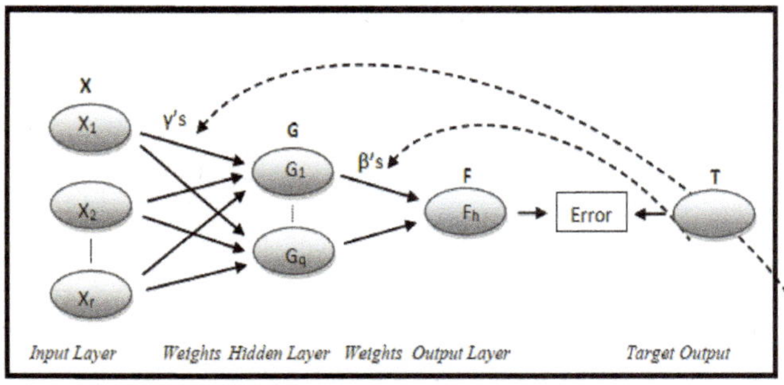

Figure 5: A multilayer ANN with 'r' input units, 'q' hidden units and one output units.

That is, the multilayer ANN mathematical model has the function of function form.

Finally, the network compares the outputs or forecasts (Fs) and the target outputs (Ts), and calculates the error (i.e., Root Mean Squared Forecast Error or RMSFE). The objective is to minimize the error; so, the computed errors are returned to the network in order to adjust the connection weights (γs and βs), hence back-propagation. The weight adjustment process, which is called learning, is done by a specific learning rule. The commonly used learning rule is the "generalized delta rule". In the delta rule, the weight is updated for each unit in the output layer as follows:

$$\beta_{hj}(t+1) = \beta_{hj}(t) + \eta \nabla_{hj} \tag{9}$$

where $\beta_{hj}(t)$ is the weight connecting unit (j) of the hidden layer to unit (h) of the output layer at time (t), (η) is the learning rate (typically less than 1), and (∇_{hj}) is the gradient vector associated with the weight (β_{hj}). The gradient vector is the set of derivatives for all weights with respect to the output error [27]. The network calculates the gradient vector on a layer-by-layer basis using the chain rule for partial derivatives. The Levenberg-Marquardt (LM) learning method which is an approximation of Gauss-Newton's optimization rule is now an improvement of the gradient descent method. It is given as:

$$\Delta W = (H'H + vI)^{-1} H'E \tag{10}$$

Where (H) is the Jacobian matrix of derivatives of each error to each weight, (v) is the scalar, and (E) is an error vector. The LM update rule approximates gradient descent if (v) is very large, and is equivalent to the Gauss-Newton's method if (v) is small. In the LM method, (v) changes as the network trains. Since the Gauss-Newton method is faster and more accurate around the minimum error, the network shifts the learning rule from the gradient descent to Gauss-Newton by decreasing v when the error declines. The network iterates the process until the error fails to decrease further, then it stops [28].

Model and Data Specifications

Data type and source

Forecasting models can be constructed with as many predictor variables as possible. From the reviewed literature, money supply growth rate and the exchange rate depreciation are found to be major determinants of the inflation. As such, to estimate and forecast inflation based on the ANN and econometric models, data on the following variables were obtained from the Bank of Ghana: inflation rate, broad money supply (M2+) growth rate and exchange rate depreciation. The data are monthly year-on-year series and cover the period 1991:01 to 2011:12: The data between 1991:01 and 2010:12 are used to estimate the models and that between 2011:01 and 2011:12 are used for the prediction. Figure 6 shows graphically the data used.

Model specification

The main objective of the study is to forecast inflation using the ANN method. However, because the performance of the ANN is compared with econometric models, the ANNs are specified on the basis of the AR and VAR specifications for a fair contest. And so, the econometric models are presented first as follows.

Time-series econometric model: The specified AR and VAR are as follows:

AR (12):
$$P_t = \varphi_0 + \sum_{i=1}^{p} \varphi_i P_{t-i} + \varepsilon_t \tag{11}$$

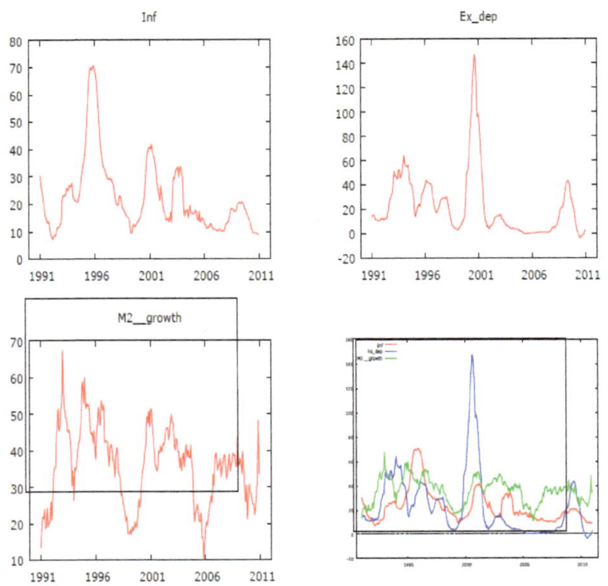

Source: Gretl (2006), Time-series data - Display levels toolbox.

Figure 6: Monthly time series data: 1991-2010.

$$\textbf{VAR (14)}: P_t = \alpha_{10} + \sum_{i=1}^{\rho}\beta_{2i}M_{t-i} + \sum_{i=1}^{\rho}\delta_{2i}P_{t-i} + \sum_{i=1}^{\rho}\nu_{2i}\varepsilon_{t-i} + \xi_{2t} \quad (12)$$

Where M_{t-i}, ε_{t-i}, and P_{t-i} are past values of: money supply growth, exchange rate and inflation rate respectively and α, β, δ, φ_i and ν are parameters to be estimated.

ANN models: The NAR and NARX models are specified based the AR (12) and VAR (14) models, respectively, in terms of the lag length and variables used. Each ANN model is constructed with twenty (20) hidden layer units and one (1) output layer unit. The ANN transfer functions are also the tan-sigmoid function in the hidden units and the linear function in the output unit. The models are specified as:

NAR (12):

$$F_h = b_h + \sum \beta_{hj}\left(tansig\left(b_j + \sum \gamma_{ji}P_{t-i}\right)\right), \quad i=1,..,12 \quad j=1,..,20 \quad h=1 \quad (13)$$

NARX (14):

$$F_h = b_h + \sum \beta_{hj}\left(tansig(b_j + \sum \gamma_{ji}x_{t-i}\right)), \quad i=1,..,14 \quad j=1,..,20 \quad h=1 \quad (14)$$

Where X_{t-i} are past values of the input and output variables, γs and βs are hidden and output layer weights respectively and the (bs) are the biases.

ANN model implementation: Designing and implementing neural network model to solve time series problems looks more like an art. However, using the MatLab (2011) neural network toolbox, standard steps are to be followed. The work flow for any of time series problem has the following primary steps.

1. Specify data
2. Create the network
3. Configure the network
4. Initialize the weights and biases
5. Train the network
6. Validate the network
7. Use the network

Data specification: This step identifies the variables that are known to be significant in predicting the target variable. In this case, omitting important variables can affect the network's performance. For simplicity and reasonable comparison, the ANN models used the same set of variables as in their econometric counterpart [29].

Creating the network: There are several neural networks for prediction; however, dynamic neural networks are good at time series prediction. The ANN models adopted in this paper are both dynamic neural networks created based on the specification of the time series econometric models presented above. That is, the nonlinear autoregressive (NAR) model and the nonlinear autoregressive with exogenous input (NARX) model were created based on the AR (12) and VAR (14) models, respectively [30].

Configuring the network: The nonlinearity of the ANN is due to the existence of the hidden layer units. Each network is configured with twenty (20) hidden neurons and one output neuron. The lags are however chosen based on their respective econometric models. The network is also set to randomly divide the input and target output data into three sets as follows: 70% are used for training the network, 15% to measure network generalization, and to halt training when generalization stops improving and the last 15% to provide an independent measure of network performance during and after training [31,32].

Initialising the weights and biases: The weight and biases of the network are randomly initialised. During training these weights and biases are adjusted in order to improve the network performance. A total of 281 weights (parameters) are estimated for the NAR network model and 881 for the NARX model. Hence, the ANNs are largely non-parametric models given the number of parameter estimates and biases [33,34].

Training the network: There are several methods or functions for training ANNs. The Levenberg-Marquardt training algorithm, a standard procedure from the literature, is used in this paper. The network is created and trained in open loop form for efficiency; but, the loop is closed for the prediction [35,36].

Validating the network: The LM training algorithm is run on the training set until the RMSE starts to increase on the validation set. The validated network can then be used for the prediction. Otherwise, the network is retrained with larger data or reconfigured to improve the results [37-39].

Using the network: After training, the network is converted to close loop form where it is used for multi-period forecasting. Finally, the training function produce forecast results on the basis of RMSE minimisation criteria.

Forecast evaluation

To evaluate the forecasting results, the Root Mean of Squared Forecast Error (RMSFE) is calculated as follows:

$$RMSFE = \sqrt{\frac{\sum_{i=0}^{T}(y_t - \hat{y}_t)^2}{T}} \quad (15)$$

where y_t and $\hat{y}_t$ are the actual and the forecast values of the dependent variable, and T is the forecast sample size.

Empirical Results

The variables for the estimation and forecasting of the models specified in the previous section are first check for stationarity. The ADF test showed that all the series have unit root, implying that they are not stationary; however, their first differences are stationary. The first difference results are shown in Figure 7.

The minimum ACF figure for the first difference of the inflation series occurs at lag twelve (12) and thus the AR (12) model is chosen for the estimation. The AIC criterion also showed that, VAR (14) is the most suitable multivariate model for the series. The estimated AR (12) model had an adjusted R^2 of 45% and that of the VAR (14) was 42%. The forecast of the econometric models for the period of 2011 based on the estimated models are shown in Table 1.

The estimated NAR (12) model had an overall R^2 of 71% and the NARX had 62%. The two ANN models forecast results for the twelve months of 2011 based on the estimated model are presented in Figure 8. It is clear that the ANN forecast results are very close to the actual results for the same period.

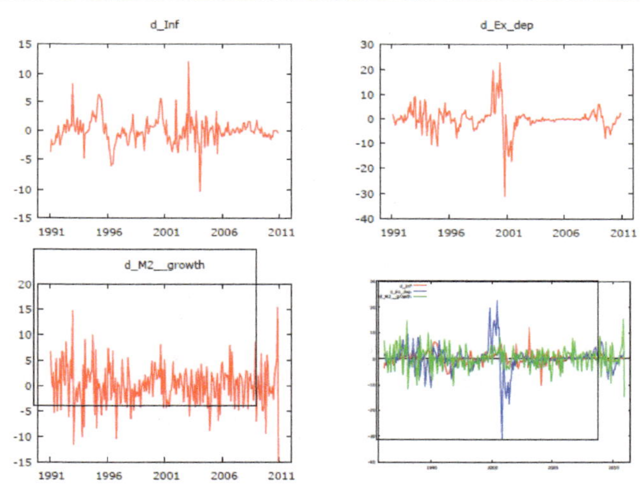

Source: Gretl 2006, Time-series data - Display first-differences toolbox.

Figure 7: First differences of the monthly time series data: 1991-2010.

Year/Month	*Actual Inflation*	*AR (12) Forecasts*	*VAR (14) Forecast*	*NAR (12) Forecasts*	*NARX (14) Forecast*
2011: 01	**9.08**	8.59	9.13	8.58	8.57
2011: 02	**9.16**	8.78	8.17	9.08	9.08
2011: 03	**9.13**	9.32	10.69	9.16	9.17
2011: 04	**9.02**	9.62	10.38	9.14	9.14
2011: 05	**8.9**	9.37	10.54	9.03	9.04
2011: 06	**8.59**	9.33	10.64	8.91	8.88
2011: 07	**8.39**	8.45	9.06	8.59	8.58
2011: 08	**8.41**	8.38	10.12	8.39	8.38
2011: 09	**8.4**	8.32	9.73	8.42	8.41
2011: 10	**8.56**	8.30	9.80	8.40	8.39
2011: 11	**8.55**	8.73	9.74	8.57	8.55
2011: 12	**8.58**	8.75	8.67	8.56	8.55
	MSFE	0.1400	1.6896	0.0377	0.0376
	RMSFE	**0.3742**	**1.2999**	**0.1943**	**0.1938**

Table 1: The summary forecast results of both econometric and ANN models.

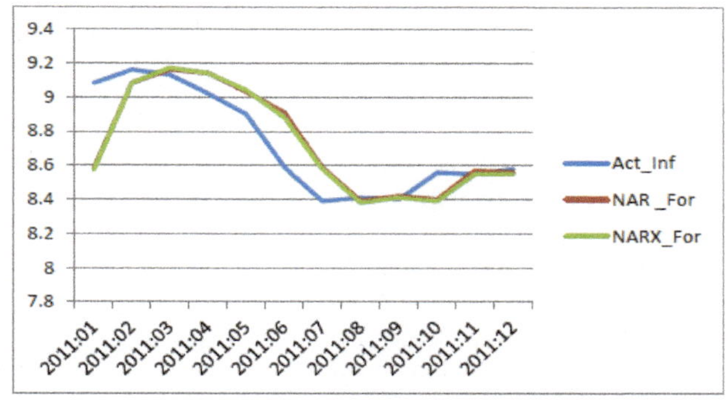

Source: Excel 2010, Spreadsheet chart display toolbox.

Figure 8: Charts of the ANN models forecast results.

Comparison of the ANN and the econometric models forecast results

The main objective of this paper is to forecast inflation using the ANN method and also to compare the forecast performance of the ANNs with the econometric models on the basis of the RMSFE criterion. The table below shows the summary forecast results of the competing models.

In general, on the basis of the RMSFE criterion, the ANN models have the lowest forecast errors in the one-period-ahead dynamic forecasts between the econometric and ANN models for the forecast period (2011: 01 to 2011:12). Precisely, in the univariate form, the NAR model has lower forecast error compared with its econometric counterpart the AR with the same specification (i.e., with lag length of 12 and the series in their first-differences). Similarly, the NARX model records the lower RMSFE in comparison with the VAR counterpart of the same specification. It is also remarkable to note that, the ANN model in the multivariate form (NARX) slightly outperforms the univariate model (NAR) in the contest. As this may be due to the inclusion of the exogenous inputs to augment the performance of the ANN model, the same cannot be said of the econometric models. Between the econometric time series models, the AR performs significantly better than the multivariate model VAR, implying that the inclusion of the additional independent variables do not improve the forecast performance of the model. In all, the NARX model has the lowest RMSFE and thus is more accurate.

Conclusion

This paper used both a univariate and multivariate artificial neural network model to forecast monthly y-o-y inflation in Ghana. The forecast was made for the period 2011 using monthly series from 1991:01 to 2010:12. The main purpose of the work was to generate forecasts that follow closely with actual data using the ANN methodology. The Nonlinear Autoregressive Network (NAR) model and Nonlinear Autoregressive with Exogenous Input Network (NARX) model were each trained with 20 hidden layer units, 1 output unit and LM back-propagation procedure. The forecast results remarkably indicate that both ANNs predict accurately with the NARX producing closer results than the NAR. Finally, the comparison of the out-of-sample forecast performance of the ANNs with their econometric counterparts showed that the RMSFE of the both ANNs are lower than those of AR (12) and VAR (14) models. And so, judging by the RMSFE criterion, forecast based on ANN are more accurate.

References

1. Arratibel O, Palenzuela DR, Thimann C (2000) Inflation Dynamics and Dual Inflation in Accession Countries: A "New Keynesian Perspective" ECB Working Paper No. 132.
2. Chauvet M (2000) Leading Indicators of Inflation for Brazil, Working Paper Series No. 7 Banco Central do Brasil.
3. AGI Business Barometer Report (2010) Overall Perception of the Business Environment, First Quarter 2010 Association of Ghana Industries, Accra.
4. Bawumia, Mahamadu (2010) Monetary Policy and Financial Sector Reform in Africa: Ghana's Experience, Combert Impressions Ghana Ltd.
5. Bialowolski P, Tomasz K, Bartosz W (2010) Business Survey Data in Forecasting Macroeconomic Indicators with Combined Forecasts. Modern Economics 4: 41-58.
6. Biswas D, Sanjay S, Arti S (2010) Forecasting Inflation and IIP Growth: Bayesian Vector Autoregressive Model, Reserve Bank of India Occasional Papers 3: Monsoon.
7. BoG (2010) Bank of Ghana Annual Report 2011, Bank of Ghana, Accra.
8. Binner JM, Bissoondeeal RK, Elger T, Mullineux AW (2005) A Comparison of Linear Forecasting Models and Neural Networks: An Application to Euro Inflation and Euro Divisa. Applied Econ 37: 665-680.
9. Binner JM, Gazely AM, Kendall G (2005) Evaluating the Performance of a EuroDivisa Index Using Artificial Intelligence Techniques. International Journal of Automation and Computing 5: 58-62.
10. Bank of Ghana (2002) Bank of Ghana Act (Act 612) Bank of Ghana, Accra.
11. Binner JM, Gazely AM, Chen S (2002) Financial Innovation and Divisia Monet in Taiwan: A Neural Network Approach. The European Journal of Finance 8: 238-247.
12. Binner JM, Gazely AM, Chen SH (2002) Financial innovation in Taiwan: An application of neural networks to the broad money aggregates. European Journal of Finance Forthcoming.
13. Chen X, Racine J, Swanson NR (2001) Semi parametric ARX neural-network models with an application to forecasting inflation. See comment in PubMed Commons below IEEE Trans Neural Netw 12: 674-683.
14. Aminian F, Suarez ED, Aminian M, Walz DT (2006) Forecasting Economic Data with Neural Networks. Computational Economics 28: 71-88.
15. Binner J, Kendall G (2003) Co-Evolving Neural Networks with Evolutionary Strategies: A New Application to Divisia Money, Nottingham Business School, The Nottingham Trent University, Nottingham, UK.
16. Abberger K (2007) Qualitative business surveys and the assessment of employment – A case study for Germany. International Journal of Forecasting 23: 249-258.
17. Muhammad AS, Shazia Salam, Feridun M (2007) Modeling and Forecasting Pakistan's Inflation by Using Time Series ARIMA Models. Economic Analysis Working Paper 6:1-10.
18. Alamsyah H (2003) Inflation forecasting in Bank Indonesia, Occasional Papers No.40. The South East Asian Central Banks, Kuala Lumpur, Malaysia.
19. Addison KE (2001) Monetary Management in Ghana. Conference on Monetary Policy Frameworks in Africa, Pretoria.
20. Allen PG, RA Fildes (2001) Econometric forecasting strategies and techniques, In J.S. Armstrong (ed.), Principles of Forecasting: A Handbook for Researchers and Practitioners. Kluwer Academic Press, USA.
21. Alnaa SE, Ahiakpor F (2011) ARIMA (Autoregressive Integrated Moving Average) Approach to predicting inflation in Ghana. Journal of Economics and Integrated Finance 3: 328-336.
22. Altiamari SN (2001) Does Money Lead Inflation In The Euro Area? European Central Bank Working Paper No.63.
23. Ang A, Bekaert G, Wei M (2007) Do Macro Variables, Asset Markets, Or Surveys Forecast Inflation Better? Journal of Monetary Economics 54: 1163-1212.
24. Appiah K, Boahene B (2006) Determinant of Inflation in Ghana–An Econometric Analysis. Working Paper Accra.
25. Atta-Mensah, Joseph, Bawumia M (2003) A Simple Vector Error Correction Forecasting Model for Ghana, Bank of Ghana. Working Paper WP/BOG-2003/01.
26. Banerjee A, Marcellino M, Masten I (2003) Leading indicators for euro-area inflation and GDP growth. Working Papers 3893, CEPR.
27. Batchelor RA Dua, Pami (1990) Forecaster Ideology, Forecasting Technique, and Forecasting Industry. International Journal of Forecasting 6: 3-10.
28. Bawumia M, Abradu-Otoo (2003) Monetary Growth, Exchange Rate and Inflation in Ghana: An Error Correction Analysis. Working paper BoG Accra.
29. Berger H, Emil S (2008) The Information Content of Money in Forecasting Euro Area Inflation. International Monetary Fund Working Paper WP/08/166.
30. Binner JM, Elger CT, Nilsson B, Tepper JA (2006) Predictable non-linearities in U.S. inflation. Economics Letters 93: 323-328.
31. Bokhari SMH, Feridun M (2006) Forecasting Inflation through Econometric Models: An Empirical Study on Pakistani Data. Dogus University Journal 7: 39-47.
32. Box GEP, Jenkins GM (1976) Time Series Analysis Forecasting and Control Operational Research Quarterly 22: 199-201.
33. Brada JG, Garrido N (2006) Exploring two inflationary Regimes in Latin-America Economics: A Binary time series analysis. International Journal of Modern Physics C 17: 343-356.
34. Campilo M, Miron JA (1996) Why does inflation differ across countries? NBER Working Paper No. 5540.
35. Caramazza F, Slawner C (1991) The relationship between money, output and prices, Working Paper 914 Bank of Canada.
36. Carlson JA (1977) A Study of Price Forecasts. Annals of Economic and Social Measurement 6: 27-56.
37. Catao L, Terrones M (2001) Fiscal Deficits and Inflation: A New Look at the Emerging Market Evidence, IMF Working Paper WP/01/74.
38. Catik AN, Karacuka M (2011) A Comparative Analysis of Alternative Univariate Time Series Models in Forecasting Turkish Inflation. Journal of Business Economics and Management 13:275- 293.
39. Cavusoglu AT (2003) The endogenous money growth: An outcome of high budget deficits in Turkey. H.U. Iktisadi ve Idari Bilimler Fakultesi Dergisi 111-127.

Rate of Interest, Money Supply, Prices and Output Interdependences in Nigeria: A Vec Approach

Obasaju BO[1] and Bowale EI[2]*

[1]Lecturer at Landmark University, Omu-aran, Nigeria
[2]Department of Economics, Covenant University, Km 10 Idiiroko Rd, Ota, Ogun State, Nigeria

Abstract

Recent developments, in the financial system in Nigeria have generated a renewed attention on the nexus between real and nominal economic variables. This study examined the relationship between nominal rate of interest, nominal money supply, prices and real output using quarterly data on these variables from 1980:1 to 2012:4. The study adopted a Vector Error-Correction Mechanism to test for the short - and long – run relationships and found out that nominal money supply has no contemporaneous effect on real output in Nigeria but does have significant impact on the latter in the long-run thereby refuting the money neutrality hypothesis. Consequent upon its bid to further examine these interdependences, Granger Causality tests, Impulse Response Functions and Variance Decompositions were carried out. The major findings are that nominal money supply and inflation rate are the most important endogenous variables in explaining variations and shocks to other variables like real output and inflation in Nigeria. The study recommends, inter alia, that money supply, not interest rate, should be used appropriately as an intermediate policy variable with real output being the final target and that appropriate inflation-targeting policies be put in place because of its significant role in explaining variations in long – run real output.

Keywords: Nominal variables; Real variables; Interdependences; Vector error correction; Impulse response; Variance decomposition

Introduction

In recent time, the interdependences between rate of interest, money supply, inflation and output have been generating a lot of interest among the academics and policy makers globally. A theory that readily comes to mind in this respect is that which was put forward by Friedman and Meiselman which related money supply to prices [1]. This theory remains popular among economists; its postulation that inflation is always and everywhere a monetary phenomenon remains noteworthy. This theory also relates money supply to output like Sim who empirically tested the money-output nexus in the United States [2]. There are other economic hypotheses like the money neutrality and Fishers which related nominal money supply to real output in the long - run and rate of interest to expected inflation rate respectively. There is also the money demand function in which money balance is a function of income and interest rate.

However, the Keynesian and Monetarists have had serious debates in the past based on the role of money and the behaviour of prices. Empirical estimates on these dynamics have also yielded varying results stemming chiefly from the use of different methodologies, data and scopes of study.

This work differs from previous works in a number of ways: unlike Vladimir and Dana who examined the relationship between money and output in the Czech Republic using a VAR analysis–this work (i) uses a VECM analysis in estimating the long and short run dynamics amongst the stated variables (ii) differs in terms of sample chosen-based on Nigeria [3]. Furthermore, Patrick and James examined the long-run monetary neutrality and long-horizon regressions, their main objective was to test the plausibility of the long-run money neutrality [4]. This work extended the scope by also testing for other dynamics amongst real variables and nominal money supply central to monetary economics. In Nigeria, Busari evaluated the money demand function and focused mainly on the long and short run money demand function while making use of real variables like real money supply, real output, inflation and other variables [5]. His scope of study was between 1979 and 2003. The scope of this study is more encompassing as it used quarterly data from 1980:1 to 2012:4 and used various techniques in assessing the dynamics amongst the four endogenous variables.

This study aims at examining these interdependences using quarterly data on these variables from the 1st quarter of 1980 to the 4th quarter of 2012, in Nigeria. In specific terms, it aims at testing the plausibility of the money neutrality hypothesis using the long and short run estimates of a Vector Error-Correction Model; assessing, based on economic theories, as stated earlier, concerning the money-output nexus, money-prices nexus and interest-inflation rates relationship. The methodologies adopted to accomplish these objectives are the Granger Causality test, Impulse Response Functions and the Variance Decomposition, both of which are based on the VECM estimates.

The remaining part of this work is divided thus: Section 2 deals with the Literature Review; section 3 presents the Research Methodology and empirical findings and section 4 gives the conclusion and areas of further studies.

Review of Literature

Employing various techniques, both for developed and developing countries, Sims [2] observed that a unidirectional causality runs from money supply to nominal income in the post war period in United States. Brillembourg and Khan [6] observed that money Granger caused prices and income. Studies like Geweke [7]; Hall and Taylor [8]; Lucas and Walsh confirmed, empirically, the strong relationship between inflation and the growth of money supply [9,10]. Strands of literature including Bernanke and Blinder, Cristiano et al. and Cushman and Zha opined that an unforeseen tightening of monetary policy in the first phase lowers monetary aggregates and various economic activities and consequently leads to a reduction in the inflation rate in the next stage

***Corresponding author:** Bowale EI, Department of economics, Covenant University, Km 10 Idiiroko Rd, Ota, Ogun State, Nigeria
E-mail: kayobowale@yahoo.co.uk

[11-13]. Hodrick stated that tests of long-horizon asset predictability based on a VAR methodology perform better than those based on OLS [14]. In India, Rangarajan and Arif discovered that changes in real output do not respond to money supply but that inflation responds to money supply [15]. According to Dutta and Gangadhar, structural factors, plus monetary factors, are very pivotal to generating and sustaining the inflation process and volatilities in economic activity [16]. In Nigeria, Busari found out that the one period past value of short-run money demand and changes in GDP have positive relationship and are positively related to movements in money demand in the short-run while the three- month deposit rate and inflation rate are both negatively linked to the movement in money demand in the short-run [5]. Saadet et al. adopted a fractional cointegration technique in examining the Fisher Hypothesis using data from thirty-three developed and developing countries [17]. They observed a long-run relationship between nominal interest rate and expected inflation rate thereby validating this hypothesis. Rudebusch and Svensson concluded that the behaviour of money, whether real or nominal, does not have any marginal significant impact on deviations of real output from its potential level [18,19]. The government of Pakistan used M_2 as an intermediate target to control inflation following from the assumptions that the demand for M_2 function is stable and has strong link with inflation rate [20].

Research Methodology and Empirical Findings

Measurement and sources of data

In this study, as stated earlier, we use quarterly data from 1980:1 to 2012:4. Quarterly values on Real Output (RGDP), Nominal Money Supply (M_2), Nominal Interest Rate (INT) and Inflation Rate (proxied by the Consumer Price Index – CPI) from 1980 to 2009 are obtained from the Central Bank of Nigeria Statistical Bulletin (2010 Golden Jubilee edition). Values for 2010 to 2012 are obtained from the World Development Indicators 2013. All variables are expressed in their logarithmic forms except for the interest rate which is in a percentage form.

This work employs the following analytical procedure sequentially: Presentation of the empirical model which consists of a four-variable (endogenous) Vector Error-Correction Model; Stationarity and Integration tests; Cointegration test; Granger Causality test; Impulse Response Functions (IRFs) and Variance Decompositions (VDCs).

The model specification

The system to be estimated is made of four endogenous variables: the nominal rate of interest(INT), nominal money supply(MS), inflation (CPI) and the real output(RGDP). The VECM is adopted for these reasons: (i) it allows for the test of the long and short run relationship among the endogenous variables (ii) it retains the advantages of a standard Vector Autoregression (VAR) and includes the fact that the statistical relationship among the variables could be detected (iii) the variables are allowed to interact with themselves without having to impose theoretical structure on the estimates (iv) the IRFs and VDCs help to trace the impact of shocks to a given variable on another and the contribution of each variable to forecast error of itself and others.

VECM is a special case of the VAR for cointegrated variables. The model for this study can be expressed thus:

$X_t = (lnRGDP_t, ln\ CPI_t, lnMS_t, INT_t)'$; *that is,* X_t is a vector of 4 endogenous variables.

The 1st objective is to test mainly for the plausibility of the long-run money neutrality hypothesis in Nigeria. Thus we aim at checking whether or not there exist contemporaneous and long run impact of nominal supply on real output.

Starting with a simple VAR model with k lags, the equation could be expressed as follows:

$$X_t=\beta_1X_{t-1} + \beta_2X_{t-2} + \ldots + \beta_kX_{t-k} + U_t$$

where $X_t'=(lnRGDP_t, lnCPI_t, lnMS_t, INT_t)$; $\beta_i=4\ X\ 4$ matrix of parameters, $i=1, 2, \ldots, k$; $U_t=4\ X\ 1$ vector of multivariate normal random variables with mean of 0 and variance-covariance matrix Σ.

A typical VECM in its simplest form could be written as:

$$\Delta X_t = \Pi X_{t-k} + \Omega_1\Delta X_{t-1} + \Omega_2\Delta X_{t-2} + \ldots + \Omega_{k-1}\Delta X_{t-(k-1)} + U_t$$

where $\Pi = (\Sigma_{i=1}{}^{k}\ \beta_i) - I_g$ and $\Omega_i = (\Sigma_{j=1}{}^{k}\ \beta_i) - I_g$; $k= 4$ *(for a 4-variable VECM)*

Stationarity and integration tests

Past studies revealed that time series data for variables like interest rate, inflation rate and money supply, be it monthly, quarterly or annual, are likely to be non-stationary [19,21]. This study adopts the Augmented Dickey Fuller (ADF) (with constant only and with both constant and trend) and the ADF GLS tests (with constant and trend) to test for the stationarity of each variable. As a necessary but not sufficient condition for cointegration, each of the variables should have the same order of integration. The results of the ADF and ADF GLS are shown in Table 1 below. The ADF GLS is a variant of the ADF test and possesses more power in handling trend components. The ADF test shows that all variables but lnRGDP are integrated of order one, I(1) while lnRGDP is integrated of order zero, I(0). The ADF GLS test however shows that all the variables have the same order of integration and are all I(1). Based on this, we proceed to test for cointegration. Since the ADF GLS test is sensitive to lag length, we use the Bayesian (Schwartz) Information Criterion in selecting the lag length. The SBC (BIC) is asymptotically consistent and has superior large sample properties. The AIC is biased towards selecting an over parametized model. Monte Carlo studies however have shown that in small samples, the AIC can work better than the SBC [22]. However, our sample is large enough and so the BIC criterion is used. The BIC suggested a lag length of 4, 1, 1 and 6 for the endogenous variables respectively.

The stationarity test and lag specification are presented in Tables 1 and 2 below:

Variables	ADF (at level)		ADF (first difference)		Order of Integration
	With Constant	With Constant and Trend	With Constant	With Constant and Trend	
Ln(RGDP)	0.1014	-3.6138	-11.8731	-11.3367	I(0)
Ln(MS)	0.6332	-2.6167	-12.6036	-12.612	I(1)
Ln(CPI)	-1.9846	-0.1919	-9.3814	-9.7041	I(1)
INT	-2.4325	-2.3720	-5.2016	-5.4549	I(1)

Table 1a: ADF test.

	LnRGDP With constant and Trend		LnMS With constant and Trend		LnCPI With constant and Trend		INT With constant and Trend	
Critical Value	**Level**	**1st Difference**	**Level**	**1st Difference**	**Level**	**1st Difference**	**Level**	**1st Difference**
1%	-3.46	-3.46	-3.46	**-3.46**	-3.46	-3.46	-3.46	-3.46
5%	-2.93	-2.93	-2.93	-2.93	-2.93	-2.93	-2.93	-2.93
10%	-2.64	-2.64	-2.64	-2.64	-2.64	-2.64	-2.64	-2.64
T Stat	**-2.33**	**-12.08**	**-1.43**	**-11.25**	**-0.46**	**-9.49**	**-1.71**	**-5.14**
Order of Integration		**I(1)**		**I(1)**		**I(1)**		**I(1)**

Table 1b: ADF GLS test.

Variables	Lags
LnRGDP	4
LnMS	1
LnCPI	1
INT	6

Table 2: SBC lag length selection.

Rank	Eigenvalue	Trace test	p-value	Lmax test	p-value
0	0.25649	61.913	0.0011	37.604	0.0010
1	0.10444	24.274	0.1952	14.009	0.3783
2	0.077306	10.265	0.2656	10.218	0.2017
3	0.00036792	0.046734	0.8288	0.046734	0.8289

Table 3: Johansen Cointegration test.
Johansen test:
Number of equations=4
Lag order=5
Estimation period: 1981:2-2012:4 (T=127)
Case 3: Unrestricted constant
Log-likelihood=1338.87 (including constant term: 978.462)

Cointegration test (Johansen)

This is the test for long run relationship amongst the variables. Existence of at least one cointegrating equation shows that the variables have a common long run trend, that is, they are cointegrated. The VECM lag length was first selected. The model was initially over specified by selecting an optimal lag order of 12 after which the BIC suggested lag order of 5.

We then tested for the number of cointegrating vector (r) present in the data by the use of the trace statistics and the Johansen full maximum likelihood test (Lmax) test. The two tests both indicate that there is 1 cointegrating vector at the 5 percent level of significance as shown in Table 3. The existence of a cointegrating vector implies that there is a long-run relationship between LnRGDP and other endogenous variables including LnMS.

Long run estimates: We imposed the rank of the cointegrating vector which in this case is 1, the normalized cointegrating vector is presented in Table 4

This long-run relationship can be expressed as:

LnRGDP – 0.4060LnMS + 0.2566 LnCPI - 1. 5348INT

The result shows that *Ln(MS) and Ln(CPI)* are not in conformity with the a priori expectation but they are both significant in explaining variations in *Ln(RGDP)* in the long-run. *INT* conforms to a priori expectation but it is not significant. However, since the cointegrating coefficient for all the variables at 5 percent significance level (other than *INT*) are non-zero, this suggests that we can retain the variables in the cointegrating space. We also chose to retain interest rate in the cointegrating space.

LnRGDP	LnMS	LnCPI	INT
1.0000	-4.060	0.2566	-1.5348
(0.0000)	(0.0323)	(0.0415)	(0.6512)

Table 4: Results for Normalized Cointegrating Vector.

Const	*Coefficient*	*Std. Error*	*t-ratio*	*p-value*	
d_l_RGDP_	2.41946	0.493124	4.9064	<0.00001	***
d_l_RGDP_2	0.0245956	0.0412456	0.5963	0.5522	
d_l_RGDP_3	-0.108987	0.0402303	-2.7091	0.00784	***
d_l_RGDP_4	-0.0118557	0.0387448	-0.306	0.76019	
d_l_RGDP_5	0.145375	0.0398158	3.6512	0.0004	***
d_l_MS_1	-0.151695	0.111109	-1.3653	0.17498	
d_l_MS_2	-0.0958487	0.110432	-0.8679	0.38733	
d_l_MS_3	-0.0012126	0.111632	-0.0109	0.99135	
d_l_MS_4	-0.054599	0.109917	-0.4967	0.62038	
d_l_CPI_1	-0.0028486	0.0791398	-0.036	0.97135	
d_l_CPI_2	-0.0700849	0.0792747	-0.8841	0.3786	
d_l_CPI_3	-0.0403569	0.0788322	-0.5119	0.60973	
d_l_CPI_4	0.196421	0.0762675	2.5754	0.01135	**
d_INT_1	0.123947	1.07354	0.1155	0.9083	
d_INT_2	-0.209319	1.32092	-0.1585	0.87438	
d_INT_3	-0.351854	1.31736	-0.2671	0.7899	
d_INT_4	-0.814304	1.07647	-0.7565	0.45101	
EC1	-0.355353	0.0728732	-4.8763	<0.00001	***
Mean dependent var		0.01263	S.D. dependent var		0.093207
Sum squared resid		0.600242	S.E. of regression		0.074208
R-squared		0.45165	Adjusted R-squared		0.366128
rho		0.04493	Durbin-Watson		1.89553

Table 5: Equation 1: d_l_RGDP.

Thus, since *LnMS* (nominal money supply) is found to be significant in explaining variations in *LnRGDP* (real output) in the long – run, the money neutrality hypothesis is thereby rejected. This result is in conformity with that of Saghaian [19].

The VECM estimates: short-run dynamics: From the long-run estimates, variables could be said to have (or not have) a common trend in the long run. According to Engle and Granger [23], existences of cointegration between non-stationary variables indicate that an error-correction representation can be specified.

The coefficient of the cointegrating equation in the VECM refers to the speed of adjustment and shows how quickly any disequilibrium in the short-run is restored after a temporary disequilibrium. Table 5 depicts this.

The VECM short run estimates show that only the 1st, 2nd and 4th lags of *LnRGDP* and the 4th lag of *LnCPI* are significant in explaining variations in *LnRGDP* in the short run at 1% level of significance. The error correction is however correctly signed and also highly significant and it shows that about 36% of the disequilibrium in *LnRGDP* is corrected in the next period. It is also observed that nominal variables such as money supply and interest rate do not have contemporaneous impact on a real variable such as real output contrary to the position of the money neutrality proponents that nominal variables do have contemporaneous impact on real variables but neutral in the long run.

Granger causality tests

Granger causality implies the presence of feedback from one variable to the other. Engle and Granger, Hendry and Granger opined that the existence of cointegration is the basis for causality [23-25]. Following from the tenets of this theory, if two variables have long-run (cointegrating) relationship, then causality must exist in at least one direction [26,27].

The relationships of particular interest in this work relate to the nexus between (i) real output (*LnRGDP*) and nominal money supply (*LnMS*) (ii) inflation rate (*CPI*) and nominal money supply and (iii) interest rate (*INT*) and inflation rate (*LnCPI*).

Since Granger causality is sensitive to lag order, the BIC & HQ criteria suggested a lag of 5. The full results of these tests are presented in Appendix A.

For (i), Granger causality between *LnRGDP* and *LnMS* show that a unidirectional causality runs from *LnMS* to *LnRGDP*. Hence, *LnMS* Granger causes *LnRGDP* at the 5% level of significance.

For (ii), a unidirectional causality also runs from *LnMS* to *LnCPI* at 5% level of significance. Thus the former Granger causes the latter.

For (iii), independence is observed between *INT* and *LnCPI*, that is, no one Granger causes the other.

The Impulse Response Functions (IRFs) based on VECM results

The IRFs obtain from the Moving Average (MA) representation of the original VAR model. They (IRFs) depict the dynamic response of a particular endogenous variable to a one-period standard deviation shock to the system. As it were, impulse responses trace out the responsiveness of dependent variables in a VAR to shocks to each of the variables. Hence, the effects upon the system consequent upon a unit shock to each variable from each separate equation are noted [28,29].

The IRFs are sensitive to lag lengths and ordering of variables. The BIC and Hannan - Quinn statistics could be used to choose the lag length [30]. Since we are basically interested in the dynamics amongst these variables, we allow shock to each variable affect others. The variables are I(1) following from the results of the unit root tests and we estimate the system as an unrestricted VAR in levels despite the fact that each variable is likely to be generated by a unit root stochastic process. This follows from Sims [31] advice. The implication of this is that we do not consider the significance of the individual coefficients in the estimated equations but the dynamics of the system can be examined by examining the IRFs [32].

With respect to the ordering, we do not have a particular theoretical basis for the ordering but we bear in mind the relevant economic theory and hypotheses as stated earlier which are the quantity theory of money, money neutrality hypothesis and Fishers hypothesis. Thus, we allow any two variables relating to the theory or any of these hypotheses to be ordered after each other.

The unrestricted VAR approach begins with a reduced form equation. The structural model that underpins this reduced form allows for a contemporaneous and lagged interaction between the variables of the system. Hence the structural model can be written as:

$$0 = B_0 + B_1X_t + B_2(L)\,X(L) + \varepsilon$$

Where $B_0 = [b_{LnRGDP}\ b_{LnMS}\ b_{LnCPI}\ b_{INT}]'$; is a vector of constants

$$B_1 = \begin{bmatrix} 1 & b_{12} & b_{13} & b_{14} \\ b_{21} & 1 & b_{23} & b_{24} \\ b_{31} & b_{32} & 1 & b_{34} \\ b_{41} & b_{42} & b_{43} & 1 \end{bmatrix};$$ is a matrix of coefficients that relate to the contemporaneous interaction between the variables in the system

$X_t = [lnRGDP\ lnMS\ lnCPI\ INT]'$ is a vector of the system variables

$$B_2(L) = \begin{bmatrix} b_{11}(L) & b_{12}(L) & b_{13}(L) & b_{14}(L) \\ b_{21}(L) & b_{22}(L) & b_{23}(L) & b_{24}(L) \\ b_{31}(L) & b_{32}(L) & b_{33}(L) & b_{34}(L) \\ b_{41}(L) & b_{42}(L) & b_{43}(L) & b_{44}(L) \end{bmatrix};$$ is a vector of coefficients that relate to the influence of variables on their current value.

$X_t(L) = [lnRGDP_{t-L}\ lnMS_{t-L}\ lnCPI_{t-L}\ INT_{t-L}]'$; is a vector of lagged variables in the system with L representing the lag length which in this case, following the BIC and HQ specifications, is 5.

$\varepsilon = [\varepsilon_{RGDP}\ \varepsilon_{lnMS}\ \varepsilon_{lnCPI}\ \varepsilon_{INT}]'$; is a vector of structural errors

The reduced form version of our structural model can be written as:

$$X_t = A_0 + A_1(L)X_{t-L} + e_t$$

where $A_0 = B_1^{-1}B_0$; $A_1(L) = B_1^{-1}B_2(L)$ and $e_t = B_1^{-1}\varepsilon$

However, the Ordinary Least Square technique can be used for the estimation since we have the same variables on the right hand side of the system. The Choleski decomposition which converts the B_1 matrix to be lower triangular is used by setting all the coefficients above the diagonal to zero.

With respect to the orderings, there are six (6) ways (2! + 2! + 2!) in which they can be arranged going by the money-output, money-price and interest-inflation relationships. Importantly, any variable that appears before others is allowed to have contemporaneous effect on them and is affected by only its own shock; and the reverse is impossible. For example, ordering 1 below shows that (LnRGDP) is allowed to have contemporaneous impact on LnMS and others, but LnMS cannot have contemporaneous effect on LnRGDP. A ten year horizon is used for the IRFs.

$X_t = [lnRGDP\ lnMS\ lnCPI\ INT]'$ .... *ordering 1*

$X_t = lnMS\ lnRGDP\ lnCPI\ INT]'$ .... *ordering 2*

$X_t = [lnCPI\ lnMS\ lnRGDP\ INT]'$ .... *ordering 3*

$X_t = [lnMS\ lnCPI\ lnRGDP\ INT]'$ .... *ordering 4*

$X_t = [INT\ lnCPI\ lnRGDP\ lnMS]'$ .... *ordering 5*

$X_t = [lnCPI\ INT\ lnRGDP\ lnMS]'$ .... *ordering 6*

The full IRFs are presented in Appendix B

IRF interpretations for orderings 1 and 2: LnRGDP and LnMS dynamics

For ordering 1, the response of *LnMS* to one standard deviation shock to *LnRGDP* has a positive and increasing impact over the years up to the 10th forecast year.

For the 2nd ordering, the response of LnRGDP to one standard deviation innovation to LnMS reduces and becomes negative up to the 3rd forecast year after which the response starts increasing and becomes positive from the 4.5th forecast year.

IRF interpretations for orderings 3 and 4: Lncpi And Lnms Dynamics

For ordering 3, the response of LnMS to a standard deviation innovation to LnCPI is positive but declines up to the 4th forecast year after which the response increases sharply up to the 5th year and then steadily up to the 10th forecast year.

For the 4th ordering, the response of LnCPI to a standard deviation innovation to LnMS is positive and sharp from the 1st to the 4th year, positive but declining between the 4th and 5th years, after which the response increases consistently up to the 8th forecast year.

IRF interpretations for orderings 5 and 6: INT and LnCPI dynamics

For the 5th ordering, the response of LnCPI to a standard deviation innovation to INT is positive but decreases sharply between the 1st and 3rd years, becomes negative between the 3rd and 7th years after which the response increases and becomes positive up to the 10th forecast year.

Considering the 6th ordering, the response of INT to a standard deviation innovation to LnCPI is positive and steadily increases between the 1st and 4th years after which it continues to decline, although still positive, up to the 10th forecast year.

Variance decompositions based on VECM results

The variance decomposition (VDCs hereafter) shows the proportion of the movements in the dependent variables as a result of their own shocks and shocks to other variables. VDCs, according to Bessler and King, may be referred to as out-of-sample causality tests. Sims stated that the variable that is optimally forecast from its own lagged values will have all the total variation in its forecast error explained by its own disturbances.

Like IRFs, VDCs are also sensitive to ordering. The table is presented in Appendix C. A ten (10) year forecast horizon is also used. We followed the 1st ordering as used in the IRF, i.e. X_t = *[lnRGDP lnMS lnCPI INT]'*. However, we experimented using different orderings and observed only marginal variations in the outputs. This might be due to the fact that the correlations among the various innovations are not large.

Shocks to LnRGDP in forecast year 1 accounted for 100% variations in itself. In the 10th year, shock to itself accounted for 71.48% variations while shock to LnCPI accounted for 17.83% variations in LnRGDP.

In the 1st year, shocks to LnMS accounted for 99.88% variations in itself while shocks to LnRGDP only accounted for 0.12%. In the 10th year, shocks to itself (LnMS) accounted for 90.01% variations in itself while shocks to LnRGDP accounted for 9.51% variations in LnMS.

For LnCPI, in the 1st year, shocks to itself explains 88.28% variations in itself while shocks to LnMS accounted for 11.08% variations in LnCPI. In the 7th year, shocks to LnCPI and LnMS respectively accounted for 71.88% and 19.89% variations in LnCPI.

For INT, in the 1st year, shocks to itself and LnCPI accounted for 98.06% and 1.35% variations in INT respectively. In the 10th year, shocks to itself and also LnCPI respectively accounted for 85.69% and 7.44% variations in INT.

From the foregoing, it is clear-cut that shocks to money supply appears to be the most important in explaining the variations in itself and inflation. This relationship between money supply and prices (inflation) seem to support (at least a bit) the Friedman's *quantity theory of money* in which he stated that inflation is always and everywhere a monetary phenomenon.

In the case of INT and CPI, CPI, other than INT itself, is the most important in explaining variations in INT. This finding is also somewhat similar to Fishers hypotheses (though not on the basis of a one-to-one relationship).

Conclusion and Areas of Future Studies

The study examined the dynamics amongst four variables, the nominal rate of interest, nominal money supply, inflation and real output. Following the results of the long run VECM estimate, Granger Causality, IRFs and VDCs, the nominal money supply proved to play the most significant role in explaining the variations and dynamics amongst these variables. The long-run money neutrality hypothesis was refuted because nominal money supply showed to be non-neutral in the long run with respect to its effect on the long run real output. Thus, policy makers need to give adequate attention to money supply as an intermediate policy variable. There is also a need for appropriate inflation - targeting policies because of the significance of the CPI in explaining variations in the long run real output as reported by the VECM and VDC estimates. These findings are consistent with that of Tahir and Mohammad (2005) who examined the relationship among same variables in Pakistan.

Further studies can focus on a methodology such as the structural VEC (unlike the theoretical standard VEC) which has theoretical underpinnings for the structural parameters of a system.

References

1. Friedman M, Meiselman D (1963) The Relative Stability of Monetary Velocity and the Investment Multiplier in the United States. The Journal of Developing Areas 41: 185-202.
2. Sim CA (1972) Money, income and causality. American Economic Review 62: 540-552.
3. Vladimir T, Dana V (2006) The relationship between money and output in the Czech Republic: Evidence from VAR analysis. Eastern European Economics 44: 23-39.
4. Patrick JC, James NM (2004) Long-Run monetary neutrality and long-horizon regressions. Journal of Applied Econometrics 19: 355-373.
5. Busari TD (2009) Money demand functions in Nigeria: Issues and further considerations. Applied econometrics and macroeconometric modelling in Nigeria. Lagos: Royal Bird Ventures Ltd.
6. Brillembourge A, Arif RR (1990) Money, output and prices: Has money mattered historically? Journal of Money, Credit and Banking 11: 358-365.
7. Geweke J (1986) The Super neutrality of Money in the United States:An Interpretation of the Evidence. Econometrica 54: 1-22.
8. Hall RE, Taylor JB (1997) Macroeconomics (5th ed.). New York: W.W. Norton.
9. Lucas RE (1980) Two Illustrations of the Quantity Theory of Money. American Economic Review 70: 1005-1014.
10. Walsh CE (2001) Monetary Theory and Policy. MIT Press, Cambridge.
11. Bernanke B, Blinder A (1992) The Federal Funds Rate and the Channels of Monetary Transmission. American Economic Review 82: 901-921.

12. Christiano L, Eichenbaum M, Evans C (1994) Identification and the Effects of Monetary Policy Shocks. FRB Chicago Working Paper.
13. Cushman D, Zha T (1997) Identifying Monetary Policy in a Small Open Economy under Flexible exchange rates. Journal of Monetary economics 39: 433-448.
14. Hodrick RJ (1992) Dividends yields and expected stock returns: alternative procedures for inference and measurement. Review of Financial Studies 5: 357-386.
15. Rangarajan C, Arif RR. (1990) Money, output and prices: A macroeconometric model. Economic and Political Weekly 25: 837-848.
16. Dutta SR, Gangadhar D (2000) Dynamics of money, output and price interaction – Some Indian evidence. Economic Modelling, 17: 559-588.
17. Saadet K, Adnan K, Evrim T (2006) Fisher hypothesis revisited: a fractional cointegration analysis. Emerging Markets Finance & Trade 42: 59-76.
18. Rudebusch GD (1998) Do Measures of Monetary Policy Shocks in a VAR Make Sense? International Economic Review 39: 907-941.
19. Saghaian SH, Reed MR, Merchant MA (2002) Monetary impacts and overshooting of agricultural prices in an open economy. American Journal of Agricultural Economics 84: 91-103.
20. Qayyum A (2008) Does Monetary Policy Play Effective Role in Controlling Inflation in Pakistan? MPRA.
21. The relative impact of national monetary policies and international exchange rate on long-term variations in relative agricultural prices (2004) Center for Agricultural Policy and Trade Studies. Department of Agribusiness and Applied Economic.
22. Walter E (2010) Applied Econometric Time Series (2nd ed.). Wiley, USA.
23. Engle RF, Granger CW (1987) Co-integration and Error Correction: Representation, Estimation, and Testing. Econometrica 55: 251-276.
24. Hendry D (1986) Econometric Modelling with Cointegrated Variables: An Overview. Oxford Bulletin of Economics and Statistics 48: 201-212.
25. Granger CWJ (1986) Developments in the Study of Cointegrated Economic Variables. Oxford Bulletin of Economics and Statistics 48: 213-228.
26. Granger CWJ (1988) Some Recent Developments in a Concept of Causality. Journal of Econometrics 39: 199-211.
27. Miller S, Russek F (1990) Cointegration and Error Correction Models: the temporal causality between government taxes and spending. Southern Economic Journal 57: 221-229.
28. Bessler D, King J (1985) A Note on Tests of Granger Causality. Applied Econometrics 16: 335-342.
29. Olayiwola K, Okodua H (2013) Foreign direct investment, non-oil exports, and economic growth in Nigeria: a causality analysis. Asian Economic and Financial Review 3: 1479-1496.
30. Lutkepohl H (1991) Introduction to Multiple Time Series Analysis. Springer-Verlag, London.
31. Sims CA (1980) Macroeconomics and reality. Econometrica 48: 1- 48.
32. Dickinson D, Liu J (2007) The real effects of monetary policy in China: An empirical analysis. China Economic Review 18: 87-111.

Is Students' Religiosity Moderating Word of Mouth in Islamic Private Higher Education?

Eko Handayanto[1]*, Tulus Haryono[2] and Hunik Sri Runing Sawitri[2]

[1]*University of Muhammadiyah Malang, East Java, Indonesia*
[2]*University of Sebelas Maret Surakarta, Central Java, Indonesia*

Abstract

Marketing communications by Word of Mouth or WOM universally important role in business success and is one of the marketing communication strategy, a strong impact on the performance of marketing, as well as playing an important role in influencing the purchasing decision back. WOM can be an alternative marketing communications for a private university based Islamic religion that have had difficulty in promoting the institution.

The research aims to analyze the influence of service quality on WOM marketing communications. Another research aim is to analyze the role of satisfaction as a mediator, and the role of religiosity as moderator effect of service quality on WOM marketing communications. Respondents are students of University of Muhammadiyah Malang and University of Islam Malang who had conducted WOM. Data collected by questionnaire and analyzed using SEM PLS.

The analysis showed that the service quality has no direct effect on WOM marketing communications. Service quality has direct effect on satisfaction, and satisfaction has direct effect on WOM. Another result is religiosity did not moderate the influence of satisfaction on WOM.

Keywords: Service quality; Satisfaction; Word of mouth

Introduction

Word of Mouth or WOM is universally seen as an important factor of business success and over 50 years of informal communication between the customers has been used as a research topic [1]. Marketing researchers and practitioners believe that WOM is one of the marketing communication strategy that had a strong impact on marketing performance [2], and played an important role in influencing the re-purchasing decision [3,4].

WOM can be done through online and offline (face to face) with a number of differences. First, offline WOM is the process of sharing information between two or more parties are mutually interested and it is voluntary, whereas the online WOM is a two-way communication that has a very wide range of opinions and experiences to share with others [5]. Second, WOM offline message's sender is closer and familiar with the receiver, so that the credibility of the sender and the message content can be easily understood by the receiver. While the nature of WOM online is to eliminate the ability of the receiver to assess the credibility of the sender and the message contents [6]. Third, offline WOM is more persuasive than the online one [7]. Differences in these characteristics indicate that the relative offline WOM is more credible and more persuasive than WOM online in influencing consumer purchasing decisions. WOM online also has its disadvantages outweigh the negative assessments offline WOM may spread rapidly and expanded in a short time, and have a negative impact on consumer attitudes [8,9]. Therefore, the research is focused on offline WOM marketing communication (face to face).

WOM sender's behavior was motivated by a variety of antecedents, such as quality of service [10,11], satisfaction, loyalty, commitment [12], and trust [13,14]. The diversity of the antecedents of WOM caused by different objects and basic theoretical research. WOM research objects include goods and services, but service research object is dominant rather than goods [15]. In terms of the theoretical foundation, a variety of theory was used to explain the phenomenon of WOM, such as cultural theory, the attribution theory [16,17], the theory of satisfaction [18,19], and the theory of personal relationships [20,21].

The object of WOM research differences has an implication for the diversity of variables in the model, it was resulted research model in a partial science expansion. Consequently, the research model has not ability to generalize. The diversity of the basic theory suggests that WOM activity can be viewed from various aspects. The results of WOM research that has been studied did not find based on the theory of causal attribution. Therefore, it is used as the theoretical basis of this research to develop a new alternative WOM models. Causal Attribution theory states that success is due to the internal and external factors. Attribution in marketing research is understood as an explanation of causality of events and consumer behavior [22]. In this study, Causal Attribution Theory is expected to explain the reasons for the success of WOM marketing of consumer communication, especially the success caused by internal factors. Empirically Babin, Bruce and Edgington, Casalo, Chaniotakis and Lymperpoulos indicate that customer satisfaction affects the WOM marketing communications. Several other studies indicate that WOM marketing communications not directly related to satisfaction [23-25]. While the study of Li [25] and Naik, Anand, and Bashir [26] indicate there is no satisfaction impact on WOM marketing communications.

The study results indicate there are three groups of previous research results. The first group is indicating the existence of a direct influence of satisfaction on WOM. The second group is indicating an indirect

***Corresponding author:** Eko Handayanto, University of Muhammadiyah Malang, East Java, Indonesia, E-mail: ehandayanto@yahoo.com

effect of satisfaction on WOM, and third group is indicating a direct effect that satisfaction has no effect on WOM. Those are demonstrates controversies in terms of the effect of satisfaction on WOM marketing communications and need to be reanalyzed. The relationship between satisfaction and WOM are expected to generate an alternative model of behavior WOM marketing communications. In the context of indirect relationships, the researchers added consumer religiosity variable as a moderator variable that is expected to strengthen the influence of satisfaction on WOM.

The object of the research is private higher education with Islamic religion background. The unit analysis of the research is student at University of Muhammadiyah University and University of Islamic Malang. Both private universities owned by the two organizations in Indonesia's largest Islamic community, namely Muhammadiyah and Nahdlatul Ulama (NU). Those are chosen because has uniqueness in communication patterns. The communication pattern in NU well known as primordial or patron-client communication where elements of Kyai or the descendants of Kyai were in institutions and the community became a central figure, whereas in Muhammadiyah uphold collegial communication links. Both the communication pattern has been a tradition among Muhammadiyah and NU [27]. Differences in patterns of communication is an interesting phenomenon to be studied from the perspective of WOM marketing communications, especially to determine whether religiosity that exists within every student is capable of moving them to do WOM marketing communications.

Literature Review

This study based on the theory of causal attribution as a basis for explaining the motivation of individual consumers to spread the information to others through word of mouth voluntarily. Attribution theory was first introduced by Fritz Heider in 1958. He suggests that if observing social behavior, the first thing you should do is determine in advance what caused it, i.e., situational factors or personal. The assumption is that people try to understand their environment and explain the causes of internal and external to an event encountered. Attribution theory is also commonly called the external and internal causality [28].

Weiner [29] states that there are three elements that underlie the causal properties that have cross situational generality that is the locus, stability, and control. First, the cause of success or failure can be caused by internal or external factors. Second, the cause of success or failure can be either stable or unstable. Third, the cause of success or failure can be either controlled or uncontrolled. Controllable factor is one of the factors that are believed to be able to change a person if he wants to do. The uncontrollable factors explain if someone does not believe him then they can easily turn. Thus, attribution theory explains that human behavior cannot be separated from the state within the individual and the environment.

Weiner attribution theory is the most influential contemporary implications on consumer behavior. Attribution theory interpreted on the success or failure of the business and the consumer tendency to do the same behavior in the future. Weiner attribution theory more widely adopted than other attribution theory by researchers in consumer behavior [30,31]. Therefore, Weiner's attribution theory was used as the theoretical basis of this research.

Effect of service quality on WOM

Athanassopoulos et al. [32] indicate that consumers' assessment of service quality is positively related to WOM. Chen and Xie [33] found that good quality services allowing consumers to recommend through the information by word of mouth (WOM). Next, Padma et al. [34] in his research indicates that consumers who are glad to be able to share information voluntarily and invite family and their friends to visit the same service provider. In the perspective of college, Hermawan [35] indicates the quality aspects of education have a significant effect on the willingness of students recommend their campus. Meanwhile, Abdullah [36] indicated that service quality is positively related to WOM.

The hypothesis is the service quality of higher education has a positive effect on WOM.

Effect of service quality satisfaction

Duggirala, Rajendran, and Anantharaman [37] indicated a positive relationship between the dimensions of service quality and satisfaction. Likewise, Bansal and Taylor, Cronin, Brady, Brand, Hightower, and Shemwell [38] study indicates the existence of a high correlation between the service quality and satisfaction. In the perspective of higher education, student satisfaction is influenced by the service quality of the college [39]. The quality of higher education has a significant effect on student satisfaction. Keong [40] indicates the quality of functional service has a significant effect on student satisfaction.

The hypothesis is the service quality of higher education has a positive effect on student satisfaction.

The influence of satisfaction on WOM marketing communications

Athanassopoulos et al. indicate that high customer satisfaction is positively related to WOM communication. Studies Babin et al., Bruce and Edgington, and Chaniotakis and Lymperopoulos also indicate that customer satisfaction has positive effect on WOM marketing communications. Hermawan indicate that significant influence satisfaction on WOM recommendations. Ahmad et al. [41] stated that the intention to encourage students doing positive WOM then universities should have a reputation for excellence and develop relationships with students is satisfactory. Bruce and Edgington stated that student satisfaction with quality of services college campus to encourage them to recommend to other prospective students voluntarily.

The hypothesis is that student satisfaction effect on WOM.

Religiosity moderating influence of satisfaction on WOM

Bloodgood [42] indicates that the higher religiosity student decreases their cheating behavior. La Barbera *et al.* [43] suggested that higher religiosity consumers looked quantity and luxury products purchased did not make them satisfied. Ariffin et al. [44] states that the level of consumer's religiosity can weaken the influence of American popular culture on conspicuous consumption. The more religious of satisfied customers will do WOM more.

The hypothesis is the student religiosity will strengthen the influence of satisfaction on WOM.

Research Methods

This research was conducted at the University of Muhammadiyah Malang (UMM) is located at Jalan Tlogomas 246, and the University of Islamic Malang (UNISMA) in Jalan MT. Haryono 193 Malang.

This study was designed to build a model of word of outh (WOM) marketing communication in the perspective of a private-higher education Islamic religion. Research type is a survey with students as an analysis unit. The study population is a registered undergraduate student at UNISMA and UMM who have ever convey information about the college to others through WOM face to face and voluntary.

Statistically, the number of students at UMM and UNISMA can be known, but the number of students who actually meet the criteria of population is not known. Therefore, the method of determining the sample follows the assumption that the Structural Equation Modeling to produce a good analysis of the size of the sample is determined at least 5 times the number of indicators used variables. The samples technique was conducted using a non-probability sampling using judgment method.

Primary data was used in this study, including service quality, satisfaction, religiosity, and WOM. Questionnaire method was used to data collection. Data that has been declared valid and reliable then analyzed using Smart PLS 2.0 version.

Results

SEM PLS analysis results

a. Model specification

1) ***Outer model:*** Outer model is a relationship specification between latent variables and the indicator that describes the characteristics of latent variables with the indicator. Outer loading value shows the value of each indicator as a measure of a variable based on the reflective value. Outer loading results were shown in Table 1.

Outer loading value of all indicators of the service quality are above 0.50 with the highest loading indicator X_{109} (certainty of time service) of 0.736. For satisfaction variable, the highest loading value was indicators X_{201} (student satisfied with their chosen), with a score of 0.764. The highest outer value on WOM is an indicator X30 (recommend to acquaintance) by a score of 0.848. The highest outer loading value indicates that the indicator has stronger reflect the latent variables compared with other indicators.

2) ***Inner model:*** Inner model is a relationship specification between latent variable (exogenous and endogenous) based on the theoretical foundation. Relationship between latent variable of service quality, satisfaction, and WOM was shown in Table 2.

b. Path diagram of SEM: Path diagram of SEM is basically a diagram that connects the structural model with the measurement model. Structural model is a model whose function is to look at the relationship between latent variables, whereas the measurement model has a function to see the connection indicator of the latent variables. Path diagram in this study connects the latent variables of service quality, satisfaction, WOM, and religiosity moderator variables and indicators of latent variables respectively as in Figures 1 and 2.

Figure 1 is the result of algorithm analysis PLS SEM that shows the outer and inner loading and also path coefficient values. It used to construct the outer and inner models. Whereas in Figure 2 is the result of bootstrapping analysis of PLS SEM showing the outer and inner significance of the model, the path model coefficients, as well as the coefficient of determination or R^2.

c. Path diagram conversion to equation

1) ***Structural equation (Inner model)***

Indicators	Original sample	Information
$X_{101} \leftarrow$ KP	0.5884	Valid
$X_{102} \leftarrow$ KP	0.5096	Valid
$X_{103} \leftarrow$ KP	0.5296	Valid
$X_{104} \leftarrow$ KP	0.6237	Valid
$X_{105} \leftarrow$ KP	0.6853	Valid
$X_{106} \leftarrow$ KP	0.66	Valid
$X_{107} \leftarrow$ KP	0.7122	Valid
$X_{108} \leftarrow$ KP	0.7233	Valid
$X_{109} \leftarrow$ KP	0.736	Valid
$X_{110} \leftarrow$ KP	0.5721	Valid
$X_{111} \leftarrow$ KP	0.6681	Valid
$X_{112} \leftarrow$ KP	0.6858	Valid
$X_{113} \leftarrow$ KP	0.6936	Valid
$X_{114} \leftarrow$ KP	0.6792	Valid
$X_{115} \leftarrow$ KP	0.6366	Valid
$X_{116} \leftarrow$ KP	0.6876	Valid
$X_{117} \leftarrow$ KP	0.5177	Valid
$X_{118} \leftarrow$ KP	0.6708	Valid
$X_{119} \leftarrow$ KP	0.5753	Valid
$X_{120} \leftarrow$ KP	0.6834	Valid
$X_{201} \leftarrow$ KEP	0.7618	Valid
$X_{202} \leftarrow$ KEP	0.7586	Valid
$X_{203} \leftarrow$ KEP	0.6622	Valid
$X_{204} \leftarrow$ KEP	0.7201	Valid
$X_{205} \leftarrow$ KEP	0.6879	Valid
$X_{401} \leftarrow$ WOM	0.7108	Valid
$X_{402} \leftarrow$ WOM	0.74	Valid
$X_{403} \leftarrow$ WOM	0.7664	Valid
$X_{404} \leftarrow$ WOM	0.7926	Valid
$X_{405} \leftarrow$ WOM	0.8277	Valid
$X_{406} \leftarrow$ WOM	0.8481	Valid
$X_{407} \leftarrow$ WOM	0.8243	Valid

Table 1: Outer Loading – Convergent Validity. Source: Smart PLS Algorithm, 2016.

Path	Original Sample (O)	Sample Mean (M)	Standard Error (STERR)
KEP → WOM	0.2673	0.1992	0.0942
KEP × REL → WOM	0.2511	0.1693	0.329
KP → KEP	0.4281	0.4577	0.0874
KP → WOM	0.1866	0.1661	0.0945
REL → WOM	0.22	0.237	0.0765

Table 2: Path coefficient. Source: Smart PLS Bootstrapping, 2016.

WOM (η_2)=0.301KP + 0.086

Kepuasan (η_1)=0.428KP + 0.087

WOM (η_2)=0.267KEP + 0.094

WOMmodKEP (η_2)=0.251 + 0.267KEP + 0.329

2) ***Measurement equation (Outer model)***

2.1) *Service quality*

$$KP=0.588KP_{01} + 0.510KP_{02} + 0.530KP_{03} + 0.624KP_{04} + 0.685KP_{05} + 0.660KP_{06} + 0.712KP_{07} + 0.723KP_{08} + 0.736KP_{09} + 0.572KP_{10} + 0.668KP_{11} + 0.686KP_{12} + 0.694KP_{13} + 0.769KP_{14} + 0.637KP_{15} + 0.688KP_{16} + 0.518KP_{17} + 0.671KP_{18} + 0.575KP_{19} + 0.683KP_{20}$$

2.2) *Satisfaction*

$$KEP=0{,}762X_{201} + 0{,}759X_{202} + 0{,}662X_{203} + 0{,}720X_{204} + 0{,}688X_{205}$$

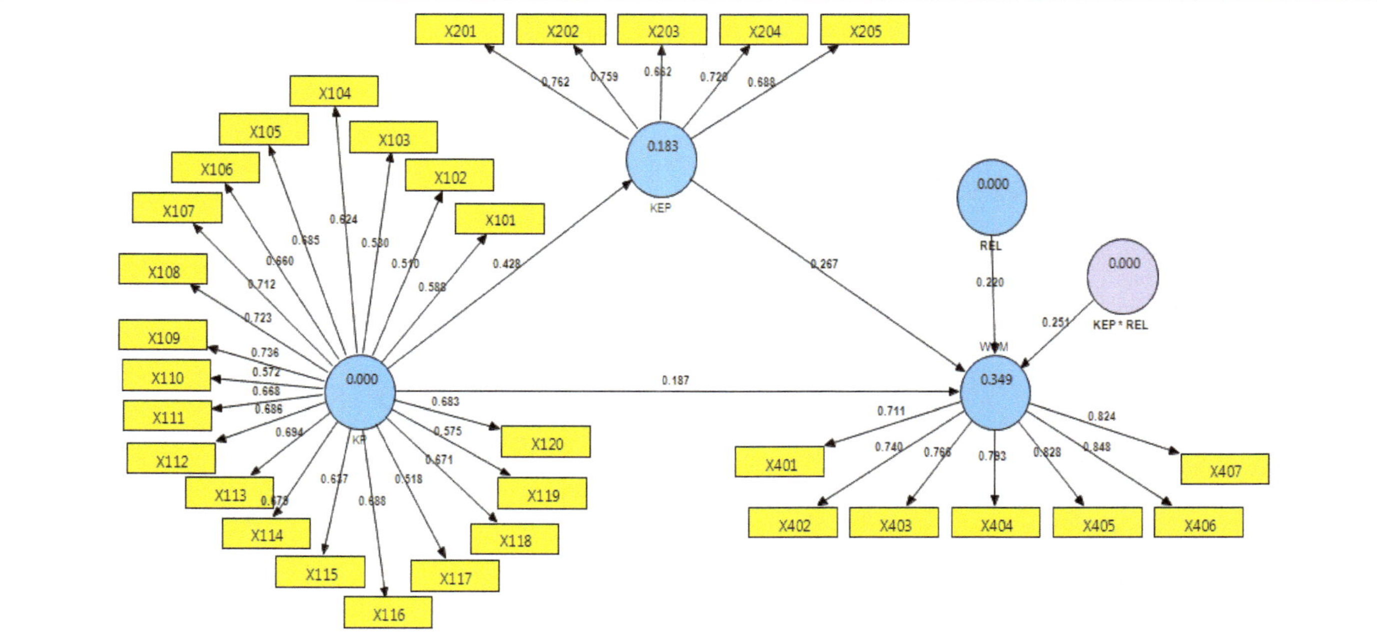

Figure 1: Diagram of algorithm structural model.

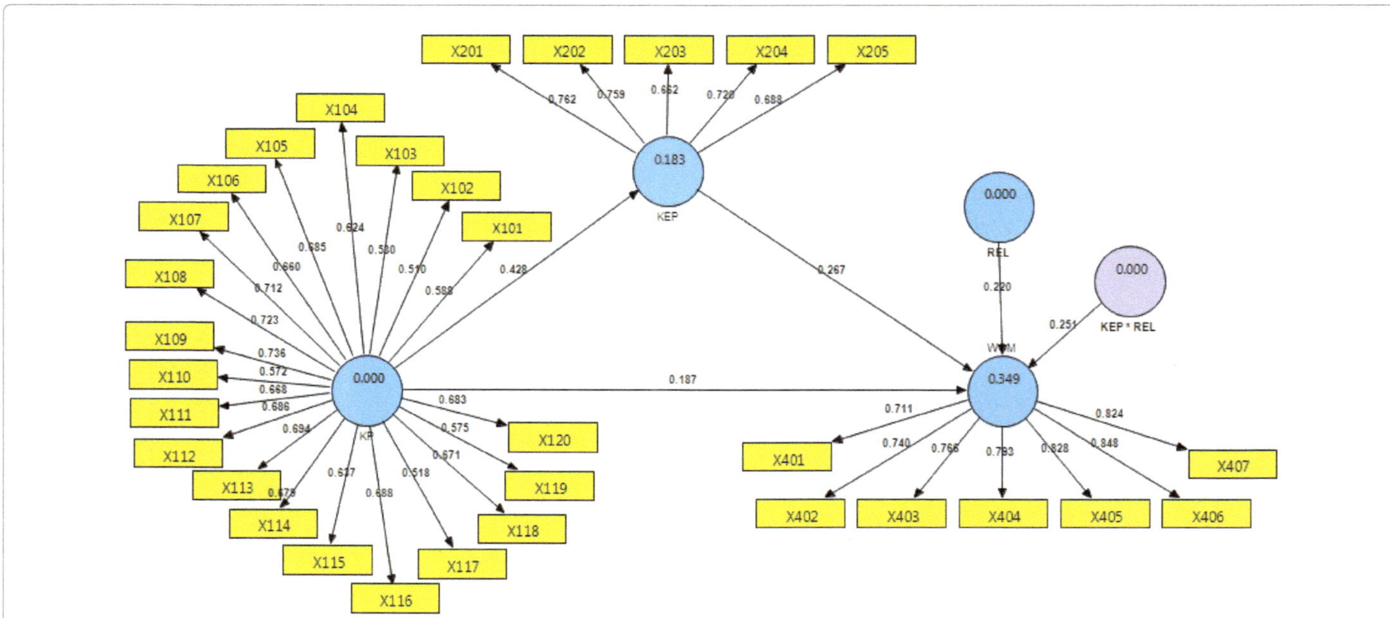

Figure 2: Diagram of Bootstrapping structural model.

2.3) *Word of mouth*

$$WOM=0{,}711X_{401} + 0{,}740X_{402} + 0{,}766X_{403} + 0{,}793X_{404} + 0{,}828X_{405} + 0{,}848X_{406} + 0{,}824X_{407}$$

d. Evaluation of goodness of fit criteria

1) ***Evaluation of measurement model (outer model)***

1.1) *Convergent validity:* The results of convergent validity analysis as in Table 1 show that all indicators of latent variables have a correlation coefficient more than 0.50. It means that all indicators of latent variables are valid as a tool to get information from respondents. Therefore, all the indicators of each latent variable statistically meets the requirements of convergent validity and valid for measuring service quality, satisfaction and WOM.

1.2) *Discriminant validity:* Discriminant validity is to measure that each indicator is a good comparator for latent variable. Indicators regarded as a good comparator if the value of cross loading greater than 0:50. Discriminant validity analysis results as in Table 2 show that all indicators of service quality, satisfaction, and WOM has cross loading greater than 0.50. Statistically all indicators considered valid, so the indicators of three latent variables are a good comparator.

Discriminant validity can also be measured by the value of the root AVE. The results of the root of AVE analysis can be seen in Table 3

Indicators considered valid if the root AVE value greater than 0.50. The value of root AVE service quality, satisfaction and WOM is greater than 0.50, which means all the latent variables meet the criteria of discriminant validity. This may imply that the measurement variable has a low correlation with variables that predicted nothing to do.

1.3) *Composite reliability:* Composite reliability function is to test the reliability of composite indicator which is reflection of latent variables in the model. Composite reliability analysis results can be seen in Table 4.

Latent variables stated reliable if the reliability value of the composite more than 0.60. The analysis showed that the composite value of each latent variable is more than 0.70. This means that each has fulfilled the criteria latent variable composite reliability and highly reliable.

2) *Evaluation of structural model (Inner model)*

GOF evaluation structural model of the inner model using R square whose function is to see the significance of latent variables. As for seeing the relevance of the predictions of endogenous latent variables and indicators reflection by looking at Q square value, where the endogenous variables are said to have a good relevance if the Q square value greater than 0. R square value generated through bootstrapping Smart PLS analysis and the results can be seen in Table 5.

Indicators	SQ	SAT	WOM	Status
X_{101}	0.5884			Valid
X_{102}	0.5096			Valid
X_{103}	0.5296			Valid
X_{104}	0.6237			Valid
X_{105}	0.6853			Valid
X_{106}	0.66			Valid
X_{107}	0.7122			Valid
X_{108}	0.7233			Valid
X_{109}	0.736			Valid
X_{110}	0.5721			Valid
X111	0.6681			Valid
X_{112}	0.6858			Valid
X_{113}	0.6936			Valid
X_{114}	0.6792			Valid
X_{115}	0.6366			Valid
X_{116}	0.6876			Valid
X_{117}	0.5177			Valid
X_{118}	0.6708			Valid
X_{119}	0.5753			Valid
X_{120}	0.6834			Valid
X_{201}		0.7618		Valid
X_{202}		0.7586		Valid
X_{203}		0.6622		Valid
X_{204}		0.7201		Valid
X_{205}		0.6879		Valid
X_{401}			0.7108	Valid
X_{402}			0.74	Valid
X_{403}			0.7664	Valid
X_{404}			0.7926	Valid
X_{405}			0.8277	Valid
X_{406}			0.8481	Valid
X_{407}			0.8243	Valid

Table 3: Cross loading. Source: Smart PLS Bootstrapping, 2016.

Variabel Laten	AVE	Akar AVE	Cut off	Keterangan
KP	0.6795	0.6454	0.5	Valid
KEP	0.5172	0.7192	0.5	Valid
WOM	0.6218	0.7885	0.5	Valid

Table 4: Average Variance Extracted (AVE). Source: Smart PLS Algorithm, 2016.

R square is the coefficient of determination that is the ability of a construct to explain the model. R-square for satisfaction is 0.232, it demonstrates the ability of service quality to explain the satisfaction as for 23.2% and 76.8% remaining is explained by other variables never analyzed in this model. The R square WOM for 0.296 shows the ability of satisfaction in explaining WOM as for 29.6%, while 70.4% is influenced by other variables never analyzed in the model. Using R square value of satisfaction and WOM, then the resulting Q square value of 0.4683. The Q square value is greater than zero, so that the structural model has predictive relevance which is able to measure both the value of the observation models and parameter estimation.

3. *Hypothesis testing*

a. *Effect of service quality and satisfaction on WOM:* To test the significance of the effect of exogenous variables on the endogenous variables seen from the inner coefficient models. Said inner coefficient models significantly if the t statistic or t-test every latent variable is greater than t-table value (1.96) at 0:05 alpha. T value on the structural model or the path diagram modeling results lies in the direction of the arrows connecting the exogenous variables of service quality with satisfaction endogenous latent variables, latent variable exogenous latent variable service quality with WOM endogenous and exogenous latent variable of satisfaction with endogenous latent variable WOM. Inner models show the meaningfulness of the relationship between the latent variables is used to test the research hypothesis. The study hypothesis was tested by comparing the value of the t statistic with a value of t table with the criteria if the value of the t statistic is greater than t table then the hypothesis is supported, and otherwise the hypothesis is not supported. Summary results of the analysis of the inner workings of the model shown by the path coefficients as set forth in Table 6.

The results of the analysis of inner models generate path coefficient is used to test the hypothesis of influence between exogenous and endogenous. To test the hypothesis service quality effect on WOM views of the coefficient paths service quality on WOM. The path coefficient was 0.1866, and significant at alpha 0.05 because the value of t statistics 3.5021 is greater than t table 1.96. This indicates the services quality has a significant positive effect on WOM. Thus the hypothesis which states that service quality effect on WOM supported.

Testing the hypothesis affect service quality on satisfaction is determined by the path coefficients and significance. Magnitude

Latent	Composite Reliability	Cut off	Information
KP	0.8423	0.7	Reliable
KEP	0.9127	0.7	Reliable
WOM	0.9339	0.7	Reliable

Table 5: Composite reliability. Source: SmartPLS Bootstrapping, 2016.

Path	R Square	Original Sample (O)/Koefisien Parameter	T Statistics (|O/STERR|)
KP → WOM	0	0.1866	3.5021
KP → KEP	0.1833	0.4281	4.9006
KEP → WOM	0.349	0.2673	2.837

Table 6: R Square. Source: Smart PLS Bootstrapping, 2016.

coefficient the path is significant at alpha 0.4281 and 0.05 for the value of t statistics 4.9006 greater than t table value of 1.96. This indicates that services quality has a significant positive effect on satisfaction. Thus the hypothesis that stated affects service quality on satisfaction is supported.

Testing the hypothesis effect satisfaction on WOM is determined by the path coefficients and significance. The path coefficient is 0.2673 and significant at alpha 0.05 for the value of t statistics of 2.837 is greater than t table 1.96. This indicates that satisfaction has a significant effect on WOM. Thus the hypothesis that satisfaction has an effect on WOM is supported.

b. *Moderating effect*: To examine the moderating of religiosity in the influence of satisfaction on WOM it is necessary to test the relationships between constructs. It is intended to obtain path coefficients between latent constructs. The result of the relationship between service quality and WOM can be seen from the estimated path coefficient and levels of significance as in Tables 7 and 8.

The first analysis was done without involving the moderator variables of religiosity in relationship path between latent variables. Analysis results showed that the path coefficient linking service quality and WOM is 0.1866 and significant, since the value of the t statistic is 1.9747 greater than t table 1.96 at the 0.05 error level. That is, the quality of services and significant positive effect on WOM. Thus the hypothesis which stated that service quality effect on WOM supported.

Coefficient path which is connecting service quality and satisfaction is 0.4281 and significant, since the value of the t statistic 4.9006 is greater than t table value at 1.96 with 0.05 error level. That is, services quality has a positive and significant effect on satisfaction. Thus the hypothesis that stated service quality has an effect on satisfaction is supported.

Coefficient path which is connecting satisfaction and WOM is 0.2673 and significant, since the t statistic value of 2,837 greater than t table value at 1.96 with 0.05 error level. That is, the customer satisfaction and significant positive effect on WOM. Thus the hypothesis stated satisfaction has a direct effect on WOM supported.

The second analysis is to examine religiosity as a moderator variable on the relationship between satisfaction and WOM. The analysis resulted path coefficient of 0.2511 and t statistics value of 0763 is smaller than 1.96 or insignificant. That is, religiosity did not significantly moderate the influence of satisfaction on WOM. Thus the hypothesis that religiosity moderates the effect of satisfaction on WOM is not supported.

Path	Original sample (O)	T Statistics (|O/STERR|)	Significance
KP → WOM	0.1866	3.5021	Significant
KP → KEP	0.4281	4.9006	Significant
KEP → WOM	0.2673	2.837	Significant

Table 7: Path coefficient. Source: Smart PLS Bootstrapping, 2016.

Path	Original Sample (O)	T Statistics (|O/STERR|)	Significance
KP → WOM	0.1866	1.9747	Sig
KP → KEP	0.4281	4.9006	Sign
KEP → WOM	0.2673	2.837	Sig
KEP × REL → WOM	0.2511	0.7631	Not Sig

Table 8: Path coefficient. Source: Smart PLS bootstrapping, 2016.

Results and Discussion

Analyzing of the first hypotheses indicated service quality at UMM and UNISMA has a positive effect on students done marketing communication through WOM. It means better service quality at UMM and UNISMA will more motivated students to inform a positive thing about the college to others. Improvements of service quality to the students will be able to encourage students to recommend or induce others to study at UMM and UNISMA.

The results support the findings of Babin et al., which indicated that service quality has a positive effect on WOM. The results also supported other studies, such as Bruce and Edgington, De Matos and Rossi, and Ferguson et al. were indicated that service quality has a positive effect on word of mouth. In the college perspective, the results support the findings of Herman, conch, and Abdullah that the higher education quality has a significant effect on the students' willingness to recommend others through WOM and the superior service quality positively increasing the word of mouth feedback.

Some reasons underlying the service quality has a significant and positive effect on WOM is derived from most respondent's responses that service quality at UMM and UNISMA meet their expectations. Most respondents considered that UMM and UNISMA had modern equipment for lecturing, luxuries campus buildings, lectures have good performance appearance, and campus facilities reflect the superior service.

In terms of reliability dimension, most responded UMM and UNISMA lecturers are always kept their promises, their science are qualified, always provided timely service, and able to deal with the problem of students' academic accurately. In terms of the dimensions of responsiveness, the majority of respondents consider that the lecturers of UMM and UNISMA always gave assurance of time service, provide faster service, concern to help students deal with academic problems and always ready to answer students' questions.

In terms of assurance dimension, most respondents considered that lecturers of UMM and UNISMA always trustworthy, always gives a sense of security, always consistent in being polite, and knowledgeable in answering questions. In terms of dimension of empathy, most respondents stated that UMM lecturers and UNISMA always give personal attention to students, always concerned with the difficulties experienced by students in the learning process, and always gives an honest concern on students.

The second hypothesis test results show that service quality has a significant and positive effect on student satisfaction. It's indicated that service quality has been satisfying UMM and UNISMA students. In other words, the more service quality of UMM and UNISMA the more student satisfaction. So, the key to building a sense of satisfaction students is UMM and UNISMA should continuously and sincerely to improve superior service quality from time to time.

The results of this study support the research Cronin et al., Hermawan, Keong, as well as Danjuma and Rasli, which indicated the quality of higher education, has a significant effect on student satisfaction. Meanwhile, this study does not support the results of research conducted by Gill and White, Wu [45], Markovic and Jankovic, as well as Fatima and Razzaque. Their results indicated that not all quality dimensions have a significant effect on satisfaction and quality of service as an exogenous variable was not able to provide customer satisfaction in several different research objects.

Some of the reasons underlying a significant effect service quality on satisfaction are derived from a variety of respondents. Most of the respondents were satisfied with the decision in choosing UMM and UNISMA and satisfied with good service. Students are also satisfied with academic program, as well as students settle into UMM and UNISMA.

The third hypothesis stated that satisfaction effect on WOM is supported. The analysis showed that satisfaction has a significant and positive effect on WOM. It's indicate that students satisfaction motivate them for communicating the institutions to others through WOM voluntarily. Thus, students who feel satisfied during their study at UMM and UNISMA will be compelled to say good things and recommend and persuade other people to choose UMM and UNISMA.

The results support research conducted by Babin et al., Bruce and Edgington, Casalo et al., Chaniotakis and Lymperopoulos, there are a direct relationship between satisfaction and WOM intention. But the results of this study do not support Wirtz and Chew Brown et al., Li, Naik, Anand, and Bashir were indicated a positive relationship between consumer satisfaction and WOM. Thus, in terms of UMM and UNISMA, students who satisfied with their decision will be motivated to voluntarily told others about good things of UMM and UNISMA.

Path analysis showed that religiosity does not significantly moderate the influence of satisfaction on WOM. It means that religiosity does not moderate the influence of satisfaction on WOM. In other words, students' religiosity did not able to strengthen WOM marketing communications even though they have been satisfied with service quality at UMM and UNISMA.

The results of this study do not support a finding Budiman [46] that religiosity moderating the intention of buying a pirated bag, as well as the findings Vitell and Paolillo [47], and Kurpis et al. [48-55] which indicated person religiosity can push a positive effect on ethical behavior. Religiosity that exists in students at private colleges Islamic religious background is not capable reinforce the students to do voluntary WOM marketing communications. Thus, both the higher education institutions in motivating students to perform WOM marketing communications simply by making the students feel satisfied with excellence service quality [56-58]. In other words, in a private college environment based on Islamic religion did not necessary to use a religiosity variable to leverage students' WOM marketing communications.

Conclusion

The service quality indicated has a positive effect on student's satisfaction and WOM marketing communications. The more service quality the more students satisfied and motivated to do voluntary WOM marketing communications. This indicates strongly that to encourage marketing communications through WOM by a student, the student must be given a more superior service in fulfilling their expectations.

Study also indicated that UMM and UNISMA's service quality had a direct impact to the students to do WOM marketing communication voluntarily. Student satisfaction has a direct positive effect on WOM marketing communications. The direct effect between latent variables indicated that students' satisfaction mediates the relationship between service quality and WOM marketing communications. Therefore, for future studies proposed to analyze the role of satisfaction as a mediator variable in the relationship between service quality and WOM marketing communications.

Students' religiosity at UMM and UNISMA did not able to strengthen WOM marketing communications although they were satisfied. This result indicated that even in the college environment based on Islamic religion, religious variables does not guarantee to bring automated students action to tell good things of institution. The important result in this study is students' religiosity cannot be played as a moderator variable to strengthen the spirit of UMM and UNISMA students to do WOM for the institution. In the neighborhood-based private colleges Islam, indicated that elements of religiosity cannot strengthen and are not able to contribute in improving the WOM marketing communications. Thus, religiosity cannot be played to strengthen the WOM marketing communications at UMM and UNISMA. For future research could examine the moderating role of religiosity in the relationship between service quality and WOM marketing communications at the college environment based private non-Islamic religion.

Inability religiosity of as moderating variable WOM marketing communications in Islamic higher education carried out a logical consequence that the variables such derived from religion are not necessarily able to support voluntarily activities. Thus the theoretical implications of this research are marketing through WOM communication can still be done without strengthening the non-material variable or variables derived from religion.

In practical terms, the management UMM and UNISMA can support their students who are satisfied to promote the campus to the community through WOM marketing communications. Service quality is the key factor of student satisfaction and encourages students doing marketing communication through WOM voluntarily. UMM management and UNISMA should be more concerned to regularly improving service quality to make student satisfaction increase and then they are more motivated to do WOM voluntarily.

References

1. Oetting M (2009) Ripple Effect: How Empowered Involvement Drives Word of Mouth, 1st Edition, Gabler, Wiesbaden, Germany.

2. Oetting M, Jacob F (2007) Empowered Involvement and Word of Mouth: An Agenda for Academic Inquiry, ESCP-EAP Working Paper 28: 1-28.

3. Money RB, Gilly MC, Graham JL (1998) Exploration of National Culture and Word-of-Mouth Behavior in the Purchase of Industrial Service in the USA and Japan. The Journal of Marketing 62: 76-87.

4. Gremler DD, Gwinner KP, Brown SW (2001) Generating Positive Word-of-Mouth Communication through Customer-Employee Relationships. International Journal of Service Industry Management 12: 44-59.

5. Dellarocas C (2003) The Digitization of Word of Mouth: Promise and Challenges of Online Feedback Mechanisms. Management Science 49: 1407-1424.

6. Sanayei A, Jokar A (2013) Determining the Effect of Electronic Services Quality on Electronic Satisfaction and Positive Word of Mouth (Case Study: Different Branches of Shiraz Mellat Bank Customers), International Journal of Academic Research in Accounting, Finance and Management Sciences. 3: 103-111.

7. Herr PM, Kardess FR, Kim J (1991) Effects of Word of Mouth and Product-Attribute Information on Persuasion: An Accessibility-Diagnostic Perspective. Journal of Consumer Research 17: 454-462.

8. Chevalier JA, Mayzlin D (2003) The Effect of Word of Mouth on Sales: Online Book Reviews, Working Paper. National Bureau of Economic Research.

9. Lee J, Park Do-H, Han I (2006) The Effect of Negative Online Consumer Reviews on Product Attitude: An Information Processing View. Electronic Commerce Research and Applications 7: 341-352.

10. Bruce G, Edgington R (2008) Factors Influencing Word-of-Mouth Recommendations by MBA Students: An Examination of School Quality, Educational Outcomes, and Value of the MBA. Journal of Marketing for Higher Education 18: 70-101.

11. Casalo LV, Flavian C, Guinaliu M (2008) The Role of Satisfaction and Website Usability in Developing Customer Loyalty and Positive Word of Mouth in the E-banking Service. The International Journal of Bank Marketing 26: 399-417.

12. Wangenheim F, Bayo´n T (2004) Satisfaction, Loyalty and Word of Mouth within the customer base of a utility provider: differences between stayers, switchers and referral switchers. Journal of Consumer Behaviour 3: 211-220.

13. Harrison-Walker LJ (2001) The Measurement of Word-of-Mouth Communication and an Investigation of Service. Journal of Service Research 4: 60-75.

14. De Matos CA, Rossi CAC (2008) Word-of-Mouth Communications in Marketing: A Meta-Analytic Review of the Antecedents and Moderators. Journal of the Academic Marketing Science 36: 578-596.

15. Mangold WG, Miller F, Brockway GR (1999) Word-of-mouth communication in the service marketplace. Journal of Services Marketing 13: 73-89.

16. Swanson SR, Kelley SW (2001) Service recovery attributions and word of mouth intentions. European Journal of Marketing 35: 194-211.

17. Laczniak RN, De Carlo TE, Ramaswami SN (2001) Consumers' Responses to Negative Word-of-Mouth Communication: An Attribution Theory Perspective. Journal of Consumer Psychology 11: 57-73.

18. Babin BJ, Lee YK, Kim EJ, Griffin M (2005) Modeling Consumer Satisfaction and Word of Mouth: Restaurant Patronage in Korea. Journal of Services Marketing 19: 133-139.

19. Chaniotakis IE, Lymperopoulos C (2009) Service Quality Effect on Satisfaction dan Word of Mouth in the Health Care Industry. Journal of Managing Service Quality 19: 229-242.

20. Bansal HS, Voyer PA (2000) Word of Mouth Processes within a Services Purchase Decision Context. Journal of Service Research 3: 166-177.

21. Ennew CT, Banerjee AK, Li (2000) Managing Word of Mouth Communication: Empirical Evidence from India. International Journal of Bank Marketing 18: 75-83.

22. Folkes VS (1988) Recent Attribution Research in Consumer Behavior: A Review and New Directions. The Journal of Consumer Research 14: 548-565.

23. Wirtz J, Chew P (2002) The Effect of Incentives, Deal Proneness, Satisfaction and Tie Strength on Word-of-Mouth Behaviour. International Journal of Service Industry Management 13: 141-162.

24. Brown TJ, Barry TE, Dacin PA, Gunst RF (2005) Spreading the Word: Investigating Antecedents of Consumers' Positive Word-of-Mouth Intentions and Behaviors in Retailing Context. Academy of Marketing Science 33: 123-138.

25. Li SC (2013) Exploring the Relationships among Service Quality, Customer Loyalty and Word-Of-Mouth for Private Higher Education in Taiwan. Asia Pacific Management Review 18: 375-389.

26. Naik JRK, Anand B, Bashir I (2013) Healthcare Service Quality and Word of Mouth: Key Drivers to Achieve Patient Satisfaction. Pacific Business Review International 5: 39-44.

27. Tafsir (2009) Simpang Jalan Muhammadiyah. MAARIF 4: 20-44.

28. Jones E, Nisbett R (1972) The actor and the observer: Divergent perceptions of the causes of behavior. In: Jones EE (ed.) Attribution: Perceiving the causes of behavior, General Learning Press, Morristown, New Jersey, United States of America.

29. Weiner B (2000) Attributional thoughts about consumer behavior. The Journal of Consumer Research 27: 382-387.

30. Burnkrant RE (1975) Teori Atribusi Dalam Penelitian Pemasaran: Masalah Dan Prospek, Asosiasi Consumer Research 465-470.

31. Wang, Yong J (2008) The application of attribution theories in marketing research: A Critique. Review of Business Research 8: 174-181.

32. Athanassopoulos A, Gounaris S, Stathakopoulos V (2001) Behavioural Responses to Customer Satisfaction: an Empirical Study. European Journal of Marketing 35: 687-707.

33. Chen Y, Xie J (2008) Online Consumer Review: Word-of-Mouth as a New Element of Marketing Communication Mix. Management Science 54: 477-491.

34. Padma P, Rajendran C, Sai LP (2009) A Conceptual Framework of Service Quality in Healthcare Perspectives of Indian Patients and Their Attendants, Benchmarking: An International Journal 16: 157-191.

35. Hermawan A (2001) The Effect of Service Cues on Perceived Service Quality, Value, Satisfaction And Word of Mouth Recommendations in Indonesian University Settings, A Dissertation, Wayne Huizenga Graduate School of Business and Entrepreneurship Nova South-eastern University, USA.

36. Abdullah F (2006) Measuring Service Quality in Higher Education: Three Instruments Compared. International Journal of Research & Method in Education 29: 71-89.

37. Duggirala M, Rajendran C, Anantharaman RN (2008) Patient-Perceived Dimensions of Total Quality Service in Healthcare. Benchmarking: An International Journal 15: 560-583.

38. Cronin JJ Jr, Brady MK, Brand RR, Hightower R Jr, Shemwell DJ (2000) A Cross-Sectional test of the effect and conceptualization of service value. The Journal of Services Marketing 11: 375-391.

39. Danjuma I, Rasli A (2012) Factors Affecting Service Quality in Nigerian Technological Universities. International Journal of Business and Management Tomorrow 2: 1-11.

40. Keong RTC (2006) Word-of-Mouth: The Effect of Service Quality, Customer Satisfaction and Commitment In A Commercial Education Context, Thesis for the Degree of Doctor of Philosophy, Graduate School of Management, University of Western Australia.

41. Ahmad SNB, Awadzb AS, Musac NC, Juhdid N (2012) Understanding The Relationship of Relational Satisfaction, Students University Identification and Positive Word of Mouth Intentions Among Students of Tun Abdul Razak University. Journal of Modern Marketing Research 1: 27-41.

42. Bloodgood JM, Turnley WH, Mudrack P (2008) The Influence of Ethics Instruction, Religiosity, and Intelligence on Cheating Behavior. Journal of Business Ethics 82: 557-571.

43. La Barbera, Priscilla A, Gurhan Z (1997) The Role of Materialism, Religiosity, and Demographics in Subjective Well-Being. Psychology & Marketing 14: 71-97.

44. Ariffin ZZ, Othman MN, Karim JA (2012) Relationship between American popular culture and conspicuous consumption: A moderating effect of religiosity. African Journal of Business Management 6: 9969-9988.

45. Wu KW (2011) Customer Loyalty Explained by Electronic Recovery Service Quality: Implications of the Customer Relationship Re-Establishment for Consumer Electronics E-Tailers. Contemporary Management Research 7: 21-44.

46. Budiman S (2012) Analysis of Consumer Attitudes to Purchase Intentions of Counterfeiting Bag Product in Indonesia. International Journal of Management, Economics and Social Sciences 1: 1-12.

47. Vitell SJ, Paolillo JGP (2003) Consumer Ethics: The Role of Religiosity. Journal of Business Ethics 46: 151-162.

48. Kurpis LV, Beqiri MS, Helgeson JG (2008) The Effects of Commitment to Moral Self-improvement and Religiosity on Ethics of Business Students. Journal of business ethics 80: 447-463.

49. Brown RM, Mazzarol TW (2009) The Importance of Institutional Image to Student Satisfaction and Loyalty Within Higher Education, Higher Education 58: 81-95.

50. Kelley HH, Michela JL (1980) Attribution Theory and Research, Annual Review Psychology 31: 457-501.

51. Ladhari R (2009) Service quality, emotional satisfaction, and behavioral intentions: A study in the hotel industry. Managing Service Quality 19: 308-331.

52. Molinari LK, Abratt R, Dion P (2008) Satisfaction, Quality and Value and Effects on Repurchase and Positive Word-of-Mouth Behavioral Intentions in A B2B Services Context. Journal of Services Marketing 22: 363-373.

53. Park DH, Kim S (2008) The Effects of Consumer Knowledge on Message Processing of Electronic Word-of-Mouth Via Online Consumer Reviews. Electronic Commerce Research and Applications 7: 399-410.

54. Ranaweera C, Prabhu J (2003) On the Relative Importance of Customer Satisfaction and Trust as Determinants of Customer Retention and Positive Word of Mouth. Journal of Targeting, Measurement and Analysis for Marketing 12: 82-90.

55. Vitell SJ, Singh JJ, Paolillo J (2007) Consumers' Ethical Beliefs: The Roles of Money, Religiosity and Attitude toward Business. Journal of Business Ethics 73: 369-379.

56. Vitell SJ, Bing MN, Davison HK, Ammeter AP, Garner BL, et al. (2009) Religiosity and Moral Identity: The Mediating Role of Self-Control. Journal of Business Ethics 88: 601-613.

57. Waemusor A (2010) The Relationship between perceived Islamic bank corporate social responsibility based customer service and customer satisfaction: The role of religiosity as a Moderator, Master Thesis, Universiti Sains Malaysia.

58. Wan Ahmad WM, Rahman AA, Ali NA, Seman AC (2008) Religiosity and Banking Selection Criteria Among Malays in Lembah Klang. Shariah Journal 16: 279-304.

The Theory and Models of Keynesian Disequilibrium Macroeconomics

Tianhao Zhi*

School of Business, The University of Technology, Sydney, New South Wales, Australia

Abstract

This paper critically reviews and examines the relationship between the origin of disequilibrium macroeconomic thinking by John Maynard Keynes, and the development of Keynesian disequilibrium macroeconomic models. Given that the two strands of literature are both plentiful, I will focus on discussing the essence of Keynesian disequilibrium thinking, and its implications of relevant models in the context of Keynes-Metzler-Goodwin and Weidlich-Haag-Lux approaches.

Keywords: Disequilibrium macroeconomics; Nonlinear economic dynamics; John Maynard Keynes; Hyman Minsky

JEL classification: B22; E5; E12; G21.

Introduction

This paper examines the interplay between the origin of disequilibrium macroeconomic thinking from John Maynard Keynes in his *General Theory*, and the subsequent development of Keynesian disequilibrium macroeconomic models. Given that these two strands of literature are both plentiful, I will focus on the essence of Keynes's disequilibrium thinking, and discuss how it influences the development of relevant disequilibrium macroeconomic models, mainly in the context of deterministic nonlinear dynamics of Keynes-Metzler-Goodwin and Weidlich-Haag-Lux approaches.

Disequilibrium macroeconomics was originally envisioned by Keynes [1]. It had once enjoyed a brief popularity in the 1970s since Leijonhufvud [2] published his famous book "On Keynesian Economics and the Economics of Keynes"[1]. Yet it had almost disappeared in the 1980s due to the popularization of theory of rational expectations and the emergence of Neo-classical synthesis.

Yet it becomes apparent in the aftermath of the 2007-2008 GFC and the subsequent world-wide recession that disequilibrium macroeconomics offers a better explanation about macroeconomic instability. Indeed, Keynes wrote the *General Theory* nearly 80 years ago in his effort to explain the Great Depression. Although his analytical framework was static in nature, he had in mind a dynamic theory, since disequilibrium is essential in understanding Keynes's *General Theory*: saving and investment are independently determined; wages and prices are rigid in the short run; and expectations are formed by the self-fulfilling sentiments and herd mentality. Later on, Minsky deepens Keynes's analysis by emphasizing the crucial role of finance in propagating macroeconomic instability.

On the other hand, the development of theories in non-linear dynamics provides a mathematical backbone for the study of disequilibrium macroeconomic models. Three areas are of particular importance: *(i)* the seminal work of Poincare [3], originally applied in the study of celestial mechanics, which had laid the foundation for the modern qualitative-geometric approach to the analysis of non-linear dynamical systems; *(ii)* the development of Bifurcation Theory, especially the Hopf Bifurcation theorem [4]; *(iii)* the discovery of chaos in deterministic dynamic system [5,6]. The use of Hopf bifurcation theorem to demonstrate the existence of a limit cycle, as a parameter of interest passes through a critical bifurcation point, has been widely applied in numerous fields in natural science. To a lesser degree in economics, it is applied in identifying and modelling endogenous business cycles of various kind[2]; the discovery of deterministic chaos, characterized by the irregular fluctuations in the Lorenz system, had inspired the study of complexity economics, which looks into the emergence of complex phenomena as a result of local interactions of heterogeneous agents with simple, deterministic laws - mimicking many complex phenomena observed in reality such as herd behaviour.

An important use of disequilibrium macroeconomic models is to understand the dynamic and heterogeneous interactions amongst the core sectors of the aggregate economy, in order to see which parameters are stabilizing or destabilizing, and which parameters, particularly parameters that are associated with policy interventions such as Tobin-type taxes, have the most influence in switching the economy between the regions of stability and instability, thus offering us an insight over the effectiveness of policy interventions in qualitative terms. In the context of deterministic models, the term "stability" (or "instability") refers to the local properties of the steady state, and the existence of transition from stability to instability (in the form of persistent, self-sustaining fluctuation) can be mathematically formulated and proven with the use of *Hopf bifurcation theorem*. Given its aggregative nature, this type of models is sometimes coined "macro-founded". It offers a particular advantage over the traditional "micro-founded" models of stochastic intertemporal optimization type such as RBC or New-Keynesian DSGE models, which are difficult to be analyzed in terms of the dynamic linkages and feedbacks between various sectors of the macro-economy [7].

This paper expounds two fundamental approaches of modelling Keynesian disequilibrium macro-dynamics: the Keynes-Metzler-Goodwin (KMG) approach and the Weidlich-Haag-Lux (WHL) approach. These two approaches represent one of the most stylized and most recent development of Keynesian disequilibrium macro-dynamics. They are also probably the most relevant in addressing

[1]Leijonhufvud is perhaps the first author that interprets Keynes in terms of disequilibrium phenomena. He argues that the traditional IS/LM formulation of Keynes's theory fails to explain phenomena such as "involuntary unemployment", which is central for Keynes's explanation of unemployment and depression. Leijonhufvud advocates a "cybernetic" approach to macroeconomics where the dynamic adjustments of prices and quantities are explicitly considered without imposing the standard Walrasian equilibrium concept.

[2]See [29] for detailed discussion.

***Corresponding author:** Tianhao Zhi, School of Business, The University of Technology, Sydney, New South Wales, Australia
E-mail: Tianhao.Zhi@student.uts.edu.au, tianhao.zhi@outlook.com

Leijonhufvud's critique of standard IS-LM interpretation of Keynes that lacked disequilibrium phenomena. The KMG model is formulated by Chiarella and Flaschel [8] and later on, Chiarella et al. [7]. "Keynes" refers to the disequilibrium between savings and investment, the sticky adjustment of prices and wages, and the causal nexus from financial to real markets; "Metzler" to inventory dynamics and "Goodwin" to the dynamics of distributive shares. It synthesizes and extends the disequilibrium macro-dynamic models in the 1960s and 1970s in a systematic and hierarchial manner. The interaction of three agents (households, firms, and government) across five markets (labour market, goods market, money market, bond market, and equities market) are considered. On the other hand, the WHL approach attempts to model the dynamics of "animal spirits". It is originally inspired by earlier work of Weidlich and Haag [9] that models the interacting population dynamics. Lux [10], in his seminal work, studies how herd behaviour and sentiment contagion contributes to asset price bubbles/crashes. The framework is further applied in Franke [11] and Charpe et al. [12], which study the dynamics of "animal spirits" and real-financial interaction in a macroeconomic setting.

The rest of the paper is organized as follows: section 4 traces back to the origin of Keynes's disequilibrium macroeconomic thinking, as well as Minsky's interpretation of Keynes. Section 5 introduces the modelling of Keynesian disequilibrium macroeconomic models in terms of KMG and WHL approaches, particularly the latter one. Section 6 concludes with a discussion regarding the interplay between these two strands of literature. It also paves a few path for future research.

The Origin of Disequilibrium Macroeconomic Thinking

The second half of the 19th century and the beginning of the 20th century had witnessed an increasing instability of capitalism, in the form of more severe economic crises and an increasing number of bankruptcies. The worsening macroeconomic instability culminates in the "Black Thursday" on the 24th of October, 1929 and the subsequent Great Depression of the 1930s, which is marked as the most prolonged and severe depression of the 20th century.

Classical economists at that time, however, believed that crises would not occur, and full employment is guaranteed due to the self-adjusting market. They based their analysis on the Say's law: goods produced will be be sold since "supply creates its own demand". Saving from household always equals business investment. Furthermore, wages and prices are assumed to be highly flexible. The increase of product prices will quickly be matched by a rise of costs, which eliminates the incentive to expand output. The belief of Say's law, coupled with the assumption of flexible price, insures that business will be able to sell their goods to either consumers or investment; full-employment is automatically maintained, as long as there is no involuntary unemployment - workers are always willing to work at any wages.

The Great Depression is clearly a significant event that had casted doubt over the myth of the self-adjusting markets. The Classical doctrines had outlived its ideological usefulness in explaining the severe depression. When it came to policy recommendations, the Classical economists could recommend nothing but a general cut in all wages. It was obvious that unconventional policies were needed to restore aggregate demand and business confidence on a scale that could only be achieved by a drastic government intervention [13].

The "disequilibrium" thinking of John Maynard Keynes

Keynes's *General Theory* was born out of the need to understand and explain the Great Depression. In a nutshell, Keynes made his departure from the Classical doctrine mainly in three aspects:

- The rejection of Say's law;
- The rejection of flexible wages and price;
- "Animal spirits".

The first departure of Keynes's analysis lies in his rejection from the Say's law. While Say's law says "supply creates its own demand", Keynes runs the causation other way around. Keynes believes that an active management of aggregate demand by means of monetary and fiscal policy is crucial in maintaining full employment. Otherwise involuntary employment would occur and the economy would reach a sub-optimal equilibrium, prevailing with prolonged unemployment. With regard to interest rate determination, Keynes refutes the concept of self-adjusting interest rates mechanism driven by saving-investment equilibrium. He argues that saving does not necessarily equal to investment, since household income is the major determinant of saving; firms' investment decisions, on the other hand, are mainly determined by profit expectations. Interest rate is primarily determined by liquidity preference in the money market.

The second departure of Keynes's analysis, which is more received and becomes the main ingredient of the New-Keynesian macroeconomics, is his rejection of flexible price and wage assumption. Price would be rigid, or in a disequilibrium dynamical adjustment process due to the existence of monopoly and the resistance of workers for cutting wages.

Perhaps the most fundamental departure of Keynes's thinking from the Classical school lies in his view over how non-rational, psychological factors play a role in influencing human behaviours and propagating aggregate business cycles, due to the presence of radical uncertainty. Keynes coined the term "animal spirits" to address this aspect in *Chapter 12 - The State of Long-term Expectation*, in which he writes:

"Even apart from the instability due to speculation, there is the instability due to the characteristic of human nature that a large proportion of our positive activities depend on spontaneous optimism rather than mathematical expectations, whether moral or hedonistic or economic. Most, probably, of our decisions to do something positive, the full consequences of which will be drawn out over many days to come, can only be taken as the result of ***animal spirits*** *- a spontaneous urge to action rather than inaction, and not as the outcome of a weighted average of quantitative benefits multiplied by quantitative probabilities."*

Akerlof and Shiller [14], in their book "Animal Spirits: How Human Psychology Drives the Economy, and Why It Matters for Global Capitalism" goes further beyond and identifies five types of animal spirits: confidence, fairness, corruption, money illusion, and stories. This paper will, however, only focus on the confidence factor given its primary importance. Akerlof and Shiller used the term "Confidence Multiplier", which is borrowed from the concept of Keynesian consumption multiplier, in describing the self-fulfilling nature of confidence: on an individual level, an optimistic attitude leads to positive actions that reinforces the confidence; on an aggregate level, confidence is contagious in the form of herd-type behaviours. This is well depicted in Keynes's famous beauty contest metaphor:

"It is not a case of choosing those [faces] that, to the best of one's judgment, are really the prettiest, nor even those that average opinion genuinely thinks the prettiest. We have reached the third degree where

we devote our intelligences to anticipating what average opinion expects the average opinion to be. And there are some, I believe, who practice the fourth, fifth and higher degrees."

"Animal spirit" alludes to a state in disequilibrium - a constant deviation of human expectations and behaviours from the ones being rationally determined. It is crucial in Keynes's explanation of economic expansion and recession: a state of over-optimism leads to inflated asset prices, over-investment and over-consumption, as well as over-expansion of credit in the financial sector, which eventually leads to its own defeat.

Although Keynes's theory is conservative in nature: his analytical framework does not deviate from the Walrasian general equilibrium theory, the three aspects of Keynes's disequilibrium thinking had clearly paved a path for the emergence of disequilibrium macroeconomics during the 1960s[1], and later on, inspired the work of Hyman Minsky.

Minsky's interpretation of Keynes

"Keynesian economics as the economics of disequilibrium is the economics of permanent disequilibrium."

Minsky HP [15].

It is the work of Hyman Minsky that brings a new light over a conventional, Hicksian IS/LM interpretation of Keynes's General Theory. Minsky views Keynes's theory as an endogenous theory of business cycle that explicitly considers the crucial role of the financial instability in propagating macroeconomic fluctuations, as he writes in his famous book "John Maynard Keynes":

"The missing step in the standard Keynesian theory is the explicit consideration of capitalist finance within a cyclical and speculative context...finance sets the pace for the economy. As recovery approaches full employment...soothsayers will proclaim that the business cycle has been banished and debts can be taken on...But in truth neither the boom, nor the debt deflation...and certainly not a recovery can go on forever. Each state nurtures forces that lead to its own destruction."

The instability and interconnection between the real and financial sector lies mainly in two aspects in Minsky's analysis: *(i)* the role of speculative and Ponzi borrowers[2]; *(ii)* the role of financial institutions. The first aspect is elaborated in Minsky's well-known "Financial Instability Hypothesis". Minsky argues that stability is inherently unstable: the economic boom in the preceding period nurtures a self-fulfilling sense of optimism that leads to an increasing portion of speculative and Ponzi borrowers in the financial market. However, the speculative boom cannot last forever. The "Minsky moment" occurs when investors are over-indebted. As they start to sell off their asset in order to meet debt repayments, asset price turns south. Consequently, the financial sector transits from stability to instability. Over the course of business cycle, it is the expansionary phase that ultimately leads to its own destruction. The financial and real cycles are inherently interconnected.

The second aspect, however, is more or less implicit in Minsky's discussion[3]. Financial institutions, particularly banks, play a crucial role in propagating credit cycle, since banks create money by creating loans that simultaneously create deposits, as is discussed by Minsky's predecessor Joseph Schumpeter and Knut Wicksell. Specifically, Minsky stresses on the role of banker's confidence over the state of credit, as he wrote:

"The state of credit reflects banker's view toward borrowers...A revision by banker of their views about the appropriate leverage to use in financing positions in capital assets will not necessarily cause an immediate revision in the market value of these assets...But such a revision of bankers' views can have a strong impact upon equity prices."

This aspect is further developed by Minsky's followers, in the Post-Keynesian literature of endogenous money theory. It can be generally categorized into three groups: the horizontalist approach, the structuralist approach, and the state money approach [16]. Horizontalist approach is initially advocated by Basil Moore[4] in the 1970s and 1980s that stresses the endogenous nature of money and reserves, arguing that "loans make deposits, deposits make reserves". Structuralists, which had emerged in 1990s and advocated by Charles Goodhart[5], on the other hand, take a more active role of banks' lending behaviour, given the profit-seeking nature of banks. The state money approach, advocated by Wray [17] and Mosler [18] amongst several other so-called *"neo-chartalists"*, agrees upon most aspects of the horizontalist and structuralist proposition. Yet it stresses the mechanism of fiat money system of the public sector and studies the macroeconomic impacts of taxation and government deficit from an accounting perspective. In a historical context, Charles [19] vividly depicts the boom/bust of credit cycles and the subsequent economic expansions/recessions over a course of historical events, which further vindicates Minsky's insights over the role of financial institutions in propagating financial and macroeconomic instability.

To sum up, the disequilibrium thinking of Keynes involves four aspects:

1. Saving $\neq$ investment;
2. Price and wages rigidity;
3. "Animal spirits";
4. Financial instability and real-financial nexus.

Models of Keynesian disequilibrium macroeconomics

The Keynes-Metzler-Goodwin model

The three decades since 1960s had witnessed an emergence of literature in the mathematical modelling of disequilibrium monetary macro-dynamics, both in Neo-classical and Keynesian schools of thought. This strand of literature is further synthesized and extended by Chiarella and Flaschel [7] and Chiarella et al. [8] in the form of Neo-classical Tobinian model, the Keynes-Wicksell model, and the textbook Keynesian AS-AD model of Turnovsky [20] and Sargent [21]. It leads to the formulation of Keynes-Metzler-Goodwin (KMG) Model that overcomes several drawbacks of these previous model types.

The (neo)-classical discussion of monetary growth can be traced

[3]See [28] for a detailed survey over the development of disequilibrium macroeconomics during the 1960s.

[4] Minsky defines three categories of borrowers, *i.e.* the hedging borrower, whose current cash flow can serve both interest and principle; the speculative borrower, who can only serve the interest payable; and the Ponzi borrower, who thrives on an inflating asset price and has to rely on borrowing in order to pay back both interest and principle.

[5] See chapter six - "Financial Institutions, Financial Instability, and the Pase of Investment", of [15], "John Maynard Keynes".

[6]See [33].

[7]See [31].

back to Tobin [22,23] and its subsequent extensions[1]. In Tobinian model, money is typically considered as an asset in addition to real capital, and the money market disequilibrium is the core driving force behind inflation and inflationary expectations. Goods market, on the other hand, is assumed to follow the Say's Law and always stays in equilibrium (Saving = Investment). These features are captured in the following equations of a prototype Tobinian model of monetary growth[2]:

$$W = M/p + K, \tag{1}$$

$$I = S = Y - \delta K - C - G = \dot{K}, \tag{2}$$

$$\hat{w} = \beta_w (V - \bar{V}) + \kappa_w \hat{p} + (1 - \kappa_w)\pi, \tag{3}$$

$$\hat{p} = \beta_p \left(\frac{M - M^d}{pK}\right) + \eta\pi + (1 - \eta)(\mu_0 - n), \tag{4}$$

$$\dot{\pi} = \beta_{\pi_1}(\hat{p} - \pi) + \beta_{\pi_2}(\mu_0 - n - \pi), \tag{5}$$

where W is the real wealth, M is the money supply (index d : demand, growth rate μ_0), p is price, K is capital stock, I (S) is investment(saving), W is nominal wage, π is expected rate of inflation, V is the rate of employment, n is the natural growth rate, and βx, Kx, and η are the adjustment parameters.

The assumption of Say's Law, coupled with the role of monetary market disequilibrium in determining inflation are surely questionable features of the Tobin-type model from a Keynesian disequilibrium perspective. The Keynes-Wicksell model, which synthesizes Goodwin [24] and Rose [25], dispenses the Say's Law by introducing independently determined saving and investment functions, and uses both the Labour and Goods market disequilibrium as the cause of inflation, as is represented by the following equations:

$$W = (M + B + p_e E)/P, \tag{6}$$

$$S = Y - \delta K - C - G, \tag{7}$$

$$I = i(\rho - r + \pi)K + nK, \tag{8}$$

$$\hat{w} = \beta_w (V - \bar{V}) + \kappa_w \hat{p} + (1 - \kappa_w)\pi, \tag{9}$$

$$\hat{p} = \beta_p \left(\frac{I - S}{K}\right) + \kappa_p \hat{w} + (1 - \kappa_p)\pi, \tag{10}$$

Where p_e is the price of equities, ρ is the rate of profit, and r is the nominal rate of interest.

The wealth function now has two additional assets (private equity and government bond) that replace the capital (K) in the prototype Tobin model. Most importantly, the investment function is independently determined by the rate of profit, rather than the saving function.

The Keynes-Wicksell model, however, still suffers from an important drawback: it is a supply-side model, since full-capacity growth is assumed. It is a problematic feature since *(i)* the price adjusts sluggishly while the quantity adjust instantly; *(ii)* for a true "Keynesian" model it requires a detailed treatment on the demand-driven mechanism. It leads to the formulation of the Keynes-Metzler-Goodwin (KMG) model, which is derived from a more traditional IS-LM approach, yet with IS disequilibrium. The Metzlerian inventory dynamics is introduced to address the Saving-Investment disequilibrium. The demand-side dynamic multiplier, coupled with Metzlerian inventory dynamics, are captured by the following equations:

$$\dot{Y} = \gamma Y^e + \beta_{y^e}(Y^d - Y^e), \tag{11}$$

$$\dot{N} = Y - Y^d = S - I, \tag{12}$$

where Y^e is the expected aggregate demand and N is the stock of inventories.

In a stylized manner, the KMG model captures the Keynesian demand-side multiplier with saving-investment disequilibrium, the Metzlerian inventory dynamics, as well as the Goodwinian profit-squeeze mechanism. The formulation of KMG model is an important development toward a rigid mathematical formalization of Keyne's disequilibrium thinking: it provides a *"macro-foundation"* as a viable alternative to the more received *micro-founded* New-Keynesian model types.

Modelling the dynamics of "animal spirits"

An important drawback of the KMG model discussed in the previous section, is that it overlooks the "animal spirits" aspect of Keynesian disequilibrium thinking, which is essential in Keynes's explanation of business cycles. In part, this is due to the "macro-founded" nature of the KMG model that overlooks certain behavioural aspects at the micro level. Arguably, however, a true Keynesian model should take into account the dynamics of "animal spirits", *i.e.* how waves of optimism and pessimism of economic agents at micro level cause speculative and herd behaviours, which ultimately lead to fluctuations at macro level.

Modelling speculative behaviour: the "fundamentalist-chartist" approach

An emerging number of empirical studies in finance literature has found abnormality in asset prices in terms of the existence of serial correlations and excess volatilities, which casts doubts over the traditional asset pricing models of efficient market hypothesis and rational expectations school. It has inspired the development of Heterogeneous Agent Models (HAMs) that was initially aimed to study speculative behaviours in the financial market and later on, it has found applications to a broader scope of issues in Keynesian disequilibrium macroeconomics[3]. In this strand of literature, agents are typically categorized into two groups: the *fundamentalists* and the *chartists*. The fundamentalists represent the rational agents that provide a stabilizing force toward the fundamental price, whereas the chartists represent trend chasers that are self-fulfilling and destabilizing.

Beja and Goldman [26] is amongst the first work that takes this "fundamentalist-chartist" approach. The stabilizing fundamentalists' excess demand is driven by the deviation of actual price from the fundamental price, while the destabilizing chartists' excess demand is driven by the perceived historical price trends:

$$\dot{p} = D_t^f + D_t^c, \tag{13}$$

$$D_t^f = a(w - p), \tag{14}$$

$$D_t^c = b(\psi - g), \tag{15}$$

where D_t^f (D_t^c) is the excess demand of fundamentalists (chartists), W is the underlying equilibrium price, P is the current price, Ψ is the speculators' assessment of the price trend, and g is the opportunity

[8]See [34] for a detailed survey.

[9]The equations presented in the following sections only describe partial structure. See [8] for full descriptions of the model.

[10]See [32] for a detailed survey of HAMs.

growth rate of alternative investments in disequilibrium trading with comparable securities.

Modelling herd behaviour and "animal spirits": the Weidlich-Haag-Lux approach: In addition to the speculative behaviour captured by Beja and Goldman [26] type model at an individual level, herd behaviour is another important aspect of self-fulfilling animal spirits, at an aggregate level. The seminal work of Lux [10] is perhaps the first work that formalizes the dynamics of herd behaviour and mutual mimetic contagion in speculative financial market. This approach has its origin from social science in the earlier work of Weidlich and Haag, which attempts to model the interacting populations in a more general context. The basic idea of Weidlich-Haag-Lux approach is to model a population of agents that choose and switch between two attitudes in probabilistic terms. The agents interact with each other based on average opinion, as well as other non-herding factors. A Master equation that captures the average opinion as a mean-field variable is applied to simplify the analysis of the stochastic system. The Lux model also inspires numerous works in macroeconomics that incorporates "animal spirits" as the core driving factor of business fluctuations.

The basic set-up in Lux model is as follows: there are $2N$ speculative traders who hold either optimistic or pessimistic sentiment. There are n_+ number of optimists and n_- number of pessimists such that $n_+ + n_- = 2N$. Let $n \equiv 0.5(n_+ - n_-)$ and $x \equiv n / N$, we have an index $x \in [-1,1]$ that describes the average opinion of traders. Hence $x > 0 (< 0)$ corresponds to a situation of predominant optimism (pessimism).

The contagion process in Lux model is modelled in terms of transitory probability. Let p_{+-} be the probability that a pessimist would switch to an optimist, and likewise for p_{-+}. It is plausible that these two transitory probabilities will depend on the average opinion: a predominant optimism will lead to a higher likelihood that pessimists switch to optimists, and vice versa. Hence at any point in time we expect $n_- p_{+-}$ to switch from n_- n_+, while $n_+ p_{-+}$ to switch from n_+ to n_-. It follows that $dn_- / dt = n_- p_{+-} - n_- p_{-+}$ and $dn_- / dt = n_+ p_{-+} - n_- p_{+-}$. Since $n = 0.5(n_+ - n_-)$ and $x = n / N$, we obtain[1]:

$$\dot{x} = (1-x)p_{+-}(x) - (1+x)p_{-+}(x). \tag{16}$$

Lux makes three assumptions over the transitory probabilities p_{+-} and p_{-+}: *(i)* they must be positive; *(ii)* the transition from pessimism to optimism is larger than the opposite direction if the predominant sentiment is already optimistic and vice versa; and *(iii)* the relative change in the probability to switch from pessimism to optimism increases linearly with changes in x, in a symmetric manner in both directions ($dp_{+-} / p_{+-} = adx$, and $dp_{-+} / p_{-+} = -adx$). Hence the most appropriate functional form would be:

$$p_{+-}(x) = v exp(ax), \tag{17}$$

$$p_{-+}(x) = v exp(-ax). \tag{18}$$

By substituting equation (17-18) into (16) we have

$$\dot{x} = v[(1-x)exp(ax) - (1+x)exp(-ax)]. \tag{19}$$

Equation (19) forms the core of the contagion mechanism. The parameter a plays a crucial role in determining the local stability condition. When $a \le 1$, equation Beja and Goldman: has a unique equilibrium at $x = 0$; when $a \ge 1$, this equilibrium becomes unstable and two additional, stable equilibria emerges.

Lux further extends the model by adding a speculative element, which is in line with Beja and Goldman: it is assumed that price is driven by the fundamental and speculative demand ($\dot{p} = \beta(D_N + D_F)$ where D_N is the speculative demand and D_Fs the fundamental demand. Lux further adds the price change to the opinion formation process, since a rising price will make pessimists more likely to switch to optimists, and vice versa. Hence,

$$p_{+-} = v exp(a_1 \dot{p} / v + a_2 x), \tag{20}$$

$$p_{-+} = v exp(-a_1 \dot{p} / v - a_2 x). \tag{21}$$

Franke adopts the Weidlich-Haag-Lux approach to model firm's sentiments in a disequilibrium macro-dynamical model. The model is characterized by a population of heterogeneous firms that constantly switch between optimistic and pessimistic attitudes. The sentiment, measured by the average opinion of firms, influences the investment decisions of firms and leads to variations of output gap. The model also incorporates a Phillips curve to capture the inflation climate and a Taylor rule equation to capture the interest rates. The two dimensional ODE system is given by Equation (22-23):

$$\dot{x} = v[(1-x)\exp(as) - (1+x)\exp(-as)], \tag{22}$$

$$\dot{\pi}^c = \alpha[\gamma\pi^* + (1-\gamma)(\pi^c + \kappa\eta x) - \pi^c], \tag{23}$$

Where π is the inflation climate, γ captures the credibility of the central bank, K is the slope of the Phillips curve, η is the proportionality factor linking the output gap to x.

The Franke paper is a highly-stylized framework that formalizes the modelling of "animal spirits" in this small-scale macroeconomic model. It can be viewed as providing an alternative micro-foundation for macro-dynamic model from a Keynesian perspective, which is fundamentally different from the dominating paradigm of representative, utility-maximizing agent approach. This approach is sufficiently simple and flexible to be applied to a broader scope of decision problem in economics.

Another stimulating work is Charpe et al. which further extended by Lux and Franke proposes a so-called *"Dynamical Stochastic General Disequilibrium (DSGD)"* model. It features the continuous dynamical adjustment process on interacting real and financial markets. The financial market is destabilizing in the presence of speculative behaviour of heterogeneous agents driven by "Animal Spirits". The financial market is populated with a changing portion of fundamentalists and chartists. The real market, on the other hand, follows a much simplified version of KMG model, in the sense that the real side is always stable in the absence of speculative activities on the financial side. The baseline 4D system is written as:

$$\dot{Y} = \beta_y[(a_y - 1)(Y - Y_o) + a_k(p_k - p_k^o)K + A], \tag{24}$$

$$\hat{p}_k = \beta_k \alpha_k [f(Y, p_k, \pi_k^e) - 1], \tag{25}$$

$$\dot{\pi}_k^e = \beta_{\pi_k^e}[\frac{1+x}{2}\hat{p}_k(Y, p_k, \pi_k^e) - \pi_k^e], \tag{26}$$

$$\dot{x} = \beta[(1-x)\exp(as) - (1+x)\exp(-as)], \tag{27}$$

where a_y is the propensity to spend, a_k asures the reaction of investment demand to deviations between the actual and the steady state, A is the autonomous consumption, α_k captures the partial demand for capital that actually enters the financial market, and π_k^e ected rate of return.

[1]This equation can also be derived more formally as an approximative mean value equation for the original stochastic system in terms of Master equation approach [10].

The DSGD approach is another viable step toward a more Keynesian macro-dynamic model that incorporates "animal spirits" in inducing financial instability and macroeconomic fluctuations. It captures the highly inter-connected real and financial markets: the former is treated as stable and the latter unstable due to a population of speculative, contagious agents with fundamentalist-chartist type interaction. This approach paves a path for numerous areas of ongoing research in Keynesian disequilibrium macro-dynamics. For example, it is subsequently adopted to an open-economy scenario in Flaschel et al. which investigates the exchange rate dynamics in a two-country framework[1] [27].

Conclusion

In his attempt to reorient economic theory and explain the Great Depression, Keynes envisioned the idea of disequilibrium macroeconomics in his *General Theory*, which consists of four crucial aspects: *(i)* the independently determined saving and investment; *(ii)* the price and wage rigidity; *(iii)* the self-fulfilling "animal spirits" and *(iv)*, the intrinsic connection and interaction between real sector and financial sector. It had inspired not only economic thinkers such as Axel Leijonhufvud (who is amongst the first economist that interprets Keynes in disequilibrium terms) and Hyman Minsky (who brings modern capitalist finance in the interpretation of Keynes), but also mathematicians and dynamic modellers who strive to formalize Keynes's disequilibrium thinking with the use of advanced tools in nonlinear dynamic systems [30-34].

This paper discusses two stylized approaches of modelling Keynesian disequilibrium macro-dynamics: the Keynes-Metzler-Goodwin (KMG) approach and the Weidlich-Haag-Lux (WHL) approach that are complementary to each other. The former emphasizes on the investment-saving disequilibrium, wage-price spiral, and sluggish inventory adjustments; whereas the latter emphasizes on the role of "animal spirits" in inducing macroeconomic fluctuations.

One particular area that could potentially benefit from this line of research is the modelling of instability from the irrational behaviours of financial institutions. It is evident that the irrational and predatory behaviours of commercial banks and investment banks, coupled with a loosening regulatory environments are the key contributors to the recent 2007-2008 GFC. It would be worthwhile to incorporate the modelling of "animal spirits" of financial institutions in the spirit of WHL approach discussed previously.

References

1. Keynes JM (1936) The General Theory of Employment, Interest, and Money. Macmillan, London.
2. Leijonhufvud A (1968) On Keynesian economics and the economics of Keynes: a study in monetary theory, Oxford University Press.
3. Poincare H (1899) The New Methods of the Mecanique Celeste, (3rd volume), Gauthier-Villars, Paris.
4. Kuznetsov YA (2004) Elements of Applied Bifurcation Theory. Applied mathematical sciences 112 Springer.
5. Lorenz EN (1963) Deterministic Nonperiodic Flow. Journal of the Atmospheric Sciences 20: 130-141.
6. Lorenz H (1993) Nonlinear dynamical economics and chaotic motion, Springer, Verlag.
7. Chiarella C, Flaschel P, Franke R (2005) Foundations for a disequilibrium theory of business cycle: qualitative analysis and quantitative assessment. Cambridge University Press.
8. Chiarella C, Flaschel P (2000) The dynamics of Keynesian monetary growth: macrofoundations. Cambridge University Press.
9. Weidlich W, Haag G (1983) Concepts and Models of a Quantitative Sociology. The Dynamics of Interacting Populations, Springer, Berlin.
10. Lux T (1995) Herd behavior, bubbles and crashes. Economic Journal 105: 881-96.
11. Franke R (2012) Microfounded animal spirits in the new macroeconomic consensus. Studies in Nonlinear Dynamics & Econometrics 16: 1-41.
12. Charpe M, Flaschel P, Hartmann F, Veneziani R (2012) Towards keynesian dsgd (isequilibrium) modelling: Real-financial market interactions with heterogeneous expectations dynamics.
13. Hunt E, Lautzenheiser M (2011) History of Economic Thought: A Critical Perspective.
14. Akerlof GA, Shiller RJ (2009) Animal spirits: how human psychology drives the economy,and why it matters for global capitalism. Princeton University Press.
15. Minsky HP (1975) John Maynard Keynes, Macmillan, New York.
16. Wray LR (2007) Endogenous Money: Structuralist and Horizontalist, Economics Working Paper Archive 512, Levy Economics Institute, USA.
17. Wray R (2012) Modern Money Theory -A Primer on Macroeconomics for Sovereign Monetary Systems, Palgrave Macmillan, New York, USA.
18. Mosler W (2010) Seven Deadly Innocent Frauds of Economic Policy, Valance Company, Incorporated.
19. Kindleberger CP, Robert ZA (1989) Manias, Panics, and Crashes: A History of Financial Crises, (6thedn), Macmillan, London.
20. Turnovsky S (1977) Macroeconomic Analysis and Stabilization Policies, Cambridge University Press.
21. Sargent T (1987) Macroeconomic Theory, Economic theory, econometrics, and mathematical economics, Academic Press.
22. Tobin J (1955) A Dynamic Aggregative Model. Journal of Political Economy 63: 103-115.
23. Tobin J (1965) Money and Economic Growth. Econometrica 33: 671-684.
24. Goodwin R (1967) A Growth Cycle. In: Feinstein C (ed.) Socialism, Capitalism, and Economic Growth. Handbook of Monetary Economics, Cambridge University Press, 54-58.
25. Rose H (1967) On the non-linear theory of the employment cycle. Review of Economic Studies 34: 153-173.
26. Beja, Goldman MB (1980) On the Dynamic Behavior of Prices in Disequilibrium. Journal of Finance 35: 235-248.
27. Flaschel P, Hartmann F, Malikane C, Proao CR (2014) A Behavioral Macroeconomic Model of Exchange Rate Fluctuations with Complex Market Expectations Formation.
28. Backhouse RE, Boianovsky M (2005) Disequilibrium macroeconomics: An episode in the transformation of modern macroeconomics, Proceedings of 33rd national meeting of economy.
29. Chiarella C (1990) The elements of a nonlinear theory of economic dynamics, Lecture notes in economics and mathematical systems, Springer, Verlag.
30. Dornbusch R (1976) Expectations and Exchange Rate Dynamics. Journal of Political Economy 84:1161-1176.
31. Goodhart C (1989) Has moore become too horizontal? Journal of Post Keynesian Economics 12: 29-34.
32. Hommes C (2005) Heterogeneous Agent Models in Economics and Finance.
33. Moore BJ (1988) Horizontalists and Verticalists: The Macroeconomics of Credit Money, Cambridge University Press.
34. Orphanides A, Solow RM (1990) Money, inflation and growth, Handbook of Monetary Economics, Elsevier pp: 223-261.

[12]This model is in line with [30].

Towards Enhancing Service Delivery in Uganda's Local Government Units: Is Fiscal Decentralization Still a Feasible Strategy?

Sudi Nangoli[1]*, Mohammed Ngoma[1], Hassan Kimbugwe[1] and Mayoka Kituyi[2]

[1]*Department of Business Administration, Makerere University Business School, Kampala, Uganda*
[2]*Department of Business Computing, Makerere University Business School, Uganda*

Abstract

The Ugandan government has for years depended on decentralization as a strategy for ensuring efficient delivery of services to its citizens. However, in the wake of obstacles like corruption, nepotism among others that have clouded fiscal decentralization, the need to re-examine its feasibility in explaining service delivery in Uganda's local governments has become apparent. This study thus examines the extent to which fiscal decentralization explains improvements in service delivery in Uganda's local government units. A quantitative survey research design was used in this study. Data were collected using a pretested questionnaire and analyzed using quantitative methods. Sampling was purposively done in three districts of Uganda and the respondents included Local Council members elected by local residents and the technical staff of the participating local governments. Correlation results revealed a positive and significant relationship between fiscal decentralization and service delivery (r=.262**, p<.01) while regression results indicated that Fiscal Decentralization can predict Service delivery in local governments (Beta =.452, Sig.=.000). This study therefore recommended that despite the current inefficiencies in fiscal decentralization, it still stands out as a feasible strategy through which the quality of services provided by local governments can be enhanced. As such, the implementation of fiscal decentralization going forward, needs to be augmented with requisite policies to help in alleviating challenges like corruption, nepotism hence improving accountability and value for money on all government contracts sourced at local government levels. This will help improve on the quality of services provided by local governments.

Keywords: Fiscal decentralization; Local governments; Service delivery; Strategy; Uganda

Introduction

A number of existence studies reveal that fiscal decentralization as implemented in developing countries is meant to improve service delivery to the people while promoting government's developmental goals [1,2]. Fiscal decentralization a strategy for enhancing service delivery has to an extent achieved good results in many African countries such as Nigeria and Uganda [3,4]. Generally, governments usually decided to decentralize so as to facilitate political, economic, social, managerial, administrative and technical empowerment of local populations to fight poverty by empowering them to participating in planning and management of their development process [1,5]. In the case of Uganda, the country's powers to create local government units are clearly enshrined in its Constitution. Article 179 of the 1995 Uganda constitution allows the government through parliament to create new districts with financial autonomy in the interest of improved service delivery.

Notwithstanding the challenges, fiscal decentralization has been seen as an effective way of promoting service delivery, especially in rural areas. The 2006 report on Annual Assessment of Minimum Conditions and Performance Measures for Local Governments in Uganda indicated that many Ugandans agitate for the creation of new districts and other local council units with hope that there will be better service delivery [6,7]. However, on deeper analysis, empirical studies reveal that there is nothing much on ground to justify all the praises heaped on decentralization at large. In Uganda for instance, a number of the decentralized units do not have capacity to run themselves as evidenced by high failure rates of many of the newly created districts that averaged 50% in 1997 with minimum standards and 45.5% for districts created by financial year 2003/04 [8-10]. As a way of curbing some the obstacles to service delivery, concerned institutions like the Inspector General of Government (IGG) and other anticorruption watchdogs have interdicted and prosecuted some of the guilty local government officials on cases of financial misappropriation, corruption and abuse of office. For example, Lambright [11] reports that on April 6, 2001, the Chief Administrative Officer (CAO) of Kasese district in western Uganda was suspend from office over allegations of corruption, financial mismanagement and misappropriation of over Ush11M district funds and that the same scenario happened in Soroti district in eastern Uganda, where the Chief Finance Officer (CFO) and the District Development Program Officer were interdicted over misappropriation of over Ush17M district funds donated by the Netherlands to implement the district's development Projects. Considering these and many other factors such as corrupt council officials and lack of accountability [12], it is pertinent to revisit the feasibility of fiscal decentralization in improving delivery of services to the people. Thus the purpose of this study was to examine the feasibility of fiscal decentralization as a strategy for enhancing service delivery in Uganda's local governments.

The remaining sections in this paper present a review of the theoretical and empirical literature, the adopted methodology, presentation and discussion of findings, conclusions, recommendations and areas for further study

Review of Theoretical and Empirical Literature

This section presents a review of theoretical and empirical literature aligned to fiscal decentralization and service delivery in Local Government Units.

***Corresponding author:** Sudi Nangoli, Department of Business Administration, Makerere University Business School, Kampala, Uganda
E-mail: nangolisudi@gmail.com

Theoretical underpinning of the study

A number of theories have been adopted and adapted in studies relating Fiscal Decentralization and Service Delivery. According to Porcelli [13], these can largely be classified under the classical theory and second generation theories. The classical theories here include three related ideas, that is, Tiebout's model of local public good provision (Tiebout, [14-17], and Leviathan's model/hypothesis. The second generation theories include but are not limited to the Decentralization Theorem with political economy by Lockwood [18] and Decentralization in principal agent model of electoral accountability [13].

The applicability of the Tiebout model and the Decentralization Theorem in LDCs like Uganda, where corruption is common place, fail on grounds that benevolence is not always assured in dealings between central government and local government units as the theories in question advance. Although also prone to certain forms of corruption, the augmented ideas of the Leviathan hypothesis tend to provide a more plausible explanation of service delivery efficiency through fiscal decentralization. According to the Leviathan hypothesis, central governments operate like leviathans who in order to increase their control over the economy's resources, favour decentralization as a plausible approach of curtailing inefficiencies of central government yet maintain ultimate power [13,17]. This model as augmented by Lockwood [18] promotes efficiency using a political model were decision-making process is implemented via majority voting over alternative levels of public good provision rather than benevolence. It can therefore be hypothesized that Fiscal decentralization enhances service delivery even under conditions where delegates are corrupt.

Conceptualization of key terms and Empirical review of the study concepts

Decentralization which was started on the principles of self-control has of now proved to be a method of choice for bringing services closer to the people with its various forms as has been widely and successfully implemented in different countries. Decentralization is understood in different ways by different scholars who have come up with varying conceptual models and frameworks purporting to explain the same concept. To this end, a debate has been ignited to clearly understand the concept and practice of decentralization [19]. According Neyapti [20], Fiscal decentralization (FD) means devolution of power and responsibilities of national (central), government towards sub-national (local), governments. This study adopted the conceptualization by Oommen [21]. According to Oommen [21], decentralization means empowering the local people through empowering the local governments. In this breath, one key strand, called political decentralization is often referred to as the transfer of authority and political functions from central to local government based on the principles of equity and political representation in those local governments. In Uganda, local governments have a political wing manned by councilors who are locally elected on a balanced basis, which allows representatives from various political parties and social-cultural affiliations [22]. Stoop [23] further observes that genuine decentralization should engulf power struggles and promote the separation of power through devolution of power, in which resources and political decision making are "transferred to a separate lower tier of government". On the other hand, COMFREL [24] and Eriksen et al. [25] urge that democratic decentralization, in which local people use an elected legislative body to solve their own problems should encourage the participation of people in the decision making process and should promote access to important information on the way business is being run by a given local government. Eriksen et al. [25] and COMFREL [24] further urge that this kind of arrangement governments more responsive to the needs of locals through prioritization and proper resource planning and allocation.

According to scholars like Dziobek, Mangas and Kufa [1], the typical reason for fiscal decentralization in developing countries is to improve service delivery to the people while promoting government's developmental goals. This has to a certain extent achieved good results in some African countries such as Nigeria and Uganda [3,4]. The government of Rwanda decided to decentralize so that they facilitate political, economic, social, managerial, administrative and technical empowerment of local populations to fight poverty by empowering them to participating in planning and management of their development process [5]. Article 179 of the 1995 Uganda constitution allows the government through parliament to create new districts with financial autonomy in the interest of improved service delivery. Notwithstanding the challenges, fiscal decentralization has been seen as an effective way of promoting service delivery, especially in rural areas. That is why many Ugandans are agitating for the creation of new districts and other local council units with hope that there will be better service delivery [7]. However, on deeper analysis, one realizes that there is nothing much on ground to justify all the praises towards decentralization at large. For instance, most of these decentralized units do not have capacity to run themselves as evidenced by high failure rates of many of the newly created districts that averaged 50% in 1997 with minimum standards and 45.5% for districts created by financial year 2003/04 [8-10]. Consideration this and many other factors such as corrupt council officials and lack of accountability [12], it is only logical for one to conclude that fiscal decentralization has failed to deliver services to the people.

Methodology

This section looks at the research methods used in the study.

Research design

A quantitative survey research design was used in this study. Data were collected using a pretested questionnaire and analyzed using quantitative methods.

Sample design

A sample of 600 respondents was picked purposively from three districts in Uganda. Two districts came from Eastern Uganda and one from Central. These include Mbale, Manafwa from East and Kampala from Central Uganda. In order to ensure well balanced opinions, one of the districts (Manafwa) was rural and one (Mbale) was urban. Kampala district was included because it is the capital city of Uganda and hosts most of the government ministries and the national parliament. At total of 250 respondents came from Mbale, 250 from Kampala and 100 respondents came from Manafwa. These numbers were based on the population density of the participating districts such that the urban districts contributed more respondents whereas a rural district with few residents contributed less.

The type of officials involved in study was Local Council members commonly referred to as LCs who are elected by local residents. These included L III (operating at sub county level), LC IV (operating at county level) and LC V (operating at district level). In addition to the council members, technical staffs of the selected local governments were also involved on the study. These included Chief Administrative Officers, the Sub-County Chiefs, Town Clerks and Assistant Town Clerks, Accountants, Revenue Collection Officers, Community Development Officers, Health Officers, Education Officers among others.

Data analysis

The data collected was coded and entered into SPSS software for analysis using quantitative methods i.e. descriptive statistics, correlations and regressions.

Findings

This section presents the findings from primary data.

Validation of research instrument

Cronbach Alpha Coefficient (CAC) and Content Validity Index (CVI) were used to test for the reliability and validity of the questionnaire respectively. The results in Table 1 below were generated for CAC and CVI: Cronbach Alpha Coefficient and Content Validity Index results in Table 1 above indicate that the questionnaire was valid and reliable since all variables scored CAC and CVI greater than 5.

Participation in revenue planning

Descriptive statistics were also used to determine whether the respondents had ever participated in revenue planning committees and/or meetings in their respective local units. The results were analyzed based on yes or no responses as seen in Table 2.

Results in Table 2 above indicate that majority respondents constituting 59.3 had never participated in revenue planning meetings and/or committees in their local units. On the other hand, 181 respondents constituting 40.7 had ever participated in revenue planning meetings and/or committees.

Planning role

Descriptive statistics including frequencies and percentages were also used to determine the role played by respondents in revenue planning meetings and/or committees in their respective local units. The results were analyzed as seen in Table 3.

Results in Table 3 above show that most respondents played the role of providing accounting services (freq=125). 95 respondent constituting 21.3% played the role of providing health services while 85 respondents representing 19.1% provided general administrative services. 75 respondents, representing 16.9% provided education services, while 31 contributing 7% played the role of providing environmental services. 29 respondents representing 6.5% played the role of providing physical and infrastructural services. Only 5 respondents representing 1.1% provided consultancy services in revenue planning committees.

Fiscal decentralization and service delivery

Descriptive statistics including means were used to determine whether and how fiscal decentralization improved service delivery in local councils. The results were analyzed as seen in Table 4 below.

Results in Table 4 above show that respondents strongly agreed that fiscal decentralization brought services nearer to the people (Mean=4.43), it was easy to get feedback from the community (Mean=4.44), and that there was better monitoring of government programmes (Mean=4.45). The respondents further agreed that fiscal decentralization made people to understand government priorities better (Mean=3.32).

The respondents however strongly disagreed that there was better quality work done by contractors due to close monitoring (Mean=2.21), there was reduced bureaucracy (Mean=2.43), there was better accountability (Mean=2.42) and also that there was value for money spent on government contracts (Mean=2.25).

Correlation for fiscal decentralization and service delivery

Correlation analysis method was used to examine the relationship between fiscal decentralization and service delivery. Table 5 presents the correlation results:

Correlation results in Table 5 above reveal that there is a positive and significant relationship between fiscal decentralization and service delivery (r=.262**, p<.01).

Regression analysis

In determining the power of fiscal decentralization in improving service delivery, regression analysis was used. The results are shown in Table 6.

Regression results seen in Table 6 above show that Fiscal Decentralization can predict Service delivery in local governments (Beta =.452). The regression model is valid given that Sig.=.000.

Discussion of Findings

This section presents a discussion of findings aimed at addressing the question 'To what extent has fiscal decentralization strategy helped achieve improved service delivery in Uganda Local Governments?' Correlation results revealed a positive and significant relationship between fiscal decentralization and service delivery. The regression of the two variables was also significant with a standardized coefficient of (0.452). These findings not only mean that enhancement in service delivery in local governments are positively related to improvements in fiscal decentralization, but that changes in fiscal decentralization

Variable	N of point	Anchor	CAC	CVI
Fiscal Decentralization	7	5 point	0.605	0.613
Service Delivery	8	5 point	0.674	0.653

Table 1: Validity and reliability tests.

Have you ever participated in revenue planning?	F	%	Valid Percent	Cumulative Percent
Yes	181	40.7	40.7	40.7
No	264	59.3	59.3	100.0
Total	445	100.0	100.0	

Source: Primary Data

Table 2: Participation in revenue planning.

Role/service	F	%	Valid Percent	Cumulative Percent
Accounting Services	125	28.1	28.1	28.1
Education Services	75	16.9	16.9	44.9
Health Services	95	21.3	21.3	66.3
General Administration	85	19.1	19.1	85.4
Physical Infrastructure	29	6.5	6.5	91.9
Environment	31	7.0	7.0	98.9
Consultant	5	1.1	1.1	100.0
Total	**445**	**100.0**	**100.0**	

Source: Primary Data

Table 3: Role played.

Descriptive statistics				
	N	Min	Max	Mean
Services are brought nearer to the people	445	1	5	4.43
People understand government priorities better	445	1	5	3.32
It is easy to get feedback from the community	445	1	5	4.44
There is better monitoring of government programmes	445	1	5	4.45
There is better quality work done by contractors due to close monitoring	445	1	5	2.21
There is reduced bureaucracy	445	1	5	2.43
There is better accountability	445	1	5	2.42
There is value for money spent on government contracts	445	1	5	2.25

Source: Primary Data

Table 4: Service delivery.

		Fiscal Decentralization	Service delivery
Fiscal Decentralization	Pearson Correlation	1	.262**
	Sig. (2-tailed)		.000
	N	442	442
Service delivery	Pearson Correlation	.262**	1
	Sig. (2-tailed)	.000	
	N	402	402
**. Correlation is significant at the 0.01 level (2-tailed).			

Table 5: Correlation.

Model		Unstandardized Coefficients		Standardized Coefficients	t	Sig^a^.
		B	Std. Error	Beta		
1	(Constant)	1.97	.029		8.111	.000
	Fiscal Decentralization	.431	.043	.452	6.024	.000
a. Dependent Variable: Service delivery						

Table 6: Regression results.

can explain about 45.2% of the changes in service delivery. In the same breath, the findings on some particular questions asked indicated that fiscal decentralization helps to improve service delivery because it brings services nearer to the people and that it is easy to get feedback from the community. The findings also indicated that there was better monitoring of government programmes, people understand government priorities better with fiscal decentralization. These findings are in line with literature. For example Akinyele [3] and Malesky [4]; Republic of Rwanda policy report [5], Republic of Uganda [7] all argued for the same points. The findings however contradicted with some literature on the suggestion that fiscal decentralization brought about better quality work done by contractors, reduced bureaucracy, improved accountability and also that there was value for money spent on government contracts. The findings pointed out corruption and nepotism as key hindrances towards the success of fiscal decentralization. The findings further indicated that there was too much political interference in the running of work, that councilors were not well educated and knowledgeable about government programmes and also that there was poor pay for technical staff. The findings further indicated that paying councilors allowances and other emoluments was too costly for local governments hence hindering service delivery. In addition, the findings indicated that local governments did not have adequate sources of revenue necessary for delivering services to the people.

Conclusion, Recommendations and Areas for Further Study

Considering the literature, findings and the discussion of the findings, it can be concluded that fiscal decentralization is still a feasible strategy for bringing about improved service delivery in local governments. It can also be concluded that fiscal decentralization most times fails to bring about better quality services because most contractors hired to provide services on behalf of government are compromised through corruption and other tendencies such as nepotism, favoritism and abnormal bureaucracies. There is was a problem of accountability and no value for money spent on government contracts. Hence, this study recommends that fiscal decentralization should be implemented along with other policies to help monitor for corruption, nepotism, accountability and value for money on all government contracts sourced at local government levels. This will help improve on the quality of services provided by local governments. The local communities should also be directly involved in evaluating the works of contractors to ensure there is value for money. In schools for example, parents can form associations that monitors the performance of teachers. The same can be done in government hospitals and health centers run by local governments such that government employees provided better services. Village communities can also form committees for monitoring government contracts in their areas of jurisdiction. For instance a village committee can monitor the monitors of services provided on borehole and report directly to the relevant authorities such as the Inspector of Government and Anti-corruption courts where a contractor has delivered poor quality services. Further studies in this area should address a bigger sample to give a reflection of the possible changes in the predictive power of the independent variable.

References

1. Dziobek C, Mangas CG, Kufa P (2011) Measuring Fiscal Decentralization – Exploring the IMF's Databases. International Monetary Fund.
2. Jutting J, Corsi E, Kauffmann C, Mcdonnell I, Osterrieder H, et al. (2005) What Makes Decentralisation in Developing Countries Pro-poor? The European Journal of Development Research 17: 626-648.
3. Akinyele RT (1996) States Creation in Nigeria: The Willink Report in Retrospect. African Studies Review 39: 71-94.
4. Malesky E (2005) Gerrymandering - Vietnamese Style: The Political Motivations behind the Creation of New Provinces in Vietnam. Paper presented at the Midwest Political Science Association 63rd Annual Conference. Measures for Local Governments, 2003. The Republic of Uganda
5. Republic of Rwanda policy Report (2000) Implementation strategy for National Decentralization Policy. Ministry of Local Government and Social Affairs, Republic of Rwanda.
6. Oguttu W, Opondo O (2007) What are the Implications of Creating More Districts? New Vision.
7. Republic of Uganda (2007) Annual Assessment of Minimum Conditions and Performance Measures for Local Governments, 2006. The Republic of Uganda
8. Tumushabe G, Mushemeza EG, Tamale LM, Lukwago D, Ssemakula E (2010) Monitoring and Assessing the Performance of Local Government Councils in Uganda; Background, Methodology and Score Card. ACODE.
9. Buwembo J (2005) What's the Fuss about New Districts? The Monitor. Clegg Nick and Greg Clark (2010). Decentralisation and the Localism Bill: an essential guide. HM Government, ISBN: 978 1 4098 2662 0
10. Republic of Uganda (2004) Annual Assessment of Minimum Conditions and Performance
11. Lambright MSG (2010) Decentralization in Uganda: Explaining Successes and Failures in Local Governance. The Journal of Politics.

12. Horng V, Pak Kimchoeun, Ann S, Ngo N (2005) Decentralization and Deconcentration Reforms in Cambodia: an Early Review', in K. Murshid and B. Ballard (eds) Annual Development Review, Phnom Penh. CDRI.

13. Porcelli F (2009) Fiscal Decentralisation and efficiency of government. A brief literature review. Department of Economics - University of Warwick (UK). Downloaded on 16th march 2015.

14. Tiebout CM (1956) A pure theory of local expenditures. The Journal of Political Economy 64: 416-424.

15. Oates WE (1985) Searching for leviathan: An empirical study. America Economic Review 75: 748-757.

16. Oates W E (1999) An essay on fiscal federalism. Journal of Economic Literature 27: 1120-1149.

17. Brennan D, Buchanan J (1980) The Power to Tax: Analytical Foundations of a Fiscal Consitution. Cambridge University Press, Cambridge.

18. Lockwood B (2007) Voting, lobbying, and the decentralization theorem. Economics and Politics 20: 416-431.

19. Yuliani EL (2004) Decentralization, deconcentration and devolution: what do they mean? Interlaken Workshop on Decentralization

20. Neyapti B (2005) Equalization via Fiscal Decentralization.

21. Oommen MA (2008) Fiscal Decentralisation to Local Governments in India. Cambridge Scholars Publishing, Newcastle, UK.

22. Rondinelli (1999) A Review of Literature of Decentralization. UNDP New York.

23. Stoop (2002) Sited by COMFREL (2007) Assessment of the First Term of Decentralization in Cambodia, 2002-2007. COMFREL.

24. COMFREL (2007) Assessment of the first term of decentralization. Decentralization in Cambodia. Commune Council Performance and Citizens' Participation, 2002-2007.

25. Eriksen (1999) Sited by COMFREL (2007) Assessment of the First Term of Decentralization in Cambodia, 2002-2007.

To Compare Information and Communication Technology on the Employment of Two Industries Yazd and Kerman (Panel Data Approach)

Ali Raeispour[1], Somayeh koochakzadeh[2] and Hajar AsnsAshari[3]*

[1]Assistant and Member of the Faculty of Kerman University, Iran
[2]Facualy Member of Vali-e-Asr University of Rafsanjan, Iran
[3]PhD Student Economics, University of Sistan and Baluchestan, Iran

Abstract

Recent decades, Information and communication technology has created inhuman life great Changes. So that all aspects of human life virtually encompass and even employment is not immune to these developments. Employment is one of the most important macroeconomic variables. In this study we compared the effects of information and communication technology on employment industries Yazd and Kerman provinces. The study included two provincial panel data from various industries since the 2009-2012. Results showed that the information and communication technology industry has a direct and significant effect on employment of the two provinces of Yazd and Kerman. This result demonstrates the importance of information and communication technology and trying to expand in the country and is helping to create jobs.

Keywords: Information and communication technology; Employment; Panel data

Introduction

OECD definition of information and communication technology is defined as the sum of manufacturing and service industries to maintain, transmit and display data and information electronically is used. Technological revolution with the rapid improvement of the quality of the equipment and the software is known by coming with a very larger education in prices. Information and communication technology has a dual role in the economy Inputs for users and outputs for producer of information technology and communications industries. Firms maximize profits by observing the relative price of their placement equipment, information and communication technology, software and services react rather than other goods and services. There for information and communication technology is achieved from distinctive three-part computer interaction, information and communication [1].

Information and communication technology has dual role in the economy. On the one hand, it is suggested as input to user and on the other hand, information and communication technology industry is output for manufacturers. Technological revolution is known with rapid improvement in the quality of equipment and software, along with a sharp decline in prices [2]. Thus, firms whose aim is the maximum profit replace the equipment, software and services so they can react to these changes with the rapid advancement of technology to enhance their own interests. The main conditions for the development to information technology is special are test and efficient, the shortage of staff is a major factor in the lack of technological development. The world is now passing and changing desirable status to the status quo. So we can expect a variety of careers in the information technology field is created. Developing countries are in urgent need for information technology specialists to have their employment. Apart from the issue of the establishment of training courses of reeducated people who can communicate in the digital age will not have sufficient skills and abilities [3]. Information and communication technology at the same time creats employment, it has been employment de bugger. The evidence indicates that acts as a catalyst for economic growth and employment. When daily activities are mechanized and productivity increases. Production costs and delivers will reduce. In other words, final price will decline for buyer. And consequently, the demand for buying increases. The information technology has led to accurate and timely information has always been available to applicants and it enables them to make timely and better decisions or decision-making. This would reduce its share of costs, Profit increases and economic growth facilitate. It is a fact that due to industrial activity, demand for labor in some industries reduces. Although the other hand, new jobs are entering the labor market. Some of these jobs include web design, expert web main tenant and management bases, expert systems, multimedia, satellite transmission technicians, technician global positioning systems, and electronic commerce professionals. These jobs require knowledge, skills and capabilities. Sometimes in some countries, there are no current or previous job description [4]. The fundamental question that this study attempted to be answered can be stated as follows: Is the development of the information and communication technology industry in the province of Yazd and Kerman to increase employment?

Basics Theoretical

To the knowledge of the technology that is used to design or manufacture a product or set of services needed [5]. Askaramvtzy defines information and communication technology technologies to build the collection, storage, exchange and use of information in various forms of business data, voice conversations, still images and an Imation's, multimedia presentations and other forms that have yet to unveil. Information and communication technology is a network of production management, knowledge processing, distribution and optimal use of information in order to enhance system performance [6]. Lucas is defined as information and communication technology information and communication technology is defined as the information and communication technology technologies to all types of processing and storing information electronically. For this purpose, the equipment, such as computers, communications equipment and

***Corresponding author:** Hajar AsnsAshari, PhD Student Economics, University of Sistan and Baluchestan, E-mail: esna.hajar@gmail.com

networks, fax machines and electronic packages used to manage [6]. Based on the theory of economic growth, increased production factors can only lead to the increased production and employment. And then, in the absence of technological progress, production efficiency will reduce; Hence, an increase in factors of production (capital) can total one increase production. But advances in technology and the law of diminishing re turns is not the transfer function can generate output and employment growth, and thus unemployment had a reduction [7].

History Research

Several studies in different countries and also in Iran to Evaluation of information and communication technology have been the case in the following. Merical in a study to evaluate the impact of in novation on employment in Estonia at the firm level and industry. Results of the study showed that the information and communication technology industry and information and communication technology firms has a positive effect on employment levels, producing has a more positive effect on employment levels. Lachenmaier [8] studied the effects of technology on employment that the study concluded that the level of technology firms has a positive effect on employment Effects of technology in the production process of its effect on the production. Product innovation creates new products in the market that creates new demand. The increased demand for labor will increase employment but the innovation process is meant to improve production processes Harrison et al. [9]. paid to investigate the impact of information and communication technology on firm-level employment (France, Germany, Spain and England). The results show that information and communication technology, changes in employment creates, But Compensation by a decline in prices caused by the impact of information and communication technology on employment is positive. Hagén and Zeed [10] using data from 2,752 firms with over 10 employees in industry and services in Sudan Using the production Cobb-Douglas function paid to study the effect of employees computer, dummy variable for broadband access as an approximation of information and communication technology. Control variables used in the study were the size of firm by number of employees, ownership type and composition skills. The results in dictate that in the industrial sector 10% increase in labor supplied to the computer makes 3/1 percent increase in labor productivity and band width increases 6/3 percent of labor productivity. Kaushalesh [11] employment growth and electronic work studied that Concluded the arrival of new technologies will not necessarily result in lost jobs. Following the arrival information and communication technology, employment in all firms surveyed had significant growth that main growth in employment was related to skilled workers Matteucc and Sterlachini [12]. The effect of information and communication technology on employment growth in the industries Italian studied, the results showed that the information and communication technology -producing industries have a Significant employment growth than industries using information and communication technology and the information and communication technology industries that do not use it. Rasully negad, and Nougy [13] studied to the effect on employment of communication technology using vector error correction model that the results of this study showed that communication technology is a short-term negative effect on employment but in the long run, this will have a positive effect. Mahmoud zadeh and Asadi [1] the effects of information and communication technology in economic growth of labor productivity was investigated. The results showed that the productivity of capital, non- information and communication technology and information and communication technology and human capital have a positive effect on labor productivity of the economy. Moshiri and jahangard [14] studied the effects of information and communication technologies on productivity and economic growth of Iran, This study consists of two parts, in the first part of the study are discussed to test the relationship between information and communication technology and economic growth. The result simply the existence of a non-significant but weak positive relationship between economic growth and information and communication technology. In addition, studies to pay about the impact of information and communication technology on firm performance conducted, Due to lack of data and information , is used Substitute or a poor approximation of them ensured application of information and communication technology. In the study, according to the census questions of industrial workshops ISC the variables used appropriate criteria to demonstrate how they are using information and communication technology in industrial enterprises.

Materials and Methods

The combined data set is called, based on cross-sectional observations by a number of variables (N) during the period (T) specified are examined. Baltagi [15] With the introduction of one-sided and two-sided error component model, joins the panel data regression model is as follows: t=1,…T æ i=1,…,N; $y_{it} = \alpha + X_{it}^{\prime}\beta + u_{it}$

In the above equation is show the cross (households, firms, countries, etc.) while t represents time. α is a scalar , β vector is $k*1$ and is X_{it} the it observation for explanatory variable k. Baltajy believes that the most regression models with panel data use, one-way error component model for disturbing elements over time. $u_{it} = \mu + \upsilon_{it}$ In the above equation μ_i is an individual specific Intangible effect and does not change with time. While shows υ_{it} the residual error and is known as part of the usual regression disturbance about the fixed effects μ_i are assumed constant parameters that must be estimated.

Diagnostic tests

Hausman test of the null hypothesis, in dictating a lack of correlation between the explanatory variables and the disturbance that if this assumption is accepted, the method of random effects is accepted too and otherwise, the fixed effects method will be accepted. To determine the type of model in combination data are used of different tests. The most common is Chow test that use for fixed effect model Against model data integration, Hausman test for fixed effects versus random effects models using LM test for random effects models using the model integration. Chow test for the merged model against the fixed effects model will perform. The assumptions for this test-is as follows: H_0: Pooled Model;

H_1: Fixed effect Model

The first hypothesis is based on the constrained values and against assumption is based on unconstrained value. Chow test statistic based on the sum of squared errors of the constrained model and unconstrained model is as follows: $\text{chow} = \dfrac{\dfrac{\text{RSSR} - \text{RSS uR}}{\text{N} - 1}}{\dfrac{\text{RSSUR}}{\text{NT} - \text{N} - \text{K}}}$

This statistic has the F distribution with degrees N-1 and NT-NK is Liberation. Static tests are the most important test for estimating the regression with reliable coefficients. To avoid the creation of spurious regression is used from static tests.

Hausman test

Based on the Hausman test, difference between fixed effects and random effects estimators approach, is considered as the null hypothesis thus rejection of the null hypothesis indicates the fixed effects method. In this test, the null hypothesis indicates a lack of correlation between the explanatory variables and the disturbance that if this assumption is accepted, the method of random effects will be accepted and fixed effects method is accepted otherwise. In this study, the following equation by Matthews and As tvlachyny conducted in Italy in 2003 is stated as follows: ln $L=C-a_1 lnW + a_2 LnR + a_3 LnQ + a_4 LnICT$ Where W is the wage, R cost of capital (interest rate), Q is the added value and information and communication technology is information technology and communications standards. The data of the years 2009-2012 as a combination of two different industries Yazd and Kerman Province is collected.

Results and Discussion

Based on the results of static tests boys and Shane, all variables, employment, wages, interest rates, value added and information and communication technology represents the unit root level and thus it is not static. First-order difference variables were statistically significant at 5 and 1% and the null hypothesis is excluded. Thus, these variables are stationary first order. F test Lymer, for industry Kerman and Yazd provinces respectively 31/5 and 02/6 obtained and show the way fixed effects model is adopted against the integrated model. Using the Hausman test to choose between fixed effects and random effects, It was clear that the null hypothesis is can be rejected based on the adjustment coefficients so this method is accepted fixed effects that are considered in Table 1.

Yazd and Kerman provinces Industry fixed effects model estimation results of the equation (1) and(2) is obtained the following:

$$LL_{kerman} = -0.40+0.63LQ+0.27LICT-0.5LR-0.52LW \quad (1)$$

t (8.27) (2.93) (-3.68) (-6.75)

The fixed effects method assumes that industries have fixed intercept and all industries have negative and different intercept but it can be seen that the absolute value of the interception Yazd, intercept is larger than Kerman industry that indicates the manufacturing sector is more advanced and more successful than Kerman and it has had the largest performance in non-oil export.

$$LL_{yazd}=-3.52+0.94LQ+0.19LICT-0.41LR-0.66LW \quad (2)$$

t (10.56) (1.56) (2.66) (-1.81)

LQ: log of value added industries provinces, LICT: log of the information and communication technology industry in two provinces, LR: log of interest rates, LW :logarithm of wages between industries, LL: log of industry employment in two provinces. As can be seen, all variables are significant. High R^2 indicates a good explanatory power of the model variables and shows the fitted regression in the Kerman province, 86% and 97% in Yazd represents the total employment of Yazd and Kerman provinces. T-statistic is significant for all four variables. And show that, for every four variables have a significant effect on the dependent variable. Thus the equations (1) and (2) can be seen, that production has a direct relation with employment. With increasing production is increasing employment too. Provinces with higher capacities, greater ability to achieve economies of scale and by increasing exports, according to the relative advantages of the two provinces can increase employment. Capacity of every province are determined based on the quantity and quality of factors of production. At any moment of time, Production capacity for constant volume of production factors, the combination and technology are fixed. But over time, factors of production are expanded. Yazd has more coefficient of production. It shows that 1 percentage change in production increases 94/0% in employment. But in Kerman province shows a percentage change in the size of production increase 63/0% in employment. Interest rate is inversely related to the employment in industries reducing the interest rate increases investment. This will lead to more employment in each province. However the impact on interest rates on employment are different. In Kerman province, a percentage reduction in interest rates increase as much as 50/0% employment. In Yazd province a percentage reduction in interest rates as of 41/0% to increase employment. Wage has had negative relationship employment in tow provinces. Reducing the wages employers demand for labor increases. It will also make employment. In province Kerman as a percent reduction in salary, 52/0 will increase the employment rate and in Yazd a percent reduction in salary as well as a 66/0 increases employment.

Hausman test	Amount	Probability
H Hausman test (Kerman equation)	14/00	0.01
Hausman test (Yazdequation)	13/5	0/03

Table 1: Hausman test to test the hypothesis of random or fixed effects model, *Source*: research findings.

In Kerman province impact of ICT on employment is direct and significant, by increasing of the ICT industry in the manufacturing sector of this province still need for labor and this variable that is associated with increasing production through innovation, demand for labor and there by employment increase. Productive innovation is changes in the mode of production is presented new products. That through offset by increased demand for labor in this province. A percentage change in ICT can be increased as much as 27% Employment rate. Innovative means to change in the production process due to the use of ICT there by increasing the demand for labor and in other words, it causes to increase in unemployment in other words, a percent increase in the size of ICT increases employment as much as 19%. Due to technical coefficients of equations (1) and (2), effect of this variable on industry employment in Kerman is more than yazd. In these two province sare considered ICT industry in the manufacturing sector as an input along with other factors of production, improves production process, capital deepening, labor quality technological progress. The implications of the effects increase the level of industrial and economic growth, productivity and consumer welfare of consumers in the province.

Suggestions

The main objective of this study was been determining the effect of ICT on employment in the two that you can see the impact of ICT on employment is positive in these two provinces. Two of these provinces should follow ICT investments with long-term prospects for creation competitive networks and developing software and hardware. This provinces also investing in ICT, infrastructure of the basis should provide for the effectiveness of ICT. In this regard, it is necessary complementary factors such as technical infrastructure, human capital, telecommunications, legislative and commercial freedom to capture the benefits of ICT to provide.

Acknowledgement

This article is drawn from are search project funded by the Research Council of Islamic Azad University we would like to thank the deputy.

References

1. Mahmoud zadeh M, Asadi F (2005) ICT infrastructure and service sector employment Iran. Journal Economy and new Trade. No3.
2. Pohjola M (2000) Information Technology and Economic Growth A Cross Country Analysis, World Institute for Development Economic Research, Research paper 173.
3. Naserzadeh H (2001) Check the status of technology in Iran, Job opportunities arising from technology. Tehran conference on information technology in employment.
4. Kurzweil R (1999) The Age of Spititual Machines: When Computers Exceed Human Intelligence, New York: Viking Publishers.
5. Fakour B, Ansary M (2010) Evaluation methods and technology resources at small firm select to Iran. Journal of Science and Technology. 2(4).
6. Hegbar Kiani K, Akhavan SH (2007) The effect of ICT on employment industries Tehran, Light Peak Humanities 5(4).
7. Afshari Z, Ramezani Fa (2006) Impact of information technology on women's employment (Cross-country). Social Studies Women's Psychological 10.
8. Lachenmaier S (2007) Effects of Innovation on Employment: A Dynamic Panel Analysis, IFO Institute Economic Research at the University of Munchen, Germany p 3.
9. Harrison R (2006) Does Innovation Stimulate Employment? A firm Level Analysis using comparable micro data from four countries.
10. Hagén HO, Zeed J (2005) Does ICT Use Matter for Firm Productivity?, Yearbook on Productivity 2005 Statistics, Sweden p 5-30.
11. Kaushalesh L (2004) Growth of employment and the adoption of E-business, Discussion Paper Series, United Nation University.
12. Matteucci N, Sterlachini A (2003) ICT and Employment Growth in Italian Indastries.
13. Rasully negad E, Nougy M (2009) Impact of ICT on employment Iran. Journal of Economic. No.89.
14. Moshiri S, Jahangard E (2004) Information and Communication Technology (ICT) and economic growth of Iran. Journal of Economic Research of Iran 6: 55-78.
15. Baltagi BH (2001) Econometric analysis of panel data, published by JhonWiely and Sons Ltd.

Throughput Port Demand Forecasting

Jeffrey E Jarrett*

Professor of Management Science and Finance, University of Rhode Island, Kingston- 02852, USA

Abstract

Forecasts are numerical estimates of the future levels of sales, demand, inventories, costs imports, exports and prices, among others. For a firm, industry, a sector of the economy or the aggregate economy let alone factors such as international trade and finance. The objective is to assist management in planning, budgeting, marketing efforts, materials requirements, sustainability, the refuse from power production and efforts to restrain the effects of pollution on climate change.

We indicate several procedures which are relatively easier to compute, more accurate and not dependent on finding predictor (or explanatory) variables which have coefficients of correlation which are small. By using one set of data, (port demand in units), we do short-term forecasting of up to twelve periods which are less data dependent and produce forecasts which do not require a huge investment in computer and personnel time.

Keywords: Time series; Autocorrelation function (ACF); Partial autocorrelation function (PACF); Forecast modeling; Ljung-box statistic; Decomposition

Introduction

Traditional methods to forecast port traffic volumes include basing projections based on GDP over time or desk and field research often how it relates to changes in the cargo port and domestic and international shipping prices. Although each method has its advantages and disadvantages, our purpose here is to determine if parsimonious forecasting models can prove to be superior to the common methods. Both of the traditional procedures laid themselves open to major error.

Importance of port traffic forecasting associated or not by political, economic

One of the best ways for successful management of certain transport companies is traffic demand planning. Demand is one of the most important aspects of business economics. Mismatch between supply and demand leads to a number of problems. Therefore, in case of port operations, higher supply than demand leads to the failure in the utilization of port infrastructure and superstructure, and to the lack of cost-effectiveness. When the demand for port services exceeds the supply, there comes to congestion of port facilities, an increase in costs of ships and losses of time due to waiting. Since the traffic capacity is not flexible and its construction and development require substantial financial resources in order to be payable, supply must be designed in accordance with the anticipated demand in the future. Therefore, to avoid the consequences of non-compliance of port supply and demand, and to create a basis for sizing supply, there is a need for demand forecasting of port services.

For future demand forecasting, the primary precondition is the construction and/or modernization of the future port infrastructure and superstructure. Since the port service cannot be stored, the port offer needs to be in line with the current demand. The analysis of relevant materials regarding traffic forecasting of demand for port services, particularly the demand for port services can change rapidly with the change relating to priorities set by governments, government agencies, demand conditions set in motion by buyers and sellers of the materials being transported by the local supply chain.

Previous study

Cargo port activity is a time series with random fluctuations associated with political, economic and natural forces affecting small deviations. Typically (noted above), one forecasts using linear or nonlinear methods associated with an important economic indicator (GDP). Typically, one focuses on port traffic demand in three areas [1,2].

First, making local improvements on the existing prediction methods, so we can obtain the prediction result which is closer to the true value. By adjusting the inflection point of the Logistic curve, researching the methods of blur compensation and estimation of optimism and pessimism on production trends including Logistic curve prediction methods.

Second, some experts predict the cargo port handling activity by referring to methods from other applications including the use of econometrics, control theory and related methods. Others have produced dynamic PHQDF models to predict the cargo port activity, which systematically combines the historical trend of cargo activity, the socio-economic development of the hinterland, politics, policy, and psychological and technical factors. The example tests show that the model has higher prediction precision and better prediction results than the models suggested above.

Third, have the raw data processed, and through selecting appropriate explanatory variables from a plurality of explanatory variables, we may obtain better forecast results. Regression models to predict the cargo port activity are not uncommon. As results often indicate, when one utilizes mathematical models to predict, the most critical aspect is that the accuracy of the model, relationship of the response variable and predictor's variables and the quality of data is most important. The complexity of the model, especially in the case of only having small amounts of historical data is of lesser importance. Some examples of forecasting port activity by many researchers [3-9]. In each application, they use very large amounts of data to predict port capacity, tonnage and other measures of activity including correlated variables.

***Corresponding author:** Jeffrey E. Jarrett, Professor of Management Science and Finance, University of Rhode Island, Kingston-- 02852, USA
E-mail: jeffreyejarrett@gmail.com

Methodology

An example using a parsimonious time series method

First, we examine the time series of a sample of data for a Chinese port to observe the dimensions of a time series plot of data. Figure 1 contains the plot of six years by month of port traffic at a river port in the People's Republic of China (PRC). The time series plot shows the ups and downs of the data indicating a long term trend in the time series with variation from month to month. Since our purpose is to simplify the forecasting to the use of a univariate autoregressive-moving- average (ARIMA) model we will further examine the data if it is necessary to do additional predictions Figure 1.

By additional steps, we will see if we can model port traffic efficiently without great time and cost associated with sophisticated models. The additional steps will identify the specification of the ARIMA model. Step 1 is to determine the ARIMA function by computing the autocorrelation function (ACF) and partial autocorrelation function (PACF). These functions are drawn in Figures 2 and 3. Figure 2 contains the autocorrelation function for the time series data for the port traffic of Figure 1. Note, the function indicates a slow decline to about lag 6 indicating that the model is AR. To determine the appropriate number of AR parameters to estimate, we draw and obtain the partial autocorrelation function (PACF) of the same data in Figure 3. The partial autocorrelation function contains a large value at lag 1 (approximately, 0.8) which is well above the 95% significant limit in Figure 3. Hence, the number of AR parameters to be estimated is 1.

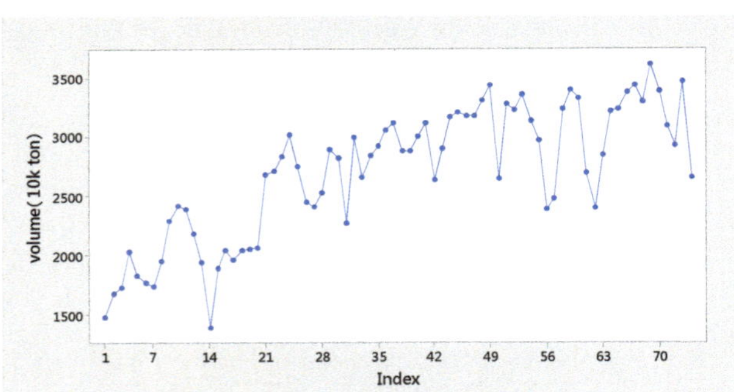

Figure 1: Time series plot of port traffic.

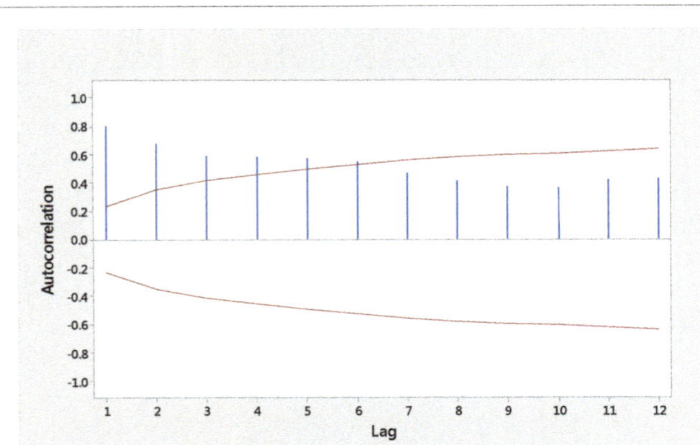

Figure 2: ACF of volume.

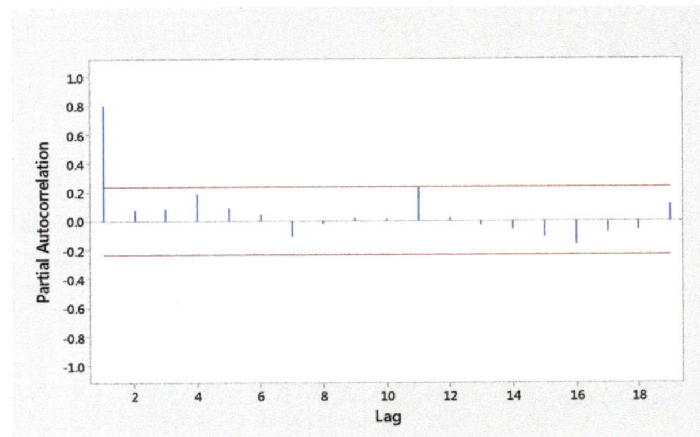

Figure 3: PACF of volume.

Type	Coefficient	St. Error	T	P
AR (1)	0.8624	0.0624	13.82	0.000
Constant	359.82	35.82	10.03	0.000
Mean	2610.6	260.2		
Modified Box-Pierce (Ljung-Box) Chi-Square statistic				
Lag	12	24	36	48
Chi-Square	12.9	21.5	32.7	46.2
DF	10	22	34	46
P-Value	0.228	0.492	0.532	0.465

Number of observations: 74
Residuals: SS = 6711497 (back forecasts excluded)
MS = 93215 DF = 72

Table 1: Final Estimates of Parameters from Minitab17.

Results

The ARIMA model and analysis

The ARIMA modeling in the first two steps are discussed in a wide amount of literature including the original developers Box and Jenkins [10] and explained also in many practitioner oriented literature include Makridakis et al. and Jarrett [11]. Using Minitab (vers 17) we find the following estimates of the final parameter of the AR (1) model.

In Table 1 of results, we obtain the model having 359.31 as the estimate of the constant and 0.8264 as the estimate of the first lag. In both the cases of the estimate of the constant and first AR coefficient , we observe p-values of 0.000 for the hypotheses that the parameters for the constant and AR (1) are equal to zero. For the modified Ljung-Box statistic indicates that the parameter test tends also to indicate there is no serial correlation in the autocorrelation of the residuals.

To finish the validation of the modeling process we calculate the autocorrelation of the residuals from forecast. Again the p-values indicate that the likelihood that we cannot reject the hypothesis that the model is adequate. What do we mean by adequate?

The above plot of time series for volume (10 k ton) indicate the direction of port demand through time period 86 (12 periods ahead. Also, 95% confidence interval estimates ahead to period 86 are also shown. Planners and managers with 95 percent certainty are able to know the limits of the prediction. In Figure 4, one observes the value of the mean square error (MS = 93215) and degrees of freedom associated with the predictive model. If we find a model that contains a smaller MS, that model could predict with uncertainty a better result. For

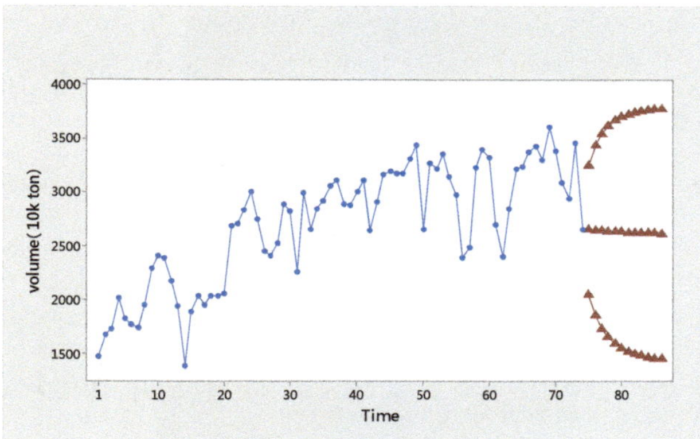

Figure 4: Time series plot for volume.

Type	Coef	SE Coef	T	P
AR (1)	0.7776	0.1229	6.33	0.000
AR (2)	0.1055	0.1222	0.86	0.391
Constant	303.40	36.11	8.40	0.000
Mean	2594.3	308.8		
Modified Box-Pierce (Ljung-Box) Chi-Square statistic				
Lag	12	24	36	48
Chi-Square	15.5	23.4	34.5	50.4
DF	9	21	33	45

Number of observations: 74

Residuals: SS = 6663734 (back forecasts excluded)

MS = 93855 DF = 71

Table 2: Result of AR (2) Model Estimation and Final Estimates of Parameters.

example, we may include a second autoregressive term in the forecast mode denoted AR (2). The result would be in Table 2 below.

Note, in Table 2, the AR (2) parameter estimates has p-value of 0.391 indication that one would not reject the hypothesis that the coefficient for this term is 0. By so doing, we would eliminate this value as an explanatory variable. Hence, we ar reduced to the AR (1) term. Also, the MS of the new model is 93855 which is larger than the MS of the AR (1) model which is 93218 [10-12]. The results noted in Table 2 if further examined by the autocorrelation function of the residuals would also indicate that the above estimated model would indicate that the model would not pass the test that autocorrelation is not present in the error terms. Hence, one would be better off by using the AR (1) model identified in the first step of the modeling process.

Forecasting with time series decomposition

Another method of forecasting which does not require finding highly correlated predictor variables is referred to as time series decomposition. Decomposition separates the time series from linear trend and seasonal components, as well as error, and to produce forecasts. For example, you might want to predict the port demand over the next twelve months data collected over the past 72 months.

You can use decomposition when you have data with either no trend or constant trend; have data with constant seasonal pattern; the seasonal component is either additive or multiplicative with the trend; and you want to make intermediate or long range forecasting. The methodology of time series decomposition developed around 1900 is one of the oldest methods for forecasting and is fully described in Jarrett [11] chapter 3 and many other books on predictive methods. Using conventional software on PC's and desk computers (Minitab), one may illustrate and compute the forecast. The result for our six years of monthly data for port traffic is illustrated in Figure 5. The figure contains the original 72 monthly data on port traffic and the 12 month period ahead forecasts. The plot contains actuals, fits, trend and forecasts and is denoted on the plot and variable definition box. Also, noting the accuracy measures is MSD (mean square deviation which MS in the previous figures) which is 92118.9. This value is smaller than the MS value. Hence the decomposition analysis is more accurate than either of the autoregressive models developed for these data previous.

Conclusions and Future Research

The analysis of the data indicates that ARIMA modeling and Time Series Decomposition produce useful results. Note in examining the final estimates of the AR (2) model (Table 2) the AR (2) parameter yielded a t-value of 0.86 corresponding to a p-value of 0.391. Hence, a second round of ARIMA modeling without the AR (2) parameter estimate would yield better results with only the constant and AR (1) parameter included in the forecasting model. Not reported in our tables but calculated the final MS estimate was smaller than for the AR (2) model. The extant of the decrease was not huge but the conclusion was that better improvement in the model forecasting was possible.

By examining Figure 5, the Time Series decomposition method also produced very good results which would fit a use trend through the data points and when reintroducing seasonality into the final forecast would result in a set of forecasts that closely model the pattern existing in the historical time series. The great ad vantages of these methodologies is that the methods do not require searching for external environmental variables which relate to throughput demand making the process of prediction and planning more difficult. Simple methods as noted in the analysis are available on common computer software. The methods do not require huge data banks or retrieval of data which may be from suspect sources. Jarrett, Zhang and Pan [11-13] noted that the use of freight rates in predicting cargo port volume but do require a very sophisticated model using a two parameter exponentially weighted moving-average model requiring much more analysis and data requirement than utilized in this study.

Our results do not stop one from seeking alternative, Jiawei, Lizhi, Xun and Shouyang [14,15] proposed in utilizing CDE-MPR methodology. Their results apply to multi-port regions in South China (PRC). They demonstrated that a feasible method to forecast and analyze maritime logistics in a multi-port regions. The methods

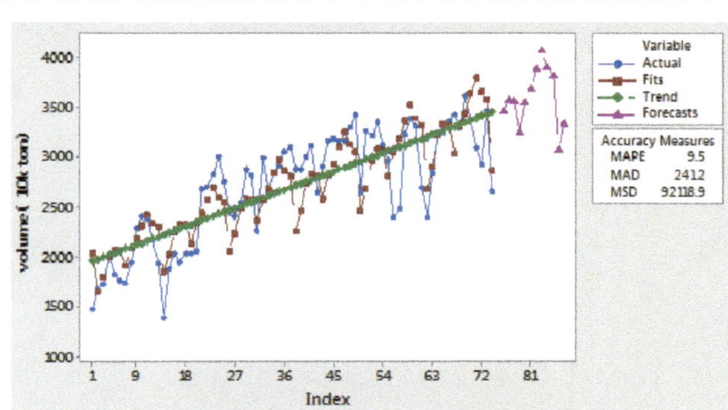

Figure 5: Time series decomposition plot for volume (10k ton) multiplicative model.

consist of many choices since there are many models to be included in the process. Their approach is promising but restricted to multi-port regions. The methods also are encouraging in designing and planning supply-chains.

References

1. Bakshi G, Panayotov G, Skoulakis G (2010) The Baltic Dry Index as a Predictor of Global Stock Returns, Commodity Returns, and Global Economic Activity.
2. Sun L (2010) The research on a double forecasting model of port cargo throughput. World Journal of Modeling and Simulation 6: 57-62.
3. Sun L, Wang Z (2007) Studying the Probability Distribution of the port handling capacity in the port. Proceedings of SSMSSD 6: 1869-1873.
4. Yuan E, Xie Y (2004) On Ports Throughput Probability Forecasting Model. Port and Waterway Engineering 33: 1028-1031.
5. Cheng L, Wong Y (1997) Port Facilities and Container Handling Services: The Hong Kong Economic Policy Studies, City University of Hong Kong Press, Hong Kong.
6. Sun Y, Zheng G (2007) Research on Forecast of Port Throughput Capacity Based on Grey Theory. China Water Transport 5: 160-162.
7. Yang S, Guan K (2005) Application of Spreadsheet to Forecasting Port Throughput. Wuhan Journal of University of Technology.
8. Hui E, Seabrooke W, Woong K (2004) Forecasting Cargo Throughput for the Port of Hong Kong: Error Correction Model Approach. Journal of Urban Planning and Development 130: 195-203.
9. Lam WHK, Pan LP Ng; Seabrooke W, Hui ECM (2004) Forecasts and Reliability Analysis of Port Cargo Throughput in Hong Kong. Journal of Urban Planning and Development 130: l33-144.
10. Box G, Jenkins G (1970, 1976) Time Series Analysis: Forecasting and Control. Operational Research Quarterly 22:199-201.
11. Jarrett J (1991) Business Forecasting Methods, (2ndedn), Basil Blackwell: Oxford.
12. Pankratz A (1983) Forecasting with Univariate Box-Jenkins Models: Concepts and Cases, John Wiley and Sons, New York.
13. Xu C, Yan Y, Zhang P (2006) Prediction Model of Port Throughput Based on System Dynamics. Port and Waterway Engineering 32: 26-29.
14. Chen N, Zhu M, Yu Z (2005) Comparing Two Forecast Models of Ports Handling Capacity. Journal of Wuhan University of Technology 27: 77-79.
15. Wang C (2006) Port Handling Capacity Forecasting Based on Unascertained Number Regressive Model Communications Standardization.

Permissions

All chapters in this book were first published in IJEMS, by OMICS International; hereby published with permission under the Creative Commons Attribution License or equivalent. Every chapter published in this book has been scrutinized by our experts. Their significance has been extensively debated. The topics covered herein carry significant findings which will fuel the growth of the discipline. They may even be implemented as practical applications or may be referred to as a beginning point for another development.

The contributors of this book come from diverse backgrounds, making this book a truly international effort. This book will bring forth new frontiers with its revolutionizing research information and detailed analysis of the nascent developments around the world.

We would like to thank all the contributing authors for lending their expertise to make the book truly unique. They have played a crucial role in the development of this book. Without their invaluable contributions this book wouldn't have been possible. They have made vital efforts to compile up to date information on the varied aspects of this subject to make this book a valuable addition to the collection of many professionals and students.

This book was conceptualized with the vision of imparting up-to-date information and advanced data in this field. To ensure the same, a matchless editorial board was set up. Every individual on the board went through rigorous rounds of assessment to prove their worth. After which they invested a large part of their time researching and compiling the most relevant data for our readers.

The editorial board has been involved in producing this book since its inception. They have spent rigorous hours researching and exploring the diverse topics which have resulted in the successful publishing of this book. They have passed on their knowledge of decades through this book. To expedite this challenging task, the publisher supported the team at every step. A small team of assistant editors was also appointed to further simplify the editing procedure and attain best results for the readers.

Apart from the editorial board, the designing team has also invested a significant amount of their time in understanding the subject and creating the most relevant covers. They scrutinized every image to scout for the most suitable representation of the subject and create an appropriate cover for the book.

The publishing team has been an ardent support to the editorial, designing and production team. Their endless efforts to recruit the best for this project, has resulted in the accomplishment of this book. They are a veteran in the field of academics and their pool of knowledge is as vast as their experience in printing. Their expertise and guidance has proved useful at every step. Their uncompromising quality standards have made this book an exceptional effort. Their encouragement from time to time has been an inspiration for everyone.

The publisher and the editorial board hope that this book will prove to be a valuable piece of knowledge for researchers, students, practitioners and scholars across the globe.

List of Contributors

Zhaofeng Chen and Huihui Chen
Science and Technology Policies and Innovation Management Research Institute, Nantong University, Nantong, Jiangsu, PR China

Raza Khan, Adeel Bukhari and Zahid Ali Channar
Department of Management Sciences, Institute of Business and Technology (IBT), Pakistan

Amutha D
Department of Economics, St. Mary's College, Tuticorin, India

Williams Agbara
Department of Economics, Benue State University, Makurdi, Nigeria

Abbott J Haron
Higher Colleges of Technology, Sharjah, United Arab Emirates

Mahsa Familmaleki
Department of Management and Accounting, College of Humanities, Hamedan Science and Research Branch, Hamedan, Iran

Alireza Aghighi
Department of Management, Faculty of Economics and Management, Payame Noor University, Hamedan, Iran

Kambiz Hamidi
Faculty Member of Management and Accounting, Islamic Azad University Hamedan Branch, Hamedan, Iran

Mohamed Bushara OA
Faculty of Agricultural Sciences, University of Gezira, Wad Medani, Sudan

Murtada KA Abdelmahmod
Faculty of Management Sciences and Economics, Department of Economics, University of AL-Butana, Rufaa, Sudan

Masoud Mohammed Albiman
Department Research Policy and Development, Zanzibar Revenue Board (ZRB) and Zanzibar Insitute of Business Research and Technology (ZIBRET), Tanzania, Zanzibar

Molla DN
Assistant Researcher, Ethiopian Public Health Institute, Addis Ababa, Ethiopia

Ariz Naqvi and Farah Naqvi
American University of the Middle East, Egaila, Al Ahmedi, Kuwait

Jeffrey E. Jarrett
College of Business Administration, University of Rhode Island, Kingston, RI 02881, USA

Md. Sajedul Islam
Begum Rokeya University, Dhaka, Bangladesh

Iftakhar Hossain Jubery
Institute of Business Administration, IBA University of Dhaka, Bangladesh

Quaisar Ijaz Khan and Abdul Shukor Shamsudin
School of Business Management, University Utara, Malaysia

Syed Soffian Syed Ismail
School of Accounting, University Utara, Malaysia

Limam Ould
Faculty of Economics and Management Sciences, International Islamic University Malaysia, Selangor, Kuala Lumpur 53100, Malaysia

Rotich Titus Kipkoech
Student, Mount Kenya University , Eldoret, Kenya

Mohammad Salhab and Ali Abu Ali
Department of Finance, University of Bradford Leeds Teaching Hospitals, UK

José G Vargas-Hernández
Lic. Ángel Tomás Wong Dan, University Center for Economic and Managerial Sciences, University of Guadalajara, Periférico Norte 799, Los Belenes, C.P. 45100, Zapopan, Jalisco, México

Hanitra Rakotondramaro
IAE-University of Perpignan, via Domitia, France

Mauro Luisetto
European Specialist Laboratory Medicine, Hospital Pharmacist manager, Italy

Luca Cabianca
Biomedical Laboratory, Torino, Italy

Ram Sahu
Columbia Institute of Pharmacy, Tekari, Raipur, India

Habtamu Lemma
Punjabi University, Business Management, Punjabi University, Patiala, Punjab 147002, India

Naeem Ali, Sagheer Abbas and Maria Shahid
National College of Business Administration and Economics, Lahore, Pakistan

Aamir Hasan
Anuna Education Network, Lucknow, Uttar Pradesh, India

Isaiah Onsarigo Miencha and Seline AO
Head of the Department, Banking and Finance, School of Business, All Nations University, Ghana

Francis KK
Lecturer Koforudua Polytechnic, Faculty of Business and Management, Koforudua, Ghana

Anane E and Twum A
Faculties Department of Banking and Finance, All Nations University, Ghana

Fanougbo Avoce Viagannou
The Benin School of Applied Economics and Management ENEAM-FASEG/University of Abomey-Calavi, 05BP 1652 Cotonou, Benin

Eugene Iheanacho
Department of Economics, Abia State University Uturu, Nigeria

Chia-Lin Chang
Department of Applied Economics, Department of Finance, National Chung Hsing University, Taiwan

Michael McAleer
Department of Quantitative Finance, National Tsing Hua University, Taiwan

Wing-Keung Wong
Department of Economics, Hong Kong Baptist University, Hong Kong, China, and Department of Finance Asia University, Taiwan

Ramin Assari and Mohammad Reza Taghva
Department of IT Management, Allameh Tabataba'i University, Tehran, Iran

Parham Azimi
Faculty of Mechanical Engineering and Industrial Engineering, Islamic Azad University, Qazvin, Iran

Victor Ushahemba Ijirshar, Fefa Joseph and Mile Godoo
Department of Economics, Benue State University, Nigeria

Mohammed HZ and Çiçek O
Girne American University, Cyprus

Yusif M Hadrat
Department of Economics, Kwame Nkrumah University of Science and Technology, Kumasi, Ghana

Eshun Nunoo Isaac K
Ghana College, Kumasi, Ghana

Effah Sarkodie Eric
University of Education, Winneba, College of Technology Education, Department of Accounting Studies Education, Kumasi, Ghana

Obasaju BO
Lecturer at Landmark University, Omu-aran, Nigeria

Bowale EI
Department of Economics, Covenant University, Km 10 Idiiroko Rd, Ota, Ogun State, Nigeria

Eko Handayanto
University of Muhammadiyah Malang, East Java, Indonesia

Tulus Haryono and Hunik Sri Runing Sawitri
University of Sebelas Maret Surakarta, Central Java, Indonesia

Tianhao Zhi
School of Business, The University of Technology, Sydney, New South Wales, Australia

Sudi Nangoli, Mohammed Ngoma and Hassan Kimbugwe
Department of Business Administration, Makerere University Business School, Kampala, Uganda

Mayoka Kituyi
Department of Business Computing, Makerere University Business School, Uganda

Ali Raeispour
Assistant and Member of the Faculty of Kerman University, Iran

Somayeh koochakzadeh
Facualy Member of Vali-e-Asr University of Rafsanjan, Iran

Hajar AsnsAshari
PhD Student Economics, University of Sistan and Baluchestan, Iran

Jeffrey E Jarrett
Professor of Management Science and Finance, University of Rhode Island, Kingston- 02852, USA

Index